P9-CFN-956

Frommer's®

Oregon

Here's what the critics say about Frommer's:

"Amazingly easy to use. Very portable, very complete."
—*Booklist*

♦

"The only mainstream guide to list specific prices. The Walter Cronkite of guidebooks—with all that implies."
—*Travel & Leisure*

♦

"Complete, concise, and filled with useful information."
—*New York Daily News*

♦

"Hotel information is close to encyclopedic."
—*Des Moines Sunday Register*

♦

"Detailed, accurate, and easy-to-read information for all price ranges."
—*Glamour Magazine*

Other Great Guides for Your Trip:

Frommer's Seattle & Portland

Frommer's Irreverent Guide to Seattle & Portland

Frommer's Vancouver & Victoria

Frommer's Washington State

Frommer's Great Outdoor Guide to Washington & Oregon

Frommer's USA

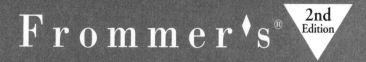

Oregon

by Karl Samson and Jane Aukshunas

IDG Books Worldwide, Inc.
An International Data Group Company
Foster City, CA • Chicago, IL • Indianapolis, IN • New York, NY

ABOUT THE AUTHOR

Husband and wife travel-writing team Karl Samson and Jane Aukshunas live in Oregon, where they spend their time juggling their obsessions with traveling, outdoor sports, and gardening. Each winter, to dry out their webbed feet, they flee the soggy Northwest to update the *Frommer's Arizona* guide, but they always look forward to their return to the land of good coffee. Karl is also the author of *Frommer's Great Outdoor Guide to Washington & Oregon* and *Frommer's Nepal*.

IDG BOOKS WORLDWIDE, INC.

An International Data Group Company
919 E. Hillsdale Blvd.
Suite 400
Foster City, CA 94404

Find us online at **www.frommers.com**

ISBN 0-02-863265-6
ISSN 1093-7455

Editors: David Gibbs and Claudia Kirschhoch
Production Editor: Robyn Burnett
Photo Editor: Richard Fox
Design by Michele Laseau
Staff Cartographers: John Decamillis and Roberta Stockwell
Page Creation: Heather Pope and Linda Quigley

SPECIAL SALES

For general information on IDG Books Worldwide's books in the U.S., please call our
Consumer Customer Service department at 1-800-762-2974. For reseller information,
including discounts, bulk sales, customized editions, and premium sales, please call our
Reseller Customer Service department at 1-800-434-3422.

Manufactured in the United States of America

5 4 3 2 1

Contents

5 The Willamette Valley: The Bread (& Wine) Basket of Oregon 110

6 The Oregon Coast 154

7 The Columbia Gorge 237

8 The Cascades 255

List of Maps

AN INVITATION TO THE READER

In researching this book, we discovered many wonderful places—hotels, restaurants, shops, and more. We're sure you'll find others. Please tell us about them, so we can share the information with your fellow travelers in upcoming editions. If you were disappointed with a recommendation, we'd love to know that, too. Please write to:

Frommer's Oregon, 2nd Edition
IDG Travel
1633 Broadway
New York, NY 10019

AN ADDITIONAL NOTE

Please be advised that travel information is subject to change at any time—and this is especially true of prices. We therefore suggest that you write or call ahead for confirmation when making your travel plans. The authors, editors, and publisher cannot be held responsible for the experiences of readers while traveling. Your safety is important to us, however, so we encourage you to stay alert and be aware of your surroundings. Keep a close eye on cameras, purses, and wallets, all favorite targets of thieves and pickpockets.

WHAT THE SYMBOLS MEAN

✪ Frommer's Favorites

Our favorite places and experiences—outstanding for quality, value, or both.

The following abbreviations are used for credit cards:

AE	American Express	EURO	EuroCard
CB	Carte Blanche	JCB	Japan Credit Bank
DC	Diners Club	MC	MasterCard
DISC	Discover	V	Visa
ER	EnRoute		

FIND FROMMER'S ONLINE

www.frommers.com offers up-to-the-minute listings on almost 200 cities around the globe—including the latest bargains and candid, personal articles updated daily by Arthur Frommer himself. No other Web site offers such comprehensive and timely coverage of the world of travel.

The Best of Oregon

Most people unfamiliar with Oregon can at least tell you that it rains a lot here. Perhaps you've heard that Oregonians have webbed feet, or that they don't tan—they rust. There's no getting around the fact that few states receive as much rain or cloudy weather as Oregon and its northern neighbor, Washington. However, the state's rainfall no longer seems to have the effect it once did. Sure, it still keeps the landscape green, but it's no longer keeping people from moving here.

Once the promised land of 19th-century pioneers, Oregon is an amalgam of American life and landscapes. Within its boundaries, the state reflects a part of almost every region of the country. Take a bit of New England's rural beauty, its covered bridges, and its steepled churches. Temper the climate with that of the upper South to avoid harsh winters. Now bring in some low, rolling mountains like the Appalachians; rugged, glaciated mountains like the Rockies; and Hawaiian-style volcanoes. Add a river as large and important as the Mississippi—complete with paddle wheel steamers—and a coastline as rugged as California's. Of course, there would have to be sagebrush and cowboys and Indians. You could even throw in the deserts of the Southwest and the wheat fields of the Midwest. A little wine country would be a nice touch, and so would some long, sandy beaches. Finally, you'll need a beautiful city, one whose downtown skyscrapers are framed by high forested hills and whose gardens are full of roses.

To explore such a diverse state takes quite a bit of advance planning, and knowing ahead of time the best that the state has to offer can make a visit much more enjoyable. After traveling the length and breadth of the state, we've chosen what we feel are the very best attractions, activities, lodgings, and restaurants. These are the places and experiences you won't want to miss. Most are described in more detail elsewhere in this book, but this chapter will give you an overview and get you started.

1 The Best Natural Attractions

- **The Oregon Coast:** Rocky headlands, offshore islands and haystack rocks, natural arches, caves full of sea lions, giant sand dunes, and dozens of state parks make this one of the most spectacular coastlines in the country. See chapter 6.
- **Columbia Gorge National Scenic Area:** Carved by Ice Age floods that were as much as 1,200 feet deep, the Columbia Gorge

is a unique feature of the Northwest landscape. Waterfalls by the dozen cascade from the basalt cliffs of the gorge. Highways on both the Washington and the Oregon sides of the Columbia River provide countless memorable views. See chapter 7.

- **Mount Hood:** As Oregon's tallest mountain and the closest Cascade peak to Portland, Mount Hood is a recreational mecca par excellence. Hiking trails, lakes and rivers, even year-round snowskiing make this the most appealing natural attraction in the state. See chapter 8.

- **Crater Lake National Park:** At 1,932 feet, Crater Lake is the deepest lake in the United States, and its sapphire-blue waters are a bewitchingly beautiful sight when seen from the rim of the volcanic crater that contains them. See chapter 8.

- **Central Oregon Lava Lands:** Throughout central Oregon and the central Cascades region, from the lava fields of McKenzie Pass to the obsidian flows of Newberry National Volcanic Monument, you'll find dramatic examples of the volcanic activity that gave rise to the Cascade Range. See chapters 8 and 10.

- **Hells Canyon:** Deeper than the Grand Canyon, this massive gorge along the Oregon-Idaho border is remote and inaccessible, and that is just what makes it fascinating. You can gaze down into it from on high, float its waters, or hike its trails. See chapter 11.

2 The Best Outdoor Activities

- **Biking the Oregon Coast:** With U.S. 101 clinging to the edge of the continent for much of its route through Oregon, this road has become one of the most popular cycling routes in the Northwest. The entire coast can be done in about a week, but there are also plenty of short sections that make good day trips. See chapter 6.

- **Windsurfing at Hood River:** Winds that rage through the Columbia Gorge whip up whitecapped standing waves and have turned this area into the windsurfing capital of the United States, attracting boardsailors from around the world. See chapter 7.

- **Fly-Fishing for Steelhead on the North Umpqua River:** Made famous by Zane Grey, the North Umpqua is the quintessential steelhead river (and for part of its length it's open to fly-fishing only). The river and the elusive steelhead offer a legendary fishing experience. See chapter 8.

- **Rafting the Rogue River:** Of all the white-water rafting rivers, none is more famous than the Rogue. Meandering through remote wilderness in the southern part of the state, this river has been popular with anglers since early in this century and attracted Zane Grey with its beauty and great fishing. Today, you can splash through roaring white water by day and spend your nights in remote lodges that are inaccessible by car. See chapter 9.

- **Mountain Biking in Bend:** Outside the town of Bend, in central Oregon, dry ponderosa pine forests are laced with trails that are open to mountain bikes. Routes pass by several lakes, and along the way you'll get great views of the Three Sisters, Broken Top, and Mount Bachelor. See chapter 10.

- **Skiing Mount Bachelor:** With ski slopes dropping off the very summit of this extinct volcano, Mount Bachelor Ski Area, in drier and sunnier central Oregon, is the state's premier ski area. Seemingly endless runs of all levels of ability make this a magnet for skiers and snowboarders from around the state, and lots of high-speed quad chairs keep people on the snow instead of standing in line. See chapter 10.

Oregon

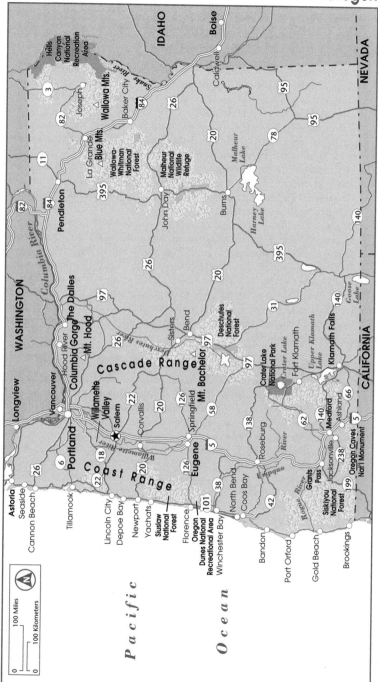

3

3 The Best Beaches

See chapter 6 for details on the beaches listed below.

- **Cannon Beach/Ecola State Park:** With the massive monolith of Haystack Rock rising up from the low-tide line and the secluded beaches of Ecola State Park just north of town, Cannon Beach offers all the best of the Oregon coast.
- **Oswald West State Park:** At this state park south of Cannon Beach, it's a 15-minute walk through the woods to the beach, which keeps the sands from ever getting too crowded. The crescent-shaped beach is on a secluded cove backed by dense forest. This also happens to be a favorite surfing spot.
- **Sunset Bay State Park:** Almost completely surrounded by sandstone cliffs, this little beach near Coos Bay is on a shallow cove. The clear waters here get a little bit warmer than unprotected waters elsewhere on the coast, so it's sometimes possible to actually go swimming.
- **Bandon:** It's difficult to imagine a more picturesque stretch of coastline than the beach in Bandon. Haystack rocks rise up from sand and sea as if strewn there by some giant hand. Motels and houses front this scenic beach, which ensures its popularity no matter what the weather.
- **The Beaches of Samuel H. Boardman State Scenic Corridor:** Within this remote south coast state park are to be found some of the prettiest, most secluded, and least visited beaches on the Oregon coast. Ringed by rocky headlands, the many little crescents of sand in this park provide an opportunity to find *the* perfect beach.

4 The Best Hikes

- **Cape Lookout Trail:** Leading 2½ miles through dense forests to the tip of this rugged cape on the north Oregon coast, this trail ends high on a cliff above the waters of the Pacific. Far below, gray whales can often be seen lolling in the waves, and the view to the south takes in miles of coastline. See chapter 6.
- **Umpqua Dunes Trail:** If you've ever dreamed of joining the French Foreign Legion or simply want to play at being Lawrence of Arabia, then the Oregon Dunes National Recreation Area is the place for you. Within this vast expanse of sand dunes, you'll find the highest dunes on the Oregon coast—some 500 feet tall. See chapter 6.
- **Eagle Creek Trail:** This trail in the Columbia Gorge follows the tumbling waters of Eagle Creek and passes two spectacular waterfalls in the first 2 miles. Along the way, the trail climbs up the steep gorge walls, and in places it is cut right into the basalt cliffs. See chapter 7.
- **Timberline Trail:** As the name implies, this trail starts at the timberline, near the famous lodge of the same name. Because this route circles Mount Hood, you can start in either direction and make a day, overnight, or multiday hike of it. Paradise Park, its meadows ablaze with wildflowers in July and August, is a favorite for both day hikes and overnight trips. See chapter 8.
- **McKenzie River Trail to Tamolitch Pool:** The McKenzie River Trail stretches for 26 miles along the banks of this aquamarine river, but by far the most rewarding stretch of trail is the 2-mile hike to Tamolitch Pool, an astounding pool of turquoise waters formed as the McKenzie River wells up out of the ground after flowing underground for several miles. The trail leads through rugged, overgrown lava fields. See chapter 8.

- **Deschutes River Trail:** The Deschutes River, which flows down from the east side of the Cascades, passes through open ponderosa pine forest to the west of Bend. Paralleling the river, and passing tumultuous waterfalls along the way, is an easy trail that's popular with hikers, mountain bikers, and joggers. See chapter 10.

5 The Best Scenic Drives

- **Gold Beach to Brookings:** No other stretch of U.S. 101 along the Oregon coast is more breathtaking than the segment between Gold Beach and Brookings. This remote coastline is dotted with offshore islands, natural rock arches, sea caves, bluffs, and beaches. Take your time, stop at the many pull-offs, and make this a leisurely all day drive. See chapter 6.
- **Historic Columbia River Highway:** Opened in 1915 to allow automobiles access to the wonders of the Columbia Gorge, this narrow, winding highway east of Portland climbs up to the top of the gorge for a scenic vista before diving into forests where waterfalls, including the tallest one in the state, pour off of basalt cliffs. See chapter 7.
- **The McKenzie Pass–Santiam Pass Scenic Byway:** This loop drive, which crosses the Cascade crest twice, takes in views of half a dozen major Cascade peaks, negotiates a bizarre landscape of lava fields, passes several waterfalls, and skirts the aptly named Clear Lake, the source of the McKenzie River. This is one of the best drives in the state for fall color. See chapter 8.
- **Crater Lake Rim Drive:** This scenic drive circles the rim of the massive caldera that holds Crater Lake. Along the way are numerous pull-offs where you can gasp in astonishment at the sapphire-blue waters and the ever changing scenery. See chapter 8.
- **Cascade Lakes Highway:** This road, formerly known as Century Drive, covers roughly 100 miles as it loops out from Bend along the eastern slope of the Cascades. Views of Broken Top and the Three Sisters are frequent, and along the way are numerous lakes, both large and small. See chapter 10.

6 The Best Museums

- **Portland Art Museum:** Having recently completed a major expansion, the Portland Art Museum is bigger and better than ever. Although it focuses on blockbuster shows, it also has a respectable permanent collection that includes many Native American artifacts. See chapter 4.
- **Jensen Arctic Museum** (Monmouth): Although this museum is not very big, it contains an amazingly diverse collection of artifacts from the Arctic. Even more surprising than the thoroughness of the collection is the fact that the museum is here and not in Alaska. See chapter 5.
- **Favell Museum of Western Art and Indian Artifacts** (Klamath Falls): This museum houses an absolutely amazing assortment of Native American artifacts, including thousands of arrowheads, spear points, and other stone tools. See chapter 9.
- **The Museum at Warm Springs** (Warm Springs Reservation): Set in a remote valley in Central Oregon, this modern museum houses an outstanding collection of artifacts from the area's Native American tribes. See chapter 10.
- **The High Desert Museum** (Bend): With its popular live-animal exhibits, this is more a zoo than a museum, but exhibits also offer glimpses into the history of

the vast and little-known desert that stretches from the Cascades eastward to the Rocky Mountains. See chapter 10.

- **Oregon Trail Interpretive Center** (Baker City): The lives of pioneers, who gave up everything to venture overland to the Pacific Northwest, are documented at this evocative museum. Set atop a hill in sagebrush country, the museum overlooks wagon ruts left by pioneers. See chapter 11.

7 The Best Family Attractions

- **Oregon Coast Aquarium** (Newport): This modern aquarium is the biggest attraction on the coast. Tufted puffins and sea otters are always entertaining, while tide pools, jellyfish tanks, and a giant octopus also contribute to the appeal of this very realistically designed public aquarium. See chapter 6.
- **Sea Lion Cave** (north of Florence): This massive cave, the largest sea cave in the country, is home to hundreds of Steller sea lions that lounge on the rocks beneath busy U.S. 101. See chapter 6.
- **West Coast Game Park** (Bandon): The opportunity to pet wild baby animals, including leopards and bears, doesn't come often, so it's hard to pass up this roadside attraction on the southern Oregon coast. See chapter 6.
- **Oregon Museum of Science and Industry** (Portland): With an OMNIMAX theater, a planetarium, a submarine, and loads of hands-on exhibits, this Portland museum is fun for kids and adults alike. See chapter 4.
- **Wildlife Safari** (Winston): Giraffes peer in your window and rhinoceroses thunder past your car doors as you drive the family through this expansive wildlife park. The savannalike setting is even reminiscent of the African plains. See chapter 9.

8 The Best Historical Sites

- **Fort Clatsop National Memorial** (Astoria): This small log fort is a reconstruction of the fort that explorers Lewis and Clark built during the winter of 1805–06. Costumed interpreters bring the history of the fort to life. See chapter 6.
- **Jacksonville:** With more than 80 buildings listed on the National Register of Historic Places, this 19th-century gold-mining town is the most historic community in Oregon. In fact, the brick buildings of Jacksonville's main street are the oldest in the state. Here you'll also find two inns housed in buildings constructed in 1861, which makes these Oregon's oldest buildings being used as inns. See chapter 9.
- **Granite** (near Baker City): This weather-beaten ghost town in the Blue Mountains is left over from a gold rush that brought miners to the region in the late 1800s. The schoolhouse, general store, and bordello are still standing. See chapter 11.
- **Oregon Trail Wagon Ruts** (Baker City): It's hard to believe that something as ephemeral as a wagon rut can last more than 150 years, but the path made by the thousands of pioneers who followed the Oregon Trail cut deep into the land. Among other places, you can see ruts near the Oregon Trail Interpretive Center. See chapter 11.
- **Kam Wah Chung & Co. Museum** (John Day): This unusual little museum is way off the beaten track but is well worth a visit if you're anywhere in the vicinity. The museum preserves the home, office, and apothecary of a Chinese doctor

who ministered to the local Chinese community in the early part of this century. See chapter 11.

9 The Best B&Bs

- **Heron Haus** (Portland; ☎ **503/274-1846**): Located in the trendiest neighborhood in Portland, this elegant old mansion is surrounded by lush grounds and has a view out over the city. If you want to sample the epitome of bathroom luxury, circa 1920, ask for the room with the multiple-head shower. See chapter 4.
- **Springbrook Hazelnut Farm** (Newberg; ☎ **800/793-8528** or 503/538-4606): Set in the midst of the Yamhill County wine country, this working hazelnut farm captures the essence of rural Oregon and distills it into a tranquil and restorative retreat. You can opt to stay in the main house, a carriage house, or a cottage. See chapter 5.
- **The Secret Garden** (Eugene; ☎ **888/484-6755** or 541/484-6755): Housed in what was once a sorority house and before that the home of one of Eugene's founding families, this very elegant inn is utterly tasteful and filled with family heirlooms and original art. The garden has some very interesting secrets. See chapter 5.
- **St. Bernards** (Cannon Beach; ☎ **800/436-2848** or 503/436-2800): Patterned after a French château, this mansion-sized B&B may seem oddly out of place on the Oregon coast, but no one staying here seems to mind. It could be the huge guest rooms and castlelike ambiance, or it could be the abundance of European antiques and original art. See chapter 6.
- **Channel House** (Depoe Bay; ☎ **800/447-2140** or 541/765-2140): Situated on the cliff above the channel into tiny Depoe Bay, this B&B offers one of the most striking settings on the Oregon coast. The contemporary design includes guest rooms made for romance—a hot tub on the balcony, a fire in the fireplace, and an unsurpassed view out the windows. See chapter 6.
- **Heceta Head Lightstation** (Yachats; ☎ **541/547-3696**): Ever dreamed of staying at a lighthouse? Well, on the Oregon coast, your dream can come true at this former lighthouse keeper's home. The Victorian B&B, which claims one of the most spectacular locations on the entire coast, is set high on a hill above Devil's Elbow State Park, and, not surprisingly, it's haunted. (Don't worry, the resident ghost is friendly.) See chapter 6.
- **Ziggurat Bed & Breakfast** (Yachats; ☎ **541/547-3925**): A boldly styled, contemporary, pyramid-shaped home built right on the beach, this is the Oregon coast's most visually stunning B&B. Its setting, near one of the most breathtaking stretches of coast, makes the inn even more recommendable. See chapter 6.
- **Bandon Beach House** (Bandon; ☎ **541/347-1196**): Set atop a 50-foot bluff overlooking the beach, this large, modern inn offers only two bedrooms, but both are huge. Wood floors, river-rock fireplaces, lots of windows, and classically elegant furnishings make this a great place to hole up for a few days. See chapter 6.
- **Chetco River Inn** (Brookings; ☎ **541/670-1645**): Want to get away from it all without sacrificing luxury and great food? Book a room at this remote B&B on the crystal-clear Chetco River. The setting in the middle of a national forest is as tranquil as you could ever wish for. See chapter 6.
- **Lakecliff Estate Bed and Breakfast** (Hood River; ☎ **541/386-7000**): Located not far from the famous Columbia Gorge Hotel, this inn is in a home built about the same time the hotel was. The view from the cliff-top location is superb, and

the shady forest setting lends the feel of the deep woods. An upscale historic atmosphere without the crowds. See chapter 7.

10 The Best Small Inns

- **Stephanie Inn** (Cannon Beach; ☎ 800/633-3466 or 503/436-2221): Combining the look of a mountain lodge with a beachfront setting in Oregon's most artistic town, the Stephanie Inn is a romantic retreat that surrounds its guests with unpretentious luxury. See chapter 6.
- **The Inn at Manzanita** (Manzanita; ☎ 503/368-6754): Although small enough to be a B&B and lacking a restaurant of its own, this inn, in what just might be the second-quaintest town on the Oregon coast, is designed for romantic getaways. Within a block you'll find both the beach and two of the state's best restaurants. See chapter 6.
- **Sylvia Beach Hotel** (Newport; ☎ 541/265-5428): Taking literature as its theme and decorating its rooms to evoke different authors—from Edgar Allan Poe to Dr. Seuss—the Sylvia Beach Hotel is the most original small inn in the Northwest. The fact that it's only a block from the beach is just icing on the cake. See chapter 6.
- **Tu Tu Tun Lodge** (Gold Beach; ☎ 541/247-6664): Though some might think of this as a fishing lodge, it's far too luxurious for anglers to keep to themselves. A secluded setting on the lower Rogue River guarantees tranquillity, and choice guest rooms provide the perfect setting for forgetting about your everyday stress. The dining room serves excellent meals. See chapter 6.
- **Steamboat Inn** (Steamboat; ☎ 800/840-8825 or 541/498-2230): Oregon's North Umpqua River is legendary for its steelhead fishing, and this is where you stay if you want to return to elegance and comfort after a day of fishing. The word is out on this inn, and many guests now show up with no intention of casting a fly into the river's waters. They'd rather just sit back and watch the river flow. See chapter 8.
- **The Winchester Country Inn** (Ashland; ☎ 800/972-4991 or 541/488-1113): Located only 2 blocks from the theaters of the Oregon Shakespeare Festival, this inn has the feel of a country inn though it's located right in town. Rooms are in three different buildings, including a modern Victorian cottage that has four spacious suites. The first floor of the main building is taken up by one of Ashland's best restaurants. See chapter 9.
- **Pine Ridge Inn** (Bend; ☎ 800/600-4095 or 541/389-6137): This luxurious inn is located on the outskirts of Bend on a bluff overlooking the Deschutes River. With its spacious rooms and suites, antiques, and regional art, it provides both elegance and a Northwest flavor. See chapter 10.
- **Pine Valley Lodge** (Halfway; ☎ 541/742-2027): Set in the tiny hamlet of Halfway just outside Hells Canyon National Recreation Area, this lodge is everything that contemporary rustic Western lodges wish they could be. Owned and operated by two artists, the lodge conjures up the image of an old stage stop with its unusual architecture, while unique details add very personal touches. See chapter 11.

11 The Best Historic Hotels & Lodges

- **The Benson** (Portland; ☎ 800/426-0670 or 503/228-2000): With its crystal chandeliers and Circassian walnut paneling in the lobby, this 1912 vintage hotel is the lodging of choice for presidents, dignitaries, and celebrities visiting Portland. See chapter 4.

- **Columbia Gorge Hotel** (Hood River; ☎ 800/345-1921 or 541/386-5566): Built in 1915 to handle the first automobile traffic up the Columbia Gorge, this mission-style hotel commands a stunning view across the gorge and is surrounded by colorful gardens. The breakfasts are legendary. See chapter 7.
- **Timberline Lodge** (Mount Hood; ☎ 800/547-1406 or 503/622-7979): Built by the WPA during the Great Depression, this stately mountain lodge is a showcase for the skills of the craftspeople who created it, with a grand stone fireplace, exposed beams, and wide plank floors. The views of Mount Hood's peak and the Oregon Cascades to the south are superb. See chapter 8.
- **Crater Lake Lodge** (Crater Lake National Park; ☎ 541/830-8700): Though only a small portion of the original structure was salvaged during its reconstruction a few years back, this place, with its stone fireplace and ponderosa pine-bark walls in the Great Hall, still maintains the feel of a classic mountain lodge. The setting, high above jewel-like Crater Lake, is breathtaking. See chapter 8.
- **Geiser Grand Hotel** (Baker City; ☎ 888/GEISERG or 541/523-1889): Opened in 1889 at the height of the Blue Mountains gold rush, this Baker City grand dame was reopened in 1997 after a 3-year renovation. With its corner turret, stained-glass ceiling, and abundance of crystal chandeliers, the hotel succeeds in capturing the feel of a Wild West luxury hotel without sacrificing any modern conveniences. See chapter 11.

12 The Best Resorts

- **The Westin Salishan Lodge** (Gleneden Beach; ☎ 888/SALISHAN or 541/764-2371): Even if it weren't the only real full-service golf resort on the Oregon coast, Salishan Lodge would likely still be the best. Set amid lush coastal forests and with plenty of holes of golf, this has long been *the* quintessential Oregon coast resort. The only drawback is that the beach is a bit of a hike. See chapter 6.
- **The Resort at the Mountain** (Mount Hood; ☎ 800/669-7666 or 503/622-3101): Located at the foot of Mount Hood, this golf resort is surrounded by dark Northwest woods and offers almost year-round golfing; yet come winter (and summer, for that matter), you can ski in the morning and play a round of golf in the afternoon. See chapter 8.
- **Black Butte Ranch** (Sisters; ☎ 800/452-7455 or 541/595-6211): This former ranch offers wide-open views and a world unto itself. The Three Sisters peaks are the backdrop for golf, horseback riding, canoeing, tennis, and numerous other activities, and in the autumn aspen trees splash the resort with bursts of golden yellow. See chapter 10.
- **Kah-Nee-Ta Resort** (North Central Oregon; ☎ 800/554-4SUN or 541/553-1112): Located miles from the nearest town yet within 90 minutes of Portland, this resort on the Warm Springs Indian Reservation is remarkable primarily for its remote sagebrush canyon setting. However, it also has an 18-hole golf course and a swimming pool fed by a natural warm spring. See chapter 10.
- **Sunriver Lodge & Resort** (Bend; ☎ 800/547-3922 or 541/593-1000): With the Three Sisters for a backdrop and the Deschutes River winding through the property, this resort is something of an institution for Oregonians. In summer, there are golf courses and miles of bike paths, and in winter the ski slopes of Mount Bachelor (Oregon's best ski area) are just up the road. It's really more of

a town than a mere vacation getaway, and once people check in, they usually decide it's just the sort of place they'd like to stay. See chapter 10.

13 The Best Portland Restaurants

For more details on all the restaurants listed below, see chapter 4.

- **Assaggio** (☎ 503/232-6151): This small neighborhood restaurant in the Sellwood district of southeast Portland captures the essence of an Italian trattoria. With a cozy lounge area, a counter overlooking the kitchen, and a dining room full of closely spaced tables, Assaggio stays packed with not only neighborhood locals but also diners from all over the city who come for the perfectly prepared pasta dishes.
- **Caprial's Bistro and Wine** (☎ 503/236-6457): Chef Caprial Pence, though a Portlander, first made a name for herself in Seattle, where she helped pioneer a distinctive regional style of cooking. In this bistro and wine shop, she continues her culinary experimentation for a loyal following of patrons from both Portland and Seattle.
- **Couvron** (☎ 503/225-1844): This tiny French restaurant took Portland by storm several years back and has, with its oh-so-Gallic decor and utterly French menu, become *the* French restaurant in the city. Don't let the unpretentious exterior of this converted home dissuade you—the menu boasts the finest of ingredients in dishes of uncompromising complexity.
- **Fiddleheads** (☎ 503/233-1547): With a menu and interior decor that draw somewhat on Native American influences, Fiddleheads offers one of Portland's most distinctive dining experiences. No, you won't be eating pemmican or dried salmon, but you might find buffalo stew or fiddleheads (fern shoots) on the menu.
- **Higgins** (☎ 503/222-9070): Chef Greg Higgins first made a name for himself just down the street at the Heathman Hotel. Here, in his eponymous restaurant, he features classic styling and a contemporary menu. Located adjacent to the Portland Center for the Performing Arts, Higgins is a favorite of theatergoers and has a lively little bar with an amazing selection of beers from around the world.
- **Ken's Home Plate** (☎ 503/236-9520): You wouldn't think a take-out restaurant would rank among the best restaurants in the city, but this little hole-in-the-wall dishes up food worthy of the city's finest restaurants, at a fraction of the cost.
- **Pazzo Ristorante** (☎ 503/228-1515): While Portland abounds in upscale contemporary Italian restaurants, Pazzo remains one of the best and most reliable. The restaurant is in the wine-themed Hotel Vintage Plaza; not surprisingly, they have a very good wine list.
- **Southpark** (☎ 503/326-1300): No, this doesn't have anything to do with the TV show, and despite the name it's one of Portland's best restaurants. Luxurious surroundings are complemented by delicious food at reasonable prices. There's also a plush little wine bar.
- **Wildwood** (☎ 503/248-WOOD): With a menu that draws on the latest culinary trends, Wildwood has been the hippest restaurant in town for several years now. The *Architectural Digest* interior is divided into various spaces to fit your mood, whether you're looking for a light bar meal or a lavish celebratory feast.
- **Zefiro Restaurant and Bar** (☎ 503/226-3394): With its chic contemporary decor, its Mediterranean-influenced menu, and its impeccably prepared dishes, Zefiro consistently ranks as one of Portland's top restaurants. The tightly packed lounge is also one of *the* places in the city to be seen sipping a martini.

14 The Best Restaurants Outside Portland

- **Jarboe's in Manzanita** (Manzanita; ☎ **503/368-5113**): With limited seating and a limited menu, this tiny restaurant, located in one of the coast's quintessential laid-back villages, serves memorable multicourse dinners with an emphasis on creatively prepared seafood. See chapter 6.
- **The Joel Palmer House** (Dayton; ☎ **503/864-2995**): Mushrooms are an obsession of the chef at this wine-country restaurant, and you'll find them in almost every dish on the menu (with the exception of the desserts). The restaurant is quite formal and is housed in an immaculately restored old home. See chapter 5.
- **Tina's** (Dundee; ☎ **503/538-8880**): Located at the base of the Red Hills, which produce some of Oregon's finest wines, this restaurant has long been a favorite wine-country dining spot for lunch or dinner. See chapter 5.
- **Zenon Café** (Eugene; ☎ **541/343-3005**): Hip decor, cases filled with desserts to tempt even the most dedicated dieter, and a long, internationally inspired menu make this the most reliable and gratifying restaurant in Eugene. See chapter 5.
- **Cascade Dining Room** (Mount Hood; ☎ **503/272-3700**): Located inside the historic Timberline Lodge, the Cascade Dining Room is Oregon's premier mountain-lodge restaurant and has long kept skiers and other hotel guests happy. Since the windows here are small, it isn't the view that keeps diners content, but rather the creative cuisine. See chapter 8.
- **Steamboat Inn** (North Umpqua Valley; ☎ **800/840-8825**): Set on the bank of the North Umpqua River, this is ostensibly a fishing-lodge dining room, but the multicourse gourmet meals served here have become the stuff of legends (and have even spawned a cookbook). See chapter 8.
- **Chateaulin** (Ashland; ☎ **541/482-2264**): Though Ashland's *raison d'être* may be Shakespeare, it is the French cuisine at Chateaulin that lingers longest in the memories of theatergoers. The dishes are hearty, and the decor is theatrically country French. See chapter 9.
- **Cucina Biazzi** (Ashland, ☎ **541/488-3739**): Slightly removed from Ashland's main restaurant district and located in a restored old house, this small Italian restaurant serves memorable and very reasonably priced multicourse dinners. Best of all, you can enjoy one of these feasts and still make it to the show on time. See chapter 9.
- **Kokanee Café** (Camp Sherman; ☎ **541/595-6420**): Located amid the ponderosa pines on the bank of the Metolius River near the Western theme town of Sisters, this rustic restaurant has the look of an upscale fishing lodge, but its clientele is much broader than just the foolish fly anglers who come to test the waters of the Metolius. The trout is, of course, always a good bet. See chapter 10.
- **The Halfway Supper Club** (Halfway; ☎ **541/742-2027**): Halfway is an unlikely town for a restaurant that can rank among the top in the state, but the imaginative, rustic Western decor combined with the chef/co-owner's love of cooking always make a meal here a highlight of a trip to the Wallowa Mountains region. See chapter 11.

15 The Best Brew Pubs

- **Bridgeport Brewery and Brew Pub** (Portland; ☎ **503/241-7179**): Since it's the oldest brew pub in Portland, you could say this is the place that got the Northwest taps flowing. It's housed in the oldest industrial building in the city, a warehouse with a very medieval look. Don't miss the cask-conditioned ales or, in winter, the Old Knucklehead barleywine ale. See chapter 4.

- **McMenamins Ringlers Pub** (Portland; ☎ **503/225-0543**): Yet another McMenamins brew pub, Ringlers is a cavernous and fantastical place filled with big old signs, Indonesian antiques, mosaic pillars, and big booths. A block away are two other associated pubs, one a below-street-level joint with a beer cellar feel and the other in a flat-iron building. Together these three pubs offer the most atmospheric ale houses in town. See chapter 4.
- **Pelican Pub & Brewery** (☎ **503/965-7007**): This brew pub, which overlooks Cape Kiwanda and is right on the beach, has the best view of any brew pub in the state. It also has a good selection of ales, including Tsunami Stout and our personal favorite, the Doryman's Dark Ale. See chapter 6.
- **Power Station Pub** (Troutdale; ☎ **503/669-8610**): Housed in the former county poor farm, this pub is part of a sprawling complex that includes a B&B, a hostel, restaurants, a beer garden, a movie theater, a winery, a distillery, and a golf course. There's always a wide selection of McMenamins ales on tap. Don't miss the little shed that now serves as a tiny pub. See chapter 7.
- **Deschutes Brewery and Public House** (Bend; ☎ **541/382-9242**): Whether you drop by après-ski, après-hike, après–fly fishing, or après–mountain bike ride, this is definitely Bend's best brew pub for downing a pint or two at the end of the day. See chapter 10.
- **Terminal Gravity Brewery & Pub** (Joseph, Enterprise, and the Wallowa Mountains; ☎ **541/426-0185**): It's small and you won't get a lot of choices here, but the IPA (India Pale Ale) is excellent and won a major award in 1998. Good nightly specials accompany the beer. See chapter 11.

16 The Best Wineries

Most of the very best wineries in the state aren't open to the public or are open on only a couple of weekends a year. Since recommending these wineries would probably only frustrate budding connoisseurs, we have listed here only wineries that are open throughout the year (or most of it). All except Foris are discussed in chapter 5.

- **Chateau Bianca Winery** (North Willamette Valley Wine Country): Good (and reasonably priced) Pinot Noirs are the specialty at this winery west of Salem, but they also do an excellent dry Riesling and a good sparkling wine.
- **Cuneo Cellars** (North Willamette Valley Wine Country): Big reds, and only big reds, including Cabernet Sauvignon, Pinot Noir, and even Nebbiolo, are the focus of this small winery in the Eola Hills outside of Salem.
- **Lange Winery** (North Willamette Valley Wine Country): While this winery produces a wide range of wines (with an emphasis on Pinot Noir), the estate-grown Pinots are the real stars. The tasting room is up in the hills at the end of a gravel road.
- **Laurel Ridge Winery** (North Willamette Valley Wine Country): Known for its sparkling wines (including an unusual sparkling Riesling) and its Sauvignon Blanc, this winery is on the site of one of Oregon's first vineyards.
- **Yamhill Valley Vineyards** (North Willamette Valley Wine Country): Reasonably priced Pinot Noirs are something of a specialty here. They also produce good dry white wines, including Chardonnay, Riesling, and Pinot Blanc.
- **Bellfountain Cellars** (Corvallis): This small family-run winery is set in a warm little valley in the foothills of the Coast Range and manages to produce very good Cabernet Sauvignon and red table wines.

- **Serendipity Cellars Winery** (Corvallis): This winery has no vineyards of its own, but it produces outstanding, full-bodied red wines from grapes purchased around the state. Noteworthy are the Maréchal Foch and Zinfandel. They also produce a dry Chenin Blanc and a Maréchal Foch port.
- **Chateau Lorane** (Eugene): Producing a greater variety of wines than just about any other winery in Oregon, Chateau Lorane is sure to have something to your liking. Some of the wines here aren't made by any other wineries in the state.
- **Hinman Vineyards** (Eugene): If you enjoy sweet dessert wines, be sure to visit this winery, which does an excellent semi-sparkling Muscat. They also do good dry whites, and even Cabernet and Merlot.
- **Foris** (Oregon Caves National Monument and the Illinois Valley): If you're a fan of Cabernet Sauvignon and Merlot, you won't want to pass up an opportunity to stop by this winery between the redwoods and Grants Pass. Big bold reds are a specialty here. See chapter 9.

2 Planning a Trip to Oregon

Planning your trip before you leave can make all the difference between having a good time and wishing you'd stayed home. In fact, for many people, planning a trip is half the fun of going. If you're one of those people, this chapter should prove useful. When should I go? What is this trip going to cost me? Can I catch a festival during my visit? Where should I head to pursue my favorite sport? These are just some of the questions we'll answer for you in this chapter. You can also contact information sources listed below to find out more about Oregon and to take a look at photos (whether in brochures or on the Web) that are certain to get you excited about your upcoming trip.

1 The Regions in Brief

Both geography and climate play important roles in dividing Oregon into its various discernible regions.

The Willamette Valley   This is Oregon's most densely populated region and site of the state's largest cities, including Portland, Eugene, and the state capital of Salem. The valley's fabled farmland, which once enticed people to walk across 2,000 miles of rugged terrain, grows the greatest variety of crops of any region of the United States. These include hops, mint, grass seed, berries, hazelnuts, irises, tulips, Christmas trees, and an immense variety of landscape plants. The Willamette Valley is also one of the nation's finest wine regions, with vineyards cropping up along its entire length.

Summer, when farm stands pop up alongside rural highways, is by far the best time of year to visit the Willamette Valley. However, if you are interested in wine, you might also want to consider October, when vineyards pick and crush their grapes. Keep in mind that summer temperatures in the valley can be in the high 90s during July and August.

The Oregon Coast   Stretching for nearly 300 miles, the Oregon coast is one of the most spectacular coastlines in the country. Backed by the Coast Range mountains and alternating sandy beaches with rocky capes and headlands, this mountainous shoreline provides breathtaking vistas at almost every turn of the road. Haystack rocks—large monoliths just offshore—lend the coast an unforgettable drama and beauty. Along the central coast, huge dunes, some as much as 500 feet high, have been preserved as the Oregon Dunes National

Recreation Area. Small towns, some known as fishing ports and some as artists' communities, dot the coast. Unfortunately, waters are generally too cold for swimming, and a cool breeze often blows even in summer.

Of course, summer is the most popular time of year on the coast, and crowds can be daunting. In Seaside, Cannon Beach, Lincoln City, and Newport, traffic backups try the patience of many vacationers. The north coast, because of its proximity to Portland, is the most visited section of the coast, and it is also one of the most dramatic. The south coast is even more spectacular than the north, and because of its distance from major metropolitan areas is not nearly as crowded as other stretches of the coast. The central coast, though it boasts the Oregon Dunes National Recreation Area, is less spectacular than the north and south coasts.

Although August is the hottest month in most of Oregon, it is often a foggy time of year on the coast. Better weather, and smaller crowds, can often be had in September.

The Columbia Gorge   Beginning just east of Portland, the Columbia Gorge is one of the region's most breathtaking attractions. Declared a national scenic area to preserve its beauty, the Gorge is the site of numerous waterfalls, including Multnomah Falls, which are the fourth highest in the United States. Winds regularly blast through the Gorge and have attracted boardsailing enthusiasts to the area. The town of Hood River is now one of the world's top boardsailing spots. Rising above the Gorge on the south side is Mount Hood, the tallest peak in Oregon.

Although the Gorge can be explored in a day or two, if you are an avid hiker or boardsailor, you might want to plan a longer visit. Springtime is the best time of year to visit. From March through May countless wildflowers, some of which grow nowhere else but the Columbia Gorge, burst into bloom, and Gorge wildflower hikes are an annual rite of spring for many Oregonians.

The Cascade Range   Stretching from the Columbia River in the north to the California state line in the south, this mountain range is a natural dividing line between eastern and western Oregon. Dominated by conical peaks of volcanic origin (all currently inactive), the Cascades are almost entirely encompassed by several national forests that serve as both sources of timber and year-round recreational playgrounds. Throughout these mountains are several designated wilderness areas in which all mechanized travel is prohibited. Among these, the Mount Hood Wilderness, the Mount Jefferson Wilderness, and the Three Sisters Wilderness are the most scenic and heavily visited. In the southern Cascades, an entire mountain once blew its top, leaving behind a huge caldera that is now filled by the sapphire-blue waters of Crater Lake, Oregon's only national park.

With little private property and few lodges other than rustic (and often run-down) cabin "resorts," the Cascades are primarily a camping destination during the warmer months. The one exception is the area stretching from Sisters to Sunriver, which abounds in upscale family and golf resorts. In winter several ski areas and many miles of cross-country ski trails attract skiers and snowboarders.

Southern Oregon   Lying roughly midway between San Francisco and Portland, southern Oregon is a jumbled landscape of mountains and valleys through which flow two of the state's most famous rivers. The North Umpqua and the Rogue Rivers have been fabled among anglers ever since Zane Grey popularized these waters in his writings. A climate much drier than that of the Willamette Valley to the north gives this region the look of parts of northern California, and, in fact, several towns in the region are very popular with retired Californians. Among these are Ashland, site of the Oregon Shakespeare Festival, and Jacksonville, a historic gold-mining town that is now the site of the Britt Festivals, an annual summer festival of music and modern dance. Also in the region are quite a few wineries that take advantage of the warm climate to produce Oregon's best Cabernet Sauvignon and Merlot.

Although summer is the most popular time of year to visit this region, with the Oregon Shakespeare Festival running through much of the spring and fall, Ashland stays busy almost year-round.

Central Oregon   For Oregonians, central Oregon is a psychological relief valve. When the rains on the west side of the Cascades become too much to bear, many of the state's residents flee to this drier and sunnier part of the state. Consisting of the east side of the Cascade Range from the Columbia River to just south of Bend, the region spans the eastern foothills of the Cascades and the western edge of the Great Basin's high desert. Known primarily for its lack of rain and proximity to the cities of the Willamette Valley, central Oregon is the state's second-most-popular summer vacation destination (after the coast), with resorts clustered around Sisters and Bend. The biggest and most popular resort is Sunriver, an entire community (complete with three golf courses, a shopping center, and thousands of vacation homes and condos) south of Bend. A volcanic legacy has left the region with some of the most fascinating geology in the state, much of which is preserved in Newberry National Volcanic Monument. Also in this region is the High Desert Museum, a combination museum and zoo that is among the state's most popular attractions.

Although summer is the peak season here, with Mount Bachelor ski area providing the best skiing in the Northwest, central Oregon is also quite popular in winter.

Eastern Oregon   Large and sparsely populated, eastern Oregon is primarily high desert interspersed with small mountain ranges. Despite the desert climate, the region is also the site of several large shallow lakes that serve as magnets for a wide variety of migratory birds. In the northeast corner of the region rise the Blue and Wallowa Mountains, which are remote, though popular, recreation areas. Carving North America's deepest gorge, and partially forming the border with Idaho, are the Snake River and Hells Canyon. Throughout this region, signs of the Oregon Trail can still be seen.

Because this region is so remote from Portland and the Willamette Valley, it is little visited. However, the breathtaking Wallowa Mountains offer some of the finest backpacking in the state. The town of Joseph, on the north side of these mountains, has also recently become one of the nation's foremost centers for casting bronze sculptures.

2 Visitor Information

Contact the **Oregon Tourism Division,** 775 Summer St. NE, Salem, OR 97310 (☎ **800/547-7842** or 986-0000; www.traveloregon.com), or the **Portland Oregon Visitors Association (POVA),** Three World Trade Center, 26 SW Salmon St., Portland, OR 97204-3299 (☎ **877/678-5263** or 503/275-9750; www.pova.com).

Also keep in mind that most cities and towns in Oregon have either a tourist office or a chamber of commerce that can provide you with information. When approaching cities and towns, watch for signs along the highway directing you to these information centers. See the individual chapters for specific addresses.

CityNet (**www.city.net/countries/united_states/oregon**) keeps excellent lists of city and some regional Web sites. For Oregon regional Web sites, try the Oregon Tourism Division's Web site at **www.traveloregon.com.**

You can also get travel information covering Oregon from the American Automobile Association (AAA) if you're a member.

To get information on outdoor recreation in the national forests of Oregon, contact the **U.S. Forest Service Recreational Information Center,** 800 NE Oregon St., Room 177, Portland, OR 97232 (☎ **503/731-4444**). For information on Crater Lake, the only national park in Oregon, contact **Crater Lake National Park** (☎ **541/594-2211;** www.nps.gov/crla).

For information on camping in Oregon state parks, call the **Oregon State Park Information Center** (☎ **800/551-6949;** www.prd.state.or.us).

3 When to Go

One of your first considerations should be when to visit. Summer is the peak season in Oregon, the season for sunshine and outdoor festivals and events. During the summer months, hotel and car reservations are almost essential; the rest of the year, they're highly advisable but not nearly as imperative. If you visit in one of the rainier months between October and May, you'll find lower hotel room rates. It will also be easier to get reservations, especially on the coast. However, you will have to bring good rain gear. Whenever you go, keep in mind that you usually get better rates by reserving at least 1 or 2 weeks in advance, whether you're booking a plane, hotel, or rental car. It goes without saying that holiday weekends in the summer are the hardest times of year to get room reservations, especially on the coast. Book months in advance for Memorial Day, Fourth of July, and Labor Day weekends.

Though Oregon is famous for its gray skies and mild temperatures, the state is actually characterized by a diversity of climates almost unequaled in the United States. For the most part, moist winds off the Pacific Ocean keep temperatures west of the Cascade Range mild year-round. Summers in the Willamette Valley and southern Oregon can see temperatures over 100°F, but on the coast you're likely to need a sweater or light jacket at night, even in August. The Oregon rains that are so legendary fall primarily as a light, but almost constant, drizzle between October and early July. Sure, there are windows of sunshine during this period, but they usually last no more than a week or so. There are also, unfortunately, occasional wet summers (blame it on La Niña), so be prepared for wet weather whenever you visit. Winters usually include one or two blasts of Arctic air, usually right around Christmas or New Year's, that bring snow and freezing weather to the Portland area. Expect snow in the Cascades any time during the winter, and even some Coast Range passes can get icy.

If you visit the coast, expect grayer, wetter weather than in the Portland area. It can be quite cool here in the summer and is often foggy or rainy throughout the year. In fact, when the Willamette Valley is at its hottest in July and August, you can be sure that the coast will be fogged in. The best month for the coast is usually September, with good weather often holding on into October.

In the Cascades and eastern Oregon's Blue and Wallowa Mountains, snowfall is heavy in the winter and skiing is a popular sport. Summer doesn't come until late in the year here, with snow lingering into July at higher elevations (for instance, the Timberline Lodge area at Mount Hood and the Eagle Cap Wilderness in the Wallowas). At such elevations, late July and on through August are the best times to see the wildflowers in alpine meadows.

The region east of the Cascades is characterized by lack of rain and temperature extremes. This high desert area can be very cold in the winter, and at higher elevations it receives considerable amounts of snow. In summer, the weather can be blazingly hot at lower elevations, though nights are often cool enough to require a sweater or light jacket.

If you're planning to go wine touring, avoid January and February, when most wineries are closed. Also keep in mind that many wineries are open daily during the summer months, but on weekends only in spring and fall.

Portland's Average Monthly Temperatures & Rainfall

	Jan	Feb	Mar	Apr	May	June	July	Aug	Sept	Oct	Nov	Dec
Temp. (°F)	40	43	46	50	57	63	68	67	63	54	46	41
Temp. (°C)	4	6	8	10	14	17	20	20	17	12	8	5
Days of Rain	18	16	17	14	12	10	4	5	8	13	18	19

Oregon Calendar of Events

February

- **Portland International Film Festival,** various theaters around the city. ☎ 503/221-1156. Mid- to late February.

- ✪ **Oregon Shakespeare Festival,** Ashland. The repertory company features about a dozen plays—some by Shakespeare and others by classical and contemporary playwrights—in three unique theaters. Backstage tours, a museum, and lectures round out the festival. Call the festival box office at ☎ 541/482-4331 for details and ticket information. February to October.

- **Newport Seafood and Wine Festival,** Newport. Taste local seafood dishes and wines while shopping for art. ☎ 800/262-7844 or 541/265-8801. Last full weekend in February.

March

- **Oregon Dune Mushers' Mail Run,** Florence. An endurance dog run over the varied terrain of the Florence coastline commemorates routes that were once used before roads were constructed. ☎ 541/269-1269. First weekend in March.

- **Winter Games of Oregon,** Mt. Hood. Competitions in several winter sports events are held at Ski Bowl and Timberline ski areas, including snowboarding, skiing, and extreme skiing. ☎ 503/658-4385. First weekend in March.

- **Spring Whale Watch Week,** Lincoln City. Interpreters are on hand at whale-watching sites to help visitors spot migrating gray whales; there's also a beach cleanup. ☎ 800/452-2151. Mid- to late March.

April

- **Hood River Blossom Festival,** Hood River. Celebration of the blossoming of the orchards outside the town of Hood River. ☎ 800/366-3530. Third weekend in April.

May

- **Cinco de Mayo Festival,** downtown Portland at Waterfront Park. Hispanic celebration with food and entertainment honoring Portland's sister city, Guadalajara, Mexico. ☎ 503/222-9807. Early May.

- **Mother's Day Rhododendron Show,** Crystal Springs Rhododendron Gardens, Portland. Blooming rhodies and azaleas transform this tranquil garden into a mass of blazing color. ☎ 503/771-8386. Mother's Day.

- **Rhododendron Festival,** Florence. Viewing of native rhododendrons, a carnival, and a car show are some of the festival events. ☎ 541/997-3128. Mid-May.

- **Azalea Festival,** Brookings. Attractions include food booths, a craft fair, and of course the colorful native azaleas, which are the main reason for this festival. ☎ 800/535-9469. Memorial Day weekend.

- **Boatnik,** Grants Pass. Jet boats and hydroplanes race on the Rogue River, and there's also a parade and carnival. ☎ **800/547-5927.** Memorial Day weekend.

June

- **Cannon Beach Sand Castle Festival,** Cannon Beach. Artistic sand-sculpted creations appear along the beach. ☎ **503/436-2623.** Early June.
- **Sisters Rodeo and Parade,** Sisters. A celebration of the West in this duded-up Western town near Bend. ☎ **800/827-7522.** Second weekend of June.
- ✪ **Portland Rose Festival.** From its beginnings back in 1888, when the first rose show was held, the Rose Festival has blossomed into Portland's biggest celebration. The festivities have now spread throughout Portland and the surrounding communities and include a rose show, a floral parade, a rose-queen contest, a juried art festival, car races, a footrace, boat races, and even an air show.

  Hotel rooms can be hard to come by; plan ahead. Contact the **Portland Rose Festival Association,** 220 NW Second Ave., Portland, OR 97209 (☎ **503/227-2681**), for information on tickets to specific events. Most events take place during the first 3 weeks of June.
- ✪ **Britt Festivals,** Jacksonville. Multiarts festival that offers world-class jazz, classical, folk, country, dance, musical theater, and pop performances in a beautiful natural setting. Bring a blanket and have a picnic supper before the performance. Call ☎ **800/88-BRITT** or 541/773-6077 for details and ticket information. June to September.
- **Oregon Bach Festival,** Eugene. One of the biggest Bach festivals around serves up Bach's big oratorio works such as the B Minor Mass, but also various other concerts including chamber music and a program for kids. ☎ **800/457-1486.** Late June to early July.

July

- **Fourth of July Fireworks,** Vancouver, Washington. Vancouver, which is part of the Portland metropolitan area, hosts the biggest fireworks display west of the Mississippi. ☎ **360/693-5481.** July 4.
- **World Championship Timber Carnival,** Albany. Logging events, parade, food, and fireworks. ☎ **800/526-2256.** Fourth of July weekend.
- **Oregon Country Fair,** Eugene. Counterculture craft fair and festival for Deadheads young and old. ☎ **800/992-8499** or 541/343-4298. Second weekend in July.
- **Yachats Smelt Fry,** Yachats. Feast on smelts (small silvery fish) as you listen to live music on the Yachats Commons. ☎ **541/547-3530.** Second Saturday in July.
- **Sisters Quilt Show,** Sisters. The entire town gets decked out in colorful handmade quilts. ☎ **541/549-0251** or 541/549-6061. Second Saturday of July.
- **Concours d'Elegance Antique Car Show,** Forest Grove. People come from all around to show off their shiny vintage cars at this show, one of the top car shows on the West Coast. ☎ **503/357-2300.** Mid-July.
- **Da Vinci Days,** Corvallis. Three-day celebration of science and technology with performances, art, interactive exhibits, children's activities, food, and wine. ☎ **800/334-8118** or 541/757-6363. Mid-July.
- **Salem Arts Festival,** Salem. The largest juried art fair in Oregon, under the trees in Bush Park, with musical entertainment and food booths. ☎ **503/581-2228.** Third weekend in July.
- **Chief Joseph Days,** Joseph. Rodeo plus exhibits and demonstrations by local Native Americans. ☎ **541/432-1015.** Last full weekend in July.

- **Oregon Brewers Festival,** Waterfront Park, Portland. Microbreweries show off their suds. ☎ **503/778-5917.** Last full weekend in July.

August

- **Mount Hood Festival of Jazz,** Mount Hood Community College, Gresham. For the serious jazz fan, this is the highlight of the summer. It features the greatest names in jazz. ☎ **503/232-3000.** First full weekend of August.
- **Astoria Regatta,** Astoria. See a fleet of boats in full sail in the historic harbor. ☎ **503/325-3984.** Mid-August.
- **Oregon State Fair,** Salem. A typical agricultural state fair. ☎ **800/833-0011** in Oregon, or 503/378-3247. The 12 days before and including Labor Day.
- **Cascade Festival of Music,** Bend. Classical and popular music in a park setting. ☎ **541/382-8381.** Last weekend in August.

September

- **Mt. Angel Oktoberfest,** Mount Angel. Biergarten, Bavarian-style oompah bands, food booths. ☎ **503/845-9440.** Second weekend after Labor Day.
- **Oregon Grape Stomp Championship and Harvest Festival,** Turner (south of Salem at Willamette Valley Vineyards). Arrive early and have a chance to stomp grapes. The winners go on to the World Championships in Santa Rosa, California. Food and music too. ☎ **503/588-9463.** Mid-September.
- **Cycle Oregon.** Bicyclists get a unique opportunity to appreciate the beauty of Oregon as they cycle across the state on a route that changes annually. ☎ **800/CYCLEOR.** Mid-September.
- **Pendleton Round-Up and Happy Canyon Pageant,** Pendleton. Rodeo, Native American pageant, country-music concert. ☎ **800/457-6336** or 541/276-2553. Mid-September.
- **Bandon Cranberry Festival,** Bandon. Cranberry bog tours, arts and crafts. ☎ **541/347-9616.** Mid-September.
- **Eugene Celebration,** Eugene. Street party celebrating the diversity of the community. Festivities include the crowning of a Slug Queen. ☎ **541/681-5108.** Third weekend in September.

October

- **International Kite Festival,** Lincoln City. Kite carnival including the world's largest spinning wind sock and lighted night kite flights. ☎ **800/452-2151.** Early October.
- **Hood River Valley Harvest Fest,** Hood River. At the Hood River Expo Center, enjoy fruit products of the region, crafts, and entertainment; drive the Fruit Loop to visit farm stands and wineries. ☎ **800/366-3530.** Mid-October.

November

- **Yamhill County Wine Country Thanksgiving,** Yamhill County. About 30 miles outside of Portland, more than 2 dozen wineries open their doors for tastings of new releases and also usually provide food and live music. Thanksgiving weekend.
- **Holiday Lights and Open House at Shore Acres State Park,** Charleston. Extravagantly decorated gardens near dramatic cliffs at the Oregon coast. ☎ **541/756-5401.** Thanksgiving to early January.

December

- **Holiday Festival of Lights,** Ashland. Thousands of lights decorate the town. ☎ **541/482-3486.** Month of December.

- **The Grotto's Festival of Lights,** The Grotto, Portland. Lighting displays and one of the largest choral festivals in the Northwest. ☎ **503/254-7371.** Month of December.
- **Holiday Parade of Ships,** Willamette and Columbia Rivers. Boats decked out in holiday lights parade along the rivers after nightfall. For more information, call ☎ **503/282-0159.** Month of December.
- **Winter Whale Watch Week,** Lincoln City. Interpreters are on hand at whale-watching sites to help visitors spot migrating gray whales; there's also a beach cleanup. ☎ **800/452-2151.** Last week in December.

4 The Active Vacation Planner

The abundance of outdoor recreational activities is one of the main reasons people choose to live in and visit Oregon. With both mountains and beaches within an hour's drive of the major metropolitan areas, there are numerous choices for the active vacationer. For more in-depth coverage on outdoor activities in Oregon, check out *Frommer's Great Outdoor Guide to Washington & Oregon.* For a directory of licensed guides and outfitters operating in Oregon, get a copy of *The Oregon Outdoor Recreation Guide* from the **Oregon Guides & Packers Association,** P.O. Box 673, Springfield, OR 97477 (☎ **541/937-3192;** fax 541/937-2819; e-mail: ogpasue@msn.com).

OUTDOOR CLASSES & ORGANIZED TRIPS

In addition to the information listed below under different activity categories, there are some places to know about that offer a wide variety of classes and outings.

In the Portland area, **Portland Parks & Recreation** (☎ **503/823-5132**) offers many seasonal outdoor sports classes and trips. Guided hikes, canoe trips, and bird-watching excursions are offered throughout the year by **Metro Regional Parks and Greenspaces** (☎ **503/797-1850;** www.metro-region.org).

In the Eugene area, **Lane Community College** (☎ **541/726-2252**) offers a wide variety of outdoor skills classes and tours throughout the year and throughout the region. Everything from sea kayaking to rock climbing to canoeing to cross-country skiing is covered. Call for a current listing of classes.

Outdoors enthusiasts with Web access will want to check out **GORP's** (Great Outdoors Recreation Pages) resource listings for online information on area parks and activities from fishing to skiing to kayaking. Head for **www.gorp.com/gorp/ location/or/or.htm** to get to the Oregon hot list.

ACTIVITIES A TO Z

BIKING/MOUNTAIN BIKING The Oregon coast is one of the most popular bicycling locales in the nation, and each summer attracts thousands of dedicated pedalers. Expect to spend about a week to pedal the entire coast if you're in good shape and are traveling at a leisurely pace. During the summer months, it's best to travel from north to south along the coast because of the prevailing winds. Also keep in mind that many state parks have designated hiker/biker campsites. You can get a free Oregon coast bicycle map, as well as other bicycle maps for the state of Oregon, by calling the Oregon Department of Transportation's **Oregon Bicycle Map Hotline** (☎ **503/986-3556**).

Other regions growing in popularity with cyclists include the wine country of Yamhill County and other parts of the Willamette Valley. Portland, Salem, Corvallis, Eugene, Cottage Grove, and Central Point all have easy bicycle trails that either are in parks or connect parks. In addition, the region's national forests provide miles of

Serious Reservations

Once upon a time on a sunny Friday morning in Oregon, it was possible to simply listen to the weekend weather forecast, then decide whether you wanted to head to the beach or to the mountains for the weekend. If you think you can still pull off this sort of weekend trip, be prepared to sleep in your car. The days of spontaneous summer weekends are a thing of the past in Oregon. If you want to be assured of getting a room or a campsite at the coast or at some of the busier destinations in the mountains, you'll need to make your reservations months in advance, especially if you're going on a weekend.

To be sure that you get the state park campsite, yurt (circular domed tents with electricity, plywood floors, and beds), cabin, teepee, houseboat, or covered wagon you want, you'll need to make your reservations as much as 11 months in advance (that's the earliest you can reserve) through **Reservations Northwest** (☎ **800/452-5687** or 503/731-3411), which handles reservations at both Oregon and Washington State Parks. Reservations are accepted for dates between April 1 and September 30, with Memorial Day, the Fourth of July, and Labor Day weekends, of course, requiring the most advance planning. A $6 reservation fee is charged.

While National Forest Service campgrounds are generally less developed and less in demand than state park campgrounds, many do stay full throughout the summer months, especially those at the beach. For reservations at forest service campgrounds, call the **National Recreation Reservation Service** (☎ **800/280-CAMP** or www.reserveusa.com), which charges a $7.50 reservation fee. These sites can be reserved up to 7 months in advance.

The same sort of advance planning also applies to such accommodations as Crater Lake Lodge (Crater Lake National Park does not, however, accept camping reservations), Timberline Lodge, and just about any lodging on the coast on a summer weekend. Making rooms even more difficult to come by are the many festivals scheduled around the state throughout the summer months. When planning an itinerary, be sure to check whether your schedule might coincide with some event that just might cause all the rooms in town to fill up that particular weekend.

Good luck, and remember, it's still possible to be spontaneous, even when you made your reservation months in advance.

logging roads and single-track trails for mountain biking. Among the most popular mountain-biking areas are the east side of Mount Hood, the Oakridge area southeast of Eugene, the Ashland area, and the Bend and Sisters areas of central Oregon.

If you're interested in a guided bike tour in the state, try **Bicycle Adventures,** P.O. Box 11219, Olympia, WA 98508 (☎ **800/443-6060** or 360/786-0989; fax 360/786-9661; www.bicycleadventures.com). This company offers road-bike trips on the Oregon coast, in the Crater Lake area, in the Columbia Gorge, and in the Oregon wine country. Tour prices range from $992 to $1,984 per person.

For less expensive bike tours through less traveled regions of the state, contact **Pathfinders,** P.O. Box 210, Oakridge, OR 97463 (☎ **800/778-4838;** www.pathfinders.com), which charges around $675 for a 7-day camping bike tour. Four-day tours are around $375. Tours are offered July through September and take in such sites as Crater Lake, covered bridges, central Oregon's lakes country, and a little bit of the coast.

Although it isn't actually an organized tour, the annual **Cycle Oregon** bike ride is a weeklong sponsored ride along some of Oregon's most scenic roads. The ride, which takes place in September, follows a different route each year. The fee is currently just under $600, which includes meals, baggage transportation, and camping or home-stays. For information, contact Cycle Oregon, 8700 SW Nimbus Ave., Suite B, Beaverton, OR 97008-7119 (☎ **800/292-5367;** www.cycleoregon.com).

BIRD WATCHING   With a wide variety of habitats, Oregon offers many excellent bird-watching spots. Malheur National Wildlife Refuge, in central Oregon, is the state's premier bird-watching area and attracts more than 300 species of birds over the course of the year. Nearby Summer Lake also offers good bird watching, with migratory waterfowl and shorebirds most prevalent. There's also good bird watching on Sauvie Island, outside Portland, where waterfowl and eagles can be seen, and along the coast, where you can see tufted puffins, pigeon guillemots, and perhaps even a marbled murrelet. The Klamath Lakes region of south-central Oregon is well-known for its large population of bald eagles, which are best seen in the winter months.

Throughout the year, the National Audubon Society sponsors expeditions and field seminars. For more information, contact the **Audubon Society of Portland** (☎ **503/ 292-6855**). You can also call this number to listen to the Rare Bird Alert hot line.

BOARDSAILING (WINDSURFING)   The Columbia River Gorge is one of the most renowned windsurfing spots in the world. Here, high winds and a strong current come together to produce radical sailing conditions. As the winds whip up the waves, skilled sailors rocket across the water and launch themselves skyward to perform aerial acrobatics. On calmer days and in spots where the wind isn't blowing so hard, there are also opportunities for novices to learn the basics. Summer is the best sailing season, and the town of Hood River is the center of the boarding scene, with plenty of wind-surfing schools and rental companies. The southern Oregon coast also has some popular spots, including Floras Lake just north of Port Orford and Meyers Creek in Pistol River State Park, south of Gold Beach.

CAMPING   Public and private campgrounds abound all across Oregon, with those along the coast among the most popular. Campgrounds on lakes also stay particularly busy. During the summer months, campground reservations are almost a necessity at most state parks, especially those along the coast. For information on making camp-site reservations, see the "Serious Reservations" box in this chapter.

Various state parks also offer a variety of camping alternatives. Tops among these are yurts (circular domed tents with electricity, plywood floors, and beds), which make camping in the rain a bit easier. Yurts, which rent for $27 a night, can be found at 14 coastal parks, as well as at 5 inland state parks (Champoeg, Valley of the Rogue, Tumalo, LaPine, and Wallowa Lake).

Log cabins can be rented at Loeb, Cape Blanco, Emigrant Springs, Farewell Bend, LaPine, Prineville Reservoir, Silver Falls, The Cove Palisades, and Umpqua Lighthouse State Parks. Nightly rates range from $35 to $65. At Farewell Bend and Deschutes River State Parks, there are covered wagons for rent ($27 per night). At Unity Lake, Farewell Bend, Lake Owyhee, Tumalo, and Clyde Holliday State Parks, there are teepees for rent ($27 per night). On Lake Billy Chinook at The Cove Palisades State Park, you can rent a houseboat for $1,049 to $1,590 per week. Make reservations through Reservations Northwest.

FISHING   The fish of Oregon enjoy near-legendary status, and while there may be few streams in the region of national importance among anglers, there are still plenty of great rivers. Salmon of half a dozen species, steelhead, and sturgeon are the favored game fish among dedicated anglers. However, wild cutthroat and redside rainbow trout also have their fans. If your idea of a great fishing trip is a skillet full of frying rainbow trout, the state's many stocked streams and mountain lakes will keep you content. Scattered throughout the state are also the odd fisheries that become the obsessions of some anglers—mackinaw trout, kokanee salmon, Atlantic salmon. Even bass anglers have plenty of places to fish for both smallmouth and largemouth. Offshore fishing for salmon, tuna, and bottom fish is also popular, and up and down the coast you'll find numerous charter boat companies that will take you for a day of fishing.

The most important thing to know about fishing in Oregon is that the rules are complicated and they're always changing. It is absolutely essential that you know all the regulations for whatever body of water you happen to be fishing in. To find out what the current regulations are, you'll need to pick up a copy of *Oregon Sport Fishing Regulations*. This publication is free and is available at sporting goods stores and bait-and-tackle shops. Alternatively, you can order copies by contacting the **Oregon Department of Fish and Wildlife,** P.O. Box 59, Portland, OR 97207-0059 (☎ 503/872-5268).

GOLF   Oregon has around 200 private and public golf courses, including numerous resort courses, most of which are in the Portland and Bend-Redmond areas. There are also quite a few excellent courses along the coast.

HANG GLIDING & PARAGLIDING   Lakeview, in south-central Oregon near the California state line, is Oregon's premier hang-gliding location. Strong, steady winds and high bluffs provide perfect conditions for experienced hang gliders. Hang gliding and paragliding (using what looks like a parachute) are also popular at Cape Kiwanda on the northern Oregon coast, where a huge sand dune and steady winds create ideal conditions for learning this sport.

HIKING & BACKPACKING   Oregon has an abundance of hiking trails, including the Pacific Crest Trail, which runs along the spine of the Cascades from Canada to the California line (and onward all the way to Mexico). The state's thousands of miles of hiking trails are concentrated primarily in national forests, especially in wilderness areas, in the Cascade Range. Along the length of the Pacific Crest Trail are such scenic hiking areas as the Mount Hood Wilderness, the Mount Jefferson Wilderness, the Three Sisters Wilderness, the Diamond Peak Wilderness, the Mount Thielsen Wilderness, and the Sky Lakes Wilderness. However, many state parks also have extensive hiking-trail systems.

The Oregon Coast Trail is a designated route that runs the length of the Oregon coast. In most places it travels along the beach, but in other places it climbs up and over capes and headlands through dense forests and windswept meadows. The longest stretches of the trail are along the southern coast in Samuel H. Boardman State Park. There's also a long beach stretch in the Oregon Dunes National Recreation Area.

Other coastal parks with popular hiking trails include Saddle Mountain State Park, Ecola State Park, Oswald West State Park, and Cape Lookout State Park. Silver Falls State Park, east of Salem, is also a popular hiking spot. The many trails of the Columbia Gorge National Scenic Area are also well trodden, with Eagle Creek Trail being a longtime favorite. For a quick hiking fix, Portlanders often head for the city's Forest Park. The trails leading out from Timberline Lodge on Mount Hood lead through forests and meadows at the tree line and are particularly busy on summer weekends.

If you'd like to do your hiking with a guide, contact Joe Whittington at **Oregon Peak Adventures,** P.O. Box 25576, Portland, OR 97298 (☎ 503/297-5100; www.oregonpeakadventures.com). Whittington leads hikes in the Columbia Gorge and on Mount St. Helens, as well as climbs to the summits of Mount St. Helens and

Before heading out to a national forest anywhere in Oregon, be sure to find out if you need a Trail Park Permit. Most trailhead parking areas in the state now require such a permit, and though they can be purchased from machines at the most popular trailheads, it's better to have one before heading out. They're available at national-forest ranger stations throughout the state and also at many outdoors supply stores, such as REI. Day passes cost $3 and annual passes are $25. In some cases such passes are required not just for trailheads but for other national-forest recreational areas as well.

Mount Adams. Prices start at around $65 per person. Nonhiking tours are also available.

KAYAKING & CANOEING   While Puget Sound, up in Washington, is the **sea kayaking** capital of the Northwest, Oregonians are also taking to this sport. However, sea kayaks in Oregon very rarely make it to the sea, where waters are usually far too rough for kayaks. There are, however, numerous protected bays along the Oregon coast that are popular paddling spots. Also, the Lewis & Clark National Wildlife Refuge on the Columbia River not far from Astoria offers miles of quiet waterways to explore.

White-water kayaking is popular on many of the rivers that flow down out of the Cascade Range in Oregon, including the Deschutes, the Clackamas, the Mollala, and the Sandy. Down in southern Oregon, the North Umpqua and the Rogue provide plenty of white-water action.

Sundance Expeditions (☎ 541/479-8508; www.sundance-kayak.com), which is located near Grants Pass, is one of the premier kayaking schools in the country. They offer a 7- or 9-day beginner's program that does a multiday trip down the wild-and-scenic section of the Rogue River after several days of initial instruction. Also in southern Oregon, you'll find the **Siskiyou Kayak School,** 4541 W. Griffin Creek Rd., Medford, OR 97501 (☎ **888/59KAYAK** or 541/772-9743; www.siskiyou-kayak.com), which offers various classes lasting from 1 to 5 days. Prices range from $85 to $575.

Canoeing is popular on many of Oregon's lakes. Some of the best are Hosmer and Sparks Lakes west of Bend, Clear Lake south of Santiam Pass, Waldo Lake near Willamette Pass southeast of Eugene, and Upper Klamath Lake (where there's a canoe trail).

MOUNTAINEERING   Mount Hood and several other Cascades peaks offer challenging mountain climbing and rock climbing for both the novice and the expert. If you're interested in learning some mountain-climbing skills or want to hone your existing skills, contact **Timberline Mountain Guides,** P.O. Box 340, Government Camp, OR 97028 (☎ **800/464-7704;** fax 503/272-3677; e-mail: climbing@ transport.com), a company that offers snow-, ice-, and rock-climbing courses. They also lead summit climbs on Mount Hood. A 2-day Mount Hood mountaineering course with summit climb costs $325.

ROCK CLIMBING   Smith Rocks State Park, near Redmond in central Oregon, is a rock-climbing mecca of international renown, and many climbers claim that sport climbing got its American start here. Smith Rock abounds in climbing routes, some of which are among the toughest in the world. If you're a serious climber, pick up a copy of Alan Watts's *Climber's Guide to Smith Rock* (Chockstone Press, 1992), an exhaustive guide to the many climbing routes here.

Educational & Volunteer Vacations

The **Nature Conservancy** is a nonprofit organization dedicated to the global preservation of natural diversity, and to this end it operates educational field trips to, and work parties at, its own nature preserves and those of other agencies. For information about field trips in Oregon, contact the Nature Conservancy, 821 SE 14th Ave., Portland, OR 97214 (☎ **503/230-1221;** www.tnc.org).

If you enjoy the wilderness and want to get more involved in its preservation, consider a **Sierra Club Service Trip.** These trips are for the purpose of building, restoring, and maintaining hiking trails in wilderness areas. It's a lot of work, but it's also a lot of fun. For more information on Service Trips, contact the **Sierra Club Outing Department,** 85 Second St., Second Floor, San Francisco, CA 94105 (☎ **415/977-5630**), or call the local chapters of the Sierra Club. In Oregon, the Portland Chapter is at ☎ **503/238-0442.**

Earth Watch, P.O. Box 9104, Watertown, MA 02172 (☎ **800/776-0188** or 617/926-8200; www.earthwatch.org), sends volunteers on scientific research projects. Contact them for a catalog listing trips and costs. Projects have included studies of orca whales, chimpanzee communication, and Oregon wildflowers.

The **Northwest School of Survival,** 39065 Pioneer Blvd., Sandy, OR 97055 (☎ **888/668-8264** or 503/668-8264; www.nwsos.com), can teach you everything from how to start a fire with a stick to how to build a snow cave to how to evaluate an avalanche hazard.

SCUBA DIVING   Although Oregon has hundreds of miles of coastline, scuba diving is not as popular a sport as it would at first seem. This is because there are very few places along the coast where shore dives are possible. Consequently, most Oregon divers head offshore to rocky reefs to do their diving, and this entails chartering a boat. Popular destinations include Tacklebuster Reef off Depoe Bay and North Pinnacle and Arch Rock off Newport.

If conditions are just right, there are a few shore dive spots along the coast. Try the jetties at the mouth of Yaquina Bay in Newport, at Sunset Bay State Park outside Coos Bay, and in Port Orford Harbor. It's a good idea to have an advanced open water or rescue diver certification in these often rough waters. You'll find dive shops in several towns along the Oregon coast.

SKIING   Because the winter weather in Oregon is so unpredictable, the state is not known as a ski destination. Most of the state's ski areas are relatively small and cater primarily to local skiers. Mount Bachelor, in central Oregon outside of Bend, is the one exception. Because of its high elevation and location on the drier east side of the Cascades, it gets a more reliable snowpack and isn't as susceptible to midwinter warming spells, which tend to bring rain to west-side ski slopes with irritating regularity.

Ski areas in Oregon include Mount Hood Meadows, Mount Hood Ski Bowl, Timberline Ski Area, Cooper Spur Ski Area, and Summit Ski Area, all of which are on Mount Hood outside Portland. Farther south, there are Hoodoo Ski Bowl (east of Salem), Willamette Pass (east of Eugene), and Mount Bachelor (outside Bend). In the eastern part of the state, Anthony Lakes and Spout Springs provide a bit of powder skiing. Down in the south, Ski Ashland is the only option. There's also snow-cat skiing north of Crater Lake on Mount Bailey.

Many downhill ski areas also offer groomed **cross-country ski trails.** Cross-country skiers will find an abundance of trails up and down the Cascades. Teacup

Lake, Trillium Basin, and Mount Hood Meadows, all on Mount Hood, offer good groomed trails. Near Mount Bachelor, there are also plenty of groomed trails. Crater Lake is another popular spot for cross-country skiing. Backcountry skiing is also popular in the Wallowa Mountains in eastern Oregon.

WHALE WATCHING   Gray whales, which can reach 45 feet in length and weigh up to 35 tons, migrate annually between Alaska and Baja California, and pass close by the Oregon coast between December and May. However, with more and more whales stopping to spend the summer off the Oregon coast, it is now possible to see these behemoths of the deep just about any month of the year.

Depoe Bay, north of Newport, is not only the smallest harbor in the world, but also a home port for several whale-watching boats that head out throughout the year to look for gray whales. It's also possible to whale watch from shore, with Cape Meares, Cape Lookout, Cape Kiwanda, Devil's Punchbowl, Cape Perpetua, Sea Lion Caves, Shore Acres State Park, Face Rock Wayside (in Bandon), Cape Blanco, Cape Sebastian, and Harris Beach State Park being some of the better places from which to watch.

WHITE-WATER RAFTING   Plenty of rain and snowmelt and lots of mountains combine to produce dozens of good white-water rafting rivers in Oregon, depending on the time of year and water levels. Central Oregon's Deschutes River and southern Oregon's Rogue River are the two most popular rafting rivers. Other popular rafting rivers include the Clackamas outside Portland, the McKenzie outside Eugene, and the North Umpqua outside Roseburg. Out in the southeastern corner, the remote Owyhee River provides adventurers with still more white water. See the respective chapters for information on rafting companies operating on these rivers.

5 Tips for Travelers with Special Needs
FOR TRAVELERS WITH DISABILITIES

When making airline reservations, always mention your disability. Airline policies differ regarding wheelchairs and Seeing Eye dogs. Almost all hotels and motels in Oregon, aside from bed-and-breakfast inns and older or historic lodges, offer accommodations accessible for travelers with disabilities. However, when making reservations, be sure to ask. Oregon lodgings that are accessible are listed in the *Oregon Traveler's Guide to Accommodations.* To get a copy of this magazine, contact the **Oregon Tourism Division,** 775 Summer St. NE, Salem, OR 97310 (☎ **800/ 547-7842**).

The public transit systems found in most Oregon cities either have regular vehicles that are accessible for riders with disabilities or offer special transportation services for people with disabilities.

Oregon State Parks has a TDD (Telephone Device for the Deaf) information line (☎ **800/858-9659**) that provides recreation and camping information.

If you plan to visit any national parks or monuments, you can avail yourself of the **Golden Access Passport.** This lifetime pass is issued free to any U.S. citizen or permanent resident who has been medically certified as disabled or blind. The pass permits free entry into national parks and monuments.

A World of Options, a 658-page book of resources for disabled travelers, covers everything from biking trips to scuba outfitters. It costs $35 ($30 for members) and is available from **Mobility International USA,** P.O. Box 10767, Eugene, OR 97440 (☎ **541/343-1284,** voice and TDD; www.miusa.org). Annual membership for Mobility International is $35, which includes their quarterly newsletter, *Over the Rainbow.*

Many of the major **car-rental** companies now offer hand-controlled cars for drivers with disabilities. Avis can provide such a vehicle at any of its locations in the United States with 48-hour advance notice; Hertz requires between 24 and 72 hours of advance reservation at most of its locations. **Wheelchair Getaways** (in the Pacific Northwest ☎ **888/376-1500** or 425/788-3718; national reservation hot line 800/642-2042; www.wheelchair-getaways.com) rents specialized vans with wheelchair lifts and other features for travelers with disabilities in more than 100 cities across the United States. Wheelchair Getaways is located near Seattle in the suburb of Woodinville.

In addition, both **Amtrak** (☎ **800/USA-RAIL;** www.amtrak.com) and **Greyhound** (☎ **800/752-4841;** www.greyhound.com) offer special fares and services for the disabled. Call at least a week in advance of your trip for details.

Travelers with disabilities may also want to consider joining a tour that caters specifically to them. Reputable specialized tour operators include **The Guided Tour, Inc.** (☎ **215/782-1370**) and **Wilderness Inquiry** (☎ **800/728-0719** or 612/379-3858), which offers sports-related vacations.

FOR GAY & LESBIAN TRAVELERS

Gay and lesbian travelers visiting Portland should be sure to pick up a free copy of *Just Out* (☎ **503/236-1252;** www.justout.com), a bimonthly newspaper for the gay community. You can usually find copies at **Powell's Books,** 1005 W. Burnside St. The newspaper covers local and national news of interest to gays. *Just Out* also publishes the *Just Out Pocketbook,* a statewide gay & lesbian business directory. Another publication to look for once you're in Portland is *Portland's Gay & Lesbian Community Yellow Pages* (☎ **503/230-7701;** www.pdxgayyellowpages.com), which is also usually available at Powell's.

FOR SENIORS

Don't be shy about asking for discounts, but always carry some kind of identification, such as a driver's license, that shows your date of birth. Mention the fact that you're a senior citizen when you first make your travel reservations, since many airlines offer discounts. Both **Amtrak** (☎ **800/USA-RAIL;** www.amtrak.com) and **Greyhound** (☎ **800/752-4841;** www.greyhound.com) offer discounts to persons over 62.

And many hotels offer seniors discounts; **Choice Hotels** (Clarion Hotels, Quality Inns, Comfort Inns, Sleep Inns, Econo Lodges, Friendship Inns, and Rodeway Inns), for example, give 30% off their published rates to anyone over 50, provided you book your room through their nationwide toll-free reservation numbers (that is, not directly with the hotels or through a travel agent). Many attractions, some theaters and concert halls, and tour companies sometimes offer senior-citizen discounts. These can add up to substantial savings, but you have to remember to ask for the discount.

Save on National Park and Monument admissions by getting a **Golden Age Passport,** which is available for $10 to U.S. citizens and permanent residents age 62 and older. This federal government pass allows lifetime entrance privileges. You can apply in person for this passport at a national park, a national forest, or any other location where it's honored, and you must show reasonable proof of age.

If you aren't already a member of the **American Association of Retired Persons (AARP),** 601 E. St. NW, Washington, DC 20049 (☎ **800/424-3410** or 202/434-2277), you should consider joining. This association provides discounts for many lodgings, car rentals, airfares, and attractions, although you can sometimes get a similar discount simply by showing your ID.

Older travelers who want to learn something from their trip to Oregon or who simply prefer the company of like-minded older travelers should look into programs by **Elderhostel,** 75 Federal St., Boston, MA 02110-1941 (☎ **877/426-8056;** www.elderhostel.org). To participate in an Elderhostel program, either you or your spouse must be 55 years old or older. In addition to 1-week educational programs, Elderhostel offers short getaways with interesting themes.

6 Getting There

BY PLANE

Almost 20 carriers service Portland International Airport from some 100 cities worldwide. The major airlines include **Air Canada** (☎ 800/776-3000; www.aircanada.com), **Alaska Airlines** (☎ 800/426-0333: www.alaskaair.com), **America West** (☎ 800/235-9292; www.americawest.com), **American Airlines** (☎ 800/433-7300; www.aa.com), **Continental** (☎ 800/525-0280, www.flycontinental.com), **Delta** (☎ 800/221-1212; www.delta-air.com), **Frontier** (☎ 800/432-1359, www.frontierairlines.com), **Hawaiian** (☎ 800/367-5320; www.hawaiianair.com), **Horizon Air** (☎ 800/547-9308; www.horizonair.com), **Northwest/KLM** (☎ 800/225-2525; www.nwa.com), **Southwest** (☎ 800/435-9792; www.southwest.com), **TWA** (☎ 800/221-2000; www.twa.com), and **United Airlines** (☎ 800/241-6522; www.ual.com).

For information on flights to the U.S. from other countries, see chapter 3.

FLY FOR LESS: TIPS FOR GETTING THE BEST AIRFARES

If you're flying to Portland from another city in the Western U.S., check with Frontier Airlines, Shuttle by United, Alaska Airlines, Horizon Airlines, or Southwest. Periodically, airlines lower prices on their most popular routes. Check your newspaper for advertised discounts or call the airlines directly and ask if any **promotional rates** or special fares are available. You'll almost never see a sale during the peak summer vacation months of July and August, or during the Thanksgiving or Christmas seasons; but in periods of low-volume travel, you should pay no more than $400 for a cross-country flight. If your schedule is flexible, ask if you can secure a cheaper fare by staying an extra day or by flying midweek. (Many airlines won't volunteer this information.) If you already hold a ticket when a sale breaks, it may even pay to exchange your ticket, which usually incurs a $50 to $75 charge.

Note, however, that the lowest-priced fares are often nonrefundable, require 1 to 3 weeks' advance purchase and a certain length of stay, and carry penalties for changing dates of travel.

Consolidators, also known as bucket shops, are a good place to find low fares. Consolidators buy seats in bulk from the airlines and then sell them back to the public at prices below even the airlines' discounted rates. Their small ads usually run in the Sunday travel section. Before you pay, however, ask for a confirmation number from the consolidator and then call the airline itself to confirm your seat. Be prepared to book your ticket with a different consolidator (there are many to choose from) if the airline can't confirm your reservation. Also be aware that bucket-shop tickets usually are nonrefundable or come with stiff cancellation penalties, often as high as 50% to 75% of the ticket price.

Council Travel (☎ **800/226-8624;** www.counciltravel.com) and **STA Travel** (☎ **800/781-4040;** www.sta.travel.com) cater especially to young travelers, but their bargain-basement prices are available to people of all ages. **Travel Bargains**

(☎ **800/AIR-FARE;** www.1800airfare.com) was formerly owned by TWA but now offers the deepest discounts on many other airlines, with a 4-day advance purchase. Other reliable consolidators include **1-800-FLY-CHEAP** (www.1800flycheap.com); **TFI Tours International** (☎ **800-745-8000** or 212/736-1140), which serves as a clearinghouse for unused seats; and "rebators" such as **Travel Avenue** (☎ **800/ 333-3335** or 312/876-1116) and the **Smart Traveller** (☎ **800/448-3338** in the U.S. or 305/448-3338), which rebate part of their commissions to you.

BY CAR

The distance to Portland from Seattle is 175 miles; from Spokane, 350 miles; from Vancouver, B.C., 285 miles; from San Francisco, 640 miles; and from Los Angeles, 1,015 miles.

If you're driving up from California, I-5 runs up through the length of the state and continues up toward the Canadian border; it will take you through both Portland and Seattle. If you're coming from the east, I-84 runs from Idaho and points east into Oregon, eventually ending in Portland.

One of the most important benefits of belonging to the **American Automobile Association** (☎ **800/222-4357**) is that they supply members with emergency road service. In Portland, AAA is located at 600 SW Market St. (☎ **503/222-6734**).

BY TRAIN

Amtrak (☎ **800/872-7245**) passenger trains connect Portland with Seattle, San Francisco, Salt Lake City, Chicago, and the rest of the country. A north-to-south Amtrak route runs between Vancouver, British Columbia and Eugene, Oregon. Both regular trains and modern European-style Talgo trains run between Seattle and Portland. The latter make the trip in 3½ hours versus 4 hours and 10 minutes for the regular train. One-way fares on either type of train run $42 to $66, and reservations are required.

7 Getting Around

BY CAR

A car is by far the best way to see Oregon. There just isn't any other way to get to the more remote natural spectacles or to fully appreciate such regions as the Oregon coast or eastern Oregon.

Portland has dozens of car-rental agencies, including branches at Portland International Airport. Prices at rental agencies elsewhere in the state tend to be higher, so if at all possible, try to rent your car in a large city such as Portland or Eugene.

You'll find the following companies at Portland International Airport: **Avis** (☎ 800/831-2847 or 503/249-6500); **Budget** (☎ 800/527-0700 or 503/249-6500); **Dollar** (☎ 800/800-4000 or 503/249-4792); **Hertz** (☎ 800/654-3131 or 503/ 249-8216); and **National** (☎ 800/227-7368 or 503/249-4900). Outside the airport, but with desks adjacent to the other car-rental desks, are **Alamo** (☎ 800/327-9633 or 503/252-7039); **Enterprise** (☎ 800/736-8227 or 503/252-1500); and **Thrifty** (☎ 800/367-2277 or 503/254-6563).

For the very best deal on a rental car, make your reservation at least a week in advance. It also pays to shop around and call the same companies a few times over the course of a couple of weeks. If you decide on the spur of the moment to rent a car, check to see whether any weekend or special rates are available. If you're a member of a frequent-flyer program, be sure to mention it; you might get mileage credit for renting a car. Keep asking about special promotions and try different combinations of where to pick up and drop off your car—car-rental agencies, like airlines, don't tell you

Driving a Bargain in Oregon

If there's any way you can arrange to pick up your car somewhere other than the Portland airport, you can save the 10% airport concession fee. If you can pick up your car in Beaverton or Hillsboro (western suburbs of Portland), you can also avoid the 10% Multnomah county tax that applies at the airport and at downtown Portland car-rental offices.

about the cheapest deals unless you ask, and they have a maze of different offerings and rates.

RENTER'S INSURANCE   Before you drive off in a rental car, be sure you're insured. If you already hold a **private auto insurance** policy, you are most likely covered in the United States for loss of or damage to a rental car, and liability in case of injury to any other party involved in an accident. Be sure to find out the details of your policy for the type of vehicle you are renting and the area you are visiting.

Most **major credit cards** provide some degree of coverage as well—provided they were used to pay for the rental. Terms vary widely, however, so be sure to call your credit-card company directly before you rent. Credit cards *will not cover liability,* or the cost of injury to an outside party and/or damage to an outside party's vehicle. If you do not hold an insurance policy, you may seriously want to consider purchasing additional liability insurance from your rental company.

The basic insurance coverage offered by most car-rental companies, known as the **Loss/Damage Waiver (LDW)** or **Collision Damage Waiver (CDW),** can cost as much as $20 a day. It usually covers the full value of the vehicle with no deductible if an outside party causes an accident or other damage to the rental car.

GASOLINE   Oregon is a big state, so keep your gas tank as full as possible when traveling in the mountains or on the sparsely populated east side of the Cascades. There are no self-service gas stations in the state.

MAPS   Maps are available at most highway tourist information centers, at the tourist information offices listed earlier in this chapter and throughout this book, and at gas stations throughout the region. For a map of Oregon, contact the **Oregon Tourism Division** (☎ **800/547-7842**). Members of AAA can get detailed road maps of Oregon by calling their local AAA office.

DRIVING RULES   You may turn right on a red light after a full stop, and if you are in the far-left lane of a one-way street, you may turn left into the adjacent left lane of a one-way street at a red light after a full stop. Everyone in a moving vehicle is required to wear a seat belt.

BREAKDOWNS/ASSISTANCE   In the event of a breakdown, stay with your car, lift the hood, turn on your emergency flashers, and wait for a police patrol car. *Do not leave your vehicle.* If you're a member of the American Automobile Association and your car breaks down, call ☎ **800/AAA-HELP** for 24-hour emergency road service.

DRIVING TIMES   It takes about 1½ hours to drive from Portland to Canon Beach on the Oregon coast; from Portland to Mt. Hood, about 1 hour; and from Portland to Bend, about 3 hours. Portland to Seattle is about a 3½-hour trip, depending on traffic conditions.

BY PLANE

Although there are airports with regular commercial service in Redmond, Eugene, and Medford, flying isn't usually a very appropriate way to get around Oregon. However,

Cruising the Columbia River

Paddle-wheel steamboats played a crucial role in the settling of Oregon, shuttling people and goods down the Columbia River before railroads came to the region. Today, the *Queen of the West,* a paddle-wheel cruise ship operated by the **American West Steamboat Company,** 601 Union St., Suite 4343, Seattle, WA 98101 (☎ **800/434-1232**), is cruising the Columbia offering a luxury never before known in Columbia River paddle wheelers. Fares for the 7-night cruise range from $1,075 to $4,200 per person. Shorter cruises are also available.

If you'd rather cruise aboard a smaller vessel, consider a trip with **Alaska Sightseeing Cruise West,** Fourth and Battery Building, Suite 700, Seattle (☎ **800/426-7702** or 206/441-8687), which offers an 8-day cruise from Portland on the Columbia and Snake Rivers. Fares range from $1,625 to $3,135 per person. Similar trips, though with naturalists and historians on board, are offered by **Special Expeditions** (☎ **800/762-0003** or 212/765-7740) at similar rates.

if you are heading to the central or southern Oregon coast, you might want to consider flying into either the Eugene or the Medford Airport. If you are headed to Bend or Sunriver, flying into Redmond might work for you. If you are headed to Ashland for some Shakespeare, you could consider the Medford airport.

BY RECREATIONAL VEHICLE (RV)

An economical way to tour Oregon is with a recreational vehicle. If you're considering renting an RV, look under "Recreational Vehicles—Rent and Lease" in the yellow pages of your local phone book. They can be rented for a weekend, a week, or longer. In Portland, you might try **Cruise America,** 2032 NW 23rd Ave. (☎ **800/327-7799** or 503/775-0538). If you're going to be traveling in the peak season of summer, it's important to make reservations for your RV at least 3 months ahead of time. The rest of the year, a couple of weeks' lead time is usually sufficient.

8 Tips on Accommodations

It's always a good idea to make hotel reservations as soon as you know your trip dates. Reservations usually require a deposit of one night's payment. Portland and the Oregon coast are particularly busy during summer months, and hotels book up in advance—especially on holiday and festival weekends. If you do not have reservations, it is best to look for a room in the midafternoon because hotels may be filled by evening. Major downtown hotels, which cater primarily to business travelers, commonly offer weekend discounts of as much as 50% to entice vacationers to fill up the empty rooms. However, resorts and hotels near tourist attractions tend to have higher rates on weekends.

For information on B&Bs in Oregon, contact the **Oregon Bed and Breakfast Guild,** P.O. Box 3187, Ashland, OR 97520 (☎ **800/944-6196;** www.obbg.org). For B&B reservations, call **Northwest Bed and Breakfast Reservation Service,** 3559 SW Valley View Dr., Redmond, OR 97756 (☎ **503/243-7616** or 541/548-2646; fax 541/548-2646; e-mail: nwbb@teleport.com). This service represents more than 400 homes throughout Oregon, Washington, British Columbia, and Northern California. All homes have been inspected. Rates range from $60 to $100 or more for doubles.

Fast Facts: Oregon

AAA   If you're a member of the American Automobile Association and your car breaks down, call ☎ **800/AAA-HELP** for 24-hour emergency road service.

American Express   In Portland, their office is at 1100 SW Sixth Ave. (☎ **503/226-2961**). Call the Portland office for information on American Express services in other outlying towns. To report lost or stolen traveler's checks, call ☎ **800/221-7282.**

ATM Networks   Automatic teller machines (ATMs) (with Star, Cirrus, Plus, Accel, and the Exchange networks widely available) are nearly ubiquitous throughout Oregon, so you can get cash as you travel; however, some small-town banks still do not have ATMs.

Car Rentals   See "Getting Around," earlier in this chapter.

Climate   See "When to Go," earlier in this chapter.

Driving Rules   See "Getting Around," earlier in this chapter.

Drugstores   United Drugs and Walgreens (☎ **800/WALGREENS** for locations) are two large pharmacy chains found in the Northwest.

Embassies and Consulates   See chapter 3.

Emergencies   Call ☎ **911** for fire, police, and ambulance.

Information   See "Visitor Information," earlier in this chapter.

Liquor Laws   The legal minimum drinking age in Oregon is 21. Bars can legally stay open until 2am. Beer and wine can often be purchased in supermarkets, but liquor can be purchased only in state-licensed liquor stores, of which there are very few.

Maps   See "Getting Around," earlier in this chapter.

Pets   Some hotels and motels in Oregon accept small well-behaved pets. However, a small fee often is charged to allow them into guest rooms. Many places, in particular bed-and-breakfast inns, don't allow pets at all. (Policies can change frequently, so always be sure to confirm.) On the other hand, many bed-and-breakfasts have their own pets, so if you have a dog or cat allergy, be sure to mention it when making a B&B reservation. Pets are usually restricted in national parks for their own safety, so call each park's ranger station to check before setting out.

Police   To reach the police, dial ☎ **911.**

Smoking   Many restaurants in Oregon are no-smoking establishments.

Taxes   Oregon is a shopper's paradise—there's no sales tax.

Time Zone   With the exception of far-eastern Oregon near Ontario, the state is on Pacific standard time (PST) and observes daylight saving time from the first Sunday in April to the last Sunday in October, making it consistently 3 hours behind the East Coast.

3 For Foreign Visitors

Although American trends have spread across Europe and other parts of the world to the extent that America may seem like familiar territory before your arrival, there are still many peculiarities and uniquely American situations that any foreign visitor will encounter.

1 Preparing for Your Trip

ENTRY REQUIREMENTS

Immigration laws are a hot political issue in the United States these days, and the following requirements may have changed somewhat by the time you plan your trip. Check at any U.S. embassy or consulate for current information and requirements. You can also plug into the **U.S. State Department's** Internet site at **www.state.gov.**

VISAS The U.S. State Department has a **Visa Waiver Pilot Program** allowing citizens of certain countries to enter the United States without a visa for stays of up to 90 days. At press time these included Andorra, Argentina, Australia, Austria, Belgium, Brunei, Denmark, Finland, France, Germany, Iceland, Ireland, Italy, Japan, Liechtenstein, Luxembourg, Monaco, the Netherlands, New Zealand, Norway, San Marino, Slovenia, Spain, Sweden, Switzerland, and the United Kingdom. Citizens of these countries need only a valid passport and a round-trip air or cruise ticket in their possession upon arrival. If they first enter the United States, they may also visit Mexico, Canada, Bermuda, and/or the Caribbean islands and return to the United States without a visa. Further information is available from any U.S. embassy or consulate. Canadian citizens may enter the United States without visas; they need only proof of residence.

Citizens of all other countries must have (1) a valid passport that expires at least 6 months later than the scheduled end of their visit to the United States, and (2) a tourist visa, which may be obtained without charge from any U.S. consulate. To obtain a visa, you must submit a completed application form (either in person or by mail) with a 1½-inch-square photo, and must demonstrate binding ties to a residence abroad. Usually you can obtain a visa at once or within 24 hours, but it may take longer during the summer rush from June through August. If you cannot go in person, contact the nearest U.S. embassy or consulate for directions on applying by mail. Your travel agent or airline office may also be able to provide you with visa applications and instructions. The U.S. consulate or embassy that issues your visa will determine whether you will be issued a multiple- or single-entry visa and any restrictions regarding the length of your stay.

British subjects can obtain up-to-date passport and visa information by calling the **U.S. Embassy Visa Information Line** (☎ **0891/200-290**) or the **London Passport Office** (☎ **0990/210-410** for recorded information).

MEDICAL REQUIREMENTS   Unless you're arriving from an area known to be suffering from an epidemic (particularly cholera or yellow fever), inoculations or vaccinations are not required for entry into the United States. If you have a disease that requires treatment with narcotics or syringe-administered medications, carry a valid signed prescription from your physician to allay any suspicions that you may be smuggling narcotics (a serious offense that carries severe penalties in the U.S.).

For HIV-positive visitors, requirements for entering the United States are somewhat vague and change frequently. For up-to-the-minute information concerning HIV-positive travelers, contact the Centers for Disease Control's **National Center for HIV** (☎ 404/332-4559; www.hivatis.org) or the **Gay Men's Health Crisis** (☎ **212/367-1000**; www.gmhc.org).

DRIVER'S LICENSES   Foreign driver's licenses are mostly recognized in the U.S., although you may want to get an international driver's license if your home license is not written in English.

CUSTOMS REQUIREMENTS   Every visitor over 21 years of age may bring in, free of duty, the following: (1) 1 liter of wine or hard liquor; (2) 200 cigarettes, 100 cigars (but not from Cuba), or 3 pounds of smoking tobacco; and (3) $100 worth of gifts. These exemptions are offered to travelers who spend at least 72 hours in the United States and who have not claimed them within the preceding 6 months. It is altogether forbidden to bring into the country foodstuffs (particularly fruit, cooked meats, and canned goods) and plants (vegetables, seeds, tropical plants, and the like). Foreign tourists may bring in or take out up to $10,000 in U.S. or foreign currency with no formalities; larger sums must be declared to U.S. Customs on entering or leaving, which includes filing form CM 4790. For more specific information regarding U.S. Customs, contact your nearest U.S. embassy or consulate, or the **U.S. Customs** office at ☎ **202/927-1770** or www.customs.ustreas.gov.

INSURANCE

Although it's not required of travelers, health insurance is highly recommended. Unlike many European countries, the United States does not usually offer free or low-cost medical care to its citizens or visitors. Doctors and hospitals are expensive, and, in most cases, they will require advance payment or proof of coverage before rendering their services. Policies can cover everything from the loss or theft of your baggage and trip cancellation to the guarantee of bail in case you're arrested. Good policies will also cover the costs of an accident, repatriation, or death. Packages such as **Europ Assistance** in Europe are sold by automobile clubs and travel agencies at attractive rates. **Worldwide Assistance Services,** Inc. (☎ **800/821-2828**), is the agent for Europ Assistance in the United States. For more information on rental car insurance, see "Getting Around" in chapter 2.

Though lack of health insurance may prevent you from being admitted to a hospital in nonemergencies, don't worry about being left on a street corner to die: the American way is to fix you now and bill the living daylights out of you later.

MONEY

CURRENCY   The U.S. monetary system has a decimal base: one American **dollar** ($1) = 100 **cents** (100¢).

Dollar bills commonly come in $1 (a "buck"), $5, $10, $20, $50, and $100 denominations (the last two are not welcome when paying for small purchases and are not accepted in taxis). There are also $2 bills (seldom encountered). Note that a newly redesigned $100 and $50 bill were introduced in 1996, and a redesigned $20 bill in 1998. Expect to see redesigned $10 and $5 notes in the year 2000. Despite rumors to the contrary, the old-style bills are still legal tender.

There are six denominations of coins: 1¢ (1 cent, or a "penny"), 5¢ (5 cents, or a "nickel"), 10¢ (10 cents, or a "dime"), 25¢ (25 cents, or a "quarter"), 50¢ (50 cents, or a "half dollar"), and, prized by collectors, the rare $1 piece (the older, large silver dollar and the newer, small Susan B. Anthony coin). A new gold $1 piece will be introduced by the year 2000. Note that U.S. coins are not stamped with their numeric value.

The foreign-exchange bureaus so common in Europe are rare even at airports in the United States, and nonexistent outside major cities. Try to avoid having to change foreign money or traveler's checks not denominated in U.S. dollars at a small-town bank, or even a branch bank in a big city. In fact, leave any currency other than U.S. dollars at home—it may prove more nuisance to you than it's worth.

TRAVELER'S CHECKS   Traveler's checks *denominated in U.S. dollars* are readily accepted at most hotels, motels, restaurants, and large stores but may not be accepted at small stores or for small purchases. The best place to change traveler's checks is at a bank. Do not bring traveler's checks denominated in other currencies. The three traveler's checks that are most widely recognized are **Visa, American Express,** and **Thomas Cook.**

CREDIT CARDS & ATMS   Credit cards are the most widely used form of payment in the United States: **Visa** (BarclayCard in Britain), **MasterCard** (EuroCard in Europe, Access in Britain, Chargex in Canada), **American Express, Diners Club, Discover,** and **Carte Blanche.** You must have a credit or charge card to rent a car. There are, however, a handful of stores and restaurants that do not take credit cards, so be sure to ask in advance. Most businesses display a sticker near their entrance to let you know which cards they accept. (*Note:* Often businesses require a minimum purchase price, usually around $10, to use a credit card.)

It is strongly recommended that you bring at least one major credit card. Hotels, car-rental companies, and airlines usually require a credit-card imprint as a deposit against expenses, and in an emergency a credit card can be priceless.

You'll find automated teller machines (ATMs) on just about every block—at least in almost every town—across the country. Some ATMs will allow you to draw U.S. currency against your bank and credit cards. Check with your bank before leaving home, and remember that you will need your personal identification number (PIN) to do so. Most accept Visa, MasterCard, and American Express, as well as ATM cards from other U.S. banks. Expect to be charged up to $3 per transaction, however. One way around these fees is to ask for cash back at grocery stores that accept ATM cards and don't charge usage fees. Of course, you'll have to purchase something first.

SAFETY

GENERAL SAFETY SUGGESTIONS   While tourist areas are generally safe, crime is on the increase everywhere, and U.S. urban areas tend to be less safe than those in Europe or Japan. You should always stay alert. This is particularly true of large U.S. cities. It is wise to ask your hotel front-desk staff or the city's or area's tourist office if you're in doubt about which neighborhoods are safe.

Avoid deserted areas, especially at night, and don't go into public parks at night unless there's a concert or similar occasion that will attract a crowd.

Travel Tip

Be sure to keep a copy of all your travel papers separate from your wallet or purse, and leave a copy with someone at home should you need it faxed in an emergency.

Avoid carrying valuables with you on the street, and don't display expensive cameras or electronic equipment. If you are using a map, consult it inconspicuously—or better yet, try to study it before you leave your room. Hold onto your pocketbook, and place your billfold in an inside pocket. In theaters, restaurants, and other public places, keep your possessions in sight.

Remember also that hotels are open to the public, and in a large hotel, security may not be able to screen everyone entering. Always lock your room door—don't assume that once inside your hotel you are automatically safe and no longer need to be aware of your surroundings.

DRIVING   Safety while driving is particularly important. Ask your rental agency about personal safety or request a brochure of traveler safety tips when you pick up your car. Obtain written directions, or a map with the route marked in red from the agency, to show you how to get to your destination. If possible, arrive and depart during daylight hours.

Park in well-lit, well-traveled areas if possible. Always keep your car doors locked, whether the vehicle is attended or unattended. Look around you before you get out of your car and never leave any packages or valuables in sight. If someone attempts to rob you or steal your car, do *not* try to resist the thief/carjacker—report the incident to the police department immediately by calling ☎ **911.**

Also, make sure that you have enough gasoline in your tank to reach your intended destination so that you're not forced to look for a service station in an unfamiliar and possibly unsafe neighborhood—especially at night.

2 Getting to the U.S.

For an extensive listing of airlines that fly into Portland, see "Getting There," in chapter 2.

A number of U.S. airlines offer service from Europe to the United States. If they do not have direct flights from Europe to Portland or Seattle (a little more than 3 hours north of Portland by car), they can book you straight through on a connecting flight. You can make reservations by calling the following numbers in Great Britain: **American** (☎ 0181/572-5555 in London), **Continental** (☎ 0800/776-464), **Delta** (☎ 0800/414-767), **Northwest/KLM** (☎ 08705/074-074), and **United** (☎ 0181/990-9900 in London, or 0800/888-555 outside London).

International carriers that fly from Europe to Los Angeles and San Francisco include **Aer Lingus** (☎ 01/886-8888 in Ireland) and **British Airways** (☎ 0345/222-111 in Great Britain), which flies direct to Seattle from London. From New Zealand and Australia, there are flights to Los Angeles on **Qantas** (☎ 2957-0111 in Sidney) and **Air New Zealand** (☎ 0800/737-000 in Auckland or 643/379-5200 in Christchurch). Continue on to Portland on a regional airline such as **Alaska** or **Southwest.**

From Toronto and Vancouver, B.C., there are flights to Portland and Seattle on **Air Canada** (☎ 800/AIR-CANADA in Canada), **Canadian Airlines** (☎ 800/665-1177 in Canada), **American** (☎ 800/433-7300), **Delta** (☎ 800/221-1212), **Northwest** (☎ 800/225-2525), and **United** (☎ 800/241-6522. Regional airlines such as **Alaska**

Airlines (☎ 800/426-0333) and **America West** (☎ 800/235-9292) fly from Vancouver to Portland and Seattle.

Travelers from overseas can take advantage of the **advance-purchase excursion (APEX)** fares offered by the major U.S. and European carriers. For more money-saving airline advice, see "Getting There," in chapter 2.

The visitor arriving by air, no matter what the port of entry, should cultivate patience before setting foot on U.S. soil. Getting through Immigration Control may take as long as 2 hours on some days, especially summer weekends. Add the time it takes to clear Customs, and you'll see that you should make a very generous allowance for delay in planning connections between international and domestic flights.

In contrast, travelers arriving by car or by rail from Canada will find border-crossing formalities streamlined practically to the vanishing point. And air travelers from Canada, Bermuda, and some places in the Caribbean can sometimes go through Customs and Immigration at the point of departure, which is much quicker.

3 Getting Around the U.S.

For specific information on traveling to and around Portland and Oregon, see "Getting There" and "Getting Around," in chapter 2.

BY PLANE   Some large airlines (for example, Northwest and Delta) offer travelers on their transatlantic or transpacific flights special discount tickets under the name **Visit USA,** allowing mostly one-way travel from one U.S. destination to another at very low prices. These discount tickets are not on sale in the United States and must be purchased abroad in conjunction with your international ticket. This system is the best, easiest, and fastest way to see the United States at low cost. You should obtain information well in advance from your travel agent or the office of the airline concerned, since the conditions attached to these discount tickets can be changed without advance notice.

BY CAR   The United States is a car culture through and through. Driving is the most cost-effective, convenient, and comfortable way to travel through the West. The interstate highway system connects cities and towns all over the country, and in addition to these high-speed, limited-access roadways, there's an extensive network of federal, state, and local highways and roads. Driving will give you a lot of flexibility in making, and altering, your itinerary and in allowing you to see some off-the-beaten-path destinations that cannot be reached easily by public transportation. You'll also have easy access to inexpensive motels at interstate highway off-ramps.

Fast Facts: For the Foreign Traveler

Automobile Organizations   Auto clubs will supply maps, suggested routes, guidebooks, accident and bail-bond insurance, and emergency road service. The **American Automobile Association (AAA)** is the major auto club in the United States. If you belong to an auto club in your home country, inquire about AAA reciprocity before you leave. You may be able to join AAA even if you're not a member of a reciprocal club; to inquire, call AAA (☎ **800/222-4357**). AAA is actually an organization of regional auto clubs, so look under "AAA Automobile Club" in the white pages of the telephone directory. AAA has a nationwide emergency-road-service telephone number (☎ **800/AAA-HELP**).

Business Hours   The following are general open hours; specific establishments may vary. **Banks** are generally open Monday through Friday from 9am to 5pm (some are also open on Sat mornings); there's usually 24-hour access to ATMs at most banks and other outlets. **Offices** are generally open weekdays from 9am to 5pm. **Stores** typically open Monday through Saturday between 9 and 10am and close between 5 and 6pm. Some department stores have later hours and are open on Sunday from 11am to 5 or 6pm, and stores in malls are usually open until 9pm. **Bars** stay open until 1 or 2am; dance clubs often stay open much later.

Climate   See "When to Go," in chapter 2.

Currency   See "Preparing for Your Trip," earlier in this chapter.

Currency Exchange   You will find currency-exchange services in major airports with international service. At Portland International Airport there is Travelex America, on the main floor across from the United Airlines desk. Seattle-Tacoma International Airport provides Thomas Cook services.

To exchange money in Portland, go to **American Express,** 1100 SW Sixth Ave. in the Standard Plaza Building (☎ **503/226-2961**), or **Thomas Cook** at Powell's Travel Store at Pioneer Courthouse Square, 701 SW Sixth Ave. (☎ **503/222-2665**).

Drinking Laws   The legal age for purchase and consumption of alcoholic beverages is 21; proof of age is required and often requested at bars, nightclubs, and restaurants, so it's always a good idea to bring ID when you go out. Beer and wine can often be purchased in supermarkets, but liquor laws vary from state to state.

Do not carry open containers of alcohol in your car or any public area that isn't zoned for alcohol consumption. The police can, and probably will, fine you on the spot. And nothing will ruin your trip faster than getting a citation for DUI ("driving under the influence"), so don't even think about driving while intoxicated.

Electricity   Like Canada, the United States uses 110 to 120 volts AC (60 cycles), compared to 220 to 240 volts AC (50 cycles) in most of Europe, Australia, and New Zealand. If your small appliances use 220 to 240 volts, you'll need a 110-volt transformer and a plug adapter with two flat parallel pins to operate them here. Downward converters that change 220-240 volts to 110-120 volts are difficult to find in the United States, so bring one with you.

Embassies & Consulates   All embassies are located in Washington, D.C. Some consulates are located in major U.S. cities, and most nations have a mission to the United Nations in New York City. If your country isn't listed below, call for directory information in Washington, D.C. (☎ 202/555-1212) for the number of your national embassy.

The embassy of **Australia** is at 1601 Massachusetts Ave. NW, Washington, DC 20036 (☎ **202/797-3000;** www.austemb.org). The nearest consulate is in **San Francisco** at 1 Bush St., San Francisco, CA 94104-4413 (☎ **415/362-6160**). There are also consulates in New York, Honolulu, Houston, and Los Angeles.

The embassy of **Canada** is at 501 Pennsylvania Ave. NW, Washington, DC 20001 (☎ **202/682-1740;** www.cdnemb-washdc.org). The regional consulate is at 412 Plaza 600 Building, Sixth Avenue and Stewart Street, Seattle, WA 98101 (☎ **206/443-1777**). Other Canadian consulates are in Buffalo (NY), Detroit, New York, and Los Angeles.

The embassy of **Ireland** is at 2234 Massachusetts Ave. NW, Washington, DC 20008 (☎ **202/462-3939**). The nearest consulate is at 44 Montgomery St., Suite 3830, San Francisco, CA 94104 (☎ **415/392-4214**). Other Irish consulates are in Boston, Chicago, and New York.

The embassy of **New Zealand** is at 37 Observatory Circle NW, Washington, DC 20008 (☎ 202/328-4800; www.nzemb.org). There is a consulate in Los Angeles at 12400 Wilshire Blvd., Suite 1150, Los Angeles, CA 90025 (☎ 310/207-1605). Other New Zealand consulates are in Salt Lake City and San Francisco, and there's an honorary consulate in Seattle.

The embassy of the **United Kingdom** is at 3100 Massachusetts Ave. NW, Washington, DC 20008 (☎ 202/462-1340). There is a consulate in Seattle at 900 Fourth Ave., Suite 3001, Seattle, WA 98164 (☎ 206/622-9255). Other British consulates are in Atlanta, Boston, Chicago, Cleveland, Houston, New York, San Francisco, and Los Angeles.

Emergencies   Call ☎ 911 to report a fire, call the police, or get an ambulance. This is a toll-free call (no coins are required at a public telephone).

If you encounter problems, check the local telephone directory to find an office of the **Traveler's Aid Society,** a nationwide nonprofit social-service organization geared to helping travelers in difficult straits. The society's services might include reuniting families separated while traveling, providing food and/or shelter to people stranded without cash, or even emotional counseling. If you're in trouble, seek it out.

Gasoline (Petrol)   Petrol is known as gasoline (or simply "gas") in the United States, and petrol stations are known as both gas stations and service stations. Gasoline costs less here than it does in Europe, and taxes are already included in the printed price. One U.S. gallon equals 3.8 liters or .85 Imperial gallons.

Holidays   Banks, government offices, post offices, and many stores, restaurants, and museums are closed on the following legal national holidays: January 1 (New Year's Day), the third Monday in January (Martin Luther King, Jr., Day), the third Monday in February (Presidents' Day, Washington's Birthday), the last Monday in May (Memorial Day), July 4 (Independence Day), the first Monday in September (Labor Day), the second Monday in October (Columbus Day), November 11 (Veterans' Day/Armistice Day), the fourth Thursday in November (Thanksgiving Day), and December 25 (Christmas). Also, the Tuesday following the first Monday in November is Election Day and is a federal government holiday in presidential-election years (held every 4 years, and next in 2000).

Legal Aid   The foreign tourist will probably never become involved with the American legal system. If you are pulled over for a minor infraction (say, speeding on the highway), never attempt to pay the fine directly to a police officer; this could be construed as attempted bribery, a much more serious crime. Pay fines by mail, or directly into the hands of the clerk of the court. If accused of a more serious offense, say and do nothing before consulting a lawyer. Here the burden is on the state to prove a person's guilt beyond a reasonable doubt, and everyone has the right to remain silent, whether he or she is suspected of a crime or actually arrested. Once arrested, a person can make one telephone call to a party of his or her choice. Call your embassy or consulate.

Mail   Generally found at intersections, mailboxes are blue with a white eagle logo and carry the inscription "U.S. Mail." If your mail is addressed to a U.S. destination, don't forget to add the five-digit postal code (or ZIP code), after the two-letter abbreviation of the state to which the mail is addressed.

At press time domestic postage rates were 20¢ for a postcard and 33¢ for a letter. For international mail, a first-class letter of up to one-half ounce costs 60¢

(46¢ to Canada and 40¢ to Mexico); a first-class postcard costs 50¢ (40¢ to Canada and 35¢ to Mexico); and a preprinted postal aerogramme costs 50¢.

Medical Emergencies   To call an ambulance, dial ☎ **911** from any phone. No coins are needed.

Newspapers/Magazines   National newspapers include the *New York Times, USA Today,* and the *Wall Street Journal.* National news weeklies include *Newsweek, Time,* and *U.S. News & World Report.* In large cities most newsstands offer a small selection of the most popular foreign periodicals and newspapers, such as *The Economist, Le Monde,* and *Der Spiegel.*

Safety   See "Safety" in "Preparing for Your Trip," earlier in this chapter.

Taxes   The United States does not have a value-added tax (VAT) or other indirect tax at a national level. Every state, and each county and city in it, is allowed to levy its own local tax on purchases (including hotel and restaurant checks, airline tickets, and so on) and services. Taxes are already included in the price of certain services, such as public transportation, cab fares, telephone calls, and gasoline. The amount of sales tax varies from about 4% to 12%, depending on the state and city, so when you're making major purchases, such as photographic equipment, clothing, or stereo components, it can be a significant part of the cost.

In Portland and the rest of Oregon, there is no sales tax. In Seattle, the sales tax rate is 8.6%. Also, you'll pay 28.3% in taxes and concession fees when you rent a car at Seattle-Tacoma Airport. At Portland International Airport, you'll pay 20% when you rent a car. You'll save 10% to 20% by renting somewhere other than the airport. Hotel room taxes range from around 9% to 15.6%. Travelers on a budget should keep both car-rental and hotel-room taxes in mind when planning a trip.

Telephone, Telegraph & Fax   The telephone system in the United States is run by private corporations, so rates, especially for long-distance service and operator-assisted calls, can vary widely. Generally, hotel surcharges on long-distance and local calls are astronomical, so you're usually better off using a **public pay telephone,** which you'll find clearly marked in most public buildings and private establishments, as well as on the street. Convenience grocery stores and gas stations always have them. Many convenience groceries and packaging services sell **prepaid calling cards** in denominations up to $50; these can be the least expensive way to call home. Many public phones at airports now accept American Express, MasterCard, and Visa credit cards. **Local calls** made from public pay phones in most locales cost either 25¢ or 35¢. Pay phones do not accept pennies, and few will take anything larger than a quarter.

Most long-distance and international calls can be dialed directly from any phone. **For calls within the United States and to Canada,** dial 1 followed by the area code and the seven-digit number. **For other international calls,** dial 011 followed by the country code, city code, and telephone number of the person you are calling.

Calls to area codes **800, 888,** and **877** are toll-free. However, calls to numbers in area codes **700** and **900** (chat lines, bulletin boards, "dating" services, and so on) can be very expensive—usually a charge of 95¢ to $3 or more per minute, and they sometimes have minimum charges that can run as high as $15 or more.

For **reversed-charge or collect calls,** and for person-to-person calls, dial 0 (zero, not the letter O) followed by the area code and number you want; an operator will then come on the line, and you should specify that you are calling collect, or person-to-person, or both. If your operator-assisted call is international, ask for the overseas operator.

For **local directory assistance** ("information"), dial 411; for long-distance information, dial 1, then the appropriate area code and 555-1212.

Telegraph services are provided primarily by Western Union. You can bring your telegram into the nearest Western Union office (there are hundreds across the country) or dictate it over the phone (☎ **800/325-6000**). You can also telegraph money or have it telegraphed to you, very quickly over the Western Union system, but this service can cost as much as 15% to 20% of the amount sent.

Most hotels have **fax machines** available for guest use (be sure to ask about the charge to use them), and many hotel rooms are wired for guests' fax machines. A less expensive way to send and receive faxes may be at stores such as Mail Boxes Etc., a national chain of packing service shops (look in the yellow pages directory under "Packing Services").

There are two kinds of telephone directories in the United States. The so-called **white pages** list private households and business subscribers in alphabetical order. The inside front cover lists emergency numbers for police, fire, ambulance, the Coast Guard, poison-control center, crime-victims hot line, and so on. The first few pages will tell you how to make long-distance and international calls, complete with country codes and area codes. Government numbers are usually printed on blue paper within the white pages. Printed on yellow paper, the so-called **yellow pages** list all local services, businesses, industries, and houses of worship according to activity, with an index at the front or back. (Drugstores/pharmacies and restaurants are also listed by geographic location.) The yellow pages also include city plans or detailed area maps, postal ZIP codes, and public transportation routes.

Time   The United States is divided into six time zones. From east to west, these are eastern standard time (EST), central standard time (CST), mountain standard time (MST), Pacific standard time (PST), Alaska standard time (AST), and Hawaii standard time (HST). Portland and Seattle run on Pacific standard time. Always keep the changing time zones in mind if you are traveling or telephoning long distances in the United States. For example, noon in New York City (EST) is 11am in Chicago (CST), 10am in Phoenix (MST), 9am in Los Angeles (PST), 8am in Anchorage (AST), and 7am in Honolulu (HST).

Tipping   Tipping is so ingrained in the American way of life that the annual income tax of tip-earning service personnel is based on how much they should have received in light of their employers' gross revenues. Accordingly, they may have to pay tax on a tip you didn't actually give them.

Here are some rules of thumb:

In hotels, tip **bellhops** at least $1 per bag ($2 to $3 if you have a lot of luggage) and tip the **chamber staff** $1 per day. Tip the **doorman** or **concierge** only if he or she has provided you with some specific service (for example, calling a cab for you or obtaining difficult-to-get theater tickets). Tip the **valet parking attendant** $1 every time you get your car.

In restaurants, bars, and nightclubs, tip **service staff** 15% to 20% of the check, tip **bartenders** 10% to 15%, tip **checkroom attendants** $1 per garment, and tip **valet-parking attendants** $1 per vehicle. Tip the **doorman** only if he has provided you with some specific service (such as calling a cab for you). Tipping is not expected in cafeterias and fast-food restaurants.

Tip **cab drivers** 15% of the fare.

As for other service personnel, tip **skycaps** at airports at least $1 per bag ($2 to $3 if you have a lot of luggage), and tip **hairdressers** and **barbers** 15% to 20%.

Tipping ushers at movies and theaters, and gas-station attendants, is not expected.

Toilets   You won't find public toilets or "rest rooms" on the streets in most U.S. cities, but they can be found in hotel lobbies, bars, restaurants, museums, department stores, railway and bus stations, and service stations. Note, however, that restaurants and bars in resorts or heavily visited areas may reserve their rest rooms for the use of their patrons. Some establishments display a notice that toilets are for the use of patrons only. You can ignore this sign or, better yet, avoid arguments by paying for a cup of coffee or a soft drink, which will qualify you as a patron. Large hotels and fast-food restaurants are probably the best bet for good, clean facilities.

4 Portland

Situated at the confluence of the Willamette and Columbia Rivers, Portland, with a population of 1.7 million people in the metropolitan area, is a city of discreet charms. That the city claims a rose garden as one of its biggest attractions should give you an idea of just how laid-back it is. Sure, Portlanders are just as attached to their cell phones and beepers as anyone, but this is the City of Roses, and people still take time to stop and smell them. Spend much time here, and you too will likely feel the city's laid-back pace seeping into your bones.

Portland does not have any major sights to pull in tourists—no Space Needle or Fishermen's Wharf. Instead, it is a quiet city that must be searched out and savored—in the shade of the stately elms in the South Park Blocks, the tranquillity of the Japanese Garden, the view from the grounds of Pittock Mansion, or the miles of hiking trails in Forest Park. Portlanders seem less proud of their recently expanded art museum and world-class science museum than of the city's many parks and public gardens. Not only does Portland claim beautiful rose gardens and the most authentic Japanese Garden in North America, but it also can lay claim to both the world's smallest city park and the largest forested urban park in the country.

The city's other claim to fame is as the nation's microbrew capital. Though espresso is the beverage that jump starts this town in the morning (this *is* the Northwest, after all), it's microbrewed beers (also called craft beers and ales) that help the city maintain its mellow character. There are so many brew pubs in Portland that the city has been nicknamed Munich on the Willamette. While in other cities craft beer has given way to cocktails, here in Portland, microbrews are still the drink of choice. Wine isn't far behind, which shouldn't come as a surprise considering how close the city is to wine country. As wineries have been proliferating to the southwest of the city, so too have wine bars in town.

Portland itself may be short on things for visitors to do, but the city's surroundings certainly are not. Within an hour and a half's drive from Portland, you can be strolling a Pacific Ocean beach, hiking beside a waterfall in the Columbia Gorge, skiing or hiking on Mount Hood (a dormant volcano as picture perfect as Mount Fuji), driving through the Mount St. Helens blast zone, or sampling world-class Pinot Noirs in the Oregon wine country. It is this proximity to the outdoors that makes Portland a great city to use as a base for exploring some of the best of the Northwest.

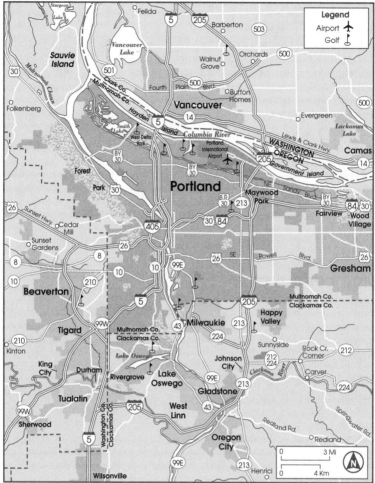

1 Orientation

ARRIVING

BY PLANE **Portland International Airport (PDX)** is located 10 miles northeast of downtown Portland, adjacent to the Columbia River. Many hotels near the airport provide courtesy shuttle service; be sure to check at your hotel when you make a reservation.

If you have rented a car at the airport and want to reach central Portland, follow the signs for downtown. These will take you first to I-205 and then to I-84 west, which brings you to the Willamette River. Take the Morrison Bridge exit to cross the river. The trip into town takes about 20 minutes and is entirely on interstate highways.

If you haven't rented a car at the airport, the best way to get into town is to take the **Gray Line Airport Shuttle** (☎ **800/422-7042** or 503/285-9845), which picks up just outside the baggage-claim area. One-way fares are $12 for adults, $10 for seniors,

$6 for children ages 4 to 12, and free for under age 4. It operates every 30 minutes almost around the clock.

Tri-Met public bus no. 12 leaves the airport approximately every 15 minutes from 5:30am to 11:50pm for the trip to downtown Portland. The trip takes about 40 minutes and costs $1.10. The bus between downtown and the airport operates between 5:15am and 12:30am and leaves from Southwest Sixth Ave. and Main Street.

A taxi to downtown generally costs between $20 and $25.

BY TRAIN　Amtrak trains stop at the historic **Union Station,** 800 NW Sixth Ave. (☎ 503/273-4866), about 10 blocks from the heart of downtown Portland. Taxis are usually waiting to meet trains and can take you to your hotel. Alternatively, you might be able to get your hotel to send a van to pick you up, or, if you are renting a car from a downtown car-rental office, you can usually get them to pick you up at the station. Public buses stop within a block of the station and are free within the downtown area if you catch the bus south of Hoyt Street (2 blks. away).

Although you could easily walk from the station into the heart of downtown, you will have to pass through a few blocks of somewhat-rough neighborhood, though this area is currently in the middle of a renaissance and is not nearly as bad an area as it once was.

VISITOR INFORMATION

The **Portland Oregon Visitors Association (POVA) Information Center,** Two World Trade Center, 25 SW Salmon St. (☎ 877/678-5263 or 503/275-9750; www.pova.com), is across the street from Tom McCall Waterfront Park in downtown Portland. There is also an information booth by the baggage-claim area at Portland Airport.

CITY LAYOUT

Portland is located in northwestern Oregon at the confluence of the Columbia and Willamette Rivers. To the west are the West Hills, which rise to more than 1,000 feet. Some 90 miles west of the West Hills are the spectacular Oregon coast and the Pacific Ocean. To the east are rolling hills that extend to the Cascade Range, about 50 miles away. The most prominent peak in this section of the Cascades is Mount Hood (11,235 ft.), a dormant volcanic peak that looms over the city on clear days. From many parts of Portland it's also possible to see Mount St. Helens, another volcano, which erupted spectacularly in 1980.

With about 1.8 million people in the entire metropolitan area, Portland is still a relatively small city. This is especially evident when one begins to explore the compact downtown area. Nearly everything is accessible on foot, and the city authorities do everything they can to encourage pedestrians.

MAIN ARTERIES & STREETS　**I-84 (Banfield Freeway or Expressway)** enters Portland from the east. East of the city is **I-205,** which bypasses downtown Portland and runs past the airport. **I-5 (East Bank Freeway)** runs through on a north-south axis, passing along the east bank of the Willamette River directly across from downtown. **I-405 (Stadium Freeway and Foothills Freeway)** circles around the west and south sides of downtown. **U.S. 26 (Sunset Highway)** leaves downtown heading west toward Beaverton and the coast. **Oregon Hwy. 217 (Beaverton-Tigard Highway)** runs south from U.S. 26 in Beaverton.

The most important artery within Portland is **Burnside Street.** This is the dividing line between north and south Portland. Dividing the city from east to west is the **Willamette River,** which is crossed by eight bridges in the downtown area. From north to south these bridges are the Fremont, Broadway, Steel, Burnside, Morrison,

No, They Didn't Just Win the Masters Tournament

If you happen to see two people walking down a Portland street wearing bright green jackets, they are probably members of the **Portland Guides** service run by the Association for Portland Progress (☎ **503/224-7383**). They'll be happy to answer any questions you have about the city.

Hawthorne, Marquam, and Ross Island. There are also additional bridges beyond the downtown area, including the Sellwood Bridge between downtown and Lake Oswego, and the St. John's Bridge from northwest Portland to north Portland.

For convenience's sake, I'll define downtown Portland as the 300-block area within the **Fareless Square.** This is the area in which you can ride free on the city's public buses and the MAX light-rail system. The Fareless Square is bounded by I-405 on the west and south, by Hoyt Street on the north, and by the Willamette River on the east.

FINDING AN ADDRESS   Finding an address in Portland can be easy if you keep a few tips in mind. Almost all addresses in Portland, and even extending for miles beyond the city, include a map quadrant—NE (Northeast), SW (Southwest), and so forth. The dividing line between east and west is the Willamette River; between north and south it's Burnside Street. Any downtown address will be labeled either SW (Southwest) or NW (northwest). An exception to this rule is the area known as North Portland, which is the area across the Willamette River from downtown going toward Jantzen Beach. Streets here have a plain "North" designation. Also, Burnside Street is designated either "East" or "West."

Avenues run north-south and streets run east-west. Street names are the same on both sides of the Willamette River. Consequently, there is a Southwest Yamhill Street and a Southeast Yamhill Street. In northwest Portland, street names are in alphabetical going north from Burnside to Wilson. Naito Parkway is the street nearest the Willamette River on the west side, and Water Avenue is the nearest on the east side. Beyond these are numbered avenues. On the west side you'll also find Broadway and Park Avenue between Sixth Avenue and Ninth Avenue. With each block, the addresses increase by 100, beginning at the Willamette River for avenues and at Burnside Street for streets. Odd numbers are generally on the west and north sides of the street, and even numbers on the east and south sides.

Here's an example. You want to go to 1327 SW Ninth Ave. Because it's in the 1300 block, you'll find it 13 blocks south of Burnside; and because it's an odd number, it will be on the west side of the street.

STREET MAPS   Stop by the **Portland Oregon Visitors Association Information Center,** Two World Trade Center, 25 SW Salmon St. (☎ **877/678-5263** or 503/275-9750; www.pova.com), for a free map of the city; they also have a more detailed one for sale. Powell's "City of Books," 1005 W. Burnside St. (☎ **800/878-7323** or 503/228-4651), has an excellent free map of downtown that includes a walking-tour route and information on many of the sights you'll pass along the way. Members of the **American Automobile Association** can obtain a free map of the city at the AAA offices at 600 SW Market St. (☎ **503/222-6734**).

The Neighborhoods in Brief

Portland's neighborhoods are, in large part, dictated by its geography. The Willamette River forms a natural dividing line between the eastern and western portions of the city, while the Columbia River forms a boundary with the state of Washington on the north. The West Hills, Portland's prime residential neighborhoods, are a beautiful backdrop for this attractive city. Covered in evergreens, the hills rise to a height of 1,000 feet at the edge of downtown. Within these hills are the Oregon Zoo, the International Rose Test Garden, the Japanese Garden, and several other attractions.

Downtown   This term usually refers to the business and shopping district south of Burnside and north of Jackson Street between the Willamette River and 13th Avenue. Within this area, you'll find a dozen or more high-end hotels, dozens of restaurants of all types, and loads of shopping (including the major department stores). Within downtown's Cultural District (along Broadway and the South Park Blocks), you'll also find most of the city's performing arts venues and a couple of museums.

Pearl District   This neighborhood of galleries, residential and business lofts, cafes, breweries, and shops is bounded by the North Park Blocks, Lovejoy Street, I-405, and Burnside Street. Crowds of people come here on First Thursday (the first Thursday of every month), when the galleries and other businesses are open late. This is currently Portland's bid for a hip urban loft scene and is one of the city's main upscale restaurant neighborhoods.

Chinatown   Portland has had a Chinatown almost since its earliest days. Today, this small area, with its numerous Chinese groceries and restaurants, is wedged between the Pearl District and the Skidmore Historic District and is entered through the colorful Chinatown Gate at West Burnside Street and Fourth Avenue. Not a great neighborhood to be in late at night.

Skidmore Historic District   Also known as Old Town, this is Portland's original commercial core, and it centers around Southwest Ankeny Street and Southwest First Avenue. Many of the restored buildings have become retail stores, but despite the presence of the Saturday Market, the neighborhood has never become a popular shopping district, mostly because of its welfare hotels, missions, street people, and drug dealing. However, with its many clubs and bars, it has become the city's main nightlife district.

Northwest/Nob Hill   Located along Northwest 23rd and Northwest 21st Avenues, this is Portland's most fashionable neighborhood. Here you'll find many of the city's most talked-about restaurants (mostly along NW 21st Ave.), as well as lots of cafes, boutiques, and ever more national chain stores such as GAP and Pottery Barn. Surrounding the two main business streets of the neighborhood are blocks of restored Victorian homes on shady tree-lined streets. This is where you'll find the city's liveliest street scene.

Irvington   Though neither as attractive nor as large as the Northwest/Nob Hill neighborhood, Irvington, centered around Broadway in northeast Portland, is almost as fashionable a neighborhood. For several blocks along Broadway (around NE 15th Ave.), you'll find interesting boutiques and numerous excellent but inexpensive restaurants.

Sellwood/Westmoreland   Situated in southeast Portland, this is the city's antiques store district and contains many restored Victorian houses. Just north of the Sellwood antiques district, surrounding the intersection of SE Milwaukie Avenue and SE Bybee Boulevard, you'll find the heart of the Eastmoreland neighborhood, which is home to numerous good restaurants.

Hawthorne/Belmont District   This enclave of southeast Portland is full of eclectic boutiques, moderately priced restaurants, and hip college students from nearby Reed College. Along Belmont Street, just north of Hawthorne Boulevard, you'll find one of the city's up-and-coming hip neighborhoods that still has a funky side to it.

2 Getting Around

BY PUBLIC TRANSPORTATION

BY BUS   Tri-Met buses operate daily over an extensive network. You can pick up the *Tri-Met Guide,* which lists all the bus routes with times, or individual route maps and time schedules, at the **Tri-Met Customer Assistance Office,** behind and beneath the waterfall fountain at Pioneer Courthouse Square (☎ **503/238-7433;** www. trimet.org). The office is open Monday through Friday from 8am to 5pm. Bus and MAX passes and transit information are also available at area Fred Meyer, Safeway, and most Albertson grocery stores. Nearly all Tri-Met buses pass through the Transit Mall on SW Fifth Avenue and SW Sixth Avenue.

Outside Fareless Square, adult fares on both Tri-Met buses and MAX are $1.10 or $1.40, depending on how far you travel. Seniors 65 years and older pay 55¢ with valid proof of age; children ages 7 through 18 pay 85¢. A day ticket costing $3.50 is good for travel to all zones and is valid on both buses and MAX. Day tickets can be purchased from any bus driver. You can also make free transfers between the bus and the MAX light-rail system.

BY LIGHT RAIL   The **Metropolitan Area Express (MAX)** is Portland's above-ground light-rail system that connects downtown Portland with the eastern suburb of Gresham and the western suburbs of Beaverton and Hillsboro. One of the most convenient places to catch the MAX is at Pioneer Courthouse Square. The MAX light-rail system crosses the Transit Mall on SW Morrison Street and SW Yamhill Street. Transfers to the bus are free.

As with the bus, MAX is free within the Fareless Square, which includes all the downtown area. However, be sure to buy your ticket and stamp it in the time-punch machine on the platform before you board MAX if you're traveling out of Fareless Square. There are ticket-vending machines at all MAX stops that tell you how much to pay for your destination; these machines also give change. The MAX driver cannot sell tickets. Fares are the same as those on buses. Ticket inspectors randomly check tickets, so be sure you get a ticket, and also get it stamped, before boarding.

A new trolley route from downtown through the Pearl District to the Nob Hill neighborhood is currently in planning and should be in operation by early 2001. There is also a new light-rail line under construction to provide service to Portland International Airport; this line is expected to be operating by late 2001.

BY CAR

Portland is a compact city, and public transit will get you to most attractions within its limits. However, if you are planning to explore outside the city—and Portland's greatest attractions, such as Mount Hood and the Columbia River Gorge, lie not in the city itself but in the countryside within an hour of the city—you'll definitely need a car.

A Free Ride

Portland is committed to keeping its downtown uncongested, and to this end it has invested heavily in its public transportation system. The single greatest innovation and best reason to ride the Tri-Met public buses and the MAX light-rail system is that they're free within an area known as the Fareless Square. That's right, *free!* The Fareless Square includes 300 blocks of downtown, and as long as you stay within the boundaries, you don't pay a cent. Fareless Square covers the area between I-405 on the south and west, Hoyt Street on the north, and the Willamette River on the east.

Park It

Parking downtown can be a problem, especially if you show up after workers have gotten to their offices on weekdays. There are a couple of very important things to remember when parking downtown:

When parking on the street, be sure to notice the meter's time limit. These vary from as little as 15 minutes (they are always right in front of the restaurant or museum where you plan to spend 2 hrs.) to long term (read "long walk"). Most common are 30- and 60-minute meters. You don't have to feed the meters after 6pm or on Sunday.

The best parking deal in town is at the **Smart Park** garages, where the cost is 95¢ per hour for the first 4 hours (but after that the hourly rate jumps considerably and you'd be well advised to move your car to another lot), $2 for the entire evening after 6pm, or $5 all day on the weekends. Look for the red, white, and black signs featuring Les Park, the friendly parking attendant. You'll find Smart Park garages at First Avenue and Jefferson Street, Fourth Avenue and Yamhill Street, Tenth Avenue and Yamhill Street, Third Avenue and Alder Street, O'Bryant Square, and Naito Parkway and Davis Street. More than 200 downtown merchants also validate parking Smart Park tickets if you spend at least $25, so don't forget to take your ticket along with you. Rates in other public lots range from about $1.50 up to about $4 per hour.

The major car-rental companies are all represented in Portland and have desks at Portland International Airport, which is the most convenient place to pick up a car. There are also many independent and smaller car-rental agencies listed in the Portland yellow pages. Currently, weekly rates for an economy car in July (high-season rates) range between $199 and $289 with no discounts. Expect lower rates in the rainy months.

On the ground floor of the airport parking deck, across the street from the baggage-claim area, you'll find the following companies: **Avis** (☎ 800/831-2847 or 503/249-6500); **Budget** (☎ 800/527-0700 or 503/249-6500); **Dollar** (☎ 800/800-4000 or 503/249-4792); **Hertz** (☎ 800/654-3131 or 503/249-8216); and **National** (☎ 800/227-7368 or 503/249-4900). Outside the airport, but with desks adjacent to the other car-rental desks, are **Alamo** (☎ 800/327-9633 or 503/252-7039); **Enterprise** (☎ 800/736-8227 or 503/252-1500); and **Thrifty,** at 10800 NE Holman St. (☎ 800/367-2277 or 503/254-6563).

You may turn right on a red light after a full stop, and if you are in the far-left lane of a one-way street, you may turn left into the adjacent left lane of a one-way street at a red light after a full stop. Everyone in a moving vehicle is required to wear a seat belt.

BY TAXI

Because most everything in Portland is fairly close, getting around by taxi can be economical. Although there are almost always taxis waiting in line at major hotels, you won't find them cruising the streets—you'll have to phone for one. **Broadway Cab** (☎ 503/227-1234) and **Radio Cab** (☎ 503/227-1212) both offer 24-hour radio-dispatched service and accept American Express, Discover, MasterCard, and Visa credit cards. Fares are $2 to $2.50 for the first mile, $1.50 for each additional mile, and $1 for additional passengers.

ON FOOT

City blocks in Portland are about half the size of most city blocks elsewhere, and the entire downtown area covers only about 13 blocks by 26 blocks. These two facts make

Portland a very easy place to explore on foot. The city has been very active in encouraging people to get out of their cars and onto the sidewalks downtown. The sidewalks are wide, and there are many small parks with benches for resting, fountains for cooling off, and works of art for soothing the soul.

Fast Facts: Portland

American Express   **American Express Travel Service Office,** 1100 SW Sixth Ave. (☎ **503/226-2961**), at the corner of Sixth and Main, is open Monday through Friday from 9am to 5pm. You can cash American Express traveler's checks and exchange major foreign currencies here.

Area Code   The main area code for the Portland and northwest Oregon is **503.** New phones in the area are also getting the **971** area code. The rest of Oregon is **541.**

Baby-sitters   If your hotel doesn't offer baby-sitting services, call **Wee-Ba-Bee Child Care** (☎ **503/786-3837**).

Car Rentals   See "Getting Around," earlier in this chapter.

Climate   See "When to Go," in chapter 2.

Dentist   If you need a dentist while you are in Portland, contact the **Multnomah Dental Society** for a referral (☎ **503/223-4731**).

Doctor   If you need a physician while in Portland, contact the **Medical Society of Metropolitan Portland** for a referral (☎ **503/222-0156**).

Driving Rules   See "Getting Around," earlier in this chapter.

Embassies/Consulates   See chapter 3.

Emergencies   For police, fire, or medical emergencies, phone ☎ **911.**

Eyeglass Repair   Check out Binyon's Eyeworld Downtown, 803 SW Morrison St. (☎ **503/226-6688**).

Hospitals   Three conveniently located area hospitals include **Legacy Good Samaritan,** 1015 NW 22nd Ave. (☎ **503/413-7711**); **Providence St. Vincent Medical Center,** 9205 SW Barnes Rd. (☎ **503/216-1234**), off U.S. 26 (Sunset Hwy.) east of Oregon Hwy. 217; and the **Oregon Health Sciences University Hospital,** 3181 SW Sam Jackson Park Rd. (☎ **503/494-8311**), just southwest of the city center.

Hot Lines   The **Portland Center for the Performing Arts Event Information Line** is ☎ **503/796-9293.** The **Oregonian's Inside Line** (☎ **503/225-5555**), operated by Portland's daily newspaper, provides information on everything from concerts and festivals to airport parking and weather.

Information   See "Visitor Information," earlier in this chapter.

Internet Access   If you need to check e-mail while you're in Portland, first check with your hotel. Otherwise, visit a **Kinkos.** There's one downtown at 221 SW Alder St. (☎ **503/224-6550**) and in Northwest at 950 NW 23rd Ave. (☎ **503/222-4133**). You can also try the **Multnomah County Library,** 801 SW 10th Ave. (☎ **503/248-5123**), which is Portland's main library and offers online services.

Liquor Laws   The legal minimum drinking age in Oregon is 21. Beer and wine can often be purchased in supermarkets, but liquor can be purchased only in state-licensed liquor stores, of which there are very few.

Maps   See "City Layout," earlier in this chapter.

Newspapers/Magazines   Portland's morning daily newspaper is *The Oregonian.* For arts and entertainment information and listings, consult the "A&E" section of the Friday *Oregonian,* or pick up a free copy of *Willamette Week* at Powell's Books and other bookstores, convenience stores, or cafes. **6th and Washington News Shop,** 617 SW Washington St. (☎ **503/221-1128**), carries a large selection of out-of-town newspapers and magazines (also at 832 SW Fourth Ave.).

Pharmacies   Convenient to most downtown hotels, **Central Drug,** 538 SW Fourth Ave. (☎ **503/226-2222**), is open Monday to Friday from 9am to 6pm, on Saturday from 10am to 4pm.

Photographic Needs   **Wolf Camera,** 900 SW Fourth Ave. (☎ **503/224-6776**), and 733 SW Alder (☎ **503/224-6775**), offers 1-hour film processing. **Camera World,** 400 SW Sixth Avenue (☎ **503/205-5900**), is the largest camera and video store in the city.

Police   To reach the police, call ☎ **911.**

Post Offices   The **main post office,** 715 NW Hoyt St., is open Monday through Friday from 7am to 6:30pm, Saturday from 8:30am to 5pm. There is also another convenient post office at 1505 SW Sixth Ave., open Monday through Friday from 7am to 6pm, Saturday from 10am to 3pm. For more information, call ☎ **800/275-8777.**

Rest Rooms   There are public rest rooms underneath Starbucks coffee shop in Pioneer Courthouse Square, in downtown shopping malls, and in hotel lobbies.

Safety   Because of its small size and emphasis on keeping the downtown alive and growing, Portland is still a relatively safe city; in fact, strolling the downtown streets at night is a popular pastime. Take extra precautions, however, if you venture into the entertainment district along West Burnside Street or Chinatown at night. Northeast Portland is the center of the city's gang activity, so before visiting any place in this area, be sure to get very detailed directions so you don't get lost. If you plan to go hiking in Forest Park, don't leave anything valuable in your car. This holds true in the Skidmore Historic District (Old Town) as well.

Taxes   Portland is a shopper's paradise—there's no sales tax. However, there is a 9% tax on hotel rooms within the city and a 10% tax on car rentals (plus an additional airport use fee if you pick up your rental car at the airport; this fee is usually an additional 10%). Outside the city, the room tax varies.

Taxis   See "Getting Around," earlier in this chapter.

Time Zone   Portland is on Pacific time, 3 hours behind the East Coast. In the summer, daylight saving time is observed and clocks are set forward 1 hour.

Transit Info   For bus and MAX information, call the **Tri-Met Customer Assistance Office** (☎ **503/238-7433**). For intercity train fares and schedules, call **Amtrak** (☎ **800/872-7245**) or, for that day's arrival and departure times, call **Union Station** (☎ **503/273-4866**).

Weather   Call **Weatherline Forecast Service** (☎ **503/243-7575**) or the Portland Oregon Visitor Association's **Weather information line** (☎ **503/275-9792**), which provides a 7- to 10-day forecast.

3 Accommodations

The past decade has seen a downtown hotel renaissance in Portland that is still underway. Several historic hotels have been renovated, and other historic buildings have been retrofitted to serve as hotels. Today these hotels offer some of Portland's most comfortable and memorable accommodations. Several other new hotels have also opened recently or are in planning stages for downtown.

The city's largest concentrations of hotels are in downtown and near the airport. If you don't mind the high prices, downtown hotels are the most convenient for visitors. However, if your budget won't allow for a first-class business hotel, try near the airport or elsewhere on the outskirts of the city (Troutdale and Gresham on the east side; Beaverton and Hillsboro on the west; Wilsonville and Lake Oswego in the south; and Vancouver, Washington in the north), where you are more likely to find inexpensive to moderately priced motels. You'll find the greatest concentration of bed-and-breakfasts in the Irvington neighborhood of northeast Portland. This area is close to downtown and is generally quite convenient even if you are here on business.

In the following listings, price categories are based on the rate for a double room (most hotels charge the same for a single or double room) in high season. Keep in mind that rates listed do not include Portland's 9% room tax. Also keep in mind that these are what hotels call "rack rates," or walk-in rates. Various discounts (AAA, senior citizen, corporate, Entertainment Book) often reduce these rates, so be sure to ask. In fact, you can often get a discounted corporate rate simply by flashing a business card (your own, that is). At inexpensive chain motels, there are almost always discounted rates for AAA members and senior citizens. You'll also find that room rates are almost always considerably lower from October through April (the rainy season), and large downtown hotels often offer weekend discounts of up to 50% throughout the year. Also be sure to ask about special packages (romance, golf, theater, and so on).

If you're planning to visit during the busy summer months, make reservations as far in advance as possible, and be sure to ask if any special rates are available.

For information on bed-and-breakfasts in the Portland area, call the **Portland Oregon Visitors Association** (☎ **877/678-5263** or 503/275-9750; www.pova.com) for a brochure put out by **Metro Innkeepers.**

DOWNTOWN
VERY EXPENSIVE

✪ **The Benson.** 309 SW Broadway, Portland, OR 97205. ☎ **800/426-0670** or 503/228-2000. Fax 503/226-4603. www.westcoasthotels.com/benson. 287 units. A/C TV TEL. $215–$225 double; $275 junior suite; $500–$900 suite. AE, DC, DISC, JCB, MC, V. Valet parking $16. Pets accepted ($50 deposit).

Built in 1912, the Benson exudes old-world sophistication and elegance. The top-hatted doorman and the fact that presidents stay here is a good clue that these are the poshest accommodations in town. The guest rooms vary considerably in size, but all are luxuriously furnished. The deluxe kings are particularly roomy, but the corner junior suites are the hotel's best deal. Not only are these rooms quite large, but the abundance of windows makes them much cheerier than other rooms.

Dining/Diversions: In the vaults below the lobby, you'll find the London Grill, one of Portland's top traditional restaurants. It features fresh seafood specialties and is well-known for its Sunday brunch. Piatto is a much more casual place, serving contemporary Italian dishes. The Lobby Court bar has live jazz in the evenings.

Amenities: Exercise room (plus access to nearby health club), 24-hour room service, concierge, valet/laundry service, daily newspaper.

Portland Accommodations

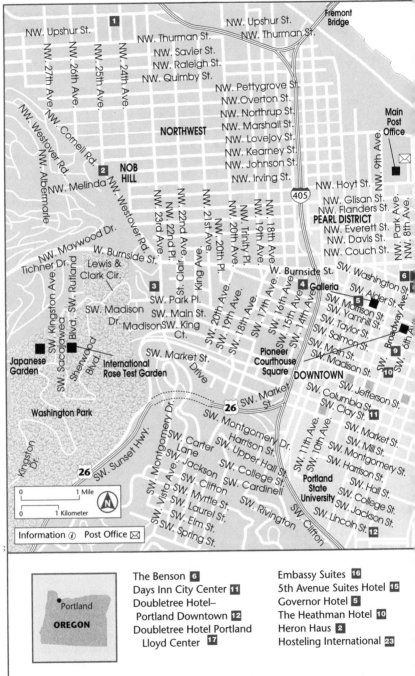

NW. Upshur St.
NW. Thurman St.
NW. Upshur St.
Fremont Bridge
NW. Thurman St.
NW. Savier St.
NW. Raleigh St.
NW. Quimby St.
NW. 27th Ave.
NW. 26th Ave.
NW. 25th Ave.
NW. 24th Ave.
NW. Pettygrove St.
NW.Overton St.
NW. Northrup St.
NORTHWEST
NW. Marshall St.
NW. Lovejoy St.
Main Post Office
NW. Kearney St.
NW. 9th Ave.
NW. Westover Rd.
NW. Cornell Rd.
NW. Johnson St.
NW. Irving St.
2 NOB HILL
NW. Melinda
NW. Westover Rd.
NW. Albermarle
NW. Hoyt St.
405
NW. Glisan St.
NW. Flanders St.
PEARL DISTRICT
NW. Everett St.
NW. Davis St.
NW. Couch St.
NW. Park Ave.
NW. 8th Ave.
NW. 22nd Ave.
NW. 22nd Pl.
NW. 23rd Ave.
NW. 21st Ave.
NW. 20th Ave.
NW. Trinity Pl.
NW. 19th Ave.
NW. 18th Ave.
NW. Maywood Dr.
Tichner Dr.
W. Burnside St.
Lewis & Clark Cir.
NW. Clair St.
King Ave.
W. Burnside St.
SW. Washington St.
6
3
SW. Park Pl.
SW. 20th Ave.
SW. 19th Ave.
SW. 18th Ave.
SW. 17th Ave.
SW. 15th Ave.
SW. 14th Ave.
SW. 10th Ave.
4 Galleria
SW. Alder St.
SW. Morrison St.
5
Broadway Ave.
SW. 6th Ave.
SW. Madison Dr.
SW. Main St.
SW. King Ct.
SW. Yamhill St.
SW. Taylor St.
SW. Salmon St.
9
SW. Kingston Ave.
SW. Rutland
SW. Sacajawea Blvd.
SW. Madison
SW. Market St.
Pioneer Courthouse Square
SW. Main St.
SW. Madison St.
10
Japanese Garden
Sherwood Blvd.
International Rose Test Garden
DOWNTOWN
SW. Jefferson St.
SW. Columbia St.
SW. Clay St.
11
Washington Park
SW. Market St.
26
SW. Market St.
SW. Market St.
SW. Mill St.
SW. Montgomery St.
SW. Montgomery Dr.
Harrison St.
SW. 11th Ave.
SW. 10th Ave.
SW. Harrison St.
SW. Carter Lane
SW. Upper Hall St.
Portland State University
SW. Hall St.
SW. College St.
SW. College St.
Kingston Dr.
26
SW. Sunset Hwy.
SW. Montgomery Dr.
SW. Jackson Ave.
SW. Clifton
SW. Myrtle St.
SW. Cardinell
SW. Rivington
SW. Clifton
SW. Jackson St.
SW. Lincoln St.
12
0   1 Mile
0   1 Kilometer
SW. Vista Ave.
SW. Laurel St.
SW. Elm St.
SW. Spring St.

Information ⓘ   Post Office ✉

Portland
OREGON

The Benson **6**
Days Inn City Center **11**
Doubletree Hotel–
 Portland Downtown **12**
Doubletree Hotel Portland
 Lloyd Center **17**

Embassy Suites **16**
5th Avenue Suites Hotel **15**
Governor Hotel **5**
The Heathman Hotel **10**
Heron Haus **2**
Hosteling International **23**

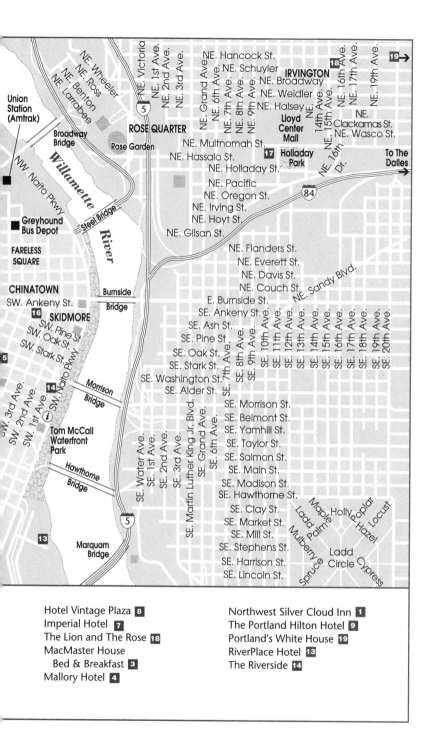

Hotel Vintage Plaza **8**
Imperial Hotel **7**
The Lion and The Rose **18**
MacMaster House
  Bed & Breakfast **3**
Mallory Hotel **4**

Northwest Silver Cloud Inn **1**
The Portland Hilton Hotel **9**
Portland's White House **19**
RiverPlace Hotel **13**
The Riverside **14**

The Governor Hotel. 611 SW 10th Ave., Portland, OR 97205. ☎ **800/554-3456** or 503/224-3400. Fax 503/241-2122. www.govhotel.com. 100 units. A/C MINIBAR TV TEL. $165–$195 double; $200 junior suite; $210–$500 suite. AE, CB, DC, DISC, JCB, MC, V. Valet parking $13.

This historic hotel is an homage to the Lewis and Clark Expedition, and throughout the hotel, you'll spot references to the famous explorers. The lobby, though small, has a classically Western feel, with a fireplace and overstuffed leather chairs. Classic styling aside, this should be the first pick in Portland for the athletically inclined since the basement houses one of the city's best athletic clubs. Guest rooms vary considerably in size, but even the smallest is beautifully decorated. Unfortunately, bathrooms are generally quite cramped and lack counter space. Suites are spacious, and some even have huge patios overlooking the city.

Dining/Diversions: Jake's Grill, a large old-fashioned restaurant with burnished wood columns and slowly turning overhead fans, is just off the lobby. There's also a complimentary evening wine tasting Monday through Friday.

Amenities: Access to the Princeton Athletic Club ($8 charge), which includes lap pool, indoor running track, whirlpool spa, steam rooms, sauna, and exercise room. Other amenities include 24-hour room service, concierge, valet/laundry service, daily newspaper, overnight shoe shine, and baby-sitting.

The Heathman Hotel. 1001 SW Broadway at Salmon St., Portland, OR 97205. ☎ **800/551-0011** or 503/241-4100. Fax 503/790-7110. www.heathmanhotel.com. 150 units. A/C MINIBAR TV TEL. $190–$210 double; $255 junior suite; $325–$775 suite. AE, CB, DC, DISC, JCB, MC, V. Parking $16. Pets accepted ($25).

The Heathman is the address of choice for visiting patrons of the arts, abutting the Portland Center for the Performing Arts and displaying an outstanding collection ranging from 18th-century oil paintings to Andy Warhol prints. Understated luxury and superb service also help make this one of the finest hotels in the city. While the marble and teak lobby is tiny, it opens onto the Tea Court, where the original eucalyptus paneling creates a warm, old-world atmosphere. The basic rooms tend to be quite small, but they are nonetheless attractively furnished and set up for business travelers. None of the rooms really has a view to speak of, but some rooms on the west side do have views of a mural done just for the hotel. Basically what you get here is luxury in a small space. Ask for a corner room; these get more light and feel more spacious.

Dining/Diversions: The Heathman Restaurant and Bar is one of Portland's finest. The menu emphasizes creatively prepared fresh local produce, seafood, and game (see "Dining" in this chapter for details). In the Mezzanine Bar or the Lobby Lounge there is usually live jazz several nights a week.

Amenities: Fitness room, access to nearby athletic club ($10), 24-hour room service, concierge, valet/laundry service, daily newspaper.

✪ **Hotel Vintage Plaza.** 422 SW Broadway, Portland, OR 97205. ☎ **800/243-0555** or 503/228-1212. Fax 503/228-3598. www.vintageplaza.com. 125 units. A/C MINIBAR TV TEL. $165–$225 double; $250–$400 suite. AE, CB, DC, DISC, MC, V. Valet parking $17. Pets accepted.

If you're a wine drinker, the Vintage Plaza should be your choice. Italianate decor and a wine theme are in evidence throughout the hotel, and complimentary evening wine tastings feature Northwest wines. Although the standard rooms have much to recommend them, the starlight rooms and bilevel suites are the real scene-stealers here. The starlight rooms in particular are truly extraordinary. They have greenhouse-style wall-into-ceiling windows that provide romantic views at night and let in lots of light during the day. The bilevel suites, some with Japanese soaking tubs, are equally attractive.

Dining/Diversions: Pazzo Ristorante, one of Portland's best Italian restaurants, is a dark and intimate trattoria (see "Dining" in this chapter for details).

Amenities: In addition to the wine tastings, the hotel offers a fitness room, 24-hour room service, valet/laundry service, shoe shine service, and daily newspaper.

RiverPlace Hotel. 1510 SW Harbor Way, Portland, OR 97201. ☎ **800/227-1333** or 503/228-3233. Fax 503/295-6161. www.riverplacehotel.com. 84 units. A/C TV TEL. $219–$239 double (from $175 weekends outside summer); $249 junior suite; from $279 suite. All rates include continental breakfast. AE, CB, DC, JCB, MC, V. Valet parking $16. Pets accepted ($100 nonrefundable cleaning fee).

With the Willamette River at its back doorstep and the sloping lawns of Waterfront Park to one side, the RiverPlace is Portland's only downtown waterfront hotel. This fact alone would be enough to recommend it, but the boutique hotel's quiet atmosphere also makes it an excellent choice. The river-view standard king rooms are the hotel's best deal, but the junior suites are only slightly more expensive and provide a bit more space. More than half of the rooms are suites, and some come with wood-burning fireplaces and whirlpool bathtubs.

Dining/Diversions: The Esplanade Restaurant overlooks the river and serves Northwest and continental fare. Just off the lobby is a comfortable bar with live piano music, a crackling fire in cool weather, and a casual menu. The bar also has a patio dining area overlooking the river.

Amenities: Whirlpool, sauna, privileges at nearby athletic club (no charge), 24-hour room service, concierge, complimentary shoe shine, valet/laundry service, in-room massage, daily newspaper, baby-sitting.

EXPENSIVE

✪ **Embassy Suites.** 319 SW Pine St., Portland, OR 97204-2726. ☎ **800/EMBASSY** or 503/279-9000. Fax 503/497-9051. www.embassy-suites.com. 276 units. A/C TV TEL. $149–$189 double. Rates include full breakfast. AE, CB, DC, DISC, JCB, MC, V.

Located in the restored Multnomah Hotel, which originally opened in 1912, this Embassy Suites is the most recent addition to the historic hotel scene in downtown Portland. The beautiful large lobby is a masterpiece of gilded plasterwork and is very successful at conjuring up the days when this hotel was new. With the exception of a handful of studio suites, the rooms here are primarily two-room suites. In keeping with the historic nature of the hotel, the suites have classically styled furnishings. More important, they give you lots of room to spread out, a rarity in downtown hotels.

Dining/Diversions: The hotel's Portland Steak and Chophouse is just what its name implies. It affects a classic dark and woody steak house decor, with a large bar area that offers nightly happy-hour specials. There's also a complimentary evening manager's reception with free drinks.

Amenities: Fitness center, indoor pool, whirlpool spa, sauna, 24-hour room service, day spa, concierge, valet/laundry service, car-rental desk, daily newspaper.

✪ **5th Avenue Suites Hotel.** 506 SW Washington St., Portland, OR 97204. ☎ **800/711-2971** or 503/222-0001. Fax 503/222-0004. 217 units. A/C MINIBAR TV TEL. $150–$185 double; $160–$300 suite. AE, DC, DISC, JCB, MC, V. Valet parking $17. Pets accepted.

Located a block from Pioneer Courthouse Square, this unpretentious yet sophisticated hotel is in a renovated department store. In the evenings, guests gather in the lobby to enjoy complimentary evening tastings of regional wines. Guest rooms, most of which are suites, are furnished in a turn-of-the-century country style but also have fax machines for 21st-century convenience. Plush chairs and beds with padded head-boards and luxurious comforters ensure that you'll be comfortable. Bathrooms have lots of counter space.

Dining/Diversions: The Red Star Tavern and Roast House is a popular and traditionally styled restaurant specializing in upscale American comfort food.

Amenities: In addition to complimentary evening wine tastings, the hotel offers an exercise room, an Aveda day spa, 24-hour room service, a concierge, and daily newspaper.

The Portland Hilton Hotel. 921 SW Sixth Ave., Portland, OR 97204-1296. ☎ **800/ HILTONS** or 503/226-1611. Fax 503/220-2565. www.hilton.com. 455 units. A/C TV TEL. $139–$200 double; $600–$1,000 suite. AE, CB, DC, DISC, JCB, MC, V. Self-parking $17, valet parking $20.

While business travelers, conventions, and tour groups compose the bulk of the business here, the Hilton is very conveniently located for vacationers as well. Within just a couple of blocks are museums and the Portland Center for the Performing Arts. An indoor pool and a health club also make this a good choice for active travelers. Rooms here tend to be fairly small, so opt for a double queen or king room if you want a bit more space. Bathrooms are also a bit small and lack counter space. Be sure to request a high floor to take advantage of the views. The corner rooms with king-size beds are our favorites.

Dining/Diversions: From its 23rd-floor aerie, Alexander's offers a striking panorama of Portland, the Willamette River, and snow-covered Mount Hood. Back down at lobby level is the informal Bistro 921 restaurant and bar, with regional and international cuisine.

Amenities: The Portland Hilton Athletic Club ($10 charge) features an indoor swimming pool, saunas, steam rooms, and lots of exercise equipment. Other amenities include room service, concierge, valet/laundry service, overnight shoe shine, daily newspaper, car-rental desk, and a beauty salon/barber shop.

MODERATE

Days Inn City Center. 1414 SW Sixth Ave., Portland, OR 97201. ☎ **800/DAYS-INN** or 503/221-1611. Fax 503/226-0447. www.daysinn.com. 173 units. A/C TV TEL. $89–$139 double. AE, CB, DC, DISC, MC, V. Free parking.

Although this 1960s vintage hotel lacks much in the way of character or charm, it's one of the few economical choices for anyone wishing to stay in downtown Portland. In the guest rooms, you'll find not only contemporary furnishings but also a small shelf of hardbound books (mostly *Reader's Digest*). There's a brass-and-wood restaurant popular at lunch with the downtown business set. Hotel amenities include valet/laundry service, room service, and daily newspaper. The hotel also has a seasonal outdoor pool.

♻ **4 Points Hotel Sheraton.** 50 SW Morrison Ave., Portland, OR 97204-3390. ☎ **800/899-0247** or 503/221-0711. Fax 503/274-0312. E-mail: riverside@transport.com. 140 units. A/C TV TEL. $99–$140 double. AE, CB, DC, DISC, MC, V. Parking $8. Pets accepted ($100 deposit).

Although this 1960s vintage hotel overlooking Waterfront Park looks very nondescript from the outside, the renovated contemporary interior makes it one of the most stylish hotels in town. The hotel is only steps from the Willamette River, close to businesses, restaurants, and shopping. Guest rooms are as boldly contemporary in design as the lobby and restaurant, sort of a downscale *Architectural Digest*. If contemporary is your style, make this your Portland choice. With its modern styling and cozy fireside lounge, the Riverside Club offers guests a very stylish place to relax over a drink or meal. Large windows look out over Waterfront Park to the river, and the menu is primarily new American. Amenities here include an exercise room, room service, valet/laundry service, and daily newspaper.

Imperial Hotel. 400 SW Broadway, Portland, OR 97205. ☎ **800/452-2323** or 503/228-7221. Fax 503/223-4551. www.hotel-imperial.com. 128 units. A/C TV TEL. $85–$110 double. AE, CB, DC, DISC, MC, V. Valet parking $10. Pets accepted ($10 fee).

Although it doesn't quite live up to its regal name, this hotel across the street from the Benson is a fine choice if you're on a budget. A recent renovation has left the rooms quite up-to-date, which makes this an excellent choice for budget travelers, and the location can't be beat. The corner king rooms, with large windows, should be your first choice, and barring this, at least ask for an exterior room. These might get a little street noise, but they are bigger than the interior rooms and get more light. Rooms have in-room safes, refrigerators, and hair dryers. Local phone calls are free. There is an upscale Thai restaurant and a jazz bar off the lobby. Amenities include access to a nearby health club, daily newspaper, and valet/laundry service.

Mallory Hotel. 729 SW 15th Ave., Portland, OR 97205-1994. ☎ **800/228-8657** or 503/223-6311. Fax 503/223-0522. www.malloryhotel.com. 130 units. A/C TV TEL. $85–$140 double; $140 suite. AE, CB, DC, DISC, JCB, MC, V. Free parking. Pets accepted ($10).

The Mallory has long been a favorite of Portland visitors who want the convenience of a downtown lodging but aren't on a bottomless expense account. This is an older hotel, and the lobby, with its ornate gilt plasterwork trim and crystal chandeliers, has a certain classic (and faded) grandeur. Time seems to have stood still here (there's a lounge straight out of the 1950s). The hotel's location right on the Westside Max line makes the Mallory convenient for exploring the city by light rail. The rooms are not as luxurious as the lobby might suggest and are smaller than comparable rooms at the Imperial or Days Inn, but they are comfortable and clean. The dining room at the Mallory continues the grand design of the lobby. Amenities include room service, free local calls, daily newspaper, and valet/laundry service.

INEXPENSIVE

✪ **Doubletree Portland Downtown.** 310 SW Lincoln St., Portland, OR 97201. ☎ **800/222-TREE** or 503/221-0450. Fax 503/226-6260. www.doubletreehotels.com. 235 units. A/C TV TEL. $79–$129 double ($69–$79 winter); $250–$350 suite. AE, CB, DC, DISC, MC, V. Free parking. Pets accepted ($25 deposit).

Situated on a shady, tree-lined street on the southern edge of downtown Portland, this low-rise hotel offers the convenience of a downtown location and the casual appeal of a resort or suburban business hotel. The design and landscaping reflect the Northwest. A free airport shuttle and free parking both add to the appeal of this hotel. The best rooms are those on the third floor overlooking the pool courtyard. All rooms have coffeemakers, hair dryers, and irons and ironing boards. There is a restaurant and a sports bar on the premises. Amenities include an outdoor pool in a pleasant garden setting, an exercise room, room service, and valet/laundry service. In the summer, this hotel makes it into the inexpensive category only on weekends.

NOB HILL & NORTHWEST PORTLAND
EXPENSIVE

✪ **Heron Haus.** 2545 NW Westover Rd., Portland, OR 97210. ☎ **503/274-1846.** Fax 503/243-1075. www.europa.com/~hhaus. 6 units. TV TEL. $135–$350 double. Rates include continental breakfast. MC, V. Free parking.

A short walk from the bustling Nob Hill shopping and dining district of northwest Portland, the Heron Haus B&B offers outstanding accommodations, spectacular

---

ⓘ Family-Friendly Hotels

Doubletree Hotel Portland Lloyd Center *(see p. below)*   Let the kids loose in the huge Lloyd Center shopping mall across the street, and they'll stay entertained for hours (there's even an ice-skating rink). The hotel has a pleasant little swimming pool, and there's a shady park across the street.

Homewood Suites Hotel Portland/Vancouver *(see p. 62)*   Although this hotel is across the Columbia River in Vancouver, Washington, its location across the street from the river, a paved riverside trail, a fun family restaurant, and a brew pub all add up to convenience for families.

---

views, and tranquil surroundings. There's even a small swimming pool with sundeck. Surprisingly, the house still features some of the original plumbing. In most places this would be a liability but not here, since the plumbing was done by the same man who outfitted Portland's famous Pittock Mansion. One shower has seven shower heads; another has two. In another room there's a modern whirlpool spa that affords excellent views of the city. All the rooms have fireplaces.

MODERATE

MacMaster House Bed and Breakfast Inn. 1041 SW Vista Ave., Portland, OR 97205. ☎ **800/774-9523** or 503/223-7362. www.macmaster.com. 8 units (2 with private bathroom). $80–$100 double with shared bathroom, $130 double with private bathroom. Rates include full breakfast. AE, DISC, MC, V.

Located adjacent to both Washington Park and the trendy shops and restaurants of the Nob Hill neighborhood, this imposing mansion sits high above the street and is surrounded by huge old rhododendrons. The inn is furnished with the sort of authentic eclecticism that characterized the Victorian era; everywhere you turn there is something interesting to catch the eye. Many of the guest rooms have interesting murals on the walls. Three rooms have fireplaces, and one of these has a clawfoot tub. Some of the rooms are on the third floor, and the inn itself is up a flight of stairs from the street; so you need to be in good shape to stay here.

Northwest Silver Cloud Inn. 2426 NW Vaughn St., Portland, OR 97210-2540. ☎ **800/205-6939** or 503/242-2400. Fax 503/242-1770. www.scinns.com. 81 units. A/C TV TEL. $90–$138 double. All rates include continental breakfast. AE, DC, DISC, MC, V.

This newer hotel is located on the edge of Portland's trendy Nob Hill neighborhood, and though it faces the beginning of the city's industrial area, it is still a very attractive and comfortable place. Reasonable rates are the main draw here, but the hotel is also within a 5-minute drive (or 15-min. walk) of half a dozen of the city's best restaurants. All rooms have refrigerators, hair dryers, irons and ironing boards, and coffeemakers; and minisuites also have wet bars, microwave ovens, and separate seating areas. Local phone calls are free, and facilities include a fitness room and a whirlpool spa. Try to get a room away from Vaughn Street. To find the hotel, take I-405 to Ore. 30 west and get off at the Vaughn Street exit.

THE ROSE QUARTER & IRVINGTON
EXPENSIVE

Doubletree Hotel Portland Lloyd Center. 1000 NE Multnomah St., Portland, OR 97232. ☎ **800/222-TREE** or 503/281-6111. Fax 503/284-8553. 476 units. A/C TV TEL. $94–$149 double; $269–$575 suite. AE, CB, DC, DISC, JCB, MC, V. Parking $9–$15. Pets accepted.

Located across the street from the Lloyd Center shopping mall, a large, shady park, and a light-rail station, this convention hotel is a very convenient choice if you don't want to be (or can't get a room) right in downtown. Best of all, if you're visiting in the summer, the hotel has a very pleasant pool in a northwest garden setting. Most rooms are quite spacious, and some have balconies. The views from the higher floors are stunning; on a clear day you can see Mount Hood, Mount St. Helens, and even Mount Rainier. Ask for a room in the south tower; these rooms are significantly larger and have full bathrooms (rather than bathrooms with showers only).

Dining: In Maxi's Restaurant, steaks and chops are the specialties; Eduardo's Margarita Grill serves Mexican; and family dining is possible in the Coffee Garden. For those seeking a quiet place for conversation and a drink, there's the Quiet Bar, which sometimes has live piano music.

Amenities: Heated outdoor swimming pool, exercise room, room service, concierge, complimentary airport shuttle, valet/laundry service.

MODERATE

The Lion and the Rose. 1810 NE 15th Ave., Portland, OR 97212. ☎ **800/955-1647** or 503/287-9245. Fax 503/287-9247. www.lionrose.com. 6 units (5 with private bathroom). A/C TV TEL. $100–$140 double. AE, MC, V.

This imposing Queen Anne–style Victorian B&B is within walking distance of several good restaurants, as well as eclectic boutiques and a huge shopping mall. Even if this inn were not so splendidly located, it would still be a gem. The living room and dining room are beautifully decorated with period antiques, and breakfasts are sumptuous affairs meant to be lingered over. Guest rooms each have a distinctively different decor and feel ranging from the bright colors and turret sitting area of the Lavonna room to the deep greens of the Starina room, which features an imposing Edwardian bed and armoire.

۞ McMenamins Kennedy School. 5736 NE 33rd Ave., Portland, OR 97211. ☎ **888/ 249-3983** or 503/249-3983. www.mcmenamins.com. 35 units. TEL. $99–$109 double. Rates include full breakfast. AE, DISC, MC, V.

Located well north of the stylish Irvington neighborhood in a slowly up-and-coming neighborhood, the Kennedy School was the second hotel/brew pub complex from the folks who turned Portland's old poor farm into the most unusual B&B in the state (see McMenamins Edgefield in chapter 7). This inn was an elementary school from 1915 to 1975, and in the guest rooms you'll still find the original blackboards and the kind of great big school clocks you used to watch so expectantly. The classrooms/guest rooms here now have their own bathrooms, so you won't have to raise your hand to get a hall pass. On the premises you'll also find a restaurant, a beer garden, a movie-theater pub, a cigar bar, and a big hot soaking pool. The inn's only real drawback is that it is surrounded by some of Portland's poorest neighborhoods.

Portland's White House. 1914 NE 22nd Ave., Portland, OR 97212. ☎ **800/272-7131** or 503/287-7131. Fax 503/249-1641. www.portlandswhitehouse.com. 9 units. A/C TEL. $98–$159 double. Rates include full breakfast. AE, DISC, MC, V.

This imposing Greek-Revival mansion bears a more-than-passing resemblance to its namesake in Washington, D.C. In the front garden, a fountain bubbles near a patio, while behind the mahogany front doors lies a huge entrance hall with original hand-painted wall murals. This hall is flanked by the parlor, with French windows and a piano, and the formal dining room, where the large breakfast is served beneath crystal chandeliers. Canopy and brass queen beds, antique furnishings, and bathrooms with clawfoot tubs further the feelings of classic luxury here. Request the balcony room and you can gaze out past the Greek columns and imagine you're in the Oval Office. Three rooms are in the old carriage house.

INEXPENSIVE

Howard Johnson Express. 3939 NE Hancock St., Portland, OR 97212. ☎ **503/288-6891.** Fax 503/288-1995. 48 units. A/C TV TEL. $55–$74 double. AE, DC, DISC, MC, V. Free parking.

Located in Northeast Portland's Hollywood District (which takes its name from its mission-revival buildings and Craftsman bungalows) about halfway between the airport and downtown, this economical choice is tucked away several blocks from the interstate. Rooms vary in size, so be sure to ask for one of the larger ones.

VANCOUVER, WASHINGTON

MODERATE

❍ **The Heathman Lodge.** 7801 NE Greenwood Dr., Vancouver, WA 98662. ☎ **888/ 475-3100** or 360/254-3100. Fax 360/254-6100. www.heathmanlodge.com. 143 units. A/C TV TEL. $89–$119 double; $159–$550 suite. AE, DC, DISC, JCB, MC, V. Free parking.

At this suburban Vancouver hotel adjacent to the Vancouver Mall, mountain lodge meets urban chic, and though it's a 20-minute drive to downtown Portland, the hotel is well placed for exploring both the Columbia Gorge and Mount St. Helens. With its log, stone, and cedar-shingle construction, this hotel conjures up the Northwest's historic mountain lodges. The hotel is filled with artwork and embellished with rugged Northwest-inspired craftwork, including totem poles, Eskimo kayak frames, and Pendleton blankets. Guest rooms feature a mix of rustic pine and peeled-hickory furniture, as well as rawhide lampshades and Pendleton-inspired bedspreads. There are also refrigerators, microwaves, coffeemakers, hair dryers, and irons and ironing boards in all the rooms. The hotel has a comfortably rustic restaurant serving regional American fare. There is also an indoor pool, a whirlpool, a sauna, and an exercise room.

Homewood Suites Hotel Vancouver/Portland. 701 SE Columbia Shores Blvd., Vancouver, WA 98661. ☎ **800/CALL-HOME** or 360/750-1100. Fax 360/750-4899. $99–$134 double (lower rates in winter). AE, DC, DISC, MC, V. Free parking. Pets accepted ($25 nonrefundable deposit plus $10 per night).

Located across the street from the Columbia River, this modern suburban all-suite hotel charges surprisingly reasonable rates for its large apartmentlike accommodations that include full kitchens. In addition, rates include both an extensive breakfast and afternoon snacks (Mon through Thurs) that are substantial enough to pass for dinner. The hotel has a swimming pool, a whirlpool, a sports court, and an exercise room, and it is right across the street from a riverside paved path that is great for walking or jogging. Also across the street are a beach-theme restaurant and a brew pub. The only drawback is that it's a 15-minute drive to downtown Portland. A great choice for families.

THE SOUTHWEST SUBURBS (INCLUDING LAKE OSWEGO & BEAVERTON)

INEXPENSIVE

❍ **Greenwood Inn.** 10700 SW Allen Blvd., Beaverton, OR 97005. ☎ **800/289-1300** or 503/643-7444. Fax 503/626-4553. www.greenwoodinn.com. 251 units. A/C TV TEL. $79–$118 double; $150–$375 suite. AE, CB, DC, DISC, MC, V. Free parking. Pets accepted ($10 deposit).

The Greenwood Inn is a resortlike, low-rise hotel with beautifully landscaped grounds that reflect the garden style of the Pacific Northwest. This is Beaverton's best hotel, located only 15 minutes from downtown Portland. An excellent restaurant and a very atmospheric lounge make this an all-around good choice, and if you're in the area to do business in the "Silicon Forest," the Greenwood is well located. Guest rooms are large and comfortable. Hotel amenities include an exercise room, a sauna, an outdoor pool, and a hot tub, as well as access to a nearby athletic club, room service, valet/laundry service, and daily newspaper.

The Pavillion Bar and Grill serves moderate to expensive Latin-influenced cuisine. There's live or recorded music 5 nights a week in the hotel's Wanigan Lounge, which is done in a sort of contemporary mountain-lodge style.

The Lakeshore Motor Hotel. 210 N. State St., Lake Oswego, OR 97034. ☎ **800/ 215-6431** or 503/636-9679. Fax 503/636-6959. www.lakeshorehotel.com. 33 units. A/C TV TEL. $69–$84 double; $84–$124 suite. AE, DC, DISC, MC, V.

The town of Lake Oswego is Portland's most affluent bedroom community, yet this motel is quite reasonably priced considering that it is located right on the shore of the lake for which this town is named. There's even a pool on a deck built right on the water's edge, which makes this a great place to stay on a summer visit. Rooms have standard motel furnishings but are large and have kitchenettes. There are also one- and two-bedroom suites. It's about 7 miles from here into downtown Portland, and the drive, along the Willamette River, is quite pleasant. There are restaurants, cafes, and a brew pub within walking distance of the motel.

NEAR THE AIRPORT

Moderately priced hotels have been proliferating in this area over the past few years, which makes this a good place to look for a room if you arrive with no reservation.

MODERATE

Courtyard by Marriott–Portland Airport. 11550 NE Airport Way, Portland, OR 97220-1070. ☎ **800/321-2211** or 503/252-3200. Fax 503/252-8921. 150 units. A/C TV TEL. $72–$98 double; $115–$118 suite. AE, DC, DISC, MC, V.

Despite the name, this modern six-story hotel has no courtyard. It does have an elegant little lobby featuring lots of marble, and modest but comfortable guest rooms with coffeemakers and irons and ironing boards. If you need some extra room, opt for one of the suites, which come with microwave ovens, wet bars, and small refrigerators. Ask for a room away from the road if you're a light sleeper. This is one of the most convenient hotels to the airport, and it offers a free shuttle. There's a comfortable lounge off the lobby, as well as a moderately priced dining room. The hotel also has a tiny outdoor swimming pool, a whirlpool spa, and a fitness room.

Silver Cloud Inn Portland Airport. 11518 NE Glenn Widing Rd., Portland, OR 97220. ☎ **800/205-7892** or 503/252-2222. Fax 503/257-7008. 110 units. A/C TV TEL. $91–$105 double; $129–$139 suite. Rates include continental breakfast. AE, DC, DISC, MC, V. Free parking.

Conveniently located right outside the airport, this hotel has the best backyard of any hotel in the Portland area. A lake, lawns, trees, and bird feeders all add up to a tranquil setting, despite the proximity of both the airport and a busy nearby road. Rooms are designed primarily for business travelers, but they offer good value, especially the king rooms with whirlpool tubs. There are refrigerators and microwaves in all the rooms, and some suites have gas fireplaces. Best of all, every room has a view of the lake. An indoor pool is another big plus. You'll also find a whirlpool and an exercise room, and local phone calls are free.

INEXPENSIVE

The **Super 8 Motel,** 11011 NE Holman St. (☎ **503/257-8988**), just off of Airport Way after you go under I-205, is conveniently located but charges a surprisingly high $64 to $75 a night for a double in summer. Not far away, in Troutdale, you'll find a **Motel 6,** 1610 NW Frontage Rd., Troutdale (☎ **503/665-2254**), charging $41 to $48 per night for a double.

4 Dining

In the past few years the Portland restaurant scene has gotten so fired up that the city has developed almost as much of a reputation as Seattle. Excellent new restaurants keep popping up around the city.

Several distinct dining districts have been developing, and though you aren't likely to choose a restaurant in one of these neighborhoods just because you're walking by (reservations are usually imperative), the close proximity of establishments makes it easy to check out a few places before making a decision for later. The Pearl District's renovated warehouses currently claim the trendiest restaurants. Nob Hill's Northwest 21st Avenue boasts half a dozen excellent restaurants within a few blocks, including two of Portland's most highly regarded places (Zefiro and Wildwood). The Sellwood/Westmoreland neighborhood of Southeast Portland is another of the city's hot restaurant districts.

DOWNTOWN (INCLUDING THE SKIDMORE HISTORIC DISTRICT & CHINATOWN)

EXPENSIVE

Atwater's Restaurant and Bar. U.S. Bancorp Tower, 111 SW Fifth Ave. ☎ **503/275-3600.** Reservations highly recommended. Main dishes $18–$32, small plates $10–$14; Fixed-price 4-course menu without wine $45, with wine $65. AE, DC, DISC, MC, V. Mon–Sat 5:30–10pm, Sun 5–9:30pm. NORTHWEST.

Atwater's whispers elegance from the moment you step off the elevator on the 30th floor. A rosy light suffuses the hall at sunset; richly colored carpets on a blond hardwood floor and large dramatic flower arrangements add splashes of color throughout the restaurant. In the middle of the dining room is a glass-enclosed wine room that would put many wine shops to shame. But the primary attractions here are the Pacific Northwest cuisine and the incredible views of the Willamette River, Portland, and Mount Hood. The combinations of regional ingredients are unexpected and delectable in such dishes as vanilla-scented Alaskan halibut with a mushroom ragout and watercress salad. The adjoining bar is a casually elegant place to have a cocktail and listen to live jazz.

۞ Couvron. 1126 SW 18th Ave. ☎ **503/225-1844.** Reservations necessary. Main courses $28–$36; tasting menu $75. AE, MC, V. Tues–Sat 5:30–9pm. CONTEMPORARY FRENCH.

Located in the Goose Hollow neighborhood at the foot of the West Hills, this small French restaurant is utterly unremarkable looking from the exterior and thoroughly French and unpretentiously sophisticated on the inside. The menu is one of the most extraordinary in the city, combining the finest of ingredients in unusual flavor combinations that almost always hit the mark. A recent menu included an exceedingly complex appetizer of sautéed Hudson Valley foie gras served with a date-studded brioche, apples, and Muscovy duck with a Sauterne sauce. Wine showed up again in the main courses in a sauce served over roasted salmon mignon with French black

Portland's Best Brunches

If you're looking for a leisurely Sunday brunch, try the **London Grill** (you'll want to dress up for this one), **Wildwood** (Portland's trendiest brunch), **Fiddleheads** (Native American–inspired cuisine), **Newport Bay** (seafood brunch at a floating restaurant), **Salty's on the Columbia** (seafood brunch with a view of the Columbia River), **Bread and Ink Cafe** (a three-course Yiddish repast), or **Papa Haydn** (brunch with an emphasis on dessert). See below for details.

truffle risotto. With dishes here being among the most memorable in the city, it is not surprising that many people opt for the six-course tasting menu so that they can sample a wide range of dishes.

MODERATE

Brasserie Montmartre. 626 SW Park Ave. ☎ **503/224-5552.** Reservations recommended. Main courses $11–$20. AE, CB, DC, MC, V. Mon–Fri 11:30am–2pm, Sat–Sun 10am–2pm; daily 5–10pm. Bistro menu available Sun–Thurs 2pm–1am and Fri–Sat 2pm–3am. NORTHWEST/FRENCH.

Though the menu lacks the creativity of other Northwest and French restaurants in Portland, and dishes are sometimes disappointing, The Bra (as it's known) is popular for its fun atmosphere. There is live jazz nightly, Tuesday through Saturday a magician performs amazing feats of digital dexterity, and on every table you'll find a paper tablecloth and a container of crayons. This playfulness is balanced out by dark, formal dining rooms, with massive faux marble pillars and silk lamp shades that lend an air of *fin de siècle* Paris. You might start your meal with a ménage à trois of pâtés, then have a cup of onion soup with three cheeses, move on to Oregon snapper with crabmeat and meunière sauce, and finish off with one of the divinely decadent pastries. The wine list is extensive but not expensive.

✪ The Heathman Restaurant and Bar. The Heathman Hotel, SW Broadway at Salmon St. ☎ **503/242-4299.** Reservations highly recommended. Main courses $13–$24. AE, CB, DC, MC, V. Mon–Fri 6:30–10:30am, Sat–Sun 6:30am–2pm; Mon–Fri 11:30am–2:30pm; Sun–Thurs 5–10pm, Fri–Sat 5–11pm. NORTHWEST/FRENCH.

The Heathman is classy and not at all pretentious, either in attitude or food presentation. This grand dame of Northwest-style restaurants has a menu that changes seasonally, but one thing remains constant: ingredients used are the very freshest of Oregon and Northwest seafood, meat, wild game, and produce with a French accent. On the walls are Andy Warhol's *Endangered Species* prints. A recent spring menu offered braised rabbit with pistachio and garlic stuffing, and grilled fillet of beef with a bourbon and black pepper demi-glace. Local fruit appears in many of the rich desserts. In the bar, Northwest microbrews are on tap, while an extensive wine list spotlights Oregon. During the theater season, a $20 three-course prix-fixe menu is offered.

✪ Higgins. 1239 SW Broadway. ☎ **503/222-9070.** Reservations highly recommended. Main courses $7–$13 at lunch, $15–$24 at dinner. AE, DC, MC, V. Mon–Fri 11:30am–2pm; daily 5–10:30pm; bistro menu served in the bar daily 2pm–midnight. NORTHWEST/MEDITERRANEAN.

Higgins, located just up Broadway from the Heathman Hotel, where chef Greg Higgins first made a name for himself in Portland, strikes a balance between contemporary and classic in both its decor and its cuisine. The menu, which changes frequently, explores contemporary culinary horizons, while the decor in the trilevel

Portland Dining

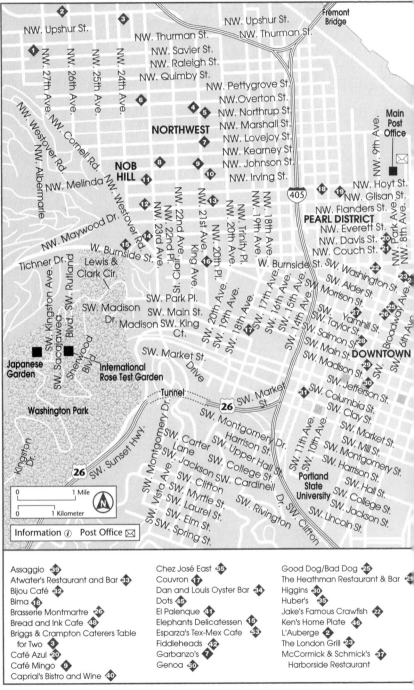

Assaggio 39
Atwater's Restaurant and Bar 33
Bijou Café 32
Bima 18
Brasserie Montmartre 26
Bread and Ink Cafe 48
Briggs & Crampton Caterers Table for Two 3
Café Azul 20
Café Mingo 9
Caprial's Bistro and Wine 40

Chez José East 55
Couvron 17
Dan and Louis Oyster Bar 34
Dots 45
El Palenque 41
Elephants Delicatessen 15
Esparza's Tex-Mex Cafe 53
Fiddleheads 42
Garbanzo's 7
Genoa 50

Good Dog/Bad Dog 25
The Heathman Restaurant & Bar 21
Higgins 30
Huber's 35
Jake's Famous Crawfish 22
Ken's Home Plate 46
L'Auberge 2
The London Grill 23
McCormick & Schmick's Harborside Restaurant 37

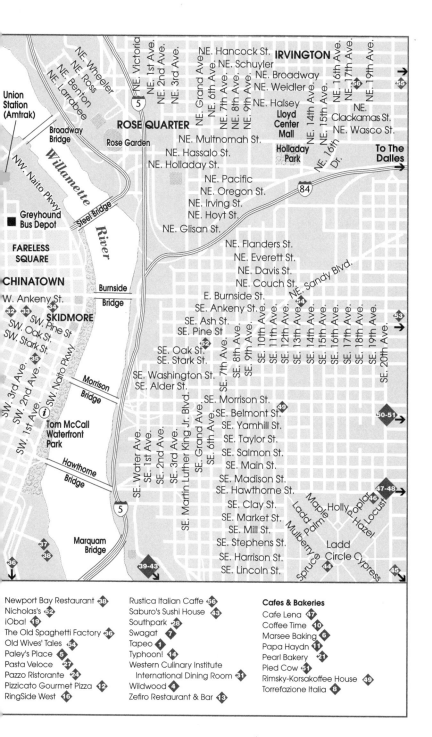

NE. Wheeler
NE. Ross
NE. Benton
NE. Larrabee
NE. Victoria
NE. 1st Ave.
NE. 2nd Ave.
NE. 3rd Ave.

Union Station (Amtrak)

Broadway Bridge

NW. Naito Pkwy

Greyhound Bus Depot

FARELESS SQUARE

CHINATOWN

W. Ankeny St.

SKIDMORE

SW. Pine St
SW. Oak St.
SW. Stark St.

SW. 3rd Ave.
SW. 2nd Ave.
SW. 1st Ave.

SW. Naito Pkwy

Tom McCall Waterfront Park

Steel Bridge

Willamette River

Burnside Bridge

Morrison Bridge

Hawthorne Bridge

Marquam Bridge

ROSE QUARTER
Rose Garden

NE. Grand Ave.
NE. 6th Ave.
NE. 7th Ave.
NE. 8th Ave.
NE. 9th Ave.

NE. Hancock St.
NE. Schuyler

IRVINGTON

NE. Broadway
NE. Weidler
NE. Halsey

Lloyd Center Mall
NE. Clackamas St.
NE. Wasco St.

NE. 14th Ave.
NE. 15th Ave.
NE. 16th Ave.
NE. 17th Ave.
NE. 19th Ave.

NE. Multnomah St.
NE. Hassalo St.
NE. Holladay St.

Holladay Park

NE. 16th Dr.

To The Dalles

NE. Pacific
NE. Oregon St.
NE. Irving St.
NE. Hoyt St.
NE. Glisan St.

NE. Flanders St.
NE. Everett St.
NE. Davis St.
NE. Couch St.

NE. Sandy Blvd.

E. Burnside St.
SE. Ankeny St.
SE. Ash St.
SE. Pine St
SE. Oak St.
SE. Stark St.
SE. Washington St.
SE. Alder St.

SE. 7th Ave.
SE. 8th Ave.
SE. 9th Ave.
SE. 10th Ave.
SE. 11th Ave.
SE. 12th Ave.
SE. 13th Ave.
SE. 14th Ave.
SE. 15th Ave.
SE. 16th Ave.
SE. 17th Ave.
SE. 18th Ave.
SE. 19th Ave.
SE. 20th Ave.

SE. Water Ave.
SE. 1st Ave.
SE. 2nd Ave.
SE. 3rd Ave.
SE. Martin Luther King Jr. Blvd.
SE. Grand Ave.
SE. 6th Ave.

SE. Morrison St.
SE. Belmont St.
SE. Yamhill St.
SE. Taylor St.
SE. Salmon St.
SE. Main St.
SE. Madison St.
SE. Hawthorne St.
SE. Clay St.
SE. Market St.
SE. Mill St.
SE. Stephens St.
SE. Harrison St.
SE. Lincoln St.

Maple
Holly
Poplar
Locust
Hazel
Mulberry
Palm
Ladd Circle
Cypress
Spruce

Ladd

Newport Bay Restaurant 38
Nicholas's 32
iOba! 19
The Old Spaghetti Factory 36
Old Wives' Tales 34
Paley's Place 5
Pasta Veloce 27
Pazzo Ristorante 24
Pizzicato Gourmet Pizza 12
RingSide West 16

Rustica Italian Caffe 26
Saburo's Sushi House 43
Southpark 28
Swagat 7
Tapeo 1
Typhoon! 14
Western Culinary Institute
  International Dining Room 31
Wildwood 4
Zefiro Restaurant & Bar 13

Cafes & Bakeries
Cafe Lena 47
Coffee Time 10
Marsee Baking 6
Papa Haydn 11
Pearl Bakery 21
Pied Cow 51
Rimsky-Korsakoffee House 49
Torrefazione Italia 8

dining room opts for wood paneling and elegant place settings. Adding a dash more classic ambiance are waiters in long white aprons. Both subtle and earthy flavors abound here. Clams steamed in white wine and red curry with spring onions was a heavenly way to begin, and grilled rockfish with baby leeks in a pool of spicy carrot sauce was inventive enough to be interesting, yet homey and satisfying. Be sure to leave room for dessert.

Huber's. 411 SW Third Ave. ☎ **503/228-5686.** Reservations recommended. Main courses $5.50–$11 at lunch, $8–$19 at dinner. AE, DC, DISC, MC, V. Mon–Fri 11:30am–4pm, Sat noon–4pm; Mon–Thurs 4–10pm, Fri–Sat 4–11pm. AMERICAN.

You'll find this very traditional establishment tucked inside the Oregon Pioneer Building. Down a quiet hallway you'll come to a surprising little room with a vaulted stained-glass ceiling, Philippine mahogany paneling, and the original brass cash register. The house specialty has been turkey since the day the first Huber's opened, so there really isn't any question about what to order. You can gobble turkey Parmesan, turkey enchiladas, turkey mushroom pie, or just plain roast turkey. The menu even has wine recommendations to accompany the different turkey dishes. Lunch prices are lower. We also love to come here for their flaming Spanish coffee.

✪ **Jake's Famous Crawfish.** 401 SW 12th Ave. ☎ **503/226-1419.** Reservations recommended. Main courses $9–$25. AE, DISC, MC, V. Mon–Thurs 11:30am–11pm, Fri 11:30am–midnight, Sat 4pm–midnight, Sun 4–10pm. SEAFOOD.

Jake's has been serving up crawfish since 1909 at an address that has housed a restaurant or bar since 1892. The back bar came all the way around Cape Horn in 1880, and much of the rest of the restaurant's decor looks just as old and well worn. The noise level after work, when local businesspeople pack the bar, can be high, and the wait for a table can be long if you don't make a reservation. However, don't let these obstacles dissuade you from visiting this Portland institution. There's a daily fresh sheet listing a dozen or more specials, but there's really no question about what to eat at Jake's: crawfish, which are always on the menu and are served several different ways. Monday through Friday from 3 to 6pm, bar appetizers are only $1.95.

McCormick and Schmick's Harborside Restaurant. 0309 SW Montgomery St. ☎ **503/220-1865.** Reservations recommended. Main courses $7–$14 at lunch, $14–$24 at dinner. AE, DC, DISC, MC, V. Mon–Fri 11:30am–2pm, Sat 11:30am–3pm, Sun 10am–3pm; Mon–Thurs 5–10pm, Fri 5–11pm, Sat 4–11pm, Sun 4–10pm. SEAFOOD.

Anchoring the opposite end of RiverPlace Esplanade from the RiverPlace Hotel, this large and glitzy seafood restaurant offers a view of the Willamette to go with its excellent seafood. Four dining levels assure everyone a view of the river and marina below, and in summer, customers head out to tables on the Esplanade. Although seafood (such as potato-encrusted Oregon lingcod, Rogue River salmon with sautéed morel mushrooms and roasted corncakes, and white prawn penne in a Dijon cream sauce) is the main attraction here, the menu is quite extensive. The clientele is mostly upscale, especially at lunch and in the after-work hours.

Newport Bay Restaurant. 0425 SW Montgomery St. ☎ **503/227-3474.** Reservations recommended. Main courses $10–$23; lunches and light entrees $6–$11. AE, CB, DC, DISC, MC, V. Summer hours Mon–Thurs 11am–11pm, Fri–Sat 11am–midnight, Sun 9am–3pm (brunch) and 3–11pm. In winter, closes 1 hr. earlier and Sun brunch opens 1 hr. later. SEAFOOD.

Though there are Newport Bay restaurants all over Portland, this one has the best location—floating on the Willamette River. Located in the marina at Portland's beautiful RiverPlace shopping and dining complex, the Newport Bay provides excellent

---

ⓘ Family-Friendly Restaurants

Chez José East *(see p. 75)* Though this place is no Taco Bell, it's definitely family friendly, so don't hesitate to bring the kids.

Dan and Louis Oyster Bar *(see p. 70)* You'll think you're eating in the hold of an old sailing ship, and all the fascinating stuff on the walls will keep kids entertained.

The Old Spaghetti Factory *(see p. 78)* This chain of inexpensive Italian restaurants got its start in Portland, and the restaurant here just might have the best location of any in the chain—right on the bank of the Willamette River.

Old Wives' Tales *(see p. 77)* This is just about the best place in Portland to eat if you've got small children. There are children's menus at all meals, and in the back of the restaurant, there's a playroom that will keep your kids entertained while you enjoy your meal.

---

views of the river and the city skyline, especially from the deck. Popular with young couples, families, and boaters, this place exudes a cheery atmosphere and service is efficient. Nearly everything on the menu has some sort of seafood in it, even the quiche, salads, and pastas. Entrees are mostly straightforward and well prepared—nothing too fancy.

✪ **Pazzo Ristorante.** Hotel Vintage Plaza, 627 SW Washington St. (at Broadway). ☎ **503/228-1515.** Reservations highly recommended. Main courses $9.50–$16 at lunch, $9.50–$23 at dinner. AE, CB, DC, DISC, MC, V. Mon–Fri 7–10:30am, Sat 8–10:30am, Sun 8–11am; Mon–Sat 11:30am–2:30pm; Mon–Fri 5–10pm, Sat 4:30–11pm; Sun noon–10pm. REGIONAL ITALIAN.

There's a warm and convivial air about this place, like walking into a country inn—in fact, if you take a seat at Pazzo's bar, you'll practically be ducking hanging hams, sausages, and garlic braids. What stands out here is not so much the complexity of dishes, but the vivid combinations of ingredients and flavors. The only complaint was that some, such as a risotto dish with clams and leeks, were on the heavy side. We started with a meaty and flavorful scallop appetizer, seared and scrumptious, accented by slivers of leeks; for an entree, deftly prepared grilled salmon with savoy cabbage in a red wine sauce is hard to beat. Dessert here is a must. We like the divine and mouth-puckering lemon-mint sorbet with a chocolate-dipped biscotti.

✪ **Southpark.** 901 SW Salmon St. ☎ **503/326-1300.** Reservations recommended. Main courses $8–$20. AE, DC, DISC, MC, V. Mon–Thurs 11:30am–3pm and 5:30–10pm, Fri 11:30am–3pm and 5:30–11pm, Sat 11am–3pm and 5:30–11pm, Sun 10:30am–3pm (brunch) and 5:30–10pm. MEDITERRANEAN.

Can it be true, an upscale restaurant/wine bar with downscale prices? Yes, that's exactly what you'll find here at Southpark (no relation to the TV show). So, what's the catch? Wine prices are not as reasonable as the food prices, so what you save on your food bill, you'll likely spend on your wine. With its high ceiling, long heavy drapes, halogen lights, and lively wall mural, the wine bar is a contemporary interpretation of a Parisian cafe from the turn of the last century. The kitchen here has a way with seafood, so don't pass up the fried calamari, shrimp, and Oregon rockfish, which is served with salt-preserved lemons bursting with flavor. Equally delicious is the ricotta-filled pasta with chanterelles, leeks, and truffle oil, which comes in a rich sauce that begs to be sopped up with crusty bread.

Quick Bites & Cheap Eats

If you're just looking for something quick, cheap, and good to eat, there are lots of great options around the city. Downtown, at **Good Dog/Bad Dog,** 708 SW Alder St. (☎ **503/222-3410**), you'll find handmade sausages. The kosher frank with kraut and onions is a good deal. Designer pizzas topped with anything from wild mushrooms to Thai peanut sauce can be had at **Pizzicato Gourmet Pizza.** Find it downtown at 705 SW Alder St. (☎ **503/226-1007**); in Northwest at 505 NW 23rd Ave. (☎ **503/242-0023**); and in Southeast at 2811 E. Burnside (☎ **503/236-6045**). **Pasta Veloce,** 1022 SW Morrison St. (☎ **503/916-4388**), which translates roughly as noodles in a hurry, really lives up to its name—it's a quick, cheap place to get an Italian-style meal in downtown Portland.

If you're in the mood for a great burger, head over to **Dots,** in southeast Portland at 2521 SE Clinton St. (☎ **503/235-0203**), which serves big, fat, juicy burgers in a setting that abounds in 1950s kitsch.

If the weather's nice and you think a picnic might be in order, **Elephants Delicatessen,** 13 NW 23rd Place (☎ **503/224-3955**), is a good place to go for your supplies, including cheeses, sandwiches, wines, and yummy desserts. Head up to nearby Washington Park to enjoy it all.

INEXPENSIVE

Bijou Café. 132 SW Third Ave. ☎ **503/222-3187.** Reservations not necessary. Breakfast and lunch $4–$9. MC, V. Mon–Fri 7am–2pm, Sat–Sun 8am–2pm. NATURAL FOODS.

The folks who run the Bijou take both food and health seriously. They'll serve you a bowl of steamed brown rice for breakfast, but you can also get fresh oyster hash or brioche French toast. However, the real hits here are the hash browns and the muffins. Don't leave without trying these two. At lunch, there are salads made with organic produce whenever possible. Keep in mind, however, that as breakfasts go, this place is pretty expensive.

Dan and Louis Oyster Bar. 208 SW Ankeny St. ☎ **503/227-5906.** Reservations recommended. Main courses $8–$15. AE, DC, DISC, MC, V. Sun–Thurs 11am–10pm, Fri–Sat 11am–11pm. SEAFOOD.

Dan and Louis has been serving up succulent oysters since 1907, and today the oysters come from Dan and Louis's own oyster farm on Yaquina Bay. Half the fun of eating here is enjoying the old-fashioned surroundings. The front counter is stacked high with candies much as it would have been in the 1920s. The walls are covered with founder Louis Wachsmuth's own collection of old and unusual plates, and nautical odds and ends are everywhere. Louis began his restaurant business serving only oyster stew and oyster cocktails, both of which are still on the menu. Fried seafood predominates, but other types of food are also available. The quality can be uneven, but the prices are great.

Western Culinary Institute International Dining Room. 1316 SW 13th Ave. ☎ **800/666-0312** or 503/223-2245. Reservations required. 5-course lunch $7.95; 6-course dinner $14–$18; Thurs buffet $15.95. AE, MC, V. Tues–Fri 11:30am–1pm and 6–8pm. CONTINENTAL/AMERICAN REGIONAL.

If you happen to be a frugal gourmet whose palate is more sophisticated than your wallet can afford, you'll want to schedule a meal here. The dining room serves five- to six-course gourmet meals prepared by advanced students at prices even a budget traveler can afford. A sample dinner menu might begin with velouté Andalouse followed by sautéed vegetables in a puff pastry, a pear sorbet, grilled ahi tuna with black-bean salsa, Chinese salad with smoked salmon, and mocha cheesecake. Remember, that's all for less than $18! The four-course lunch for only $7.95 is just as good a deal.

NORTHWEST PORTLAND (INCLUDING THE PEARL DISTRICT & NOB HILL)
EXPENSIVE

Briggs & Crampton Caterers Table for Two. 1902 NW 24th Ave. ☎ **503/223-8690.** Reservations several months in advance. 4-course lunch for 2 people $75. MC, V. Tues–Fri 12:30pm. INTERNATIONAL.

At an atmospheric old house in Northwest Portland, Briggs & Crampton Caterers puts on a special lunch for two people only (make reservations well in advance). This pampering experience, which occurs in a screened-off area in the front parlor, begins with an appetizer, followed by a sorbet, breads, the main course with side dishes, dessert, and coffee. Dishes are influenced by whatever is in season, be it a certain type of fish, morel mushrooms, or fresh berries. The chef doubles as the waiter, so attention is concentrated on your special needs and desires. The wine list has some fine selections, but wine is not included in the price, nor is the gratuity. Reservations are taken quarterly, in January, April, July, and October.

MODERATE

Bima. 1338 NW Hoyt St. ☎ **503/241-3465.** Reservations recommended. Main courses $14–$19. AE, MC, V. Mon–Sat 11:30am–3pm and 6–10:30pm. Lounge menu served between lunch and dinner and from kitchen close until midnight. AMERICAN REGIONAL/CARIBBEAN.

This was one of the first upscale restaurants to venture into the Pearl District, and with its contemporary decor and new Southern and Caribbean food, it remains a popular place. A barely noticeable entryway leads into the cavernous converted warehouse space, which is softened and romanticized with indirect lighting and oversize booths. Now, if the words "Southern food" have you thinking collard greens and grits, think again. This is new Southern. The catfish fillets covered in crushed pecans are served with chipotle-flavored polenta cakes, and the grilled pork tenderloin comes with lemongrass risotto cakes.

✪ **Café Azul.** 112 NW Ninth Ave. ☎ **503/525-4422.** Reservations recommended. Main courses $13–$25. DISC, MC, V. Tues–Sat 5–10pm. MEXICAN.

Located in the Pearl District in what is clearly an old warehouse, Café Azul is a long and narrow space softened by expanses of warm yellow and terra-cotta walls. The food here includes some of the best regional Mexican dishes you're likely to find on this side of the border. Tasty margaritas are generous and can be made with various tequilas. Start by spreading some dangerously tasty chili butter on a crusty roll, and then follow this with *caldo tlalapeño,* a full-flavored broth-based soup with chicken, *chipotle* chile, and avocado. From Oaxaca, Mexico, comes the inspiration for Café Azul's *mole,* a rich and spicy sauce made with more than two dozen ingredients, which is served over chicken. This is the most expensive Mexican food you're likely to ever encounter, but it's well worth it.

✪ **Café Mingo.** 807 NW 21st Ave. ☎ **503/226-4646.** Reservations accepted only for parties of 6 or more. Main courses $8–$16. AE, DISC, MC, V. Sun–Thurs 5–10pm, Fri–Sat 5–11pm. ITALIAN.

If there's any problem with this intimate little cafe, which is immensely popular and doesn't take reservations, it's that you almost always have to wait for a table. The solution? Get here as early as possible. The interior is as attractive as that of any other upscale restaurant here on Restaurant Row, but the prices are less expensive. The short

When Your Sweet Tooth Calls . . .

When you've just got to have something gooey and rich, there's no better place to get it than **Marsee Baking,** 1323 NW 23rd Ave. (☎ **503/295-5900**). The cases are crammed to overflowing with cakes, tarts, pastries, bagels, and breads, and they also make sandwiches. Other locations are at 845 SW Fourth Ave., near Pioneer Place shopping center (☎ 503/226-9000), 935 NE Broadway (☎ 503/280-8800), 1220 SW Fifth Ave.(☎ 503/294-6000), and the Portland International Airport shopping mall.

Pearl Bakery, 102 NW Ninth Ave. (☎ **503/827-0910**) in the heart of the Soho-like Pearl district, is famous for its breads and European-style pastries. The gleaming bakery cafe is a good place for such sandwiches as mozzarella and tomato on crusty bread.

The **Rimsky-Korsakoffee House,** 707 SE 12th Ave. (☎ **503/232-2640**), a classic tearoom with mismatched chairs, has been Portland's favorite dessert hangout for more than a decade. There's no sign on the old house, but you'll know that this is the place once you open the door. Open after 7pm.

Papa Haydn, 701 NW 23rd Ave. (☎ **503/228-7317**) is legendary for such desserts as lemon chiffon torte, raspberry gâteau, black velvet, and tiramisu. Also at 5829 SE Milwaukie Ave. (☎ 503/232-9440) in Sellwood.

Located in Ladd's Addition, an old neighborhood full of big trees and craftsman's bungalows, **Palio Dessert House,** 1996 SE Ladd Ave. (☎ **503/232-9412**), is a very relaxed place with a timeless European quality. To get there, take Hawthorne Boulevard east to the corner of 12th and Hawthorne, and then go diagonally down Ladd Avenue.

---

menu focuses on painstakingly prepared Italian comfort food. Just about all the items on the menu are winners, from the *inslata caprese,* a salad with tomato, house-made fresh mozzarella, basil, and extra-virgin olive oil, to grilled Italian sausage with braised savoy cabbage and cannellini beans. We love the *panna cotta* dessert: "cooked cream" with poached fruit.

L'Auberge. 2601 NW Vaughn St. ☎ **503/223-3302.** Reservations highly recommended. Bistro menu $8–$14, main dishes $19–$24; 4-course, fixed-price dinner $38. AE, CB, DISC, MC, V. Mon–Fri 11:30am–2:30pm; Sun–Thurs 5pm–midnight, Fri–Sat 5pm–1am. NORTHWEST/FRENCH.

Located at the edge of the industrial district, L'Auberge has stood the test of time—while other restaurants have come and gone, it's been around for 30 years. It offers some of the best French and Northwest cuisine in Portland and is a favorite special-occasion restaurant. There are two venues for dining here: the bistro, which features a more casual and less expensive menu, and the dining room, which offers a more formal experience. Both feature French cuisine with a Northwest accent. In the bistro, such fare as mussels steamed with *pastis* (an anisette-flavored liquor) or *coq au vin* are good choices, while the dining room offers dishes such as citrus marinated salmon with olive-oil mashed potatoes, or chestnut and honey smoked duck breast.

¡Oba! 555 NW 12th Ave. ☎ **503/228-6161.** Reservations recommended. Main courses $12–$24. AE, DISC, MC, V. Sun–Mon 5:30–9pm, Tues–Thurs 5:30–10pm, Fri–Sat 5:30–10:30pm. Bar opens at 4:30pm and stays open later than restaurant. NUEVO LATINO.

Lively, with a Latin American feeling in both color and design, ¡Oba! is currently the most trendy watering hole in the Pearl District, and oh what a rumbling buzz of conversation fills the air. The big bar is guaranteed to be filled with people wearing requisite black and sipping fresh-fruit mango margaritas. Service is polished and personable, something you wouldn't expect from the latest hip restaurant. Get away from some of the ambient noise by asking for one of the cozy and romantic booths. Memorable dishes include crispy coconut prawns with jalapeño-citrus marmalade and anything with a sauce, such as the *pepian* sauce made with pumpkin seeds, which spices up rotisserie chicken. Desserts are most unusual. Some hit, some miss, but they are all pretty extravagant.

Paley's Place. 1204 NW 21st Ave. ☎ **503/243-2403.** Reservations highly recommended. Main courses $14–$24. AE, MC, V. Mon–Thurs 5:30–10pm, Fri–Sat 5:30–11pm, Sun 5–9pm. NORTHWEST/FRENCH.

Paley's is located in a turn-of-the-century Victorian house, and in good weather, the front porch is the preferred place to dine. This porch also doubles as an open-air storage area for some of the restaurant's fresh produce, which lends a traditional European flavor to the surroundings. Inside, the restaurant is small and stylishly comfortable, but it can be quite noisy. Chef Vitaly Paley combines the best of Northwest produce with other ingredients to make such vibrantly flavorful dishes as a watercress salad with Oregon blue cheese, caramelized pears, and toasted walnuts. Choices for entrees might include a melt-in-your-mouth tender slow-roasted halibut with thyme-infused risotto and wilted greens. Signature *frites*, with a mustard *aïoli*, are not to be missed. Big on wines, Paley's offers wine-tasting and wine-maker dinners. For dessert, we can't pass up the warm chocolate soufflé with ice cream.

RingSide West. 2165 W. Burnside St. ☎ **503/223-1513.** Reservations highly recommended. Steaks $13–$22; seafood main dishes $18–$38. AE, DC, DISC, MC, V. Mon–Sat 5pm–midnight, Sun 4–11:30pm. Ringside East Mon–Thurs 11:30am–2:30pm and 5–11pm, Fri 11:30am–2:30pm and 5pm–midnight, Sat 5pm–midnight, Sun 4–10:30pm. STEAK/SEAFOOD.

RingSide has long been a favorite Portland steak house. Though boxing is the main theme, the name also refers to the incomparable onion rings that should be an integral part of any meal here. Have your rings with a side order of one of their perfectly cooked steaks for a real knockout meal. There is also a RingSide East at 14021 Northeast Glisan St. (☎ **503/255-0750**), on Portland's east side, with basically the same menu but not as much atmosphere. See above for hours.

✪ **Tapeo.** 2764 NW Thurman St. ☎ **503/226-0409.** Reservations not accepted. Tapas $2–$9. DISC, MC, V. Tues–Sat 5:30–10pm. SPANISH/TAPAS.

With the feeling of an old European restaurant, this small neighborhood spot located deep in the Northwest Portland area seems intimate, but it can get loud when the place is full, which is often. People wait around for the tables, which are placed so close together that you could shake hands with your neighbor. But it's worth the wait for authentic Spanish tapas like the excellent grilled eggplant, thinly sliced and stuffed with goat cheese, or deliciously crispy fried calamari served with aïoli. The flan is the richest you'll ever taste. Prices on wines, both by the glass and by the bottle, are decent. With a setting that is simple, small-scale, and plush, this place has a more intimate feel than downtown Fernando's Hideaway.

✪ **Wildwood.** 1221 NW 21st Ave. ☎ **503/248-WOOD.** Reservations highly recommended. Main courses $10–$16 at lunch, $18–$23 at dinner. AE, MC, V. Mon–Sat 11:30am–2:30pm; Mon–Thurs 5:30–10pm, Fri–Sat 5:30–11pm; Sun brunch 10am–2pm, Sun family-style supper 5–9:30pm. AMERICAN REGIONAL.

With a menu that changes daily and an elegant and spare interior decor straight out of *Architectural Digest*, Wildwood has for many years been one of the best and most talked-about restaurants in Portland. Fresh seasonal ingredients are the basis for chef

Cory Schreiber's simple yet imaginative dishes (often no more than four ingredients are used in order to let the flavors shine through). Results are artful, not pretentious. Roll a few of these flavors over on your imaginary taste buds: cornmeal-encrusted razor clams with a saffron and mustard aïoli; skillet-roasted Washington mussels with garlic, dried tomato, and a saffron-infused Chardonnay vinaigrette; or a Dungeness crab salad served with *lavosh* (Middle Eastern crackers). If you can't get a reservation, you can still get a couple of delicious appetizers or a crispy pizza at the bar.

✪ **Zefiro Restaurant and Bar.** 500 NW 21st Ave. ☎ **503/226-3394.** Reservations highly recommended. Main courses $16–$23. AE, DC, MC, V. Tues–Thurs 5:30–10pm, Fri–Sat 5:30–10:30pm. MEDITERRANEAN.

An initiator of the explosion of upscale restaurants on Northwest 21st Avenue, Zefiro has for many years now been considered one of the best restaurants in Portland. A chic place to see and be seen, many patrons begin their experience here in the small and crowded bar, where it is *de rigueur* to wear black and sip melon-infused vodka. Where the cuisine at Zefiro's really shines is in the appetizers, salads, and desserts. For a starter, arugula and red comice pear salad with pecorino cheese and champagne vinaigrette pops with contrasting flavors. Grilled ahi tuna is perfectly cooked and comes with grilled eggplant and a Moroccan sauce of cilantro, parsley, and lemon. Truly memorable are the desserts, worthy of the cover of a magazine. Standouts include a chocolate tower with layers of chocolate cake, and chocolate ganache layered with mint ice cream and decorated with gold foil. The setting for this dining experience is an elegantly stark room with huge flower displays.

INEXPENSIVE

Garbanzo's. 922 NW 21st Ave. ☎ **503/227-4196.** Reservations not accepted. Sandwiches $3.75–$5; dinners $7–$9. AE, DISC, MC, V. Sun–Thurs 11:30am–1:30am, Fri–Sat 11:30am–3am (closed 1 hr. earlier Oct–June). MIDDLE EASTERN/LATE-NIGHT DINING.

This casual little place calls itself a falafel bar and is a popular spot for a late-night meal (but it's also good for lunch or dinner). The menu includes all the usual Middle Eastern offerings, most of which also happen to be American Heart Association approved. You can eat at one of the tiny cafe tables or get your order to go. They even serve beer and wine. There's another Garbanzo's at 3433 SE Hawthorne Blvd. (☎ 503/239-6087) and also at 6341 SW Capitol Hwy. (☎ **503/293-7335**).

✪ **Swagat.** 2074 NW Lovejoy St. ☎ **503/227-4300.** Reservations not accepted. Main courses $8–$12. AE, DISC, MC, V. Daily 11:30am–2:30pm and 5–10pm. INDIAN.

Around the corner from Garbanzo's (see above) is an exceptionally good Indian restaurant. The *dosas,* crepes made of lentil flour, stuffed with vegetable curry, and served with a variety of sauces, are deliciously savory. We like to begin with vegetable *samosas,* crisp turnovers stuffed with potatoes and peas, and follow up with the *thali* dinner, a multicourse meal available in vegetarian or nonvegetarian. Don't forget to order some of the puffy *nan* (Indian bread). Lunch here is typically a buffet, and it's a good deal.

Another Swagat, the original one, is located on the west side in Beaverton at 4325 SW 109th Ave. (☎ **503/626-3000**).

Typhoon! 2310 NW Everett St. ☎ **503/243-7557.** Reservations recommended. Main courses $8–$15. AE, CB, DC, DISC, MC, V. Mon–Thurs 5–9pm, Fri–Sat 5–10pm, Sun 4:30–9pm (closes 1 hr. later in winter). THAI.

Located just off Northwest 23rd Avenue, this trendy Thai restaurant is a bit pricey (for Thai food), but the unusual menu offerings generally aren't available at other Portland Thai restaurants. Be sure to start a meal with the *miang kum,* which consists of dried shrimp, tiny chiles, ginger, lime, peanuts, shallots, and toasted coconut drizzled with a sweet-and-sour sauce and wrapped up in a spinach leaf. The eruption of flavors that takes place on your taste buds is absolutely astounding (we first had this in Thailand and waited years to get it here in the United States). Also not to be missed is the *hor mok*, a sort of shrimp and coconut pudding appetizer. An extensive tea list is composed of Asian teas, even more of which are available at the second location, **Typhoon! on Broadway** at 400 SW Broadway at the Imperial Hotel (☎ **503/224-8285**).

NORTHEAST PORTLAND (INCLUDING IRVINGTON)
EXPENSIVE
Salty's on the Columbia. 3839 NE Marine Dr. ☎ **503/288-4444.** Reservations highly recommended. Main courses $12–$16 at lunch, $17–$27 at dinner. AE, CB, DC, DISC, MC, V. Mon–Sat 11:15am–3pm, Sun brunch 9:30am–2:30pm; Mon–Thurs 5–10pm, Fri–Sat 5–10:30pm, Sun 4:30–9:30pm. SEAFOOD.

Located out on the Columbia River near the airport, Salty's is one of Portland's best waterfront restaurants and offers views that take in the river, mountains, and forests. Preparations here are creative, especially on the daily specials menu, and portions are large. Salmon is particularly popular. Try it smoked over alder wood (a traditional Northwest preparation). A few choice offerings of steak and chicken dishes provide options to those who don't care for seafood. *A warning:* Though the decks look appealing, the noise from the airport can make conversation difficult.

INEXPENSIVE
✪ **Chez José East.** 2200 NE Broadway. ☎ **503/280-9888.** Reservations not accepted. Main courses $5–$10. MC, V. Mon–Thurs 11:30am–11pm, Fri–Sat 11:30am–midnight, Sun 5–10pm. MEXICAN.

It's immediately obvious from both the hip decor and the menu that this isn't Taco Bell. While a squash enchilada with peanut sauce (spicy and sweet with mushrooms, apples, jicama, and sunflower seeds) sounds weird, it actually tastes great. Don't worry, though, there's plenty of traditional fare on the menu too (and at traditional cheap prices too). Because the restaurant doesn't take reservations, it's a good idea to get here early, before the line starts snaking out the door. This is a family-friendly place, so don't hesitate to bring the kids. There's also a Chez José West, 8502 SW Terwilliger Blvd. (☎ **503/244-0007**).

Rustica Italian Caffe. 1700 NE Broadway. ☎ **503/288-0990.** Reservations recommended. Main courses $9–$14. AE, DC, MC, V. Mon–Thurs 11:30am–2:30pm and 5–9:30pm, Fri 11:30am–2:30pm and 5–10:30pm, Sat 5–10:30pm, Sun 5–9pm. ITALIAN.

If you're looking for good, moderately priced Italian food in Northeast Portland, look no further than Rustica. The menu is long, portions are large, and they have a nice selection of Chianti wines and great bread. What more could you ask for, right? In addition, the atmosphere is unpretentious, the space is light and airy, and it's a popular spot for families. There is also a small pizzeria adjacent to the main restaurant. Among our favorite dishes here are the *al ceppo* pasta with grilled prawns wrapped in pancetta and the lasagna rustica made with rock shrimp, bay scallops, and Dungeness crab.

HAWTHORNE, BELMONT & INNER SOUTHEAST PORTLAND
EXPENSIVE
Genoa. 2832 SE Belmont St. ☎ **503/238-1464.** Reservations required. Fixed-price 4-course dinner $45, 7-course dinner $55. AE, CB, DC, DISC, MC, V. Mon–Sat 5:30–9:30pm; (4-course on Fri–Sat limited to 5:30 and 6pm seatings only). REGIONAL ITALIAN.

This is one of the best Italian restaurants in Portland, and with only 10 tables, it's also one of the smallest, an ideal setting for a romantic dinner. Everything is made fresh in the kitchen with the best of local seasonal ingredients, from the breads to the luscious desserts, and service is quite attentive. The fixed-price menu changes every couple of weeks, but a typical dinner might start with *prosciutto* ham accompanied by balsamic-infused vegetables, followed by a creamy wild mushroom soup. The pasta course could be a lasagne, followed by sautéed calamari. Main courses offer such choices as quail stuffed with juniper berries and sage, or baked halibut with a sauce of clams, white wine, and parsley. Following a dessert such as a chocolate and nut torte, the finishing touch is a fresh fruit course.

MODERATE

Bread and Ink Cafe. 3610 SE Hawthorne Blvd. ☎ **503/239-4756.** Reservations recommended. Main courses $6–$9 at lunch, $12–$20 at dinner; Sun brunch $15 or à la carte. AE, DISC, MC, V. Mon–Thurs 7am–9pm, Fri 7am–10:30pm, Sat 8am–10:30pm, Sun 9am–2pm and 5–9:30pm. NORTHWEST/MEDITERRANEAN.

This is funky Hawthorne Boulevard's most upscale restaurant, yet it is still more of a casual neighborhood cafe. Every meal here is carefully and imaginatively prepared using fresh Northwest ingredients, and consequently, flavors change considerably with the seasons. A recent spring menu included chicken breast provençal with kalamata olives and roasted garlic, and spinach and feta cheese ravioli. Desserts are a mainstay of Bread and Ink's loyal patrons, so don't pass them by. The Yiddish Sunday brunch is one of the most filling in the city.

INEXPENSIVE

Esparza's Tex-Mex Café. 2725 SE Ankeny St. ☎ **503/234-7909.** Reservations not accepted. Main courses $8.75–$14.50. AE, CB, DC, DISC, MC, V. Tues–Sat 11:30am–10pm (in summer Fri–Sat until 10:30pm). TEX-MEX.

With red-eyed cow skulls on the walls and stuffed iguanas and armadillos hanging from the ceiling, the decor here can only be described as Tex-eclectic, an epithet that also applies to the menu. Sure there are tamales and tacos, but they might be filled with ostrich, buffalo meat, or smoked salmon. Rest assured you can also get standard ingredients such as chicken and beef. Main courses come with some of the best rice and beans we've ever had. The *nopalitos* (fried cactus) are worth a try, and the margaritas just might be the best in Portland. While you're waiting for a seat (there's almost always a wait), check out the vintage tunes on the jukebox.

✪ **Ken's Home Plate.** 1852 SE Hawthorne Blvd. ☎ **503/236-9520.** Plates and sandwiches $7–$8. MC, V. Tues–Sat 11am–7pm. AMERICAN REGIONAL.

It's just a tiny take-out place, but chef/owner Ken Gordon turns out dishes that would do justice to the best restaurants in town. More than a dozen entrees are available daily, such as salmon-mushroom strudel, seafood and andouille sausage gumbo, Moroccan chicken pie, and Asian barbecued ribs. That's if you can get past the incredibly delicious grilled sandwiches that come with a side of any of the more than half a dozen different salads. Desserts such as marble cheesecake brownies and luscious fruit cobblers, prominently displayed on the countertop, are very difficult to ignore.

Nicholas's. 318 SE Grand Ave. (between Pine and Oak sts.). ☎ **503/235-5123.** Reservations not accepted. Main courses $3–$9. No credit cards. Mon–Sat 10am–9pm, Sun 11am–7pm. LEBANESE.

This little hole-in-the-wall on an ugly stretch of Grand Avenue is usually packed at mealtimes, and it's not the decor or ambiance that pulls people in. The big draw is the great food at cheap prices. Our favorite dish is the *Manakishe,* Mediterranean pizza with thyme, oregano, sesame seeds, olive oil, and lemony-flavored sumac. Also available are a creamy *humous, baba ghanouj,* kabobs, *falafel,* and *gyro* sandwiches.

Old Wives' Tales. 1300 E. Burnside St. ☎ **503/238-0470.** Reservations recommended for parties of 5 or more. Breakfasts $5–$7; lunch and dinner main courses $6–$14. AE, DISC, MC, V. Sun–Thurs 8am–9pm, Fri–Sat 8am–10pm. INTERNATIONAL/VEGETARIAN.

Old Wives' Tales is a sort of Portland countercultural institution. The menu is mostly vegetarian, with multiethnic dishes such as spanakopita and burritos, with a smattering of chicken and seafood dishes. Breakfast here is a popular meal and is served until 2pm daily. Old Wives' Tales's other claim to fame is as the city's best place to eat out with kids if you aren't into the fast-food scene. There are plenty of meal choices for children, and they love the playroom.

WESTMORELAND & SELLWOOD
MODERATE

✪ **Assaggio.** 7742 SE 13th Ave. ☎ **503/232-6151.** Reservations accepted only for parties of 6 or more. Main courses $10–$14. MC, V. Tues–Thurs 5–9:30pm, Fri–Sat 5–10pm. RUSTIC ITALIAN.

This tiny trattoria in the Sellwood neighborhood offers 15 pastas and more than 100 wines, almost all of which are Italian. The atmosphere is theatrical, with indirect lighting, dark walls, and the likes of Mario Lanza playing in the background. Don't be surprised if after taking your first bite, you suddenly hear a Verdi aria. While pastas are the main attraction, this does not mean the flavors are not robust. *Assaggio* means a sampling or a taste, and that is exactly what you get if you order salad, bruschetta, or pasta Assaggio—a sampling of several dishes all served family style. This is especially fun if you're here with a group. For dessert, we wouldn't miss the *semifreddo al torrone* (frozen chocolate-almond mousse) or the tiramisu.

✪ **Caprial's Bistro and Wine.** 7015 SE Milwaukie Ave. ☎ **503/236-6457.** Reservations highly recommended. Main courses $7.50–$9.75 at lunch, $18–$22 at dinner. MC, V. Tues–Fri 11am–3pm, Sat 11:30am–3pm; Tues–Thurs 5–9pm, Fri–Sat 5–9:30pm. NORTHWEST.

If you're a foody, you're probably already familiar with celebrity chef Caprial Pence, who helped put the Northwest on the national restaurant map and has since written several cookbooks and hosted TV and radio food shows. Because of Caprial's popularity, you should make your reservation here as soon as you know you'll be in town. Entrees combine perfectly cooked meats and seafoods with vibrant sauces such as onion compote or coriander-yogurt sauce. Pork loin is always a good bet here, as are the seasonal seafood dishes. Desserts are usually rich without being overly sweet. There is also a small wine bar and a superb selection of wines that are sold for only $3 over retail price.

✪ **Fiddleheads.** 6716 SE Milwaukie Ave. ☎ **503/233-1547.** Reservations recommended. Main courses $6.75–$8.75 at lunch, $14–$23 at dinner. AE, DISC, MC, V. Mon–Sat 11:30am–11pm, Sun 11am–10pm. PAN-AMERICAN.

Drawing on Native American cooking and indigenous ingredients of the Americas, Fiddleheads is one of the most unusual restaurants in Portland. We're not talking Indian fry bread here; the food at Fiddleheads is inventive and flavorful. You might find wild rice and corn fritters served with crab and crayfish and *tatonka,* a buffalo stew that's a bit like chili and is served with corn dumplings. For less unusual fare, look for the likes of beef tenderloin with Pinot Noir sauce. For dessert, you might try a warm bing-cherry dumpling. Wine choices are many, and the prices are moderate.

Half a dozen vegetarian dishes appear on the menu, and brunch is served on Saturday and Sunday.

Saburo's Sushi House. 1667 SE Bybee Blvd. ☎ **503/236-4237.** Reservations not accepted. Main courses $7.50–$15; sushi $2.50–$7. DC, JCB, MC, V. Mon–Thurs 5–9:30pm, Fri 5–10:30pm, Sat 4:30–10pm, Sun 4:30–9pm. JAPANESE.

This tiny sushi restaurant is so enormously popular that there is almost always a line out the door, and as people linger over their sushi, frequently ordering "just one more," the line doesn't always move very fast. However, when you do finally get a seat and your sushi arrives, you'll know it was worth it. Our favorite is the *sabu* roll with lots of fish, and the *maguro* tuna sushi with generous slabs of tuna. Most Westerners don't care for the sea urchin, but you can try it if you're brave.

INEXPENSIVE

○ **El Palenque.** 8324 SE 17th Ave. ☎ **503/231-5140.** Main courses $5–$13. MC, V. Sun–Wed 11am–9:30pm, Thurs–Sat 11am–11pm. SALVADORIAN/MEXICAN.

Though El Palenque also bills itself as a Mexican restaurant, the Salvadoran dishes are the real reason to come. If you've never had a *pupusa,* this is your chance; it's basically an extra-thick corn tortilla with a meat or cheese filling inside, accompanied by spicy shredded cabbage. Instead of the filling being added after the tortilla is cooked, the filling goes in beforehand, so you end up with a sort of griddle-cooked turnover. Accompany your pupusa with some fried plantains and a glass of horchata (sweet and spicy rice drink) for a typically Salvadoran meal.

SOUTHWEST PORTLAND & THE SOUTHWEST SUBURBS (INCLUDING BEAVERTON)

Also see the listings under "Northwest Portland" for information on Swagat, an Indian restaurant also located in Beaverton.

MODERATE

The Pavillion Grill. Greenwood Inn, 10700 SW Allen Blvd., Beaverton. ☎ **503/626-4550.** Reservations recommended. Main courses $11–$20. AE, DC, DISC, MC, V. Mon 6:30am–9pm, Tues–Fri 6:30am–10pm, Sat 7am–10pm, Sun 7am–9pm. REGIONAL AMERICAN.

The food in Beaverton at the Greenwood Inn's Pavillion Grill is so good that even urban residents are willing to make the drive out here to eat. There's no denying the superb quality of the meals served at this quintessentially Northwestern restaurant; just try to make a reservation for after rush hour. The dining room looks like a gazebo, and in the center of the room, three large columns of basalt have been turned into a bubbling water fountain. The menu is varied and creative, with the likes of fried squid with chili aïoli and a salad with grilled pears, spiced hazelnuts, and goat cheese showing up on a recent appetizer list. Yucatan-style chicken with ancho chile sauce sports a lively combination of flavors.

INEXPENSIVE

The Old Spaghetti Factory. 0715 SW Bancroft St. ☎ **503/222-5375.** Reservations not accepted. Main courses $5.25–$9. AE, DISC, MC, V. Mon–Thurs 11:30am–2pm and 5–10pm, Fri 11:30am–2pm and 5–11pm, Sat noon–11pm, Sun noon–10pm. ITALIAN.

Sure this is a chain restaurant, but incredibly low prices, great decor, a fabulous water-front location on the bank of the Willamette River, and the fact that the chain had its start right here in Portland are reason enough to give this place a chance. This is the best waterfront restaurant in town for kids, and it's a lot of fun for adults too. Sort of a cross between a church, a trolley depot, and a Victorian brothel, this restaurant will keep you entertained and won't cost much more than McDonald's. To find it, watch for the big building with the blue tile roof.

CAFES

The following cafes not only serve the full range of coffee drinks, but also have atmosphere to boot:

- **Café Lena,** 2239 SE Hawthorne Blvd. (☎ **503/238-7087**), located in the funky Southeast Hawthorne neighborhood, has live music and tasty food but is best known for its poetry nights.
- **Coffee Time,** 712 NW 21st Ave. (☎ **503/497-1090**), is a favorite Northwest neighborhood hangout with tables outside, and a variety of atmospheres inside, including a cafe with big wooden booths and a dark Victorian drawing room. Take your pick.
- **Pied Cow,** 3244 SE Belmont St. (☎ **503/230-4866**), is in a Victorian house decorated in Bohemian chic, where there are couches for lounging and an outdoor garden. Soups and snacky-type foods are served, too.
- **Torrefazione Italia,** 838 NW 23rd Ave. (☎ **503/228-1255**), serves its classic brew in hand-painted Italian crockery and has a good selection of pastries to go with your drink. Also at 1430 NE Weidler (☎ 503/288-1608) and 1140 NW Everett (☎ 503/224-9896).

5 Seeing the Sights

While most American cities boast of their museums and historic buildings, shopping, and restaurants, Portland, as always, is different. Ask a Portlander about the city's must-see attractions and you'll likely be directed to the Japanese Garden, the International Rose Test Garden, and the Portland Saturday Market. Portland's weather produces some of the finest gardens in the country. And all the rain seems to keep artists indoors creating beautiful art and crafts for much of the year, work that many artists sell at the Portland Saturday Market.

DOWNTOWN PORTLAND'S CULTURAL DISTRICT

Any visit to Portland should start at the corner of Southwest Broadway and Yamhill Street on ✪ **Pioneer Courthouse Square,** which doubles as Portland's outdoor living room and the heart of the city. The brick-paved square is an outdoor stage for everything from flower displays to concerts to protest rallies, but not too many years ago this beautiful brick-paved square was nothing but a parking lot. The parking lot was created by the controversial razing in 1951 of the Portland Hotel, an architectural gem of a Queen Anne–style château. Today the square, with its tumbling waterfall fountain and freestanding columns, is Portland's favorite gathering spot, especially at noon, when the *Weather Machine,* a mechanical sculpture, forecasts the upcoming 24 hours. Amid a fanfare of music and flashing lights, the Weather Machine sends up clouds of mist and then raises either a sun (clear weather), a dragon (stormy weather), or a blue heron (clouds and drizzle). Keep your eyes on the square's brick pavement. Every brick contains a name (or names) or statement, and some are rather curious. Also on the square, you'll find a Starbucks espresso bar and Powell's Travel Store, and in 1999 Portland Oregon Visitors Association (POVA) had plans to open a visitor information center here, possibly in the year 2000.

Also not to be missed in this neighborhood are ***Portlandia* and the Portland Building,** 1120 SW Fifth Ave. Symbol of the city, *Portlandia* is the second-largest hammered bronze statue in the country (the largest, of course, is the Statue of Lib-

Portland Attractions

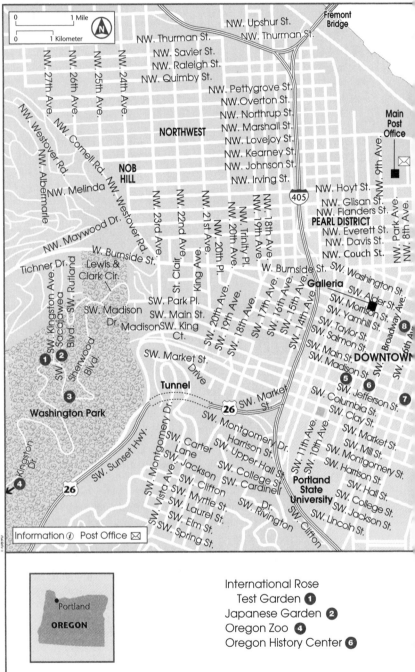

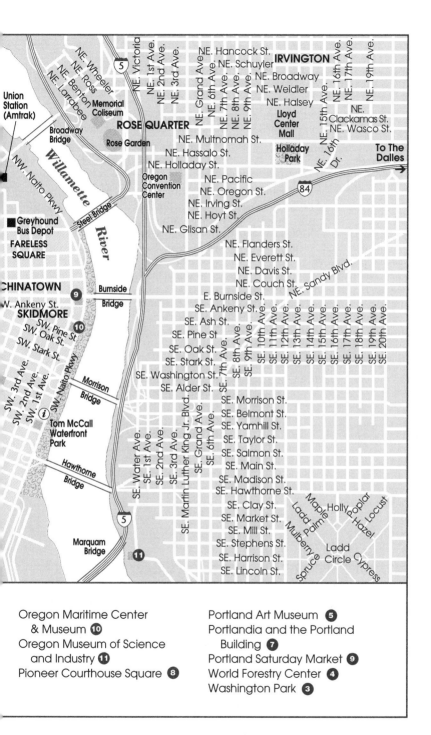

Oregon Maritime Center
  & Museum ⑩
Oregon Museum of Science
  and Industry ⑪
Pioneer Courthouse Square ⑧

Portland Art Museum ⑤
Portlandia and the Portland
  Building ⑦
Portland Saturday Market ⑨
World Forestry Center ④
Washington Park ③

erty). The massive kneeling figure holds a trident in one hand and with the other reaches toward the street. Strangely enough, this classically designed figure reminiscent of a Greek goddess perches above the entrance to one of Portland's most controversial buildings: the Portland Building, built in the early 1980s and considered the first post-modern structure in the country. Today anyone familiar with the bizarre constructions of Los Angeles architect Frank Gehry would find it difficult to understand how such an innocuous and attractive building could have ever raised such a fuss, but it did.

Oregon History Center. 1200 SW Park Ave. ☎ **503/222-1741.** Admission $6 adults and seniors (free for seniors on Thurs.), $3 students, $1.50 children 6–12, free for children under 6. Tues–Sat 10am–5pm (Thurs until 8pm), Sun noon–5pm. Bus: 6. MAX: Library Station.

In the middle of the 19th century, the Oregon Territory was a land of promise and plenty. Thousands of hardy individuals set out along the Oregon Trail, crossing a vast and rugged country to reach the fertile valleys of this region. Others came by ship around the Horn. Today the state of Oregon is still luring immigrants, and those who wish to learn about the people who discovered Oregon before them should visit this well-designed museum, where Oregon history from before the arrival of the first Euro-peans to well into this century is chronicled in educational and fascinating exhibits. The displays incorporate Native American artifacts, a covered wagon, nautical and surveying instruments, and contemporary objects such as snow skis, dolls, and bicy-cles. Museum docents, with roots stretching back to the days of the Oregon Trail, are often on hand to answer questions. There is also a research library that includes many journals from early pioneers. You can't miss this complex, with its eight-story trompe l'oeil mural stretching across the front.

✪ **Portland Art Museum.** 1219 SW Park Ave. ☎ **503/226-2811.** www.pam.org. Admis-sion $7.50 adults, $6 seniors and students (half-price for seniors every Thurs.), $4 ages 5–18, under 5 free, seniors Tues–Sat 10am–5pm, Sun noon–5pm; first Thurs of each month 10am–9pm. Bus: 6. MAX: Library Station.

While this relatively small art museum has a respectable collection of European, Asian, and American art, the museum has recently been positioning itself as the Northwest stop for touring "Blockbuster" exhibits. New galleries will be opening in 2000 with the staging of an exhibit of Russian treasures from the Stroganoff collection. Other new galleries will include one for Native American art and another for works by Northwest artists. An outdoor sculpture garden is also being added. On Wednesday nights (except in summer), the Museum After Hours program presents live music. The adjacent Northwest Film Center is affiliated with the Art Museum and shows an eclectic mix of films.

SKIDMORE HISTORIC DISTRICT & THE WILLAMETTE RIVER WATERFRONT

If Pioneer Courthouse Square is the city's living room, **Tom McCall Waterfront Park,** along the Willamette River, is the city's party room and backyard play area. There are acres of lawns, shade trees, sculptures, and fountains, and the paved path through the park is popular with in-line skaters and joggers. This park also serves each summer as the site of numerous festivals, and it houses the Waterfront Story Garden and the Japanese-American Historical Plaza, which is dedicated to Japanese Americans who were sent to internment camps during World War II.

Oregon Maritime Center and Museum. 113 SW Naito Pkwy. ☎ **503/224-7724.** www.teleportcom/~omcm. Admission $4 adults, $3 seniors, $2 students 8 and older, free for children under 8. Fri–Sun 11am–4pm (sometimes also open Wed and Thurs in summer). Bus: 12, 19, 20. MAX: Skidmore Fountain Station.

Inside this museum you'll find models of ships that once plied the Columbia and Willamette, along with early navigation instruments, artifacts from the battleship *Oregon*, old ship hardware, and other maritime memorabilia. The historic steam-powered sternwheeler *Portland*, moored across Waterfront Park from the museum, is also open to the public. Inside the old steam-powered paddle-wheel tugboat there are more displays about maritime history, and docents are on hand to answer questions about the boat.

✪ **Oregon Museum of Science and Industry (OMSI).** 1945 SE Water Ave. ☎ **800/ 955-6674** or 503/797-4000. www.omsi.edu. Museum or OMNIMAX $6.50 adults, $4.50 seniors and children 4–13; submarine tours $3; planetarium shows $3; laser light shows $6.50; discounted combination tickets available. Thurs 3pm until closing all tickets are 2-for-1. Memorial Day–Labor Day daily 9:30am–7pm (Thurs until 8pm); Labor Day–Memorial Day Tues–Sun 9:30am–5:30pm (Thurs until 8pm; also open on holiday Mondays). Closed Dec 25. Bus: 63.

Located on the east bank of the Willamette River across from the south end of Waterfront Park, this modern science museum has six huge halls, and both kids and adults find the exhibits fun and fascinating. This is a hands-on museum and everyone is urged to get involved with displays, from a discovery space for toddlers to physics and chemistry labs for older children. Simulated earthquakes and tornadoes are perennial favorites. There's plenty of pure entertainment at an OMNIMAX theater and the Murdock Sky Theater, which features laser-light shows and astronomy presentations. The USS *Blueback* submarine (used in the film *The Hunt for Red October*) is docked here and tours are given daily. Mechanical dinosaurs make frequent appearances here. Between May and late September, Samtrak (☎ **503/659-5452**), a small open-air train, runs between OMSI and Oaks Park Amusement Center. OMSI is also the departure point for several different boat cruises up and down the Willamette River.

✪ **Portland Saturday Market.** Underneath the Burnside Bridge between SW First Ave. and SW Ankeny St. ☎ **503/222-6072.** www.saturdaymarket.org. Free admission. 1st weekend in Mar–Christmas Eve, Sat 10am–5pm and Sun 11am–4:30pm. Bus: 12, 19, 20. MAX: Skidmore Fountain Station.

Portland Saturday Market (held on both Sat and Sun) is arguably the city's single most important and best loved event. For years the Northwest has attracted artists and craftspeople, and every Saturday and Sunday nearly 300 of them can be found selling their exquisite creations here. In addition to the dozens of crafts stalls, you'll find unusual ethnic foods and lots of free entertainment. This is the single best place in Portland to shop for one-of-a-kind gifts. The atmosphere is always cheerful and the crowds are colorful. At the heart of the Skidmore District, Portland Saturday Market makes an excellent starting or finishing point for a walk around Portland's downtown historic neighborhood—don't miss it. On Sunday, on-street parking is free.

WASHINGTON PARK & PORTLAND'S WEST HILLS

Portland is justly proud of its green spaces, foremost of which are Washington Park and Forest Park. Within Washington Park, you'll find the Japanese Garden and International Rose Test Garden, which are adjacent to one another on the more developed east side of the park. On the west side of the park (farther from the city center), you'll find the Hoyt Arboretum, the Oregon Zoo, and the World Forestry Center. By 2001, this will also be the site of the new Portland Children's Museum.

The 175-acre **Hoyt Arboretum,** which is planted with 900 species of trees from temperate regions around the world, is immediately adjacent to the Oregon Zoo and World Forestry Center. The arboretum has 10 miles of hiking trails and is a great place for a quick hike. Between April and October, there are guided tours of the arboretum on Saturday and Sunday at 2pm. At the south end of the arboretum, adjacent to the World Forestry Center and the Oregon Zoo, is the Vietnam Veterans Living Memorial.

To the north of Hoyt Arboretum is **Forest Park,** which, with 4,900 acres of forest, is the largest forested city park in the United States. There are 60 miles of trails and old fire roads for hiking, jogging, and mountain biking. More than 100 species of birds call these forests home, making this park a bird-watcher's paradise. Along the forest trails, you'll find huge old trees and quiet picnic spots. One of the most convenient park access points is at the top of Northwest Thurman Street (just keep heading uphill until the road dead-ends).

You can pick up a map of Forest Park at the Hoyt Arboretum Visitor Center, or at **Portland Parks & Recreation headquarters,** 1120 SW Fifth Ave., Room 1302 (☎ **503/823-5122**).

By car, the easiest route to the Washington Park attractions is straight up Southwest Main Street from downtown Portland. Alternatively, you can drive west on West Burnside Street and watch for signs, or take the zoo exit off U.S. 26. All of these attractions can also be reached via Bus 63. You can also take the MAX line to the Washington Park Station, which is adjacent to the Oregon Zoo, World Forestry Center, and Hoyt Arboretum. From here, it is possible (in the summer months) to take a bus shuttle to the Japanese Garden and International Rose Test Garden. There is also a miniature train that runs from the zoo to a station near the two public gardens.

✪ **International Rose Test Garden.** 400 SW Kingston Ave., Washington Park. ☎ **503/823-3636.** Free admission (donations accepted). Daily dawn to dusk. Bus: 63.

Covering 4½ acres of hillside in the West Hills above downtown Portland, these are among the largest and oldest rose test gardens in the United States and are the only city-maintained test gardens to bestow awards on each year's best roses. The gardens were established in 1917 by the American Rose Society and are used as a testing ground for new varieties of roses. Though you will likely see some familiar roses in the Gold Medal Garden, most of the 400 varieties on display here are new hybrids being tested before marketing. Among the roses in bloom from late spring to early winter, you'll find a separate garden of miniature roses. There is also a Shakespeare Garden that includes flowers mentioned in the Bard's works. After seeing these acres of roses, you will certainly understand why Portland is known as the City of Roses and why the Rose Festival in June is the city's biggest annual celebration. In July and August each year, there are also concerts (from classical to rock) in the Rose Garden Amphitheater. Admission varies.

✪ **Japanese Garden.** Off Kingston Ave. in Washington Park. ☎ **503/223-1321.** www.japanesegarden.com. Admission $6 adults, $3.50 students, $4 seniors, free for children under 6. Apr 1–May 31 and Sept 1–Sept 30 daily 10am–6pm; June 1–Aug 31 daily 9am–8pm; Oct 1–Mar 31 daily 10am–4pm. Closed Thanksgiving, Christmas, and New Year's Day. Bus: 63. MAX: Washington Park Station (then, in summer months, take the shuttle bus or the Zoo Train).

Considered the finest example of a Japanese garden in North America, Portland's Japanese Garden is one of the city's most popular attractions and should not be missed. Not only are there five styles of Japanese gardens scattered over 5½ acres, but there also is a view of Mount Hood, which looks surprisingly like Mount Fuji (they're both volcanoes). While Japanese gardens are traditionally not designed with colorful floral displays in mind, this garden definitely has its seasonal highlights. In early spring there are the cherry trees, in mid-spring there are the azaleas, in late-spring a huge wisteria bursts into bloom, and in early summer, huge Japanese irises color the banks of a pond. Among the gardens here there's a beautiful and very realistic waterfall (rebuilt after a landslide a couple of years ago). This is a very tranquil spot that is even more peaceful on rainy days when the crowds stay away, so don't pass up a visit just because it's raining. Also, on the third Saturday of each of the summer months, a demonstration of the Japanese tea ceremony is given in the garden's tea house. Many special events and exhibitions are also held here throughout the year (ikebana, bonsai, Japanese-inspired art).

Oregon Zoo. 4001 SW Canyon Rd., Washington Park. ☎ **503/226-1561.** www.zoooregon.org. Admission $6.50 adults, $5 seniors, $4 children ages 3–11, free for children under 2; free second Tues of each month from 3pm to closing. Apr 1–Sept 30 daily 9am–6pm; Oct 1–Mar 31 daily 9:30am–4pm. Bus: 63. MAX: Washington Park Station.

Best known for its elephant breeding program, the Oregon Zoo has the largest breeding herd of elephants in captivity. However, in recent years, the zoo has been continually adding new exhibits and has been branching out beyond the world of pachyderms. The Africa exhibit, which includes a very lifelike rain forest and a savannah populated by zebras, rhinos, giraffes, hippos, and other animals, is one of the most lifelike habitats you'll ever see in a zoo. Equally impressive is the Alaskan tundra exhibit, with grizzly bears, wolves, and musk oxen. The Cascade Exhibit is currently in the middle of an ongoing expansion that has added a mountain-goat habitat and will by summer 2000 also include a Northwest coastal environment. Other residents of this area include otters and beavers.

The Washington Park and Zoo Railway travels between the zoo and the International Rose Test and Japanese Gardens. Tickets for the miniature railway are $2.75 for adults, $2 for seniors and children 3 to 11. In the summer, there are outdoor concerts 2 nights a week; most concerts are free with zoo admission.

Pittock Mansion. 3229 NW Pittock Dr. ☎ **503/823-3624.** Admission $5 adults, $4.50 seniors, $2.50 ages 6–18. Daily noon–4pm. Closed 3 days in late Nov, most major holidays, and the month of Jan.

At nearly the highest point in the West Hills, 1,000 feet above sea level, stands the most impressive mansion in Portland. Once slated to be torn down to make way for new housing, this grand château built by the founder of Portland's *Oregonian* newspaper has been fully restored and is open to the public. Built in 1914 in a French Renaissance style, the mansion featured many innovations, including a built-in vacuum system and amazing multiple showerheads in the showers. Today it is furnished with 18th- and 19th-century antiques, much as it might have been at the time the Pittocks occupied the building. Lunch is served in the **Gate Lodge,** the former caretaker's cottage (☎ **503/823-3627**). Reservations are required.

World Forestry Center. 4033 SW Canyon Rd. ☎ **503/228-1367.** www.worldforest.org. Admission $3.50 adults, $2.50 seniors and children under 6. Daily 9am–5pm (10am–5pm in winter). Closed Christmas Day. Bus: 63. MAX: Washington Park Station.

Although with each passing year Oregon depends less and less on the timber industry, the World Forestry Center is still busy educating visitors about the importance of our forest resources. Step inside the huge wooden main hall and you come face to bark with a very large and very lifelike tree. Press a button at its base and it will tell you the story of how trees live and grow. In other rooms you can see exhibits on forests of the world, old-growth trees, a petrified wood exhibit, and a rain-forest exhibit from the Smithsonian. There are also interesting temporary exhibits staged here throughout the year, from photographic exhibits to displays of the woodworker's art.

OTHER IN-TOWN ATTRACTIONS

American Advertising Museum. Location pending, call for address. ☎ **503/226-0000.** www.admuseum.org. Admission $3 adults, $2 seniors and children 12 and under. Wed–Sat 11am–5pm, Sun noon–5pm.

Like it or not, advertising seems here to stay. In this small museum, you'll learn about its history through displays on historic advertisements, celebrities, and jingles from the 1700s to the present. Tapes of old TV commercials provide a popular trip down memory lane. At press time, the museum was close to finally establishing a permanent exhibit space after years of moving around the city; however, the address had not yet been established.

24-Hour Church of Elvis/Where's the Art? 720 SW Ankeny St. ☎ **503/226-3671;** www.churchofelvis.com. Free admission, coin-operated installations. Hours are very flexible; almost always open on weekends.

This is Portland's longtime temple of kitsch and is the city's most bizarre attraction. Coin-operated art, a video psychic, cheap (though not legal) weddings, and other absurd assemblages, interactive displays, and kitschy contraptions (such as the Vend-O-Matic Mystery Machine with whirling dolls' heads) cram this second-floor oddity. As celebrity-spokesmodel/minister S. G. Pierce says, "The tour *is* the art form." If you pass the customer test, you can even buy a Church of Elvis T-shirt. Great fun if you're a fan of Elvis, tabloids, or the unusual. If you've seen Elvis anytime in the past decade, a visit is absolutely mandatory.

PORTLAND'S OTHER PUBLIC GARDENS

For Portland's two best-loved public gardens, the **International Rose Test Garden** and the **Japanese Garden,** see "Washington Park & Portland's West Hills," earlier in this chapter.

If roses are your passion, you'll also want to check out the **Peninsula Park Rose Garden** at the corner of North Portland Boulevard and North Albina Avenue (take the Portland Blvd. exit of I-5 and go 2 blks. east), which has more rose bushes than the International Rose Test Garden.

The Berry Botanic Garden. 11505 SW Summerville Ave. ☎ **503/636-4112.** www.berrybot.org. Adults $5. Open daylight hours by appointment. Bus: 35 or 36.

Originally founded as a private garden, the Berry Botanic Garden is now one of Portland's favorite public gardens. Among the highlights is a large collection of mature rhododendron shrubs that create a forest. There is also a native plant trail, a fern garden, and rock gardens with unusual plants. Open by reservation only.

Crystal Springs Rhododendron Garden. SE 28th Ave. (1 blk. north of SE Woodstock Blvd.). ☎ **503/777-1734** or 503/771-8386. Admission $3 Mar 1–Labor Day, Thurs–Mon 10am–6pm; free at other times. Open year-round daily dawn to dusk. Bus: 19.

Nowhere do rhododendrons do better than in the cool, rainy Northwest, and nowhere in Portland is there a more impressive planting of rhodies than this one. Eight months out of the year this is a tranquil garden, with a waterfall, a lake, and ducks to feed. But when the rhododendrons and azaleas bloom from March to June, it becomes a spectacular mass of blazing color. The Rhododendron Show and Plant Sale is held here on Mother's Day weekend.

✪ **Elk Rock Garden of the Bishop's Close.** 11800 SW Military Lane. ☎ **503/636-5613.** Free admission. Daily 8am–5pm. Bus: 35 or 36.

Set on a steep hillside above the Willamette River between Portland and Lake Oswego, this garden is another that started out as a private garden. This one was donated to the local Episcopal bishop of Oregon on the condition that it be opened to the public. The mature gardens are at their best through the spring and early summer. There's also an excellent view of Mount Hood from the grounds.

✪ Frommer's Favorite Portland Experiences

Strolling the Grounds at the Japanese Garden. This is the best Japanese Garden in the United States, perhaps the best anywhere outside of Japan. My favorite time to visit is in June when the Japanese irises are in bloom. There's no better stress-reducer in the city.

Beer Sampling at Brew Pubs. They may not have invented beer here in Portland, but they certainly have turned it into an art form. Whether you're looking for a cozy corner pub or an upscale tap room, you'll find a brew pub where you can feel comfortable sampling what local brewmeisters are concocting. Try a raspberry hefeweizen for a true Northwest beer experience.

Kayaking Around Ross Island. Seattle may be the sea-kayaking capital of the Northwest, but Portland is not a bad spot either for pursuing this sport. You can paddle on either the Columbia or the Willamette River, but my favorite easy paddle is around Ross Island in the Willamette. You can even paddle past the submarine at the Oregon Museum of Science and Industry and pull out at Tom McCall Waterfront Park.

Mountain Biking the Leif Ericson Road. Forest Park is the largest forested city park in the country. Running its length is the unpaved, 12-mile Leif Ericson Road, which is closed to cars and offers occasional views of the Columbia River. This is a pretty easy ride, without any strenuous climbs.

Hanging Out at Powell's. They don't call Powell's the City of Books for nothing. Selling both new and used books, this place is so big you have to get a map at the front door. No matter how much time I spend here, it's never enough. A large cafe makes it even easier to while away the hours as you sample from the shelves.

Free Rides on the Vintage Trolleys. Tri-Met buses and MAX light-rail trolleys are all free within a large downtown area known as the Fareless Square. That alone should be enough to get you on some form of public transit while you're in town, but if you're really lucky, you might catch one of the vintage trolley cars. There aren't any San Francisco–style hills, but these old trolley cars are still fun to ride.

An Afternoon at the Portland Saturday Market. This large arts-and-crafts market is an outdoor showcase for hundreds of the Northwest's creative artisans. You'll find fascinating one-of-a-kind clothes, jewelry, kitchen wares, musical instruments, and much more. The food stalls serve up some great fast food, too.

Summertime Concerts at the Washington Park Zoo. Summertime in Portland means partying with the pachyderms. Two to three evenings a week throughout the summer, you can catch live music at the zoo's amphitheater. Musical styles include blues, bluegrass, folk, ethnic, and jazz. For the price of zoo admission, you can catch the concert and tour the zoo (if you arrive early enough). Picnics are encouraged, but no alcohol is allowed in the zoo. (However, beer and wine are on sale during concerts.)

First Thursday Art Walk. On the first Thursday of every month, Portland goes on an art binge. People get dressed up and go gallery hopping from art opening to art opening. Hors d'oeuvres and wine are usually available, and sometimes there's even live music. The galleries stay open until 9pm.

The Grotto—National Sanctuary of Our Sorrowful Mother. NE 85th Ave. and Sandy Blvd. ☎ **503/254-7371.** Free admission; elevator $1.50. Open daily summer 9am–8pm, winter 9am–5:30pm. Closed Christmas and Thanksgiving. Bus: 12.

Although, with its marble replica of Michelangelo's Pietà set in a shallow rock cave at the foot of a cliff, this forested 62-acre sanctuary is primarily a Catholic religious shrine, the gardens are also quite beautiful. This retreat is at its best in the summertime and during the Christmas season, when the grounds are decorated with thousands of lights and a choral festival is held. An elevator ride to the top of the bluff offers panoramic views of the Cascade Range, the Columbia River, and Mount St. Helens. There is also a couple of chapels on the grounds, a gift shop, and a coffee shop. The Grotto is open to visitors of all faiths.

6 Especially for Kids

In addition to the attractions listed below (described earlier in this chapter), the kids will likely enjoy the **Oregon Museum of Science and Industry,** which has lots of hands-on exhibits, and the **Oregon Zoo,** known for its elephant-breeding program. From inside the zoo, it's possible to take a small train through Washington Park to the International Rose Test Garden, below which there is the Rose Garden Children's Park, a colorful play area for younger children.

Oaks Park Amusement Center. East end of the Sellwood Bridge. ☎ **503/233-5777.** Free (all activities are on individual tickets). Memorial Day–Labor Day Tues–Thurs noon–9pm, Fri–Sat noon–10pm, Sun noon–7pm (separate hours for skating rink); May and Sept (before Memorial Day and after Labor Day) Sat–Sun noon–5pm. Bus: 40.

What would summer be without the screams of happy thrill-seekers risking their lives on a roller coaster? Pretty boring, right? Just ask the kids. They'll tell you that the real Portland excitement is at Oaks Park. Covering more than 44 acres, this amusement park first opened in 1905 to coincide with the Lewis and Clark Exposition. Beneath the shady oaks for which the park is named, you'll find waterfront picnic sites, miniature golf, music, and plenty of thrilling rides. The largest roller-skating rink in the Northwest is also here.

Portland Children's Museum. 3037 SW Second Ave. ☎ **503/823-2227.** Admission $4 adults and children, free for children under 1. Tues–Sun 9am–5pm (open school-holiday Mondays). Closed some national holidays. Bus: 1, 5, 12, 40, 43, 45, or 55.

Although this museum is small, it's loads of fun. Visitors can shop in a kid-size grocery store or play waiter or diner in a restaurant. In the Clayshop, children can make things with clay and even take home their creations. In H2 Oh! kids can blow giant bubbles and pump water. Listening to seashells, sculpting clay, blowing bubbles—there's plenty to entertain kids at this big little museum. The museum has plans to move to Washington Park, across from the Oregon Zoo, in late 2000 or early 2001. This move will give the museum lots more space and all new exhibits and will make for a full day's kid-oriented outing in combination with the zoo.

7 Organized Tours

WALKING TOURS   Peter's Walking Tours of Portland (☎ **503/665-2558** or 503/310-9837; famchausse@aol.com), led by university instructor Peter Chausse, are a great way to learn more about Portland. The walking tour of downtown takes 2½ to 4 hours, covers about 2 miles, and takes in the fountains, parks, historic places, art, and architecture that make Portland the energetic city it is. Tours are by reservation and cost $10 for adults (children are free with a paying adult).

BUS TOURS   If you want to get a general overview of Portland, **Gray Line** (☎ 800/422-7042 or 503/285-9845) offers several half-day and full-day tours. One tour visits the International Rose Test Garden and the grounds of Pittock Mansion; another stops at the Japanese Gardens and the World Forestry Center. There are also tours to see the waterfalls in the Columbia Gorge (one tour includes an excursion on the stern-wheeler *Columbia Gorge*), to Mount Hood, to the Oregon coast, and to Mount St. Helens. Tour prices range from $25 to $55 for adults, and from $12.50 to $27.50 for children.

BOAT TOURS   With two rivers, the Columbia and the Willamette, Portland has a lot of water running through it, and if you'd like to see the city from the water, you've got plenty of options. Traditionalists will want to book a tour on the **stern-wheeler** *Columbia Gorge* (☎ 503/223-3928), which offers stern wheeler cruises on the Willamette River between October and late June. During the summer months, this boat operates out of Cascade Locks on the Columbia River and does trips in the scenic Columbia Gorge. While it's fun to see the city from the water, the summer trips beneath the towering cliffs of the Columbia Gorge are far more impressive—a definite must on a summertime visit to Portland. Two-hour cruises are $12.95 for adults and $7.95 for children. Call for information on brunch, dinner, and dance cruises.

If a modern yacht is more your speed, try the ***Portland Spirit*** (☎ 800/224-3901 or 503/224-3900; www.portlandspirit.com). This 75-foot yacht specializes in dinner cruises and seats 350 people on two decks. Lunch, brunch, and dinner cruises feature Northwest cuisine with views of the city skyline out the cabin windows. Saturday nights the *Portland Spirit* becomes a floating nightclub with live bands or a deejay, and there are also Friday-afternoon cocktail cruises in the summer. Call for reservations and schedule. Prices range from $14 to $49 for adults and $9 to $18 for children.

Rose City Riverboat Cruises (☎ 503/234-6665) offers a variety of boat excursions between May and October. There are Portland harbor tours, moonlight cruises, dinner and Sunday-brunch cruises, and historical river tours, including a trip that goes through the historic Oregon City Locks at Willamette Falls. Prices range from $9 to $45 for adults, $8 to $40 for seniors, and $6 to $20 for children 12 and under. Tours leave from OMSI.

For high-speed tours up the Willamette River, there are the **Willamette Falls Jetboats** (☎ 503/231-1532 or 888/JETBOAT; www.jetboatpdx.com). The high-powered open-air boats blast their way from downtown Portland to the impressive Willamette Falls at Oregon City. The 2-hour tours, which start at OMSI, are $22 for adults and $14 for children ages 4 to 11, free for children under 4. Tours are offered May through mid-October.

TROLLEY & TRAIN EXCURSIONS   In 1998, after years of construction, the Westside MAX line finally opened from downtown Portland to Hillsboro. This line passes under the West Hills in a tunnel that stops at the deepest subway station in the country. All the stations along the route have lots of public art, which makes a ride on the light rail an interesting excursion. The trip to Hillsboro takes about an hour, and after walking around downtown Hillsboro for a bit, you can catch the MAX back to Portland. A guide to art on the Westside MAX is available. A day pass for the MAX costs $3.50. MAX also operates vintage trolleys between downtown Portland and the Lloyd Center shopping mall on the east side of the Willamette River. For information call **Vintage Trolley Inc.** (☎ 503/323-7363).

While Portland is busy reviving trolleys as a viable mass-transit option, the **Willamette Shore Trolley** (☎ 503/222-2226) is offering scenic excursions along the Willamette River in historic trolley cars (including a double-decker) from the early part of this century. The old wooden trolleys rumble over trestles and through a tunnel as they cover the 7 miles between Portland and the prestigious suburb of Lake Oswego (a 45-min. trip). Along the way, you pass through shady corridors with lots of views of the river and glimpses into the yards of posh riverfront homes. The trip takes about 45 minutes each way. In Lake Oswego, the trolley station is on State Street, between "A" Avenue and Foothills Road. In downtown Portland, the station is just south of the RiverPlace Athletic Club on Harbor Way (off Naito Pwy. at the south end of Tom McCall Waterfront Park). The round-trip fare is $6 for adults, $5 for seniors, and $3 for children ages 3 to 12. Call for a schedule. They also do an annual Fourth of July fireworks run from Oaks Park on the east bank of the Willamette River.

One other option that is sure to appeal to families is **Samtrak** (☎ 503/653-2380), which uses a restored 1942 locomotive to pull an open-air excursion car and a miniature caboose between the neighborhood of Sellwood and the Oregon Museum of Science and Industry. What makes these train rides a hit with kids is that not only is there a fun museum at one end of the run, but the train also stops at the Oaks Park Amusement Center. Along the way, the train also passes a wetland that is a bird sanctuary. Trains run from May to late September (when Oaks Park has its big Oktoberfest). Round-trip fares are $5 adults, $4 seniors, $3 ages 7 to 11, $2 ages 2 to 6. Call for schedule.

A BREWERY TOUR   If craft beers and ales are your passion, consider the **Portland Brew Bus** (☎ 888/BIG-BREW). The Brew Bus does 3- to 4-hour tours that usually stop at three brew pubs. You'll get to sample 15 to 20 brews (served in 2- to 3-oz. samples)—and you don't have to worry about who's going to be the designated driver. This is less a pub crawl than a way to learn about the process of craft brewing while visiting some of Portland's best brew pubs. Tours are $29.95 and are usually scheduled on Saturdays.

OTHER TOURS   **Ecotours of Oregon** (☎ 503/245-1428; www.ecotours-of-oregon. com), operated by Jeff Davies, offers a variety of tours and hikes. They travel to the Columbia River Gorge, Mount Hood, Mount St. Helens, the Oregon coast, ancient forests, and places to whale watch or experience Native American culture. Visits to wineries, microbreweries, and custom tours can all be arranged. Tour prices range from $30 for a city tour to $59.50 for a whale-watching excursion to the Oregon coast.

8 Outdoor Pursuits

If you're planning ahead for a visit to Portland, contact **Metro Regional Parks and Greenspaces,** 600 NE Grand Ave., Portland, OR 97232 (☎ 503/797-1850; www.metroregion.org), for its *Metro Green Scene* publication that lists tours, hikes, classes, and other outdoor activities and events being held in the Portland metro area.

BIKING   You'll notice many bicyclists on Portland streets. If you want to get rolling with everyone else, head over to **Fat Tire Farm,** 2714 NW Thurman St. (☎ 503/222-3276), to rent a mountain bike for $40 a day. Straight up Thurman Street, you'll find the trailhead for the **Leif Erikson Trail,** Forest Park's favorite route for cyclists and runners (the road is closed to motor vehicles); the trail is 12 miles long.

Bikes can also be rented downtown at **Bike Central,** 732 SW First Ave. (☎ 503/227-4439), where rental fees are about $30 per day (reservations recommended), or at **The Bike Gallery,** 1001 Tenth Ave. (☎ 503/222-3821), which is on the corner of Salmon Street and rents bikes for $40 per day. Once you have your bike, there are a number of good options for rides. The city puts out a map of Portland bike trails and routes, and you can pick up a copy of this map at bike shops. The most convenient trail starts downtown at **Tom McCall Waterfront Park** and heads south along the Willamette River through the Johns Landing area and almost to the Sellwood Bridge. If you crossed this bridge, you could visit the antiques stores in Sellwood, stop at one of the many area restaurants, and then head back. For a more strenuous ride with lots of hills, try the **Terwilliger Path,** which starts at the south end of Portland State University and travels for 10 miles through Portland's West Hills to Tryon Creek State Park. The views from the top are breathtaking. The newest Portland bike trail is the Springwater Corridor Trail through southeast Portland. This trail used to be a railroad line. Stop by a bike shop to pick up a bicycling map for the Portland metro area.

FISHING   The Portland area is salmon, steelhead, sturgeon, and trout country. You can find out about licenses and seasons from the **Oregon Department of Fish and Wildlife,** P.O. Box 59, Portland, OR 97207-0059 (☎ **503/872-5268**). If you prefer to have a guide take you where the big ones are biting, contact **Page's Northwest Guide Service** (☎ **503/760-3373**), which will take you out fishing for salmon, steelhead, walleye, and sturgeon on the Columbia or Willamette Rivers, on Nehalem or Tillamook Bay, or on other area waters ($100 to $125 per person per day). **Reel Adventures** (☎ **503/622-5372** or 503/789-6860) offers a similar fishing guide service ($125 per person per day).

GOLF   If you're a golfer, don't forget to bring your clubs along on a trip to Portland. There are plenty of public courses around the area, and greens fees at municipal courses are as low as $19 for 18 holes on a weekday and $21 on weekends and holidays. Municipal golf courses operated by the Portland Bureau of Parks and Recreation include **Progress Downs Golf Course,** 8200 SW Scholls Ferry Rd. (☎ **503/ 646-5166**); **Eastmoreland Golf Course,** 2425 SE Bybee Blvd. (☎ **503/775-2900,** or 503/292-8570 for tee-time reservations); **Heron Lakes Golf Course,** 3500 N. Victory Blvd. (☎ **503/289-1818** or 503/292-8570); and **Rose City Golf Course,** 2200 NE 71st Ave. (☎ **503/253-4744,** or 503/292-8570 for tee-time reservations).

HIKING   Hiking opportunities in the Portland area are almost unlimited, and you don't even have to leave the city for shorter hikes. Bordered by West Burnside Street on the south, Newberry Road on the north, St. Helens Road on the east, and Skyline Road on the west, **Forest Park** is the largest forested city park in the country. You'll find more than 50 miles of trails through this urban wilderness. One of the best access points is at the top of NW Thurman Street in northwest Portland.

South of downtown, you'll find **Tryon Creek State Park** on Terwilliger Road. This park is similar to Forest Park and is best known for its displays of trillium flowers in the spring. There are several miles of walking trails within the park, and a bike path to downtown Portland starts here.

SEA KAYAKING   If you want to check out the Portland skyline from water level, arrange for a sea-kayak tour through the **Portland River Company,** 0315 SW Montgomery St. (☎ **888/238-2059** or 503/229-0551; www.portlandrivercompany.com), which operates out of the Riverplace Marina at the south end of Tom McCall Waterfront Park. A 2½-hour tour that circles nearby Ross Island costs $35 per person. All-day trips on the lower Columbia River are also offered ($80 per person) and will get you off an urban river and into a wildlife refuge. This company also rents sea kayaks for $15 for the first hour and $10 per hour after that.

Photo Op

If you've seen a photo of Portland, it probably had snow-covered Mount Hood looming in the background. If you want to snap a similar photo while you're in town, there are several places to try. Most popular are probably the terraces of the International Rose Test Garden and from behind the pavilion at the Japanese Garden. Another great view can be had from the grounds of the Pittock Mansion. All three of these places are described in detail elsewhere in this chapter.

One other viewpoint is located atop Council Crest, a hilltop park in Portland's West Hills. To reach this park, take the Sylvan exit off U.S. 26 west of downtown Portland, turn south and then east (left) on Humphrey Boulevard, and then follow the signs. Alternatively, you can follow SW Broadway south out of downtown Portland. This road winds through the hills for a ways; watch for signs to the park.

9 Spectator Sports

Tickets to most sporting events, including those of the Trail Blazers, the Portland Winter Hawks, and the Portland Rockies, are sold through **TicketMaster** (☎ **503/224-4400**). Tickets to events at the Rose Garden arena and Memorial Coliseum are also sold through the **Rose Quarter** box office (☎ **503/797-9617** for tickets; 503/321-3211 event information hot line). The Rose Garden arena is home to the Portland Trail Blazers and the Portland Winter Hawks and is the main focal point of Portland's **Rose Quarter,** a sports and entertainment neighborhood that is still more an idea than a reality; but it does include the Rose Garden, Memorial Coliseum, and several restaurants and bars. To reach the Rose Garden or adjacent Memorial Coliseum, take the Rose Quarter exit off I-5. Parking is expensive, so you might want to consider taking the MAX light-rail line from downtown Portland.

AUTO RACING   **Portland International Raceway,** West Delta Park, 1940 N. Victory Blvd. (☎ **503/823-RACE**), hosts road races, drag races, motocross and other motorcycle races, go-kart races, and even vintage-car races. February to October are the busiest months here.

BASEBALL   The **Portland Rockies Baseball Club** (☎ **503/223-2837**) plays class-A minor-league ball at Civic Stadium, SW 20th Avenue and Morrison Street. The box office is open Monday through Friday from 9am to 6pm and from 8am the day of the game. Tickets are $2.50 to $7 for adults, $1 to $5 for ages 12 and under.

BASKETBALL   The NBA's **Portland Trail Blazers** (☎ **503/231-8000**) do well enough each year that they have a very loyal following. Unfortunately, they have a habit of not quite making it all the way to the top. The Blazers pound the boards at the Rose Garden arena. Call for current schedule and ticket information. Tickets are $10 to $96. If the Blazers are doing well, you can bet that tickets will be hard to come by.

HORSE RACING   **Portland Meadows,** 1001 N. Schmeer Rd. (☎ **503/285-9144**), is the place to go if you want a little horse-racing action. The race season runs from October to April, with post time at 6pm on Thursday and Friday and 12:30pm on Saturday. By car, take I-5 north to the Delta Park exit. Admission is free.

ICE HOCKEY   The **Portland Winter Hawks** (☎ **503/238-6366**), a junior-league hockey team, carves up the ice at Memorial Coliseum and the Rose Garden from October to March. Call for schedule and ticket information. Tickets are $11 to $19.

10 Day Spas

If you'd prefer a massage to a hike in the woods, consider spending a few hours at a day spa. These facilities typically offer massages, facials, seaweed wraps, and the like. Portland day spas include **Aveda Lifestyle Store and Spa,** 5th Avenue Suites Hotel, 500 Washington St. (☎ **503/248-0615**); **Urbaca,** 120 NW Ninth Ave., Suite 101 (☎ **503/241-5030**); and **Salon Nyla–The Day Spa,** 327 SW Pine St. (☎ **503/228-0389**). Expect to pay $55 to $75 for a 1-hour massage and $150 to $365 for a multitreatment spa package.

11 Shopping

Portland may not be the shopping mecca that Seattle is, but it has one thing going for it that Seattle can't claim: There's no sales tax here. This fact alone makes Portland a popular shopping destination with Washingtonians who cross the Columbia River to avoid paying their state's substantial sales tax.

GREAT SHOPPING AREAS

The blocks around Pioneer Courthouse Square are the heartland of upscale shopping in Portland. It is here that you will find Nordstrom, NIKETOWN, Saks Fifth Avenue, Pioneer Place shopping mall, and numerous other upscale boutiques and shops.

New Market Village (120 SW Ankeny St.), **Morgan's Alley** (515 SW Broadway), and **Skidmore Fountain Building** (28 SW First Ave.) are all outstanding examples of how Portland has preserved its historic buildings by turning them into unusual and very attractive shopping centers.

Portland's most "happening" area for shopping is the **Nob Hill/Northwest** neighborhood along Northwest 23rd Avenue beginning at West Burnside Street. Here you'll find block after block of unusual boutiques that are unfortunately rapidly being replaced by such chains as GAP and Pottery Barn. For shops with a more downbeat and funky flavor, head out to the **Hawthorne District,** which is the city's counterculture shopping area (lots of tie-dye and imports). In the **Pearl District,** centered around Northwest Glisan Street and Northwest 10th Avenue, you'll find the city's greatest concentration of art galleries.

SHOPPING FROM A TO Z
ANTIQUES

The **Sellwood** neighborhood (at the east end of the Sellwood Bridge) is Portland's main antiques shopping district and has around 30 antiques shops and antiques malls along 12 blocks of Southeast 13th Avenue. With its old Victorian homes and turn-of-the-century architecture, Sellwood is an ideal setting for these shops. There are plenty of good restaurants in the area in case it turns into an all day outing.

ART GALLERIES

If you're in the market for art, try to arrange your visit to coincide with the first Thursday of the month. On these days galleries in downtown Portland schedule coordinated openings in the evening.

An art gallery guide listing almost 60 Portland galleries is available at the **Portland Oregon Visitors Association Information Center,** Two World Trade Center, 25 SW Salmon St. (☎ **877/678-5263** or 503/275-9750; www.pova.com), or at galleries around Portland.

Augen Gallery. 817 SW Second Ave. ☎ **503/224-8182.**

When it opened 16 years ago, the Augen Gallery focused on internationally recognized artists such as Dine, Warhol, and Hockney. Today, the gallery has expanded its repertoire to regional contemporary painters and printmakers as well.

Butters Gallery Ltd. 520 NW Davis St. ☎ **503/248-9378.**

The Butters Gallery now has a beautiful and airy loft space on the second floor, where regional and national painters and high-quality artworks in metal, natural fibers, and glass are featured.

✪ The Laura Russo Gallery. 805 NW 21st Ave. ☎ **503/226-2754.**

Laura Russo has been on the Portland art scene for a long time and is highly respected. The focus here is on Northwest contemporary artists, showcasing talented emerging artists, as well as the estates of well-known artists.

Margo Jacobsen Gallery. 1039 NW Glisan St. ☎ **503/224-7287.**

In the heart of the Pearl District, this gallery is where you'll find most of the crowds milling about on First Thursdays. Margo Jacobsen promotes contemporary painters, printmakers, and photographers, with a focus on ceramics and glass.

Quartersaw Gallery. 528 NW 12th Ave. ☎ **503/223-2264.**

With an emphasis on figurative and expressionistic landscape, Quartersaw is a showcase for progressive Northwest art. Located in the Pearl District.

✪ Quintana Galleries. 501 SW Broadway. ☎ **503/223-1729.**

This large bright space is virtually a small museum of Native American art, selling everything from Northwest Indian masks to contemporary painting and sculpture by various Northwest coast and Inuit Native American artists. They also carry a smattering of Northwest and Southwest Indian antiquities. The jewelry selection is outstanding. Prices, however, are not cheap.

ART GLASS GALLERIES
The Bullseye Connection. 1308 NW Everett St. ☎ **503/227-2797.**

Located in the Pearl District, the Bullseye Connection is a large open exhibition and sales space for glass artists. Pieces sold here include sculptures, delightful glass jewelry, paperweights, and even marbles. At press time, the gallery was planning to move its display and sales area to a new space across the street.

Gallery Glass & Gift. 522 SW Yamhill St. ☎ **503/223-2688.**

Located across from Pioneer Square, this small shop represents more than 50 artists from the U.S. and Europe and sells whimsical and exquisite glass objects, including vases, candle holders, plates, and other pieces, from Bohemia, Poland, Germany, Italy, and Egypt.

CRAFTS
For the largest selection of local crafts, visit the **Portland Saturday Market** (see "Markets," below). This entertaining outdoor market is a showcase for local crafts.

✪ Contemporary Crafts Gallery. 3934 SW Corbett Ave. ☎ **503/223-2654.**

In business since 1937, this is the nation's oldest nonprofit art gallery that shows exclusively artwork in clay, glass, fiber, metal, and wood. It's located in a residential area between downtown and the John's Landing neighborhood, and it has a spectacular

The City of Books

Though Seattle claims the largest library system in the country, Portland has
✪ **Powell's City of Books,** 1005 W. Burnside St. (☎ **503/228-4651;** www.
powells.com), the bookstore to end all bookstores. Covering an entire city block three
floors deep, Powell's sells more than 3 million volumes each year. Though there are
arguments over whether the City of Books is the biggest bookstore in the country,
most people agree that Powell's has more titles on its shelves than any other bookstore
in the United States. In any case, there's no denying Powell's is a contender for the
claim to America's biggest bookstore.

Powell's has its origins in two used bookstores, one in Chicago and one in Portland,
both of which opened in the early 1970s. It's different from many other bookstores
in that it shelves all its books, new and used, hardback or paperback, together. At any
given time, there are usually around three-quarters of a million new and used books
on the shelves. You never know what you'll find on the shelves here.

Browsing is what Powell's is really all about. Once inside you can pick up a store
map that will direct you to color-coded rooms containing different collections of
books. Serious book collectors won't want to miss a visit to the Rare Book Room,
where you might run across a copy of the writings of Cicero published by the Aldine
Press in 1570. The most expensive book ever sold here was a Fourth Folio Shakespeare
with archival repairs for $6,000.

Satellite stores include **Powell's Technical Bookstore,** 33 NW Park St. (☎ **503/
228-3906**); **Powell's Books for Cooks and Gardeners,** 3747 SE Hawthorne Blvd.
(☎ **503/235-3802**); **Powell's Travel Store,** Pioneer Courthouse Square, Southwest
Sixth Avenue and Yamhill Street (☎ **503/228-1108**); **Powell's Books at Cascade
Plaza,** at the Progress exit off Ore. 217 in Beaverton (☎ **503/643-3131**); and
Powell's Books at PDX, Portland International Airport (☎ **503/249-1950**).

tree-shaded porch overlooking the Willamette River. The bulk of the gallery is taken
up by glass and ceramic pieces, with several cabinets of designer jewelry.

Graystone Gallery. 3279 SE Hawthorne Blvd. ☎ **503/238-0651.**

This gallery in the Southeast Hawthorne neighborhood is full of fun and whimsical
artwork and home furnishings, including paintings, jewelry, furniture, and greeting
cards.

Hoffman Gallery. 8245 SW Barnes Rd. ☎ **503/297-5544.**

The Hoffman Gallery is located on the campus of Oregon College of Art and Craft,
which has been one of the nation's foremost crafts education centers since 1906. The
gallery hosts installations and group shows by local, national, and international artists.
The adjacent gift shop has a good selection of handcrafted items. The grounds are
serene and relaxing, and there is also a cafe open to the public.

✪ **The Real Mother Goose.** 901 SW Yamhill St. ☎ **503/223-9510.**

This is Portland's premier crafts shop, and actually one of the better craft shops in the
United States. It showcases only the very finest contemporary American crafts,
including imaginative ceramics, colorful art glass, intricate jewelry, exquisite wooden
furniture, and sculptural works. Hundreds of craftspeople and artists from all over the
United States are represented here, and even if you're not buying, you should stop by
to see the best of American craftsmanship.

Other locations include Washington Square; Tigard (☎ **503/620-2243**); and Portland International Airport, Main Terminal (☎ **503/284-9929**).

Twist. 30 NW 23rd Place. ☎ **503/224-0334.**

This large store has quite a massive selection of wildly colorful and imaginative furniture, crockery, glassware, and lamps, and also a limited but intense selection of handmade jewelry from artists around the United States.

DEPARTMENT STORES

Meier and Frank. 621 SW Fifth Ave. ☎ **503/223-0512.**

Meier and Frank has been a Portland institution for more than 100 years. Their flagship store on Pioneer Courthouse Square was built in 1898 and, with 10 stories, was at one time the tallest store in the Northwest. Today those 10 stories of consumer goods and great sales still attract crowds of shoppers. The store is open daily, with Friday usually the latest night. Other locations include 1100 Lloyd Center (☎ **503/281-4797**) and 9300 SW Washington Square Rd. in Tigard (☎ **503/620-3311**).

Nordstrom. 701 SW Broadway. ☎ **503/224-6666.**

Directly across the street from Pioneer Courthouse Square and a block away from Meier and Frank, Nordstrom is a top-of-the-line department store that originated in the Northwest and takes great pride in its personal service and friendliness. This pride is well founded—the store has devoutly loyal customers who would never dream of shopping anywhere else. There is even a pianist playing a baby grand to accompany shoppers on their rounds. Other Nordstroms in the area are at 1001 Lloyd Center (☎ **503/287-2444**) and 9700 SW Washington Square Rd. in Tigard (☎ **503/620-0555**).

FASHION

Sportswear

Columbia Sportswear Company. 911 SW Broadway and Taylor St. ☎ **503/226-6800.**

This flagship store is surprisingly low-key, given that the nearby Nike flagship store and the new REI in Seattle are designed to knock your socks off. Displays showing the Columbia line of outdoor clothing are rustic, with lots of natural wood. The most dramatic architectural feature of the store is the entryway, in which a very wide tree trunk seemingly supports the roof, and a mini-video light show plays upon the floor.

Columbia Sportswear Company Outlet Store. 1323 SE Tacoma St. ☎ **503/238-0118.**

This outlet store in the Sellwood neighborhood south of downtown and across the river sells well-made outdoor clothing and sportswear from one of the Northwest's premier outdoor clothing manufacturers. You'll pay 30% to 50% less here than you will at the downtown flagship store (though the clothes will likely be last year's models).

The Jantzen Store. 921 SW Morrison St. (in the Galleria). ☎ **503/221-1443.**

Jantzen is another sports-apparel manufacturer located in Portland. The company got its start when a local rowing team requested wool outfits to keep out the chill, but nowadays, Jantzen is supplying outfits for warmer weather. You can shop their full line of attractive and innovative swimsuit styles right here, and there are even occasional sales.

Nike Factory Outlet. 3044 NE Martin Luther King Jr. Blvd. (¾ mile north of Broadway). ☎ **503/281-5901.**

The Nike outlet is one season behind the current season at NIKETOWN, selling swoosh brand running, aerobic, tennis, golf, basketball, kids, and you-name-it sports clothing and accessories at discounted prices.

✪ **NIKETOWN.** 930 SW Sixth Ave. ☎ **503/221-6453.**

This superglitzy, ultracontempo showcase for Nike products blasted onto the Portland shopping scene with all the subtlety of a Super Bowl celebration. Matte black decor, George Segal–style plaster statues of athletes, and videos everywhere give NIKE-TOWN the feel of a sports museum or disco. A true shopping experience.

Men's & Women's
Langlitz Leathers. 2443 SE Division St. ☎ **503/235-0959.**

This family-run shop produces the Rolls-Royce of leather jackets. Even though there may be a wait for a handmade motorcycle jacket (the shop turns out only six a day), motorcyclists ride their Harleys from the East Coast to be fitted for one. It's rumored that Jay Leno bought a jacket here before he became famous.

Norm Thompson. 1805 NW Thurman St. ☎ **503/221-0764.**

Known throughout the rest of the country from its mail-order catalogs, Norm Thompson is a mainstay of the well-to-do in Portland, offering classic styling for men and women. There's also a store at Portland International Airport (☎ **503/249-0170**).

The Portland Pendleton Shop. 900 SW Fifth Ave. (entrance is actually on Fourth Ave. between Salmon and Taylor). ☎ **503/242-0037.**

Pendleton wool is as much a part of life in the Northwest as forests and salmon. This company's fine wool fashions for men and women define the country-club look in the Northwest and in many other parts of the country. Pleated skirts and tweed jackets are de rigueur here, as are the colorful blankets that have helped keep generations of northwesterners warm through long chilly winters.

Men's Clothing
Mario's. 921 SW Morrison St. ☎ **503/227-3477.**

Located inside the Galleria, Mario's sells self-consciously stylish European men's fashions straight off the pages of upscale men's fashion magazines. Prices are as high as you would expect. If you long to be European but your birth certificate says otherwise, here you can at least adopt the look.

Women's Clothing
Changes. 927 SW Yamhill St. ☎ **503/223-3737.**

Located next door to The Real Mother Goose gallery, this shop specializes in hand-made clothing, including handwoven scarves, jackets, shawls, hand-painted silks, and other wearable art.

✪ **The Eye of Ra.** 5331 SW Macadam Ave. ☎ **503/224-4292.**

Women with sophisticated tastes in ethnic fashions will want to visit this shop in The Water Tower at John's Landing shopping center. Silk and rayon predominate, and there is plenty of ethnic jewelry by creative designers to accompany any ensemble you might put together here. Ethnic furniture and home decor are also for sale.

Mercantile. 735 SW Park St. (across the street from Nordstrom). ☎ **503/223-6649.**

This specialty store for women carries modern classic clothing from blue jeans to black tie. Designers represented are both European and American, from Zannela Italian separates to the whimsical fashions of Nicole Miller. You'll find stylish purses, exquisite formal wear, and cashmere sweaters. The occasional sale yields some good selections at marked-down prices.

M. Sellin Ltd. 3556 SE Hawthorne Blvd. ☎ **503/239-4605.**

Located in the relaxed and low-key Hawthorne district, this shop carries women's "soft dressing" clothing made of natural fabrics with comfortable styling along the lines of designers such as Mishi and Amanda Gray. There's also a good selection of jewelry at reasonable prices.

FOOD

The Made in Oregon shops offer the best selection of local food products such as hazelnuts, marionberry and raspberry jam, and smoked salmon. See "Gifts & Souvenirs," below, for details.

GIFTS & SOUVENIRS

For unique locally made souvenirs, your best bet is Portland Saturday Market (see "Markets," below, for details).

Made in Oregon. 921 SW Morrison St. (in the Galleria). ☎ **800/828-9673** or 503/241-3630.

This is your one-stop shop for all manner of made-in-Oregon gifts, food products, and clothing. Every product they sell is either grown, caught, or made in Oregon. This is the place to visit for salmon, filberts, jams and jellies, Pendleton woolens, and Oregon wines.

Other Portland-area branches can be found in Portland International Airport's Main Terminal (☎ **503/282-7827**); in Lloyd Center, Southeast Multnomah Street and Southeast Broadway (☎ **503/282-7636**); and in Old Town at 10 NW First Ave. (☎ **503/273-8354**). All branches are open daily, but hours vary from store to store.

MALLS/SHOPPING CENTERS

Jantzen Beach SuperCenter. 1405 Jantzen Beach Center. ☎ **503/286-9103.**

This large shopping mall is located on the site of a former amusement park where an old 1920s carousel still operates. There are several major department stores and more than 80 other shops. You'll also find the REI co-op recreational-equipment store here. This mall has long been popular with residents of Washington State, who come to shop where there is no sales tax.

Lloyd Center. Bounded by SE Multnomah St., NE Broadway, NE 16th Ave., and NE Ninth Ave. ☎ **503/282-2511.**

Lloyd Center was the largest shopping mall on the West Coast when it opened in 1960. In 1991, an extensive renovation was completed to bring it up to current standards. There are five anchor stores and more than 200 specialty shops here, including a Nordstrom and a Meier and Frank. A food court, ice-skating rink, and eight-screen cinema complete the mall's facilities.

Pioneer Place. 700 SW Fifth Ave. ☎ **503/228-5800.**

Located only a block from Pioneer Courthouse Square, Portland's newest downtown shopping center is also its most upscale. Anchored by a Saks Fifth Avenue, Pioneer Place is where the elite shop for high fashions and expensive gifts. You'll also find Portland's branch of the Nature Company and the city's only Godiva chocolatier here.

The Water Tower at Johns Landing. 5331 SW Macadam Ave. ☎ **503/228-9431.**

As you're driving south from downtown Portland on Macadam Avenue, you can't miss the old wooden water tower for which this unusual shopping mall is named. Standing high above the roof of the mall, it was once used as a storage tank for fire-fighting water. Hardwood floors, huge overhead beams, and a tree-shaded courtyard paved with Belgian cobblestones from Portland's first paved streets give this place plenty of character. There are about 40 specialty shops and restaurants here.

MARKETS

✪ **Portland Saturday Market.** Underneath the Burnside Bridge between SW First Ave. and SW Ankeny St. ☎ **503/222-6072.** www.saturdaymarket.org.

The Portland Saturday Market (held on both Sat and Sun) is arguably the city's single most important and best loved event. For years the Northwest has attracted artists and craftspeople, and every Saturday and Sunday nearly 300 of them can be found selling their exquisite creations here. In addition to the dozens of crafts stalls, you'll find flowers, fresh produce, ethnic and unusual foods, and lots of free entertainment. This is the single best place in Portland to shop for one-of-a-kind gifts. The atmosphere is always cheerful and the crowds are always colorful. Don't miss this unique market. On Sunday, on-street parking is free. Open first weekend in March through Christmas Eve, Saturday 10am to 5pm, Sunday 11am to 4:30pm; closed January and February.

TOYS

✪ **Finnegan's Toys and Gifts.** 922 SW Yamhill St. ☎ **503/221-0306.**

We all harbor a small child within ourselves, and this is the sort of place that has that inner child kicking and screaming in the aisles if you don't buy that silly little toy you never got when you were young. Kids love this place, too. It's the largest toy store in downtown Portland.

WINE

Great Wine Buys. 1515 NE Broadway. ☎ **503/287-2897.**

Oenophiles who have developed a taste for Oregon wines will want to stock up here before heading home. One of the best little wine shops in Portland, this store has a tasting bar, and the staff is always very helpful. Open Monday through Saturday 10:30am to 6:30pm, Sunday noon to 5pm.

Oregon Wines on Broadway. 515 SW Broadway. ☎ **503/228-4655.**

This cozy wine bar/shop is located diagonally across from the Hotel Vintage Plaza. Here you can taste some of Oregon's fine wines, including Pinot Noirs, Chardonnays, and Gewürztraminers, as well as Washington state Cabernet Sauvignons and Merlots. It's very difficult to walk out of here without buying a bottle or two.

12 Portland After Dark

Portland is the Northwest's second cultural center. Its symphony orchestra, ballet, and opera are all well regarded, and the many theater companies offer classic and contemporary plays. If you're a jazz fan, you'll feel right at home—there's always a lot of live jazz being played around town. In summer, festivals move the city's cultural activities outdoors.

To find out what's going on during your visit, pick up a copy of *Willamette Week* (www.wweek.com), Portland's free weekly arts-and-entertainment newspaper. The *Oregonian* (www.oregonian.com), the city's daily newspaper, also publishes lots of entertainment-related information in its Friday "A&E" section and also in the Sunday edition of the paper. The *Oregonian's* Inside Line (☎ **503/225-5555**) provides information on upcoming concerts and festivals.

Many theaters and performance halls in Portland offer discounts to students and senior citizens, who can often save money by buying their tickets on the day of a performance or within a half hour of curtain time.

Tickets for many of the venues listed below can be purchased through either **TicketMaster** (☎ 503/224-4400; www.ticketmaster.com), which has outlets at area G.I. Joe's and Meier & Frank stores, or **Fastixx** (☎ 800/992-TIXX or 503/224-TIXX), which has outlets at area Fred Meyer stores. More convenient for many visitors will be the **Ticket Central–Portland** desk at the Portland Oregon Visitors Association's visitor center, 25 SW Salmon St. This one-stop, walk-up ticket-shopping desk sells tickets to events and performances at almost all Portland venues, including tickets otherwise sold through Ticketmaster or Fastixx. Phone purchases are currently not available.

THE PERFORMING ARTS

For the most part, the Portland performing-arts scene revolves around the **Portland Center for the Performing Arts,** 1111 SW Broadway (☎ **503/248-4335**), which comprises four theaters in three different buildings (☎ **503/796-9293** for upcoming events). The **Arlene Schnitzer Concert Hall,** Southwest Broadway and Southwest Main Street, known locally as the Schnitz, is an immaculately restored 1920s movie palace that still displays the original Portland theater sign and marquee out front and is home to the Oregon Symphony. This hall also hosts popular music performances, lectures, and many other special performances. Directly across Main Street from the Schnitz, at 1111 SW Broadway, is the sparkling glass jewel box known as the **New Theater Building.** This building houses both the **Intermediate** and the **Winningstad** theaters. The Intermediate Theatre is home to Portland Center Stage, while the two theaters together host stage productions by local and visiting companies. A few blocks away from this concentration of venues is the 3,000-seat **Portland Civic Auditorium,** Southwest Third Avenue and Southwest Clay Street, the largest of the four halls and the home of the Portland Opera and the Oregon Ballet Theatre. In addition to resident companies mentioned above, these halls together host numerous visiting companies each year, including touring Broadway shows.

For occasional avant-garde performances, check the schedule of the **Portland Institute for Contemporary Art (PICA)** (☎ **503/242-1419**), which presents innovative performances by both well-known and less-established performance artists and musicians.

OPERA & CLASSICAL MUSIC

Founded in 1896, the **Oregon Symphony** (☎ **800/228-7343** or 503/228-1353), which performs at the Arlene Schnitzer Concert Hall, 1111 SW Broadway, is the oldest symphony orchestra on the West Coast. Under the expert baton of conductor James de Preist, the symphony has achieved national recognition and each year between September and June stages several series, including classical, pops, Sunday matinees, and children's concerts. Ticket prices range from $15 to $60 (Sat and Sun nights seniors and students may purchase half-price tickets 1 hr. before a classical or pops concert; Mon nights there are $5 student tickets).

Each season, the **Portland Opera** (☎ **503/241-1802;** www.portlandopera.org), which performs at the Portland Civic Auditorium, Southwest Third Avenue and Southwest Clay Street, offers five different productions of grand opera and light opera. The season runs from October to May. Ticket prices range from $25 to $125.

Summer is the time for Portland's annual chamber music binge. **Chamber Music Northwest** (☎ **503/294-6400;** www.cmnw.org) is a 5-week-long series that starts in late June and attracts the world's finest chamber musicians. Performances are held at Reed College and Catlin Gable School (tickets $16 to $29).

THEATER

Portland Center Stage (☎ **503/274-6588**), at the Portland Center for the Performing Arts, 1111 SW Broadway, is Portland's largest professional theater company. A combination of six classic and contemporary plays are staged during their October to April season (tickets $10 to $38).

The play's the thing at **Tygres Heart Shakespeare Co.** (☎ **503/288-8400**), which performs at the Dolores Winningstad Theatre, 1111 SW Broadway, and old Will would be proud. Tygres Heart remains true to its name and stages only works by the bard himself. The three-play season runs from October to May (tickets $9 to $30).

If it's musicals you want, you've got a couple of options in Portland. At Civic Auditorium, you can catch the latest touring Broadway shows brought to town by the **Portland Opera Presents KeyBank Best of Broadway series** (☎ **503/241-1802**). Tickets range from $16 to $65. For other classics from Broadway's past, check the schedule of the **Musical Theatre Company** (☎ **503/224-8730; 503/224-5411** for tickets), a semiprofessional company that performs at the Eastside Performance Center, Southeast 14th Avenue and Southeast Stark Street. The season runs October to May (tickets $21 to $27).

For more daring theater productions, see what's on tap at the **Artists Repertory Theater,** 1516 SW Alder St. (☎ **503/241-1278**); **IMAGO Theatre,** 17 SE Eighth Ave. (☎ **503/231-9581**); or the **Miracle Theater/Teatro Milagro,** 425 SE Sixth Ave. (☎ **503/236-7253**), which specializes in Latino-inspired theater. Also, at 3430 SE Belmont Street, you'll find Theater! Theatre!, which is home to two of Portland's more adventurous theater companies: **Stark Raving Theater** (☎ **503/232-7072**) and **triangle productions** (☎ **503/239-5919**).

DANCE

Although the **Oregon Ballet Theatre** (☎ **503/222-5538**), which performs at the Portland Civic Auditorium, is best loved for its sold-out performances each December of *The Nutcracker,* this company also stages the annual American Choreographers Showcase. This latter performance often features world premieres. Rounding out the season are performances of classic and contemporary ballets (tickets $12.50 to $76.50).

SUMMER CONCERT SERIES

When summer hits, Portlanders like to head outdoors to hear music. Most of this music is popular rock, reggae, jazz, blues, and folk, and most of these series schedule enough variety over the summer that they'll eventually appeal to almost every music listener in the city.

Outdoor music series to check on in the summer include performances at **The Showplace at Portland Meadows** in north Portland, **Rose Garden Concerts** (national acts) at the Washington Park Rose Garden Amphitheater, and **Rhythm and Zoo** and **Zoo Beat Concerts** at Washington Park Zoo (national acts; ☎ **503/226-1561**). With the exception of the zoo concerts and Music by Blue Lake, tickets for shows in these series are available through either **TicketMaster** (☎ **503/224-4400**) or **Fastixx** (☎ **503/224-8499**).

THE CLUB & MUSIC SCENE
ROCK, BLUES & FOLK

Aladdin Theater. 3017 SE Milwaukie Ave. ☎ **503/233-1994;** www.showman.com. Tickets $10–$20.

This former movie theater now serves as one of Portland's main venues for touring performers (such as John Prine, Chick Corea, Michelle Shocked) from a very diverse musical spectrum that includes blues, rock, ethnic, country, folk, and jazz. Regular singer-songwriter programs.

Berbati's Pan. 231 SW Ankeny St. ☎ **503/248-4579.** Cover $1–$15.

Located in Old Town and affiliated with a popular Greek restaurant, this is currently one of Portland's most popular rock clubs. A wide variety of acts, often those on the verge of breaking into the national limelight, play here.

✪ **Crystal Ballroom.** 1332 West Burnside St. ☎ **503/778-5625;** www.mcmenamins. com. Cover $5–$17.

The Crystal Ballroom has a long and not-so-illustrious history. It first opened before 1920, and since then it has seen performers from the early jazz scene to James Brown, Marvin Gaye, and The Grateful Dead. The McMenamin Brothers (of local brewing fame) renovated the Crystal Ballroom a few years back and refurbished its dance floor, which is made to feel like it's floating. The ballroom is now host to a variety of performances and special events nearly every night of the week. Ringlers Pub (a brew pub) is downstairs.

Roseland Theater & Grill. 8 NW Sixth Ave. ☎ **503/224-2038.** Cover $5–$35.

Roseland Theater, though it isn't all that large, is currently Portland's premier live music club for touring national name acts. You might encounter the likes of John Mayall, Joe Satriani, John Hiatt, Sugar Ray, Little Feat, or Mickey Hart. There's also a restaurant affiliated with the club.

Jazz

✪ **Atwater's Restaurant and Bar.** 111 SW Fifth Ave. ☎ **503/275-3600.**

Up on the 30th floor of the pale-pink U.S. Bancorp Tower is one of Portland's most expensive restaurants, and certainly the one with the best view. However, if you'd just like to sit back and sip a martini while gazing out at the city lights below, they have a splendid bar, perfect for a romantic nightcap. Tuesday through Saturday evenings there is live jazz. The lounge menu is one of the most creative in Portland.

Brasserie Montmartre. 626 SW Park Ave. ☎ **503/224-5552.** No cover.

Located just a block off Broadway and a block away from Pioneer Courthouse Square, this is downtown Portland's most popular spot for live jazz. The Bra, as it's known by regulars, is also a favorite French restaurant, and customers tend to dress up. There's live jazz nightly.

Jazz De Opus. 33 NW Second Ave. ☎ **503/222-6077.** Cover $5 on weekends.

Located in the Old Town nightlife district, this restaurant/bar has long been one of Portland's bastions of jazz, with a cozy room and smooth jazz on the stereo. You can also catch live performances nightly by jazz musicians.

Cabaret

Darcelle's XV. 208 NW Third Ave. ☎ **503/222-5338.** Cover $10. Reservations recommended Fri–Sat.

In business since 1967 and run by Portland's best-loved cross-dresser, this cabaret is a campy Portland institution, with a female-impersonator show that has been a huge hit for years. There are shows Wednesday through Saturday.

Dance Clubs

In addition to the two clubs listed here, you can catch contemporary and retro dance music at **Panorama,** 341 SW Tenth Ave. (☎ **503/221-7262**), which is popular primarily with a gay clientelle, though it also attracts lots of straights. See "The Gay & Lesbian Nightlife Scene," below, for details.

Fernando's Hideaway. 824 SW First Ave. ☎ **503/248-4709.** Cover $3.

Located upstairs from a popular Spanish tapas restaurant and bar, this is currently the hottest Latin dance spot in Portland. The dance floor is tiny and the place gets packed, but that's just fine with the cruising singles who hang out here.

Red Sea. 318 SW Third Ave. ☎ **503/241-5450.** Cover $4.

By day this is a barbecue/Ethiopian restaurant, but by night it's the busiest Afro-Caribbean dance club in Portland. The dance floor is small and the place gets stiflingly hot, but the music, a mix of Afro-pop, reggae, soca, and calypso, is imminently danceable. There's live reggae on Thursday nights and sometimes on Friday night as well.

THE BAR & PUB SCENE
BARS

Bima. 1338 NW Hoyt St. ☎ **503/241-3465.**

One of the first warehouse remakes to appear in the Pearl District, Bima is ostensibly a Southern/Caribbean restaurant, but as everyone knows, folks in the islands and in the South enjoy a good stiff drink too. The bar is dark and the clientele well dressed.

✪ **The Brazen Bean.** 2075 NW Glisan St. ☎ **503/294-0636.**

What started out as a late-night coffeehouse has now become a very hip cocktail and cigar bar with a *fin de siècle* European elegance. This is mainly a man's domain, but cigar-puffing women will appreciate it as well. Try the special Brazen Bean martini.

Jake's Famous Crawfish. 401 SW 12th Ave. ☎ **503/226-1419.**

In business since 1892, Jake's is a Portland institution and should not be missed (see "Dining" above). Although the historic fish house is best known for its crawfish, the bar here also happens to be one of the busiest in town when the downtown offices let out.

The Lobby Court. The Benson Hotel, 309 SW Broadway. ☎ **503/228-2000.**

Hands down the most elegant and old-world bar in Portland, the Lobby Court is in the city's most luxurious hotel. The Circassian walnut paneling and crystal chandeliers will definitely put you in the mood for a martini or single malt. Several nights a week there's live jazz.

McCormick and Schmick's Pilsner Room. 0309 SW Montgomery St. ☎ **503/220-1865.**

Located at the south end of Tom McCall Waterfront Park overlooking the Willamette River and RiverPlace Marina, the Pilsner Room keeps more than 20 local microbrews on tap, but it also does a brisk cocktail business. The crowd is upscale, and the view is one of the best in town.

✪ **iOba!** 555 NW 12th Ave. ☎ **503/228-6161.**

Currently the trendiest bar in Portland, this big Pearl District bar and nuevo Latino restaurant has a very tropical feel, despite the warehouse-district locale. After work, the bar is always packed with the stylish and the upwardly mobile. Don't miss the tropical-fruit margaritas!

Saucebox. 214 SW Broadway. ☎ **503/241-3393.**

Popular with the city's scene-makers, this hybrid restaurant-bar is a large, dramatically lit dark box that is joining the trend toward noisy dining spaces. If you want to talk,

A Portland Original: The Theater Pub

Portland brew-pub magnates, the McMenamin brothers, have hit upon a novel way to sell their craft ales—in movie pubs. The movies shown are recent releases that have not yet made it onto video. Theaters include the **Bagdad Theater,** 3702 SE Hawthorne Blvd. (☎ **503/236-9234**), a restored classic Arabian Nights movie palace; the **Mission Theater,** 1624 NW Glisan St. (☎ **503/223-4031**), which was the McMenamin brothers' first theater pub; and the **Kennedy School Theater,** 5736 NE 33rd Ave. (☎ **503/288-2180**).

you'd better do it before 10pm, which is when the deejay arrives to turn this place from restaurant into dance club. Great cocktails.

Veritable Quandary. 1220 SW First Ave. ☎ **503/227-7342.**

This tiny old brick building sits alone in the shadow of the Hawthorne Bridge and looks like a relic from the past. Inside you'll find a lively bar scene popular with the young cigar-and-martini crowd.

PUBS

If you're a beer connoisseur, you'll probably find yourself with little time left from your brew tasting to see any of Portland's other attractions. They're brewing beers in Portland the likes of which you won't taste anywhere else this side of the Atlantic. This is the heart of the Northwest craft brewing explosion, and Portland has more brew pubs and microbreweries than any other city in the United States. Although many of Portland's craft beers are available in restaurants, you owe it to yourself to go directly to the source.

Brew pubs have become big business in Portland, and there are now glitzy upscale pubs as well as funky warehouse-district locales. What this means is that no matter what vision you have of the ideal brew pub, you're likely to find your dream come true here in Portland. Whether you're wearing bike shorts or a three-piece suit, there's a pub in Portland where you can get a handcrafted beer, a light meal, and a vantage for enjoying the convivial atmosphere that only a pub can provide.

With almost three dozen brew pubs in the Portland metropolitan area, the McMenamins chain is Portland's biggest brew pub empire, and its owners style themselves as the court jesters. McMenamins pubs tend to mix brewing fanaticism with a Deadhead aesthetic. Throw in a bit of historic preservation and a strong belief in family-friendly neighborhood pubs, and you'll understand why these places are so popular.

Downtown, Pearl District & Nob Hill Pubs

✪ **Bridgeport Brewery and Brew Pub.** 1313 NW Marshall St. ☎ **503/241-7179** or 888/8FIRKIN.

Located in the trendy Pearl District, Portland's oldest microbrewery was founded in 1984 and is housed in the city's oldest industrial building (where workers once produced rope for sailing ships). The old ivy-draped brick building has loads of character, just right for enjoying craft ales, of which there are usually four to seven on tap on any given night (including several cask-conditioned ales). The pub also makes great pizza—the crust is made with wort, which is produced during the brewing process. Brewery tours are offered daily and there is occasional live music.

✪ **McMenamins Ringlers Pub.** 1332 West Burnside St. ☎ **503/225-0543.**

With mosaic pillars framing the bar, Indonesian antiques, and big old signs all around, this cavernous place is about as eclectic a brew pub as you'll ever find. A block away

Portland Is Brewing Up a Microstorm

Though espresso is the drink that drives Portland, it is the city's dozens of brew pubs that educated beer drinkers head to when they want to relax over a flavorful pint of ale. No other city in America has as great a concentration of brew pubs, and it was here that the craft brewing business got its start in the mid-1980s. Today, brew pubs continue to proliferate, with cozy neighborhood pubs vying for business with big polished establishments.

To fully appreciate what the city's craft brewers are concocting, it helps to have a little beer background. There are four basic ingredients in beer: malt, hops, yeast, and water. The first of these, malt, is made from grains, primarily barley and wheat, which are roasted to convert their carbohydrates into the sugar needed to grow yeast. The amount of roasting the grains receive during the malting process will determine the color and flavor of the final product. The darker the malt, the darker and more flavorful the beer or ale. There is a wide variety of malts, each providing its own characteristic flavor. Yeast in turn converts the malt's sugar into alcohol. There are many different strains of yeast that all lend different characters to beers. The hops are added to give beer its characteristic bitterness. The more "hoppy" the beer or ale, the more bitter it becomes. The Northwest is the nation's only commercial hop-growing region, with 75% grown in Washington and 25% grown in Oregon and Idaho.

Lagers, which are cold-fermented, are the most common beers in America, made from pale malt with a lot of hops added to give them their characteristic bitter flavor. **Pilsener,** a style of beer that originated in the mid–19th century in Czechoslovakia, is a type of lager. **Ales,** which are the most common brews served at microbreweries, are made using a warm fermentation process and usually with more and darker malt than is used in lagers and pilsners. **Porters** and **stouts** get their characteristic dark coloring and flavor from the use of dark, even charred, malt.

To these basics, you can then add a few variables. Fruit-flavored beers, which some disparage as soda-pop beer, are actually an old European tradition and, when considering the abundance of fresh fruits in the Northwest, are a natural here. If you see a sign for nitro beer in a pub, it doesn't mean they've got explosive brews, it means they've got a keg charged with nitrogen instead of carbon dioxide. The nitrogen gives the beer an extra creamy head. A nitro charge is what makes Guinness Stout so distinctive. Cask-conditioned ales, served almost room temperature and with only their own carbon dioxide to create the head, are also gaining in popularity. While some people think these brews are flat, others appreciate them for their unadulterated character. What all this adds up to is a lot of variety in Portland pubs. Cheers!

are two associated pubs, one below street level and with a beer-cellar feel and the other in a flat-iron building. These three pubs are the most atmospheric ale houses in town.

Portland Brewing Company's Brewhouse Tap Room and Grill. 2730 NW 31st Ave. ☎ **503/228-5269.**

With huge copper fermenting vats proudly displayed and polished to a high sheen, this is by far the city's most ostentatious, though certainly not its largest, brew pub. We aren't particularly fond of their brews, but decide for yourself.

Tugboat Brewing Co. 711 SW Ankeny St. ☎ **503/226-2508.**

This tiny brew pub on an alleylike street just off Broadway near The Benson hotel is just what a good local pub should be. With its picnic-table decor, it's decidedly casual, but the shelves of books lend the place a literary bent. Good brews too.

Southeast Pubs
Hawthorne Street Ale House. 3632 SE Hawthorne St. ☎ **503/233-6540.**

This neighborhood pub is a satellite of the ever-popular Bridgeport Brew Pub in the Pearl District, with the same great beers. It has a very California feel, with lots of wood and an upscale bar. There are lots of cask-conditioned ales, as well as standard taps. Good menu.

Lucky Labrador Pub. 915 SE Hawthorne Blvd. ☎ **503/236-3555.**

With a warehouse-size room, an industrial feel, and picnic tables on the loading dock out back, this brew pub is a classic southeast Portland local. The crowd is young, and dogs are welcome (even non-Labradors).

Northeast & North Portland Pubs
Alameda Brewhouse. 4765 NE Fremont St. ☎ **503/460-9025.**

With its industrial chic interior, this high-ceilinged neighborhood pub brews up some of the most unusual beers in Portland. How about a rose-petal bock, a juniper-berry porter, or a heather-flower ale made without hops? Some work, some don't, but fans of craft beers have to appreciate the willingness to experiment.

✪ **McMenamin's Kennedy School.** 5736 NE 33rd Ave. ☎ **503/249-3983.**

Never thought they'd start serving beer in elementary school, did you? In the hands of the local McMenamins brew-pub empire, an old northeast Portland school has been transformed into a sprawling complex complete with brew pub, beer garden, movie theater/pub, cigar-and-cocktails room, and even a bed-and-breakfast inn. Order up a pint and wander the halls checking out all the cool artwork.

McMenamins St. Johns Pub. 8203 N. Ivanhoe St. ☎ **503/283-8520.**

Housed in a pavilion built for the 1905 Lewis & Clark Exposition, this building was another great score for the McMenamins, who have been snapping up historic buildings left and right over the past few years. Unusual chandeliers and tapestries give this place a unique atmosphere.

Widmer Brewing and Gasthaus. 955 N. Russell St. ☎ **503/281-3333.**

Located in an industrial area just north of the Rose Garden arena, this place has the feel of a classic workingman's pub. It's Portland's largest craft brewery, best known for its hefeweizen. German and American food are served.

IRISH & ENGLISH PUBS
✪ **Horse Brass Pub.** 4534 SE Belmont St. ☎ **503/232-2202.**

If not for this eastside pub, the local microbrew scene may never have developed. It was here that many of Portland's big-name brewers used to hang out way back in the days when people could only dream of European-quality beers. There are 46 beer taps here, and you'll find some obscure and delicious brews. There's an adjacent store selling all things beer related, including lots of imported bottled beers.

Kells. 112 SW Second Ave. ☎ **503/227-4057.**

Located in Old Town, Kells is a traditional Irish pub and restaurant. In addition to pulling a good pint of Guinness, the pub has one of the most extensive Scotch whiskey lists on the West Coast. You can hear live music here every night.

THE GAY & LESBIAN NIGHTLIFE SCENE

The area around the intersection of Southwest Stark and West Burnside streets has the largest concentration of gay bars in Portland.

BARS

The Egyptian Club. 3701 SE Division St. ☎ **503/236-8689.**

Billing itself as a "girl's bar," this place sponsors everything from "Southpark" night to retro dance nights to a nude revue (women dancing for women).

Scandal's Tavern. 1038 SW Stark St. ☎ **503/227-5887.**

In business for more than 20 years, this bar/restaurant is at the heart of the gay bar scene, and there always seems to be some special event going on here. Currently, Tuesdays are dollar drink night.

DANCE CLUBS

Embers. 110 NW Broadway. ☎ **503/222-3082.** Cover $4 Thurs, $5 Fri–Sat, free Sun–Wed.

Though this is still primarily a gay disco, it's also popular with straights. There are always lots of flashing lights and sweaty bodies until the early morning, with drag shows 7 nights a week.

Panorama/Boxxes/The Brig. 341 SW Tenth Ave. ☎ **503/221-7262.** Cover $5 before 2am Fri–Sat , $7 after 2am.

Open only on Friday and Saturday, Panorama is a cavernous dance club playing a mix of retro disco and current dance music. Under the same roof you'll also find The Brig, a smaller dance club, and Boxes, a video club. The admission allows you into all three. With several different environments and a mixed crowd, an evening here can be quite entertaining. The crowd is mostly gay but everyone is welcome.

13 Side Trips to Vancouver, Washington & Oregon City

VANCOUVER, WASHINGTON

The city of Vancouver, Washington, was one of the first settlements in the Northwest and consequently has a long pioneer and military history. After the British in the guise of the Hudson's Bay Company (HBC) gave up Fort Vancouver, it became the site of the Vancouver Barracks U.S. military post. The stately homes built for the officers of the post and their attractive surroundings are now preserved as the **Vancouver National Historic Reserve.** You'll find the tree-shaded row of 21 homes, as well as Fort Vancouver, in the 1-square-mile Central Park, located just east of I-5 (take the East Mill Plain Boulevard exit just after you cross the bridge into Washington).

Start a visit to Officer's Row at the **Howard House,** 750 Anderson St. (☎ **360/ 992-1820**), a restored Victorian mansion that was once an NCO club for the military post and now serves as the information center for the national historic reserve. After learning a bit about the history of this area, you can stroll the grounds admiring the well-kept homes, two of which are open to the public. The **Grant House Folk Art Center/Grant House Gallery,** 1101 Officer's Row (☎ **360/694-5252**), was the first commanding officer's quarters and is named for President Ulysses S. Grant, who was stationed here as quartermaster in the 1850s (admission is free; open Tues through Sun from 11am to 3pm). In addition to the art center, this old home houses **Sheldon's Cafe** (☎ **360/699-1293**), which is a good place to stop for lunch.

Farther along Officers' Row, you'll find the **George C. Marshall House,** 1301 Officers' Row (☎ 360/693-3103), a Victorian-style building that replaced the Grant House as the commanding officer's quarters. This home is furnished much the way it might have looked when it was built in the late 1800s (admission is free; open Mon through Fri 9am to 5pm, Sat and Sun 11am to 6pm).

Fort Vancouver National Historic Site. 1501 E. Evergreen Blvd. ☎ **360/696-7655.** Admission $2 in summer, free in winter. Daily 9am–5pm (until 4pm in winter).

It was here in Vancouver that much of the Northwest's important early pioneer history unfolded at the Hudson's Bay Company's Fort Vancouver. The HBC, a British company, came to the Northwest in search of furs and, for most of the first half of the 19th century, was the only authority in this remote region. Fur trappers, mountain men, missionaries, explorers, and settlers all made Fort Vancouver their first stop in Oregon. Today Fort Vancouver houses several reconstructed buildings that are furnished as they might have been in the middle of the 19th century. In summer, there are period cultural demonstrations on Saturday and Sunday at 3pm.

Pearson Air Museum. 1115 E. Fifth St. ☎ **360/694-7026.** Admission $4 adults, $3 seniors, $1.50 students. Tues–Sun 10am–5pm.

A very different piece of history is preserved at this small air museum on the far side of Fort Vancouver from Officers' Row. This airfield was established in 1905 and is the oldest operating airfield in the United States. Dozens of vintage aircraft, including several World War I–era biplanes and the plane that made the first transpacific flight, are on display in a large hangar.

OREGON CITY

When the first white settlers began crossing the Oregon Trail in the early 1840s, their destination was Oregon City and the fertile Willamette Valley. At the time Portland had yet to be founded, and Oregon City, set beside powerful Willamette Falls, was the largest town in Oregon. However, with the development of Portland and the shifting of the capital to Salem, Oregon City began to lose its importance. Today this is primarily an industrial town, though one steeped in Oregon history and well worth a visit.

To get to Oregon City from Portland, you can take I-5 south to I-205 east, or you can head south from downtown Portland on Southwest Riverside Drive and drive through the wealthy suburbs of Lake Oswego and West Linn. Once you're in Oregon City, your first stop should be just south of town at the **Willamette Falls overlook** on Ore. 99E. Though the falls have been much changed by industry over the years, they are still an impressive sight.

Oregon City is divided into upper and lower sections by a steep bluff. A free municipal elevator connects the two halves of the city and affords a great view from its observation area at the top of the bluff. You'll find the 100-foot-tall elevator at the corner of Seventh Street and Railroad Avenue. It's in the upper section of town that you will find the town's many historic homes, including those listed below and the **Ermatinger House,** Sixth and John Adams streets (☎ 503/557-9199), which is Oregon City's oldest house and is open to the public Friday through Sunday from 11am to 4pm. Admission $2 adults.

Clackamas County Museum of History. 211 Tumwater Dr. ☎ **503/655-5574.** Admission $4 adults, $3 seniors, $2 ages 6–18. Mon–Fri 10am–4pm, Sat–Sun 1–5pm.

This small museum houses collections of historic memorabilia and old photos from the area. There's the obligatory covered wagon, as well as a display of Native American petroglyphs. Your admission ticket to this museum will also get you into the **Stevens Crawford House,** 603 Sixth St., a foursquare-style home that is furnished with late-19th-century antiques and looks as if the family just stepped out.

End of the Oregon Trail Interpretive Center. 1726 Washington St. ☎ **503/657-9336.** Admission $5.50 adults, $4.50 seniors, $3 ages 5–12, free for children under 5. Mon–Sat 9am–5pm, Sun 10am–5pm. Tour hours vary with day and season.

With its three Paul Bunyon–size wagons parked in the middle of Abernethy Green (the official end of the Oregon Trail), this interpretive center is impossible to miss. Inside the first of the giant wagons, you'll find an exhibit hall, a hands-on area, and a gift shop. After looking around this first wagon, visitors are then led through the next one by costumed interpreters who explain the difficulties of provisioning for the overland trek. The third wagon houses a multimedia presentation based on three Oregon Trial diaries.

McLoughlin House. 713 Center St. ☎ **503/656-5146.** Admission $4 adults, $3 seniors, $2 children ages 6–12, free for children under 6. Tues–Sat 10am–4pm, Sun 1–4pm. Closed Jan and major holidays.

Oregon City's most famous citizen was retired Hudson's Bay Company chief factor John McLoughlin, who helped found Oregon City in 1829. By the 1840s, immigrants were pouring into Oregon, and McLoughlin provided food, seeds, and tools to many of them. Upon retirement in 1846, McLoughlin moved to Oregon City, where he built what was at that time the most luxurious home in Oregon. Today McLoughlin's house is a National Historic Site and is furnished as it would have been in McLoughlin's days. Many of the pieces on display are original to the house.

5

The Willamette Valley:
The Bread (& Wine) Basket
of Oregon

For more than 150 miles, from south of Eugene to the Columbia River at Portland, the Willamette River (pronounced Wih-*lam*-it) flows between Oregon's two major mountain ranges. Protected from winter winds by the Cascade Range to the east and tempered by cool moist air from the Pacific Ocean, to the west of the Coast Range, the Willamette Valley enjoys a mild climate that belies its northerly latitudes. It was because of this relatively benign climate and the valley's rich soils that the region's first settlers chose to put down roots here, and it was along the banks of the Willamette that Oregon's first towns sprang up. Today the valley is home to Oregon's largest cities, its most productive farmlands, the state capital, and the state's two major universities.

The Willamette Valley was the Eden at the end of the Oregon Trail, a fabled land of rich soils, mild winters, and plentiful rains. Families were willing to walk 2,000 miles across the continent for a chance at starting a new life here. The valley became the breadbasket of the Oregon country, and today, despite the urban sprawl of such cities as Portland, Salem, and Eugene, the Willamette Valley still produces an agricultural bounty unequaled in its diversity. Although the region offers history and culture, its idyllic rural scenery and prolific farms are what enchant most visitors. Throughout the year, you can sample the produce of the region at farms, fruit stands, and wineries. In spring, commercial fields of tulips and irises paint the landscape with bold swaths of color. In summer, there are farm stands near almost every town, and many farms will let you pick your own strawberries, raspberries, blackberries, peaches, apples, cherries, and plums. In the autumn, you can sample the filbert and walnut harvest, and at any time of year, you can do a bit of wine tasting at dozens of wineries.

1 The North Willamette Valley Wine Country

McMinnville: 38 miles SW of Portland, 26 miles NW of Salem

If it hadn't been for Prohibition, wine connoisseurs might be comparing California wines to those of Oregon rather than vice versa. Oregon wines had already gained a national reputation back in the days when the Oregon became one of the earlier states to vote in

The Willamette Valley

Prohibition. It would be a few years before more liberal California would outlaw alcohol, and in the interim, the Golden State got the upper hand. When Prohibition was rescinded, California quickly went back to wine production, but no one bothered to revive Oregon's wine potential until the 1970s. By then, Napa Valley had sealed the cork on its wine dominance. Perhaps someday Willamette Valley wineries will be as well-known as those down in California. Actually, those days have already arrived for fans of Pinot Noir. Oregon's Pinot Noirs have gained such international attention that even some French wineries have planted vineyards here and begun producing their own Oregon wines.

The Willamette Valley is on the same latitude as the great wine regions of France, and the weather is quite similar—plenty of spring rains, then long, hot summer days and cool nights. Unfortunately, wineries here must contend with the potential specter of dark clouds and early autumn rains. These rains can sometimes wreak havoc on Willamette Valley wines, but most years the grapes get harvested before the rains begin to fall.

The North Willamette Valley wine country begins in the town of Newberg and extends south to the Salem area. The majority of the region's wineries flank the rural Ore. 99W; you'll see dozens of blue signs pointing to wineries a few miles off the highway. To the south of Salem, there are more wineries in the Corvallis and Eugene areas, which are listed later in this chapter. To the north of Ore. 99W, there are still more wineries in Washington County, which is actually in the drainage of the Tualatin River, which flows into the Willamette. These latter wineries are included below.

The two most important wine growing areas within this region, and the areas that produce the best wines, are the Red Hills above the town of Dundee and the Eola Hills northwest of Salem. In Dundee, you'll find the greatest concentration of good restaurants, while in McMinnville, the largest town in the area, you'll find plenty of hotel rooms and more good restaurants.

AREA ESSENTIALS

GETTING THERE   You'll find the heart of wine country between Newberg and McMinnville along Ore. 99W, which heads southwest out of Portland.

VISITOR INFORMATION   Contact the **McMinnville Chamber of Commerce,** 417 N. Adams St., McMinnville, OR 97128 (☎ **503/472-6196**), or the **Newberg Area Chamber of Commerce,** 115 N. Washington St., Newberg, OR 97132 (☎ **503/538-2014**).

FESTIVALS   The most prestigious festival of the year is the **International Pinot Noir Celebration** (☎ **800/775-4762**), held each year on the last weekend in July or first weekend in August. The 3-day event, which is usually sold out months in advance, includes tastings, food, music, and seminars. Registration forms are mailed out in February each year, and tickets are currently $625 per person.

TOURING THE WINERIES

The first thing you need to know about the Willamette Valley wine country is that this is not the Napa Valley. Forget pretentiousness, grand villas, celebrity wineries, snobbish waiters, or high prices for tastings. Oregon wineries are, for the most part, still small establishments. Even the new wineries that have been opening up right on Ore. 99W (and that seem calculated to provide beach-bound vacationers with a bit of distraction and some less-than-impressive wine for the weekend) are still small affairs compared to the wineries of Napa Valley. Although in recent years more and more corporate wineries have been opening with the sole purpose of producing high-priced Pinot Noir, many of the region's wineries are still family owned and operated and produce moderately priced wines.

Second, forget about Cabernet Sauvignon and Zinfandel. With the exception of southern Oregon wineries and a few Willamette Valley wineries that buy their grapes from warmer regions, the Willamette Valley just doesn't get hot enough to produce these two varietals. The wines of the Willamette Valley are primarily the cooler-climate varietals traditionally produced in Burgundy, Alsace, and Germany. Pinot Noir is the uncontested leader of the pack, with Pinot Gris running a close second these days. Gewürztraminer and Riesling are also produced, and with the recent introduction of early-ripening Dijon-clone Chardonnay grapes, the region is finally beginning to produce Chardonnays that can almost compete with those of California. Other wines you'll likely encounter in this area include Müller-Thurgau (a usually off-dry white wine), Muscats (dessert wines), and sparkling wines (often made from Pinot Noir and Chardonnay grapes).

Wine country begins only a few miles southwest of Portland on Ore. 99W. Approaching the town of Newberg, you leave the urban sprawl behind and enter the rolling farm country of Yamhill County. These hills form the western edge of the Willamette Valley and provide almost ideal conditions for growing wine grapes. Consequently, a patchwork quilt of vineyards, interspersed with orchards and woodlands, now blankets the slopes. The views from these hills take in the Willamette Valley's fertile farmlands, as well as the snowcapped peaks of the Cascades.

Between Newberg and Rickreall, you'll find more than 2 dozen wineries and tasting rooms that are open on a regular basis. There are concentrations of wineries in Dundee's Red Hills and in the Eola Hills northwest of Salem, and if you head north from Ore. 99W, you'll find another dozen or so wineries near Carlton, Yamhill, Hillsboro, and Forest Grove. Each of these groupings of wineries makes a good day's tasting route, and they have been organized here so that you can easily link them together.

Most, but not all, wineries maintain tasting rooms that are open to the public, usually between 11am or noon and 5pm. During the summer, most tasting rooms are open daily, but in other months they may be open only on weekends or by appointment. Wineries located right on Ore. 99W are usually open throughout the year. Many wineries also have a few picnic tables, so if you bring some goodies with you and then pick up a bottle of wine, you'll be set for a great picnic.

For anyone simply interested in tasting a little Oregon wine, the wineries along the highway are a good introduction. It will prove to be a very educational experience, and you'll likely find a few wines that agree with you. If you have a more-than-passing interest in wine, you'll want to explore the wineries located a few miles off Ore. 99W.

Many of the best wineries, however, are open only by appointment or on Memorial Day and Thanksgiving weekends (see "The Twice-a-Year Wineries" box for a list).

Tasting Tips

Although few Oregon wineries have regularly scheduled winery tours, if you're interested and there is someone on hand to show you around, you're usually welcome to tour the facilities.

So as not to get pulled over by the local police, you might want to limit the number of wineries you visit to between three and five in an afternoon. This will also allow you time to stop and enjoy the countryside. Even better: Have a designated driver.

The Twice-a-Year Wineries

Harvest season aside, Memorial Day weekend and Thanksgiving weekend are the two most important days of the year in wine country. On these weekends, wineries often introduce their new releases and sometimes offer barrel tastings of wines that haven't yet been bottled.

Many of the area's best boutique wineries are open to the public *only* on these two weekends. So if you're serious about wine, you won't want to pass up a Willamette Valley wine tour on one or the other of these holidays.

Area wineries open only Thanksgiving and Memorial Day weekends include the following:

Newberg, Dundee & Carlton Area

Adelsheim Vineyard, 22150 NE Calkins Lane, Newberg (☎ **503/538-3652**), is one of Oregon's oldest wineries and now does several vineyard-designate wines.

Belle Pente, 12470 NE Rowland Rd., Carlton (☎ **503/852-6389**), is one of the newer wineries in the region and produces Pinot Noir, Pinot Gris, and Chardonnay at moderate prices.

Cameron Winery, 8200 Worden Hill Rd., Dundee (☎ **503/538-0336**), focuses on Pinot Noir and produces the best nonvintage Pinot in the state (around $10).

Carlo & Julian Vineyard and Winery, 1000 E. Main St., Carlton (☎ **503/852-7432**), which is one of the newer wineries in the area and produces Pinot Noir and Sauvignon Blanc.

Chehalem, 31190 NE Veritas Lane, Newberg (☎ **503/538-1470**), produces a range of wines that includes Cerise (a Gamay Noir/Pinot Noir blend) and good Pinot Noir.

If you're serious about your wine, plan accordingly; Pinot Noir fans especially are likely to uncover some rare gems this way.

At some wineries, you'll be asked to pay a tasting fee, but at most Oregon wineries there is no charge (although there is often a fee of a few dollars to taste select or reserve vintages or older "library" wines). Many wineries have celebrations, festivals, music performances, and picnics throughout the summer, and sometimes they charge a fee to cover the cost of the appetizers and wine served.

For more information about the Oregon wine scene, including a calendar of winery events, pick up a copy of *Oregon Wine,* a monthly newspaper available at area wine shops and wineries, or contact the **Oregon Wine Magazine,** 644 SE 20th Ave., Portland, OR 97214 (☎ **503/232-7607**). The **Yamhill County Wineries Association,** P.O. Box 25162, Portland, OR 97298 (☎ **503/646-2958;** www.yamhillwine.com), publishes a free map and guide to the local wineries. You can pick up copies at almost any area winery.

THE YAMHILL COUNTY WINERIES
THE NEWBERG & DUNDEE AREA

Argyle. 691 Ore. 99W. ☎ **503/538-8520.** Daily 11am–5pm.

Located right on the highway in Dundee, this winery specializes in sparkling wines, and it started out as a joint venture between an Australian winemaker and France's

McMinnville & Amity Area

Panther Creek Cellars, 455 N. Irvine Rd., McMinnville (☎ **503/472-8080**), which is known for its excellent Pinot Noir and Chardonnay, but which also is one of the few Oregon wineries to produce Melón, a wine made from Muscadet grapes.

Tempest Vineyards, 6000 Karla's Rd., Amity (☎ **503/835-2600**), which produces all the expected area varietals but also does Zinfandel and Cabernet Sauvignon.

Youngberg Hill Vineyards, 10660 SW Youngberg Hill Rd., McMinnville (☎ **503/472-2727** or 888/657-8668), which is affiliated with a B&B and makes an excellent base of operations for exploring this region.

Eola Hills & Salem

Evesham Wood Vineyard, 3795 Wallace Rd. NW, Salem (☎ **503/371-8478**), which produces Pinot Noir, Pinot Gris, Chardonnay, and Gewürtztraminer and offers some of the best values in the state (good Pinot Noir for under $20).

St. Innocent Winery, 2701 22nd St. SE, Salem (☎ **503/378-1526**), which does very drinkable white wines as well as some good Pinot Noirs. St. Innocent also has a year-round tasting room in Portland: Oregon Wines on Broadway, 515 SW Broadway (☎ **503/228-4655**).

Hillsboro Area

Helvetia Vineyards & Winery, 22485 NW Yungen Rd., Hillsboro (☎ **503/647-5169**), which is located far north of most other wineries and does very respectable Pinot Noir.

Bollinger Champagne house. Although prices for most wines here are fairly reasonable ($12 to $14 range), the wines themselves seem harsh. Bruts and Chardonnays are the specialty, and for these you'll pay a premium. Given the traffic congestion in Dundee, this winery is best visited on the way back from the Oregon coast.

Champoeg Wine Cellars. 10375 Champoeg Rd. NE, Aurora. ☎ **503/678-2144.** May–Sept 11am–6pm; Oct–Apr Sat–Sun noon–5pm. From Newberg, go south on Ore. 219 and turn left on Champoeg Rd.

Located southeast of Newberg several miles, this small winery is a bit off the main Yamhill winery circuit. They do a wide range of wines, including Pinot Noir, Pinot Gris, Chardonnay, White Riesling, Gewürtztraminer, and Müller-Thurgau. The Pinot Gris is very drinkable.

Duck Pond Cellars. 23145 Ore. 99W. ☎ **503/538-3199.** May–Oct daily 10am–5pm; Nov–Apr daily 11am–5pm.

With its strategic location right on the highway, large parking lot, and tasting room full of gourmet food products and wine accessories, this winery aims to snag beach-bound traffic, and on summer weekends the tasting room is often too crowded to be an enjoyable place for sampling wines. So far none of their wines has impressed us, but because they're so convenient to the highway, you might as well drop by and see if anything strikes your fancy.

Dundee Springs. Ore. 99W and Fox Farm Rd. ☎ **503/554-8000.** Summer daily 11am–5pm; winter Wed–Sun 11am–5pm. Tasting fee $2.

Although this small winery produces Pinot Noir, Pinot Gris, and Pinot Blanc, the Pinot Noirs are the main focus and production is quite limited. If you're lucky, they might be tasting some of their "library" wines when you visit (the 1992 and 1994 Pinot Noirs were very good). The tasting room is housed in a little white house with purple shutters.

Erath Vineyards. 9009 NE Worden Hill Rd. ☎ **800/539-9463** or 503/538-3318. May 15–Oct 15 daily 10:30am–5:30pm; Oct 16–May 14 daily 11am–5pm. Closed Thanksgiving, Christmas, and New Year's Day. In Dundee, go north on Ninth St., which becomes Worden Hill Rd.

In business since 1972, Erath Vineyards, set high in the Red Hills of Dundee, was founded by Dick Erath, one of the pioneers of modern Oregon wine making. A wide variety of wines is produced here, and you can usually taste 10 or more during your visit to the tasting room. With so many wines to choose from, you're almost certain to find one you like. There's a pretty little public park, just right for a picnic, at the foot of the winery's driveway.

✪ **Lange Winery.** 18380 NE Buena Vista Rd., Dundee. ☎ **503/538-6476.** June–Nov Wed–Mon 11am–6pm; Dec–May Sat–Sun noon–5pm. Tasting fee $2–$3. In Dundee, go north on Ninth St. and follow signs.

Good Pinot Noirs are the hallmark of this small winery in Dundee's Red Hills, and although these usually fall in the $30 to $50 price range, they are usually competitive with comparable premier Oregon Pinots. Lange also produces quite a few wines, mostly whites, in the under-$20 range. The Pinots here are usually among the best in the state, making this a good place to develop a taste for them. We prefer the estate-grown Pinot Noirs.

Maresh Red Barn. 9325 NE Worden Hill Rd. ☎ **503/537-1098.** Mar–Nov Fri–Sun noon–5pm. In Dundee, go north on Ninth St., which becomes Worden Hill Rd.

Although the grapes of Maresh Vineyards are managed primarily for Rex Hill Vineyards, they do get some grapes custom crushed by Rex Hill under the Maresh label. There are generally only three or four varietals available, with the emphasis on Pinot Noir. Rex Hill seems to do a better job with these grapes when processing them for their own label. The setting is picturesque, with a tasting room in an old red barn.

Ponzi Vineyards/Ponzi Wine Bar. 100 SW Seventh St. ☎ **503/554-1500.** Sun–Thurs 11am–5pm, Fri–Sat 11am–6pm.

Ponzi Vineyards was one of the Oregon wine pioneers, and though it has its winery north of here near Beaverton, this new tasting room/wine bar is a more convenient place to sample Ponzi wines. Expect excellent Pinot Gris and Chardonnay (in the $20 range) and be sure to sample the Arneis, an Italian varietal dry white wine that is aged in oak and is rarely planted in this area. Also don't miss the Vino Gelato, a dessert wine made from frozen grapes. Wines from other wineries are also available here.

Rex Hill Vineyards. 30835 N. Ore. 99W. ☎ **503/538-0666.** Daily 11am–5pm (Fri–Sun 10am–5pm in summer).

One of the oldest and largest wineries in Oregon, Rex Hill is also the first winery you'll come to in the Yamhill County wine country. The hillside setting just off the highway is impressive, with attractive landscaping. Inside the tasting room, you'll find antiques, contemporary art, and a large fireplace that together set a very toney mood. Pinot Noirs are the main focus here, but with more than 200 acres of grapes, Rex Hill also does respectable Pinot Gris, Sauvignon Blanc, Chardonnay, and Riesling.

Sokol Blosser Winery. 5000 Sokol Blosser Lane. ☎ **503/864-2282.** May–Oct daily 10:30am–5:30pm; Nov–Apr 11am–5pm. West of Dundee off Ore. 99W.

Another of the big Oregon wineries, Sokol Blosser sits high on the slopes above the west end of Dundee. Off-dry whites are a strong point here, and the Evolution No. 9, a blend of 10 different grapes, shouldn't be missed. A walk-through showcase vineyard provides an opportunity to learn about the growing process. Every summer, the winery hosts concerts by well-known folk, rock, and jazz performers.

Torii Mor Winery. 18325 NE Fairview Dr. ☎ **503/434-1439.** May–Nov Sat–Sun noon–5pm. In Dundee, go north on Ninth St., and follow the signs.

With the Japanese-inspired name (*torii* means "gate" in Japanese) and gardens, you might expect this winery to produce *sake*, but instead they limit their production to Pinot Noir and Chardonnay (for sake, you'll have to drive north to Forest Grove and the Saké One brewery—see the box later in this chapter). Their better Pinot Noirs tend to be very expensive (around $50) and don't quite warrant the high price. However, less expensive Pinots are usually available, and the Chardonnay comes in at under $20.

THE AMITY & DAYTON AREA

Amity Vineyards. 18150 Amity Vineyards Rd. SE. ☎ **503/835-2362.** Feb–Dec 23 daily noon–5pm. Closed Dec 24–Jan 31. In Amity, go east on Rice Lane.

This was one of the earlier wineries in Oregon, and the winemaker here is not a fan of oaky wines. Consequently, Amity doesn't do a Chardonnay, instead offering a Pinot Blanc. They also do an unusual sulfite-free Pinot Noir made from organically grown grapes. Their late-harvest and dessert wines are a strong point. Amity also operates the Oregon Wine Tasting Room near Sheridan and the Oregon Wine Tasting Room Too in Pacific City.

Kristin Hill Winery. 3330 SE Amity-Dayton Hwy. ☎ **503/835-0850.** Mar–Dec 21 daily noon–5pm; Dec 26–Feb Sat–Sun noon–5pm. Closed Thanksgiving, Christmas, and New Year's Day. Just north of Amity at the junction with Ore. 233.

"Méthode champenoise" sparkling wines are a specialty here and make this winery well worth a visit. The Fizzy Lizzy, a cherry-infused dry sparkling wine, is one of Kristin Hill's most popular wines.

THE MCMINNVILLE AREA

For a selection of area wines (several of which can be tasted on any given day), visit **Noah's–A Wine Bar,** 525 NE Third St., McMinnville (☎ **503/434-2787**), or the **Third Street Grill & Wine Shop,** 729 NE Third St. (☎ **503/435-1745**), both of which are in downtown McMinnville. West of McMinnville on Ore. 18, you'll also find the **Oregon Wine Tasting Room,** 19702 SW Ore. 18, Sheridan (☎ **503/ 843-3787**), which is adjacent to the Lawrence Gallery.

✪ **Yamhill Valley Vineyards.** 16250 Oldsville Rd. ☎ **800/825-4845.** Mid-Mar to June 1 Sat–Sun 11am–5pm; June 2–Thanksgiving weekend daily 11am–5pm.

This is one of our favorite area wineries, located west of McMinnville near Sheridan on a 200-acre estate in the foothills of the Coast Range. Pinot Noirs are the strong point here, and prices for younger Pinots are often quite reasonable (under $20). You can sometimes also find older "library" wines here at prices comparable to or slightly less than those of the region's high-end boutique wineries. The Chardonnay here represents an especially good deal, and good Pinot Blancs and dry Rieslings are also produced.

THE YAMHILL & CARLTON AREA

In the town of Carlton, you'll find **The Tasting Room,** 105 W. Main St. (☎ **503/852-6733**), which specializes in wines from wineries that are not usually open to the public, making this an absolute must if you can't be around on Memorial Day or Thanksgiving weekend. Most wines featured here are from wineries in the immediate vicinity of Carlton.

✪ **Autumn Wind Vineyard.** 15225 NE North Valley Rd., Newberg. ☎ **503-538-6931.** June–Aug daily noon–5pm; Mar–May and Sept–Dec Sat–Sun noon–5pm. Closed Jan–Feb. From Yamhill, go east on Ore. 240, turn left on Ribbon Ridge Rd. and left again on North Valley Rd.

This small winery between Carlton and Newberg is one of the area's more reliable producers of moderately priced wines (mostly in the $10 to $15 range). Although the majority of the vineyard is planted in Pinot Noir grapes, they also produce good dry whites (Sauvignon Blanc, Pinot Gris, and Chardonnay) and a sweet Müller-Thurgau. You'll find a couple of different styles of Pinot Noir in the $20 to $30 range. It's worth the drive.

Chateau Benoit. 6580 NE Mineral Springs Rd. ☎ **800/248-4835** or 503/864-2991. Daily 10am–5pm. Take Ore. 99W to Lafayette and go north on Mineral Springs Rd.

Located high on a hill with one of the best views in the area, this winery, amid nearly 100 acres of vines, has a large and impressive tasting room and does quite a few respectable white wines. Dry Gewürztraminers and Müller-Thurgaus are among the more reliable dry whites here. The winery's new Dijon-clone Chardonnay grapes are also producing better Chardonnays than ever before. Look for decent inexpensive Pinot Noirs too.

Willakenzie Estate. 19143 NE Laughlin Rd., Yamhill. ☎ **503/662-3280.** Memorial Day–Labor Day daily 11am–5pm.

Situated on a 400-acre estate above the Chehalem Valley, this winery produces primarily Pinot Noir, Pinot Gris, Pinot Blanc, and Chardonnay in its gravity-fed facility. There's a nice picnic area with good views.

THE MARION & POLK COUNTY WINERIES
THE EOLA HILLS

Some people claim that the best Pinot Noirs in Oregon come from the Eola Hills northwest of Salem. Why not decide for yourself?

Bethel Heights Vineyards. 6060 Bethel Heights Rd. NW. ☎ **503/581-2262.** June–Aug Tues–Sun 11am–5pm; Mar–May and Sept–Dec Sat–Sun 11am–5pm. Closed Dec 24–Feb. From Ore. 221 in Lincoln, take Zena Rd. west and turn right on Bethel Heights Rd.

Set high on a hill and surrounded by more than 50 acres of grapes, Bethel Heights produces primarily Chardonnays and Pinot Noirs, though they also offer Pinot Gris and Pinot Blanc. Their less expensive Pinot Noirs can be good buys, and while their best Chardonnays are up around $20, they're very good. The tasting room was new as of summer 1999.

Cristom Vineyards. 6905 Spring Valley Rd. NW. ☎ **503/375-3068.** Tues–Sun 11am–5pm. Closed Jan–Feb. From Ore. 221 in Lincoln, take Zena Rd. west and turn right on Spring Valley Rd., or take Spring Valley Rd. west from Ore. 221 north of Lincoln.

With a beautiful setting high in the Eola Hills, this winery is an ideal place for a picnic (they have several tables just outside the tasting room). The Chardonnays here, from both estate-grown grapes and grapes grown elsewhere in the region, are quite good. They fall within the standard $20 price range you would expect to pay for a good Oregon Chardonnay. Cristom is one of the few wineries in the region producing a Viognier wine, which has a Rieslinglike nose but is peppery like a Gewürtztraminer.

✪ **Cuneo Cellars.** 9360 SE Eola Hills Rd. ☎ **503/835-2782.** Apr–Nov Sat noon–5pm. From the Lafayette Hwy. south of Ore. 18, go west on Eola Hills Rd.

Big reds are the specialty of this winery on the northern edge of the Eola Hills. Winemaker Gino Cuneo does only red wines, with his Cana's Feast Cabernet-Merlot blend a favorite of fans of complex, full-bodied red wines. Cabernet Sauvignon, Pinot Noir, and even Nebbiolo all get the same treatment. If you like assertive red wines, don't miss this small winery. The only drawback is the limited hours.

Redhawk Vineyard. 2995 Michigan City Rd. NW. ☎ **503/362-1596.** May–Nov daily noon–5pm. Closed Dec–Apr. 3 miles north of Ore. 22 off Ore. 221.

Best known for its "Grateful Red" Pinot Noir, Redhawk brings a welcome dose of humor to wine making and wine tasting. Other noteworthy vintages include Chateau Mootom (with a cow on the label), Rat Race Red, and Punk Floyd (with an alien punk rocker on the label). Plenty of serious wines are also available. Most table wines run $5 to $10; varietals run $12 to $25. Definitely not for wine snobs.

Stangeland Cellars. 8500 Hopewell Rd. NW. ☎ **503/581-0355.** May–Nov Sat–Sun noon–5pm; Dec–Apr first weekend of each month noon–5pm. Off Ore. 221 north of Lincoln; from I-5, take exit 263 and the Wheatland Ferry.

Located on the northeast side of the Eola Hills, this small family-run winery produces Chardonnay, Pinot Gris, and Pinot Noir, as well as a fun and inexpensive picnic wine made with Chenin Blanc. The estate Pinot Noir can be a good value.

Witness Tree Vineyard. 7111 Spring Valley Rd. NW. ☎ **503/585-7874.** June–Aug Tues–Sun 11am–5pm; Mar–May and Sept–Dec Sat–Sun 11am–5pm. Closed Jan–Feb. From Ore. 221 in Lincoln, take Zena Rd. west and turn right on Spring Valley Rd., or take Spring Valley Rd. west from Ore. 221 north of Lincoln.

Located right next door to Cristom and named for a tree used by surveyors in the 19th century, this unpretentious winery produces estate-grown Chardonnays and Pinot Noirs. In a region of high-priced Pinots, Witness Tree is noteworthy for offering very drinkable Pinot Noirs for under $20 (though they also produce pricier vintage select Pinots). Winemaker Bryce Bagnall is often on hand to answer questions.

THE RICKREALL & DALLAS AREA

✪ **Chateau Bianca Winery.** 17485 Ore. 22, Dallas. ☎ **503/623-6181.** Feb–Dec daily 11am–6pm. Closed Jan, Dec 25, and Jan 1. On Ore. 22 about 10 miles west of Rickreall and Ore. 99W.

This family-run winery does a wide range of wines, most of which are excellent. (But you'd expect no less from a family that brought its wine-making skills over from Germany.) The Pinot Noirs here are great values, with bottles usually available in both the $10 and the $20 range. The dry Riesling is proof that a German-style wine can be just as good as the much-touted Burgundian-style wines so prevalent in Oregon. A good sparkling wine is also available, and a port was in the works in 1999. The winery also has a B&B.

Eola Hills Wine Cellars. 501 S. Pacific Hwy., Rickreall. ☎ **503/623-2405.** Daily 11am–5pm. On Ore. 99W between Rickreall and Monmouth.

Well-known in the area for its Sunday brunches, this winery is located on the outskirts of Rickreall and offers everything from Cabernet Sauvignon to Zinfandel (and almost all at very reasonable prices). However, the reason Eola Hills has such a wide variety of wines is that they bring their grapes in from as far away as California. This makes for lower prices too.

Flynn Winery. 2200 Pacific Hwy. W., Rickreall. ☎ **503/623-8683.** Sat–Sun 11am–5pm. Closed Easter, Dec 23–25, and Jan 1. On Ore. 99W north of Rickreall.

This winery is known primarily for its sparkling wines, and they do both a Brut (75% Pinot Noir and 25% Chardonnay) and a Blanc de Blanc (100% Chardonnay), both of which are quite good and usually sell for less than $15. The tasting room is in the winery's aging room, where you can observe the steps involved in the classic "méthode champenoise." They also do decent Chardonnays and Pinot Noirs in the $8 to $12 range.

Oak Grove Orchards Winery. 6090 Crowley Rd., Rickreall. ☎ **503/364-7052.** Tues–Sun noon–6pm. From Ore. 99W between Amity and Rickreall, go east on Crowley Rd. or the road on the north side of Flynn Vineyards.

This casual little winery on the west side of the Eola Hills specializes in dessert wines, particularly various types of Muscat wines. If you're a fan of Muscats, you won't want to pass up the opportunity to stop here.

Van Duzer Vineyards. 11975 Smithfield Rd. ☎ **503/623-6420.** Sat–Sun 11am–5pm. North of Rickreall off Ore. 99W; take graveled Smithfield Rd. 3 miles west.

Producing primarily Pinot Noirs and Chardonnays in the Burgundian style, this winery is built on the side of an oak-shaded knoll with a commanding view across the valley to the Eola Hills. The tasting room is small, and only a few wines are available at any given time. Van Duzer also does a well-balanced Riesling and a sparkling wine.

WASHINGTON COUNTY WINERIES
THE GASTON & FOREST GROVE AREA

Although Gaston is little more than a wide spot in the road, it is home to a great little wine and sandwich shop. **24° Brix,** 108 Mill St. (☎ **503/985-3434**), specializes in good local wines for under $20. Several of the wines sold here are from tiny wineries that are never open to the public; in fact, some of them don't even have their own winery facilities, but produce their wines elsewhere. By the way, the Brix is the scale by which sugar in grapes is measured.

Elk Cove Vineyards. 27751 NW Olson Rd., Gaston. ☎ **503/985-7760.** Daily 11am–5pm. Closed Dec 24–25 and Jan 1. From Ore. 47 in Gaston, go west on Olson Rd.

Located in the hills above the community of Gaston, this is another of the state's larger wineries. The La Sirene is an unusual blend that is quite balanced and drinkable. They also do a good dry Riesling and a sparkling wine (around $20). Some of their Pinot Noirs are good values.

Kramer Vineyards. 26830 NW Olson Rd., Gaston. ☎ **503/662-4545.** June–Sept daily noon–5pm; Mar–May and Oct–Dec Fri–Sun noon–5pm. Closed Easter, Thanksgiving, and Christmas. From Ore. 47 in Gaston, go west on Olson Rd.

Located a little farther along the same road as Elk Cover Vineyards, this small winery does a decent Chardonnay. Don't miss the raspberry wine; it's the absolute essence of berries—a perfect summer dessert wine. Prices are fairly reasonable. There's a wine and weird food festival the first weekend in April, plus other celebrations throughout the year.

✪ **Laurel Ridge Winery.** 46350 David Hill Rd. ☎ **503/359-5436.** Feb–Dec daily noon–5pm. Closed Jan. West of Forest Grove off Ore. 8.

This winery, up a gravel road, overlooks the forested foothills of the Coast Range and has its tasting room in a picturesque yellow farmhouse. Here you'll usually find around

Sake It to Me, Baby

When you've just had it with fruity Pinot Noirs and oaky Chardonnays and you've got to have something a little bit different, why not try a little sake?

In Forest Grove, you'll find one of North America's few sake breweries, **Saké One Brewery,** 820 Elm St. (☎ 503/357-7056). But this Japanese-style rice wine is probably unlike any you've tasted before. This is premium sake and is meant to be served cold—the traditional way to serve premium sake in Japan. (Cheaper sakes are served hot to cover up the inferior quality.) To make things even more unusual, this sake brewery also bottles several very untraditional flavored sakes made with citrus, hazelnut, Asian pear, and raspberry flavoring. Think sake latte and you've got a pretty good idea of what these rice wines are like. You'll find Saké One on the south side of Forest Grove off Ore. 47.

2 dozen wines available for tasting. Laurel Ridge is best known for its excellent Brut sparkling wines and its very drinkable Sauvignon Blanc. The winery also does an unusual sparkling Riesling and a couple of ports, one of which is made from Pinot Noir grapes ($1 to taste the ports).

Montinore Vineyards. 3663 SW Dilley Rd. ☎ **503/359-5012.** Jan–Mar Sat–Sun noon–5pm; Apr–Dec daily noon–5pm. Closed major holidays. South of Forest Grove off Ore. 47 at Dilley.

As at other large Oregon wineries, the wines here seem to be somewhat lacking, though prices are generally quite reasonable. Exceptions include reasonably priced Pinot Noirs, Chardonnays, and their late-harvest Riesling (which isn't too sweet). The setting, an old farmhouse straight out of the antebellum South, is quite picturesque. There are outdoor jazz concerts in the summer.

Shafer Vineyard Cellars. 6200 NW Gales Creek Rd. ☎ **503/357-6604.** Mar–Dec Sat–Sun 11am–5pm. Closed Jan–Feb. From Forest Grove, go 4.5 miles west on Ore. 8.

This winery is small enough that the owners still work the tasting room, but large enough to have a dozen or more wines available for tasting on any given day. They're strong on whites, which they sell at very reasonable prices. The 1998 Müller-Thurgau and 1998 Gewürztraminer were both very tasty, and the Rieslings are very consistent. Adjacent to the tasting room is a Christmas shop.

Tualatin Vineyards. NW 10850 Seavey Rd. ☎ **503/357-5005.** Mar–Dec Sat–Sun noon–5pm. Closed Thanksgiving, Christmas, and Jan–Feb. From Forest Grove, go west on Ore. 8, turn north on Thatcher Rd. and then west on Clapshaw Hill Rd.

Under the same ownership as the huge Willamette Valley Vineyards, this winery is a bit off the beaten track but is worth searching out. Their 1997 Riesling was distinctive for a strong citrus flavor, which also came through in their 1997 late harvest Gewürztraminer, a sweet dessert wine. The 1997 Pinot Noir was also good but was selling for more than $20 a bottle. They also do a semisparkling Muscat dessert wine.

THE HILLSBORO & BEAVERTON AREA

Cooper Mountain Vineyards. 9480 SW Grabhorn Rd., Beaverton. ☎ **503/649-0027.** May–Oct Fri–Sun noon–5pm; Feb–Apr and Nov Sat–Sun noon–5pm. Closed Dec–Jan. From Ore. 217 on the west side of Portland, take Ore. 210 (Scholls Ferry Rd.) west approximately 5 miles, turn right on Tile Flat Rd. and right again on Grabhorn Rd.

Now nearly surrounded by wealthy suburbs, this mountain-top winery is one of the few in the state that uses only organic grapes. The Pinot Gris is moderately priced and quite tasty, as are the Chardonnays, which go light on the oak. Pinot Noirs are decent,

---

Wine Tasting by Appointment

For the serious oenophile only, there are quite a few wineries that are open only by appointment. These wineries aren't really set up to handle visitors, but if you are seriously interested in wine and are looking to purchase a case for your wine cellar, they're usually happy to let you drop by. Alternatively, wines from most of these wineries can be had at **The Tasting Room,** Main and Pine Streets, Carlton (☎ **503/852-6733**).

Area wineries open by appointment only include the following:

Archery Summit, 18599 NE Archery Summit Rd., Dayton (☎ **503/864-4300**), which does hearty Pinot Noirs reminiscent of Cabernet Sauvignon.

Brick House Vineyards, 18200 Lewis Rogers Lane, Newberg (☎ **503/538-5136**), which is an organic vineyard.

Ken Wright Cellars, 236 N. Kutch St., Carlton (☎ **503/852-7070**), one of the region's top Pinot Noir producers.

Raptor Ridge Winery, 29090 SW Wildhaven Lane, Hillsboro (☎ **503/887-5595**), which does a very good Pinot Noir.

Stag Hollow, 7930 Blackburn Rd., Yamhill (☎ **503/662-4022**), which is a small family winery producing Pinot Noir.

---

and for those who like a light wine, there is a Pinot Noir Blanc that makes a great picnic wine. There's also a fruity yet dry Brut that weighs in at around $20.

Lion Valley Vineyards. 35040 SW Unger Rd., Cornelius. ☎ **503/628-5458.** Sat–Sun noon–5pm. Take Ore. 219 south 5 miles from Hillsboro, then go 3 miles west on SW Unger Rd.

One of the region's newer wineries and located off the usual wine route, this small winery does very good and reasonably priced (under $20) Pinot Noirs. (Serious Burgundy drinkers sometimes find the Pinots a bit too untraditional, though.) It's worth searching out.

✪ **Oak Knoll Winery.** 29700 SW Burkhalter Rd., Hillsboro. ☎ **503/648-8198.** Daily noon–5pm. From Hillsboro, go south on Ore. 219 and turn left on Burkhalter Rd.

Although the only grape they actually grow here is a Niagara—which makes for a fruity but very drinkable wine—Oak Knoll manages each year to acquire some of the best grapes from area vineyards. Their wines are consistently excellent; in fact, this is one of the few wineries we know of where we've liked every wine we've tasted.

Ponzi Vineyards. 14665 SW Winery Lane, Beaverton. ☎ **503/628-1227.** Feb–Dec Sat–Sun noon–5pm, Mon–Fri 10am–5pm. Closed Thanksgiving, Christmas, New Year's, and Jan. From Ore. 217 on the west side of Portland, take Ore. 210 (Scholls Ferry Rd.) west 4.5 miles to a left on Vandermost Rd.

Although Ponzi's new tasting room/wine bar on Ore. 99W in Dundee is more convenient for most people touring wine country, it's still possible to taste wines here at the source. See "The Yamhill County Wineries," above, for a description of this pioneering Oregon winery.

ALTERNATIVE WINE COUNTRY TOURING

If you're interested in learning more about Oregon wines and want to tour the nearby wine country, contact **Grape Escape** (☎ **503/282-4262**), which offers an in-depth winery tour of the Willamette Valley. The all-day tour includes stops at several wineries, with an elegant picnic lunch, and pickup and drop-off at your hotel ($75 per person). For those with less time, there are half-day afternoon trips that take in two or three wineries ($50 per person). A number of other tours are also available.

You can also see the wine country from the air on a hot-air balloon ride with **Vista Balloon Adventures** (☎ **800/622-2309** or 503/625-7385), which charges $179 per person for a 1-hour flight (with hot breakfast and sparkling wine toast), or through **Rex Hill Vineyards** (☎ **503/538-0666**), which charges $180 per person or $350 per couple for a 1-hour flight followed by a sparkling wine brunch at the vineyard. Alternatively, you can opt for a flight over the region in a glider. Contact **Cascade Soaring,** McMinnville Airport (☎ **503/472-8805**), which offers a variety of flights ranging in duration from 15 to 55 minutes and in price from $40 to $150. Gliders carrying one or two passengers are used.

Want to see wine country from a saddle? Give the **Wine Country Farms Bed & Breakfast,** 6855 Breyman Orchards Rd. (☎ **503/538-8249**), a call. They offer 2- to 4-hour horseback rides ($38 to $75). The longer ride goes through vineyards while the shorter ride is on a forest trail.

MORE THINGS TO SEE & DO

Seven miles south of Newberg off Ore. 219, on the banks of the Willamette River, is **Champoeg State Park** (pronounced Sham-*poo*-ee) (☎ **503/678-1251**). It was here, in the area known as French Prairie (home to several families of French Canadian settlers), that the region's first pioneers voted in 1843 for the formation of a provisional American government. This occurred at a time when the British, in the form of the Hudson's Bay Company, exercised a strong control over the Northwest. The park includes a campground, a bike path, a picnic area, a historic home, a log cabin, and a visitor center that traces Champoeg's history from its days as a Native American village up through its pioneer farming days. Park admission is $3.

Near downtown Newberg, the **Hoover-Minthorn House Museum,** 115 S. River St. (☎ **503/538-6629**), preserves the childhood home of Herbert Hoover, the 31st president of the United States. It's open March to November, Wednesday through Sunday from 1 to 4pm; December and February, Saturday and Sunday from 1 to 4pm (closed Jan). Admission is $2 for adults, $1.50 for seniors, and $1 for students.

It has been many years since Howard Hughes's famous **"Spruce Goose"** flying boat left Long Beach, California, to take up residence in McMinnville, but as of yet the plane's new home has still not been completed. Currently, it looks as though the new museum may open in the summer of 2001. Check with the McMinnville Chamber of Commerce.

SHOPPING IN THE AREA

If you're interested in picking up some local art or crafts, there are several places worth visiting in the area. West of McMinnville near Sheridan, you'll find the **Lawrence Gallery** (☎ **503/843-3633**). This large art gallery has a sculpture garden, a water garden, and several rooms full of artworks by regional artists; it's open daily.

If you enjoy shopping for antiques and collectibles, there are several places in the area you may want to visit. In Lafayette, there is the **Lafayette Schoolhouse Antique Mall,** 784 Ore. 99W (☎ **503/864-2720**), located in a 1910 schoolhouse and filled with more than 100 dealers.

To stock up on local jams, wines, and other gourmet food items, visit **Your Northwest,** Ore. 99W and Seventh Street, Dundee (☎ **503/554-8101**), which is in the same building as the Ponzi Wine Bar and Dundee Bistro restaurant. This little shop is crammed full of all manner of gourmet foods and Northwest crafts. **Firestone Farms,**

18400 N. Ore. 99W (☎ 503/864-2672), which is located just west of Dundee, also sells a wide selection of produce and gourmet foods from around the area. This shop also sells area wines. If you like chocolate, you might want to head down to Amity and stop in at the **Brigittine Monastery,** 23300 Walker Lane (☎ 503/835-8080), which is known for making a heavenly fudge. The fudge and truffles are on sale at the guest reception area, which is open daily from 9:30am to 5:30pm (closed from 10:30am to 1:30pm on Sun).

WHERE TO STAY
THE NEWBERG & DUNDEE AREA

Partridge Farm Bed & Breakfast. 4300 E. Portland Rd., Newberg, OR 97132. ☎ 503/538-2050. 3 units. $70–$90 double; $90–$110 suite. Rates include full breakfast. MC, V.

Under the same ownership as the nearby Rex Hill Winery, this old yellow farmhouse feels secluded even though it's right on busy Ore. 99W (and gets a bit of traffic noise). Shade trees, beautiful gardens full of perennials, berry hedges, and fruit trees give Partridge Farm a relaxing country atmosphere that, on a sunny summer afternoon, positively begs to be enjoyed with a glass of wine and a good book. Inside, there's a hint of French country sophistication. The one room and two suites are all quite large and are furnished with period antiques that complement the mood of this turn-of-the-century home.

✪ **Springbrook Hazelnut Farm.** 30295 N. Ore. 99W, Newberg, OR 97132. ☎ 800/793-8528 or 503/538-4606. 5 units. $95 double; $175 suite; $175 cottage; $160 carriage house. Rates include full breakfast. No credit cards.

Only 20 miles from Portland, this 70-acre working farm is a convenient rural getaway for anyone who craves a vacation with a slower pace. The four craftsman-style buildings here are all listed on the National Register of Historic Places and include the main house with its two rooms and a suite, a carriage house, and a cottage. Original artwork abounds in the boldly decorated and very colorful main house. Both of the main buildings overlook the farm's pond and lovely back garden. There are also tennis courts and a swimming pool, and through the hazelnut orchard is Rex Hill Vineyards. The little white cottage, with its antique fireplace mantle, fir floors, and tiled bathroom, overlooks the farm's pond and a meadow that's filled with daffodils in the spring.

Wine Country Farm. 6855 Breyman Orchards Rd., Dayton, OR 97114. ☎ 800/261-3446 or 503/864-3446. Fax 503/864-3109. www.winecountryfarm.com. 7 units. A/C. $85–$125 double; $125 suite. Rates include full breakfast. MC, V.

Located high in the hills between Dundee and Lafayette, this B&B has one of the best views in the area, and with its wine-tasting room and 5 acres of grape vines, it should satisfy all those wishing to steep themselves in the atmosphere of wine country. When this 1910 farmhouse was renovated and converted into a B&B, the owners even gave the facade the look of a French farmhouse. Although the decor is nothing fancy, two of the rooms have good views, as do the breakfast room and the deck that runs the entire length of the house. The Courtyard Room and the Vineyard Suite are the two best choices here. A croquet lawn and horseshoe pit provide traditional rural recreational activities when guests aren't out wine tasting.

THE MCMINNVILLE AREA

Best Western—The Vineyard Inn. 2035 S. Ore. 99W, McMinnville, OR 97128. ☎ 800/285-6242 or 503/472-4900. Fax 503/434-9157. 65 units. A/C TV TEL. $76–$115 double. Rates include continental breakfast. AE, CB, DC, DISC, MC, V.

This modern hotel was the first in the area to actively cater to the growing numbers of oenophiles who are touring Oregon's wine country. Purple and lavender are the predominant colors here, and there are wine posters throughout the hotel. The guest rooms are very comfortable and most are quite spacious. You'll find a microwave and a refrigerator in every room. An indoor pool, an exercise room, and a whirlpool provide a bit of exercise and relaxation in the evening. You'll find the Vineyard Inn at the west end of McMinnville.

Mattey House. 10221 NE Mattey Lane, McMinnville, OR 97128. ☎ **503/434-5058.** Fax 503/434-6667. www.matteyhouse.com. 4 units. $90–$110 double. Rates include full breakfast. MC, V.

Located between Lafayette and McMinnville, this restored 1892 Queen Anne Victorian farmhouse sits on 10 acres of farmland behind 1½ acres of grape vines. This is a grand old house, and up on the second floor, you'll find a tiny balcony overlooking the vineyard. It's the perfect spot for a glass of wine in the afternoon. Guest rooms are decorated in country Victorian style, with antique beds. The Riesling Room, with its clawfoot bathtub, is our favorite. Innkeepers Jack and Denise Seed are British and keep copies of magazines from their homeland scattered about the inn.

✪ McMenamins Hotel Oregon. 310 NE Evans St., McMinnville, OR 97128. ☎ **888/ 472-8427** or 503/472-8427. www.mcmenamins.com. 42 units (6 with private bathroom). $75–$110 double with shared bathroom, $95–$125 double with private bathroom. Rates include full breakfast. AE, DISC, MC, V.

In 1999, this historic hotel in downtown McMinnville was reopened after an extensive renovation and remodeling by McMenamins, a Portland-based chain of brew pubs, nightclubs, and unusual hotels that are all filled with interesting artwork. Guest rooms are done in a simple and classic style, with antique and reproduction furniture. The corner kings with private bathrooms are the nicest rooms here, with big windows on two sides. However, keep in mind that most rooms here have shared bathrooms. Despite this inconvenience, this hotel has a genuinely historic feel. What makes it imminently recommendable, however, are its ground-floor brew pub/dining room and its rooftop bar and deck overlooking McMinnville and the Yamhill Valley. There's also a Cellar Bar and a Kitchen Bar. There are also a couple of good restaurants within a few blocks.

Steiger Haus. 360 Wilson St., McMinnville, OR 97128. ☎ **503/472-0821** or 503/ 472-0238. Fax 503/472-0100. www.steigerhaus.com. 5 units. A/C. $70–$110 double; $130 suite. Rates include full breakfast. DISC, MC, V.

Set on tree-shaded grounds just a few blocks from downtown McMinnville, this inn makes a good base for exploring the surrounding wine country. The contemporary three-story building sports lots of windows and decks and has a multilevel, parklike yard. Depending on which room you choose, you may enjoy a superb view of the garden through a bay window or perhaps have a nice deck for afternoon lounging. We like the treetop room the best, though there is also a room with a fireplace and a suite with a kitchen. This inn is within walking distance of several good restaurants.

✪ Youngberg Hill Vineyard & Inn. 10660 SW Youngberg Hill Rd., McMinnville, OR 97128. ☎ **888/657-8668** or 503/472-2727. Fax 541/472-1313. www.youngberghill.com. 7 units. A/C. $110–$125 double; $195–$225 suite. Rates include full breakfast. MC, V.

Set on a 50-acre farm that includes 12 acres of vineyards, this is the quintessential wine country inn. A long gravel driveway leads to the large modern inn, which sits atop a hill with commanding views of the Willamette Valley, snowcapped Cascades peaks, and the Coast Range. Large decks wrap around both floors of the inn, and two of the guest rooms (and one of the suites) have their own fireplaces. Big farm breakfasts, often using produce from the farm, get visitors off to a good start each morning. Pull up a chair on the porch, pour a glass of the inn's own Pinot Noir, gaze out over the rolling hills, and you'll likely start thinking about cashing in the mutual funds to start a vineyard of your own.

THE EOLA HILLS

Bethel Heights Farm Bed & Breakfast. 6055 Bethel Heights Rd. NW, Salem, OR 97304. ☎ **503/364-7688.** 2 units. Apr–Oct $90 double; Nov–Mar $80 double. MC, V.

Set high on a hill overlooking the Willamette Valley, the Coast Range, and the distant Cascades (including Mount Jefferson), this inn is in the middle of a 20-acre farm and vineyard. Outside the front door are a rock garden, small pond, and gazebo, while down the hill and into the oak woods, you'll find a much larger farm pond. Inside, all is spotless and modern. The two rooms both have outstanding views west to the Coast Range. One room has a patio and the other has a balcony. The gourmet breakfasts include homemade jams and syrups and homemade pastries. If you're in the area specifically to do a bit of wine touring, there is no better location than this contemporary inn in the middle of the Eola Hills wine region.

WHERE TO DINE
THE NEWBERG & DUNDEE AREA

The Dundee Bistro. 100-A SW Seventh St. ☎ **503/554-1650.** Reservations recommended. Main courses $14–$20. AE, MC, V. Tues–Sat 11:30am–9pm, Sun 10am–3pm. NORTHWEST.

Located in the same building as the Ponzi Wine Bar and the Your Northwest gift shop, this chic eatery would fit right in in Portland's hip Pearl District. That it's here in the wine country only adds to the appeal and has made it quite popular with people touring the area wineries. The menu is relatively short and changes on a regular basis. However, the emphasis is on fresh regional ingredients, which translates into the likes of pork loin with hazelnut dumplings, roast chicken with a dried cherry barbecue sauce, or smoked duck breast salad with wax beans, watercress, and marionberries. Sunday brunch is especially popular since most people choose to do their wine touring on the weekends. Bring a big appetite if you opt for the baked brioche French toast or the smoked trout hash. Accompany any meal with some local wine and you have the perfect wine country meal.

Red Hills Provincial Dining. 276 Ore. 99W. ☎ **503/538-8224.** Reservations recommended. Main courses $16.50–$22.50; lunch $6.75–$9.50. MC, V. Tues–Fri 11:30am–2pm and 5–9pm, Sat–Sun 5–9pm. MEDITERRANEAN.

Located in a 1920s craftsman bungalow on the east side of Dundee, this restaurant sums up the Oregon wine country appeal with both its setting and its food. The dinner menu changes daily, but you can be sure it will always include plenty of fresh local produce, as well as Northwest meats and seafood. If you enjoy a mix of traditional French fare (escargot bourguignonne, frog's legs in garlic butter, steak Diane) and more creative cookery (pork tenderloin in nigella seeds with tomato and cucumber salsa or sautéed chicken breast with fresh figs, walnuts, and pastis), you'll find plenty to tempt you here. Lunches display a welcome creativity too, with focaccia sandwiches a mainstay. A very good selection of wines is available (local wines are featured). Dishes are calculated to pair well with the wines of the region.

✪ **Tina's.** 760 Ore. 99W. ☎ **503/538-8880.** Reservations recommended. Dinner $20–$26.50; lunch $8–$10. AE, MC, V. Tues–Fri 11:30am–2pm and 5–9pm, Sat–Sun 5–9pm. CONTINENTAL/NORTHWEST.

Despite its rather small and nondescript building right on the highway in Dundee, Tina's has long been one of the Yamhill County wine country's premier restaurants. The menu here changes regularly and usually has around half a dozen entrees and fewer appetizers. However, a balance between the traditional (grilled New York steak with Roquefort butter and fries) and the less familiar (roasted duck breast with corn soufflé and ginger-fig sauce) keeps a wide variety of diners content. There are usually almost as many desserts available as entrees, and the wine selection, of course, emphasizes local wines.

THE AMITY & DAYTON AREA

✪ **The Joel Palmer House.** 600 Ferry St., Dayton. ☎ **503/864-2995.** Reservations highly recommended. Main courses $15.50–$23.50. AE, DISC, MC, V. Tues–Fri 11:30am–2pm and 5–9pm, Sat 5–9pm. FRENCH/NORTHWEST.

If you love mushrooms in all their earthy guises, then in this downtown Dayton restaurant you will find your culinary Nirvana. Chef/owner Jack Czarnecki is a man obsessed with mushrooms (they're the reason he moved to Oregon to open this restaurant), and nearly every item on the menu (with the exception of the desserts, of course) has mushrooms in it. Start your meal with the extraordinary wild-mushroom soup made with suillis mushrooms or, if you're not a mushroom fan, the crab cakes, which, though small, might be the best you'll ever taste. Also expect the unexpected; a recent menu included a fiddlehead fern salad and a side dish of braised sea beans (a wild plant of the salt marsh). Though the rack of lamb doesn't feature any mushrooms, with its Pinot-hazelnut sauce it is the quintessential wine country entree. The extensive wine list features Oregon wines, especially those from the immediate area. Should the chocolate-lavender ice cream be available, don't miss the opportunity to sample one of the richest and most unique desserts you will ever find. The restaurant is in a house built in the 1850s and is quite formal.

THE MCMINNVILLE AREA

For casual and inexpensive meals, try the **McMenamins Pub,** Hotel Oregon, 310 NE Evans St. (☎ 503/472-8427), which serves decent pub fare, plus good microbrews and regional wines. More of the same can also be had at the **Golden Valley Brewery & Pub,** 980 E. Fourth St. (☎ 503/472-2739). For espresso, drop by **Union Block Coffee,** 403 NE Third St. (☎ 503/472-0645), or **Cornerstone Coffee Roasters,** 216 NE Third St. (☎ 503/472-6622). For baked goods, it's **Piontek's Bakery and Cafe,** 411 NE Third St. (☎ 503/434-6256).

The Fresh Palate Cafe. 19706 SW Ore. 18 (between McMinnville and Sheridan). ☎ **503/843-4400.** Reservations recommended on weekends. Main courses $5–$10. MC, V. Daily 9am–3pm. SANDWICHES/PASTA.

This bright little lunch spot is located upstairs from the Lawrence Gallery west of McMinnville and is popular both with people touring the wine country and with families headed to or from the beach. The menu is simple and straightforward. Because this is the best place for miles around, there is usually a wait for a table on summer weekends.

Nick's Italian Café. 521 E. Third St. ☎ **503/434-4471.** Reservations recommended. 5-course fixed-price dinner $35–$37. AE, MC, V. Tues–Thurs 5:30–9pm, Fri–Sat 5:30–10pm, Sun 5–8pm. NORTHERN ITALIAN.

There's nothing in Nick's narrow storefront windows to indicate that this is one of the best restaurants in the region. However, when you step through the door and are immediately confronted by the rich tones of carved and polished wood, you'll know that this is someplace special. Each evening, there's a fixed-price five-course dinner (although à la carte meals are also available if you aren't hungry enough for five courses). Dinner might start with an artichoke served with tarragon mayonnaise, followed by minestrone soup. A salad of Belgian endive, apples, port-glazed walnuts, and gorgonzola might be followed by a spinach ravioli. For the entree, there's always a choice between three dishes—say, grilled salmon; pork loin with fennel-seed sauce and polenta; or top sirloin stuffed with prosciutto, garlic, and lappi cheese. If you still have room after all that, there are desserts such as tiramisu, chocolate brandy torte, and crème brûlée.

Third Street Grill. 729 E. Third St. ☎ **503/435-1745.** Reservations recommended. Main courses $14.50–$19.50. AE, MC, V. Mon–Sat 5–9pm. NORTHWEST.

Down at the east end of Third Street, in an old Victorian home surrounded by a white picket fence, you'll find an elegant little restaurant serving some of the more creative meals in the region. Expect appetizers the likes of crab and smoked salmon cakes with caper-basil aïoli, and entrees such as pork tenderloin stuffed with dried cherries and in a sweet Bourbon sauce, or Columbia River sturgeon with a black pepper–artichoke sauce. Salads also get the creative treatment here, so don't overlook the greens when contemplating a starter. The restaurant also has its own little wine shop.

THE CARLTON & YAMHILL AREA

✪ **Caffé Bisbo.** 214 Main St., Carlton. ☎ **503/852-RAGU.** Reservations required for dinner. Main courses $14–$16. MC, V. Mon–Tues 6am–2pm, Wed–Fri 6am–2pm and 5:30–9pm, Sat 5:30–9pm, Sun 5–8pm. ITALIAN.

This family-run restaurant in downtown Carlton is small and features a short menu, but each dish is lovingly prepared by chef Claudio Bisbocci, while his wife, Joanne, works the front. If you're lucky, you just might find Claudio's pesto lasagna on the day's menu; but even if you don't, the lasagna, with homemade noodles, is always excellent. The chicken cacciatore, bathed in olives and olive oil, is also excellent. However, the very best is held out for last. Caffé Bisbo's tiramisu is absolutely heavenly.

THE GASTON & FOREST GROVE AREA

If you're up in the northern end of wine country and need a light lunch, drop by **24° Brix,** 108 Mill St. (☎ **503/985-3434**), a small sandwich shop and wine-tasting room that sells focaccia sandwiches, breads, pastries, and cheeses.

EN ROUTE TO THE BEACH

It used to be almost impossible to get beach-bound traffic on Ore. 18 west of McMinnville to stop for anything, but that was before the **Spirit Mountain Casino** (☎ **800/760-7977** or 503/879-2350) opened in the town of Grand Ronde. These days a lot of the traffic on this highway isn't even going to the beach, it's headed to this large glitzy temple of luck. Locals swear that the food here is the best around, and the prices can't be beat.

2 Salem & the Mid-Willamette Valley

47 miles S of Portland, 40 miles N of Corvallis, 131 miles W of Bend, 57 miles E of Lincoln City

Though it's the state capital and home to Willamette University (the oldest university west of the Rockies), Salem feels more like a small Midwestern college town than a Pacific Rim capital. Sure, Salem, with just over 100,000 residents, is the third-largest city in the state, but it still feels like a small town. True to its origins (it was founded by a Methodist missionary), the city still wears its air of conservatism like a minister's collar. No one has ever accused Salem of being too raucous or rowdy. Even when both the school and the legislature are in session, the city hardly seems charged with energy. The quiet conservatism does, however, give the city a certain charm that's not found in the other cities of the Willamette Valley. Though there are some interesting museums and the state capitol building to be visited here, it is the countryside surrounding Salem that is the real attraction. Within 20 to 25 miles of town, you'll find the Oregon Garden (the state's newest major attraction), Silver Falls State Park (one of the most popular state parks in Oregon), wineries, commercial flower fields, and several quaint small towns (Aurora, Silverton, Mount Angel, Independence, Monmouth) that conjure up the Willamette Valley's pioneer past.

Salem's roots date from 1834, when Methodist missionary Jason Lee, who had traveled west to convert the local Indians, founded Salem, making it the first American settlement in the Willamette Valley. In 1842, 1 year before the first settlers crossed the continent on the Oregon Trail, Lee founded the Oregon Institute, the first school of higher learning west of the Rockies. In 1857, the first textile mill west of the Mississippi opened here, giving Salem a firm industrial base. However, despite all these historic firsts, Oregon City and Portland grew much faster and quickly became the region's population centers. Salem seemed doomed to backwater status until the year 1859, when Oregon became a state and Salem was chosen to become the state capital.

ESSENTIALS

GETTING THERE   Salem is on I-5 at the junction of Ore. 22, which heads west to connect with Ore. 18 from Lincoln City and southeast to connect with U.S. 20 from Bend.

Amtrak has passenger rail service to Salem. The station is at 13th and Oak streets.

VISITOR INFORMATION   Contact the **Salem Convention & Visitors Association,** 1313 Mill St. SE, Salem, OR 97301 (☎ **800/874-7012** or 503/581-4325; fax 503/581-4540; www.scva.org). For more information on the Silverton area, contact the **Silverton Chamber of Commerce,** 421 S. Water St., Silverton, OR 97381 (☎ **503/873-5615;** www.teleport.com/~cast). For Mount Angel, contact the **Mt. Angel Chamber of Commerce,** P.O. Box 221, Mt. Angel, OR 97362 (☎ **503/845-9440**).

GETTING AROUND   Car rentals are available from **Hertz, Budget,** and **National.** If you need a taxi, contact **Yellow Cab** (☎ **503/362-2411**). Public bus service throughout the Salem area is provided by **Salem Area Transit** (☎ **503/588-BUSS**), which goes by the name of Cherriots.

FESTIVALS   Two of the biggest events of the year in Salem are the **Oregon State Fair** (☎ **800/833-0011** or 503/378-3247), which is held from late August to Labor Day, and the **Salem Arts Festival,** which is the largest juried art fair in Oregon and is held the third weekend in July.

Each year on the second weekend after Labor Day, the town of Mt. Angel is the site of the huge ♦ **Mt. Angel Oktoberfest** (☎ **503/845-9440**). With polka bands from around the world, beer and wine gardens, loads of German food, and dancing in the streets, this is just about the biggest party in the state.

SALEM
SEEING THE SIGHTS

Though it is sometimes easy to forget, Salem is a river town. On the western edge of downtown, you'll find Salem's **Riverfront Park,** which features a state-of-the-art playground, amphitheater, and meandering pathways. It is also home to the **A.C. Gilbert Discovery Village** (see "Especially for Kids," below).

Also worth a visit is **Willamette University's Martha Springer Botanical Garden and Rose Garden,** located near the gymnasium in the southeast corner of the campus. These gardens feature not only a rose garden full of modern hybrids and heirloom roses, but also a Japanese garden, an alpine rock garden, and an English perennial garden.

Oregon State Capitol. 900 Court St. (Visitor Services Center). ☎ **503/986-1388.** Free admission. Building open year-round; tours offered mid-June through Labor Day Mon–Fri 7:30am–5:30pm, Sat 9am–4pm, Sun noon–4pm. Tours by appointment other months. Closed national holidays.

Where's the dome? That's the first thing that strikes most visitors to the Oregon State Capitol, which looks as if builders forgot to complete the building. It was actually designed without a dome, and consequently, the building, which opened in 1938, has a stark appearance, not unlike that of a mausoleum. If you look closer, though, you'll recognize the pared-down lines of art deco design aesthetics in this building. Sort of a modernistic Greek revival building of white Italian marble, the capitol is topped by *The Oregon Pioneer,* a 23-foot-tall gilded statue. Outside the building, there are numerous sculptures and attractive gardens; inside, there are murals of historic Oregon scenes. Tours of the capitol are available during the summer, with separate tours up into the building's tower. There are also changing art exhibits and videos about the history of the building and the state.

Bush House and Bush Barn Art Center. 600 Mission St. SE. ☎ **503/363-4714** (Bush House) and 503/581-2228 (Bush Barn Art Center). www.oregonlink.com/bushhouse/. Bush House, $3 adults, $2.50 students and seniors, $1.50 children ages 6–12; Bush Barn Art Center, free. Bush House, May–Sept Tues–Sun noon–5pm; Oct–Apr Tues–Sun 2–5pm. Bush Barn Art Center, Tues–Fri 10am–5pm, Sat–Sun 1–5pm. Closed major holidays.

Set at the top of a shady hill in the 100-acre Bush's Pasture Park, this imposing Italianate Victorian home dates back to 1878. Inside, you can see the original furnishings, including 10 fireplaces and even the original wallpaper. At the time it was built, this home had all the modern conveniences, including indoor plumbing with hot and cold water, gas lights, and central heating. Also on the grounds are the oldest greenhouse conservatory in Oregon and the Bush Barn Art Center. The latter includes a sales gallery as well as exhibition spaces that feature changing art exhibits. Each year on the third weekend in July, Bush's Pasture Park is the site of the Salem Art Fair and Festival, one of the most popular art festivals in the Northwest.

✪ **Hallie Ford Museum of Art.** 700 State St. ☎ **503/370-6855.** Admission $3, $2 seniors and students, free for children under 13. Tues–Sat noon–5pm.

Opened in 1998, this is the second-largest art museum in Oregon and features collections of Native American baskets and Northwest, European, and Asian art. The first floor galleries are devoted to contemporary art and feature changing exhibitions. Upstairs, you'll find one gallery filled with more than 70 Native American baskets, the finest collection of such baskets on display in the state. Other galleries hold artifacts ranging from an ancient Egyptian coffin mask to 19th-century Chinese porcelain to a 3rd-century Buddhist stone bas relief from Pakistan.

Historic Deepwood Estate. 1116 Mission St. SE. ☎ **503/363-1825.** www.oregonlink.com/deepwood/. Admission $4 adults, $3 seniors, $2 children ages 6–12. Grounds daily dawn–dusk; guided house tours May–Sept Sun–Fri noon–5pm, Oct–Apr Tues–Sat noon–5pm.

Set on 5½ acres of English-style gardens and woodlands, this Queen Anne Victorian home is a delicate jewel box of a house. Although the house, with its many stained-glass windows, golden-oak moldings, and numerous lightning rod–topped peaked roofs and gables, was built in 1894, the gardens weren't added until the 1930s, designed by the Northwest's first women-owned landscape architecture firm. Many of the garden structures have been recently restored, as has the second floor of the house.

Mission Mill Museum. 1313 Mill St. SE. ☎ **503/585-7012.** Admission $4 adults, $3 seniors, $1.50 children. Tues–Sat 10am–4:30pm. Closed major holidays.

The sprawling red **Thomas Kay Woolen Mill,** a water-powered mill built in 1889, has become one of the most fascinating attractions in Salem. The restored buildings house exhibits on every stage of the wool-making process, and in the main mill building the water-driven turbine is still in operation, producing electricity for these buildings. Also on the neatly manicured grounds are several other old structures, including the **Jason Lee House,** which was built by Salem's founder in 1841 and is the oldest frame house in the Northwest. There is also a cafe and a collection of interesting shops. The **Marion County Historical Society Museum,** also on the grounds, houses exhibits on the history of the area with a particularly interesting exhibit on the local Kalapuyan Indians. Because this complex also houses the **Salem Visitors Information Center,** it should be your first stop in town. The old mill has been undergoing a $2 million renovation that has made it an even more interesting place to visit than it was before. There is now a new orientation room and a large gift shop.

A NEARBY STATE PARK & TWO WILDLIFE REFUGES

Eight miles north of Salem you'll find **Willamette Mission State Park** (☎ **503/393-1172**), which preserves the site of the first settlement in the Willamette Valley. It was here that Methodist missionary Jason Lee and four assistants established their first mission in 1834. Today, there are many miles of walking, biking, and horseback riding paths through the park, which is also home to the largest black cottonwood tree in the country. Horseback rides are offered Friday through Sunday during the summer for $20 per hour (reservations recommended). To make a horseback-riding reservation, call ☎ **503/393-1611.**

If it's bird watching that interests you, there are two national wildlife refuges in the area that are excellent places to observe ducks, geese, swans, and raptors. **Ankeny National Wildlife Refuge** is 12 miles south of Salem off I-5 at exit 243. **Basket Slough National Wildlife Refuge** is northwest of the town of Rickreall on Ore. 22. Fall through spring is the best time of year for birding at these refuges.

ESPECIALLY FOR KIDS

A.C. Gilbert Discovery Village. 116 Marion St. NE. ☎ **503/371-3631.** www.acgilbert.org. Admission $4. Tues–Sat 10am–5pm, Sun noon–5pm (also open Mon Feb–Sept).

Known as the "man who saved Christmas," Salem's A.C. Gilbert may not be familiar to most people, but the toy he invented, the Erector Set, certainly is. Erector Sets have inspired generations of budding engineers, and it was during World War I that Gilbert saved Christmas. It seems Congress wanted to turn his toy factory into a munitions factory, but after taking Erector Sets to Congress, he convinced the solons that America needed to prime its next generation of inventors just as much as it needed to prime its war machine. Here, in two Queen Anne Victorian homes and a half-acre outdoor play/recreation center, the 21st century's inventors can let loose their own creative energies. Among the many interactive exhibits here are a 53-foot-tall Erector Set tower and a simulated mammoth excavation for budding paleontologists.

Enchanted Forest. 8462 Enchanted Way SE. ☎ **503/363-3060.** Admission $6.95 adults, $6.25 children 3–12. Mar 15–Labor Day daily 9:30am–6pm; Sept Sat–Sun 9:30am–6pm. Closed Oct–Mar 14. Take I-5 7 miles south of Salem to Exit 248.

Classic children's stories come to life at this amusement park for kids. In addition to Storybook Land, English Village, and a mining town, there's a haunted house, a bobsled run, a log-flume ride, and a comedy theater. Rides cost extra. Adjacent to Enchanted Village is **Thrill-Ville USA** (☎ 503/363-4095), a small amusement park with a roller coaster, water slides, and other rides and activities. It's open in summer from 11am to 6:30pm; rides cost $2 to $3 and an all-day water-slide pass is $8.

WHERE TO STAY

✪ **Marquee House.** 333 Wyatt Ct. NE, Salem, OR 97301. ☎ **800/949-0837** or 503/ 391-0837. www.marqueehouse.com/rickiemh. 5 units (3 with private bathroom). A/C. $65 double without bathroom, $75–$90 double with bathroom. Rates include full breakfast. DC, DISC, MC, V.

Fans of old movies will want to make this their address in Salem. All the rooms are named for well-known movies and are furnished to reflect the theme. We like the Topper Room with its black-tie theme, and the Blazing Saddles Room with its Wild West decor. This B&B is located on a narrow lane in a quiet residential neighborhood and has Mill Creek running through the back yard. The gardens are quite impressive.

Phoenix Inn. 4370 Commercial St. SE, Salem, OR 97302. ☎ **800/445-4498** or 503/ 588-9220. Fax 503/585-3616. www.phoenixinn.com. 88 units. A/C TV TEL. $70–$115 double. Rates include continental breakfast. AE, DC, DISC, MC, V. Pets accepted ($10 fee).

Of Salem's many corporate business hotels, the modern Phoenix Inn is just about the best and is popular with legislators and business travelers. The rooms (called "minisuites" here) are in fact quite large and well designed for both business and relaxation. There are two phones (free local calls), hair dryers, microwave ovens, refrigerators, and wet bars in all the rooms. The top-end rooms also have whirlpool tubs. Facilities include an indoor pool, a whirlpool, and an exercise room. You'll find the hotel south of downtown Salem.

WHERE TO DINE

If you have a sweet tooth, you won't want to miss **Gerry Frank's Konditorei,** 310 Kearney St. SE (☎ 503/585-7070), which sells an amazing selection of extravagant cakes and pastries. For a good cup of espresso (or a sandwich), head to **The Beanery,** 220 Liberty St. NE (☎ 503/399-7220). If you're looking for a microbrew and a burger, try **The Ram Border Cafe & Big Horn Brewery,** 515 12th St. SE (☎ 503/363-1904), or **Thompson Brewery & Pub,** 3575 Liberty Rd. S (☎ 503/363-7286). For Sunday brunch, consider **Eola Hills Wine Cellars,** 501 S. Ore. 99W, Rickreall (☎ 503/623-2405), which serves gourmet omelets, panfried oysters, pasta, Belgian waffles, sparkling wine, and more for $21.95. Reservations are required.

Alessandro's 120. 120 Commercial St. NE. ☎ 503/370-9951. Reservations recommended. Main courses $9.50–$23; set dinners $32–$43; lunch $6.50–$10. AE, DISC, MC, V. Mon–Thurs 11:30am–2pm and 5:30–9pm, Fri 11:30am–2pm and 5:30–10pm, Sat 5:30–10pm. ITALIAN.

Long located just south of downtown, the ever-popular Alessandro's has now moved to an older downtown building that, with its old wooden floors, exposed brick walls, and player piano, has both a historic and a romantic feel. The move also meant that the restaurant could add a full bar, which is very popular with Salem's moneyed set and its politicos. There's a good range of prices here, so no matter what your budget, you should be able to enjoy a dinner here, though the set menus, which showcase the chef's skills, are a bit pricey. Sauces are made fresh daily from the finest of ingredients, including fresh herbs and the best of Northwest seafood. The wine list features moderately priced Italian and Oregon wines.

Court Street Dairy Lunch. 347 Court St. ☎ **503/363-6433.** Meals $3–$7. AE, MC, V. Mon–Fri 6am–2pm. BURGERS.

In business since the 1920s, the Court Street Dairy Lunch is the quintessential burger place and a Salem institution. Burgers and sandwiches "just like Mom used to make" are the attraction. The specialties of the house are the ranch burger and ranch dog, marionberry pie, and chocolate malts.

DaVinci Ristorante. 180 High St. SE. ☎ **503/399-1413.** Reservations recommended. Main courses $14–$19. AE, DISC, MC, V. Mon–Thurs 11:30am–1:30pm and 5–9pm, Fri 11:30am–1:30pm and 5–10pm, Sat 5–10pm, Sun 5–9pm. ITALIAN.

Competing directly with Alessandro's for the title of reigning upscale Italian restaurant in Salem, DaVinci abounds in early-20th-century ambiance, with a pressed-tin ceiling and lots of oak and exposed brick. Wonderful aromas (including a very pronounced scent of garlic) greet you as you step through the door of this casual yet elegant restaurant in a restored downtown building. Menu offerings run the gamut from traditional fare (spaghetti carbonara) to more contemporary Italian offerings such as beef tenderloin with portobello mushroom and a roasted garlic demi-glace. Traditionalists can even start with some escargots or carpaccio. There's live jazz or classical music nightly.

Karma's Café. 1313 Mill St. SE. ☎ **503/370-8855.** Meals $4.50–$6.50. DISC, MC, V. Mon 10am–2pm, Tues–Sat 10am–4:30pm. DELI.

We can't imagine a more pleasant place to lunch on a sunny summer afternoon in Salem. The deck in front of Karma's sandwich shop is right in the middle of Mission Mill Village and overlooks the big red mill. You can hear water flowing through the stream and are almost completely surrounded by history. Soups, salads, and sandwiches are the fare here.

✪ **Morton's Bistro Northwest.** 1128 Edgewater St. W. ☎ **503/585-1113.** Reservations recommended. Main courses $16–$22. MC, V. Tues–Sat 5–10pm. AMERICAN REGIONAL.

This romantic little bistro on the west side of the Willamette River serves up the most imaginative meals in Salem. The menu changes regularly depending on the whim of the chef, the availability of ingredients, the season, and even the weather. On a recent summer evening, flavors ranged from the subtle scents of ale-steamed clams to the fiery flavors of penne diablo made with crab and andouille sausage. Other summer standouts included a mango, tiger prawn, and scallop sauté and a three-chili rubbed pork tenderloin.

SALEM AFTER DARK

The Oregon Symphony performs in Salem between September and May, with concerts held at Smith Auditorium on the campus of Willamette University. For more information, contact the **Oregon Symphony Association in Salem** (☎ **503/364-0149**). Classical music lovers can also catch the **Salem Chamber Orchestra;** for ticket information, contact the Mid-Valley Arts Council (☎ **503/370-7469**). There are also regularly scheduled performances by touring companies at the historic **Elsinore Theater,** 170 High St. SE (☎ **503/375-3574** or 503/581-8810). Since 1954, **Pentacle Theatre** (☎ **503/364-7121**), located in the West Salem hills, has been bringing live theater to the state capital; for ticket information, contact the Mid-Valley Arts Council (☎ **503/370-7469**).

SILVERTON
THE OREGON GARDEN

Silverton, long known as the gateway to the waterfall-filled Silver Falls State Park (see "A Nearby State Park & Two Wildlife Refuges," above) has now acquired what many people expect will eventually be an equally popular destination. ✪ **The Oregon Garden** (☎ 877/ORGARDEN or 503/874-8100; www.oregongarden.org) is located on Main Street just outside of town; at press time it was scheduled to open in May 2000 for a preview season. Though most of the plantings should be in the ground by the summer of 2000, the gardens aren't expected to be completely finished until sometime in 2001.

The Oregon Garden is to be a world-class display garden showcasing the incredible variety of plants grown in the commercial plant nurseries of Oregon (nursery plants are currently Oregon's leading crop and are shipped all over the country). The dream is to make this into an Oregon equivalent of Victoria, British Columbia's famed Butchart Gardens, and at 70 acres of plantings in the first phase, the gardens are already much larger. There will be an incredible array of plantings and numerous distinctive gardens, including several water features and ponds, terraced gardens, a sensory garden, a children's garden, and a native oak grove. During the summer months, concerts will be held in the garden's amphitheater. Call for hours and admission information.

SILVER FALLS STATE PARK

Located 26 miles east of Salem on Ore. 214, ✪ **Silver Falls State Park** (☎ 503/873-8681) is the largest state park in Oregon and one of the most popular. Hidden in the lush canyons and dark old-growth forests of this park are 10 silvery waterfalls ranging in height from 27 to 178 feet. A 7-mile trail links all the falls, but it is also possible to do shorter hikes. The trails here are some of the most enjoyable in the state, and the many waterfalls will make it clear why these mountains are called the Cascades. You can even walk behind South, Lower South, and North Falls. You can spend an afternoon or several days exploring the park. Popular activities include camping (for reservations, call **Reservations Northwest,** ☎ 800/452-5687), swimming, picnicking, bicycling, and horseback riding. Park admission is $3.

Guided horseback rides are available Memorial Day through Labor Day ($25 for a 1-hr. ride, $40 for 2 hrs., $60 for 3 to 4 hrs.). For reservations, call ☎ 503/873-3890. It's also possible to lead a llama through the woods for 1 to 3 hours on guided llama treks offered by **Wiley Woods Ranch** (☎ 503/362-0873; www.oregonlink. com/llama/). Rates range from $10 to $25. Just don't expect to ride the llamas—they carry gear, not people.

OTHER AREA ATTRACTIONS & ACTIVITIES

While in Silverton, be sure to wander around town and admire the town's many murals. Some of these murals were painted by local artists who display their work at the **Lunaria Gallery,** 216 E. Main St. (☎ 503/873-7734), an artists' cooperative featuring fine arts and crafts. Also worth a visit is the **Silver Creek Gallery,** 119A N. Water St. (☎ 503/873-6767), which features works by regional artists, as well as jewelry designed by the gallery's owners. If you want to learn more about local history, drop by the **Silverton Country Museum,** 428 S. Water St. (☎ 503/873-4766), open Thursday and Sunday from 1 to 4pm. Admission is $1 for adults and 50¢ for children.

North of Silverton about 8½ miles you'll find **Marquam Hill Vineyards,** 35803 S. Ore. 213 (☎ 503/829-6677), a family-run winery that produces a wide range of white wines, as well as good Pinot Noir. Watch for the winery about 1.5 miles north of the community of Marquam. Memorial Day through September, the winery is open daily from noon to 6pm; other months, it's open Saturday and Sunday from 11am to 5pm (closed in Jan).

WHERE TO DINE

Silver Grille Cafe & Wines. 206 E. Main St. ☎ **503/873-4035.** Reservations recommended. Main courses $10–$14. DISC, MC, V. Wed–Sun 4–9pm. MEDITERRANEAN.

This classy little restaurant in an old storefront is a welcome outpost of urban culinary aesthetics in downtown Silverton. The menu emphasizes daily specials, which might include bruschetta with gorgonzola, basil, and pine nuts; a spinach salad with warm bacon-and-cheese dressing; or beef tenderloin. Wine is also a very important part of a meal here, which you'll probably guess when you see all the bottles around the dining room. The walls are even wine-colored, and wine quotes are painted on the front windows.

MOUNT ANGEL

Mount Angel is best known as the site of Oregon's most popular Oktoberfest celebration, but should you be here any other time of year besides the second weekend after Labor Day, you might want to visit the **Mount Angel Abbey** (☎ **503/845-3030**), which stands atop a 300-foot bluff on the edge of town and has peaceful gardens, an architecturally interesting library, and a collection of rare books. The abbey, which was established by Benedictine monks in 1882, also has a gift shop and offers tours by appointment. It's also the site of the annual Abbey Bach Festival, which takes place each year on the last Wednesday, Thursday, and Friday in July and sells out months in advance. It is also possible to stay here on religious retreats.

WHERE TO DINE

Mt. Angel Brewing Company. 210 N. Monroe St. ☎ **503/845-9624.** Main courses $6–$17. MC, V. Mon–Thurs 11am–8:30pm, Fri–Sat 11am–9:30pm, Sun 11am–8:30pm. AMERICAN/GERMAN.

Located in an old potato warehouse that now looks surprisingly like a Munich Oktoberfest beer hall, this brew pub carries the German torch for all those long months that the Mount Angel Oktoberfest is but a memory. In addition to a wide variety of microbrew ales, you can get anything from German sausages to pizza to burgers here. Smoked meats are a specialty.

AURORA & CANBY

An interesting chapter in Oregon pioneer history is preserved 13 miles south of Oregon City in the town of **Aurora,** which was founded in 1855 as a Christian communal society. Similar in many ways to more famous communal experiments like the Amana Colony and the Shaker communities, the Aurora Colony lasted slightly more than 20 years. Today Aurora is a National Historic District, and the large old homes of the community's founders have been restored. Many of the old commercial buildings now house antiques stores, which are the main reason most people visit the town. You can learn about the history of Aurora at the **Old Aurora Colony Museum,** Second and Liberty streets (☎ **503/678-5754**). Between April and October, the museum is open Tuesday through Saturday from 10am to 4pm and on Sunday from noon to 4pm; other months the schedule varies. Admission is $3.50 for adults, $3 for seniors, and $1.50 for ages 6 to 18.

A few miles north of Aurora toward Canby, you'll find **St. Josef's Wine Cellar,** 28836 S. Barlow Rd. (☎ **503/651-3190**). This is one of the older wineries in the state, and with its half-timbered buildings it has a very European feel. This winery is one of the few in the area that produces Cabernet Sauvignon, while its sweet Gewürztraminer is an excellent dessert wine. To reach the winery, go north on

Ore. 99E to a right on Barlow Road. Between May and September, the winery is open Thursday through Monday from 11am to 5pm; between October and April, it's open Saturday and Sunday from 11am to 5pm. Closed in January. Tasting fee $1.50.

WHERE TO STAY

The Inn at Aurora. 15109 NE Second St. (P.O. Box 249), Aurora, OR 97002. ☎ **888/ 799-1374** or 503/678-1932. www.innataurora.aurora.or.us. 4 units. A/C TV TEL. $89–$119 double. Rates include full breakfast. AE, MC, V.

Set on the edge of Carlton's historic district behind big shade trees, this inn looks as if it's been here for a century or more, but it's actually a modern home. A big front porch and a second-floor veranda draped with red, white, and blue buntings sum up the small-town American style that this inn aims to capture. All the rooms have king beds. One has a whirlpool spa and two have fireplaces. The Aurora Colony Museum and the town's many antiques stores are within 2 blocks.

WHERE TO DINE

Chez Moustache. 21527 Ore. 99E. ☎ **503/768-1866.** Reservations recommended. Main courses $13–$19. MC, V. Tues–Sat 11am–2:30pm and 5–10pm, Sun 10am–2pm and 5–9pm. CONTINENTAL.

Located right in downtown Aurora, this restaurant is not in the most attractive of buildings, but that has not lessened its popularity over the years. Though unassuming, the restaurant serves reliable continental fare. For starters you could opt for the escargot in mushroom caps, grape leaves stuffed with feta and roasted garlic, or simple sautéed mushrooms. Main courses include such dishes as filet mignon with caramelized onions on spinach bordelaise, panfried razor clams flamed with sherry, and *poulet le Havane* (chicken with pineapple and dark rum). Sunday brunch is particularly popular.

MONMOUTH

Monmouth, located about 10 miles southwest of Salem, is home to Western Oregon University, and despite the presence of the university, it feels more like a small farm town than a college town.

✪ **Jensen Arctic Museum.** 590 W. Church St., Monmouth. ☎ **503/838-8468.** Admission $2 adults, $1 children. Wed–Sat 10am–4pm.

While Monmouth may seem an unlikely location for a museum dedicated to the natural and cultural history of the Arctic, it is here that the museum's founder lived while working with Alaskan Eskimo peoples. The core of the museum's exhibits is Dr. Jensen's personal collection, but over the years the museum has become a repository for more than 60 other collections. Though small, this museum has fascinating displays, including a parka made from cormorant feathers, salmon-skin mukluks, a waterproof seal-intestine jacket, and woven baleen baskets.

BROOKS

Although Brooks is little more than a freeway off-ramp, it is home to one of the valley's unusual little historical museums.

Antique Powerland Museum. 3995 Brooklake Rd. NE, Brooks. ☎ **503/393-2424.** Admission $1. Apr–Oct daily 10am–6pm. Nov–Mar daily 10am–4pm.

Dedicated to the preservation of old farm equipment and related items, this sprawling open-air museum just off the Interstate is home to lots of old tractors and steam-driven mills. For the kids, there's a miniature railroad. This museum is best known as

Blossom Time

Each year between mid-May and early June, the countryside around Salem bursts into color as commercial iris fields come into bloom. The two biggest growers open their farms during bloom time. **Cooley's Gardens,** 11553 Silverton Rd. NE (☎ **503/873-5463**), with approximately 250 acres and more than three million irises, is the world's largest bearded iris grower. To reach the gardens, take the Market Street exit and drive east to Lancaster Road; at Lancaster, turn left and drive north to Silverton Road. Turn right onto Silverton, and it's less than 10 miles. **Schreiner's Iris Gardens,** 3625 Quinaby Rd. NE, Brooks (☎ **503/393-3232**), has more than 200 acres of irises and is an equally impressive sight. To reach Schreiner's, take the Brooks exit off I-5 north of Salem. Also in the area are **Adelman Gardens,** 5690 Brooklake Rd. NE (☎ **503/393-6185**), which has more than 60 varieties of peonies in bloom between mid-May and mid-June. They're open daily from 9am to 7pm. From the Brooks exit, go east on Brooklake Road.

From late March to late April, you can see more than 90 acres of tulips in bloom at **Wooden Shoe Bulb Company,** 33814 S. Meridian Rd., Woodburn (☎ **800/711-2006** or 503/634-2243). Throughout the blossom season, there are wooden shoe–making seminars, hot-air balloon rides, vintage car shows, live music, and lots of other activities.

---

the site of the annual Great Oregon Steamup ($5 adults, $4 seniors, $2 children), which is held each year on the last weekend in July and the first weekend in August. Also on the grounds is the **Pacific Northwest Truck Museum** (☎ **503/463-8701**), which is open on weekends throughout the summer.

WINE TOURING

For information on the many wineries west and northwest of Salem, see "The North Willamette Valley Wine Country" section, above.

Honeywood Winery. 1350 Hines St. SE. ☎ **800/726-4101** or 503/362-4111. Mon–Fri 9am–5pm, Sat 10am–5pm, Sun 1–5pm. South of downtown at the corner of 13th St.

This large winery, located right in Salem, has been in business since 1933 and is the oldest producing winery in the state. The focus here is on sweet fruit wines made from the region's abundant berries. They also do mead (honey wine) and wines from American grapes such as Niagara and Concord (which have recently been found to be even better for the heart than the much-touted "noble" red wines made from European vinifera grapes).

Willamette Valley Vineyards. 8800 Enchanted Way SE, Turner. ☎ **503/588-9463.** Daily 11am–6pm. Take exit 248 or 244 off I-5.

Willamette Valley Vineyards, the second-largest wine producer in the state, sits high on a hill overlooking the Willamette Valley. With its huge facility and fabulous views, it's about as close to a Napa Valley wine-tasting experience as you'll find in Oregon. With nearly 20 wines usually available for tasting and three separate labels, Willamette Valley manages to produces wines to please almost every palate. Be sure to try the reserve wines, for which there is a small tasting fee. There are monthly jazz concerts here for most of the year and numerous other special events, including a September wine stomp. Good Chardonnays and Pinot Noirs.

3 Corvallis & Albany

40 miles S of Salem, 45 miles N of Eugene, 55 miles E of Newport

Corvallis, whose name is Latin for "heart of the valley," is set amid flat farmlands in the center of the Willamette Valley and is home to Oregon State University, a noted center for agricultural research. The fields around Corvallis produce much of the nation's grass-seed crop, and in late summer, after the seed has been harvested, the remaining stubble has traditionally been burned. These field burnings have been scaled back in recent years, but they still can blanket the valley with dense black smoke, making driving quite difficult along certain roads. Grapes for area wines are also grown in the Corvallis area.

Nearby Albany, 13 miles northeast, was a prosperous town in territorial days. Located on the banks of the Willamette River, the town made its fortune as a shipping point in the days when the river was the main transportation route for the region. More than 500 historic homes make Albany the best-preserved historic town in the state.

ESSENTIALS

GETTING THERE   Albany is on I-5 at the junction with U.S. 20, which heads east to Bend and west to Newport. Corvallis is 12 miles west of I-5 at the junction of U.S. 20, Ore. 99W, and Ore. 34.

VISITOR INFORMATION   Contact the **Corvallis Convention & Visitors Bureau,** 420 NW Second St., Corvallis, OR 97330 (☎ **800/334-8118** or 541/757-1544; www.visitcorvallis.com), or the **Albany Convention & Visitors Association,** 300 SW Second Ave. (P.O. Box 965), Albany, OR 97321 (☎ **800/526-2256** or 541/928-0911; www.albanyvisitors.com).

GETTING AROUND   Public bus service around the Corvallis area is provided by the **Corvallis Transit System** (☎ **541/757-6998**). Adult fare is 50¢

FESTIVALS   DaVinci Days (☎ **800/334-8118**), held each year in mid-July, is Corvallis's most fascinating festival. The highlight of this celebration of art, science, and technology is the **Kinetic Sculpture Race,** in which competitors race homemade, people-powered vehicles along city streets, through mud, and down the Willamette River. Prizes are given for engineering and artistry. The **World Championship Timber Carnival,** held each year on the Fourth of July, is Albany's biggest celebration. This festival is the largest of its kind and attracts logging contestants from around the world.

OUTDOOR ACTIVITIES   If you're a bird-watcher, the **William L. Finley National Wildlife Refuge,** 12 miles south of Corvallis on Ore. 99W, is a good place to add a few more birds to your life list. Head west 16 miles from Corvallis on Ore. 34 and you'll come to **Mary's Peak,** the highest peak in the Coast Range. A road leads to the top of the mountain, but there is also a trail that leads from the campground up through a forest of old-growth noble firs to the meadows at the summit.

CORVALLIS
SEEING THE SIGHTS

The stately old building in downtown Corvallis is the historic **Benton County Courthouse,** 120 NW Fourth St. (☎ **541/757-6831**), which was built in 1888 and is still in use today. It's open Monday through Friday from 8am to 5pm, and tours are available by appointment. A few blocks away, housed in an old church, the **Corvallis Arts Center,** 700 SW Madison Ave. (☎ **541/754-1551**), schedules changing exhibits of works by regional artists, and its gift shop has a good selection of fine crafts. The center is open Tuesday through Sunday from noon to 5pm; admission is free.

If you're interested in the area's history, drop by the **Benton County History Center,** 110 NW Third St. (☎ 541/758-3550), open Tuesday through Saturday from 10am to 5pm; admission by donation. To learn more of the history of the area, take U.S. 20 6 miles west to **Philomath,** where you'll find the **Benton County Historical Museum,** 1101 Main St. (☎ 541/929-6230). The museum building itself was built in 1867 as part of Philomath College. The museum contains primarily exhibits on early pioneer life but also includes a collection of Native American artifacts. Open Tuesday through Saturday from 10am to 4:30pm; admission by donation.

WHERE TO STAY

✪ **Hanson Country Inn.** 795 SW Hanson St., Corvallis, OR 97333. ☎ **541/752-2919.** 4 units (including a cottage). TV TEL. $85–$135 double. Rates include full breakfast. AE, DC, DISC, MC, V. Take Western Blvd. to West Hills Rd.; Hanson St. is on the right just past the fork onto West Hills Rd.

Situated atop a knoll on the edge of town and surrounded by 5 acres of fields and forests, this B&B feels as if it's out in the country yet is within walking distance of the university. The Dutch Colonial–style farmhouse was built in 1928 and features loads of built-in cabinets, interesting woodwork, and lots of windows. The decor is in a pastel country motif, and two of the rooms have large balconies. The two-bedroom cottage, ideal for families, sits behind the main house and is tucked back in the trees.

Super 8 Motel. 407 NW Second St., Corvallis, OR 97330. ☎ **800/800-8000** or 541/ 758-8088. Fax 541/758-8267. 101 units. AC TV TEL. $59–$68 double. AE, CB, DC, DISC, MC, V.

It may seem hard to believe that a Super 8 Motel could be one of the best accommodations in town, but Corvallis just doesn't have too many places to stay. This budget motel has a great location on the bank of the Willamette River only a few blocks from downtown. There is an indoor pool and a whirlpool spa, and local calls are free.

WHERE TO DINE

When you just have to have a jolt of java, drop by **The Beanery,** Second Street (☎ 541/753-7442). For good microbrews and pub fare, try **McMenamins,** 420 NW Third St. (☎ 541/758-6044). For deli sandwiches and a large selection of Oregon wines to go, check out **The Wine Cellar & Delicatessen,** Cannery Mall, 777 NW Ninth St. (☎ 541/758-3585).

Big River. 101 Jackson St. ☎ **541/757-0694.** Reservations accepted only for parties of 8 or more. Main courses $12–$17. AE, MC, V. Mon–Thurs 11am–2pm and 5–9pm, Fri 11:30am–2:30pm and 5–10pm, Sat 5–10pm. INTERNATIONAL.

The concept of the modern American bistro, a mainstay of big-city dining scenes, has finally come to Corvallis. Housed in a renovated warehouselike space across the street from the Willamette River, this big, lively place serves everything from designer brick-oven pizzas and Asian-inspired pastas to steaks and even Northwest-Mexican fusion food (smoked salmon Vera Cruz). The owners of this restaurant have a commitment to fresh local produce (often organic), local wines, Oregon-caught seafood (when possible), and organic meats. The rustic breads are baked on the premises. Though this is a big space, you probably won't be able to miss the case full of tempting desserts.

Le Bistro. 150 SW Madison Ave. ☎ **541/754-6680.** Reservations recommended. Main courses $10–$18. MC, V. Tues–Sat 4:40–9:30pm. FRENCH.

Located right in the heart of downtown Corvallis, this sparsely decorated restaurant focuses on country French preparations, and with its surprisingly low prices, the restaurant manages to attract students as well as professors and local high-tech employees. Although there are daily specials, the main menu offers no surprises, just down-home French country cooking. Among other dishes, you'll find coq au vin, oven-roasted quail with brandy and orange essence, and pork medallions with a light mustard velouté. The restaurant is only half a block from the river and the waterfront pathway, so before or after dinner you can go for a stroll.

Nearly Normal's. 109 NW 15th St. ☎ **541/753-0791.** Reservations not accepted. Main courses $5–$9. No credit cards. Mon–Fri 8am–9pm, Sat 9am–9pm (shorter hours Mon–Wed in winter). VEGETARIAN/INTERNATIONAL.

Housed in an old bungalow half a block from campus, Nearly Normal's is your basic college-town vegetarian hippie cafe. They serve up filling portions of food that spans the globe, from pad Thai to tempehchangas to a fakin-bakin burger to garlic-gorgonzola ravioli. If it's sunny out, try to get a seat out back in the patio area planted with apple trees and kiwi vines. As often as possible, ingredients are organically grown. Good iced teas in summer, plus regional microbrews on tap.

Sweet's Bar-B-Que. 225 SW Fourth St. ☎ **541/754-3663.** Main courses $6.75–$17.50. MC, V. BARBECUE.

Barbecue joints seem to be springing up all over the place lately, and in Corvallis, everyone knows that Sweet's is the place. Boasting "old school taste," this downtown rib joint does not only succulent bones, but also barbecued chicken, beef brisket, and hot links. True barbecue fanatics can get a full rack of ribs or a four-meat combo dinner, with all the usual side orders (baked beans, cole slaw, potato salad, and corn). Several sandwiches are also available. Wash it all down with a Northwest microbrew.

ALBANY
SEEING THE HISTORIC SIGHTS

Albany is a hidden jewel that lies right on I-5 but is overlooked by most motorists because the only thing visible from the Interstate is a smoke-belching wood-pulp mill. Behind the industrial screen lies a quiet town that evokes days of starched crinolines and straw boaters. Throughout the mid– to late 19th century, Albany experienced prosperity as it shipped agricultural and wood products downriver to Oregon City and Portland. Though every style of architecture popular during that period is represented in the buildings of downtown Albany's historic districts, it is the town's many elegant Victorian homes that capture the attention of visitors. Stop by the **Albany Convention & Visitors Association** or the **information gazebo** at the corner of Eighth and Ellsworth streets and pick up a guide to the town's historic buildings. Each year, on the last Saturday of July, many of the historic homes are opened to the public for a **Summer Historic Homes Tour;** and on the third Sunday in December, homes are opened for a **Christmas Parlour Tour.** For information on these homes' tours, contact the Albany Convention & Visitors Association.

Among the town's more noteworthy historic buildings are two sparkling-white 1890s churches—the **Whitespires Church** and **St. Mary's Church**—which were both built in the Gothic Revival style. The **Monteith House,** 518 Second Ave. SW (☎ 541/928-0911), built in 1849, is the town's oldest frame building. It was here that the Oregon Republican party was formed. The house is open mid-June to mid-September Wednesday through Saturday from noon to 4pm; admission is free.

To learn more about Albany's past, stop in at the **Albany Regional Museum,** Second Avenue and Lyon Street (☎ 541/967-6540). It's open Monday through Sunday from noon to 4pm. Admission is free.

The most educational and entertaining way to delve into Albany's past is by attending one of the living history dinner-theater programs presented by **Flinn's Tours,** 222 W. First Ave. (☎ **800/636-5008** or 541/928-5008). Vaudeville shows, tales of women's lives in pioneer days, and murder mysteries from the turn of the century and Prohibition days are currently in the repertoire at this downtown theater, which also doubles as a tearoom. There are several special programs at Christmas.

While touring the historic district, you can stop in at more than a dozen antiques stores, most of which are on First and Second avenues downtown.

One other interesting way to experience historic Albany is aboard the *Willamette Queen* (☎ **541/928-4090** or 503/371-1103), a paddle wheeler that cruises the Willamette River offering lunch, brunch, and dinner cruises, as well as excursions and even melodrama cruises. Prices range from $5 ($3 children 12 and under) for a half-hour cruise to $35 ($17.50 for children 12 and under) for a brunch cruise.

WHERE TO STAY

Brier Rose Inn. 206 Seventh Ave. SW, Albany, OR 97321. ☎ **541/926-0345.** 5 units (4 with private bathroom). $59–$89 double with shared bathroom, $89–$125 double with private bathroom. Rates include full breakfast. AE, MC, V.

This turreted Queen Anne–style Victorian B&B is on a busy corner in the heart of Albany's historic district and surprisingly is the only historic B&B in town. With its balconies, bay windows, curving porches, stained glass, and numerous styles of siding, it's a classic example of Victorian excess. Common areas are filled with period antiques, though the guest rooms are more simply furnished.

WHERE TO DINE

If you need a good cup of coffee, try **Boccherini's Coffee & Tea House,** 208 SW First Ave. (☎ **541/926-6703**), in a downtown historic building with exposed brick walls. For quick deli meals accompanied by Oregon wine, try the **Wine Depot & Deli,** Two Rivers Market, 300 Second Ave. (☎ **541/967-9499**). If it's a good pint of ale and some pub food you crave, there's **Wyatt's Eatery & Brewhouse,** 211 NW First Ave. (☎ **541/917-3727**).

Capriccio Ristorante. 442 First Ave. W. ☎ **541/924-9932.** Reservations recommended. Main courses $12.50–$21.50. AE, CB, DC, DISC, MC, V. Tues–Thurs 5–9pm, Fri–Sat 5–10pm. ITALIAN.

Located in historic downtown Albany, this restaurant is cavernous, but with its sparkling halogen lights high overhead, it still manages to feel romantic. The menu here is surprisingly sophisticated for Albany. For an antipasto, you can opt for shrimp grilled on rosemary skewers or calamari stuffed with herbs, garlic, three cheeses, and bread crumbs. For an entree, it's hard to pass up the Ligurian seafood stew, made with walnuts, pine nuts, and lots of seafood. There's a good selection of wines from Italy, Oregon, and California. If you feel like splurging, check out the reserve wine list.

✪ **Novak's Hungarian Restaurant.** 2835 Santiam Hwy. SE. ☎ **541/967-9488.** Reservations recommended. Main courses $8–$15. DISC, MC, V. Sun–Fri 11am–9pm, Sat 4–9pm. HUNGARIAN.

From the outside, Novak's looks like it could be a car-repair garage, especially given the neighborhood it's in. As soon as you walk through the door, though, you're hit with gracious Hungarian hospitality. The tongue-twisting dishes on the menu challenge the long-held belief that Eastern European cuisine means meat and potatoes. More often than not, Hungarian pearl noodles or fresh bread accompany dishes here. The homemade pork sausage is very good, though the chicken paprika, in its creamy red sauce, is probably the restaurant's most popular dish.

A Covered Bridge Tour

If you're a fan of covered bridges, you won't want to miss the backroads east of Albany. Here you'll find nine wooden covered bridges dating mostly from the 1930s. For a map to these covered bridges, contact the **Albany Convention & Visitors Association,** 300 SW Second Ave. (P.O. Box 965), Albany, OR 97321 (☎ **800/ 526-2256** or 541/928-0911; www.albanyvisitors.com). A 10th covered bridge, the Irish Bend Bridge, can be found in Corvallis on a pedestrian/bicycle path on the west side of the university campus.

WINE TOURING

The Corvallis area is about the upper limit of Cabernet Sauvignon production in Oregon, so if you aren't headed down to southern Oregon but want to sample an Oregon Cabernet, you might want to stop by some of the area wineries.

Airlie Winery. 15305 Dunn Forest Rd., Monmouth. ☎ **503/838-6013.** Mid-Mar to mid-Dec Sat–Sun noon–5pm. Closed Jan–Feb. From Ore. 99W between Corvallis and Monmouth, go 7 miles west on Airlie Rd., turn left on Maxfield Creek Rd., and continue another 3 miles.

Located northwest of Corvallis, this winery is quite a ways off the main wine-touring routes, but it has an idyllic setting in a narrow valley surrounded by forested hills. The large pond and covered picnic area on the premises make this a good place to stop for a picnic lunch. They produce a wide variety of wines, but their Müller-Thurgaus and their Gewürztraminer are definite strong points.

✪ **Bellfountain Cellars.** 25041 Llewellyn Rd., Corvallis. ☎ **541/929-3162.** Sat–Sun 11am–5pm. Closed Dec 24–Jan 31. From Corvallis, go south on Ore. 99W, then go west on Llewellyn Rd. and watch for the sign west of the Fern Rd. intersection.

Located at the end of a long gravel driveway in a remote heat pocket of the Coast Range foothills, Bellfountain is a family operation producing exceptional wines, the reds of which are still made by foot stomping. Because this little valley has such a long growing season, Bellfountain's vineyards are able to ripen Cabernet Sauvignon grapes, though these are sometimes bottled as red table wine when they don't meet winemaker Rob Mommsen's high standards. A good spot for a picnic.

✪ **Serendipity Cellars Winery.** 15275 Dunn Forest Rd., Monmouth. ☎ **503/838-4284.** May–Sept Wed–Mon noon–6pm; Apr, Oct–Nov Sat–Sun noon–6pm; Dec–Mar by appointment. Follow directions for Airlie Winery.

Located right next door to Airlie Winery, this tiny winery has no vineyards of its own but instead buys grapes from vineyards around the state. Winemaker Glen Longshore bucks Oregon wine trends by producing an excellent Maréchal Foch, a full-bodied dry red wine. If you like reds but aren't a fan of Pinot Noir, then you won't want to miss Serendipity. Dry Chenin Blanc and Zinfandel (from southern Oregon grapes) are also produced and are generally all quite good. They also do a Maréchal Foch port.

Springhill Cellars. 2920 NW Scenic Dr., Albany. ☎ **541/928-1009.** Memorial Day weekend–Christmas Sat–Sun 1–5pm. Closed rest of year. From Ore. 20 west of Albany, go north on Scenic Dr.

You'll find this winery just outside Albany, somewhat removed from most of the other area wineries and slowly being encroached upon by suburbs. Pinot Noir, Pinot Gris, Chardonnay, and Riesling are all produced.

Tyee Wine Cellars. 26335 Greenberry Rd., Corvallis. ☎ **541/753-8754.** Apr–June and Sept–Dec Sat–Sun noon–5pm; July and August Fri–Mon noon–5pm. Jan–Mar by appointment only. From Corvallis, go 7 miles south on Ore. 99W and then 2.3 miles west on Greenberry Rd.

Tyee Wine Cellars is located on a 460-acre farm established in 1885, and the tasting room is in an old milking barn from the days when this was a dairy farm. Although Tyee does a decent, peppery Pinot Noir, their real strength lies in the consistency of their whites—Pinot Gris, Pinot Blanc, Chardonnay, and Gewürztraminer—all of which tend to be dry and light. Be sure to walk the winery's 1.5-mile trail through farm and forest.

4 Eugene

40 miles S of Salem, 71 miles N of Roseburg, 61 miles E of Florence

Although Eugene, with more than 100,000 residents, is the second-largest city in Oregon, tie-dyed T-shirts are still a more common sight than silk ties here. The town's lively laid-back character is due in large part to the presence of the University of Oregon, the state's liberal arts college. The U of O, as it's known here in Oregon, has helped the city develop a well-rounded cultural scene, at the heart of which is the grandiose, glass-gabled **Hult Center for the Performing Arts.** On the university's tree-shaded 250-acre campus, you'll also find an art museum, a natural-history museum, and a science museum. Since this is still the Willamette Valley, you'll also find several wineries not far from the city.

Eugene has been known for years as a home to liberal-minded folks and alternative lifestyles. Though 1960s nostalgia has produced a new wave of hippies all over the country, many flower children here in Eugene never grew up. At the **Saturday Market,** a weekly outdoor craft market, you can see the works of many of these colorful and creative spirits.

Throw in a couple of beautiful riverfront parks with miles of bike paths, numerous excellent restaurants, and proximity to both the mountains and the coast, and you have a great base for exploring this part of the state.

ESSENTIALS

GETTING THERE   Eugene is located just off I-5 at the junction with I-105, which connects Eugene and Springfield, and Ore. 126, which leads east to Bend and west to Florence. Ore. 58 leads southeast to connect with U.S. 97 between Klamath Falls and Bend. Ore. 99W is an alternative to I-5.

The **Eugene airport** is located 9 miles northwest of downtown off Ore. 99W. It's served by Horizon and United/United Express. There's nonstop service to Portland, Seattle, San Francisco, Denver, and Phoenix.

Amtrak passenger trains stop in Eugene. The station is at East Fourth Avenue and Willamette Street. The new European-style high-speed Talgo train (called The Cascades) services this route.

VISITOR INFORMATION   Contact the **Convention & Visitors Association of Lane County Oregon,** 115 W. Eighth Ave., Suite 190 (P.O. Box 10286), Eugene, OR 97440 (☎ **800/547-5445** or 541/484-5307; www.cvalco.org/visit.html).

GETTING AROUND   Car rentals are available at the Eugene airport from **Hertz, Budget, Avis,** and **National.** If you need a taxi, contact **Yellow Cab** (☎ **541/ 343-7711**). **Lane Transit District (LTD)** (☎ **541/687-5555**) provides public transit throughout the metropolitan area and out to a number of nearby towns, including McKenzie Bridge, which is up the scenic McKenzie River; some routes do not run on Sunday. You can pick up bus-route maps and other information at the **LTD Customer Service Center** at the corner of 11th Avenue and Willamette Street. LTD fares are 50¢ to $1 for adults and youths ages 12 to 17, and 25¢ to 50¢ for seniors and children 5 to 11.

FESTIVALS Eugene's two biggest and most important music festivals are the **Oregon Bach Festival** (☎ 800/457-1486 or 541/346-5666) and the **Oregon Festival of American Music** (☎ 541/687-6526). The former, held the last week in June and the first week in July, is just what its name implies. The latter, held in August, is a celebration of everything from blues to gospel to jazz. Most performances for both festivals are held at the Hult Center in downtown Eugene. The **Eugene Celebration** (☎ 541/681-4108), held the third weekend in September, is a 3-day celebration that includes a wacky parade and the crowning of the annual Slug Queen. In mid-July, all the region's hippies, young and old, show up in nearby Veneta for the ✪ **Oregon Country Fair** (☎ 800/992-8499), a showcase for music and crafts. Also of note is **Junction City's Scandinavian Festival** (☎ 541/998-9372), which celebrates the region's Scandinavian heritage and is held each year on the second weekend in August. Junction City is 14 miles northwest of Eugene.

SEEING THE SIGHTS
MUSEUMS & HISTORIC BUILDINGS

Lane County Historical Museum. 740 W. 13th Ave. ☎ **541/682-4239.** Admission $2 adults, $1 senior citizens, 75¢ children 3–17. Wed–Fri 10am–4pm, Sat noon–4pm. Adjacent to the Lane County Fairgrounds 6 blks. from downtown Eugene.

The Willamette River valley was one of the first regions of the Northwest to be settled, and at this museum you'll find displays on the Oregon Trail and early pioneer life along the river. There are also period rooms, old vehicles, and children's exhibits.

Maude Kerns Art Center. 1910 E. 15th Ave. ☎ **541/345-1571.** Admission $2. Mon–Fri 10am–5:30pm, Sat noon–5pm.

The works of contemporary local, regional, and national craftspeople are the subjects of changing exhibits at this small gallery. You'll find this art center just up the street from the Museum of Natural History.

Oregon Air and Space Museum. 90377 Boeing Dr. ☎ **541/461-1101.** Admission $4 adults, $1 children 6–11. Wed–Fri and Sun noon–4pm, Sat 10am–4pm.

Located near the Eugene airport, the museum focuses on the history of aviation in Oregon. Numerous aircraft, including a World War I Fokker triplane, an F-4 Phantom, an F-86 Sabre Jet, and a Russian YAK-50, are on display. At press time, the museum was building a new hangar bay to display more of its aircraft.

Shelton-McMurphey-Johnson House. 303 Willamette St. ☎ **541/484-0808.** Admission $3 adults, $1 children under 12. Tues, Thurs, and Sun noon–4pm.

Built in 1888, this ornate Queen Anne Victorian home stands on the south slope of Skinner Butte on the north edge of downtown Eugene. It was long referred to as the Castle on the Hill. Tours of the beautiful old home focus on the families who lived here over the century that it was a private residence.

Springfield Museum. 590 Main St., Springfield. ☎ **541/726-3677.** Admission $1 adults. Wed–Fri 10am–4pm, Sat noon–4pm.

More area historical artifacts, here focusing on the region's industrial, logging, and agricultural heritage, are on display in this renovated 1908 Pacific Power & Light building in nearby Springfield. The collection of old photos is very evocative.

University of Oregon Museum of Art. 1430 Johnson Lane. ☎ **541/346-3027.** www.uoma.oregon.edu. Admission $3 adults, free for students. Wed noon–8pm, Thurs–Sun noon–5pm. Just east of 14th Ave. and Kincaid St. on the U of O campus.

The Asian art collection here is one of the finest in the Northwest and is the museum's main attraction. Included in this impressive collection is an astoundingly detailed

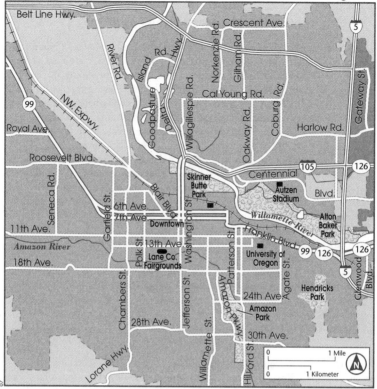

18th-century miniature jade pagoda. There are also rooms of Japanese woodblock prints and Cambodian sculptures. Keep an eye out for the case full of Chinese jewelry made from kingfisher feathers. Contemporary art of the Northwest is also represented. Exhibits change throughout the year.

University of Oregon Museum of Natural History. 1680 E. 15th Ave. ☎ **541/ 346-3024.** Admission $2 adults, $1.50 ages 3–18. Tues–Sun noon–5pm.

This small museum is housed in a building designed to vaguely resemble a traditional Northwest Coast Indian longhouse. Ancient peoples and even more ancient animals that once roamed the Northwest are the main focus of the museum, which also has exhibits on pre-Columbian ceramics from western Mexico and Australian aboriginal art and mythology. Temporary exhibits cover worldwide traditional cultures.

Willamette Science & Technology Center (WISTEC). 2300 Leo Harris Pkwy. ☎ **541/682-7888.** www.wistec.org. Admission $4 adults, $3 seniors and children 3–17. Wed–Fri noon–5pm, Sat–Sun 11am–5pm.

With loads of cool hands-on exhibits, this is the place to bring the kids to teach them about science. You might even learn something yourself. The building also houses the Lane Education Service District Planetarium, which offers changing features throughout the year.

PARKS & GARDENS
Alton Baker Park, on the north bank of the Willamette River, is Eugene's most popular park and offers jogging and biking trails. Across the river, **Skinner Butte Park** on

The Bridges of Lane County

In Robert James Waller's runaway hit novel *The Bridges of Madison County,* photographer Robert Kincaid hales from the Puget Sound area, but *National Geographic* sends him all the way to Madison County, Iowa, to photograph covered bridges. Kincaid could have saved himself a lot of miles on that beat-up old pickup truck if he had just headed south into Oregon, where he would have found the largest concentration of covered bridges west of the Mississippi.

Today, there are more than 50 covered bridges still standing in Oregon, down from more than 300 as recently as the 1930s. The oldest covered bridge is the Drift Creek Bridge near Lincoln City, which dates from 1914, and the newest (a reconstruction of a bridge destroyed by fire) dates to as recently as 1998. Built of wood and covered to protect them from the rain and extend their life, the covered bridges of Oregon are found primarily in the Willamette Valley, where early farmers needed safe river and stream crossings to get their crops to market. The highest concentration of covered bridges is found in Lane County, which stretches from the crest of the Cascade Range all the way to the Pacific Ocean and is home to 20 covered bridges.

You can get a map and guide to Lane County's covered bridges from the **Convention & Visitors Association of Lane County Oregon,** 115 W. Eighth Ave., Suite 190 (P.O. Box 10286), Eugene, OR 97440 (☎ **800/547-5445** or 541/484-5307; www.cvalco.org/visit.html).

---

the north side of downtown Eugene includes a 12-mile bike path. Nearby are the **Owen Memorial Rose Gardens.** At the **Mount Pisgah Arboretum,** Frank Parish Road, south of town off Seavey Loop Road, you can hike 7 miles of trails through meadows and forests. Set beneath towering fir trees high on a hill overlooking the city, **Hendricks Park and Rhododendron Garden** is one of the prettiest parks in the city, especially in the spring when the rhododendrons bloom. You'll find this park in southeast Eugene off Franklin Boulevard (U.S. 99). Take Walnut Street to Fairmount Boulevard and then turn east on Summit Avenue.

WINE TOURING

Eugene is at the southern limit of the Willamette Valley wine region, and there are half a dozen wineries within 30 miles of the city. With the exception of LaVelle Vineyards' downtown Eugene tasting room and High Pass Winery, all of these wineries are west of the city near Veneta and Lorane. To spend an afternoon wine tasting, head west out of Eugene on Ore. 126.

✪ **Chateau Lorane.** 27415 Siuslaw River Rd., Lorane. ☎ **541/942-8028.** June–Sept daily noon–5pm; Oct–Dec and Mar–May Sat–Sun noon–5pm. Closed Jan–Feb (or by appointment). Take Ore. 126 west to Veneta and go south through Crow to Lorane.

Located in a wooded setting overlooking its own lake, Chateau Lorane produces a greater variety of wines than just about any other winery in the state. Many of these are wines you won't find produced at any other Oregon wineries, and several are made from organic grapes. Some of the more unusual wines available here include a Viognier, a Flora (a cross between a Gewürztraminer and a Semillon), an organic Maréchal Foch (and a late harvest wine from this same grape), and several meads (honey wine), including a huckleberry mead. They also do a good Pinot Noir for under $20.

High Pass Winery. 24757 Lavell Rd., Junction City. ☎ **541/998-1447.** Memorial Day and Thanksgiving weekends only. From Junction City, on Ore. 99W, go west on High Pass Rd.

This is one of the few Willamette Valley wineries to attempt Cabernet Sauvignon and Merlot this far north, so if you're a fan of red wines, you might want to keep it in mind. They also produce Pinot Noir and lots of whites.

✪ **Hinman Vineyards.** 27012 Briggs Hill Rd., Eugene. ☎ **541/345-1945.** Daily noon–5pm. Closed Thanksgiving and Dec 24–Jan 1. Take Ore. 126 west to Veneta and go south through Crow.

If you enjoy sweet wines, you'll want to drop by this winery. Sure it's easy to do good sweet wines, but the semisparkling Muscat here is outstanding, the perfect dessert wine. Hinman also does respectable Merlots and Cabernet Sauvignons with grapes from southern Oregon. The Pinot Gris, Chardonnay, and Riesling also tend to be quite good. All in all, one of the best and most reliable wines in the state.

King Estate. 80854 Territorial Rd. ☎ **800/884-4441** or 541/942-9874. June–Sept daily noon–5pm; Oct–May Sat–Sun noon–5pm. Take Ore. 126 west to Veneta and go south through Crow almost to Lorane.

This is one of the largest wineries in the state, set in an idyllic hidden valley southwest of Eugene. The winery, part of an 820-acre estate, is surrounded by 250 acres of vineyards and features a huge chateaulike facility. The tasting room, however, is just about the smallest in the state. This winery feels more like a corporate endeavor than a work of love, and the wines are generally not among the state's better ones. However, in terms of touring a winery, this is one of the best to visit.

LaVelle Vineyards. 89697 Sheffler Rd., Elmira. ☎ **541/935-9406.** Memorial Day–Oct daily noon–6pm; Nov–May Sat–Sun noon–5pm. Closed Thanksgiving, Christmas, and New Year's. Off Ore. 126 west of Eugene.

Consistently good white wines (fruity but not too sweet) are the hallmark of this winery. The Pinot Gris and Riesling are outstanding. The vineyards here were first planted as test vineyards back in 1972 and are the oldest in the southern Willamette Valley. Special events are held throughout the summer, including first-Sunday music performances. LaVelle also has a tasting room in downtown Eugene at the Fifth Street Public Market, 296 E. Fifth Ave. (☎ **541/338-9875**), a good place to start a wine tour of the area.

Secret House Vineyards Winery. 88324 Vineyard Lane, Veneta. ☎ **541/935-3774.** June–Dec 23 Wed–Mon 11am–5pm; Mar–May Thurs–Mon 11am–5pm. Closed Dec 24–Feb. Off Ore. 126 west of Eugene.

Located adjacent to the grounds of the Oregon Country Fair, this is a small and casual winery that is known for its many special events, including the Wine and Blues Festival on the second weekend of August and the Long Tom Music Festival on the first Saturday after Labor Day. Chardonnay, Pinot Noir, and Riesling wines are produced, but the sparkling wines are what make this winery noteworthy.

OUTDOOR ACTIVITIES

Eugene has long been known as Tracktown, USA, and if you want to follow in the footsteps of Steve Prefontaine, there are plenty of routes around town for doing some running. At the Convention & Visitors Association of Lane County Oregon (see "Visitor Information," above), you can pick up a map of area running trails, including the popular **Pre's Trail,** a 3.87-mile system of loops in Alton Baker Park, which is just across the Willamette River from downtown Eugene. When the university's track team isn't practicing, it's possible to use the track at the University of Oregon's **Hayward Field,** where Pre and other Eugene runners have trained. You'll find Hayward Field off Agate Street in the southeast corner of the campus. Runners will also want to drop by the **Nike Store,** Fifth Street Public Market, 296 E. Fifth Ave. (☎ **541/342-5155**), which has an interesting little exhibit about Prefontaine, Bill Bowerman, and Phil Knight, who together laid the foundations for Nike's later success.

With two rivers, the McKenzie and the Willamette, flowing through the area, it isn't surprising that Eugene has quite a number of water-oriented activities. You can rent canoes, kayaks, rafts, and pedal boats at **River Runner Supply,** 78 G Centennial Loop (☎ **800/223-4326** or 541/343-6883; www.riverrunnersupply.com), which is across the street from Alton Baker Park. Rates are $8 and up per hour. This company also offers guided white-water rafting trips on the McKenzie ($45 to $65). For more exciting river running, contact **The Oregon Paddler** (☎ **888/297-9922** or 541/ 741-8661), which offers a quick and easy Willamette River float trip right through Eugene ($24.50). This company also does longer and more exciting rafting trips on both the Willamette and the McKenzie Rivers ($75). See the "The Santiam Pass, McKenzie Pass & McKenzie River" section of chapter 8 for more information on rafting the McKenzie River.

The calmer waters of **Fern Ridge Reservoir,** 12 miles west of Eugene on Ore. 126, attract boardsailing enthusiasts. Sailing, powerboating, waterskiing, and swimming are also popular. **Orchard Point Rentals** (☎ **541/689-4926**), at the north end of the lake off Clear Lake Road, rents 24-foot pontoon boats, paddleboats, canoes, and rowboats. Sailboats (☎ **541/688-6908**), sailboards (☎ **541/484-2588**), and jet skis (☎ **541/954-7895**) can also be rented here.

Eugene is Oregon's best bicycling city, and if you'd like to see why, you can rent a bike at **High Street Bicycles,** 535 High St. (☎ **541/687-1775**), which is located only a couple of blocks from the city's extensive riverside network of bike paths. The store has road bikes, mountain bikes, and tandems. Rates start at $5 per hour or $20 per day. Another great place for a bike ride is the paved Row River Trail, which starts just east of the nearby town of Cottage Grove and follows an abandoned railroad grade past Dorena Lake.

Golfers have plenty of Eugene options, including the **Emerald Valley Golf Club,** 83301 Dale Kuni Rd., Creswell (☎ **541/895-2174**), a championship daily-fee course; **Fiddler's Green Golf Club,** 91292 Ore. 99 (☎ **541/689-8464**), an 18-hole par-three course; **Laurelwood Golf Club,** 2700 Columbia St. (☎ **541/687-5321**), a 9-hole city-owned course; the **Oakway Golf Course,** 2000 Cal Young Rd. (☎ **541/ 484-1927**), an 18-hole executive course; and the **Riveridge Golf Course,** 3800 N. Delta Hwy. (☎ **541/345-9160**), which is located along the Willamette River.

SHOPPING

You can shop for one-of-a-kind crafts at Eugene's ✪ **Saturday Market** (☎ **541/ 686-8885**), which covers more than two downtown blocks beginning at the corner of Eighth Avenue and Oak Street. The bustling outdoor arts and crafts market was founded in 1970. Good, inexpensive food, fresh produce, and live music round out the offerings of this colorful event. The market is held every Saturday from 10am to 5pm between April and December.

Other days of the week, you can explore the **Market District,** a 6-block area of restored buildings that now house unusual shops, galleries, restaurants, and nightclubs. The **Fifth Street Public Market,** 296 E. Fifth St. at the corner of Fifth Avenue and High Street, is the centerpiece of the area. In this recently expanded shopping center, you'll find **Twist,** selling fine crafts and wildly artistic jewelry; **French Quarter,** selling fine linens; **Watches by Gosh,** with an amazing variety of watches and clocks; **Destinations,** a travel store; and **The Nike Store,** selling you know what. Directly across Fifth Avenue is the **5th & Pearl building,** which houses a couple of restaurants, a couple of music stores, and an antiques shop, among others. **Station Square,** a block west on Fifth Avenue, is a modern upscale mall designed to look like an old train station. Also nearby is **Down to Earth,** 532 Olive St. (☎ **541/342-6820**), a fascinating garden and housewares shop housed in an old granary building. A few blocks farther away, you'll find **Real Goods,** 77 W. Broadway (☎ **541/334-6960**), which sells products for sustainable living and energy independence (including photovoltaic cells and solar appliances).

Also well worth a visit, if you're here during the summer, is the **Tuesday Farmer's Market,** held at the corner of Eighth Avenue and Oak Street. Also, if you're interested in art, there is a monthly **First Friday Artwalk,** during which downtown art galleries have openings and stay open late.

WHERE TO STAY

Best Western New Oregon Motel. 1655 Franklin Blvd., Eugene, OR 97403. ☎ **800/ 528-1234** or 541/683-3669. Fax 541/484-5556. 128 units. A/C TV TEL. $68–$84 double. AE, CB, DC, DISC, EC, MC, V. Pets accepted.

Located across the street from the university campus, this Best Western is a convenient and fairly economical choice. Although the motel looks a bit old from the outside, guest rooms are in good shape and come with refrigerators and hair dryers. If you're in need of a bit of exercise or relaxing, you'll find racquetball courts, an indoor swimming pool, a whirlpool tub, saunas, an exercise room, and a sundeck.

✪ **The Campbell House.** 252 Pearl St., Eugene, OR 97401. ☎ **800/264-2519** or 541/343-1119. Fax 541/343-2258. www.campbellhouse.com. 18 units. A/C MINIBAR TV TEL. June–Oct $86–$289 double. Nov–May $79–$229. AE, DISC, MC, V. Rates include full breakfast.

Located only 2 blocks from the Market District and set at the base of Skinner's Butte overlooking the city, this large Victorian home was built in 1892 and now offers luxury, convenience, and comfort. The guest rooms here vary considerably in size and price, so there's something to fit all tastes and budgets. Breakfasts are served in a cheerful room with a curving wall of glass, and there's also a parlor with a similar glass wall. Several of the guest rooms on the first floor have high ceilings, and on the lower level there's a pine-paneled room with a fishing theme and another with a golf theme. The upstairs rooms have plenty of windows, and in the largest room you'll find wood floors and a double whirlpool tub. A separate carriage house now houses some of the inn's most luxurious and most thoughtfully designed rooms.

Eugene Hilton Hotel. 66 E. Sixth Ave., Eugene, OR 97401. ☎ **800/937-6660** or 541/ 342-2000. Fax 503/342-6661. www.eugene.hilton.com. 272 units. A/C TV TEL. $115–$160 double; $175–$325 suite. AE, CB, DC, DISC, MC, V.

This is Eugene's only downtown corporate high-rise convention hotel, catering primarily to business travelers and convention-goers. However, with the Hult Center for the Performing Arts right next door and dozens of restaurants and cafes within a few blocks, it also makes a good choice if you are in town to take in a show or get to know downtown Eugene. Try to get a room on an upper floor so you can enjoy the views. Although the lobby area and restaurants recently underwent a $5 million renovation, the rooms are still in need of refurbishing.

Dining/Diversions: A restaurant just off the lobby features a Northwest fishing theme and serves moderately priced meals. The Lobby Bar is a convenient place for an after-work drink.

Amenities: Indoor pool, exercise room, whirlpool, saunas, room service.

✪ **McKenzie View.** 34922 McKenzie View Dr., Springfield, OR 97478. ☎ **888/MCK-VIEW** or 541/726-3887. Fax 541/726-6968. 4 units. A/C. Apr–Oct $90–$250 double. Nov–Mar $75–$200 double. Rates include full breakfast. AE, MC, V.

Located on 6 acres of woodlands overlooking the McKenzie River, this country inn is located between Springfield and Eugene. Beautiful perennial gardens surround the inn, and there are decks and a gazebo from which guests can enjoy the property. The inn itself is an expansive contemporary home that is comfortably furnished—not over-done or too full of antiques for guests to feel comfortable. Three of the rooms are quite large (two are actually suites) and have views of the river through large windows. The smallest room doesn't have a river view, but the rates are quite economical. Avid gardeners will love this place. It's about a 15- to 20-minute drive from downtown Eugene.

✪ **The Secret Garden.** 1910 University St., Eugene, OR 97403. ☎ **888/484-6755** or 541/484-6755. Fax 541/431-1699. www.secretgardenbbinn.com. 10 units. May–Oct $115–$235 double. Nov–Apr $105–$215 double. Rates include full breakfast. MC, V.

This B&B is housed in what was once a sorority house, though before that it was the home of Eugene pioneer Alton Baker, for whom the city's waterfront park is named. Today, the large inn is run by the granddaughter of Portland shipping and steel magnate Henry Kaiser and is filled with family heirlooms and other European and Asian art and antiques. Guest rooms are beautifully and very tastefully decorated with interesting touches here and there to add visual interest. One of our favorite rooms is the Scented Garden, which has floor lamps made from Tibetan horns and a gorgeous sitar on display. Yes, there is a secret garden as well as a not-so-secret one. The former is a unique outdoor room with living walls that hide a whirlpool tub.

Valley River Inn. 1000 Valley River Way, Eugene, OR 97401. ☎ **800/543-8266** or 541/687-0123. Fax 541/683-5121. www.valleyriverinn.com. 257 units. A/C TV TEL. $180–$225 double; $225–$350 suite. Occasionally lower rates in winter. AE, CB, DC, DISC, MC, V. Pets accepted.

Although this lushly landscaped low-rise hotel boasts an envious location on the bank of the Willamette River and on Eugene's extensive riverfront path system, the rates are obviously aimed at expense accounts and not vacationers. If you can get any sort of substantial discount, this might be a good choice. The hotel is only a few minutes' drive from downtown and the university, and is adjacent to Eugene's largest shopping mall. All the rooms are large and have a balcony or patio, but the riverside rooms have the best views.

Dining/Diversions: Sweetwater's Restaurant has a long wall of glass overlooking the river and serves primarily Northwest cuisine. In the same large room is a more casual bar and grill.

Amenities: Outdoor pool, whirlpool, saunas, exercise room, concierge, room service, bicycle rentals.

WHERE TO DINE

For rustic breads, breakfast pastries, and desserts, drop by the **Palace Bakery,** 844 Pearl St. (☎ **541/484-2435**), an offshoot of the ever-popular Zenon Café. For espresso, drop by **Cafe Paradiso,** 115 W. Broadway (☎ **541/484-9933**), one of Eugene's most popular coffeehouses.

EXPENSIVE

Adam's Place. 30 E. Broadway. ☎ **541/344-6948.** Reservations recommended. Main courses $16–$23. AE, MC, V. Tues–Thurs 11:30am–2pm and 5–9pm, Fri 11:30am–2pm and 5–10pm, Sat 5–10pm. NORTHWEST.

Located downtown on the pedestrian mall, this restaurant conjures up the atmosphere of an old English inn and is now one of the most elegant dining establishments in the city. The menu is short and changes frequently, but on a recent summer evening the appetizer menu included fragrant salmon-and-dill potato pancakes as well as *mieng kum,* a Thai dish of spinach leaves wrapped around an assortment of flavorful ingredients that you assemble yourself. Entree flavors tend to the simpler end of creative cookery, with emphasis on subtle flavors and perfect preparation. Salmon might be coated with a citrus-infused breading and served with an apricot-brandy beurre blanc, and rack of lamb might be crusted in herbs and served with a morel demi-glace. In the summer, you can also dine under the stars out on the patio. Several nights each week there is live jazz.

Chanterelle. 207 E. Fifth St. ☎ **541/484-4065.** Reservations highly recommended. Main courses $15–$22. AE, DISC, MC, V. Tues–Thurs 5–10pm, Fri–Sat 5–11pm. Closed Mar 14– Apr 5 and Aug 17–Sept 6. CONTINENTAL.

This small continental restaurant is located in one of downtown Eugene's many restored old industrial buildings that have been turned into chic shopping centers. There are few surprises on the menu, just tried-and-true recipes prepared with reliable expertise and served with gracious attentiveness. Escargots bourguignonne, oysters Rockefeller, tournedos of beef, and steak Diane are just some of the familiar dishes on the Chanterelle menu. You'll also sometimes find emu, moose, and buffalo on the menu. A long wine list offers plenty of choices for the perfect accompaniment to your meal.

Marché. 296 E. Fifth Ave. ☎ **541/342-3612.** Reservations recommended. Main courses $13.50–$22.50. AE, DISC, MC, V. Mon–Thurs 11:30am–2pm and 5:30–10pm, Fri–Sat 11:30am–2pm and 5:30–11pm, Sun 10:30am–2pm and 5:30–10pm. MEDITERRANEAN.

After many years of coasting along on a handful of reliable standby establishments, Eugene's restaurant scene is slowly going more upscale. Marché, in the Fifth Street Public Market, is at the forefront of this movement. With its hip decor, tiny but popular bar, patio, and display kitchen with a few settings for solo diners, the restaurant pulls in a wide range of customers, from couples on dates to pretheater parties and even families. The menu, though it at times seems a bit pretentious, is as creative as you'll find in Eugene, and preparations are fairly reliable. There's an extensive wine list with plenty of reasonably priced wines, plus nearly 20 wines by the glass.

MODERATE

✪ **The LocoMotive.** 291 E. Fifth Ave. ☎ **541/465-4754.** Reservations recommended. Main courses $12.50–$13.75. MC, V. Wed–Thurs 5–9pm, Fri–Sat 5–10pm. VEGETARIAN.

Eugene has long been a magnet for countercultural types, so it should come as no surprise that the city has an excellent gourmet vegetarian restaurant. (Think white tablecloths, not hippie hangout.) Located across the street from the Fifth Street Public Market and next to the railroad tracks, this restaurant not only serves excellent vegetarian fare influenced by international cuisines, but also uses organic ingredients as often as possible. A recent menu included a very spicy Indian eggplant dish on basmati rice and a very flavorful Middle Eastern chickpea stew. Desserts, ranging from an organic blueberry pie (in season) to apples poached in red wine and calvados, are well worth saving room for. A lavender ice cream was absolutely unforgettable.

Waterfront. 2210 Centennial Ave. ☎ **541/465-4506.** Reservations recommended. Main courses $10–$22. AE, DISC, MC, V. Mon–Thurs 11:30am–2pm and 5–9pm, Fri 11:30am–2pm and 5–10pm, Sat 5–10pm, Sun 5–9pm. AMERICAN.

Although the water that this large contemporary restaurant overlooks is the old mill race and not the Willamette River, the parkside setting is still quite pleasant. (Don't be discouraged by all the car dealers surrounding it.) The interior decor would fit right in in Portland's Pearl District or Seattle's Belltown, but the menu is surprisingly simple. There are just a few basic salads (Caesar, spinach, Greek), a handful of pasta dishes, a half dozen steaks, and a few miscellaneous other entrees. The owner is Lebanese, and there are even a couple of dishes "the way my mother used to make it." In summer a tranquil patio overlooks the water. There is also a bar, a separate bar patio, and even a cigar room.

✪ **Zenon Café.** 898 Pearl St. ☎ **541/343-3005.** Reservations not accepted. Main courses $6.75–$16.25. MC, V. Sun–Thurs 8am–11pm, Fri–Sat 8am–midnight. INTERNATIONAL.

Located in downtown Eugene, Zenon has long been the city's top outpost for cutting-edge cookery. If you've read about it in the latest *Gourmet* or *Bon Appétit*, you'll probably find it on the menu here. The setting is fairly stark, though with some raw wood for warmth, and the menu, which changes daily, is long and emphasizes East Indian and Middle Eastern flavors. The globe-trotting menu assures all adventurous eaters of finding something they've never before tried. Before you ever reach your table, though, you'll have to run the gamut of the dessert case, which usually flaunts about 20 irresistible cakes, pies, tortes, and other pastries.

INEXPENSIVE

Mekala's Thai Restaurant. 296 E. Fifth Ave. ☎ **541/342-4872.** Reservations recommended. Main courses $8–$15. AE, DISC, MC, V. Mon–Thurs 11am–9pm, Fri 11am–10pm, Sat noon–10pm, Sun noon–9pm. THAI.

Located on the second floor of the Fifth Street Public Market, Mekala's has for years been Eugene's favorite Thai restaurant, and though the setting is strictly American, the aromas that fill the restaurant and its small patio dining area are all Thai. The menu is quite long and includes a substantial vegetarian section (this is, after all, the Northwest's countercultural capital). If you like your Thai food spicy, be sure to say so, since they tend to go extremely light on the peppers here for sensitive American palates.

Mona Lizza/West Brothers Bar-B-Que. 830 & 844 Olive St. Mona Lizza ☎ **541/345-1072.** West Brothers ☎ **541/345-4026.** Main courses $8–$20. AE, DC, MC, V. Daily 11:30am–11:30pm. ITALIAN.

With two restaurants and a brew pub all under one roof, this place may have a split personality, but it keeps Eugene's residents happily supping and sipping. Though you can't get barbecue on the Mona Lizza side or Italian on the West Brothers side, you can get the same good Eugene City Brewery beers at either restaurant. Mona Lizza's offers primarily wood-oven pizzas and pasta, while West Brothers serves up half a dozen types of barbecue, including Carolina pork shoulder and Memphis baby-back pork ribs. The dessert case just inside the front door of Mona Lizza may have you thinking about a salad instead of a big plate of pasta. For decor, there are Mona Lisa paintings in contemporary poses, and at West Brothers photos of barbecue joints around the country. As you might have guessed, both places are pretty casual.

EUGENE AFTER DARK

With its two theaters and nonstop schedule, the **Hult Center for the Performing Arts,** One Eugene Center, Seventh Avenue and Willamette Street (☎ **541/682-5000;** www.hultcenter.org), is the heart and soul of this city's performing arts scene. The center's huge glass gables are an unmistakable landmark of downtown Eugene, and each year this sparkling temple of the arts manages to put together a first-rate schedule of performances by the Eugene Symphony, the Eugene Ballet Company, the Eugene Opera, and other local and regional companies, as well as visiting companies and performers. Tickets range from about $6 to $40. During the summer, the center hosts the Oregon Bach Festival and the Oregon Festival of American Music. Summer concerts are also held at the **Cuthbert Amphitheater** in Alton Baker Park.

To find out what's happening in town, pick up a copy of the free *Eugene Weekly,* available at restaurants and shops around town.

BREW PUBS

In addition to the places listed below, you'll find plenty of microbreweries in Eugene. These include the **High Street Brewery & Cafe,** 1243 High St. (☎ **541/345-4905**); the **East 19th Street Cafe,** 1485 E. 19th St. (☎ **541/342-4025**); **Eugene City Beer,** 844 Olive St. (☎ **541/345-8489**); **Steelhead Brewing Co.,** 199 E. Fifth Ave. (☎ **541/686-2739**); and the **Wild Duck Restaurant & Brewery,** 169 W. Sixth Ave. (☎ **541/485-DUCK**). Over in Springfield, adjacent to the Gateway shopping mall, there's **Spencer's,** 980 Kruse Way (☎ **541/726-1726**), which does a very good organic pale ale, as well as lots of other brews.

NIGHTCLUBS & BARS

✪ **Jo Federigo's Café & Bar.** 259 E. Fifth Ave. ☎ **541/343-8488.**

Housed in a historic granary building, Jo Federigo's is both a popular restaurant and Eugene's favorite jazz club. There's live music nightly.

Oregon Electric Station. 27 E. Fifth Ave. ☎ **541/485-4444.**

This building dates from 1914, and with a wine cellar in an old railroad car, lots of oak, and a back bar that requires a ladder to access all the various bottles of premium spirits, it's the poshest bar in town.

WOW Hall. 291 W. Eighth Ave. ☎ **541/687-2746.**

The historic Woodmen of the World Hall now serves as a sort of community center for the performing arts and hosts an eclectic array of concerts and performances by alternative bands.

6 The Oregon Coast

Extending from the mouth of the Columbia River in the north to California's redwood country in the south, the Oregon coast is a shoreline of stunning natural beauty. Yes, it's often rainy or foggy, and yes, the water is too cold for swimming, but the coastline more than makes up for these shortcomings with its drama and grandeur. Wave-pounded rocky shores; dense, dark forests; lonely lighthouses; rugged headlands—these are what set this shoreline apart from any other in America.

In places, the mountains of the Coast Range rise straight from the ocean's waves to form rugged, windswept headlands that still bear the colorful names given them by early explorers—Cape Foulweather, Cape Blanco, Cape Perpetua. With roads and trails that scale these heights, these capes provide ideal vantage points for surveying the wave-washed coast. Between the rocky headlands stretch miles of sandy beaches. In fact, on the central coast there's so much sand that dunes rise as high as 500 feet, providing Saharalike hiking trails and playgrounds for dune buggies.

Wildlife viewing opportunities here are outstanding. From the beaches and the waters just offshore rise countless haystack rocks, rocky islets, monoliths, and other rock formations that serve as homes to sea birds, sea lions, and seals. Harbor seals loll on isolated sandspits, and large colonies of Steller sea lions lounge on rocks and docks, barking incessantly and entertaining people with their constant bickering. The best places to observe sea lions are at Sea Lion Caves north of Florence and at Cape Arago State Park outside of Coos Bay. Hundreds of gray whales also call these waters home, and each year thousands more can be seen during their annual migrations. Twice a year, in late winter and early spring, gray whales migrate between the Arctic and the waters off Baja California. They pass close by the coast and can be easily spotted from headlands such as Tillamook Head, Cape Meares, Cape Lookout, and Cape Blanco. In coastal meadows, majestic elk graze contentedly, and near the town of Reedsport, the Dean Creek meadows have been set aside as an elk preserve. It's often possible to spot 100 or more elk grazing here. The best introduction to the aquatic flora and fauna of the Oregon coast is Newport's Oregon Coast Aquarium, where you can learn more about the myriad animals and plants that inhabit the diverse aquatic environments of the Oregon coast.

The Cost of the Coast

State parks, county parks, national-forest recreation areas, outstanding natural areas—along the Oregon coast, there are numerous state and federal access areas that now charge day-use fees. You can either pay these fees wherever you encounter them or purchase an Oregon Pacific Coast Passport for $10. These passes are good for 5 days and get you into all state and federal parks and recreation areas along the coast (however, you'll still have to pay campsite fees). A $35 annual pass is also available.

Rivers, bays, and offshore waters are also home to some of the best **fishing** in the country. The rivers, though depleted by a century of overfishing, are still home to salmon, steelhead, and trout, most of which are now hatchery raised. Several charter-boat marinas up and down the coast offer saltwater fishing for salmon and bottom fish, and few anglers return from these trips without a good catch. **Crabbing** and **clamming** are two other productive coastal pursuits that can turn a trip to the beach into a time for feasting.

To allow visitors to enjoy all the beauties of the Oregon coast, the state has created nearly 80 state parks, waysides, recreation areas, and scenic viewpoints between Fort Stevens State Park in the north and McVay Rock State Recreation Site in the south. Among the more popular activities at these parks are kite flying and beachcombing (but not swimming; the water is too cold). For information on **camping** in area state parks, call the state parks information line at ☎ **800/551-6949;** to make a camping reservation, contact **Reservations Northwest,** 2501 SW First St. (P.O. Box 500), Portland, OR 97207 (☎ **800/452-5687** or 503/731-3411).

As we've already mentioned, it rains a lot here. Bring a raincoat, and don't let a little moisture prevent you from enjoying one of the most beautiful coastlines in the world. In fact, the mists and fogs add an aura of mystery to the coast's dark, forested mountain slopes. Contrary to what you might think, the hot days of July and August are not always the best time to visit. When it's baking inland, the coast is often shrouded in fog. The best months to visit tend to be September and October, when the weather is often fine and the crowds are gone.

1 Astoria

95 miles NW of Portland; 20 miles S of Long Beach, WA; 17 miles N of Seaside

The oldest American community west of the Mississippi, Astoria abounds in history. In the winter of 1805–06, Lewis and Clark, having crossed the continent by boat and on foot, built a fort near here and established an American claim to the region. Five years later, in 1811, fur traders working for John Jacob Astor arrived at the mouth of the Columbia River to set up a fur-trading fort that was named Fort Astoria. During the War of 1812, the fort was turned over to the British, but by 1818 it reverted to American hands. By the mid–19th century, the town boasted the state of Oregon's first brewery. When the salmon-canning boom hit in the 1880s, Astoria became a bustling little city—the second largest in Oregon—and wealthy merchants began erecting ornate, Victorian-style homes here.

Today, with no beach to call its own, Astoria's greatest attraction lies in its many blocks of restored Victorian homes and its riverfront setting near the mouth of the mighty Columbia River. While it still has its seamy sections of waterfront, it is also developing something of a tourist-oriented waterfront character. But fish-packing plants still outnumber ice-cream parlors.

ESSENTIALS

GETTING THERE   From Portland, take U.S. 30 west. From the north or south, take U.S. 101.

VISITOR INFORMATION   Contact the **Astoria-Warrenton Area Chamber of Commerce,** 111 W. Marine Dr. (P.O. Box 176), Astoria, OR 97103 (☎ **800/ 875-6807** or 503/325-6311; www.oldoregon.com).

GETTING AROUND   Car rentals are available through **Enterprise Rent-a-Car** (☎ **800/RENTACAR** or 503/325-6500). If you need a taxi, contact **Yellow Cab** (☎ **503/325-3131**).

FESTIVALS   The **Astoria Regatta,** held each year in early August, is the city's biggest festival and includes lots of sailboat races. As part of the festival, you can catch a performance of the Astor Street Opry Company's *Shanghaied in Astoria,* a musical melodrama staged at the Astoria Eagles Lodge, Ninth and Commercial streets (☎ **503/325-6104**). This usually runs from early July to late August.

DELVING INTO ASTORIA HISTORY

Columbia River Maritime Museum. 1792 Marine Dr. ☎ **503/325-2323**. Admission $5 adults, $4 seniors, $2 children 6–17. Daily 9:30am–5pm. Closed Thanksgiving and Dec 25.

The Columbia River, the second-largest river in the United States, was the object of centuries of exploration in the Northwest, and since its discovery in 1792, this river has become as important to the region as the Mississippi is to the Midwest. This boldly designed museum, built to resemble waves on the ocean, tells the story of the river's maritime history. Displays of shipwrecks, lighthouses, and lifesaving are all testament to the dangerous waters at the mouth of the Columbia. Here, high seas and the constantly shifting sands of the Columbia Bar conspire to make this one of the world's most difficult rivers to enter (over the centuries hundreds of ships have sunk here). Fishing, navigation, and naval history are also subjects of museum exhibits. Docked beside the museum and open to museum visitors is the lightship *Columbia,* the last seagoing lighthouse ship to serve on the West Coast.

Flavel House Museum. 441 Eighth St. ☎ **503/325-2203**. Admission $5 adults, $2.50 children 6–17. May–Sept daily 10am–5pm; October–April daily 11am–4pm.

The Flavel House, owned and operated by the Clatsop County Historical Society, is the grandest and most ornate of Astoria's many Victorian homes. This Queen Anne–style Victorian mansion was built in 1885 by Capt. George Flavel, who made his fortune operating the first pilot service over the Columbia River Bar and was Astoria's first millionaire. When constructed, this house was the envy of every Astoria resident. The high-ceilinged rooms are filled with period furnishings that accent the home's superb construction, and throughout the house there is much ornate woodworking.

Admission to the Flavel House also gets you into the nearby **Heritage Museum,** 1618 Exchange St., which is housed in Astoria's former city hall and chronicles the history of Astoria and surrounding Clatsop County. Native American and pioneer artifacts compose the main exhibits, but there is also an art gallery and a collection of historic photos dating from the 1880s to the 1930s.

Flavel House tickets also get you into the **Uppertown Fire Fighters Museum,** on the corner of 30th Street and Marine Drive. Housed in a former brewery building that was closed by Prohibition, the museum includes fire-fighting equipment dating from between 1877 and 1921.

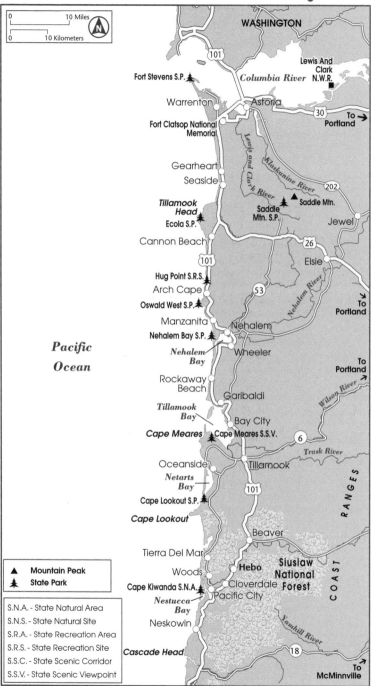

The Northern Oregon Coast

0 ___ 10 Miles
0 ___ 10 Kilometers

N

WASHINGTON

101

Fort Stevens S.P.

Columbia River

Lewis And Clark N.W.R.

Warrenton

Astoria

30
To Portland

Fort Clatsop National Memorial

Lewis and Clark River

Klaskanine River

202

Gearheart

Seaside

Tillamook Head

Saddle Mtn.

Ecola S.P.

Saddle Mtn. S.P.

Jewel

Cannon Beach

101

26

Elsie

Hug Point S.R.S.

Arch Cape

53

Nehalem River

Oswald West S.P.

To Portland

Manzanita

Nehalem

Nehalem Bay S.P.

Wheeler

Nehalem Bay

To Portland

Rockaway Beach

Garibaldi

Wilson River

Tillamook Bay

Bay City

Cape Meares

Cape Meares S.S.V.

6

Trask River

Tillamook

Oceanside

Netarts Bay

101

Cape Lookout S.P.

Cape Lookout

Beaver

C O A S T   R A N G E S

Tierra Del Mar

Woods

Hebo

Siuslaw National Forest

Cape Kiwanda S.N.A.

Cloverdale

Pacific City

Nestucca Bay

Neskowin

Yamhill River

Cascade Head

18

To McMinnville

Pacific Ocean

▲ Mountain Peak
🌲 State Park

S.N.A. - State Natural Area
S.N.S. - State Natural Site
S.R.A. - State Recreation Area
S.R.S. - State Recreation Site
S.S.C. - State Scenic Corridor
S.S.V. - State Scenic Viewpoint

✪ **Fort Clatsop National Memorial.** Off U.S. 101, 5 miles southwest of Astoria. ☎ **503/861-2471.** Admission $2 per person or $4 per car. Labor Day to mid-June daily 8am–5pm; mid-June to Labor Day daily 8am–6pm. Closed Dec 25.

During the winter of 1805–06, Meriwether Lewis, William Clark, and the other members of the Corps of Discovery, having crossed the continent from St. Louis, camped at a spot near the mouth of the Columbia River. They built a log stockade and named their encampment Fort Clatsop after the local Clatsop Indians who had befriended them. Today's Fort Clatsop is a reconstruction of Lewis and Clark's winter encampment and is built near the site of the original fort. The 50-foot-square compound contains seven rooms, each of which is furnished much as it may have been during Lewis and Clark's stay. From late spring to Labor Day, park rangers clad in period clothing give demonstrations of activities pursued by the explorers, from candle making and firearms use to buckskin sewing and food preparation. In the visitor center you can learn the history of the Corps of Discovery and Fort Clatsop before visiting the stockade itself.

OTHER ASTORIA ACTIVITIES & ATTRACTIONS

Atop Coxcomb Hill, which is reached by driving up 16th Street and following the signs and painted "column" markings on the road, you'll find the **Astoria Column.** Built in 1926, the column is patterned after Trajan's Column in Rome and stands 125 feet tall. On the exterior wall of the column, a mural depicts the history of the area. It's 164 steps up to the top of the column, and on a clear day the view is well worth the effort. The column is open daily from dawn to dusk and admission is free. On the way to the Astoria Column, stop by **Fort Astoria,** on the corner of 15th and Exchange streets. A log blockhouse and historical marker commemorate the site of the trading post established by John Jacob Astor's fur traders.

There are several places in downtown where you can linger by the riverside atop the docks that once composed much of the city's waterfront. Stop by the **Sixth Street Viewing Dock,** where there is a raised viewing platform as well as a fishing dock. From here you can gaze out at the massive Astoria-Megler Bridge, which stretches for more than 4 miles across the mouth of the Columbia River. Also keep an eye out for sea lions, which like to feed in the waters here. A few blocks away, you'll find the **14th Street River Park.** You can see all the Astoria waterfront with a ride on the restored **vintage trolley** that now operates on a short stretch of dockside track. If you'd like to see the waterfront from an offshore perspective, you can book a river cruise by **Tiki Charters** (☎ 503/325-7818). Cruises of the Astoria waterfront are $15 per person, and trips upriver to Cathlamet are $50 per person.

Right in downtown Astoria, you'll find one of the most unusual wineries in the state. **Shallon Winery,** 1598 Duane St. (☎ 503/325-5978), specializes in fruit wines, including vintages made from Himalayan blackberries, evergreen blackberries, black raspberries, and apples. However, it is the winery's unique whey wines that are the greatest achievement of winemaker Paul van der Veldt. The Cran du Lait, made with local cranberries and whey from the Tillamook cheese factory, is a surprisingly smooth and drinkable wine. However, the most amazing wine here is the chocolate-orange wine, a thick nectar that will make a chocoholic of anyone.

If you'd like to see what local artists are up to, stop by the **Pacific Rim Gallery,** 108 Tenth St. (☎ 503/325-5450), which also has an espresso bar and cafe. For more regional art, visit the **RiverSea Gallery,** 1160 Commercial St. (☎ 503/325-1270). And right next door, the **Hide & Silk Co.,** 1164 Commercial St. (☎ 503/325-2766), sells handmade clothing made of natural fabrics.

Shot in Astoria

Over the past decade or so, several popular movies have been shot in Astoria, including *Kindergarten Cop, Free Willy, Goonies, Short Circuit,* and *Teenage Mutant Ninja Turtles III*. If you're interested in seeing some of the sites where these films were shot, you can pick up a booklet called *Shot in Astoria* for $1 at the chamber of commerce visitor center.

OUTDOOR ACTIVITIES

Fort Stevens State Park, 8 miles from Astoria at the mouth of the Columbia (☎ 503/861-1671), preserves a fort that was built during the Civil War to protect the Columbia River and its important port cities. Though Fort Stevens had the distinction of being the only mainland military reservation to be fired on by the Japanese, the fort was deactivated after World War II. Today the fort's extensive grounds include historic buildings and gun emplacements, a museum housing military artifacts, miles of bicycle paths and beaches, and a campground and picnic area. Admission is $3. At the north end of the park, you can climb to the top of a viewing tower and get a good look at the South Jetty, which was built to make navigating the mouth of the Columbia easier. Also within the park you can see the wreck of the *Peter Iredale,* one ship that did not make it safely over the sandbars at the river's mouth. During the summer, **Bikes & Beyond,** 1089 Marine Dr. (☎ 503/325-2961), rents bikes inside the state park at Coffenbury Lake.

If you're interested in exploring the waters of the Astoria area, you can rent a kayak from **Pacific Wave Ltd.,** 21 U.S. 101, Warrenton (☎ 503/861-0866; www.pacwave.net), which also offers classes and guided tours.

Several charter fishing boats operate out of nearby Warrenton. Trips can be arranged through **Tiki Charters** (☎ 503/325-7818) and **Charlton Deep Sea Charters** (☎ 503/861-2429). Expect to pay around $70 per person.

A few miles outside of town on Ore. 30, bird-watchers will find a roadside viewing platform overlooking the marshes of the **Twilight Creek Eagle Sanctuary.** Take Burnside Road off Ore. 30 between the John Day River and Svenson.

WHERE TO STAY

✪ **Clementine's Bed and Breakfast.** 847 Exchange St., Astoria, OR 97103. ☎ 800/521-6801 or 503/325-2005. Fax 503/325-7056. www.clementines-bb.com. 7 units. $60–$100 double; $125 suite. AE, DISC, MC, V. Pets accepted in suites.

Located across the street from the Flavel House Museum, this eclectic little inn is surrounded by a beautiful flower garden. The inn, built in 1888 in the Italianate Victorian style, is now filled with Asian arts and antiques, and in summer it is always filled with fresh cut flowers from the gardens. Rooms vary considerably in size. Two rooms have their own little balconies, and several have expansive views of the river and town. The two suites are quite large and are great for families. With backgrounds in music and river guiding on the Colorado River, innkeepers Judith and Cliff Taylor keep guests entertained and informed about what there is to see and do in the area.

Columbia River Inn Bed & Breakfast. 1681 Franklin Ave., Astoria, OR 97103. ☎ 800/953-5044 or 503/325-5044. www.moriah.com/columbia. 4 units. $75–$125 double. Rates include full breakfast. AE, DC, MC, V.

With a classic "painted lady" exterior, this Victorian house overlooks downtown Astoria and the Columbia River and is surrounded by colorful gardens in summer.

Inside, reproduction Victorian-era furnishings and country decor set the stage for a stay with friendly proprietor Karen Nelson. The Victorian Rose and River Queen rooms have the best views. In order to get private bathrooms into every room, some strange remodeling had to be done. In Amanda's Room, an odd little shower was tucked into one corner. However, in the honeymoon suite, you'll find a whirlpool tub. Much of the inn's country decor was done by the owner, and if you see something you like, you just might find a similar item at the inn's Krafty's Korner gift shop.

Crest Motel. 5366 Leif Erickson Dr. (about 2 miles east of town on U.S. 30), Astoria, OR 97103. ☎ **800/421-3141** or 503/325-3141. Fax 503/325-3141. www.crest-motel.com. 40 units. TV TEL. $52.50–$89.50 double. AE, CB, DC, DISC, MC, V. Pets accepted.

Located a few miles from downtown Astoria, the Crest Motel sits high on a hillside overlooking the town and the river. The views, congenial atmosphere, and comfortable refurbished rooms have made this motel immensely popular. Keep in mind that the lower-priced rooms have no views—and since the views are the main reason to stay here, it's worth a bit of a splurge for a better room even if you're on a tight budget. The deluxe-view rooms are very large and have sliding glass doors and a patio or balcony. There's also a whirlpool tub in a gazebo overlooking the river.

Franklin Street Station Bed and Breakfast Inn. 1140 Franklin St., Astoria, OR 97103. ☎ **503/325-4314.** 5 units. $80–$135 double. Rates include full breakfast. MC, V. Closed Oct–Apr.

Though from the exterior this B&B 3 blocks from downtown Astoria doesn't seem to epitomize Victorian ornateness, inside you'll find rich wood accents and trim in every room. The innkeepers, Maurizio Bassini and Darcy Urell, are from Milan. Built in 1900, the large house has been completely renovated, and each of the guest rooms now has a private bathroom. The best room in the house, if you don't mind the climb, is the attic Captain's Quarters, which has a great view of the Columbia, as well as a clawfoot tub, TV, VCR, stereo, and wet bar. The Columbia Room, with its river-view deck, is another of our favorites.

Officer's Inn Bed and Breakfast. 540 Russell Place, Hammond, OR 97121. ☎ **800/377-2524** or 503/861-2524. Fax 503/861-1784. www.moriah.com/officersinn. 8 units. June–Oct $75–$95 double. Nov–May $55–$75 double. MC, V.

Housed in the former Fort Stevens officers' quarters built in 1905, this sprawling 8,000-square-foot B&B is located just around the corner from the Fort Stevens Museum and about 10 minutes' drive from Astoria. The inn captures the essence of small-town America with its long front porch overlooking the old parade grounds. Inside, you'll find simple, classic decor. However, it is the perfectly preserved pressed-tin ceilings of the parlors and dining rooms that are the inn's finest feature. Guest rooms vary in size and come with king, queen, or double beds. There are even two rooms set up for families. Any time of year, but especially in spring and fall, you might see elk grazing in the field behind the inn.

✪ **Rosebriar Hotel.** 636 14th St., Astoria, OR 97103. ☎ **800/487-0224** or 503/325-7427. Fax 503/325-6937. www.oregoncoastlodgings.com. 11 units (including 1 cottage). TV TEL. $49–$149 double. Rates include full breakfast. Two-night minimum on weekends. AE, CB, DC, DISC, MC, V.

Originally built as a private home, the Rosebriar became a convent in the 1950s before being renovated and turned into a small hotel in the 1990s. In its current incarnation, the Rosebriar is decorated in the style of a 1920s hotel. Ornate wainscoting, scrollwork ceilings, and lots of wood trim show the quality of workmanship that went into this home when it was built in 1902. The grand old Georgian mansion sits high above the river and high above the street, with commanding views from the two front rooms. If

---

Camping on the Beach

Fort Stevens State Park, on the beach at the mouth of the Columbia River, is one of the largest and most popular state park campgrounds on the Oregon coast. For reservations, contact **Reservations Northwest (☎ 800/452-5687**).

---

you're seeking that extra bit of privacy for a special occasion, ask for the carriage-house cottage, which has its own fireplace, whirlpool tub, and private patio.

WHERE TO DINE

In addition to the restaurants listed below, you might want to check out **Josephson's,** 106 Marine Dr. (☎ **800/772-3474** or 503/325-2190), which is a local seafood-smoking company that sells smoked salmon by the pound, but that also has a take-out deli counter where you can get clam chowder, smoked seafood on rolls, and the like. If you're looking for some local ale, stop by **The Wet Dog Cafe,** 144 11th St. (☎ **503/325-6975**), the town's only brew pub. For airy baked goods and light lunch fare, the **Home Spirit Bakery Café,** housed in a peach and green Victorian at 1585 Exchange St., is the place to go (☎ **503/325-6846**).

MODERATE

Gunderson's Cannery Cafe. Sixth St. at the Columbia River. ☎ **503/325-8642.** Reservations recommended. Main dishes lunch $5–$9, dinner $9.50–$18. DC, DISC, MC, V. Mon 11am–3pm, Tues–Sat 11am–8pm. In summer Sun 11am–4pm. SEAFOOD/NORTHWEST.

Housed in a restored salmon cannery, this small, bright restaurant provides a more contemporary dining alternative to the aging Pier 11. You get the same views and are just as likely to see sea lions out the window, but the food is much more creative. For nightly specials, chefs draw upon world cuisines for inspiration; and on a recent evening the special included baked halibut with fruit chutney, garlic- and pepper-crusted pork loin, and crab and shrimp cakes. Lunches are mostly grilled sandwiches, salads, and good chowder.

Pier 11 Feed Store Restaurant. At the foot of Tenth and Eleventh streets. ☎ **503/325-0279.** Reservations recommended. Main dishes lunch $6–$11; dinner $12.50–$21. DISC, MC, V. Sun–Thurs 7am–9pm, Fri–Sat 7am–10pm (until 10pm nightly in summer). SEAFOOD.

Originally a freight depot for river cargo and one of the few buildings in town that was not destroyed by a fire in 1922, Pier 11 now houses a few small shops and this popular, though touristy, seafood restaurant. Nearly everyone gets a great view of the river through the restaurant's wall of glass, and if you're lucky, you might spot some seals or sea lions frolicking just outside the window. Meals are simply prepared and are usually quite good, although the restaurant does have an occasional off night. Garlic and butter steamed little neck clams and blackened prime rib are both usually reliable.

Someplace Else. 965 Commercial St. ☎ **503/325-3500.** Reservations recommended. Main dishes lunch $5, dinner $7–$14. AE, DISC, MC, V. Wed–Mon 11:30am–2pm and 4–9pm. Closed 2 weeks over Christmas holidays. INTERNATIONAL.

A mannequin outside the door on Astoria's main downtown commercial street is a sign that you've arrived at Someplace Else. The restaurant's owner is a born traveler and has been to the places from which she draws her recipes, although since her family is from Sicily, it's no surprise that the emphasis is on southern Italian cuisine. An international dish, such as Moroccan meatball stew with couscous or German sauerbraten, is featured daily. Some of the dishes are more successful than others. Homey treatments of pastas such as ravioli are satisfying, and sliced tomatoes with onions and anchovies

Biking the Oregon Coast

The Oregon coast is one of the nation's most fabled bicycle tour routes, ranking right up there with the back roads of Vermont, the Napa Valley, and the San Juan Islands. Its fame is in no way overrated. Cyclists will find not only breathtaking scenery, but also interesting towns, parks and beaches to explore, wide shoulders, and well-spaced places to stay. You have the option of staying in campgrounds (all state park campgrounds have hiker/biker campsites) or hotels. If you can afford it, an inn-to-inn pedal down this coast is the way to go; as you slowly grind your way up hill after hill, you'll appreciate not having to carry camping gear.

The entire route, from Astoria to California, covers between 368 and 378 miles (depending on your route) and includes a daunting 16,000 total feet of climbing. While most of the route is on U.S. 101, which is a 55 m.p.h. highway for most of its length, the designated coast route leaves the highway for less crowded and more scenic roads whenever possible.

During the summer, when winds are generally out of the northwest, you'll have the wind at your back if you ride from north to south. In the winter (when you'll likely get very wet), you're better off riding from south to north to take advantage of winds out of the southwest. Planning a trip along the coast in winter is not advisable though because, although there is less traffic, winter storms frequently blow in with winds of up to 100 m.p.h.

For a map and guide to bicycling the Oregon coast, contact the **Oregon Bicycle Map Hotline** (☎ **503/986-3556**). You might also want to get a copy of the *Umbrella Guide to Bicycling the Oregon Coast* (1991, Umbrella Books), by Robin Cody.

---

make a tasty salad. This cozy neighborhood restaurant has red-checked tablecloths and a twinkle light–decorated ceiling, and even an e-mail station for customers to use.

INEXPENSIVE

✪ **Columbian Café.** 1114 Marine Dr. ☎ **503/325-2233.** Breakfast or lunch $4–$8; dinner $8–$20. No credit cards. Mon–Tues 8am–2pm, Wed–Thurs 8am–2pm and 5–9pm, Fri 8am–2pm and 5–10pm, Sat 9am–3pm and 5–10pm, Sun 9am–3pm (dining hours may change with the season). VEGETARIAN/SEAFOOD.

With an offbeat and eclectic decor, this tiny place looks a bit like a cross between a college hangout and a seaport diner, and indeed the clientele reflects this atmosphere. There are only three or four booths and a lunch counter, and the cafe's reputation for good vegetarian fare keeps the seats full. Crepes are the house specialty and come with a variety of fillings, including avocado, tomato, and cheese, or curried bananas. Dinner offers a bit more variety, with an emphasis on seafood, and there are always a few specials. Even the condiments here, including pepper jelly and garlic jelly, are homemade.

2 Seaside

17 miles S of Astoria, 79 miles W of Portland, 7 miles N of Cannon Beach

Seaside is the northern Oregon coast's favorite family vacation destination. Although the town is one of the oldest beach resorts on the coast (dating from 1899) and is filled with quaint historic cottages and tree-lined streets, it is better known for its miniature golf courses, bumper boats, video arcades, and souvenir shops.

This is not the sort of place most people imagine when they dream about the Oregon coast, and if you're looking for a quiet, romantic weekend getaway, don't head here. As one of the closest beaches to Portland, crowds and traffic are a way of life on summer weekends. The town is also a very popular conference site, and several of the town's largest hotels cater primarily to this market (and have the outrageous rates to prove it). However, the nearby community of Gearhart, which has long been a retreat for wealthy Portlanders, is as quiet as any town you'll find on this coast.

ESSENTIALS

GETTING THERE   Seaside is on U.S. 101 just north of the junction with U.S. 26, which connects to Portland.

VISITOR INFORMATION   Contact the **Seaside Chamber of Commerce,** 7 N. Roosevelt (P.O. Box 7), Seaside, OR 97138 (☎ **800/444-6740** or 503/738-6391; www.seasideor.com).

FESTIVALS   The weekend before Labor Day weekend, the **Hood to Coast Run** celebration is held in Seaside.

ENJOYING THE BEACH & SEASIDE'S OTHER ATTRACTIONS

Seaside's centerpiece is its 2-mile-long beachfront **Promenade** (or Prom), built in 1921. At the west end of Broadway, the Turnaround divides the walkway into the North Prom and the South Prom. Here a bronze statue marks the official end of the trail for the Lewis and Clark expedition. South of this statue on Lewis & Clark Way between the Promenade and Beach Drive, 8 blocks south of Broadway, you'll find the **Lewis and Clark Salt Works,** a reconstruction of a fire pit used by members of the famous expedition. During the winter of 1805–06, while the expedition was camped at Fort Clatsop near present-day Astoria, Lewis and Clark sent several men southwest 15 miles to a good spot for making salt from seawater. It took three men nearly 2 months to produce four bushels of salt for the return trip east. Five kettles were used for boiling seawater, and the fires were kept stoked 24 hours a day. Ironically, Captain Clark felt no need for salt, though Lewis and the rest of the men felt it was necessary for the enjoyment of their meager rations.

History is not what attracts most people to Seaside, though. Miles of **white-sand beach** begin just south of Seaside at the foot of the imposing Tillamook Head and stretch north to the mouth of the Columbia River. Though the waters here are quite cold and only a few people venture in farther than knee-deep, there are lifeguards on duty all summer, which is one reason Seaside is popular with families. At the south end of Seaside beach is one of the best surf breaks on the north coast. You can rent a board and wetsuit at **Cleanline Surf,** 719 First Ave. (☎ **503/738-7888**). A complete rental package runs $35 a day for adults. You can also rent bodyboards here.

However, because the waters here never warm up to comfortable swimming temperatures, kite flying, beach cycling, and other nonaquatic activities prove far more popular than swimming or surfing. All over town there are places that rent in-line skates, four-wheeled bicycles called surreys, and three-wheeled cycles (fun cycles) for pedaling on the beach. The latter are the most popular and the most fun, but can really be used only when the tide is out and the beach is firm enough to pedal on. Skates rent for $6 an hour, cycles go for between $6 and $10 an hour, and multi-passenger surreys rent for between $13 and $36 an hour. Try **Iron Coach,** 151 Ave. A (☎ **503/717-4337**), or any of the other shops on Avenue A 1 block south of Broadway near the beach, or **Outdoor Fun for All!** at 407 S. Holladay Dr. (☎ **503/738-8447**).

If you prefer hiking over cycling, head south of town to the end of Sunset Boulevard, where you'll find the start of the **Tillamook Head Trail,** which leads 6 miles over the headland to Indian Beach in **Ecola State Park.** This trail leads through shady forests of firs and red cedars with a few glimpses of the Pacific along the way.

If it's horseback riding that interests you, there are several stables just south of Seaside on U.S. 101 that offer rides. Try **Faraway Farms** (☎ 503/738-6336), which offers rides both on its own property and on the beach.

Golfers can play a round at the **Seaside Golf Club,** 451 Ave. U (☎ 503/738-5261), **The Highlands at Gearhart,** 1 Highlands Rd. (☎ 503/738-5248), or the **Gearhart Golf Links,** on North Marion Street in Gearhart (☎ 503/738-3538). Expect to pay about $30 or under for 18 holes at these courses.

In addition to the miles of sandy beach, the **Seaside Aquarium,** 200 N. Promenade (☎ 503/738-6211), where you can feed the seals, is also popular. Admission is $5.50 for adults and $2.75 for children. Kids will also enjoy the gaudily painted **carousel** at the Seaside Town Center Mall at 300 Broadway.

At the **Seaside Museum,** 570 Necanicum Dr. (☎ 503/738-7065), you can see Native American artifacts dating from A.D. 230, as well as more recent items of historic significance. It's open daily from 10am to 4pm; admission is $2. The adjacent **Butterfield Cottage** is decorated much as a summer cottage would have looked in 1912.

One of Seaside's oddest new attractions is **Butterflies Forever,** at the corner of Broadway and U.S. 101. This greenhouse features about 200 butterflies and displays illustrating the butterfly's life cycle. You'll find the greenhouse garden across from the Seaside Chamber of Commerce. Hours are daily from 10am to 6pm; adult admission is $4, and children 4 to 12 are $1.50.

WHERE TO STAY
IN SEASIDE
Moderate
Ebb Tide. 300 N. Promenade, Seaside, OR 97138. ☎ 800/468-6232 or 503/738-8371. 83 units. TV TEL. May–Sept $90–$150 double. Oct–Apr $70–$125 double. AE, DISC, MC, V.

With a wide variety of rooms and a location right on the Promenade, this older motel is one of the best values in Seaside. The best rooms, however, don't have ocean views, but instead are in a new wing on the inland side of the hotel. Most rooms have fireplaces and kitchenettes. Some rooms also have whirlpool tubs. All the rooms have refrigerators. An indoor swimming pool, a whirlpool, a sauna, and an exercise room are available.

✪ **The Gilbert Inn.** 341 Beach Dr., Seaside, OR 97138. ☎ 800/410-9770 or 503/738-9770. Fax 503/717-1070. www.gilbertinn.com. 10 units. TV TEL. $89–$99 double; $105 suite. Rates include full breakfast. AE, DISC, MC, V.

One block from the beach and 1 block south of Broadway, on the edge of both the shopping district and one of Seaside's old residential neighborhoods, stands the Gilbert Inn, a big yellow Queen Anne–style Victorian house with a pretty little yard. Alexander Gilbert, who had this house built in 1892, was once the mayor of Seaside, and he built a stately home worthy of someone in such a high position. Gilbert made good use of the plentiful fir trees of the area; the interior walls and ceilings are constructed of tongue-and-groove fir planks. The current owners, Dick and Carole Rees, have decorated the house in country French decor that manages to enhance the Victorian ambiance.

Shilo Inn—Seaside Oceanfront Resort. 30 N. Promenade (at Broadway), Seaside, OR 97138-5823. ☎ **800/222-2244** or 503/738-9571. Fax 503/738-0674. 112 units. TV TEL. $65–$229 double. AE, CB, DC, DISC, MC, V.

Located right on the Turnaround that marks the end of the trail for the Lewis and Clark expedition, the Shilo Inn is a very comfortable and modern beachfront convention/resort hotel. However, high prices in summer are a bit out of line for what you get. But if you expect to spend more time in the pool than on the beach, you might want to consider this hotel—the recreation facilities here are the best in town. The indoor swimming pool, whirlpool tub, steam room, sauna, and exercise room all overlook the beach and are separated from the lobby by a wall of glass that lets people in the lobby look out at the ocean as well. Oceanfront guest rooms all have large balconies, fireplaces, and kitchenettes, so you can enjoy your stay no matter what the weather, but these are the most expensive and overpriced rooms here. The hotel's dining room has a splendid view of the beach and serves entrees in the $10 to $23 range. Sunday brunch is especially popular. Expect some form of live entertainment in the lounge on summer nights.

Inexpensive

Hillcrest Inn. 118 N. Columbia St., Seaside, OR 97138. ☎ **800/270-7659** or 503/738-6273. 26 units (including 3 cottages). TV TEL. $49–$99 double to 6 people. AE, DC, MC, V.

This lodging has a mix of older cottages and newer motel-style units, and prices are some of the best in town. All the units cluster around a small lawn and flower-filled gardens beneath a few shady pine trees. Our favorites here are the two-bedroom cottages, which manage to capture a bit of the old Seaside atmosphere. However, some of the newer rooms are more comfortable and include whirlpool tubs, fireplaces, or both. It's only 2 blocks to the beach or Broadway.

Riverside Inn Bed & Breakfast. 430 S. Holladay Dr., Seaside, OR 97138. ☎ **800/826-6151** or 503/738-8254. Fax 503/738-7375. www.riversideinn.com. 11 units. TV. $55–$99 double. Rates include full breakfast. AE, DISC, MC, V.

Though it's located on busy Holladay Drive, the Riverside Inn is an oasis amid the traffic and businesses. Beautiful gardens frame the restored 1907 home and its attached cottages. Through the backyard flows the Necanicum River, and a sprawling multilevel deck lets you enjoy the riverside location. Inside, all the rooms are a bit different, with antique country decor and an emphasis on fishing collectibles. The Captain's Quarters room, way up on the third floor, features a skylight directly over the bathtub and has the feel of a well-appointed artist's garret. Another of our favorite rooms here is the Old Seaside, a two-room unit with its own private deck. If you're planning a long stay, there are some rooms with kitchenettes.

IN GEARHART

Gearhart by the Sea. 1157 N. Marion Ave. (P.O. Box 2700), Gearhart, OR 97138. ☎ **800/547-0115** or 503/738-8331. Fax 503/738-0881. www.gearhartresort.com. 85 condos. TV TEL. $126–$148 1-bedroom; $158–$194, 2-bedroom. AE, DISC, MC, V. Pets accepted ($10 per night).

Although this four-story condominium hotel isn't the most attractive building on the coast (stark cement exterior), it is an ideal accommodation for golfers. The Gearhart Golf Links are directly across the street. Condos all have full kitchens, fireplaces, and ocean views; but the best views go to the two-bedroom units, which makes this a good choice for families or pairs of golfing couples. While the golf course is right across the street, the beach is actually a bit farther across the sand dunes. Amenities include an indoor swimming pool; whirlpool; coffee shop; restaurant, and lounge.

Gearhart Ocean Inn. 67 N. Cottage St. (P.O. Box 2161), Gearhart, OR 97138. ☎ **800/ 352-8036** or 503/738-7373. www.oregoncoastlodgings.com/gearhart. 11 units. TV TEL. $39–$99 double. AE, CB, DC, DISC, MC, V. Pets accepted ($10 fee).

This old motor court–style motel has been fully renovated with all the care that's usually lavished on Victorian homes. A taupe exterior with white trim gives the two rows of wooden buildings a touch of sophistication, and roses and Adirondack chairs add character to the grounds, though a wide expanse of gravel parking lot does detract somewhat from the effect. The rooms all have lots of character and have been fully renovated. The most expensive rooms are two stories with wood floors, a kitchen, and even a garage. The decor is a combination of country cute and casual contemporary.

WHERE TO DINE

If you're looking for a quick meal, some picnic food, or something to take back and cook in your room, drop by the old-timey **Bell Buoy Crab Co.,** 1800 S. Holladay Dr. (☎ **503/738-2722**), which sells not only cooked Dungeness crabs, but award-winning chowder, smoked salmon, fresh seafood, and shrimp or crab melts.

IN SEASIDE

Dooger's Seafood & Grill. 505 Broadway. ☎ **503/738-3773.** Reservations not accepted. Meals $5–$20. AE, DISC, MC, V. Daily 8am–10pm. SEAFOOD.

For no-frills, simple, decent seafood in a family atmosphere, try Dooger's. Prices are reasonable, especially at lunch, when you can order from a list of specials that includes steamers, calamari, or petrale sole accompanied by a salad topped with bay shrimp. Try their tasty clam chowder. In case you've already eaten too much, the dinner menu includes alternative smaller-portion servings of all the main dishes.

Vista Sea Café. 150 Broadway. ☎ **503/738-8108.** Pizzas $12–$24; sandwiches $5–$6. MC, V. Summer daily 11:30am–10pm (open fewer days and shorter hours in winter). PIZZA/SANDWICHES.

Whether you're in the mood for pizza or soup and a sandwich, you can't go wrong here. High-backed antique booths and a few tables in a bright and artistically decorated dining room give the cafe a touch of class, and big windows let in plenty of sunshine in the summer. Whatever you do, don't leave without trying the clam chowder, which is served with a delicious homemade beer bread. On the pizza menu you'll find such creations as pesto pizza and a veggie and blue-cheese pizza.

IN GEARHART

Pacific Way Cafe and Bakery. 601 Pacific Way, in Gearhart. ☎ **503/738-0245.** Main dishes $7–$18. MC, V. Thurs–Mon 11:30am–3pm and 5–9pm. Shorter hours in winter. SANDWICHES/NORTHWEST.

You'll find this former mom-and-pop grocery store in the center of nearby Gearhart. The present owners will admit they are stuck in the 1930s, as the vintage interior of the restaurant will attest. At lunch, there are appetizing sandwich and salad concoctions, and in the evening, rib-eye steak, salmon, and ahi tuna occur in various permutations, along with the likes of razor clams or seafood pasta. The only thing wrong with this place is that it isn't open daily.

3 Cannon Beach

7 miles S of Seaside, 112 miles N of Newport, 79 miles W of Portland

When most people dream of a vacation on the Oregon coast, chances are they're thinking of a place like **Cannon Beach:** weathered cedar-shingle buildings, picket fences behind drifts of nasturtiums, quiet gravel lanes, interesting little art galleries, and massive rock islands rising from the surf just off the wide sandy beach. If it weren't for all the other people who think Cannon Beach is a wonderful place, this town would be perfect. However, Cannon Beach is suffering from its own quaintness and the inevitable upscaling that ensues when a place begins to gain national recognition. Once the Oregon coast's most renowned artists' community, Cannon Beach is now going the way of California's Carmel—lots of upscale shopping tucked away in utterly tasteful little plazas along a neatly manicured main street. Oh well, we still love it.

Cannon Beach was named for several cannons that washed ashore after the warship *Shark* wrecked on these rocks in 1846. The most famous of the area's monoliths is **Haystack Rock,** which rises 235 feet above the water at the edge of the beach. Because of their resemblance to piles of hay, such offshore rocks are known generically as haystack rocks or sea stacks, but this is *the* Haystack Rock—the most photographed on the Oregon coast.

One glance up and down the beach at the many offshore sea stacks, and it's easy to understand what has attracted artists and vacationers alike to tiny Cannon Beach. Despite the crowds, it still has a village atmosphere, and summer throngs and traffic jams can do nothing to assault the fortresslike beauty of the rocks that lie just offshore.

ESSENTIALS

GETTING THERE Cannon Beach is on U.S. 101 just south of the junction with U.S. 26.

VISITOR INFORMATION Contact the **Cannon Beach Chamber of Commerce,** 207 N. Spruce St. (P.O. Box 64), Cannon Beach, OR 97110 (☎ **503/436-2623;** www.cannonbeach.org).

GETTING AROUND The **Cannon Beach Shuttle,** which provides free van service up and down the length of town, operates daily in the summer from 9am to 1pm and 2 to 7pm. Watch for signed shuttle stops. Donations for the ride are accepted.

FESTIVALS Each year in late April, the **Puffin Kite Festival** fills the skies over Cannon Beach with colorful kites and features stunt kite-flying exhibitions. In early June, the **Sand Castle Day** contest turns the beach into one vast canvas for sand sculptors from all over the region, and in early November, the **Stormy Weather Arts Festival** celebrates the arrival of winter storms. On summer Sunday afternoons, the **Concerts in the Park** series stages free concerts in a variety of musical styles at City Park on the corner of Second and Spruce streets.

EXPLORING THE TOWN, THE COAST & NEARBY STATE PARKS

Seven miles of wide sandy **beach** stretch south from Cannon Beach, but it's the offshore rocks, most protected as nesting grounds for sea birds, and not the abundance of sand that have made this stretch of coast so popular. Watch for **tufted puffins** sitting on the area's haystack rocks. With their large colorful beaks, these birds are something of a Cannon Beach mascot. Though Haystack Rock is the area's most famous monolith, Tillamook Rock, a mile offshore, has an interesting history. This rocky islet serves as the site of the **Tillamook Rock Lighthouse,** which began operation in 1881 and was decommissioned in 1957. Known as "Terrible Tilly," the lighthouse was subject to huge storm waves that occasionally sent large rocks crashing through the light, which is 133 feet above sea level. Today the lighthouse is used as a columbarium, a vault for the interment of the ashes of people who have been cremated.

Kite flying, surf fishing, and beachcombing are all popular Cannon Beach pastimes. If you've always dreamed of riding a horse on the beach, your dream can come true here. Guided rides to Cove Beach and Haystack Rock are offered by **Sea Ranch Stables.** The price is $30 per trip, and reservations are accepted in person at 415 N. Old Hwy. 101 (Hemlock St.) at the north entrance to Cannon Beach.

✪ **Ecola State Park,** which marks the southernmost point that Lewis and Clark explored on the Oregon coast, is just north of Cannon Beach, and it offers the most breathtaking vantage point from which to soak up the view of Cannon Beach, Haystack Rock, and the Tillamook Rock Lighthouse. The park also has several picnic areas perched on bluffs high above the crashing waves and a trail that leads 6 miles over Tillamook Head to Seaside. The 1-mile stretch of trail between the main bluff-top picnic area and Indian beach is particularly rewarding, passing through old-growth forests and offering good views of the ocean and beaches far below. Admission is $3 per vehicle on weekends and holidays.

One of the best ways to see the beach here is from a funcycle, a three-wheeled beach cycle. These cycles allow you to ride up and down the beach at low tide. Funcycles can be rented from **Manzanita Fun Merchants,** 1160 S. Hemlock St. (☎ **503/436-1880**), and **Mike's Bike Shop,** 284 N. Spruce St. (☎ **503/436-1266**). Mountain bikes are also available for rent from these shops. Rental rates for bikes are around $5 to $7 per hour.

For many Cannon Beach visitors, **shopping** is the town's greatest attraction. In the heart of town, along Hemlock Street, you'll find dozens of densely packed small shops and galleries offering original art, fine crafts, unusual gifts, and casual fashions. Galleries worth seeking out include **Jeffrey Hull Gallery,** 172 N. Hemlock St. (☎ **503/436-2600**), specializing in Oregon coast landscapes; **The White Bird Gallery,** 251 N. Hemlock St. (☎ **503/436-2681**), a respectable gallery for contemporary work; **Northwest by Northwest Gallery,** 239 N. Hemlock St. (☎ **503/436-0741**); and **Windridge Gallery,** 224 N. Hemlock St. (☎ **503/436-2406**). South of downtown, you'll find **Icefire Glassworks,** 116 E. Gower St. (☎ **503/436-2359**), a glassblowing studio that features beautiful pieces of art glass. Across the street from this studio is the **Cannon Beach Arts Association Gallery,** 1064 S. Hemlock St. (☎ **503/436-0744**), which mounts shows in a wide variety of styles not usually seen in other Cannon Beach galleries, and which tend to be heavy on beach landscapes.

Also in downtown Cannon Beach, you'll find the **Coaster Theater Playhouse,** 108 N. Hemlock St. (☎ **503/436-1242**), one of the best little playhouses in Oregon. In addition to plays, the theater stages performances of classical music and jazz. Tickets are $15.

WHERE TO STAY

If you're heading here with the whole family or plan to stay a while, consider renting a house, a cottage, or an apartment. Offerings range from studio apartments to large luxurious oceanfront houses, and prices span an equally wide range. Contact **Cannon Beach Property Management** (☎ **503/436-2021;** www.cbpm.com) or **Arch Cape Property Services** (☎ 503/436-1607) for more information.

✪ **Cannon Beach Hotel Lodgings.** 1116 S. Hemlock St., Cannon Beach, OR 97110. ☎ **800/238-4107** or 503/436-1392. Fax 503/436-1396. 26 units. TV TEL. June–Sept $49–$155 double. Oct–May $45–$139 double.. Rates include continental breakfast (for rooms in hotel only). AE, CB, DC, DISC, MC, V.

With its white picket fence, green shutters, and cedar-shingle siding, the Cannon Beach Hotel seems to have been on the Cannon Beach scene for ages and fits in perfectly with the town's atmosphere. The rooms vary in size, which means that even those on a budget can afford something here. However, the best rooms are those with fireplaces and whirlpool tubs, and two of these rooms have partial ocean views. Though it's not in the best location in Cannon Beach (there are parking lots all around the hotel), it is one of the best deals and has the ambiance of a small European inn. Also available are rooms in the rustic Hearthstone Inn, in the renovated and updated

McBee Motel Cottages (perhaps the best value in town), and in a third building called the Courtyard.

Hallmark Resort. 1400 S. Hemlock St., Cannon Beach, OR 97110. ☎ **888/448-4449** or 503/436-1566. Fax 503/436-0324. www.hallmarkinns.com. 131 units. TV TEL. May–Sept $114–$239 double; $165–$269 suite. Oct–Apr $59–$229 double; $95–$249 suite. AE, CB, DC, DISC, MC, V. Pets accepted ($5 per night).

Situated on a bluff at the south end of town and with a head-on view of Haystack Rock, the Hallmark appeals to both families and couples on romantic getaways, and the wide range of rates reflects the variety of rooms available. The lowest rates are for nonview standard rooms, and the highest rates are for oceanfront two-bedroom suites. In between these extremes are all manner of rooms, studios, and suites. The best values are the limited-view rooms, many of which have fireplaces and comfortable chairs set up to take in what little view there might be. Most rooms have a small refrigerator and a coffeemaker, and some have kitchenettes. Though the grounds aren't spacious, there are several little Japanese gardens tucked in some unlikely spots, so be sure to stroll around.

Facilities: Indoor swimming pool, two whirlpool spas, sauna, meeting rooms.

✪ **St. Bernards.** 3 E. Ocean Rd. (P.O. Box 102), Arch Cape, OR 97102. ☎ **800/436-2848** or 503/436-2800. www.pacifier.com/~bernards. 7 units. TV TEL. $139–$199 double. Rates include full breakfast. AE, MC, V.

If you can't find time in your schedule for that trip to France this year, a stay at St. Bernard's will provide a reasonable facsimile. Although the setting, just off U.S. 101 between Cannon Beach and Manzanita, won't convince you that you're in Provence, the building itself is as grand a manor house as any château in the south of France. Newly built and incorporating elements from castles and châteaux, this inn is straight out of a fairy tale. European antiques and original art fill the house, which has tile floors and an abundance of tapestry-cloth furnishings. Each of the rooms is designed to fulfill a different fantasy of the perfect romantic escape. There is the Provence room, of course, but there is also the circular Tower room, with its own soaking tub; the Gauguin, filled with paintings by you-know-who; and the Tapestry room, with a stained-glass ceiling and an ocean view from the soaking tub. Get the picture? Lavish, multicourse breakfasts are served in the conservatory, and evening social hour is usually held by the fireplace.

The Sea Sprite. 280 Nebesna St. (P.O. Box 933), Cannon Beach, OR 97110. ☎ **503/ 436-2266.** Fax 503/436-0715. www.beachlodgings.com/seasprite. 6 units. TV TEL. $85–$185 double. Lower rates in off-season. MC, V.

This small motel is located in the Tolovana Park area south of Cannon Beach, and though it has been around for quite a few years, it still makes a great choice for families. All the rooms have kitchens and most have woodstoves. However, it's the views of Haystack Rock that convince most people that the Sea Sprite is aging gracefully.

✪ **Stephanie Inn.** 2740 S. Pacific St., Cannon Beach, OR 97110. ☎ **800/633-3466** or 503/436-2221. Fax 503/436-9711. www.stephanie-inn.com. 56 units. A/C TV TEL. $159–$359 double; $349–$429 suite. Rates include full breakfast. AE, CB, DC, DISC, MC, V. Children 12 and over are welcome.

Simply stated, the Stephanie Inn is the most classically romantic inn on the Oregon coast (the perfect place for an anniversary or other special weekend away). With flower boxes beneath the windows and neatly manicured gardens by the entry, the inn is reminiscent of New England's country inns, but the beach out the back door is definitely of Pacific Northwest origin. Inside, the lobby feels warm and cozy with its river-rock fireplace, huge wood columns, and beamed ceiling. The guest rooms, all individually decorated, are equally cozy. All come with small refrigerators, wet bars, and VCRs, and most also have double whirlpool tubs and fireplaces. The higher you go in the three-story inn, the better the views and the more spacious the outdoor spaces (patios, balconies, and decks). Smoking is not permitted.

Dining/Entertainment: A bounteous buffet breakfast is served each morning in the second-floor dining room, which surprisingly does not have a view of the water. Creative four-course prix-fixe dinners ($34.95) are also served (reservations are required).

Services: Room service, complimentary afternoon wine, morning newspaper, video library, complimentary shuttle to downtown Cannon Beach, massages.

The Waves/The Argonauta Inn/White Heron Lodge. 188 W. Second St. (P.O. Box 3), Cannon Beach, OR 97110. ☎ **800/822-2468** or 503/436-2205. Fax 503/436-1490. www.thewavesmotel.com. 55 units. TV TEL. $89–$295 double. 3-night minimum July and Aug; 2-night minimum on weekends Sept–June. DISC, MC, V.

Variety is the name of the game in eclectic Cannon Beach, and The Waves plays the game better than any other accommodation in town. This lodge, only a block from the heart of town, consists of more than 4 dozen rooms, suites, cottages, and beach houses at The Waves and two other jointly managed lodges, The Argonauta Inn and the White Heron Lodge. The Garden Court rooms (with no ocean views) are the least expensive. Our favorites, however, are the cottages of The Argonauta Inn. Surrounded by beautiful flower gardens in the summer, these old oceanfront cottages capture the spirit of Cannon Beach. For sybarites and romantics, there are fireplaces in some rooms and whirlpool spas overlooking the ocean. If you want to get away from the crowds, ask for an apartment at the White Heron Lodge. The Waves itself offers contemporary accommodations, some of which are right on the beach and have great views.

CAMPGROUNDS

At the north end of town, the **Sea Ranch R.V. Park,** 415 N. Hemlock St. (P.O. Box 214), Cannon Beach, OR 97110 (☎ **503/436-2815**), offers sites for RVs and tents. The campground is green and shady and is right across the street from the road to Ecola State Park. Rates range from $18 to $20 per night. You can also try **Wright's for Camping,** P.O. Box 213, Cannon Beach, OR 97110 (☎ **503/436-2347**), which is set back in the trees on the inland side of the road at the second Cannon Beach exit off U.S. 101 and charges $16 for campsites. At either of these, you'll need to make reservations at least a month in advance for summer weekends.

WHERE TO DINE

If you've got a weakness for good bakeries as we do, check out **Hane's Bakerie,** 1064 S. Hemlock St. (☎ **503/436-0120**). For a nice cup of joe, stop in at the **Espresso Bean,** 1235 S. Hemlock St. (☎ **503/436-0522**). **Osburns Ice Cream & Espresso** at 240A Hemlock St. is the best place to overindulge in fabulous ice-cream treats (some even combined with espresso, as the name implies). You want a simple sandwich out in the sun? **Heather's Café,** 271 N. Hemlock St. (☎ **503/436-9356**), makes up some tasty chicken salad or smoked turkey sandwiches, and you can eat them outside or inside, or get them to go.

✪ **Bistro Restaurant.** 263 N. Hemlock St. ☎ **503/436-2661.** Reservations highly recommended. Main courses $12.75–$20.75. MC, V. Daily 4–9:30pm. Closed Tues in winter. Closed 2 or 3 weeks at the beginning of Jan. NORTHWEST.

The best of Cannon Beach is rarely in plain view. Such is the case with the Bistro Restaurant. You'll see the restaurant's sign toward the north end of the shopping district, but the restaurant itself is set back a bit from the street behind a small garden and down a brick walkway. Step through the door and you'll think you've just stepped into a French country inn. Stucco walls, old prints of flowers, and fresh flowers on the tables are all the decor this tiny place can afford without growing cramped. Dining choices here are focused on the likes of exquisitely prepared seafood and pasta dishes such as sautéed oysters in lemon sauce or a seafood bisque with saffron risotto. There's live guitar music on Friday and Saturday evenings, and even a tiny bar. If you're searching for atmosphere and good food, this is the place.

Kalypso. 140 N. Hemlock St. ☎ **503/436-1585.** Reservations recommended. Main courses $15.50–$19.75. MC, V. Summer daily 5–9pm. Closed Wed in spring and fall; closed Wed and Thurs in winter. REGIONAL/INTERNATIONAL.

Along with the Bistro Restaurant (see above), this is one of the few places in town where people get dressed up, but you don't have to. Decor in this small and quiet restaurant is pleasantly minimal, with twinkle lights and colorful walls. There's a patio out back, but not much of a view there. For starters, a great focaccio bread is served with olive oil and balsamic vinegar. We prefer to stick with the fish dishes, which have interesting accompaniments and sauces. Grilled tuna is perfectly done with braised greens and house-made *kimchee* (spicy pickled vegetables), and Pacific snapper is served over crayfish hash with a warm and flavorful tomatillo chili sauce. Go for the coconut crunch cake with vanilla bean ice cream and caramel sauce—it's the signature dessert.

Lazy Susan Café. 126 Hemlock St. ☎ **503/436-2816.** Breakfast main courses $3.50–$8.25; salads, soups, sandwiches $6–$9.75. No credit cards. Winter hours Mon and Wed 8am–2:30pm, Thurs 8am–5pm, Fri–Sat 8am–8pm, Sun 8am–5pm; summer hours Wed–Mon 8am–8pm. BREAKFAST/SALADS/LIGHT DINNER.

Cannon Beach is a great place to be for breakfast. The air is invigorating and you can linger over the delicious waffles or omelets at the Lazy Susan. Tucked into the back of a little brick courtyard shared with the Coaster Theater, the Lazy Susan is a quaint little cottage with unpainted siding, window boxes full of flowers in summer, and white Victorian railings leading up to the front door. If you sleep in, don't worry; breakfast is available all day. Nightly dinner specials include a choice of dessert.

✪ **Midtown Café.** 1235 S. Hemlock St. ☎ **503/436-1016.** Breakfast, lunch, and dinner $4–$9. No credit cards. Mon, Wed–Fri 7am–2pm, Sat–Sun 8am–2pm. NATURAL/INTERNATIONAL.

You'll find some of the most innovative dishes on this stretch of the coast at this little diner for health-conscious gourmands. How about a burrito for breakfast, or eggs scrambled with Kosher salami? If you need a kick-start in the morning, try the chocolate-espresso smoothie. Authentic Mexican food is served at dinner. You can be sure that anything you order will be as fresh as possible, since these folks even grind their own flour and make their own jams, marmalades, ketchup, and salsa. One meal and we're sure you'll be hooked.

EN ROUTE TO OR FROM PORTLAND

If you'd like to see a large herd of **Roosevelt elk,** watch for the Jewell turnoff about 37 miles before reaching Cannon Beach on U.S. 26. From the turnoff, continue 10 miles north following the wildlife viewing signs to the ✪ **Jewell Meadows Wildlife Area,** where there's a large meadow frequented most of the year by anywhere from 75 to 200 elk. In June, you may see elk calves, and in the September and October rutting season, big bulls can be heard bugling and seen locking antlers.

Twelve miles past the U.S. 26 turnoff for Jewell, you'll find ✪ **Saddle Mountain State Natural Area,** which is a favorite day hike in the area. A 2½-mile trail leads to the top of Saddle Mountain, from which there are breathtaking views up and down the coast. In the spring, rare wildflowers are abundant along this trail. The trail is steep and rocky, so wear sturdy shoes or boots and carry water.

WHERE TO DINE

Camp 18 Restaurant. In Elsie 22 miles east of Seaside on U.S. 26. ☎ **503/755-1818.** Main courses lunch $4–$8, dinner $12–$20. AE, DISC, MC, V. Daily 7am–9pm. AMERICAN.

If you're interested in learning about how logging was done in the days before clear-cutting, there is no better place than this combination restaurant and logging museum. The restaurant is in a huge log lodge with lots of chain-saw art, axes for door handles, and a hollowed-out stump for a hostess desk. The 85-foot-long ridge pole in the restaurant is the largest of its kind in the country and weighs 25 tons. There are also a pair of stone fireplaces and lots of old logging photos. After tucking into logger-size meals (don't miss the marionberry cobbler), you can wander the grounds studying old steam logging equipment. A gift shop sells logging-oriented souvenirs.

SOUTH FROM CANNON BEACH

Three miles south of Cannon Beach is ✪ **Arcadia Beach Wayside,** one of the prettiest little beaches on the north coast; and another mile farther south you'll find **Hug Point State Recreation Site,** which has picnic tables, a sheltered beach, and the remains of an old road that was cut into the rock face of this headland. ✪ **Oswald West State Park,** 10 miles south of Cannon Beach, is one of our personal favorites of all the parks on the Oregon coast. A short paved trail leads to a driftwood-strewn cobblestone beach on a small cove. Headlands on either side of the cove can be reached by hiking trails that offer splendid views. The waves here are popular with surfers. There's also a walk-in campground.

4 Tillamook County

Tillamook: 75 miles W of Portland, 51 miles S of Seaside, 44 miles N of Lincoln City

Tillamook is a mispronunciation of the word *Killamook,* which was the name of the Native American tribe that once lived in this area. The name is now applied to a county, a town, and a bay. While this is one of the closest stretches of coast to Portland, it is not a major destination because there are no large beachfront towns in the area. The town of Tillamook, which lies inland from the Pacific at the south end of Tillamook Bay, is the area's commercial center, but it is the surrounding farmland that has made the biggest name for Tillamook County. Ever since the first settlers arrived in Tillamook in 1851, dairy farming has been the mainstay of the economy, and large herds of contented cows graze in the area's fragrant fields. These cows provide the milk for the Tillamook County Creamery Association's cheese factory, which turns out a substantial share of the cheese consumed in Oregon. With no beaches to attract visitors, the town of Tillamook has managed to turn its dairy industry into a tourist attraction. No, this isn't the cow-watching capital of Oregon, but the town's cheese factory is now one of the most popular stops along the Oregon coast, annually attracting more than 800,000 visitors.

There are a few beachside hamlets in the area that offer a variety of accommodations, activities, and dining options. Tillamook is also the starting point for the scenic Three Capes Loop, which links three state parks and plenty of great coastal scenery.

ESSENTIALS

GETTING THERE   Tillamook is on U.S. 101 at the junction with Ore. 6, which leads to Portland.

VISITOR INFORMATION   For more information on the area, contact the **Tillamook Chamber of Commerce,** 3705 U.S. 101 N., Tillamook, OR 97141 (☎ **503/842-7525**); the **Nehalem Bay Area Chamber of Commerce,** P.O. Box 159, Nehalem, OR 97131 (☎ **503/368-5100**); or the **Garibaldi Chamber of Commerce,** P.O. Box 915, Garibaldi, OR 97118 (☎ **503/322-0301**).

MANZANITA

As the crowds have descended on Cannon Beach, people seeking peace and quiet, a slower pace, and smaller crowds have migrated south to the community of Manzanita. Located south of Neahkanie Mountain, Manzanita enjoys a setting similar to Cannon Beach but without the many haystack rocks. There isn't much to do here except walk on the beach and relax, which is exactly why most people come here. If you absolutely must do something, try renting a beach bike from **Manzanita Fun Merchants,** 186 Laneda Ave. (☎ **503/368-6606**). The low-slung, three-wheel beach bikes are a great way to explore the beach, and they cost about $7 an hour. You could also play a round of golf on the meandering fairways of the nine-hole **Manzanita Golf Course,** Lake View Drive (☎ **503/368-5744**), which charges $14 for 9 holes. One other great reason to stay in Manzanita is that this little community has a couple of the north coast's best restaurants (see "Where to Dine" below).

   The beach at Manzanita stretches for 5 miles from the mouth of the Nehalem River to the base of Neahkanie Mountain. This beach is a favorite of both surfers and sailboarders. The latter have the option of sailing either in the waves or in the quieter waters of Nehalem Bay. Access to both the bay and the beach is provided at **Nehalem Bay State Park** (☎ **503/368-5154**), which is just south of Manzanita and encompasses all of Nehalem Spit. The park, which includes a campground (and an airstrip), has a 2-mile paved bike path, a horse camp, and horse trails. The day-use fee is $3. Out at the south end of the spit, more than 50 harbor seals can often be seen lounging on the beach. To reach the seal area requires a 5-mile round-trip hike. The **Jetty Fishery** (see below) offers seal-watching trips by ferry to the spit.

WHERE TO STAY

If you want to rent a vacation house in Manzanita, contact **Manzanita Rental Company,** 32 Laneda Ave. (P.O. Box 162), Manzanita, OR 97130 (☎ **800/579-9801** or 503/368-6797).

✪ **The Inn at Manzanita.** 67 Laneda Ave. (P.O. Box 243), Manzanita, OR 97130. ☎ **503/368-6754.** Fax 503/368-5941. www.neahkahnie.net. 13 units. TV TEL. $100–$145 double (lower off-season midweek rates available). 2-night minimum on weekends and July 1–Labor Day; 3 nights on some holidays. MC, V.

Searching for an unforgettably romantic spot for a weekend getaway? This is it. Right in the heart of Manzanita and within steps of a couple of the best restaurants on the Oregon coast, the Inn at Manzanita is a great place to celebrate an anniversary or any other special event. Double whirlpool tubs sit between the fireplace and the bed in every room, and most rooms have balconies that look out through shady pines to the ocean. The weathered cedar-shingle siding blends unobtrusively with the natural vegetation, and the grounds are planted with beautiful flowers for much of the year. A wet bar and small refrigerator let you chill a bottle of wine.

Ocean Inn. Manzanita Rental Company, 32 Laneda Ave. (P.O. Box 162), Manzanita, OR 97130. ☎ **800/579-9801** or 503/368-6797. www.doormat.com/mr/mr-cov.htm. 10 units. TV TEL. May–Sept $95–$145 double. Oct–Apr $85–$135 double. MC, V. 2- to 7-night minimum. Pets accepted.

With four remodeled apartments right on the beach and six more new apartments set back a bit from the sand, this inn is a good choice if you want the space of a one-bedroom apartment and appreciate modern amenities and comfortable, new furnishings. All but one of the rooms have an ocean view. Of the newer apartments, five are on the second floor and have balconies overlooking the beach. Several rooms have woodstoves, most have kitchens, and one has a whirlpool tub.

WHERE TO DINE

✪ **Blue Sky Café.** 154 Laneda Ave. ☎ **503/368-5712.** Reservations highly recommended. Main courses $11–$24. No credit cards. Daily 5:30–9:30pm. NORTHWEST.

On the left as you approach the beach on the main street through town, you'll see a pale-gray beachy building with colorful raised flower beds in front. Inside, the decor is more casual than Jarboe's across the street. We could make a dinner of thick slabs of fresh-baked bread smeared with the Blue Sky's potted Montrachet cheese with fresh herbs, sun-dried tomatoes, roasted garlic, and olive oil, but that would mean never making it past the appetizer list. Entrees show influences from around the globe, particularly well integrated in the numerous fresh-fish dishes. Salmon might be prepared with Thai red and green curries and served with Vietnamese cabbage, or rock shrimp might be sautéed with black beans, cilantro–pumpkin seed pesto, and orange peel. For dessert, who could pass up a s'more made with homemade graham crackers?

Cassandra's Pizza. 60 Laneda Ave. ☎ **503/368-5593.** Pizzas $8–$24. No credit cards. Sun–Thurs 4:30–9:30pm, Fri–Sat 4:30–10pm. Hours vary off-season. PIZZA.

With a surfboard for a counter and other boards hanging from the walls, there's no question of who likes to grab their pizzas here. Even if you don't surf, though, you'll enjoy the hand-thrown pizzas, of which there are no fewer than three Hawaiian styles (the North Shore, the Waikiki, and the Pipeline), most of which have pineapples and Canadian bacon (go figure).

✪ **Jarboe's in Manzanita.** 137 Laneda Ave. ☎ **503/368-5113.** Reservations highly recommended. Main courses $17.50–$18.50; 3-course fixed-price dinner $30.50. MC, V. Summer Thurs–Mon 5–9pm (shorter hours other months). NORTHWEST.

Housed in a tiny restored beach cottage, Jarboe's is about as intimate as a restaurant gets. There are only a few tables in the two tiny dining rooms, which makes reservations imperative. The menu changes daily but is always reliable, and while the prix-fixe dinners are really the way to go here, if you aren't that hungry, you can still order à la carte. On any given day, four appetizers, four entrees, and four desserts will be available, which helps to reduce decision-making time. On a recent evening, a complete dinner might have consisted of a warm Reggiano Parmesan cheese tart with basil; mesquite grilled silver salmon with crab, fennel, and artichoke hearts; and a chocolate cake with strawberries to finish things off.

WHEELER

Located on Nehalem Bay, this little wide spot in the road has long been popular for crabbing and fishing. However, in recent years it has also become a favorite north-coast sea kayaking locale. The marshes of the bay provide plenty of meandering waterways to explore, and several miles of the Nehalem River can also be easily paddled if the tides are in your favor. There are now two places in town where you can rent a kayak: **Nehalem Bay Kayak Co.,** 395 Hwy. 101 (☎ 877/KAYAKCO or 503/ 368-6055), and **Wheeler on the Bay Lodge & Marina,** 580 Marine (☎ 800/ 469-3204 or 503/368-5858). Rates are $12 to $21 per hour or $32 to $38 per day; higher rates are for double kayaks.

If you're interested in trying your hand at crabbing, contact **Jetty Fishery** (☎ 800/ 821-7697 or 503/368-5746), which is located just south of Wheeler at the mouth of the Nehalem River. They rent boats and crab rings and offer dock crabbing. The folks here also offer a ferry service ($5 per person) across the river to Nehalem Bay State Park, where you can often see lots of harbor seals lying out on the beach. Interestingly enough, the seals will let people get a lot closer in a motorized boat than in a kayak. You can also sometimes see seals close up if you sit on the jetty rocks at nearby Neadonna.

Although we personally don't care for the wines at **Nehalem Bay Winery,** 34965 Ore. 53 (☎ 503/368-WINE), many people do; and there is no denying that the fruit wines here are interesting, if a bit overpriced. It's worth a stop just to visit the historic half-timbered building that houses the tasting room. This building was constructed in 1909 as part of the Tillamook Creamery Association (think Tillamook cheese factory).

WHERE TO STAY

The Nehalem River Inn. 34910 Ore. 53 (P.O. Box 421), Nehalem, OR 97131. ☎ 800/ 368-6499 or 503/368-7708. www.river-inn.com. 5 units. TV TEL. $79–$129 double. AE, DISC, MC, V.

The Oregon coast is not just about beaches and rocky headlands, it's also about meandering tidal rivers, and this country inn is set on one. Situated a couple of miles off U.S. 101 between Nehalem and Wheeler, the inn is a hideaway par excellence, with its own restaurant and wines bottled under its own label. Guest accommodations range from the cozy Kingfisher Room to the two-room Riverside Cottage, but one thing all have in common is decks or views of the river and mountains. The cottage has a private spa and the Cormorant's Watch has a fireplace. The inn rents kayaks ($20 to $26 for a half day) and has a riverside hot tub.

Wheeler on the Bay Lodge. U.S. 101 and 580 Marine (P.O. Box 580), Wheeler, OR 97147. ☎ 800/469-3204 or 503/368-5858. www.mkt-place.com/wheeler. 10 units. TV TEL. $75–$115 double. AE, DISC, MC, V.

It would be easy to pass off this renovated lodge as just another fisherman's motel, but that would be a big mistake. Located right on the shore of Nehalem Bay, this lodge has one of our favorite rooms on the coast. The Honeymoon room here has walls of glass looking onto the bay, a private deck, a fireplace, and, best of all, a whirlpool tub that's situated to grab the best views. Six of the rooms here have spas, and most of these have water views. Other rooms sport distinctive decor: a "Mess O' Trout" string of lights, bold sunflower patterns everywhere, tropical fish motifs. Although this isn't a bed-and-breakfast, all the rooms are different and have that individualized touch. A great spot for a romantic weekend.

WHERE TO DINE

Nehalem Dock Restaurant. 35815 U.S. 101. ☎ 503/368-5557. Main courses $6–$13. DISC, MC, V. Mon–Sat 11:20am–4pm and 5–9pm, Sun 11:30am–4pm and 5–8pm. AMERICAN.

With a pleasant deck on the Nehalem River, this casual restaurant is a great place for lunch if you are exploring the area. It also makes a good sunset dinner spot if you happen to be staying nearby. Tasty sandwiches and local seafood are the mainstays. It's a fun destination if you happen to have rented a kayak in nearby Wheeler.

✪ **The Nehalem River Inn Restaurant.** 34910 Ore. 53, off U.S. 101. ☎ **503/368-7708.** Reservations highly recommended. Main courses $15–$26.50. AE, DISC, MC, V. Daily 6–10pm (Fri–Sun 6–10pm in winter). NORTHWEST/MEDITERRANEAN.

Set on the bank of the Nehalem River a couple of miles off U.S. 101, this restaurant is part of a country inn, and it serves some of the best food on the Oregon coast. The menu is contemporary and relies heavily on wild ingredients and organic produce. Although it changes with the seasons, you might start your meal with shell-baked scallops with wild tidewater greens or a salad of wild sorrel and organic greens. For an entree, you might opt for salmon fillet with capers, dill, and lemon baste; or roast confit of duck with honey, gooseberry, and kumquat sauce. For dessert? How about wild huckleberry cheesecake with berry sauce and citrus crème fraîche? The inn's wines are produced for them at Eola Hills Winery, and tastings are available daily.

Treasure Café. 92 Rorvik St. ☎ **503/368-7740.** Reservations not accepted. Breakfast $4.50–$8.50, main courses $13–$17. No credit cards. Thurs–Fri 9am–1pm, Sat–Sun 8am–1pm. Dinner served Fri–Sat in summer 6–9pm. BREAKFAST/INTERNATIONAL.

This hidden jewel is in a small cottage up a side street from downtown Wheeler, with a view of Nehalem Bay and Neahkanie Mountain from the small deck out front. The focus here is on breakfast, which draws in locals and visitors alike for the likes of airy hazelnut waffles, oysters and eggs, and strawberry smoothies. Dinner, served on weekends in the summer, features fresh local ingredients with international touches, such as grilled halibut with a soy and ginger sauce, pasta with smoked salmon, and pork carnitas.

ROCKAWAY BEACH

Rockaway Beach has little of the picturesque scenery of Cannon Beach or Manzanita, but it does have plenty of wide sandy beach. The town has a rather run-down feel to its narrow strip of aging cottages but is still quite popular with families who rent beach houses for their summer vacation.

WHERE TO DINE

If you like smoked salmon, don't miss ✪ **Karla's Smokehouse,** 2010 U.S. 101 N. (☎ **503/355-2362**), which sells the best smoked fish and oysters on the coast and has been doing so for more than 30 years. The smoked oysters are particularly succulent, and anything here makes great picnic food. Karla's is open daily from 10am to 5pm in summer and on weekends only in the winter.

GARIBALDI

Named (by the local postmaster) in 1879 for Italian patriot Giuseppi Garibaldi, this little town is located at the north end of Tillamook Bay and is the region's main sportfishing and crabbing port. Even before the arrival of white settlers in the region, this spot was a fishing and whaling village of the Tillamook Indians. If you've got an urge to do some salmon or bottom fishing, this is the place to book a trip. Try **Troller Charters** (☎ **880/546-3666** or 503/322-3666), **Siggi-G Ocean Charters** (☎ **503/322-3285**), **Kerri Lin Charters** (☎ **503/355-2439**), or **Garibaldi/D&D Charters** (☎ **800/900-HOOK** or 503/322-0007). Fishing rates are around $65 for a full day of salmon fishing. Deep-sea halibut fishing will run you about $140 for a full day.

If bay and river fishing for salmon and steelhead is more your speed, contact **No-How Salmon Fishing** (☎ **503/322-3369**), which offers salmon fishing trips on Tillamook and Nehalem Bays for around $125 per person per day. Spring and fall are salmon season.

These companies also offer **whale-watching** and **bird-watching** trips, and **Troller Charters** (☎ **800/546-3666** or 503/322-3666) offers quick trips (known as ocean eco-tours) around Tillamook Bay for $10. At the **Garibaldi Marina,** 300 Mooring Basin Rd. (☎ **503/322-3312**), you can rent boats, tackle, and crab rings, if you want to do some fishing or crabbing on your own.

If scuba diving is your sport, you'll find all your diving needs met at **Garibaldi Aqua Sports,** 108 Seventh Ave., Garibaldi (☎ **503/322-0113**).

Garibaldi is also where you'll find the depot for the **Fun Run Express** (☎ **800/685-1719**), an excursion train that runs along some of the most scenic portions of this section of coast. Unfortunately, at press time the train wasn't running, but they hope to have it up again soon. Call to see if it's back on track when you visit.

If you're in the market for some fresh seafood to cook for dinner, visit **Smith's Pacific Shrimp Co.,** in the boat basin on Mooring Basin Road (☎ **503/322-3316**).

TILLAMOOK

Tillamook has long been known as one of Oregon's foremost dairy regions, and Tillamook cheese is ubiquitous in the state. So it's no surprise that the **Tillamook Cheese Factory,** on U.S. 101 just north of Tillamook (☎ **503/842-4481**), is the most popular tourist attraction in town. Not only can visitors observe the cheese-making process (cheddars are the specialty), but there's also a large store where all manner of cheeses and other edible gifts are available. The factory is open daily from 8am to 8pm in summer and 8am to 6pm in winter.

If the Tillamook Cheese Factory seems too crowded for you, head back toward town a mile and you'll see the **Blue Heron French Cheese Company,** 2001 Blue Heron Dr. (☎ **503/842-8281**), which is on the same side of U.S. 101 as the Tillamook Cheese Factory. Located in a big old dairy barn with a flagstone floor, this store stocks the same sort of comestibles as the Tillamook Cheese Factory, though the emphasis here is on brie (which, however, is not made locally). Farm animals make this a good stop for kids. Blue Heron is open daily from 8am to 8pm in summer and 9am to 6pm in winter.

If you'd like to find out more about the cows that produce the milk for the cheese factories, the **Tillamook County Creamery Association** (☎ **503/815-1300**) offers tours of local dairy farms. Tours cost $8 for adults, $6 for children 4 to 16 (or $25 for a family of four). Tours, which are led by area farmers, leave from the cheese factory daily at 3pm between mid-June and the end of August.

At the **Tillamook County Pioneer Museum,** 2106 Second St. (☎ **503/842-4553**), you'll find the expected hodgepodge of antique cars, old kitchen appliances, blacksmith's tools, and the like, as well as dioramas on natural history. The museum is open Monday through Saturday from 8am to 5pm and on Sunday from 11am to 5pm. Admission is $2 for adults, $1.50 for seniors, 50¢ for students 12 to 17.

A hangar built during World War II for a fleet of navy blimps is 2 miles south of town off U.S. 101 and lays claim to being the largest freestanding wooden building in the world. Statistics bear out the impressiveness of this building: 250 feet wide, 1,100 feet long, and 170 feet high. The blimp hangar now houses the **Tillamook Naval Air Station Museum,** 6030 Hangar Rd. (☎ **503/842-1130**), which contains a respectable collection of old planes, including a P-51 Mustang, a B-25 Mitchell, an F4U Corsair, and a PBY-5A Catalina. Of course, there are exhibits on lighter-than-air flight as well. The museum is open Memorial Day to Labor Day daily from 9am to 6pm; other months daily from 10am to 5pm. Admission is $8 for adults, $7 for seniors, $4.50 for youths ages 13 to 17, and $2.50 for children ages 7 to 12.

Although no blimp rides are being offered, you can go up in a small plane to see this section of the coast. Contact **Tillamook Air Tours** (☎ 503/842-1942), which charges $25 per person for a 20-minute flight and $35 for a 30-minute flight. Tours are in a restored 1942 Stinson Reliant V-77 plane. You may even see whales from the plane.

If you're a quilter, be sure to stop in at the **Latimer Quilt and Textile Center,** 2105 Wilson River Loop Rd. (☎ 503/842-8622), which is housed in an old wooden schoolhouse. This center not only has quilting supplies, but also has a reference library and exhibits. It also offers classes, does quilt restorations, and serves as a repository for important regional textiles.

Golfers can play a round at the 18-hole **Alderbrook Golf Course,** 7300 Alderbrook Rd. (☎ 503/842-6413), which charges $24 for 18 holes, or the much less challenging 9-hole **Bay Breeze Golf Course,** 2325 Latimer Rd. (☎ 503/842-1166), which is located near the cheese factory.

If you're interested in outdoor activities, you can hike to **Munson Falls,** the tallest waterfall in the Coast Range, at Munson Creek County Park, 7 miles south of Tillamook off U.S. 101. The trail to the falls is only about ¼ mile long and leads through a stand of old-growth forest.

Anglers interested in going after salmon or steelhead in Tillamook Bay or area rivers should contact **Oregon Alaska Sportfishing** (☎ 503/842-5171), **The Guide Shop** (☎ 800/24-FISH'S), **Coastal Hook-R's Guide Service** (☎ 503/842-6563), or **Ted Wade River Guide Service** (☎ 503/245-0206).

WHERE TO DINE

Stop by **Debbie D's Sausage Factory** on 2210 Main St. N. in Tillamook (☎ 888/485-4277) for such potential picnic items as smoked salmon, salmon jerky, or summer sausage.

If you need to stock up your larder for the beach house or are on your way back from a weekend at the beach, don't miss an opportunity to stop in at **Bear Creek Artichokes** (☎ 503/398-5411), which is located 11 miles south of Tillamook on U.S. 101. This is one of the only commercial artichoke farms in Oregon and usually has fresh artichokes throughout the summer and fall. The farm stand also has lots of other great produce, as well as jams, mustards, and salsas to sample. The display gardens offer a pleasant break from driving.

La Casa Modelo. 1160 U.S. 101 N. ☎ **503/842-5768.** Main dishes $6–$12. MC, V. Daily 11:30am–9pm. MEXICAN.

If you're passing through Tillamook and haven't already filled up on cheese samples and ice cream at the cheese factory, La Casa Modelo, in an old cedar-shingled house on the north side of town, is a good bet for a full meal. With hardwood floors and a college-town feel, this casa serves up surprisingly authentic burritos, tacos, and tostadas. Be sure to try the guacamole and tamales with a molé sauce.

In Nearby Bay City

If you want to try some Tillamook Bay oysters, stop in at **Pacific Oyster Co.** (☎ 503/377-2323), which is just off U.S. 101 at the end of the boardwalk. Here you can order up oyster shooters at the oyster bar and watch the oyster shuckers at work.

Artspace. U.S. 101 and Fifth St. ☎ **503/377-2782.** Reservations recommended. Main courses $6.25–$16.75. No credit cards. Thurs–Sat noon–8pm. SEAFOOD/SANDWICHES.

You just can't miss this unusual place as you drive through the hamlet of Bay City. Just watch for the building with Matisselike murals on the outside walls. Located just off U.S. 101 several miles north of Tillamook, Artspace is both an art gallery and a small

Camping in Tillamook County

Despite the fact that **Oswald West State Park** is a walk-in campground, the sites are closer together than those at most car campgrounds. Don't say I didn't warn you if the guy in the next campsite keeps you up all night with his snoring. Surfers and boardsailors will likely prefer **Nehalem Bay State Park,** where they can keep a closer eye on their equipment. **Roy Creek County Park** is a nearby, though inland, alternative to the area's state parks.

On the Three Capes Loop, west of Tillamook, there are several campgrounds. **Cape Lookout State Park** is the largest of these. **Whalen Island County Park,** on the south side of Sand Lake just off Sand Lake Road, is a smaller and less crowded alternative (though it's not right on the ocean).

Inland alternatives in this area include **Kilchis River County Park,** north of Tillamook at the end of Kilchis River Road; six Tillamook State Forest campgrounds along the Wilson River; **Trask County Park,** 12 miles east of Tillamook on Trask River Road; **Rocky Bend Campground,** 15½ miles east of Beaver up Blaine Road; **Hebo Lake Campground,** 5 miles east of Hebo; and **Mount Hebo Campground,** 3 miles past Hebo Lake Campground.

---

restaurant with a view of Tillamook Bay. The ambiance is laid back, and offerings from the kitchen range from oysters Italia to lemon chicken to vegetarian fettuccine. For lunch we like the oyster burgers and fish burgers. Be sure to ask about dessert before you eat too much to indulge. The high-quality art here is mostly by contemporary Northwest artists.

THE THREE CAPES SCENIC LOOP

The Three Capes Scenic Loop begins just west of downtown Tillamook and leads past Cape Meares, Cape Lookout, and Cape Kiwanda. Together these three capes offer some of the most spectacular views on the northern Oregon coast. All three capes are state parks, and all make great whale-watching spots in the spring or storm-watching spots in the winter. To start the loop, follow Third Street out of town and watch for the right turn for Cape Meares State Scenic Viewpoint. This road will take you along the shore of Tillamook Bay and around the north side of Cape Meares, where the resort town of Bayocean once stood. Built early in this century by developers with a dream to create the Atlantic City of the West, Bayocean was constructed at the end of a sand spit that often felt the full force of winter storms. When Bayocean homes began falling into the ocean, folks realized that this wasn't going to be the next Atlantic City. Today there's no sign of the town, but the long sandy beach along the spit is a great place for a walk and a bit of bird watching.

Just around the tip of the cape, you'll come to **Cape Meares State Scenic Viewpoint,** which is the site of the **Cape Meares Lighthouse.** The lighthouse is open to the public and houses a small museum. The views from atop this rocky headland are superb. Continuing around the cape, you come to the residential community of **Oceanside,** from where you have an excellent view of the **Three Arch Rocks** just offshore. The beach at Oceanside is a popular spot and is often protected from the wind in the summer. Oceanside is a popular lunch stop for people doing the Three Capes Loop.

Three miles south of Oceanside, you'll come to tiny **Netarts Bay,** which is well-known for its excellent clamming and crabbing. Continuing south, you come to **Cape Lookout State Park,** which has a campground, picnic areas, beaches, and several miles of hiking trails. The most breathtaking ✪ **trail** leads 2½ miles out to the end of Cape Lookout, where, from several hundred feet above the ocean, you can often spot gray whales in the spring and fall.

✪ **Cape Kiwanda,** which lies just outside the town of Pacific City, is the last of the three capes and is preserved as Cape Kiwanda State Natural Area. At the foot of the cape's sandstone cliffs, you'll find sand dunes and tide pools, and it's possible to scramble up a huge sand dune to the top of the cape for dramatic views of this rugged piece of shoreline. At the base of the cape is the staging area for Pacific City's beach-launched dory fleet. These flat-bottomed commercial fishing boats are launched from the beach and plow through crashing breakers to get out to calmer waters beyond. When the day's fishing is done, the dories roar into shore at full throttle and come to a grinding stop as high up on the beach as they can. This is Oregon's only such fishing fleet and is celebrated each year during the annual Dory Derby on the third weekend in July.

The beach at the base of Cape Kiwanda is also one of the north coast's best surfing spots, and the high sand dune behind the beach has perfect conditions for paragliding. **Over the Hill Paragliding** (☎ **503/667-4557**) and the **Hang Gliding and Paragliding School of Oregon** (☎ **503/223-7448**) offer paragliding classes here.

If you'd like to do a bit of horseback riding in the area, contact **Into the Sunset** (☎ **503/965-6326**).

WHERE TO STAY

In Oceanside

House on the Hill. 1816 Maxwell Mountain Rd. (P.O. Box 187), Oceanside, OR 97134. ☎ **503/842-6030.** 16 units. TV. May–Oct $75–$125 double. Nov–Apr $65–$115 double. DISC, MC, V. No pets accepted.

Set 250 feet above Oceanside's beach on a promontory jutting into the ocean, the House on the Hill is a collection of two-story buildings, several of which look like truncated A-frames. The rooms here are large and the views are stunning, with the Three Arch Rocks directly offshore. In many rooms you can even lie in bed and soak up the views. With too much asphalt around the buildings, the grounds leave a bit to be desired, but, oh, those views. You won't find a more beautiful setting; cliffs drop off from the edge of the property. Consequently, this is not a good choice for families with small children.

Ocean Front Cabins. 1610 Pacific Ave. NW (P.O. Box 203), Oceanside, OR 97134. ☎ **503/842-6081.** 7 units. $50–$75 double. MC, V.

Ocean Front Cabins is a collection of funky old cabins, but if you don't mind swapping cramped quarters, paneled walls, and low ceilings for being only 100 feet from the beach with an unobstructed view of the waves and the Three Arch Rocks, then you might find these cabins perfect. Be forewarned, however, that there's nothing standardized or fancy about these cabins. Young people, especially surfers, will be right at home here. A few have kitchenettes, which is a definite plus in a town with only one restaurant (and a cafe that's attached to the cabins). These cabins are very popular, so call in February for summer reservations.

Oceanside Inn. 1440 Pacific Ave. NW, Oceanside, OR 97134. ☎ **800/347-2972** or 503/842-2961. TV. 9 units. $50–$95 double. MC, V.

Located right next door to Roseanna's Oceanside Café (see "Where to Dine" below), this restored older inn sits at the top of a steep stairway down to the beach and has five rooms with ocean views. Of these, room 6 is our favorite. It's up on the second floor and has three walls of windows to take in the great views. This room also has a whirlpool tub, and at $80 it is a real bargain for the area. If you opt for an econom-ical room without a view, you can still hang out on the large deck that's perched high above the beach. This place isn't fancy, but it is comfortable.

Sea Rose. 1685 Maxwell Mountain Rd. (P.O. Box 122), Oceanside, OR 97134. ☎ **503/ 842-6126.** www.moriah.com/searose. 2 units. TEL. $95–$115 double. Rates include full breakfast. MC, V.

Located about halfway up the very steep Maxwell Mountain Road, you'll find one of Oceanside's newest B&Bs. Although this inn isn't very large, it is cozy and has out-standing ocean views. Interesting antiques fill the common areas, while a simple country decor prevails in guest rooms. Both rooms do, however, have clawfoot tubs, and the Antoinette room has a private deck.

In Cloverdale

✪ **Sandlake Country Inn.** 8505 Galloway Rd., Cloverdale, OR 97112. ☎ **503/965-6745.** Fax 503/965-7425. www.sandlakecountryinn.com. 4 units. $90–$135 double. DISC, MC, V.

Although the Sand Lake area is best known as a playground for noisy all-terrain vehi-cles and dune buggies, this inn, with its white picket fence, cottage garden, and fairy-tale feel, is a quiet and very romantic retreat surrounded by colorful gardens. The Starlight Suite, which takes up the inn's entire second floor, is the most spacious room here and includes both a double whirlpool tub and a clawfoot tub. It also has a fire-place visible both from the bedroom and the sitting room. Downstairs in the Timbers room, which is almost as large, you'll find a fireplace and a double whirlpool as well, but you'll also get a rustic lodge atmosphere complete with exposed 3-by-12 timbers that were salvaged from a shipwreck and used to build this home in 1894. For even greater privacy, there is a separate cottage alongside a little creek.

In Pacific City

✪ **Inn at Cape Kiwanda.** 33105 Cape Kiwanda Dr., Pacific City, OR 97135. ☎ **888/ 965-7001** or 503/965-7001. Fax 503/965-7002. www.InnAtCapeKiwanda.com. 35 units. TV TEL. $109–$179 double; $189–$239 suite. Lower rates in winter. AE, DISC, MC, V.

For many years Pacific City was a sleepy little fishing village, but all that started to change with the opening a few years ago of the Inn at Cape Kiwanda. Although it's across the street from the beach (and Cape Kiwanda State Natural Area), this modern cedar-shingled three-story hotel has one of the best views on the Oregon coast: Directly offshore rises Haystack Rock, a huge jug-handled monolith. Since a great view isn't quite enough, the hotel was designed with luxurious, contemporary rooms, all of which have balconies and fireplaces. A few of the rooms have whirlpool tubs, and there is also a very luxurious suite. The corner rooms are our favorites. The inn is affil-iated with the Pelican Pub & Brewery, which is right across the street, and on the inn's ground floor there is an art gallery and an espresso bar that also sells wine and books. The inn has a fitness room, and there are plans to add a pool and whirlpool spa in the fall of 2000.

WHERE TO DINE
In Oceanside
Roseanna's Oceanside Café. 1490 Pacific Ave. ☎ **503/842-7351.** Reservations highly recommended. Main courses lunch $6–$11.50, dinner $10–$17. MC, V. Mon–Fri 11am–9pm, Sat 10:30am–10pm, Sun 8am–9pm. SEAFOOD/INTERNATIONAL.

When you're the only restaurant in town, you can't help staying busy, but Roseanna's is such a Scenic Loop legend that people come from miles around to eat here and don't seem to mind long waits to get a table. What brings them are the reliable meals and the view of the beach and offshore rocks. The menu mixes the traditional with international influences without getting overly creative. Lunch prices are reasonable, with such offerings as a full-flavored cioppino soup or oyster sandwich. Angels on horseback (oysters wrapped in bacon and broiled) are one of our favorite appetizers here. Entrees offer a choice of shellfish or fish with a choice of sauces (apricot-ginger glaze, aïoli, or spicy garlic-chile, for example). The wait for a table can be long, so make a reservation if possible. If you just want a quick snack, there are bar stools at the front counter.

In Pacific City
For tasty baked goods and lunches, stop in at **The Grateful Bread Bakery & Restaurant,** 34805 Brooten Rd. (☎ 503/965-7337), which has tables both inside and out on a deck. If you enjoy good books, coffee, and wine, you'll appreciate **Migrations,** a small shop located on the ground floor of the Inn at Cape Kiwanda, 33105 Cape Kiwanda Dr. (☎ 503/965-4661).

✪ **Pelican Pub & Brewery.** 33180 Cape Kiwanda Dr. ☎ **503/965-7007.** Reservations not accepted. Main courses $7–$15. AE, CB, DISC, MC, V. Sun–Thurs 8am–9pm, Fri–Sat 8am–10pm. Later closing times in the summer. PUB FOOD.

With hands down the best view of any brew pub in Oregon, the Pelican is the only brew pub in all of Tillamook County. The building overlooks Cape Kiwanda and is right on the beach, with its own beach volleyball court in back, lots of windows for taking in the views, and a good selection of ales, including Tsunami Stout and our personal favorite, the Doryman's Dark Ale. Sandwiches, burgers, fish-and-chips, and pizzas are the menu mainstays here, but the steamed clams served with barley bread made from beer grain are divine. This is a good place for families, since kids are welcome.

The Riverhouse. Brooten Rd. ☎ **503/965-6722.** Reservations not accepted. Main courses $8–$20. MC, V. Sun–Thurs 11am–9pm, Fri–Sat 11am–10pm (closes 1 hr. earlier in winter). AMERICAN.

This tiny place is built on the bank of the Nestucca River and has great river views out its many windows. Because there is nothing but forest across the river, the Riverhouse feels as if it's miles out in the country, though it is only a few blocks from Pacific City's main intersection and a couple more from the beach. With a timeless roadside diner feel and a casual, friendly atmosphere, this is a nice spot for a splurge dinner. While burgers and sandwiches are the order of the day at lunch, the dinner menu features prawns in a creamy wine sauce; fresh fish amandine; halibut basted with butter, lemon pepper, and dill; as well as filet mignon and crepes Florentine.

NESKOWIN
The quaint little community of Neskowin is nestled at the northern foot of Cascade Head, 12 miles north of Lincoln City. The tiny cottages and tree-lined lanes have for decades been the summer retreats of inland families. Quiet vacations are the rule in Neskowin, where you'll find only condominiums and rental houses. Beach access here is provided at **Neskowin Beach State Recreation Site,** which faces Proposal Rock, a tree-covered haystack rock bordered by Neskowin Creek.

If you'd like to go for a horseback ride on the beach, contact **Neskowin Stable,** 48490 Hawk Ave. (☎ 503/392-3277), which charges about $20 per hour. The stable is open mid-May through September. In Neskowin, you'll also find two nine-hole golf courses. The **Hawk Creek Golf Course,** 48480 U.S. 101 (☎ 503/392-4120), plays up the valley of Hawk Creek with mountains rising on three sides. The greens fee is $12 for 9 holes. Across the highway, in a wide flat area, is the **Neskowin Beach Golf Course,** Hawk Avenue (☎ 503/392-3377), which isn't quite as scenic and charges the same price.

If you're interested in art, check out the **Hawk Creek Gallery,** 48460 U.S. 101 S. (☎ 503/392-3879), which is open in the summer and features the paintings of Michael Schlicting, a master watercolorist.

Just to the south of Neskowin is the rugged and unspoiled **Cascade Head.** Rising 1,770 feet from sea level, this is one of the highest headlands on the coast, and it creates its own weather: rain falls here more than 180 days a year. Lush forests of Sitka spruce and windswept cliff-top meadows thrive in this rainy climate and are home to such a diversity of flora and fauna that the Nature Conservancy purchased much of the land here. Trails onto Cascade Head start about 2 miles south of Neskowin. The Nature Conservancy's preserve has been set aside primarily to protect the habitat of the rare Oregon silverspot butterfly; the upper trail is closed from January 1 to July 15 due to the nature of the butterflies' life cycle. However, a lower trail, reached from Three Rocks Road (park at Knight Park and walk up Savage Rd. to the trailhead) is open year-round.

On the south side of Cascade Head, you'll find the **Sitka Center for Art and Ecology,** Neskowin Coast Foundation, P.O. Box 65, Otis, OR 97368 (☎ **541/ 994-5485;** www.oregonvos.net/~sitka), which, during the summer, offers classes on various subjects from writing to wood carving to painting to ecology.

WHERE TO STAY

In addition to the condominium resort listed here, there are numerous vacation cottages and beach houses for rent in Neskowin. Contact **Sea View Vacation Rentals,** P.O. Box 1049, Pacific City, OR 97135 (☎ **503/965-7888),** or **Grey Fox Vacation Rentals,** P.O. Box 364, Neskowin, OR 97149 (☎ **503/392-4355).** Rates range from about $85 to $300 per night. The first company also rents homes in nearby Pacific City and Oceanside.

Neskowin Resort. 48990 U.S. 101 S. (P.O. Box 447), Neskowin, OR 97149. ☎ **503/ 392-4850.** Fax 503/392-4264. 25 condos. TV. July 1–Sept 15 $49–$139 double; $165–$325 4 to 6 people. Sept 16–June 30 $35–$79 double; $89–$249 4 to 6 people. No credit cards. Pets accepted.

Most units at this condominium resort have views of Proposal Rock, and the views, combined with the tranquillity of Neskowin, set this place apart from hotels in nearby Lincoln City. Most of the units have kitchens, which makes this a popular choice with families. Hawk Creek runs along the back of the resort, and just across the parking lot is a good little cafe. The views from the rooms here are among the best on the Oregon coast.

5 Lincoln City/Gleneden Beach

88 miles SW of Portland, 44 miles S of Tillamook, 25 miles N of Newport

Lincoln City is not really a city, but a collection of five small towns that stretch for miles along the coast. Over the years these towns all grew together as this became the most popular beach destination for vacationers, especially families, from Portland and Salem. Today there's no specific downtown area, and though there may be more motel rooms here than anywhere else on the Oregon coast, there's little to distinguish most of the thousands of rooms. However, family vacationers looking for a long beach with lots of sand and steady winds for flying kites will find Lincoln City to their liking. Motel rates here, though often high for what you get, are generally better than those in beach towns that are longer on charm, and you'll find an abundance of vacation homes for rent. Likewise, restaurants catering to large families and small pocketbooks proliferate here. Such restaurants purvey hot meals rather than haute cuisine, and you can eat your fill of seafood without going broke.

Once referred to as "20 miracle miles," Lincoln City is no longer the miracle it once was. Miracle miles have become congested urban sprawl, and a summer weekend in Lincoln City can mean coping with bumper-to-bumper traffic. Not surprisingly, many have come to think of this as "20 miserable miles." If at all possible, come during the week or during the off-season to avoid the crowds.

Once you get off U.S. 101, though, Lincoln City has neighborhoods as charming as any on the coast. It is also here, in the Gleneden Beach area just south of Lincoln City, that you'll find the coast's most prestigious resort. Also to be found in this area are some of Oregon's best art galleries and some interesting artists' studios.

ESSENTIALS

GETTING THERE   Ore. 22 from Salem merges with Ore. 18 before reaching the junction with U.S. 101. From Portland, take Ore. 99W to McMinnville and then head west on Ore. 18.

VISITOR INFORMATION   For more information on the area, contact the **Lincoln City Visitor and Convention Bureau,** 801 SW U.S. 101, Lincoln City, OR 97367 (☎ **800/452-2151** or 541/994-8378).

GETTING AROUND   Car rentals are available from **Robben Rent-A-Car** (☎ **800/305-5530** or 541/994-5530). If you need a taxi, contact **Lincoln Cab Co.** (☎ **541/996-2003**). Public bus service between the Rose Lodge on Ore. 18 and Newport, south of Lincoln City, is provided by **Lincoln County Transit** (☎ **541/ 765-2177,** ext. 4900) but is available on weekdays only.

FESTIVALS   Annual **kite festivals** include the Spring Kite Festival in early May and the Fall International Kite Festival in early October. In addition, Lincoln City hosts the annual **Cascade Head Music Festival** on the first three weekends in June, and in July there's the annual **Sandcastle Building Contest.** On the nearby Siletz Indian Reservation, the **Nesika Illahee,** the annual Siletz Pow Wow takes place on the second weekend in August.

ENJOYING THE BEACH & THE OUTDOORS

Lincoln City's 7½-mile-long **beach** is its main attraction. However, cold waters and constant breezes conspire to make swimming a pursuit for Polar Bear Club members only. The winds, on the other hand, make this beach the best kite-flying spot on the Oregon coast. If you didn't bring your own kite, you can buy one at **Catch the Wind,** 266 SE U.S. 101 (☎ **541/994-9500**). Among the better beach-access points are the D River State Wayside on the south side of the river and the Road's End State Wayside up at the north end of Lincoln City. Road's End is also a good place to explore some tide pools. You'll find more tide pools on the beach at Northwest 15th Street and at Southwest 32nd Street.

Adding to the appeal of Lincoln City's beach is **Devil's Lake,** which drains across the beach by way of the D River, the world's shortest river. Formerly called Devil's River (Christians didn't like the name), the D River is only 120 feet long, flowing from the outlet of Devil's Lake, under U.S. 101 and across the beach to the Pacific Ocean. Boating, sailing, waterskiing, boardsailing, swimming, fishing, and camping are all popular Devil's Lake activities. Access points on the west side of the lake include **Devil's Lake State Park (West),** NE Sixth Street (☎ **541/994-2002**), which has a campground, and **Regatta Grounds Park** and **Holmes Road Park,** both of which are off West Devil's Lake Road and have boat ramps and picnic tables. On the east side you'll find **Devil's Lake State Park (East)** 2 miles east on East Devil's Lake Road and

The Central Oregon Coast

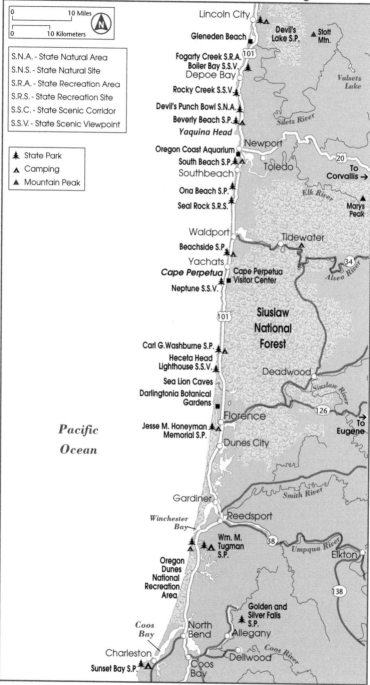

0   10 Miles

0   10 Kilometers

S.N.A. - State Natural Area
S.N.S. - State Natural Site
S.R.A. - State Recreation Area
S.R.S. - State Recreation Site
S.S.C. - State Scenic Corridor
S.S.V. - State Scenic Viewpoint

🌲 State Park
△ Camping
▲ Mountain Peak

Lincoln City
Devil's Lake S.P.
Stott Mtn.
Gleneden Beach
Fogarty Creek S.R.A.
Boiler Bay S.S.V.
Depoe Bay
Valsetz Lake
Rocky Creek S.S.V.
Devil's Punch Bowl S.N.A.
Beverly Beach S.P.
Siletz River
Yaquina Head
Newport
Oregon Coast Aquarium
To Corvallis →
South Beach S.P.
Toledo
Southbeach
Ona Beach S.P.
Elk River
Seal Rock S.R.S.
Marys Peak
Waldport
Tidewater
Beachside S.P.
Yachats
Cape Perpetua
Cape Perpetua Visitor Center
Neptune S.S.V.
Alsea River
Siuslaw National Forest
Carl G. Washburne S.P.
Heceta Head Lighthouse S.S.V.
Deadwood
Sea Lion Caves
Darlingtonia Botanical Gardens
Siuslaw River
Florence
To Eugene
Jesse M. Honeyman Memorial S.P.
Dunes City
Pacific Ocean
Gardiner
Smith River
Reedsport
Winchester Bay
Wm. M. Tugman S.P.
Umpqua River
Elkton
Oregon Dunes National Recreation Area
Golden and Silver Falls S.P.
Coos Bay
North Bend
Allegany
Charleston
Dellwood
Coos River
Sunset Bay S.P.
Coos Bay

1-1356

185

Sand Point Park on View Point Lane near the north end of East Devil's Lake Road. Both of these parks have picnic tables and swimming areas. If you don't have your own boat, you can rent canoes, kayaks, paddleboats, aquabikes, and various motorboats at **Blue Heron Landing,** 4008 W. Devil's Lake Rd. (☎ **541/994-4708**). Rates range from $10 an hour for a kayak up to $35 an hour for a runabout or pontoon boat. You'll also find bumper boats here at Blue Heron Landing.

If you're a gardener or enjoy visiting public gardens, schedule time to visit the **Connie Hansen Garden,** 1931 NW 33rd St. (☎ **541/994-6338**). This cottage garden was created over a 20-year period and abounds in primroses, irises, and rhododendrons, making it a great place to visit in the spring. The gardens are open on Tuesday and Saturday from 10am to 2pm or by appointment.

Golfers have two Lincoln City options. The top choice is the Scottish-inspired (though solidly Northwestern in character) ✪ **Salishan Golf Links,** on U.S. 101 in Gleneden Beach (☎ **541/764-3632**), which charges $55 to $65 for 18 holes of golf in the summer months. This resort course is a longtime Oregon coast favorite. Other than this, it's the **Lakeside Golf & Fitness Club,** 3245 Club House Dr. (☎ **541/994-8442**), which charges $30 for 18 holes.

If you want to challenge the waves, you can rent a surfboard or bodyboard at the **Oregon Surf Shop,** 4933 SW U.S. 101 (☎ **541/996-3957**).

Hikers searching for an interesting trail should head inland approximately 10 miles to ✪ **Drift Creek Falls Trail,** which leads through coastal forest to a 240-foot-long suspension bridge above a 75-foot-tall waterfall. From the bridge you have a bird's-eye view not only of the falls but of the treetops as well. It's 1¼ miles in to the bridge and the route is moderately difficult. To find the trailhead (TrailPark permit required), head east from U.S. 101 on Drift Creek Road, which is just north of the Westin Salishan lodge at the south end of Lincoln City. Turn right onto South Drift Creek Road and then left onto Forest Road 17 (not Anderson Creek Rd.) and continue 10 miles on this single-lane road.

INDOOR PURSUITS

These days the hottest thing in town is the **Chinook Winds Casino,** 1777 NW 44th St. (☎ **888/CHINOOK**), a massive gambling palace run by the Confederated Tribes of Siletz Indians and located right on the beach at the north end of town. The casino offers bingo, blackjack, poker, slot machines, and keno. Of course, there's also plenty of cheap food available, as well as a video-games room for the kids. Big-name entertainers (Bill Cosby, B.B. King, Loretta Lynn, Ray Charles) help attract folks who might not otherwise consider visiting a casino.

The casino may actually be second in popularity to the **Factory Stores @ Lincoln City,** 1500 SE East Devils Lake Rd. (☎ **888/SHOP333** or 541/996-5000), which is on the corner of U.S. 101.

Perhaps because the Westin Salishan attracts some well-heeled visitors to the area, Lincoln City has a surprising number of interesting art galleries and artists' studios. At the north end of town, the first gallery you'll come to is the **Ryan Gallery,** 4270 N. U.S. 101 (☎ **541/994-5391**). Right in the heart of Lincoln City's main business strip, watch for the **Earthworks Gallery,** 620 NE U.S. 101 (☎ **541/557-4148**), which has an emphasis on ceramic and glass art but also carries a wide variety of other types of art and fine crafts. Gardening enthusiasts will also want to visit **Garden Art & Gifts,** 3001 SW U.S. 101 (☎ **541/994-2660**), a store full of beautiful garden accessories and garden-oriented art.

South of Lincoln City proper, you'll find the impressive **Freed Gallery,** 6119 SW U.S. 101 (☎ **541/994-5600**), which has an excellent selection of art glass and ceramic work, as well as sculptures and paintings in a wide variety of styles. Just off

U.S. 101, north of the Westin Salishan, you'll find **Alder House III,** 611 Immonen Rd. (no phone), which is the oldest glassblowing studio in Oregon. The shop and studio are open daily from 10am to 5pm between March 15 and November 30. Also on Immonen Road (which is just north of the Westin Salishan) is **Mossy Creek Pottery** (☎ **541/996-2415**), with an imaginative selection of porcelain and stoneware by Oregon potters. Also not to be missed by art collectors is the **Gallery at Salishan** (☎ **800/764-2318**), which is in the Marketplace at Salishan shopping plaza opposite the entrance to the Westin Salishan.

The only museum in town is the **North Lincoln County Museum,** 4907 SW U.S. 101 (☎ **541/996-6614**), which has rooms decorated with historic artifacts and antiques from pioneer days. It's open Tuesday through Saturday from noon to 4pm (until 5pm in summer); admission by donation.

WHERE TO STAY

In addition to the town's many hotels and motels, Lincoln City has plenty of vacation rental houses and apartments offering good deals, especially for family vacations. For information on renting a house or an apartment, contact **Horizon Rentals** (☎ **800/995-2411** or 541/994-2226; www.wwte.com/horizon.htm) or **Pacific Retreats** (☎ **800/473-4833;** www.pacificretreats.com). Rates generally range from around $100 up to $250 for houses for anywhere from 4 to 12 people.

EXPENSIVE

The Inn at Spanish Head. 4009 SW U.S. 101, Lincoln City, OR 97367. ☎ **800/452-8127** or 541/996-2161. Fax 541/996-4089. www.spanishhead.com. 155 units. TV TEL. $135–$165 double; $209–$289 suite. Lower rates in winter. AE, DC, DISC, MC, V. Free valet parking.

Located toward the south end of Lincoln City, this hotel is the only high-rise hotel on the Oregon coast, but you'd never know it from the parking lot. From the entry, the hotel appears to be only two stories tall. What isn't readily apparent is that the lobby is on the ninth floor (there are eight stories below the parking-lot level) due to the fact that the hotel is built into a steep cliff that rises up from the beach. This is a condominium resort and all the rooms are individually owned, which means there's a different decor in every room. However, the furnishings are reliably comfortable. Many rooms have kitchens, and there are larger suites for family vacationers. Best of all, all the rooms have an ocean view.

Dining/Entertainment: The Ocean View restaurant and lounge, on the 10th floor, provides a dizzying view and fresh seafood with Northwest flavorings and is one of Lincoln City's better restaurants. Sunday brunch ($16.95) is also served here.

Services: Room service.

Facilities: Beachside outdoor pool, whirlpool, sauna, exercise room, coin laundry, games room.

The O'dysius Hotel. 120 NW Inlet Court, Lincoln City, OR 97367. ☎ **800/869-8069** or 541/994-4121. Fax 541/994-8160. www.odysius.com. 30 units. MINIBAR TV TEL. $139–$169 double; $194–$289 suite. Rates include continental breakfast. AE, DISC, MC, V.

Although it seems a bit out of place, this new hotel offers the sort of luxury you would expect from a downtown Portland historic hotel—with a beach right across the street. Traditional European styling dominates, and the lobby, with its antique furniture, has a very luxurious living room feel. It's here that the hotel serves its complimentary afternoon wine. Guest rooms have lots of nice touches, including slate entries, down comforters, art nouveau lamps, gas fireplaces, and VCRs. All the rooms have ocean views, and some have balconies. If you enjoy luxury but aren't into the golf-resort scene, this is definitely the place for you.

✪ **The Westin Salishan Lodge.** 7760 U.S. 101, Gleneden Beach, OR 97388. ☎ **888/725-4742** or 541/764-2371. Fax 541/764-3681. www.salishan.com. 205 units. MINIBAR TV TEL. Jan–Apr $119–$169 double. May–Sept $159–$279 double. Oct–Dec $119–$249 double. AE, CB, DC, DISC, MC, V. Pets accepted ($25 per night).

The largest and most luxurious resort on the coast, the Salishan Lodge is nestled amid towering evergreens on a hillside at the south end of Siletz Bay. Unfortunately, the resort is almost half a mile from the beach and on the inland side of U.S. 101. However, since most guests are here to play golf, few seem to mind this inconvenience. Guest rooms, which are spread out around just a portion of the resort's 750 acres, come in three sizes. However, whichever size room you opt for, try to get a second-floor room. Most of these have cathedral ceilings and stone fireplaces. For breathtaking views, you'll have to shell out top dollar for a deluxe or premier room. In 1997, the resort underwent a complete renovation that gave both the lobby and the guest rooms a fresh lodge look (think Eddie Bauer), and in 1999, it became a Westin resort.

Dining/Entertainment: The **Salishan Dining Room** is the most upscale restaurant on the entire coast. See "Where to Dine" below for details. There's also a less expensive restaurant, as well as a coffee shop. The Attic Lounge is a quiet upscale spot for a late-night cocktail or a game of pool.

Services: Concierge, room service, valet/laundry service, baby-sitting, in-room massages.

Facilities: 18-hole golf course, driving range, pro shop, indoor pool, indoor and outdoor tennis courts, whirlpool, exercise room, saunas, children's games room, playground, walking trails, beach access.

MODERATE

Cozy Cove. 515 NW Inlet Ave., Lincoln City, OR 97367. ☎ **800/553-COVE** or 541/994-2950. Fax 541/996-4332. 69 units. TV TEL. $55–$175 double. DC, DISC, MC, V.

Located near the mouth of the D River, the Cozy Cove offers some good deals among its wide range of guest rooms. The hotel is on a long, wide stretch of beach with easy access, and only a short walk away you'll find several good restaurants. Some rooms have fireplaces and balconies, while others have kitchens or whirlpool tubs or some combination of all of these amenities. There's a seasonal outdoor pool and a year-round whirlpool. While the best (and most expensive) rooms are those facing the beach, there are very economical nonview rooms as well. Our favorite rooms are the oceanfront rooms with fireplaces and whirlpool tubs in the windows.

Siletz Bay Lodge. 1012 SW 51st St. (P.O. Box 952), Lincoln City, OR 97367. ☎ **888/430-2100** or 541/996-6111. Fax 541/996-3992. www.siletzbaylodge.com. 44 units. A/C TV TEL. Summer $98–$145 double; $145 suite. Other months $69–$125 double; $125 suite. Rates include continental breakfast. 3-night minimum on holidays. AE, DISC, MC, V.

Located at the south end of Lincoln City right on Siletz Bay, this modern motel is a good choice for both families and couples. Although the motel isn't on the ocean, it is on a driftwood-strewn beach that has quiet waters that are perfect for kids, and across the bay you can often see harbor seals lounging on the beach. About half of the standard rooms here have balconies, and all the rooms have microwaves, refrigerators, and coffeemakers. Spa rooms and spa suites are also available if you happen to be in town for a romantic getaway.

CAMPGROUNDS

There's a campground at **Devil's Lake State Park,** just off U.S. 101 north of the D River.

WHERE TO DINE

If you're looking for some good smoked salmon or smoked oysters while you're in town, stop by **Mr. Bill's Village Smokehouse,** 2981 SW U.S. 101 (☎ **888/MR-BILLS** or 503/994-4566). If you're looking for a good cup of espresso, stop in the combination coffeehouse/bookstore **Café Roma,** 1437 NW U.S. 101 (☎ **541/994-6616**).

EXPENSIVE

✪ **Bay House.** 5911 SW U.S. 101. ☎ **541/996-3222.** Reservations recommended. Main courses $18–$28. AE, DISC, MC, V. May–Sept Sun–Fri 5:30–9pm, Sat 5–9pm. Closed Mon–Tues Oct–Apr. NORTHWEST.

With a big wall of glass overlooking the Siletz Bay and Salishan Spit, the Bay House, between Lincoln City and Gleneden Beach, provides fine dining and dramatic sunsets (and good bird watching if you're interested). There are snowy linens on the tables, and service is gracious. For starters, we have a weakness for the bay shrimp wontons with the zesty lime dipping sauce. Entrees include such unusual creations as panfried oysters in a lemon grass and ginger broth. The Bay House also has a wine shop and a bistro lounge area for cocktails and appetizers. If you have time for only one dinner while in the area, make it here.

Chez Jeanette. 7150 Gleneden Beach Loop, Gleneden Beach. ☎ **541/764-3434.** Reservations highly recommended. Main courses $20–$28. MC, V. Daily 5:30–8 or 8:30pm. FRENCH/NORTHWEST.

With the Westin Salishan in the neighborhood, it's obvious that Gleneden Beach is the Oregon coast's poshest destination. So you won't be surprised to learn that this little French restaurant is one of the most expensive dining establishments on the coast. Housed in a quaint little cottage tucked under the trees, Chez Jeanette does a commendable job of duplicating the feel of a French country inn and is the perfect spot for a romantic dinner. While there is always plenty of seafood on the menu, wild game is the real specialty here. The venison chops and tenderloin are both good choices. Every night there are also different seafood specials, as well as a pasta du jour. You'll find Chez Jeanette south of Salishan Lodge on a side road that leads to Gleneden Beach.

✪ **The Dining Room at Salishan Lodge.** U.S. 101, Gleneden Beach. ☎ **541/764-2371.** Reservations highly recommended. Main courses $22–$34. AE, CB, DC, DISC, MC, V. Daily 6–10pm. NORTHWEST.

The Westin Salishan Lodge is the Oregon coast's premier full-service resort, and it also boasts one of the coast's best restaurants. The menu is as creative as any you'll find in the region and can hold its own with popular restaurants in Portland. The menu changes regularly to take advantage of the ever-changing offerings of fresh Northwest ingredients, and regional wines are often emphasized. Expect plenty of seafood-based appetizers the likes of oysters on the half shell with Champagne-dill mignonette, or Dungeness crab cakes with jicama-fennel slaw and lemon-walnut aïoli. The main courses are more evenly split among meats and seafood. Expect daring preparations such as espresso and brown-sugar crusted loin of lamb with dried cherry and Pinot Noir beurre rouge. Lots of windows assure every diner at this ever-popular restaurant a tranquillity-inducing view of the lush forest outside. Service is professional and unobtrusive, and the wine cellar, with more than 15,000 bottles, is positively legendary.

MODERATE

✪ **Kyllo's Seafood Grill.** 1110 NW First Court. ☎ **541/994-3179.** Reservations not accepted. Main courses lunch $4.50–$11, dinner $8–$19. AE, DISC, MC, V. Sun–Thurs 11am–9pm, Fri–Sat 11am–10pm. SEAFOOD.

Providing a touch of urban chic on a family-oriented beach, Kyllo's is housed in a architecturally striking contemporary building that features concrete floors and walls, a big copper fireplace, plenty of deck space, and walls of glass to take in the view of the D River and the ocean. A colorful, narrow mural winds around the dining room, and there are unusual deconstructivist wall lamps. If all this sounds like you're going to be paying for the atmosphere, think again. Prices for such dishes as large and tasty crab cakes, halibut with lemon-garlic butter, or Cajun-style panfried oysters are quite reasonable. You'll almost certainly have to wait for a table if you come here on a summer evening.

INEXPENSIVE

Chameleon Cafe. 2145 NW U.S. 101. ☎ **541/994-8422.** Reservations for 5 or more people only. Main courses $7–$15. DISC, MC, V. Mon–Sat 11:30am–9pm (until 8pm in winter). INTERNATIONAL/VEGETARIAN.

This tiny cafe is cheerful and bustling, and a surprising find in downtown Lincoln City. Although the main influence is Mediterranean, the Chameleon lives up to its name by offering cuisines from around the globe. There are lots of veggie options, but you'll also find a few fish dishes, such as spicy fish tacos or prawns in an orange chili sauce. No matter what you choose, it's bound to be healthful and well prepared. And don't resist dessert—it takes a Herculean effort to say no to chocolate ganach or reliably fine carrot cake.

✪ **Otis Café.** Ore. 18, Otis. ☎ **541/994-2813.** Reservations not accepted. Breakfast, lunch, and dinner $4–$10. DISC, MC, V. June–Sept daily 7am–9pm; Oct–May Mon–Thurs 7am–3pm, Fri–Sun 7am–9pm. AMERICAN.

If you've ever seen the determination with which urbanites head for the beach on summer weekends, you can understand what a feat it is to get cars to stop before they've got sand in the treads of their tires. This tiny roadside diner 5 miles north of Lincoln City and 4 miles shy of the beach manages to do just that with its black bread, cinnamon rolls, and fried red potatoes. The homemade mustard and killer salsa also have their loyal fans. Pies—marionberry, strawberry/rhubarb, or walnut—have crusts for the noncholesterol conscious and are memorable even in this land of perfect pies. Expect a line out the screen door. Otis made national news in late 1999 when the whole town was put up for sale for $3 million.

Salmon River Cafe. Lincoln City Plaza, 4079-B NW Logan Rd. ☎ 541/996-FOOD. Main courses lunch $5.50–$7.50, dinner $10–$13.50. No credit cards. Mon–Tues 9am–4pm, Wed–Thurs 9am–9pm, Fri–Sat 8am–9pm, Sun 8am–8pm. AMERICAN/ITALIAN.

Located in a nondescript shopping plaza at the north end of town, this combination casual restaurant and deli is run by Barbara Lowry, who got her Lincoln City start at the upscale Bay House. The menu is short and simple, but everything is made fresh daily and is available either in the dining room or to go from the deli. While lunches consist mainly of burgers and sandwiches, the dinner menu might include pork tenderloin with roasted sweet bell peppers or rock shrimp in a reduced cream sauce with nutmeg, garlic, and lemon juice. Italian and Northwest wines are available to accompany meals. Families are always welcome at this casual spot. On weekends there are free wine tastings.

SOUTH TO DEPOE BAY

Two miles north of Depoe Bay, you'll come to **Fogarty Creek State Recreation Area,** a beautiful little cove with basalt cliffs at one end and a creek flowing across the beach.

The parking area is on the east side of U.S. 101. A mile south of this beach, you'll find **Boiler Bay State Scenic Viewpoint,** where there are tide pools among the rocks in some small coves. Although the beach itself is not accessible from the state park pull-off, about midway between Fogarty Creek and Bolier Bay there's a trail that leads down to it.

6 Depoe Bay

13 miles S of Lincoln City, 13 miles N of Newport, 70 miles W of Salem

Depoe Bay calls itself the smallest harbor in the world, and once you've seen it you'll have to agree. Though the harbor covers only 6 acres, it's home to more than 100 fishing boats. As fascinating as the harbor itself is the narrow channel, little more than a crack in the coastline's solid rock wall, that leads into Depoe Bay. During stormy seas, it's almost impossible to get in or out of the harbor safely. Storm waves also bring on the impressive fountains of Depoe Bay's famous spouting horns, which are produced when waves break in narrow fissures in the area's rocky coastline.

Shell mounds and kitchen middens around the bay indicate that Native Americans long called this area home. In 1894, the U.S. government deeded the land surrounding the bay to a Siletz Indian known as Old Charlie Depot, who had taken his name from an army depot at which he had worked. Old Charlie later changed his name to DePoe, and when a town was founded here in 1927, it took the name Depoe Bay. Though most of the town is located a bit off the highway, you'll find, right on U.S. 101, a row of garish souvenir shops, which sadly mar the beauty of this rocky section of coast. Among these shops are several family restaurants and charter-fishing and whale-watching companies.

ESSENTIALS

GETTING THERE   From the north, the most direct route is Ore. 99W/18 to Lincoln City and then south on U.S. 101. From the south take U.S. 20 from Corvallis to Newport and then go north on U.S. 101.

VISITOR INFORMATION   Contact the **Depoe Bay Chamber of Commerce,** 214 SE U.S. 101 (P.O. Box 21), Depoe Bay, OR 97341 (☎ **541/765-2889**).

FESTIVALS   Memorial Day is time for the **Fleet of Flowers,** during which local boats carry flower wreaths out to sea in memory of loved ones. In mid-September, the town holds its annual **Salmon Bake,** which is a great opportunity to enjoy some traditionally prepared salmon. Contact the Chamber of Commerce for details.

DEPOE BAY ACTIVITIES & ATTRACTIONS

Aside from watching the boat traffic passing in and out of the world's smallest harbor, the most popular activity here, especially when the seas are high, is watching the spouting horns across U.S. 101 from Depoe Bay's souvenir shops. Spouting horns, which are similar to blowholes, can be seen all along the coast, but nowhere are they more spectacular than here at Depoe Bay. These geyser-like plumes occur in places where water is forced through narrow channels in basalt rock. As the channels become more restricted, the water shoots skyward under great pressure and can spray 60 feet into the air. If the surf is really up, the water can carry quite a ways, and more than a few unwary visitors have been soaked.

Sportfishing and ✪ **whale watching** draw most visitors to town these days. You can arrange for either at **Tradewinds** (☎ **800/445-8730** or 541/765-2345), at the north end of the bridge; **Joan-E Charters** (☎ 800/995-FUNN or 541/765-2222), at the south end of the bridge; or **Dockside Charters** (☎ 800/733-8915 or 541/765-2545), down by the marina. Whale-watching trips run $12 for 1 hour and $18 for 2 hours, and fishing trips run $55 for 5 hours up to $150 for 12 hours of halibut or tuna fishing.

WHERE TO STAY

✪ **Channel House.** 35 Ellingson St., Depoe Bay, OR 97341. ☎ **800/447-2140** or 541/765-2140. Fax 541/765-2191. www.channelhouse.com. 12 units. TV TEL. $85–$100 double ocean-view, $170 oceanfront; $200–$245 suite. Rates include continental breakfast. AE, DISC, MC, V.

The narrow, cliff-bordered channel into diminutive Depoe Bay is one of the most challenging harbor entrances in Oregon, and perched above it is the Channel House, one of the coast's most luxurious and strikingly situated small inns. A contemporary building with lots of angles and windows, the Channel House offers large rooms, most of which have gas fireplaces and private decks with whirlpool tubs. You can sit and soak as fishing boats navigate their way through the channel below you. There are few lodgings with as dramatic a view anywhere on the Oregon coast.

Inn at Arch Rock. P.O. Box 1516, Depoe Bay, OR 97341. ☎ **800/767-1835** or 541/765-2560. 13 units. TV. $59–$119 double; $139–$249 suite/cottage. Slightly lower rates in winter. AE, DISC, MC, V.

You just won't find a better view from any hotel on the Oregon coast. This collection of old but recently renovated Cape Cod–style buildings sits above the cliffs on the north side of Depoe Bay. You can sit in your room and watch the waves crashing against the rocks or walk down a flight of stairs to a tiny beach. Guest rooms have a sort of simple, modern cottage decor, and most have big windows, microwaves, and coffeemakers. Out on the lawns overlooking the ocean you'll find white Adirondack chairs. The inn also happens to be just around the corner from the Tidal Raves restaurant.

✪ **Inn at Otter Crest.** Otter Crest Loop Rd. (P.O. Box 50), Otter Rock, OR 97369. ☎ **800/452-2101** or 541/765-2111. Fax 541/765-2047. www.ottercrest.com. 120 units. TV TEL. $99–$139 double; $159–$299 suite. 2-night minimum on holidays and weekends in July and Aug. DISC, MC, V.

Few hotels on the Oregon coast boast as spectacular a setting as the Inn at Otter Crest, which is one of the Oregon coast's premier resorts and reflects the region in both architecture and setting. The inn's numerous weathered-cedar buildings are surrounded by 35 acres of forests and beautifully landscaped gardens on a rocky crest above a secluded cove. If you want to get away from it all and enjoy a bit of forest seclusion on the beach, there's no better spot. Most rooms have excellent ocean views through a wall of glass that opens onto a balcony. Our favorite rooms are the loft suites, which have fireplaces, kitchens, and high ceilings. Service here is rather casual, in keeping with Northwest attitudes, and you'll have to leave your car in a parking lot that's removed from the guest rooms (staff will shuttle you around in golf carts).

Dining/Entertainment: The Flying Dutchman restaurant, which has a rather uninspired menu, is located downhill from the guest rooms near the resort's swimming pool. The menu focuses on local seafood, and there's even an affiliated winery.

Facilities: Outdoor swimming pool, hot tub, sauna, tennis, hiking trails.

The Surfrider. 3115 NW U.S. 101 (P.O. Box 219), Depoe Bay, OR 97341. ☎ **800/ 662-2378** or 541/764-2311. www.surfriderresort.com. 42 units. TV TEL. Mid-June to Sept 30 $75–$115 double. Lower rates in off-season. AE, DC, DISC, MC, V.

Though it has been around for many years and is nothing fancy, this low-rise motel just north of Depoe Bay claims an enviable location and view and has long been a family favorite on the Oregon coast. It's hidden from the highway, which gives it a secluded feel, and there are great views from the open bluff-top setting. You can choose between basic motel rooms and rooms with fireplaces, kitchens, or whirlpool tubs. At the foot of a long staircase is the wide beach of Fogarty Creek State Recreation Area, which is on a pretty little cove. The dining room and lounge offer a great view of this cove. The hotel also has an indoor swimming pool and a hot tub.

WHERE TO DINE

At the **Siletz Tribal Smokehouse,** on U.S. 101 south of the bridge (☎ **800/ 828-4269** or 541/765-2286), you can buy smoked salmon and other seafood. The Smokehouse is run by the Confederated Tribes of the Siletz and is a great place to buy picnic fixings as you head out to the beach.

✪ **Tidal Raves.** 279 NW U.S. 101. ☎ **541/765-2995.** Reservations highly recommended (4–5 days in advance for summer weekends). Main courses lunch $6.50–$10.50, dinner $11.50–$18. MC, V. Daily 11am–9pm. SEAFOOD.

If you're searching for the most dramatic restaurant setting on the Oregon coast, your search is over.

Located at the north end of Depoe Bay's strip of tourist shops, this place has had folks raving for years now. With its bright, uncluttered decor and big windows for taking in the view of wave-carved sandstone cliffs, Tidal Raves offers Depoe Bay diners a contemporary restaurant with a view. On days when the surf is up, it's hard to take your eyes off the wave-pounded cliffs outside the window. The menu offers plenty of straightforward seafood, but it also includes some creative preparations such as smoked seafood with penne pasta and Thai barbecued prawns. For light eaters, there are even small portions of many menu favorites.

SOUTH TO NEWPORT

The road south from Depoe Bay winds its way through grand scenery of rugged splendor as it passes several small, picturesque coves. Just south of town, **Rocky Creek State Scenic Viewpoint,** with windswept lawns, picnic tables, and great views of buff-colored cliffs and spouting horns, is a good place for a picnic. In a few more miles you'll come to the **Otter Crest State Scenic Viewpoint** on Cape Foulweather. This cape was named by Capt. James Cook in 1778. This was Cook's first glimpse of land after leaving the Sandwich Islands (Hawaii), and the sighting initiated the first English claims to the region. The cape frequently lives up to its name, with winds often gusting to more than 100 miles per hour. However, the views here are quite stupendous. Keep an eye out for the sea lions that sun themselves on offshore rocks near Cape Foulweather. Although the Otter Crest Scenic Loop is no longer open due to a landslide that closed part of the road, there is a historic building now used as a gift shop that provides a protected glimpse of the sea from atop Cape Foulweather.

At the south end of the Otter Crest Scenic Loop, you'll find an overlook at ✪ **Devil's Punchbowl State Natural Area.** The overlook provides a glimpse into a collapsed sea cave that during high tides or stormy seas becomes a churning cauldron of foam. Adjacent to Devil's Punchbowl, in a small cove, you'll find the **Marine Gardens,** where numerous tide pools can be explored at low tide. From this cove, you can also explore inside the Devil's Punchbowl. South of Devil's Punchbowl State Natural Area lies **Beverly Beach State Park,** which has a large campground and is a popular surfing spot.

7 Newport

23 miles S of Lincoln City, 58 miles W of Corvallis, 24 miles N of Yachats

As Oregon coast towns go, Newport has a split personality. Dockworkers unloading fresh fish mingle with vacationers licking ice-cream cones, and both fishing boats and pleasure craft ply the waters of the bay. The air smells of fish and shrimp, and freeloading sea lions doze on the docks while they wait for their next meal from the processing plants along the waterfront. Directly across the street from these, art galleries and souvenir shops stand side by side. Across Yaquina Bay from the waterfront, you'll also find the Oregon Coast Aquarium (the coast's top tourist attraction) and the Hatfield Marine Science Center. If you're looking for a balance of the old and the new on the Oregon coast, Newport is the place.

Newport got its start in the late 1800s as both an oystering community and one of the earliest Oregon beach resorts, and many of the old cottages and historic buildings can still be seen. While the town's Nye Beach area has the feel of a turn-of-the-century resort, the downtown bayfront is, despite its souvenir shops, galleries, and restaurants, still a working port and home to the largest commercial fishing fleet on the Oregon coast. Oysters are also still important to the local economy and are raised in oyster beds along Yaquina Bay Road east of town.

Though in recent years it has come close to matching the overdevelopment of Lincoln City, this fishing port on the shore of Yaquina Bay still manages to offer a balance of industry, history, culture, beaches, and family vacation attractions.

ESSENTIALS

GETTING THERE Newport is on U.S. 101 at the junction with U.S. 20, which leads to Corvallis. **Lincoln County Transit** (☎ 541/265-4900) provides bus service from Lincoln City in the north and Yachats in the south. Newport's small airport is served with regular flights from Portland and Corvallis on **Harbor Air** (☎ 800/359-3220). Round-trip fares from Portland range from $125 to $187.

VISITOR INFORMATION Contact the **Newport Chamber of Commerce,** 555 SW Coast Hwy., Newport, OR 97365 (☎ 800/262-7844 or 541/265-8801; www.newportnet.com).

GETTING AROUND Public bus service is provided by **Lincoln County Transit** (☎ 541/265-4900), which operates north to Lincoln City and south to Yachats. If you need a taxi, call **Yaquina Cab** (☎ 541/265-9552).

FESTIVALS In late July each year, the music of composer Ernest Bloch, who once lived in this area, is celebrated during the **Ernest Bloch Music Festival** (☎ 541/265-ARTS). In August, the **Jazz on the Water Festival** (☎ 541/265-4074) brings world-class jazz to the Newport Marina.

FINS AND FLIPPERS

Hatfield Marine Science Center. 2030 Marine Science Dr. ☎ **541/867-0100.** Admission by donation. Memorial Day–Oct 1 daily 10am–5pm; Oct 1–Memorial Day Thurs–Mon 10am–4pm.

Before the Oregon Coast Aquarium was built, Newport was already known as a center for marine science research. This facility, though primarily a university research center, also contains displays that are open to the public. Exhibits, though not quite as impressive as those at the Oregon Coast Aquarium, highlight current topics in marine research and include an octopus aquarium and a "touch" tank. Interpretive exhibits explain life in the sea. Definitely a worthwhile adjunct to a visit to the Oregon Coast Aquarium.

✪ **Oregon Coast Aquarium.** 2820 SE Ferry Slip Rd. ☎ **541/867-3474.** www. aquarium.org. Admission $8.75 adults, $7.75 seniors and children 13–18, $4.50 children 4–12. Memorial Day–Labor Day daily 9am–6pm; Labor Day–Memorial Day daily 10am–5pm. Closed Dec 25.

Considered one of the top aquariums in the country, the Oregon Coast Aquarium focuses its exhibits on sea life along the Oregon coast. There are so many fascinating displays here that it's easy to spend the better part of a day at the aquarium. The stars here (now that Keiko the orca whale has moved on) are the playful sea otters, but the clown-faced tufted puffins, which are kept in a walk-through aviary, are big favorites as well. The sea lions sometimes rouse from their naps to put on impromptu shows, and the lucky visitor even gets a glimpse of a giant octopus with an arm span of nearly 20 feet. Artificial waves surge in a tank that reproduces, on a speeded-up scale, life in a rocky intertidal zone. And so far, you haven't even made it to the indoor aquarium displays. In the summer of 2000, the aquarium will also be opening a walk-through deep-sea shark tank featuring a 200-foot-long acrylic walkway. Indoors, you'll also find "At the Jetty," a 35,000-gallon tank that spotlights salmon and the issues surrounding their continued survival in the Northwest. Other indoor exhibits focus on various coastal habitats and the life-forms that inhabit them. There are examples of sandy beaches, rocky shores, salt marshes, kelp forests, and even the open ocean, where diaphanous jellyfish drift lazily on the currents.

Because this is the most popular attraction on the Oregon coast, lines to get in can be very long. Arrive early if you're visiting on a summer weekend.

SEEING THE LIGHTS

Newport is home to two historic lighthouses, which are located only 3 miles apart. The Yaquina Bay Lighthouse began operation in 1871, but in 1874 was replaced by the Yaquina Head Lighthouse. This latter lighthouse was supposed to be built on Cape Foulweather farther to the north, but heavy seas made it impossible to land there. Instead, the light was built on Yaquina Head, and so powerful was the light that it supplanted the one at Yaquina Bay. Today both lights can be visited by the public.

At 93 feet tall, the **Yaquina Head Lighthouse,** 3 miles north of Newport, is the tallest lighthouse on the Oregon coast and is still a functioning light. The lighthouse, open to the public whenever volunteers are available to man it (usually daily from 10am to 4pm in summer), lies within the **Yaquina Head Outstanding Natural Area** (☎ **541/574-3100**). Adjacent to the lighthouse, you'll find the **Yaquina Head Interpretive Center,** which houses displays covering everything from the life of lighthouse keepers and their families to the sea life of tide pools. Here, you'll learn that the headland is the remains of an ancient volcano and is home to thousands of nesting sea birds, something you will undoubtedly have already noticed from the raucous cries of glaucous-winged and western gulls. Cormorants and pigeon guillemots can be seen roosting on the steep slopes here, and harbor seals can also be seen lounging on the rocks. In early winter and spring, gray whales can be spotted migrating along the coast. On the cobblestone beach below the lighthouse, you can explore tide pools at low tide, and there is even a wheelchair-accessible tide-pool trail in a cove that once was the site of a rock quarry. Admission to Yaquina Head is $5 per car.

The older of the two lighthouses, **Yaquina Bay Lighthouse,** is now part of Yaquina Bay State Recreation Site, 846 SW Government St. (☎ **541/265-5679**), which can be found just north and west of the Yaquina Bay Bridge. This lighthouse, built in 1871, is the oldest building in Newport, and it is unusual in that the light is in a tower atop a two-story wood-frame house. The building served as both home and lighthouse, and supposedly is haunted. The lighthouse is open Memorial Day through the end of September daily from 11am to 5pm; October through Memorial Day it's open daily from noon to 4pm.

BEACHES

Beaches in the Newport area range from tiny rocky coves where you can search for agates to long, wide stretches of sand perfect for kite flying. Right in town, north and west of the Yaquina Bay Bridge, you'll find the **Yaquina Bay State Recreation Site,** which borders on both the ocean and the bay. North of Newport is **Agate Beach,** which was once known for the beautiful agates that could be found there. However, in recent years sand has covered the formerly rocky beach, hiding the stones from rock hunters. This beach has a stunning view of Yaquina Head. Two miles south of Newport, you'll find **South Beach State Park,** a wide sandy beach with picnic areas and a large campground (that also rents yurts).

THE BAYFRONT

The Bayfront is tourist central for Newport, where you'll find ice-cream parlors, salt-water taffy stores, chowder houses, and souvenir shops. However, it is also home to commercial fishermen, seafood processing plants, and art galleries. The waters of the Bayfront are also home to numerous sea lions, which love to sleep on the floating docks adjacent to Undersea Gardens. From the adjacent pier, you can observe the sea lions at close range. Their bickering and barking provides great free entertainment.

As one of the coast's most popular family vacation spots, Newport has all the tourist traps one would expect. Billboards up and down the coast advertise the sorts of places that kids demand to be taken to. Tops on this list are **Ripley's Believe It or Not** and the **Wax Works Museum.** Across the street from these you'll find **Undersea Gardens,** where a scuba diver feeds fish in a large tank beneath a boat moored on the Bayfront. All three attractions are on the Bayfront and share the same address and phone number: Mariner Square, 250 SW Bay Blvd. (☎ 541/265-2206). Admission for each is $6.95 for adults, $3.95 for children; or $13.80 for adults and $7.80 for children to visit all three attractions.

Adults will likely be more interested in the Bayfront's numerous art galleries, which oddly are directly across the street from the fish and shrimp processing plants. **Breach the Moon Gallery,** 434 SW Bay Blvd. (☎ 541/265-9698), features art glass and art with ocean and whale themes. Nearby is **Oceanic Arts,** 444 SW Bay Blvd. (☎ 541/265-5963), which sells interesting crafts, including wind chimes and lots of ceramics. The **Wood Gallery,** 818 SW Bay Blvd. (☎ 541/265-6843), specializes in wooden items, including boxes and musical instruments.

The Bayfront is also the place to arrange **whale-watching tours** and **fishing trips.** Whale-watching tours are offered throughout the year by **Marine Discovery Tours,** 345 SW Bay Blvd. (☎ 800/903-BOAT or 541/265-6200), which charges $18 for a 2-hour cruise. You can charter a fishing boat on the Bayfront at **Bayfront Charters,** 1000 SE Bay Blvd. (☎ 800/828-8777 or 541/265-7558); **Newport Tradewinds,** 653 SW Bay Blvd. (☎ 800/676-7819 or 541/265-2101); or **Sea Gull Charters,** 343 SW Bay Blvd. (☎ 800/865-7441 or 541/265-7441). Salmon, tuna, halibut, and bottom fish can all be caught off the coast here depending on the season. Fishing trips run anywhere from $50 to $140 depending on what you're fishing for and how long you stay out. These last three companies also offer whale-watching trips.

Newport claims to be the Dungeness crab capital of the world, and if you'd like to find out if this claim is true, you can rent crab rings and boats. At **Sawyer's Landing,** 4098 Yaquina Bay Rd. (☎ 541/265-3907), a boat and two crab rings (with bait) rent for $37.50 for 3 hours or $50 for the whole day. At the **Embarcadero Marina,**

1000 SE Bay Blvd. (☎ **541/265-5435**), a boat rents for $45 for 3 hours or $75 for the entire day, and crab rings rent for an additional $8 each. **Clamming** is also popular, and sometimes productive, in the Newport area. Pick up a tide table at a local business and head out on the flats with your clam shovel and a bucket.

NYE BEACH
Newport was one of the earliest beach vacation destinations in Oregon, and it was in the area of Nye Beach that the first beach hotels and vacation cottages were built. Today this neighborhood, north of the Yaquina Bay Bridge along the beach, is slowly being renovated and now has both historic and hip hotels, good restaurants, some interesting shops, and, of course, miles of sandy beach to explore. You'll find public parking at the turnaround on Beach Drive.

The works of local and regional artists are showcased at the **Newport Visual Arts Center,** 777 NW Beach Dr. (☎ **541/265-6540**). The center is open Tuesday through Sunday: April to September from noon to 4pm and October to March from 11am to 3pm. Just a few blocks away, the **Newport Performing Arts Center,** 777 W. Olive St. (☎ **541/265-ARTS**), hosts local and nationally recognized performers throughout the year and also runs a film series. Tickets run $5 to $30.

At the **Nye Beach Gallery,** 715 NW Third St. (☎ **541/265-3292**), you'll find the nature-oriented sculptures of Lon Bruselback, as well as an interesting selection of wines for sale. A block away, you'll find natural-fiber women's fashions, with an emphasis on ethnic styles, at **Toujours,** 704 NW Beach Dr. (☎ **541/574-6404**). On this same street, you'll find several other interesting gift shops.

OTHER NEWPORT ACTIVITIES & ATTRACTIONS
If you'd like to delve into local history, stop by the **Oregon Coast History Center,** 545 SW Ninth St. (☎ **541/265-7509**), which consists of two historic buildings—the Burrows House and the Log Cabin. The Burrows House was built in 1895 as a boardinghouse and now contains exhibits of household furnishings and fashions from the Victorian era. The Log Cabin houses Siletz Indian artifacts from the area, as well as exhibits on logging, farming, and maritime history. The museum is open Tuesday through Sunday, June to September from 10am to 5pm and October to May from 11am to 4pm.

Golfers can head out to the nine-hole **Agate Beach Golf Course,** 4100 N. Coast Hwy. (☎ **541/265-7331**), north of town.

If you'd like to see this area from the air, book a scenic flight with **Central Oregon Coast Air Services,** 135 SE 84th St. (☎ **800/424-3655** or 541/867-3655), which charges $50 for a 30-minute flight for three people.

There are a couple of popular dive sites off Newport, and if you're a certified diver and are interested in checking out these sites, contact **Newport Water Sports,** South Jetty Road, Newport (☎ **541/867-3742**).

WHERE TO STAY
EXPENSIVE
Newport Belle Bed & Breakfast. P.O. Box 685, South Beach, OR 97366. ☎ **800/348-1922** or 541/867-6290. Fax 541/867-6291. www.NewportBelle.com. 5 units. $125–$145 double. Rates include full breakfast. 2-night minimum on weekends and during summer. MC, V.

This 100-foot-long modern stern-wheeler is one of the most unusual B&Bs on the Oregon coast and is docked in the Newport Marina in Yaquina Bay across from Newport's Bayfront. The guest rooms (staterooms) here are small, as you'd expect on any boat, but they all have big windows, private bathrooms, and wood floors. A parlor on the main deck provides a space for gathering to meet other guests or just enjoy the feel of being aboard an old-fashioned riverboat.

✪ Starfish Point. 140 NW 48th St., Newport, OR 97365. ☎ **541/265-3751.** Fax 541/265-3040. 6 units. $155–$180 for 2 to 6 people. Off-season rates available. 2-night minimum on weekends. AE, DISC, MC, V.

Located north of town in a grove of fir trees on the edge of a cliff, the Starfish Point condominiums are our favorite rooms in the area. Each of the six condos has two bedrooms and two baths spaced over two floors. Between the two floors you'll find a cozy sitting area in an octagonal room that's almost all windows. This room is in addition to the spacious living room with its fireplace, stereo, and VCR. The bathrooms here are extravagant affairs with two-person whirlpool tubs and skylights or big windows. A path leads down to the beach, and to the north is Yaquina Head, one of the coast's picturesque headlands. You're a ways out of town here, so you might want to cook your own meals and savor the solitude.

MODERATE

Elizabeth Street Inn. 232 SW Elizabeth St., Newport, OR 97365. ☎ **877/265-9400** or 541/265-9400. Fax 541/265-9551. 74 units. TV TEL. $89–$196 double. Rates include continental breakfast. AE, DISC, MC, V.

Located in the Nye Beach area and walking distance from Yaquina Bay State Recreation Site, this is Newport's newest beachfront hotel, and with its stone foundation wall, cedar-shingle facade, and white trim, it has a classic beachy feel. Inside, you'll find a nautical theme throughout. All the guest rooms have ocean views, balconies, and fireplaces, and some also have whirlpool tubs. The hotel is perched up on a bluff above the beach and has an indoor pool, a whirlpool spa, and a fitness room. Several restaurants are within walking distance.

Embarcadero. 1000 SE Bay Blvd., Newport, OR 97365. ☎ **800/547-4779** or 541/265-8521. www.embarcadero-resort.com. 150 units. TV TEL. Summer $70–$97 double; $99–$190 suite. Lower rates Oct–May. AE, CB, DC, DISC, MC, V.

Located on Yaquina Bay, a 10-minute walk from the touristy Bayfront area, the Embarcadero is an older condominium resort with a very Northwestern feel. The modern three-story cedar-shingle buildings angle back from the water, so everyone gets a private balcony overlooking the marina. Guest rooms feel somewhat dated, though in the larger one- and two-bedroom suites, you get lots of space plus fireplaces and kitchens. The resort is particularly popular with the boating set, who tie up at the resort's marina.

The Embarcadero dining room has a good view of the bay and serves primarily Mediterranean fare. Facilities include an indoor pool, a whirlpool, and saunas, and sportfishing charters and boat rentals are available.

✪ Nye Beach Hotel & Cafe. 219 NW Cliff St., Newport, OR 97365. ☎ **541/265-3334.** www.nyebeach.com. 18 units. $65–$145 double. AE, DISC, MC, V.

Located on the same block as the literary Sylvia Beach Hotel, the Nye Beach has adopted the visual and performing arts as its theme; and instead of having a resident cat, it has resident tropical birds. The wide-open combination lobby and dining room has a warehouselike feel, though just outside lie the beach and the roaring ocean waves. A funky urban chic pervades this hotel, appealing most to young urbanites for whom there are very few hip beach retreats on the Oregon coast. While all the guest rooms have balconies and ocean views, room decor diverges wildly from that of most oceanfront hotels in the area. Bent-willow love seats, tubular metal bed frames, old movie and theater posters, and Indonesian masks all add up to a decidedly eclectic style here. The best rooms are the oceanfront spa rooms with gas fireplaces ($105 to $145 a night). The restaurant in the lobby serves mostly snacks and simple meals.

✪ **Sylvia Beach Hotel.** 267 NW Cliff St., Newport, OR 97365. ☎ **541/265-5428.** www.sylviabeachhotel.com. 20 units. $63–$157 double. Rates include full breakfast. 2-night minimum on weekends. AE, MC, V.

This eclectic four-story cedar-shingled hotel pays homage to literature and is one of the Oregon coast's most famous lodgings. The guest rooms are named for different authors, and in each you'll find memorabilia, books, and decor that reflect their lives, times, and works. The Agatha Christie Room, the hotel's most popular, seems full of clues, while in the Edgar Allan Poe Room, a pendulum hangs over the bed and a stuffed raven sits by the window. Among the writers represented are Tennessee Williams, Colette, Hemingway, Mark Twain, Jane Austen, F. Scott Fitzgerald, Emily Dickinson, and even Dr. Seuss. If you happen to be allergic to cats, you'll want to pass on this inn since there is one in residence. The Tables of Content restaurant downstairs is a local favorite (see "Where to Dine" below). Hot wine is served in the library at 10pm each evening.

Tyee Lodge. 4925 NW Woody Way, Newport, OR 97365. ☎ **888/553-8933** or 541/ 265-8953. www.newportnet.com/tyee. 5 units. $100–$125 double. Rates include full breakfast. AE, DISC, MC, V.

Located just south of Yaquina Head, this oceanfront bed-and-breakfast sits atop a high bluff surrounded by tall trees. Guest rooms here are large and all have good ocean views, as do the living and dining rooms. Although the first floor of the inn dates back more than 50 years, the upper floor, which houses all the guest rooms, was only recently added on. A complete interior renovation has left the entire house looking very fresh and modern. In the breakfast room, you'll find a telescope for whale watching, and on cooler days, a fireplace warms the living room. A stylish Eddie Bauer look predominates.

The Vikings Cottages and Condos. 729 NW Coast St., Newport, OR 97365. ☎ **800/ 480-2477** or 541/265-2477. Fax 541/574-6202. www.vikingsoregoncoast.com. 14 cabins, 22 condo apts. TV. $65–$80 1-bedroom cabin for 2; $70–$95 2-bedroom cabin for 2; $95–$225 condo for 2. AE, DC, DISC, MC, V. Pets accepted in cottages.

Though there are more of the new condominiums here than old cabins, the cabins are still most appealing, especially if you're on a budget. Certainly not for everyone, these rustic old places are rather dark and eclectically furnished but are right on the beach and are comfortable nonetheless. Most cabins come with kitchens, which makes them an even better deal. Built in 1925 and modeled after Cape Cod cottages, the cabins are reminiscent of times gone by when families spent their annual vacation clamming, fishing, and beachcombing. The most popular accommodation here is a room called the Crow's Nest, which has a great view. The condos are clean, modern, and individually decorated, and all have kitchens.

CAMPGROUNDS

If you're looking for a place to pitch a tent or are interested in renting a yurt, try to get into **South Beach State Park** (☎ **541/867-4715**), which is located 2 miles south of Newport at the mouth of Yaquina Bay. With 244 campsites and 16 yurts, this is one of the biggest state-park campgrounds on the coast. Make reservations through **Reservations Northwest** (☎ **800/452-5687**).

WHERE TO DINE
MODERATE

April's at Nye Beach. 749 NW Third St. ☎ **541/265-6855.** Reservations recommended. Main courses $10–$18. DISC, MC, V. Tues–Thurs 11am–2pm and 5–9pm, Fri 11am–2pm and 5–10pm, Sat 5–10pm, Sun 5–9pm. Closed in Jan. MEDITERRANEAN.

Located in the historic Nye Beach neighborhood, this restaurant provides an alternative to the Tables of Content restaurant, which is across the street in the Sylvia Beach Hotel. Popular with a hip crowd and patrons of the nearby Newport Center for the Performing Arts, the restaurant dishes up good contemporary Italian fare amid artistic surroundings. The afternoon light here is fabulous, so try to schedule your dinner for sunset (and try to get a table with a view of the ocean). At lunch there's an assortment of panini (Italian sandwiches)—turkey sausage and sun-dried tomato, grilled chicken, black forest ham. There's an excellent selection of Oregon and California wines at very reasonable prices.

Canyon Way Restaurant & Bookstore. 1218 SW Canyon Way. ☎ **541/265-8319.** Reservations recommended. Main courses lunch $4.25–$11, dinner $14–$23. DISC, MC, V. Tues–Thurs 11am–3pm and 5–9pm, Fri–Sat 11am–3pm and 5:30–9:30pm (sometimes longer hrs. in summer). NORTHWEST/INTERNATIONAL.

Located just up the hill from Bay Boulevard (and off the main tourist drag), this big pink building is a combination restaurant, deli, bookstore, and gift shop and has long been a Newport favorite. With a very extensive lunch menu and some of Newport's best food at dinner, Canyon Way is a good bet throughout the day. For dinner you might start with ahi carpaccio or spicy prawns with tomato chutney and then move on to hazelnut-crusted ling cod or couscous-crusted oyster sauté. At lunch, although you'll find the likes of fish-and-chips, you'll also find Szechuan shrimp and shrimp in pesto cream sauce. If you'd rather get your food to go, there's a deli just inside the building's front door. Early dinners ($12), available between 5 and 6pm, are a good deal.

✪ Tables of Content. Sylvia Beach Hotel, 267 NW Cliff St. ☎ **541/265-5428.** Reservations required. Fixed-price 4-course dinner $17.95. AE, MC, V. Seatings Sun–Thurs 7pm, Fri–Sat 6 and 8:30pm. INTERNATIONAL.

Located downstairs in the Sylvia Beach Hotel, an homage to the literary arts, this cleverly named restaurant serves delicious and very reasonably priced four-course dinners. While on any given night you'll have limited choices, if you enjoy creative cookery and eclectic combinations, you'll likely leave your table perfectly content. Expect the likes of black-bean soup, Greek salad, scallops in saffron sauce, wild rice, fresh vegetables, a chocolate-berry trifle, and coffee or tea.

The Whale's Tale. Bay Blvd. and Fall St. ☎ **541/265-8660.** Reservations not accepted. Breakfast and lunch $5–$9.50; dinner main courses $11–$19. AE, CB, DC, DISC, MC, V. Sun–Tues and Thurs 8am–9pm, Fri–Sat 9am–10pm. Open Wed Jun–Sept. BREAKFAST/SEAFOOD.

Opened in the 1970s and still owned by its founder, the Whale's Tale is a tried-and-true place for locals who seek it out for the clam chowder and such great breakfasts as corned-beef hash or huevos rancheros. Lunch and dinner include Greek salads, catch of the day with fruit salsa, veggie lasagna, or grilled oysters. Service is friendly, whether you're a longtime customer or just visiting. On summer days, there is usually a line out the door both at lunch and at dinner.

INEXPENSIVE

Cosmos Cafe & Gallery. 740 W. Olive St. ☎ **541/265-7511.** Main courses $5–$7. DISC, MC, V. Mon–Sat 8am–8pm (Thurs until 9pm). INTERNATIONAL.

Located in the historic Nye Beach neighborhood across the street from the Newport Performing Arts Center, this combination counter-service cafe and art gallery is in a modern building that has limited ocean views both from the main dining room and from a small front porch. Sandwiches and baked goods predominate here, with pita sandwiches being especially popular. On Thursday nights, there is live music. This is also a good place to warm up with a latte after a stroll on the beach. Casual and hip.

Lighthouse Deli & Fish Company. 3650 SW Coast Hwy. ☎ **541/867-6800.** Main dishes $5–$9. DISC, MC, V. Daily 8am–8pm.

If you're looking for the best fish-and-chips on the Oregon coast, be sure to sample the offerings at this little roadside fish-and-chips stand in Newport's South Beach area (near the Oregon Coast Aquarium). You can get salmon and chips, halibut and chips, oysters and chips, shrimp and chips, or the basic house fish-and-chips, which is made with whatever fresh inexpensive fish is available that day. Okay, so the chips aren't the best, but the fish is very lightly battered, which lets its flavor shine through.

Mo's. 622 SW Bay Blvd. ☎ **541/265-2979.** Reservations not accepted. Complete dinner $7–$11. AE, DISC, MC, V. Daily 11am–9pm. SEAFOOD.

Established in 1942, Mo's has become so much of an Oregon coast institution that it has spawned not only an annex across the street but several other restaurants up and down the coast as well. Clam chowder is what made Mo's famous, and you can get it by the bowl, by the cup, or family style. Be forewarned, though: Some people think this clam chowder is the best and others think it's awful (we'd put it somewhere in between the two extremes). Basic seafood dinners are fresh, large, and inexpensive, and the seafood-salad sandwiches are whoppers. There are also such dishes as cioppino, oyster stew, and slumgullion (clam chowder with shrimp). Expect a line out the door.

✪ **Rogue Ales Public House.** 748 SW Bay Blvd. ☎ **541/265-3188.** Sandwiches $4.75–$11.50; pizzas $8–$21. AE, DC, DISC, MC, V. Daily 11am–11:30pm (beer until 2am). PUB FOOD.

This microbrewery's fresh ales, of which there can be as many as a dozen on tap at any given time, not only are delicious to drink, but also end up in a number of the pub's most popular dishes. The chili is made with amber ale. The pizza dough is made with stout. The English bangers are served with a beer mustard, and the oyster shooters come with an ale sauce. You'll find the pub downtown on the bay. There's a second Rogue brew pub across the bay near the Oregon Coast Aquarium at 2320 OSU Dr. (☎ 541/867-3660). The main pub also has some apartments that can be rented on a nightly basis (one-bedrooms are $80 and two-bedrooms are $120 for 1 night; lower rates for 3 nights or more).

SOUTH TO YACHATS

Six miles south of Newport, you'll find **Ona Beach State Park,** a sandy beach with a picnic area under the trees. Beaver Creek, a fairly large stream, flows through the park and across the beach to the ocean. Another 2 miles south will bring you to **Seal Rock State Recreation Site,** where a long wall of rock rises from the waves and sand and creates numerous tide pools and fascinating nooks and crannies to explore.

Here in the community of Seal Rock, you'll find **Triad Gallery** (☎ 541/ 563-5442), which has an eclectic array of fine arts and crafts and is the most strikingly designed art gallery on the Oregon coast.

Waldport, located at the mouth of the Alsea River 8 miles north of Yachats, is popular with anglers who head upriver to catch salmon, steelhead, and cutthroat trout. **Crabbing** and **clamming** are also good here in the Alsea Bay. To learn a little more about the area, visit the **Historic Alsea Bay Bridge Interpretive Center,** 620 NW

Spring St., Waldport, at the south end of the new Alsea Bay Bridge on U.S. 101
(☎ 541/563-2002).

A B&B WITH A VIEW
Cliff House Bed & Breakfast. 1450 Adahi Rd. (P.O. Box 436), Yaquina John Point, Waldport, OR 97394. ☎ **541/563-2506.** Fax 541/563-4393. 4 units. TV. $120–$150 double;
$245 suite. 2-night minimum on weekends, 3-night on holidays. Rates include continental
breakfast on weekdays and full breakfast on weekends. DISC, MC, V.

The setting of this B&B, perched on the edge of a cliff overlooking the mouth of the
Alsea River and 8 miles of beach, should be enough to take your breath away. The
guest rooms are beautifully decorated. Depending on which room you take, you may
find a four-poster bed; a wood stove; huge skylights; a wall of windows overlooking
the ocean; or, should you stay in the Bridal Suite, a huge bathroom with mirrored
ceiling, double whirlpool tub, and double shower. There's a hot tub and massages are
available.

8 Yachats

26 miles S of Newport, 26 miles N of Florence, 138 miles SE of Portland

Located on the north side of 800-foot-high Cape Perpetua, the village of Yachats (pronounced *Yah*-hots) is known as something of an artists' community. When you get
your first glimpse of the town's setting, you, too, will likely agree that there's more than
enough beauty here to inspire anyone to artistic pursuits. Yachats is an Alsi Indian
word meaning "dark waters at the foot of the mountains," and that sums up perfectly
the setting of this small community, one of the few on the Oregon coast that could
really be considered a village. The tiny Yachats River flows into the surf on the south
edge of town, and to the east stand steep, forested mountains. The shoreline on which
the town stands is rocky, with little coves here and there where you can find agates
among the pebbles paving the beach. Tide pools offer hours of exploring, and in
winter, storm waves create a spectacular show. Uncrowded beaches, comfortable
motels, and one of the coast's best restaurants all add up to a great spot for a quiet
getaway.

ESSENTIALS
GETTING THERE   From the north, take Ore. 34 west from Corvallis to Waldport
and then head south on U.S. 101. From the south, take Ore. 126 west from Eugene
to Florence and then head north on U.S. 101.

VISITOR INFORMATION   Contact the **Yachats Area Chamber of Commerce,**
441 U.S. 101 (P.O. Box 728), Yachats, OR 97498 (☎ **541/547-3530;**
www.yachats.org).

YACHATS AREA ACTIVITIES & ATTRACTIONS
Looming over tiny Yachats is the impressive bulk of Cape Perpetua, which, at 800 feet
high, is the highest spot on the Oregon coast. Because of the cape's rugged beauty and
diversity of natural habitats, it has been designated the ✪ **Cape Perpetua Scenic Area.**
The **Cape Perpetua Interpretive Center** (☎ **541/547-3289**) is located up a steep
road off U.S. 101 and houses displays on the natural history of the cape and the Native
Americans who harvested its bountiful seafood for thousands of years. The visitor center is
open daily from 9am to 5pm between Memorial Day and Labor Day and on weekends
from 10am to 4pm the rest of the year; admission is $3 per vehicle. Within the Scenic
Area are 18 miles of hiking trails, tide pools, ancient forests, scenic overlooks, and a

campground. During the summer, guided hikes are offered twice a day. If you're here on a clear day, be sure to drive to the top of the cape for one of the finest vistas on the coast. Waves and tides are a year-round source of fascination along these rocky shores, and Cape Perpetua's tide pools are some of the best on the coast. However, it is the more dramatic interactions of waves and rocks that attract most people to walk the oceanside trail here: At the Devil's Churn, a spouting horn caused by waves crashing into a narrow fissure in the basalt shoreline sends geyserlike plumes of water skyward, and waves boil through a narrow opening in the rocks.

Right in Yachats, **Smelt Sands State Recreation Site** has a ¾-mile trail along a rocky stretch of coastline. Along the route of the trail, there are little pocket beaches (where smelts spawn) and tide pools. At the north end of the trail, a wide, sandy beach stretches northward.

Between April and October each year, **fishing** in Yachats takes on an unusual twist. It's during these months that thousands of smelts, sardinelike fish, spawn in the waves that crash in the sandy coves just north of Yachats. The fish can be caught using a dip net, and so popular are the little fish that the town holds an annual **Smelt Fry** each year on the second Saturday in July.

Gray whales also come close to shore near Yachats. You can see them in the spring from Cape Perpetua, and throughout the summer several take up residence at the mouth of the Yachats River. South of Cape Perpetua, Neptune State Wayside at the mouth of Cummins Creek, and Strawberry Hill Wayside are other good places to spot whales, as well as sea lions, which can be seen lounging on the rocks offshore at Strawberry Hill.

A couple of historic buildings in the area are also worth a visit if you're spending any amount of time in Yachats. Built in 1927, the **Little Log Church by the Sea,** on the corner of Third and Pontiac streets, is now a museum housing displays on local history. Nine miles up Yachats River Road, you'll find a **covered bridge** that was built in 1938 and is one of the shortest covered bridges in the state.

The Yachats area has several crafts galleries, the most interesting of which is **Earthworks Gallery,** 2222 U.S. 101 N. (☎ **541/547-4300**), which is located north of town and has a strong focus on glass and ceramic art.

WHERE TO STAY

In addition to the hotels listed below, plenty of rental homes are also available in Yachats. Contact **Ocean Odyssey,** P.O. Box 491, Yachats, OR 97498 (☎ **800/800-1915** or 541/547-3637), or **Yachats Village Rentals,** 230 Aqua Vista Loop (P.O. Box 44), Yachats, OR 97498 (☎ **541/547-3501**). Rates range from around $110 to $215 per night.

The Adobe. 1555 U.S. 101 N. (P.O. Box 219), Yachats, OR 97498. ☎ **800/522-3623** or 541/547-3141. www.adoberesort.com. 104 units. TV TEL. $58–$95 double; $110–$150 suite. Lower rates off-season. AE, CB, DC, DISC, MC, V. Pets accepted ($5 per night).

This older motel has long been a favorite family vacation spot, and though the accommodations aren't as up-to-date as those at the nearby Overleaf Lodge, the setting, on a windswept stretch of rocky coastline on the edge of town, is just as spectacular. In front of the hotel at low tide there are tide pools to explore and tiny beaches where you can find agates among the pebbles. Our favorite rooms here are the fireplace rooms, which also have some of the best ocean views. Other rooms have balconies or whirlpool tubs. The least expensive rooms are those facing the hills to the east of town. There's no pool but there is a whirlpool. The Adobe dining room is a circular space with the best ocean views for miles around. The menu is primarily seafood. A separate lounge offers similar views.

✪ **Overleaf Lodge.** 2055 U.S. 101 N., Yachats, OR 97498. ☎ **800/338-0507** or 541/547-4880. Fax 541/547-4888. www.overleaflodge.com. 42 units. TV TEL. July 1–Sept 30 $110–$190 double; $225 suite. Oct 1–June 30 $85–$190 double; $225 suite. Rates include continental breakfast. DISC, MC, V.

Situated overlooking the rocky shoreline at the north end of Yachats, this small hotel is the newest lodging in the area and offers some of the most luxurious and tastefully decorated rooms on the central coast. Built in a sort of modern interpretation of the traditional Victorian beach cottage, this lodge caters primarily to couples seeking a romantic escape. Guest rooms all have ocean views, VCRs, refrigerators, and microwaves, and most have patios or balconies. However, for a truly memorable stay, book one of the Restless Waters rooms, which have whirlpool tubs overlooking the crashing waves below. If you don't want to spring for one of these rooms, you can still curl up in a sunny little window nook beside your balcony and watch the waves in relative comfort. Many rooms also have fireplaces. Throughout the hotel you'll find artwork by Oregon artists. Should you be so inclined, you can even work out in a small exercise room, and massages are available. The Overleaf also manages the adjacent Fireside Resort Motel, which is much less expensive and not nearly as elegant (though it does have the same oceanfront setting).

Shamrock Lodgettes. 105 U.S. 101 S. (P.O. Box 346), Yachats, OR 97498. ☎ **800/845-5028** or 541/547-3312. Fax 541/547-3843. 19 units (including 6 cabins). TV TEL. $71–$95 double; $95–$112 cabin for 2. AE, CB, DC, DISC, MC, V. Pets accepted in cabins only ($3).

This collection of classic log cabins at the mouth of the Yachats River bewitched us the first time we saw it. Spacious lawns and old fir trees give the rustic cabins a relaxed old-fashioned appeal that just begs you to kick back and forget your cares for the duration. Each log cabin has a tile entry, hardwood floors, a kitchenette, a stone fireplace, and a big picture window that takes in a view of either the beach or the river. Otherwise, however, these cabins are pretty basic. The motel rooms are more up-to-date and also have fireplaces and views. Some rooms also have whirlpool tubs. A health spa features an exercise room, a hot tub, and a sauna. Massages are also available at very reasonable rates.

CAMPGROUNDS
Just north of Yachats you'll find **Beachside State Park** right on U.S. 101, but it's not particularly recommendable. For exploring the rugged Cape Perpetua area, the Forest Service's **Cape Perpetua Campground,** in a wooded setting set back a little ways from the water, is your best option.

WHERE TO DINE
One of Yachats' most popular restaurants is the dining room at **The Adobe** (see "Where to Stay" above for details). For a quick sandwich, check out **Yachats Natural Foods,** 84 Beach Ave. (☎ 541/547-4065), which also happens to have a nice view. The **Yachats Crab & Chowder House,** in town at 131 U.S. 101 (☎ 541/547-4132), makes chowders you wouldn't normally expect, such as smoked salmon or Dungeness crab chowder, along with the usual New England style.

✪ **La Serre.** Second Ave. and Beach St. ☎ **541/547-3420.** Reservations highly recommended. Main courses $13.50–$24. AE, MC, V. Mon and Wed–Sun 5–9pm. Closed Jan. CONTINENTAL.

For years, La Serre has served up the best food in the area, and although the greenhouse setting is attractive, if you're like us, you'll be immediately distracted by the dessert table just inside the front door. Hanging from the ceiling are more plants and lots of old Japanese glass floats, the sort that frequently wash up on the shores of this coast. You could start your dinner with some Manhattan clam chowder, a delicious surprise here on the West Coast. The entree menu includes everything from a simple shrimp sandwich to filet mignon to fisherman's stew, a gentle tomato-flavored cioppino with so much fish, shrimp, clams, crab, and oysters in it that you don't know where to start. The desserts are as good as they look: tiramisu, berry cobbler, and a wickedly rich flourless chocolate cake.

Traveler's Cove Cafe. 373 U.S. 101. ☎ **541/547-3831.** Main courses $5–$12. MC, V. Summer daily 9am–8pm; other months Mon–Fri 11am–3pm, Sat 11am–4pm, Sun 9am–3pm. INTERNATIONAL.

For years this location has been *the* place in Yachats for breakfast, pastries, and espresso, and now with new ownership the cafe also serves light meals. The menu is an eclectic melange of flavors ranging from hot crab or shrimp on toast to black-bean and chicken chile to vegetarian quiche. The little weather-beaten shack of a place has loads of character, with an abundance of wood, a loft dining area, and an outdoor deck. If you're looking for a casual, inexpensive meal amid laid-back surroundings, this is the place.

SOUTH TO FLORENCE

More wide sandy beaches can be found south of Yachats at (in order from north to south) Stonefield Beach State Recreation Site, Muriel O. Ponsler Memorial State Scenic Viewpoint, and Carl G. Washburne Memorial State Park. The latter offers 2 miles of beach, hiking trails, and a campground.

The next park to the south, **Heceta Head Lighthouse State Scenic Viewpoint** (formerly **Devils Elbow State Park**), offers the most breathtaking setting. Situated on a small sandy cove, the park has a stream flowing across the beach and several haystack rocks just offshore. As the new park name implies, the park is also home to **Heceta Head Lighthouse,** the most photographed lighthouse on the Oregon coast. Heceta (pronounced Huh-*see*-tuh) Head is a rugged headland that's named for Spanish explorer Capt. Bruno Heceta. The old lighthouse keeper's home is now a bed-and-breakfast (see below).

Another 7 miles south is the **Darlingtonia Botanical Gardens,** a small botanical preserve protecting a bog full of *Darlingtonia californica* plants, insectivorous pitcher plants also known as cobra lilies. You'll find this interesting preserve on Mercer Lake Road.

✪ **Sea Lion Caves,** 91560 U.S. 101, 1 mile south of Heceta Head Lighthouse. ☎ **541/547-3111.** Admission $6.50 adults, $4.50 children ages 6–15. Daily from 8am in July through August, 9am other months; closes 1 hour before darkness in the cave.

At more than 300 feet long and 120 feet high, this is the largest sea cave in the United States. The cave was discovered in 1880, and since 1932 it has been one of the most popular stops along the Oregon coast. The cave and a nearby rock ledge are the only year-round mainland homes for Steller's sea lions, hundreds of which reside here throughout the year. This is the larger of the two species of sea lion that frequent this coast, and bulls can weigh almost a ton. The sea lions spend the day lounging and barking up a storm, and the bickering of the adults and antics of the pups never fail to entertain visitors. Although at any time of year you're likely to find quite a few of the sea lions in the cave, it is during the fall and winter that the majority of the sea lions move into the cave. Today, a combination of stairs, pathways, and an elevator leads down from the bluff-top gift shop to a viewpoint in the cave wall. The best time to visit is late in the afternoon, when the sun shines directly into the cave and the crowds of people are smaller.

WHERE TO STAY

✪ **Heceta Head Lightstation.** 92072 U.S. 101 S., Yachats, OR 97498. ☎ **541/ 547-3696.** www.hecetalighthouse.com. 3 units (1 with private bath). $132.50–$167 double. Rates include full breakfast. MC, V.

Thanks to its spectacular setting on a forested headland, the Heceta Head Lighthouse is the most photographed lighthouse on the Oregon coast. While you can't spend the night in the lighthouse itself, you can stay in the former lighthouse keeper's home, a white clapboard Victorian building high atop an oceanfront bluff and set behind a picket fence. Because the house is a national historic site, it has been preserved much the way it might have looked when it was still active. Breakfasts are elaborate seven-course meals that will take at least an hour, so leave plenty of time in your day's schedule. This is one of the most popular B&Bs on the coast, so you'll need to book your room 2 to 3 months in advance for a weekday stay and 5 to 6 months in advance for a weekend stay. Oh, and by the way, this old house is haunted.

Ocean Haven. 94770 U.S. 101, Florence, OR 97498. ☎ **541/547-3583.** Fax 541/ 547-3583. www.oceanhaven.com. 7 units. $40–$95 double. MC, V.

Rustic and cozy, the Ocean Haven is a great place to hole up with family or friends. Opt for either the North View or the South View room, and you'll find yourself ensconced in a room with two walls of glass overlooking the ocean. When the weather's good, you're only a short trail away from the beach and some of the best tide pools around; when it's stormy, you can retreat to your room and watch the waves through the big windows (binoculars are provided). The Shag's Nest cottage is the lodge's most popular room. This private elfin cottage, located across the grass from the main lodge and perched on the edge of the bluff, allows you to lie in bed gazing out to sea with a fire crackling in the fireplace. If you're looking for a good value and rooms that are a little bit out of the ordinary, this is the place.

Sea Quest Bed and Breakfast. 95354 U.S. 101, Yachats, OR 97498. ☎ **800/341-4878** or 541/547-3782. Fax 541/547-3719. www.seaq.com. 5 units. $145–$170 double. MC, V.

Set on a low bluff above the beach, this sprawling contemporary inn is about as luxurious a place as you'll find on the central Oregon coast. All the rooms have private entrances and whirlpool tubs, so obviously privacy and romance are high priorities here. All the rooms also have ocean views. In the second-floor great room, you'll find expansive views and a convivial atmosphere most evenings. There's also a huge deck if you want to take in the salt air. Miles of beach stretch away from the inn in both directions.

✪ **Ziggurat Bed & Breakfast.** 95330 U.S. 101 S., Yachats, OR 97498. ☎ **541/ 547-3925.** www.newportnet.com/ziggurat. 1 unit, 2 suites. $140 double. Rates include full breakfast. No credit cards. Closed Christmas.

Located 6½ miles south of Yachats on a wide, flat stretch of beach, the Ziggurat is an architectural gem on this jewel coast. The four-story pyramidal contemporary home rises beside a salmon stream on the edge of the dunes. The interior is every bit as breathtaking, with contemporary art and international artifacts on display. A maze of rooms and stairways lead to the two huge first-floor suites, the larger of which covers more than 700 square feet. In these fascinating spaces you'll find slate floors, walls of windows, spacious bathrooms, private saunas, and contemporary furnishings—in short, they're the most stunning rooms on the coast. Up at the apex of the pyramid is the third room, which has a half bath in the room plus a full bath two flights below. This room has two decks and the best views in the house. If you like contemporary styling, this will be your favorite lodging on the coast.

Campgrounds

Just south of Cape Perpetua, there are a couple of campgrounds within Siuslaw National Forest. **Tillicum Beach Campground** is right on the beach and is popular with RVs. **Rock Creek Campground** is tucked back in the woods along a pretty creek and is a good choice for tenters and anyone who dislikes crowds. The area's state park option is **Carl G. Washburne Memorial State Park,** which is one of only a few coastal state parks that do not take reservations. Campsites are across the highway from a pretty beach just north of Heceta Head.

9 Florence

50 miles S of Newport, 50 miles N of Coos Bay, 60 miles W of Eugene

Florence and its environs, which lie at the northern end of the Oregon Dunes National Recreation Area (see section 10, below), have long been a popular summer vacation spot for families. Sand dunes, beaches, the Siuslaw River, and 17 freshwater lakes combine to provide an abundance of recreational opportunities. However, with few roads providing access to the ocean's shore, this area is known more for its lakes than for its beaches. Many area lakes are ringed with summer homes, while on others you'll find state-park and national-forest campgrounds. Tops among area recreational activities are probably waterskiing, riding off-road vehicles (ORVs) through the sand dunes, and fishing. (This area is not especially popular for romantic weekend getaways.)

All this said, Florence does have quite a bit of charm. Along the town's Siuslaw River waterfront, many old wooden buildings have been restored. Today, there are interesting shops to explore and waterfront seafood restaurants in which to dine. The charming character of this neighborhood is all the more appealing when compared to the unsightly sprawl along U.S. 101.

Keep in mind, however, that the area's popularity means crowds, and in the summer months campgrounds and hotels around here stay full and traffic can be bumper to bumper through town. Luckily, with miles and miles of protected shoreline, sand dunes, and forests within the national recreation area and nearby Jessie M. Honeyman Memorial State Park, there are plenty of opportunities for escaping the crowds.

ESSENTIALS

GETTING THERE   Florence is on U.S. 101 at the junction with Ore. 126 from Eugene.

VISITOR INFORMATION   Contact the **Florence Area Chamber of Commerce,** 270 U.S. 101 (P. O. Box 26000), Florence, OR 97439 (☎ **800/524-4864** or 541/997-3128; www.florencechamber.com).

FESTIVALS   Each spring, rhododendrons blossom profusely throughout this region, and they have become so much a symbol of Florence that the town holds a **Rhododendron Festival** each year on the third weekend of May.

ENJOYING THE OUTDOORS

At the north end of the Siuslaw Estuary Scenic Drive, just past the Driftwood Shores Resort, you'll find **Heceta Beach County Park,** which provides Florence's best beach access. From here, miles of wide sand beach stretch north.

If you'd like to ride a horse along the beach, head north to **C&M Stables,** 90241 U.S. 101 N. (☎ **541/997-7540**), which is located 8 miles north of Florence and offers rides either on the beach and through the dunes or into the coast range. Shorter rides last 1½ to 2 hours, and prices range from about $30 to $40.

If you want to get on or in the water, you can rent surfboards, bodyboards, sea kayaks, canoes, and scuba-diving equipment from **Central Coast Watersports,** 1560 Second St. (☎ 800/789-DIVE or 541/997-1812), which also offers lessons.

If golf is your sport, try the 18-hole **Sandpines Golf Course,** 1201 35th St. (☎ 541/997-1940), which plays through dunes and pine forest and is one of Oregon's most popular courses. You'll pay $35 to $48 for a round. Or you can try the 18-hole **Ocean Dunes Golf Links,** 3345 Munsel Lake Rd. (☎ 800/468-4833 or 541/997-3232), which also plays through the dunes and charges $28 to $35 for 18 holes.

OTHER AREA ACTIVITIES & ATTRACTIONS

Florence's **Old Town,** on the north bank of the Siuslaw River, is one of the most charming historic districts on the Oregon coast. The restored wood and brick buildings capture the flavor of a 19th-century fishing village, and many of them now house interesting shops, galleries, and restaurants. Shops worth checking out include **bonjour!,** 1336 Bay St. (☎ 541/997-8194), featuring high-style fashions for women made from both natural and exotic fabrics, and **Grape Leaf,** 1368 Bay St. (☎ 541/997-1646), where you can pick up a bottle of Oregon wine.

South of town, the **Siuslaw Pioneer Museum,** 85294 U.S. 101 S. (☎ 541/997-7884), which looks a bit like an old bar, displays pioneer and Native American artifacts from this area. It's open Tuesday through Sunday from 10am to 4pm (closed in Dec); admission is by donation.

Pioneer days are also conjured up by the *Westward Ho!* (☎ 541/997-9691), a half-scale replica of an 1850s stern-wheeler. Regular cruises cost $12 for adults, $8 for children 4 to 12; the dinner cruise is $28 to $31. The *Westward Ho!* leaves from a dock on the Old Town waterfront and operates daily between April and October.

If you'd like to see the area's sand dunes and lakes from the air, contact **M&M Seaplane Operations,** 83595 U.S. 101 S., 4 miles south of the Florence Bridge (☎ 541/997-6567), or **Florence Aviation,** 2001 Airport Way (☎ 541/997-8069). Fares start around $40. The former company operates floatplanes that fly off of Woahink Lake.

WHERE TO STAY

Blue Heron. 6563 Ore. 126 (P.O. Box 1122), Florence, OR 97439. ☎ **541/997-4091.** www.virtualcities.com. 6 units. May 15–Sept 30 $65–$120 double. Oct 1–May 14 $55–$100 double. Rates include full breakfast. DISC, MC, V.

Located just a few minutes' drive up the Siuslaw River from Old Town Florence, this casual inn has nice views of the river. In the living room you'll find a spotting scope that lets you get close-up looks at the herons, cormorants, and bald eagles that are often seen here. The Raspberry Cream room has an unusual sunken tub, and the Heron's Nest has a river view. The best room in the house is the bridal suite, which has a river view and a double whirlpool tub. Innkeeper Maurice Souza whips up delicious multicourse breakfasts and helps guests plan their visits to the area.

Driftwood Shores Resort & Conference Center. 88416 First Ave., Florence, OR 97439. ☎ **800/422-5091** or 541/997-8263. Fax 541/997-5857. www.driftwoodshores.com. 136 units. TV TEL. $86–$130 double; $198–$261 suite. AE, CB, DC, DISC, MC, V.

Located several miles north of Florence's Old Town district, this is the only oceanfront lodging in the area. It's popular year-round, so be sure to book early. The rooms vary in size and amenities, but all have ocean views and balconies. Most also have kitchens, which makes this a great place for a family vacation (and three-bedroom suites are as large as many vacation homes). There is an indoor pool and a whirlpool, and the Surfside Restaurant and Lounge serves reasonably priced seafood and steaks with a view from every table.

The Edwin K Bed & Breakfast. 1155 Bay St. (P.O. Box 2687), Florence, OR 97439. ☎ **800/8-EDWIN-K** or 541/997-8360. Fax 541/997-1424. www.edwink.com. 6 units. May–Oct $85–$125 double. Lower rates other months. Rates include full breakfast. DISC, MC, V.

Located only 2 blocks from Old Town Florence, this vintage 1914 home is one of the most luxurious B&Bs on the coast. The four upstairs rooms are the most spacious, and two overlook the Siuslaw River, which is just across the street and has a huge sand dune rising up on its far shore. One of these two front rooms has a clawfoot tub on a raised tile platform beside the bed, while the other has a double whirlpool tub in the room. Other rooms are not quite as plushly appointed but are quite comfortable nevertheless. Decor draws on early American styles. In the living room and dining room, you'll find beautiful original paneling. Breakfasts are lavish formal affairs with fine china and crystal.

✪ **The Johnson House.** 216 Maple St. (P.O. Box 1892), Florence, OR 97439. ☎ **800/768-9488** or 541/997-8000. www.touroregon.com/thejohnsonhouse. 5 units (3 with private bath). $95–$125 double. Rates include full breakfast. DISC, MC, V.

A white house behind a white picket fence conjures up classic images of small-town America, and with Old Town's Bay Street only a block away, it's easy to maintain the image (if you can tune out the summer crowds). The Johnson House is the oldest home in Florence, and it has been completely renovated. Today, it's filled with antiques and surrounded by beautiful perennial gardens. The guest rooms are bright and cozy, and there's a comfortable parlor where guests can gather to swap stories of their day's outings. Our favorite room is the little cottage at the back of the gardens. The breakfasts are elaborate and filling.

River House Motel. 1202 Bay St., Florence, OR 97439. ☎ **541/997-3933.** 40 units. Summer $69–$120 double. Lower rates off-season. AE, DISC, MC, V.

Overlooking the Siuslaw River drawbridge and sand dunes on the far side of the river, the River House is only 1 block from the heart of Florence's Old Town district. This modern motel offers comfortable and attractive rooms, most of which have views and balconies. The largest and most expensive rooms are those with a double whirlpool tub. An indoor hot tub is also available to all guests.

CAMPGROUNDS

North of Florence are the first of this region's many campgrounds, **Sutton** and **Alder Dune,** both of which are operated by the Forest Service. These campgrounds are linked by a hiking trail through the dunes. Just outside Florence at the Siuslaw River's north jetty is the relatively quiet **Harbor Vista County Park** (☎ 541/997-5987), with nice campsites and day-use areas, an alternative to ever-crowded Honeyman State Park.

WHERE TO DINE

When you need a good cup of espresso, stop in at **Old Town Coffee Co.,** 1269 Bay St. (☎ **541/902-9336**). For great ice cream, everyone swears by **BJ's Ice Cream,** 1441 Bay St. (☎ **541/902-7828**), which makes 48 of its own flavors, many of which use old family recipes dating from 1917.

Bridgewater Seafood Restaurant. 1297 Bay St. ☎ **541/997-9405.** Reservations recommended. Main courses $7–$18. DISC, MC, V. Daily 8:30am–8:30pm (shorter hours in the off-season). AMERICAN/SEAFOOD.

Located in a restored building in Old Town, this eclectic eatery combines a Wild West storefront facade with a tropical interior complete with wicker furniture and potted plants. In the summer there's patio dining, and any time of year the lounge area is a cozy place to wait out the rain. The menu is long and includes everything from jambalaya and turkey enchiladas to pasta, burgers, and chowders.

International C-Food Market. 1498 Bay St. ☎ **541/997-7978.** Reservations recommended. Main courses $7–$20. DISC, MC, V. Daily 11am–10pm (may close earlier in seasons other than summer). SEAFOOD.

Located on a dock on the old waterfront, this restaurant also happens to be a fish processing facility, which means the seafood served here is as fresh as you'll find anywhere on the coast. The warehouselike space has loads of windows providing views of the river, and interesting undersea murals on every wall that doesn't have a window. The owners of this restaurant also have a clam processing facility, so don't pass up the teamed Manila clams. Order up a pot and be sure to ask for some "tiger's milk," a drink made from the clam broth, lemon juice, Tabasco sauce, and cracked pepper. After this, you can hardly go wrong. The crab cakes are another good bet and, together with the steamed clams, make a great meal.

Lovejoy's. Best Western Pier Point Inn, 86525 U.S. 101 S. (just south of the Florence Bridge). ☎ **541/902-0502.** Reservations recommended. Main dishes $6–$30. AE, DISC, MC, V. Daily 11am–9pm; tea daily 2–4pm. BRITISH.

Although Florence seems an unlikely location for a traditional British restaurant and tearoom, Lovejoy's is a big hit. While lunch consists primarily of fish-and-chips and other classic pub fare, dinner leans toward continental with an English bent, ranging from filet mignon stuffed with pâté and chicken Oscar to the adventurous domain of wild boar and kangaroo. (If this sounds like too much for you, you'll be happy to know that the lunch menu is served all day.) Dinners are multicourse affairs, making the prices pretty reasonable. Of course, tea, with all the traditional sandwiches, crumpets, scones, and double Devon cream, is very popular here.

Windward Inn. 3757 U.S. 101 N. ☎ **541/997-8243.** Reservations recommended. Main courses $7–$20. MC, V. Daily noon–9pm (sometimes later Fri–Sat). AMERICAN/ CONTINENTAL.

With the sophistication of an elegant historic hotel, the Windward is Florence's biggest "fine dining" restaurant, but way back in 1932 it was just a roadside diner and gas station. Today a small dining room and a few decorative antique gas pumps are all that remain of these humble beginnings. Each of the current dining rooms has a slightly different atmosphere, but in each the ambiance is generally sedate. Most everything on the menu is well prepared. The blackened Cajun oysters make a good starter, and among the entrees, good choices are the charbroiled ling cold over linguine with roasted red pepper sauce, and salmon fillet poached in Riesling, butter, and dill. In the high-ceilinged lounge you'll find a marble floor and a long bar.

10 Dune Country

Winchester Bay: 91 miles SW of Eugene, 23 miles N of Coos Bay, 25 miles S of Florence

The **Oregon Dunes National Recreation Area,** which is the largest area of sand dunes on the West Coast and includes more than 14,000 acres of dunes, stretches for more than 40 miles along the coast between Florence and Coos Bay. Within this vast area of shifting sands, there are dunes more than 500 feet tall, numerous lakes both large and small, living forests, and skeletal forests of trees that were long ago "drowned" beneath drifting sands. It is also here that you'll find the longest unbroken, publicly owned stretches of coastline on the Oregon coast.

The national recreation area is divided roughly at its midway point by the Umpqua River, on whose banks you'll find the towns of Gardiner, Reedsport, and Winchester Bay, each of which has a very distinct character. **Gardiner** was founded in 1841 when a Boston merchant's fur-trading ship wrecked near here, and it is the oldest of the three towns. An important mill town in the 19th century, Gardiner has several stately Victorian homes, as well as a huge pulp mill on the edge of town.

Reedsport is the largest of these three communities and is the site of numerous cheap motels, as well as the Umpqua Discovery Center, a museum focusing on the history and natural history of this region.

The town of **Winchester Bay** is almost at the mouth of the Umpqua River and is known for its large fleet of charter-fishing boats. The fishing boats are moored at Salmon Harbor marina, where a stroll along the docks is almost certain to turn up a boat willing to take you out fishing for salmon, bottom fish, steelhead, striper, or sturgeon.

ESSENTIALS

GETTING THERE   Gardiner, Reedsport, and Winchester Bay are all on U.S. 101 at or near the junction with Ore. 38 from Elkton, which in turn is reached from I-5 by taking either Ore. 99 from Drain or Ore. 138 from Sutherlin.

VISITOR INFORMATION   For more information on the dunes, contact the **Oregon Dunes National Recreation Area,** 855 U.S. 101, Reedsport, OR 97467 (☎ **541/271-3611**). At this address, you'll find a visitor center where you can pick up a map of the region and learn about various camping and recreational opportunities within the national recreation area. The visitor center is open daily from 8am to 4:30pm in summer, and November to May it's open Monday through Friday from 8am to 4:30pm and Saturday from 10am to 4pm.

Housed in this same building is the **Reedsport/Winchester Chamber of Commerce,** 855 U.S. 101 (P.O. Box 11), Reedsport, OR 97467 (☎ **800/247-2155** or 541/271-3495), which can provide you with more area information.

THE OREGON DUNES NATIONAL RECREATION AREA

The first Oregon dunes were formed between 12 and 26 million years ago by the weathering of inland mountain ranges. Though the dunes are in constant flux, they reached their current size and shape about 7,000 years ago after the massive eruption of the Mount Mazama volcano, which emptied out the entire molten-rock contents of the mountain, and in the process created the caldera that would become Crater Lake.

Water currents and winds are the factors responsible for the dunes. Currents move the sand particles north each winter and south each summer, while constant winds off the Pacific Ocean blow the sand eastward, piling it up into dunes that are slowly marching east. Over thousands of years, the dunes have swallowed up forests, leaving some groves of trees as remnant tree islands.

Fresh water trapped behind the dunes has formed numerous freshwater lakes, many of which are now ringed by campgrounds and vacation homes. These lakes are popular for fishing, swimming, and boating. The largest of the lakes lie outside the national recreation area and are, from north to south, Woahink Lake, Siltcoos Lake, Tahkenitch Lake, Clear Lake, Eel Lake, North Tenmile Lake, and Tenmile Lake. Smaller lakes that are within the recreation area include Cleawox Lake, Carter Lake, Beale Lake, and Horsfall Lake. Traditionally, these lakes have been in a constant state of change; however, with the construction of homes around the lakeshores, the lakes must be maintained at their current shape and size.

European beach grass is playing an even greater role in changing the natural dynamics of this region. Introduced to anchor sand dunes and prevent them from inundating roads and river channels, this plant has been much more effective than anyone ever imagined. Able to survive even when buried under several feet of sand, European beach grass has covered many acres of land and formed dunes in back of the beach. These dunes effectively block sand from blowing inland off the beach, and as winds blow sand off the dunes into wet, low-lying areas, vegetation takes hold, thus eliminating areas of former dunes. Aerial photos have shown that where once 80% of the dunes here were open sand, today only 20% are. It is predicted that within 50 years, these dunes will all have been completely covered with vegetation and will no longer be the barren, windswept expanses of sand seen today. In an attempt to restore at least a small area of the dunes, National Guard engineers bulldozed 50 acres of dunes near the Dunes Overlook in 1998 in an attempt to eliminate European beach grass from this much-visited area.

There are numerous options for exploring the dunes. ✪ **Jessie M. Honeyman Memorial State Park** (☎ 541/997-3641), 3 miles south of Florence, is a unique spot with a beautiful forest-bordered lake and towering sand dunes. The park offers camping, picnicking, hiking trails, and access to Cleawox and Woahink Lakes. On Cleawox Lake, there is a swimming area and a boat-rental facility. The dunes adjacent to Cleawox Lake are used by off-road vehicles.

The easiest place to get an overview of the dunes is at the **Dunes Overlook,** 10 miles south of Florence. Here you'll find viewing platforms high atop a forested sand dune that overlooks a vast expanse of bare sand. Another easy place from which to view the dunes is the viewing platform on the Taylor Dunes Trail, which begins at the **Carter Lake Campground,** 7½ miles south of Florence. It is an easy ½-mile walk to the viewing platform.

If you want to get your shoes full of sand and wander among these Saharan sand dunes, there are several places to try. If you have time only for a quick walk in the sand, head to **Carter Lake Campground,** where you can continue on from the Taylor Dunes viewing platform. The beach is less than a mile beyond the viewing platform, and roughly half this distance is through dunes. From this same campground, you can hike the **Carter Dunes Trail.** The beach is 1½ miles away through dunes and forest and meadows known as a deflation plain. A 3½-mile loop trail leads from the **Dunes Overlook** (see above) out to the beach by way of Tahkenitch Creek, a meandering stream that flows through the dunes and out to the ocean. Another mile south of the Dunes Overlook, you'll find the **Tahkenitch Trailhead,** which accesses an 8-mile network of little-used trails that wander through dunes, forest, marshes, and meadows. Continuing south from here, you'll find several more trails starting from the **Tahkenitch Campground.** Here, the **Dunes Trail** leads 2 miles across the dunes to the beach, while the **Threemile Lake Trail** leads 3 miles through forest to Threemile Lake (and also connects to the beach and eventually makes a loop with the Dunes Trail). However, for truly impressive dunes, the best route is the ✪ **Umpqua Dunes Trail,** which has its trailhead ½ mile south of **Eel Creek Campground,** which is 10½ miles south of Reedsport. This 2½-mile round-trip trail leads through an area of dunes 2 miles wide by 4 miles long. Don't get lost!

Bird-watchers will find several decent **birding spots** within the recreation area. Just south of Florence, the South Jetty area is a good place to spot shore birds. Other good birding areas include the Lagoon Trail at Lagoon Campground on the Siltcoos River, Eel Creek Trail at Eel Creek Campground, and Bluebill Trail at the Bluebill Campground.

About 30% of the sand dunes are open to **off-road vehicles (ORVs),** and throngs of people flock to this area to roar up and down the dunes. If you'd like to do a little off-roading, you can rent a miniature dune buggy for around $30 to $40 an hour from **Sandland Adventures,** 85366 U.S. 101 S. (☎ **541/997-8087**), 1 mile south of Florence; or **Sand Dunes Frontier & Theme Park** (☎ **541/997-3544**), which has its facilities 4 miles south of Florence. Both of these companies also offer guided tours of the dunes in a variety of vehicles from dune buggies to four-wheel-drive trucks. Both companies also have little amusement parks as well. Down at the southern end of the recreation area, you can rent vehicles or take tours from **Spinreel Dune Buggy Rentals,** 9122 Wildwood Dr. (☎ **541/759-3313**), located just off U.S. 101, 13 miles south of Reedsport; or **Pacific Coast Recreation,** 4121 U.S. 101 (☎ **541/756-7183**), located 5 miles north of North Bend. The latter company operates its tours in World War II military surplus transport vehicles. The tours cost about $12 for adults and $8 for children. Off-road vehicles rent for $30 to $35 per hour.

If you'd rather avoid the dune buggies and ORVs, stay away from the dunes between the South Jetty area (just south of Florence) and Siltcoos Lake; the area adjacent to Umpqua Lighthouse State Park just south of Winchester Bay; and the area from Spinreel Campground south to the Horsfall Dune & Beach Access Road, which is just north of the town of North Bend.

Currently there is a $3-per-car day-use fee within the recreation area. The fee covers use of all facilities and parking lots. If you just want to stop at the Dunes Overlook, there is a $1 fee.

OTHER AREA ACTIVITIES & ATTRACTIONS

In downtown Reedsport on the Umpqua River waterfront, you can visit the **Umpqua Discovery Center,** 409 Riverfront Way (☎ **541/271-4816**). This modern museum contains displays on the history and ecology of the area. It's open in summer, daily from 9am to 5pm; in winter, Wednesday through Sunday from 10am to 4pm. Admission is $3 for adults, $1.50 for children 5 to 12. Outside the discovery center, you'll find an observation tower that is sometimes a good place to do a little bird watching.

If you want to get out on the water, you can take a jet-boat tour with **Umpqua Jet Adventures,** 423 Riverfront Way (☎ **800/353-8386** or 541/271-5694), which offers 2-hour trips at $15 for adults and $8 for children ages 4 to 11.

At the ✪ **Dean Creek Elk Viewing Area,** 1 mile east of town on Ore. 38, you can spot 120 or more elk grazing on 1,000 acres of meadows that have been set aside as a preserve. During the summer months, the elk tend to stay in the forest, where it's cooler.

In Winchester Bay, you can visit the historic **Umpqua River Lighthouse.** The original lighthouse was at the mouth of the Umpqua River and was the first lighthouse on the Oregon coast. It fell into the Umpqua River in 1861 and was replaced in 1894 by the cur-

---

Iditarod in the Sand?

The area's most unusual annual event is the **Dune Musher's Mail Run,** which takes place each year in March and attracts dogsled teams from all over the United States and Canada. Teams race from Horsfall Beach near Coos Bay all the way to Florence, with miniteams of three or four dogs covering 55 miles in 3 days, and full-size teams of 5 to 12 dogs covering 72 miles in 2 days. For this race, dogsleds with fat tires (instead of skids) are used. Racers carry special commemorative envelopes that are canceled at both Horsfall Beach and Florence. For more information, contact Beverly Meyers at ☎ **541/269-1269.**

rent lighthouse. Adjacent to the lighthouse is the **Visitors Center & Museum,** 1020 Lighthouse Rd. (☎ 541/271-4631), which is housed in a former coast-guard station and contains historical exhibits and an information center. Here at the museum, you can arrange to join a tour of the lighthouse. Tours are offered in the summer from Wednesday through Sunday between 10am and 4pm and other months more irregularly.

Across the street from the lighthouse is a **whale-viewing platform** (best viewing months are Nov to June). Also nearby is the very pretty **Umpqua Lighthouse State Park,** the site of the 500-foot-tall sand dunes that are the tallest in the United States. The park offers picnicking, hiking, and camping amid forests and sand dunes.

On U.S. 101 just south of Reedsport, you'll find a Wayfinding Viewpoint, with lots of informative interpretive signs. This is also the only place between north of Florence and Port Orford where you can see the Pacific from U.S. 101.

WHERE TO STAY

You'll find numerous cheap motels in Reedsport and Winchester Bay that cater primarily to anglers and off-roading enthusiasts.

CAMPGROUNDS

You'll find 13 Forest Service campgrounds and three state park campgrounds within the Oregon Dunes National Recreation Area. **Jesse M. Honeyman Memorial State Park,** just a few miles south of Florence, is one of the most popular state parks in Oregon, and it stays full throughout the summer. With its two lakes, swimming, canoeing, sand dunes, and shady forests, it's easy to understand the park's popularity. Just south of this state park you'll find the Siltcoos Recreation Area, where **Lagoon Campground** and **Waxmyrtle Campground** are the better choices (Driftwood II Campground is an ORV staging area). Nearby, **Tyee Campground** is set on the bank of the Siltcoos River and is popular with boaters. **Carter Lake Campground,** on a popular swimming and boating lake, is another quiet choice in this area. The **Tahkenitch Campground,** however, is probably the best choice in the area. It's set in the forest on the edge of the dunes. Nearby is lakefront **Tahkenitch Landing Campground,** which is popular with anglers.

South of Reedsport and Winchester Bay, you'll find **Umpqua Lighthouse State Park,** in the forest just south of Winchester Bay, and **William M. Tugman State Park,** at the south end of Eel Lake. **Eel Creek Campground,** adjacent to the Umpqua Dunes, is a quiet choice down at this end of the national recreation area. The southern end of the Oregon Dunes NRA has been given over to dune buggies and ORVs. Campgrounds catering to off-roaders include **Spinreel, Horsfall, Horsfall Beach, Bluebill,** and Umpqua Lighthouse State Park.

For reservations at the state park campgrounds, contact **Reservations Northwest** (☎ 800/452-5687). National-forest campgrounds in the area that accept reservations are Driftwood II, Horsfall, and Wild Mare Horse Camp. For reservations, call the **National Forest Reservation Service** (☎ 800/280-2267).

WHERE TO DINE IN WINCHESTER BAY

If you're craving some smoked salmon or other type of fish, drop by **Sportsmen's Cannery & Smokehouse** (☎ 541/271-3293), on Bayfront Loop in Winchester Bay.

Bayfront Bistro. 208 Bayfront Loop, Winchester Bay. ☎ **541/271-9463.** Reservations recommended. Main courses lunch $4–$10, dinner $9–$17. AE, MC, V. Daily 11am–9pm (closes at 8pm in winter). AMERICAN.

While the menu is none too French at this cozy little place in the Salmon Harbor Marina area, the Bayfront does a respectable job of conjuring up the atmosphere of a

Parisian bistro. Whatever you order, be sure it's oysters, which come from right here in the Umpqua River. You can get them panfried, Cajun-style, on the half shell, as shooters, in burgers, or as an entree. Friday and Saturday nights are prime-rib nights, but you could still start with an oyster appetizer. There's a modest selection of Oregon wines and microbrews. On cool days, you can curl up on the couch by the fireplace before or after a meal. At lunch, simple sandwiches dominate (including those oyster burgers). The clam chowder is pretty good, too.

Cafe Français. U.S. 101, Winchester Bay. ☎ **541/271-9270.** Reservations recommended. Main courses $15–$20. MC, V. Wed–Sun 5–10pm. COUNTRY FRENCH.

A town known as one of the fishing capitals of Oregon hardly seems the place to find a country French restaurant, but there it is, right on busy U.S. 101. With flower boxes in the windows and fine linens on the tables, this place is a world away from the family restaurants that line the roads in this area (nothing here is deep-fried; amazing!). The menu consists of a handful of daily specials, which might include lingcod with capers, filet mignon flambéed with cognac, or scallops sautéed with garlic, parsley, and wine. There is a good selection of wines from Oregon, France, and California. For a starter, you can usually opt for escargot, oysters on the half shell, or stuffed mushrooms.

11 Coos Bay, North Bend & Charleston

85 miles NW of Roseburg, 48 miles S of Florence, 24 miles N of Bandon

Coos Bay, North Bend, and Charleston are together known as Oregon's bay area, and with a combined population of 35,000, this bay area is the largest urban center on the Oregon coast. Coos Bay and North Bend are the bay's commercial center and have merged into a single large town, while nearby Charleston maintains its distinct character as a small fishing port.

As the largest natural harbor between San Francisco and Puget Sound, Coos Bay has long been an important port. Logs, wood chips, and wood products are the main export, but with the controversy over raw log shipments to Japan and the continuing battle to save old-growth forests in the Northwest, Coos Bay's days as a timber-shipping port may be numbered. In response to the economic downturn of the port, the bay area is gearing up to attract both more tourists and more industry. In downtown Coos Bay, there is an attractive waterfront boardwalk, complete with historical displays, and what was once a huge lumber mill is now the site of the equally large **Mill Resort & Casino.**

Even if it isn't the most beautiful town on the Oregon coast, Coos Bay has a lot of character and also quite a few tourist amenities, including several good restaurants, moderately priced motels, and even a few B&Bs. However, what makes Coos Bay a town not to be missed is its proximity to a trio of state parks that are, in our opinion, the most beautiful on the coast.

The beauty of these parks was threatened in early 1999 by the wreck of the *New Carissa,* a wood-chip freighter that ran aground just outside Coos Bay. Repeated attempts to ignite the ship's heavy "bunker oil" fuel (to burn it off before it leaked into the water) proved unsuccessful, despite attempts to set it on fire with napalm. Eventually, the ship broke in two and the bow was towed out to sea and sunk. At press time, the stern was still stuck in the sands just offshore. More than 70,000 gallons of oil leaked from the stricken freighter and coated beaches for miles up and down the coast.

Coos Bay and North Bend are also the southern gateway to the **Oregon Dunes National Recreation Area** (see section 10 of this chapter), and from North Bend you can see the dunes on the far side of Coos Bay.

ESSENTIALS

GETTING THERE From the north, take Ore. 99 from just south of Cottage Grove. This road becomes Ore. 38. At Reedsport, head south on U.S. 101. From the south, take Ore. 42 from just south of Roseburg.

The North Bend–Coos Bay Municipal Airport is served by **Horizon Air** (☎ 800/547-9308).

VISITOR INFORMATION Contact the **Bay Area Chamber of Commerce & Visitor Bureau,** 50 E. Central Ave. (P.O. Box 210), Coos Bay, OR 97420 (☎ 800/824-8486 or 541/269-0215; www.ucinet.com/~bacc). North of the city of Coos Bay off U.S. 101, there's the **North Bend Information Center,** 1380 Sherman St., N. Bend, OR 97459 (☎ 541/756-4613; www.coos.or.us/~nbend).

GETTING AROUND If you need a taxi, contact **Coos Yellow Cab** (☎ 541/267-3111). Car rentals are available in the Coos Bay area from **Hertz** and **Enterprise Rent-a-Car.**

FESTIVALS Each year during the last 2 weeks of July, the **Oregon Coast Music Festival** (☎ 541/269-2720) brings a wealth of music to the area. Classical, jazz, bluegrass, Celtic, blues, and pop are all part of the festival, which is held in different locations around the bay area.

A TRIO OF STATE PARKS & MORE

Southwest of Coos Bay you'll find three state parks and a county park that together preserve some of the most breathtaking shoreline anywhere in the Northwest. Walkers should note that the three state parks are connected by a trail that makes an excellent day hike.

Start your exploration of this beautiful stretch of coast by heading southwest on the Cape Arago Highway. In 12 miles you'll come to ✪ **Sunset Bay State Park** (☎ 541/888-4902). This park has one of the few beaches in Oregon where the water actually gets warm enough for swimming (although folks from warm-water regions may not agree). Sunset Bay is almost completely surrounded by sandstone cliffs, and the entrance to the bay is quite narrow, which means the waters here stay fairly calm. Together these two factors allow the waters of the bay to warm up a bit more than the waters of other beaches on the coast. Picnicking and camping are available in the park, and there are lots of tide pools to explore.

Another 3 miles brings you to ✪ **Shore Acres State Park** (☎ 541/888-3732), once the estate of local shipping tycoon Louis J. Simpson, who spent years developing his gardens. His ships would bring him unusual plants from all over the world, and eventually the gardens grew to include a formal English garden and a Japanese garden with a 100-foot lily pond. The gardens and his home, which long ago was torn down, were built atop sandstone cliffs overlooking the Pacific and a tiny cove. Rock walls rise up from the water and have been sculpted by the waves into unusual shapes. During winter storms, wave watching is a popular pastime here. The water off the park is often a striking shade of blue, and **Simpson Beach,** in the little cove, just might be the prettiest beach in Oregon. A trail leads down to this beach.

✪ **Cape Arago State Park** (☎ 541/888-4902) is the third of this trio of parks. Just offshore from the rugged cape lie the rocks and small islands of Simpson Reef, which together offer sunbathing spots for hundreds of seals (including elephant seals) and sea lions. Their barking can be heard from hundreds of yards away, and though you can't get very close to the seals, with a pair of binoculars you can see them quite well. The best viewing point is at **Simpson Reef Viewpoint.** On either side of the cape are coves with

The Southern Oregon Coast

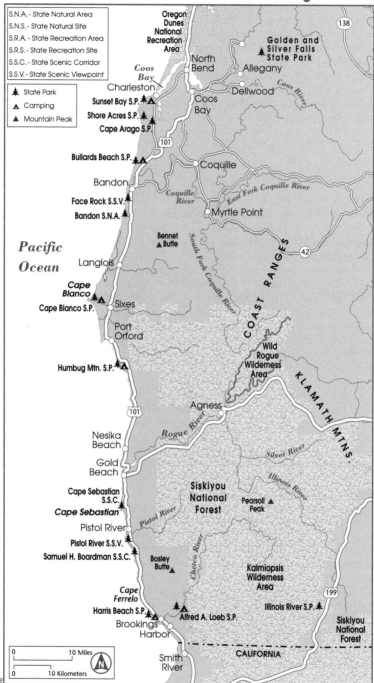

S.N.A. - State Natural Area
S.N.S. - State Natural Site
S.R.A. - State Recreation Area
S.R.S. - State Recreation Site
S.S.C. - State Scenic Corridor
S.S.V. - State Scenic Viewpoint

🌲 State Park
▲ Camping
▲ Mountain Peak

Oregon Dunes National Recreation Area

Golden and Silver Falls State Park

North Bend

Allegany

Coos Bay

Charleston

Coos Bay

Dellwood

Coos River

Sunset Bay S.P.

Shore Acres S.P.

Cape Arago S.P.

101

Bullards Beach S.P.

Coquille

Bandon

Coquille River

East Fork Coquille River

Face Rock S.S.V.

Bandon S.N.A.

Myrtle Point

42

Pacific Ocean

Bennet ▲ Butte

South Fork Coquille River

Langlois

COAST RANGES

Cape Blanco

Cape Blanco S.P.

Sixes

Port Orford

Wild Rogue Wilderness Area

KLAMATH MTNS.

Humbug Mtn. S.P.

Agness

Rogue River

Nesika Beach

Silver River

Gold Beach

Illinois River

Cape Sebastian S.S.C.

Siskiyou National Forest

Pearsoll ▲ Peak

Cape Sebastian

Pistol River

Pistol River

Pistol River S.S.V.

Samuel H. Boardman S.S.C.

Bosley Butte ▲

Chetco River

Kalmiopsis Wilderness Area

199

Cape Ferrelo

Harris Beach S.P.

Illinois River S.P.

Brookings Harbor

Alfred A. Loeb S.P.

Siskiyou National Forest

0   10 Miles

N

0   10 Kilometers

CALIFORNIA

Smith River

217

quiet beaches, although the beaches are closed from March 1 to June 30 to protect young seal pups. Tide pools along these beaches offer hours of fascination during other months.

Also in the vicinity of these three state parks, you'll find **Bastendorff Beach County Park** (☎ 541/888-5353), north of Sunset Bay at the mouth of Coos Bay, which offers a long, wide beach that's popular with surfers.

Four miles down Seven Devils Road from Charleston, you'll find the **South Slough National Estuarine Research Reserve** (☎ 541/888-5558). An interpretive center (open from 8:30am to 4:30pm, daily in summer and Mon through Fri in other months) set high above the slough provides background on the importance of estuaries. South Slough is in the process of being restored after many years of damming, diking, and reclamation of marshlands by farmers. A hiking trail leads down to the marshes, and there is good canoeing or sea kayaking in the slough. Ask at the interpretive center for information.

OTHER AREA ACTIVITIES & ATTRACTIONS

Charleston is the bay area's charter-fishing marina. If you'd like to do some sport-fishing, contact **Bob's Sport Fishing** (☎ 800/628-9633 or 541/888-4241) or **Betty Kay Charters** (☎ 800/752-6303 or 541/888-9021). Expect to pay around $55 for a 6-hour bottom-fishing trip and $150 for a 12-hour halibut-fishing trip.

Golfers can choose between the 18-hole **Kentuck Golf Club,** 675 Golf Course Lane (☎ 541/756-4464), north of North Bend off East Bay Drive, and the **Sunset Bay Golf Course,** 11001 Cape Arago Hwy. (☎ 541/888-9301), a nine-hole course near Sunset Bay State Park.

In addition to all the outdoor recreational activities around the bay area, there are also a few small museums. The **Coos Art Museum,** 235 Anderson Ave., Coos Bay (☎ 541/267-3901), is a highly regarded little museum that hosts changing exhibits in a wide variety of styles and media. It's open Tuesday through Saturday from 10am to 4pm; admission is by $2.50 donation. The **Coos County Historical Society Museum,** 1220 Sherman Ave., North Bend (☎ 541/756-6320), contains artifacts pertaining to the history of Coos County and southern coastal Oregon. Here you can also pick up copies of walking-tour brochures that will guide you to the historic buildings of both North Bend and Coos Bay. It's open Tuesday through Saturday from 10am to 4pm; admission is $2 for adults, $1 for children 5 to 12. At the **Marshfield Sun Printing Museum,** Front Street and Bayshore Drive, Coos Bay (☎ 541/269-0215), you can see a preserved 19th-century newspaper office and exhibits on printing in the region and around the country. The museum is open Tuesday through Saturday from 1 to 4pm in summer (other times by special arrangement).

At Coos Bay you enter **myrtle-wood** country. The myrtle tree grows only along a short section of coast in southern Oregon and northern California and is prized by woodworkers for its fine grain and durability. A very hard wood, it lends itself to all manner of platters, bowls, goblets, sculptures, and whatever. All along this section of coast, you'll see myrtle-wood factories and shops where you can see how the raw wood is turned into finished pieces. The **Oregon Connection,** on U.S. 101 south of Coos Bay (☎ 541/267-7804), is one of the bigger myrtle-wood factories. The **Real Oregon Gift,** 3955 U.S. 101 (☎ 541/756-2582), 5 miles north of North Bend, is another large factory and showroom. If you'd like to see some myrtle trees in their natural surroundings, visit **Golden and Silver Falls State Natural Area** (☎ 541/888-8867), which is 25 miles northeast of Coos Bay on Coos River Road (take the Allegany exit off U.S. 101). Here, in addition to seeing myrtle trees, you can hike to two 100-foot-high waterfalls.

Part of the renovation of the Coos Bay waterfront has been the construction of **The Mill Resort & Casino,** 3201 Tremont Ave., North Bend (☎ 800/953-4800 or

541/756-8800). Here you can play slot machines, blackjack, poker, and bingo. There are also several restaurants and a lounge.

WHERE TO STAY

Coos Bay Manor Bed & Breakfast Inn. 955 S. Fifth St., Coos Bay, OR 97420. ☎ **800/269-1224,** or 541/269-1224. www.virtualcities.com. 5 units (3 with private bathroom). TV TEL. $79 double with shared bath, $100 double with private bath. Rates include full breakfast. DISC, MC, V. Pets accepted ($10 per animal).

Built in the colonial style in 1912, this restored home in a quiet residential neighborhood in downtown Coos Bay is your best bet in the area if you're looking for a bed-and-breakfast. The guest rooms are large and vary from a Victorian room full of ruffles and lace to the masculine Cattle Baron's Room, which has bear and coyote rugs.

Edgewater Inn. 275 E. Johnson Ave., Coos Bay, OR 97420. ☎ **800/233-0423** or 541/267-0423. Fax 541/267-4343. www.edgewater-inns.com. 82 units. A/C TV TEL. $80–$139 double. Rates include continental breakfast. AE, DC, DISC, MC, V.

This is Coos Bay's only waterfront hotel, and though the water it fronts on is only a narrow stretch of the back bay, you can sometimes watch ships in the harbor. The guest rooms are large, and the deluxe rooms are particularly well designed and spacious, with a breakfast bar, a coffeemaker, a refrigerator, and an extra large TV. Other deluxe rooms have in-room spas. Most rooms also have balconies overlooking the water (and industrial areas). Facilities include an indoor pool, a hot tub, an exercise room, and a fishing and ship-viewing dock.

CAMPGROUNDS

About 12 miles outside Coos Bay, you'll find **Sunset Bay State Park,** which has the only beach on this coast where people actually go in the water much and is on one of the prettiest stretches of coastline in the state. However, it doesn't make a very good base for exploring due to its location well off U.S. 101. **Bastendorff Beach County Park** (☎ **541/888-5353**), north of Sunset Bay at the mouth of Coos Bay, is an alternative to the crowded, frequently full Sunset Bay State Park campground.

WHERE TO DINE

In addition to the restaurants listed below, you might want to check out **Kaffe 101,** 134 S. Broadway (☎ **541/267-4894**), which serves espresso and pastries. If you're looking for a nice bottle of wine to take back to your room, or perhaps some snacks for a picnic, drop by **Oregon Wine Cellars,** 155 S. Broadway (☎ **541/267-0300**), which stocks a wide selection of Oregon wines.

Bank Brewing Company. 201 Central Ave., Coos Bay. ☎ **541/267-0963.** Reservations not accepted. Main courses $5–$15. MC, V. Mon 4–11pm, Tues–Thurs 11:30am–11pm, Fri 11:30am–2am, Sat noon–2am, Sun noon–11pm. AMERICAN.

Housed in a 1923 bank building in downtown Coos Bay, this is the area's only brew pub and is a great place for pizza and a pint. Of the 10 brews produced here, there are usually four or so on tap at any given time. While pizza seems to be the meal of choice here, there are also a variety of sandwiches, as well as such dinners as seafood fettuccine, barbecued baby-back ribs, and vegetarian selections. Occasional live music.

Benetti's. 260 S. Broadway, Coos Bay. ☎ **541/267-6066.** Reservations for 6 or more people only. Main courses $8–$16. MC, V. Sun–Thurs 5–9pm, Fri–Sat 5–10pm. ITALIAN.

Dark and candlelit, this is the best Italian restaurant in town and usually has a line out the door at dinnertime. As soon as you step through the door, the aromas of an Italian kitchen wash over you. Straightforward southern Italian fare dominates the menu, and for those who can't decide what to order, there's a combination plate that includes spaghetti with ravioli, lasagna, and cannelloni. A downstairs dining room accommodates families.

Blue Heron Bistro. 100 Commercial Ave., Coos Bay. ☎ **541/267-3933.** Reservations recommended. Main courses $6–$15.50. AE, DISC, MC, V. July–Aug daily 11am–10pm; other months Mon–Sat 11am–9pm. INTERNATIONAL.

A casual cafe, espresso bar, deli, and international restaurant all rolled up in one—that's what you'll find at the Blue Heron, which is in the heart of downtown Coos Bay and right on U.S. 101. Add to this one of the largest assortments of imported beers on the coast, and you have the sort of place that's perfect for lunch, dinner, or just a quick bite to eat over a newspaper or magazine from the restaurant's extensive library. Blue Heron chefs cruise the world in search of tantalizing dishes, from German bratwurst (nitrite free) to chicken fajitas to blackened red snapper. If you've got some friends with you, don't miss the Greek antipasto plate.

Portside. 8001 Kingfisher Dr., Charleston. ☎ **541/888-5544.** Reservations recommended. Main courses $11–$25. AE, DC, MC, V. Daily 11:30am–11pm. SEAFOOD.

Charleston is home to Coos Bay's charter and commercial fishing fleets, so it should come as no surprise that it's also home to the area's best seafood restaurant. Under different names, this restaurant has been in business for more than 30 years and has developed quite a reputation. Check the daily fresh sheet to see what just came in on the boat. Preparations tend toward traditional continental dishes, of which the house specialty is a bouillabaisse Marseilles that's just swimming with shrimp, red snapper, lobster, crab legs, butter clams, prawns, and scallops—a seafood symphony. The restaurant overlooks the boat basin and is popular with families.

12 Bandon

24 miles S of Coos Bay, 85 miles W of Roseburg

Once known primarily as the cranberry capital of Oregon (you can see the cranberry bogs south of town along U.S. 101), Bandon is now better known as an artists' colony, and there are several art galleries downtown. It's also set on one of the most spectacular pieces of coastline in the state. Just south of town, the ✪ **beach** is littered with boulders, monoliths, and haystack rocks that seem to have been strewn by some giant hand. Sunsets are stunning—it's easy to see why artists have been drawn here.

Just north of town the Coquille River empties into the Pacific, and at the river's mouth stands a picturesque and historic lighthouse. The lighthouse was one of only a handful of Bandon buildings to survive a fire in 1936 that destroyed nearly the entire town. Even though most buildings downtown date only from the 1930s, Bandon has a quaint seaside village atmosphere.

ESSENTIALS

GETTING THERE From Roseburg, head west on Ore. 42 to Coquille, where you take Ore. 42S to Bandon, which is on U.S. 101.

VISITOR INFORMATION Contact the **Bandon Chamber of Commerce,** 300 SE Second St. (P.O. Box 1515), Bandon, OR 97411 (☎ **541/347-9616;** www.bandon.com).

FESTIVALS Bandon is the cranberry capital of Oregon, and each year in September the impending harvest is celebrated with the **Bandon Cranberry Festival.** Other festivals include the **Seafood and Wine Festival** held over Memorial Day weekend and the **Festival of Lights,** held each year during the Christmas season.

OUTDOOR ACTIVITIES

Head out of Bandon on Beach Loop Road and you'll soon see why rock watching is one of the area's most popular pastimes. Wind and waves have sculpted monoliths along the shore into contorted spires and twisted shapes. The first good place to view the rocks is at **Coquille Point,** at the end of 11th Street. From here you can see Table Rock and the Sisters. From the **Face Rock Viewpoint** you can see the area's most famous rock, which resembles a face gazing skyward. Nearby stand a dog, a cat, and kittens. An ancient Chinook tribal legend tells how a young woman, Ewauna, swam into the sea and, while gazing at the moon, was seized by a sea monster. Her dog, cat, and kittens tried to save her but to no avail, and they were all turned into stone. A trail leads down to the beach from the Viewpoint, so you can go out and explore some of the rocks that are left high and dry by low tide. South of the rocks, along a flat stretch of beach backed by sand dunes, there are several beach access areas, all of which are within **Bandon State Natural Area.**

Across the river from downtown Bandon, you'll find **Bullards Beach State Park** (☎ **541/347-2209**). Within the park are beaches, a marsh overlook, hiking and horseback-riding trails, a picnic area, a campground, and a boat ramp. Fishing, crabbing, and clamming are all very popular in the park. Also within the park, you'll find the historic **Coquille River Lighthouse,** which was built in 1896. This lighthouse is one of the only lighthouses to ever be hit by a ship—in 1903 an abandoned schooner plowed into the light. In December the lighthouse is decorated with Christmas lights. Between April and October, tours of the lighthouse are generally offered daily from 10am to 4pm.

At Bandon, as elsewhere on the Oregon coast, **gray whales** migrating between the Arctic and Baja California, Mexico, pass close to the shore and can often be spotted from land. The whales pass Bandon between December and February on their way south and between March and May on their way north. Gray days, and early mornings, before the wind picks up, is the best time to spot whales. Coquille Point, at the end of 11th Street, and the bluffs along Beach Loop Road are the best vantage points.

More than 300 species of birds have been spotted in the Bandon vicinity, making this one of the best sites in Oregon for **bird watching.** The **Oregon Islands National Wildlife Refuge,** which includes 1,400 rocks and islands off the state's coast, includes the famous monoliths of Bandon. Among the birds that nest on these rocks are rhinoceros auklets, storm petrels, gulls, and tufted puffins. These latter birds, with their large colorful beaks, are the most beloved of local birds, and their images show up on all manner of local souvenirs. The **Bandon Marsh National Wildlife Refuge,** at the mouth of the Coquille River, is another good spot for bird watching. In this area you can expect to see grebes, mergansers, buffleheads, plovers, and several birds of prey.

Anglers can head offshore for bottom fish, salmon, tuna, and halibut with **Port O' Call,** 155 First St. (☎ **541/347-2875**), which charges $50 to $150 for a fishing trip. If you're interested in exploring the Coquille River, you can rent a sea kayak from **Adventure Kayak,** on the waterfront in Bandon at 315 First St. (☎ **541/347-3480**), which also offers kayak tours and lessons. Boats rent for $20 to $30 for the first 2 hours, and tour prices range from $35 to $65. If you'd rather ride a horse down the beach, contact **Bandon Beach Riding Stables** (☎ **541/347-3423**), on Beach Loop Drive south of Face Rock. A 1-hour ride is $25.

In 1999, Bandon became a major golfing destination with the opening of the world-class ✪ **Bandon Dunes Golf Course,** Round Lake Dr. (☎ **888/345-6008** or 541/347-4380; www.bandondunesgolf.com), a classic Scottish-style links course and Oregon's only oceanfront golf course. The course has been compared to Pebble Beach and St. Andrews and is already notorious for its blustery winds. The greens fee is $100 ($50 for your second 18 holes). This is a walking course and no golf carts are allowed; but caddies are available for an additional $35 per golfer.

If that's out of your price range, there is always the **Bandon Face Rock Golf Course,** 3235 Beach Loop Dr. (☎ 541/347-3818), which offers a scenic 9 holes not far from the famous Face Rock. The greens fee is $10 for 9 holes.

OTHER AREA ACTIVITIES & ATTRACTIONS

The ✪ **West Coast Game Park,** 7 miles south of Bandon on U.S. 101 (☎ 541/347-3106), bills itself as America's largest wild-animal petting park and is a must for families. Depending on what young animals they have at the time of your visit, you might be able to play with a leopard, tiger or bear cub. It's open daily from 9am to 7pm in summer, with shorter hours other months; call for hours. Admission is $8.50 for adults, $7.50 for seniors, $6.50 for children 7 to 12, $4.50 for children 2 to 6.

Animals of a different sort are the attraction at **Free Flight Bird and Marine Mammal Rehabilitation Center,** 1185 Portland Ave. (☎ 541/347-3882), which takes in and cares for injured birds and other animals. At any given time, the center might be caring for seals, sea lions, an elk calf, a bear cub, a bald eagle, or tiny songbirds. During the summer, volunteers are on hand daily from 2 to 4pm; other months, call for an appointment.

If you're interested in local history, stop in at the **Coquille River Museum** (☎ 541/347-2164), right on U.S. 101 at the corner of Fillmore Street (1 blk. from Bandon Cheese). The museum contains Native American artifacts, historic photos (including ones of the fire that burned Bandon to the ground), displays on lifesaving, and other examples of Bandon history. During the summer, it's open Monday through Saturday from 10am to 4pm; winter hours may vary. Admission is $2. If you're a fan of old architecture, head over to the nearby town of Coquille, known for its turn-of-the-century Victorian homes.

Shopping is one of Bandon's main attractions, and in Old Town Bandon, just off U.S. 101, you'll find some interesting shops and galleries. A couple of galleries sell artworks by regional artists. One of the better ones is the **Bandon Glass Art Studio** at 240 U.S. 101 (☎ 541/347-4723), a short walk across the highway from Old Town. Here you can watch glass direct from the furnace being made into the paperweights or fluted glass bowls the gallery sells.

At the **Bandon Cheese Factory,** located right on U.S. 101 in the middle of town (☎ 800/548-8961), you can watch cheese being made, try some samples, and maybe pick up some fixings for a picnic on the beach. A few blocks away, **Cranberry Sweets,** on the corner of First Street and Chicago Avenue (☎ 541/347-9475), sells handmade candies. Some of the candies are made from cranberries, but there are also many noncranberry candies among the 200 varieties available. At **Classic Gourmet and Faber Farms,** 519 Morrison Rd. (☎ 541/347-1166), a working cranberry farm, you can see how cranberries are grown and sample a variety of products made from cranberries. If you visit in October, you'll be there for the harvest. To reach the farm, drive 1½ miles north of Florence, turn east on Morrison Road, and continue another mile.

If you haven't yet visited a myrtle-wood factory and showroom, you can visit **Zumwalt's Myrtlewood Factory** (☎ 541/347-3654), 6 miles south of Bandon on U.S. 101, or **Pacific Myrtlewood** (☎ 541/347-2200), 1 mile farther south on the same side of the road. The former shop seems to have better selection and prices.

WHERE TO STAY

✪ **Bandon Beach House.** 2866 Beach Loop Rd., Bandon, OR 97411. ☎ **541/347-1196.** Fax 541/347-1204. www.bandonbeach.com. 2 units. $160 double. Rates include full breakfast. No credit cards.

Although this modern, lodgelike oceanfront home is quite large, it has only two rooms for rent, which means that you can expect plenty of space here. The setting, atop a 50-foot-high bluff overlooking the beach, is among the most dramatic in the area, and the inn more than lives up to this sense of drama. Each guest room is huge and has a river-rock fireplace, a beautiful maple floor, and walls of windows with ocean views, and one of the rooms has its own deck. Classically elegant furnishings, including leather chairs and oriental carpets, set the tone.

✪ **Bandon Dunes.** Round Lake Dr., Bandon, OR 97411. ☎ **888/345-6008** or 541/347-4380. Fax 541/347-8161. www.bandondunesgolf.com. 68 units. A/C TV TEL. $115–$185 double; $165–$800 suite. AE, DC, DISC, MC, V.

While this is one of the most tasteful and luxurious accommodations on the Oregon coast, the emphasis is so entirely on the golf course that anyone not interested in the game will most certainly feel like an interloper. However, if golf is your game and you're here because you've heard the hype, then you'll love this place. The lodge itself sits up on the dunes and looks out over the course to the Pacific. Rooms are also available in what are called "Lily Pond Cottages," not really cottages but rather multiunit buildings arranged around a pretty little pond. These rooms don't have the golf course views, but they are very comfortable.

Dining/Diversions: The restaurant here is quite formal and classic country club fare. There's also a sports lounge.

Amenities: 18-hole golf course, pro shop, exercise room, sauna, whirlpool spa, massages available.

Best Western Inn at Face Rock Resort. 3225 Beach Loop Dr., Bandon, OR 97411. ☎ **800/638-3092** or 541/347-9441. Fax 541/347-2532. www.facerock.net. 55 units. June 15–Sept 30 $85–$185 double. Oct 1–June 14 $59–$159 double. AE, DC, DISC, MC, V.

Located about a mile south of Face Rock, this modern hotel is Bandon's original golf resort, and it is adjacent to the nine-hole Bandon Face Rock Golf Course. Guest rooms here are the best on Beach Loop Drive (aside from a few B&B rooms), and you get the added bonus of an indoor pool, a fitness room, a whirlpool spa, and a sauna. Although the hotel is across the street from the beach, many of the rooms have ocean views. There's also a full-service restaurant (with ocean views) on the premises. A short path leads down to the beach.

Lighthouse Bed and Breakfast. 650 Jetty Rd. SW (P.O. Box 24), Bandon, OR 97411. ☎ **541/347-9316.** www.moriah.com/lighthouse. 5 units. $105–$175 double. MC, V.

Located on the road that leads to the mouth of the Coquille River, this riverfront B&B has a view of the historic Bandon Lighthouse. With its weathered cedar siding, large decks, and small sunroom, this is the quintessential beach house. Guest rooms range from a small room with the private bath across the hall to a spacious room with views of the ocean and lighthouse, a wood-burning stove, and a double whirlpool tub overlooking the river. Both the beach and Old Town Bandon are within a very short walk.

Sunset Motel. 1755 Beach Loop Rd. (P.O. Box 373), Bandon, OR 97411. ☎ **800/842-2407** or 541/347-2453. Fax 541/347-3636. www.sunsetmotel.com. 71 units (including 14 cabins/condos). TV TEL. $52–$110 double; $95–$165 cabin/condo. AE, DISC, MC, V.

Nowhere in Oregon will you find a better ocean view than here at the Sunset Motel. Dozens of Bandon's famous rock spires, sea stacks, and monoliths rise from the beach or just offshore in front of the motel, making sunsets from the Sunset truly memorable. Though the rooms aren't nearly as good as the views, guests don't seem to mind the dated furnishings or paneled walls, and this place stays full all summer. You'll find everything from economy motel rooms to contemporary condos, rustic cabins, and

Stormy Weather

"And the weather at the coast this weekend will be high winds and heavy rain, as another storm front moves in off the Pacific Ocean." This sort of forecast would keep most folks cozily ensconced at home with a good book and a fire in the fireplace, but in Oregon, where storm watching has become a popular winter activity, it's the equivalent of "Surf's up!"

Throughout the winter, Oregon's rocky shores and haystack rocks feel the effects of storms that originate far to the north in cold polar waters. As these storms slam ashore, sometimes with winds topping 100 m.p.h., their huge waves smash against the rocks with breathtaking force, sending spray flying. The perfect storm-watching days are those rare clear days right after a big storm, when the waves are still big but the sky is clear. After a storm is also the best time to go beachcombing—it's your best chance to find the rare hand-blown Japanese glass fishing floats that sometimes wash ashore on the Oregon coast.

So popular is storm watching that some bed-and-breakfast inns keep lists of people who are interested in storms and will give potential guests a call when the waves reach impressive proportions.

Among the best storm-watching spots on the coast are the South Jetty at the mouth of the Columbia River in Fort Stevens State Park, Cannon Beach, Cape Meares, Depoe Bay, Cape Foulweather, Devil's Punchbowl on the Otter Crest Scenic Loop, Seal Rock, Cape Perpetua, Shore Acres State Park, Cape Arago State Park, Face Rock Viewpoint outside Bandon, and Cape Sebastian.

Among the best lodgings for storm watching are the Inn at Otter Crest north of Depoe Bay, the Channel House in Depoe Bay, the Cliff House in Waldport, the Adobe Motel Resort in Yachats, and the Sunset Motel in Bandon. The coast's best restaurants for storm watching are Tidal Raves in Depoe Bay, the dining room of the Adobe Motel Resort in Yachats, and Lord Bennett's Restaurant in Bandon.

classic cottages. If you want modern accommodations, opt for the Vern Brown addition rooms; and if you want something rustic and private, try to get one of the cottages, several of which were built back in the 1930s or 1940s. The adjacent Lord Bennet Restaurant has *the* view in Bandon. A hot tub, video rentals, and a guest laundry round out the motel's amenities.

Windermere by the Sea Motel. 3250 Beach Loop Rd., Bandon, OR 97411. ☎ **541/ 347-3710.** www.windermerebythesea.com. 24 units. TV. $64–$125 double. Lower rates off-season. AE, MC, V.

Turning into the Windermere's driveway on a gray blustery day, you can almost hear a voice calling, "Heathcliff, Heathcliff." The *Wuthering Heights* setting is a combination of moorlike surroundings and the English cottage–style architecture of this 60-year-old beach getaway. Set on the edge of a wide sand beach, the Windermere has seen better years; but for families on a budget or anyone who enjoys old-fashioned accommodations, the rooms here are quite adequate. All the rooms have oceanfront decks, and some have sleeping lofts or kitchens. Several rooms were built recently, and these are definitely the best here, though they're also the most expensive.

CAMPGROUNDS

Bullards Beach State Park, across the Coquille River from downtown Bandon, has 190 campsites and 13 yurts for rent. To make reservations, call **Reservations Northwest** (☎ 800/452-5687).

WHERE TO DINE

When it's time for espresso, stop in at **Rayjen Coffee Company,** 365 Second St. SE (☎ **541/347-1144**), in a cottage on the edge of Old Town. For a quick meal of incredibly fresh fish-and-chips, you can't beat **Bandon Fish Market,** 249 First St. (☎ **541/347-4282**), which is right on the waterfront and has a few picnic tables out front. Most Oregon towns of any size have a brew pub these days, but **Brewmaster's,** 375 Second St. (☎ **541/347-1195**) in Florence, has to be the smallest. You can't get food here, but you can down a pint or two of cranberry ale, of which there are often three types on tap.

Aside from Keefer's, all the restaurants listed below have good views of either the bay or the haystack rocks and monoliths on the beach.

Bandon Boatworks. 275 Lincoln Ave. SW. ☎ **541/347-2111.** Reservations recommended both lunch and dinner. Main courses lunch $5–$9.50, dinner $11–$30. AE, DISC, MC, V. Mon–Sat 11:30am–9pm, Sun 11am–8:30pm. SEAFOOD.

Located directly across the Coquille River from the historic Bandon Lighthouse, this large seafood restaurant has a view similar to Harp's (see below), although you'll find the menu here more traditional and the atmosphere not nearly as romantic. This said, views are great. You can watch the waves crashing on the jetties at the mouth of the river while you dine on the likes of shrimp scampi or steak and lobster. Fish-and-chips, burgers, and sandwiches predominate on the lunch menu, and they also have a seniors' menu.

✪ **Harp's On The Bay.** 480 First St. SW. ☎ **541/347-9057.** Reservations recommended. Main courses $10–$20. AE, DC, DISC, MC, V. Sun–Thurs 5–9:30pm, Fri–Sat 5–10pm. SEAFOOD/AMERICAN.

Harp's, located in a restored historic building on the Coquille River, is probably the most sophisticated and romantic restaurant in Bandon. Although casual dress is certainly acceptable (as are families with children), it's a place where people are more likely to dress for dinner. Ask for a table with a view of the Coquille Light House. There's no easy-listening music or fried food here, but there is some of the best clam chowder we've had on the Oregon coast. House-made pasta with garlic and olive oil comes with entrees such as halibut charbroiled with an unusual spicy pistachio sauce or grilled oysters. Rounding out the experience are candles on the tables, Oregon wines by the glass, and such tantalizing desserts as pumpkin cheesecake or bread pudding with bourbon sauce.

Keefer's Old Town Café. 160 Baltimore Ave. ☎ **541/347-1133.** Reservations recommended. Main courses $6.50–$16. MC, V. Daily 11am–9pm. Sunday brunch 11am–4pm. HAWAIIAN/PACIFIC RIM.

Though it looks like a well-worn natural-foods college cafe on the inside, this laid-back spot in the center of Old Town serves food that's many steps above college cuisine. Though there are no views here, the seafood dishes are a good reason to come. Many incorporate Hawaiian and Asian influences, such as grilled halibut with fruit salsa or seafood stir-fry. Breads here are delicious. Try the cheese soup with rye bread, or the roasted garlic Caesar salad.

Lord Bennett's Restaurant and Lounge. 1695 Beach Loop Dr., next to the Sunset Motel. ☎ **541/347-3663.** Reservations recommended. Main courses lunch $5–$9, dinner $11–$30. AE, DISC, MC, V. Daily 11am–3pm and 5–10pm (until 9pm in winter). AMERICAN.

Lord Bennett's is the only restaurant in Bandon overlooking the bizarre beachscape of contorted rock spires and sea stacks, and this fact alone makes it a must for a meal. This isn't as casual as the Bandon Boatworks or as attractive a setting as Harp's (see above), but the sunsets here are an absolute must. Good meals make the restaurant doubly worthwhile, and since sunsets come late in the day in the summer, you might want to eat a late lunch the day you plan to come here. We suggest starting dinner with some crab cakes before moving on to such main courses as New York steak with peppercorns or lamb chops with a hazelnut crust. There's a decent wine list, and the desserts are both beautiful and delicious.

SOUTH TO PORT ORFORD

In Langlois, north of Port Orford, you'll find **Raincoast Arts,** 48358 U.S. 101 (☎ **541/348-9992**), a gallery housed in an old wooden commercial building that features works in a wide variety of styles (woodcraft, weaving, pottery, photography) and media by local artists.

If you're interested in boardsailing, check out the **Floras Lake Windsurfing School,** at the Floras Lake House Bed & Breakfast, 92870 Boice Cope Rd. (☎ **541/ 348-2573**), which offers rentals and lessons. You'll find Floras Lake west of U.S. 101 south of the community of Langlois. Equipment is also available at **Big Air Windsurfing,** 48435 U.S. 101, Langlois (☎ **541/348-2213**). Surfers will want to check out the break at Hubbard Creek, south of town.

WHERE TO STAY

Floras Lake House Bed & Breakfast. 92870 Boice Cope Rd., Langlois, OR 97450. ☎ **541/348-2573.** Fax 541/348-9912. www.floraslake.com. 4 units. $100–$130 double. Rates include full breakfast. DISC, MC, V.

Located north of Port Orford near the community of Langlois, this contemporary B&B is close to the shore of Floras Lake, which is popular for boardsailing (the inn offers sailboard rentals and lessons). The guest rooms all have views of the lake, and the two more expensive rooms have fireplaces. Across the back of the house are several large decks that provide plenty of lounging areas.

Campgrounds

Camping is available at **Boice-Cope County Park** on Floras Lake in Langlois.

13 The Port Orford Area

27 miles S of Bandon, 79 miles N of Crescent City, 95 miles W of Grants Pass

Port Orford, today little more than a wide spot in the road, actually has an older history than any other town on the coast other than Astoria. Named by Capt. George Vancouver on April 5, 1792, this natural harbor in the lee of Port Orford Heads became the first settlement right on the Oregon coast when, in 1851, settlers and soldiers together constructed Fort Orford. A fort was necessary due to hostilities with the area's native population. Eventually the settlers fled inland, crossing the Siskiyou Mountains. Today, Port Orford's biggest claim to fame is as the westernmost incorporated town in the contiguous 48 states.

While the first settlers made camp here because there was something of a natural harbor, these days the area's fishing fleet is hauled out of the water nightly by a large crane. The fact is that this really isn't a harbor at all, but just a slightly protected cove on a very wave-swept coastline. Working out of this tiny port are a fishing fleet and sea-urchin harvesting industry. The roe of sea urchins is considered a delicacy in Japan, but American palates have yet to develop a taste for the slimy, smelly eggs.

Perhaps because of the remote location and perhaps because bad weather keeps the hordes at bay, this area has become something of a magnet for artists. You'll find several art galleries in town showcasing the works of local artists.

Nearby Cape Blanco, just north of Port Orford and discovered and named by Spanish explorer Martín de Aguilar in 1603, once made an even grander claim than Port Orford when it was heralded as the westernmost point of land in the lower 48. Today, that claim has been laid to rest by Cape Flattery, Washington, and Cape Blanco now only claims to be the westernmost point in Oregon.

ESSENTIALS

GETTING THERE   Port Orford is on U.S. 101 between Bandon and Gold Beach and has no direct connecting roads to I-5.

VISITOR INFORMATION   For more information on this area, contact the **Port Orford Chamber of Commerce** (P.O. Box 637), Battle Rock Park, U.S. 101 S., Port Orford, OR 97465 (☎ **541/332-8055;** www.portorfordoregon.com). You'll also find a wayfinding station here.

PORT ORFORD AREA ACTIVITIES & ATTRACTIONS

For a good view of Port Orford and this entire section of coast, drive up to the **Port Orford Heads Wayside,** where you'll find a short trail out to an overlook. This is the site of a former coast-guard lifesaving station, and the old buildings are in the process of being renovated and turned into an interpretive center and history museum, which should be opening in spring of 2000. The route to the wayside is well marked. Right in Port Orford, you can visit **Battle Rock Park** and learn the history of the rock refuge that rises out of Port Orford's beach. If you want to walk the beach, this is a good one, as is the beach at the end of Paradise Point Road just north of town.

Cape Blanco now lends its name to **Cape Blanco State Park** (☎ 541/332-6774), where you'll find miles of beaches and hiking trails through windswept meadows, a campground, picnic areas, and a boat ramp on the Sixes River. This high headland is also the site of the **Cape Blanco Lighthouse,** which was built in 1870 and is the oldest continuously operating lighthouse in Oregon. Not far from the lighthouse is the **Hughes House Museum,** a restored Eastlake Victorian home that was built in 1898 and is furnished with period antiques. It's open May to September only, Thursday through Saturday and Monday from 10am to 3:30pm and Sunday from noon to 3:30. In this same area north of Port Orford, you'll find the Elk River and the Sixes River, which are both well-known for their fall and winter steelhead and salmon runs.

Six miles south of Port Orford, you'll find **Humbug Mountain State Park** (☎ 541/332-6774), where Humbug Mountain rises 1,756 feet from the ocean's waves. A pretty campground is tucked into the forest at the base of the mountain, and a trail leads to the summit.

Art galleries in Port Orford include the **Cook Gallery,** 705 Oregon St. (☎ 541/332-0045), which features beautiful handcrafted wood furniture and sculptures, as well as prints and ceramics; **Port Orford Pottery Studio,** 917 U.S. 101 (☎ 541/332-0313), which specializes in unusual pottery wall sculptures made from molds of fish; and **Laughing Baskets,** 330 W. Fifth St. (☎ 541/332-4101), where the proprietor makes baskets from sea grass.

WHERE TO STAY

The Castaway. P.O. Box 844, Port Orford, OR 97465. ☎ **541/332-4502.** Fax 541/332-9303. www.castawaybythesea.com. 13 units. TV TEL. $45–$80 double. Lower rates in off-season. DISC, MC, V. Pets accepted ($5 per night and must be attended).

Located on a hill high above Port Orford harbor and commanding a sweeping panorama of the southern Oregon coast, this modest motel is far more comfortable than it appears from the outside. All the rooms take in the superlative view, and most have comfy little sunrooms from which to gaze off to sea. The rooms are also quite large and well maintained, and some have kitchenettes. Out back there is a lawn with a few benches overlooking the harbor.

Home by the Sea. 444 Jackson St. (P.O. Box 606), Port Orford, OR 97465. ☎ **541/ 332-2855.** www.homebythesea.com. 2 units. TV TEL. $95–$105 double. Rates include full breakfast. MC, V.

Set high atop a bluff overlooking the beach and Battle Rock, this contemporary B&B offers large guest rooms with some of the best views on the coast. In the downstairs living room you'll still get the same million-dollar view that's to be had from the guest rooms. The inn is a block off U.S. 101 and is within walking distance of several restaurants and art galleries. The innkeepers also offer a shuttle service for people walking sections of the Oregon Coast Trail.

Sixes River Hotel. 93316 Sixes River Rd. (P.O. Box 327), Sixes, OR 97476. ☎ **800/ 828-5161** or 541/332-3900. www.sixeshotel.com. 5 units. $85 double. Rates include full breakfast. AE, MC, V.

About 6 miles north of Port Orford, near the turnoff to Cape Blanco State Park, stands the last remaining building in Sixes, once an active logging and mining community. Built in 1895, the fully restored Sixes River Hotel is surrounded by farmland and makes a good base for exploring the coast and nearby state parks. The guest rooms are simply furnished and sport a country decor. The inn also has a small restaurant that serves reasonably priced reservation-only five-course dinners.

CAMPGROUNDS
Cape Blanco State Park is the most popular camping spot in this area, and reservations aren't accepted. There are also campsites up the Sixes River at **Edson Creek Park,** which is 4 miles off U.S. 101. Farther up this same road, you can camp at the **Sixes River Recreation Site.**

WHERE TO DINE
In addition the restaurant listed below, you can get simple vegetarian fare at **Seaweed Natural Grocery & Cafe,** 832 Oregon St. (U.S. 101) (☎ **541/332-3640**).

Spaghetti West. 236 Sixth St. (U.S. 101). ☎ **541/332-9378.** Main courses $11.50–$17. AE, MC, V. Daily 5–9pm. ITALIAN.

Located right across from the beach and Battle Rock, this fun restaurant has a playful atmosphere that includes colorful western accents and a chipboard floor. The menu features not only Italian food but also barbecue. There are also daily seafood specials that aren't always Italian in heritage (salmon in a beurre blanc sauce, for example). Pastas run the gamut, served with the likes of grilled chicken with Gorgonzola cheese or just plain spaghetti with meatballs. For dessert opt for the blueberry cobbler.

SOUTH TO GOLD BEACH
About 12 miles south of Port Orford is a place the kids aren't going to let you pass by. The **Prehistoric Gardens,** 36848 U.S. 101 S. (☎ **541/332-4463**), is a lost world of life-size dinosaur replicas. Though they aren't as realistic as those in *Jurassic Park,* they'll make the kids squeal with delight. The gardens are open in the summer daily from 8am to dusk; other months, call for hours. Admission is $6 for adults, $5 for seniors and youths 12 to 18, $4 for children 4 to 11.

14 Gold Beach

54 miles N of Crescent City, Calif.; 32 miles S of Port Orford

In California, gold prospectors of the mid–19th century had to struggle through rugged mountains in search of pay dirt, but here in Oregon they could just scoop it up off the beach. The black sands at the mouth of the Rogue River were high in gold (as were the river and other nearby streams), and it was this gold that gave the town its name. The white settlers attracted by the gold soon came in conflict with the local Rogue River (or TuTuNi) Indians. Violence erupted in 1856, but within the year the Rogue River Indian Wars had come to an end and the TuTuNis were moved to a reservation.

The TuTuNis had for centuries found the river to be a plentiful source of salmon, and when the gold played out, commercial fishermen moved in to take advantage of the large salmon runs. The efficiency of their nets and traps quickly decimated the local salmon population, and a hatchery was constructed to replenish the runs. In the 20th century, sportfishing on the Rogue River became legendary enough to attract the attention of Western author Zane Grey, whose novel *Rogue River Feud* chronicles the conflict that arose between the sportfishermen and the commercial fishermen.

Today the area is more peaceful, but it's still the Rogue River that draws visitors to Gold Beach.

ESSENTIALS

GETTING THERE   From the north, take Ore. 42 west from Roseburg to Bandon and then head south on U.S. 101. From the south, the only route to Gold Beach is from California via U.S. 101. There is also a narrow, winding road over the mountains to Gold Beach from Galice (near Grants Pass).

VISITOR INFORMATION   Contact the **Gold Beach Visitor's Center & Chamber of Commerce,** 29279 Ellensburg Ave., Suite 3, Gold Beach, OR 97444 (☎ **800/525-2334** or 541/247-7526; www.goldbeach.org).

OUTDOOR ACTIVITIES & MORE

While there is of course a beach at Gold Beach, it is surprisingly not the area's main attraction. That distinction goes to the Rogue River, which empties into the Pacific at the town of Gold Beach. This is the most famous fishing and rafting river in the state, and since 1895, mail boats have been traveling up the Rogue River from Gold Beach to deliver mail and other freight to remote homesteads. Back when this route was initiated, it took 4 days to make the 64-mile round-trip run. Today you can cover the same length of river in just 6 hours in powerful hydrojet boats; these use water jets instead of propellers and have a very shallow draft, which allows them to cross rapids and riffles only a few inches deep. Along the way you may see deer, black bear, river otters, and bald eagles. A running narration covers the river's colorful history. Three different trips are available, ranging in length from 64 to 104 miles. Two companies operate these trips. **Rogue River Mail Boat Trips** (☎ **800/458-3511** or 541/ 247-7033) leaves from a dock ¼ mile upriver from the north end of the Rogue River Bridge. **Jerry's Rogue Jets** (☎ **800/451-3645** or 541/247-4571) leaves from the Port of Gold Beach on the south side of the Rogue River Bridge. Fares range from $30 to $75 for adults and $12 to $35 for children.

An alternative to the hydrojet trips is to do a white-water rafting trip down the Rogue. These are offered May through August by **Rogue River Rafting** (☎ **800/ 525-2161** or 541/247-6022). The 4-hour float costs $75 for adults and $35 for children 4 to 11.

Fighting salmon and steelhead are what have made the Rogue River famous, and if you'd like to hire a guide to take you to the best **fishing** holes, you have plenty of options. Some guides to check out include **Rogue River Outfitters** (Denny Hughson) (☎ 888/420-6582 or 541/247-2684) and **Russell McCall Guide Service** (☎ 541/247-2061). Or call the fishing and referral line at Curry Guide Association (☎ 800/775-0886 or 541/247-3476; www.curryguides.com). A half day of fishing will cost you around $125 and a full day will cost around $150. Clamming and crabbing can also be quite productive around Gold Beach.

Whale-watching trips can be arranged through **Sea Level Tours!** (☎ 888/780-9470 or 541/247-0915). A 2-hour trip, where you might see not only gray whales but also sea lions and possibly an Orca whale, costs about $45.

Jerry's Rogue River Museum (☎ 541/247-4571), located at the Port of Gold Beach and affiliated with Jerry's Jet Boat Tours, is actually the more modern and informative of the town's two museums. It focuses on the geology and cultural and natural history of the Rogue River. It's open daily in summer from 7:30am to 9pm and other months daily from 8am to 6pm; admission is free. At the diminutive **Curry County Historical Museum,** 29410 Ellensburg Ave. (☎ 541/247-6113), you can learn more about the history of the area and see plenty of Native American and pioneer artifacts. The museum is open June to October, Tuesday through Saturday from noon to 4pm; the rest of the year, on Saturday from noon to 4pm. Admission is by donation.

Golfers can play a round at **Cedar Bend Golf Course,** 34391 Squaw Valley Rd. (☎ 541/247-6911), 12 miles north of Gold Beach off U.S. 101. If you'd like to go horseback riding, contact **Hawk's Rest Ranch** (☎ 541/247-6423) in Pistol River, 10 miles south of Gold Beach. Expect to pay between $20 and $30 for a 1- to 2-hour ride.

Hikers have an abundance of options in the area. At the **Schrader Old-Growth Trail,** 10 miles up Jerry's Flat Road/South Bank Rogue Road near the Lobster Creek Campground, you can hike through an ancient forest and see for yourself the majestic trees that so many people in the Northwest are fighting to save. In this same area, you'll also find the **Myrtle-Tree Trail.** Along this short trail, you'll find the world's largest myrtle tree, which is 88 feet tall and 42 feet in circumference. In spring, the **Lower Illinois River Trail,** 27 miles up South Bank Road and another 3¼ miles up County Road 450, is abloom with wildflowers. Backpackers can hike the **Rogue River Trail,** which is 40 miles long and parallels the river most of the way. If you don't want to carry a heavy pack, lodges along the river provide meals and accommodations. This hike is most often started at the upper end and hiked downstream. The **Oregon Coast Trail,** which extends (in short sections) from California to Washington, has several segments both north and south of Gold Beach. The most spectacular sections of this trail are south of town at Cape Sebastian and in **Samuel H. Boardman State Scenic Corridor.** For more information on hiking in the Gold Beach area, contact the Gold Beach Visitor's Center & Chamber of Commerce (see "Visitor Information," above) or the **Siskiyou National Forest,** Gold Beach Ranger District, 29279 Ellensburg Rd., Gold Beach, OR 97444 (☎ 541/247-6651). If you'd like to hike this region with a guide, contact **Rogue Quest** (☎ 888/517-1614 or 541/247-0915), which offers a variety of guided hikes ranging in price from $55 for a half day to $80 for a full day.

WHERE TO STAY

✪ **Inn at Nesika Beach.** 33026 Nesika Rd., Gold Beach, OR 97444. ☎ **541/247-6434.** www.moriah.com/nesika. 4 units. $100–$130 double. Rates include full breakfast. No credit cards.

Located 5½ miles north of Gold Beach, this modern Victorian-style inn is set on a bluff above the beach and has expansive ocean views from its many windows. All four guest rooms have whirlpool tubs and feather beds, making this one of the coziest and most romantic lodgings on the south coast. Three of the guest rooms also have gas fireplaces, and two have private decks. Needless to say, every room has a great view. Hardwood floors throughout the three-story inn provide a classic feel. Hostess Ann Aresnault provides guests with sumptuous, large breakfasts each morning.

Ireland's Rustic Lodges. 29330 Ellensburg Ave. (P.O. Box 774), Gold Beach, OR 97444. ☎ **541/247-7718.** Fax 541/247-0225. 40 units (including 9 cottages and 3 houses). TV. $50–$70 double. Lower rates off-season. MC, V.

The name sums it all up—rustic cabins set amid shady grounds that are as green as Ireland (and beautifully landscaped too). Though there are some modern motel rooms here, they just can't compare to the quaint old cabins, which have stone fireplaces, paneled walls, and unusual door handles made from twisted branches. Built in 1922, the cabins are indeed rustic and are not for those who need modern comforts. The mature gardens surrounding the cabins are beautiful any time of year but particularly in late spring.

Jot's Resort. 94360 Waterfront Loop (P.O. Box 1200), Gold Beach, OR 97444. ☎ **800/ 367-5687** or 541/247-6676. Fax 541/247-6716. www.jotsresort.com. 140 units. TV TEL. Summer $85–$95 double; $135–$295 suite/condo. Off-season $50–$75 double; $100–$250 suite/condo. AE, CB, DC, DISC, MC, V.

Stretching along the north bank of the Rogue River, Jot's has a definite fishing orientation and is very popular with families. The resort offers a wide variety of room sizes and rates, but every room has a view of the water and the Rogue River Bridge. The deluxe rooms here are the most attractively furnished, while the condos are the most spacious (some have spiral staircases that lead up to loft sleeping areas). The dining room and lounge offer reasonably priced meals. Fishing guides, deep-sea charters, boat and bicycle rentals, and jet-boat trips can all be arranged; and there are indoor and outdoor pools, a whirlpool, a sauna, and a boat dock and marina.

✪ **Tu Tu Tun Lodge.** 96550 North Bank Rogue Rd., Gold Beach, OR 97444. ☎ **800/ 864-6357** or 541/247-6664. Fax 541/247-0672. www.tututun.com. 20 units (including 2 houses). TEL. $135–$200 double; $190–$225 suite; $210–$235 house. Lower rates in winter. MC, V.

Tu Tu Tun, located 6 miles up the Rogue River from Gold Beach, is the most luxurious lodging on the south coast, and it can hold its own against any luxury lodge anywhere in the country. In fact, it has developed something of a national reputation in recent years as much for its sophisticated styling as for its idyllic setting, which together make this the quintessential Northwest luxury lodge. The main lodge building incorporates enough rock and natural wood to give it that rustic feel without sacrificing any modern comforts, and the immense fireplace in the lounge is the center of activity. On warm days, the patio overlooking the river is a great spot for relaxing and sunning, and on cold nights logs crackle in a fire pit. The guest rooms are large and beautifully furnished with slate-topped tables and tile counters. Each room has a private patio or balcony, and should you get an upstairs room, you'll have a high ceiling and an excellent river view. Some rooms also come with a fireplace or an outdoor soaking tub.

Dining/Entertainment: The dining room overlooks the river and serves four-course fixed-price dinners ($35.50) focusing on Northwest cuisine. For those heading out on the river, box lunches are available.

Amenities: Outdoor pool, four-hole pitch-and-putt golf course, horseshoe pits, games room with pool table, dock, hiking trails. Fishing guides and boat rentals can be arranged.

NEARBY FISHING LODGES

The Rogue River is one of the most famous fishing rivers in the United States and was also one of the first designated National Wild and Scenic Rivers in the country. Along the river's length are a number of rustic fishing lodges, several of which can be reached only by boat. These lodges are popular with rafting companies and fishing guides heading downstream from the Grants Pass area. Fishing lodges are, in general, rustic riverside retreats with small guest rooms and dining rooms serving fixed menus. However, in the tiny rural community of **Agness,** at the end of a 35-mile winding road from Gold Beach, you'll find several lodges that can be reached by car.

Paradise Bar Lodge. P.O. Box 456, Gold Beach, OR 97444. ☎ **800/525-2161**, 541/247-6022, or 541/247-6504. Fax 541/247-7714. 14 units. $154–$390 double. Rates include all meals. MC, V.

You can fly in, hike in, raft in, or jet-boat in, but you can't drive in; and as far as we're concerned, that's reason enough for a trip to the Paradise Bar Lodge. Located 52 miles upriver from Gold Beach and 13 miles from the nearest road access, the lodge was built in the early 1960s, but the area was first homesteaded in the early 1900s. The lodge buildings are up above the river on an open hill and command a sweeping view of the river's turbulent waters. Basic rooms and more spacious cabins, some with loft sleeping areas, are available. Though steelhead and salmon fishing and white-water rafting are the main topics of discussion here, hiking trails lead along the banks of the river and up to the top of nearby Deak's Peak.

Santa Anita Lodge. 36975 Agness-Illahe Rd., Agness, OR 97406. ☎ **541/247-6884.** 8 units, 3 with bath. $200 double. Rates include all meals. AE, MC, V.

Built in the 1930s, the Santa Anita Lodge captures the essence of the Rogue River experience in its classic fishing-lodge decor. Though the exterior is unremarkable, step through the door and you'll enter a different world—massive timbers, wood stoves and stone fireplaces, and a trophy room filled with the mounted heads of the original owner's big-game hunting expeditions around the world. A huge deck overlooks the river and a meadow where elk and bear are often seen. Deer and wild turkeys are regular visitors to the lodge grounds, and best of all, the fishing is great right in front of the lodge. The three guest rooms with private baths also have walls of glass and wood stoves in the rooms. Even if you aren't into fishing, these rooms would be ideal for a quiet getaway.

CAMPGROUNDS

Up the Rogue River between Gold Beach and Agness, you'll find two campgrounds: **Lobster Creek** and **Quosatana.** A third, **Illahee,** is another 6 miles past Agness, though not on the river. At Foster Bar, above Agness, there is an unofficial campground right on the river.

WHERE TO DINE

The best meals in Gold Beach are served in the dining room at **Tu Tu Tun Lodge** (see "Where to Stay," above for details). If you're looking for a good cup of espresso, drop by the **One Horse Coffee Co.,** 29964 Ellensburg Ave. (☎ **541/247-2760**), at the north end of town on U.S. 101. For a town this size, dining options are pretty slim.

Grant's Pancake & Omelette House. 94682 Jerry's Flat Rd. (½ mile east off U.S. 101). ☎ **541/247-7208.** Breakfast and lunch $3–$8.50. DISC, MC, V. Daily 5:30am–2pm. AMERICAN

While you can get burgers and sandwiches here at lunch, this is really a breakfast place. In fact, it's the most popular breakfast joint for miles around, and you're likely to find a line out the door on any summer morning. Boysenberry waffles, corned beef hash, and smoked pork chops are the sort of hearty fare that pulls the masses in.

Nor'wester Seafood. Port of Gold Beach. ☎ **541/247-2333.** Reservations for 5 or more people only. Main courses $14–$40. AE, MC, V. Daily 5–9pm. SEAFOOD/STEAK.

Large portions of simply prepared fresh seafood are the mainstay of the menu at this dockside restaurant where you can watch fishing boats in the mouth of the Rogue River. Fish-and-chips are good, and the steak-and-seafood combinations are popular choices for big appetites; but we prefer such dishes as pasta and shrimp tapenade or scallops and prawns sautéed in garlic. Most entrees are around $18.

SOUTH TO BROOKINGS

Gold Beach itself is a wide sandy beach, but just a few miles to the south, the mountains once again march into the sea, creating what many say is the single most spectacular section of coastline in Oregon. Though it's only 34 miles from Gold Beach to the town of **Brookings,** you can easily spend the whole day making the trip. Along the way are numerous viewpoints, picnic areas, hiking trails, and beaches.

The first place you'll come to is **Turtle Rock Wayside,** just south of Gold Beach. Although this is little more than a roadside pull-off, it does have a nice view. The next place to stop is at **Cape Sebastian,** 5 miles south of Gold Beach. This headland was named by a Spanish explorer in 1603 and towers 700 feet above the ocean. Between December and March, this is a good vantage point for whale watching. A 2-mile trail leads down to the water. In another 2 miles you come to ☼ **Meyers Creek,** which is in Pistol River State Scenic Viewpoint. Here you can get a closer look at some of the rugged monolithic rock formations scattered on the beach that make this coastline so breathtaking. This is the most popular boardsailing and surfing beach on the south coast and is also a good clamming beach.

About 2 miles farther south, you'll come to the sand dunes at the mouth of Pistol River. This was the site of a battle during the Rogue River Indian Wars of 1856. In another 6 miles, you come to the **Arch Rock Viewpoint,** a picnic area with a stunning view of an offshore monolith that has been carved into an arch by the action of the waves. Two miles beyond this, you come to the **Natural Bridge Viewpoint.** These two arches were formed when a sea cave collapsed. In 2 more miles you cross the **Thomas Creek Bridge,** which at 345 feet high is the highest bridge in Oregon. In a little more than a mile, you come to **Whalehead Beach Viewpoint,** where a pyramidal rock just offshore bears a striking resemblance to a spy-hopping whale. There's a better view of Whalehead Rock half a mile south.

In another 1½ miles you'll come to **House Rock Viewpoint,** which offers sweeping vistas to the north and south. At **Cape Ferrelo Viewpoint** and **Lone Ranch Viewpoint** just to the south, you'll find a grassy headland. Just south of here, watch for the **Rainbow Rock Viewpoint,** which has a panorama of a stretch of beach strewn with large boulders. Three more miles brings you to **Harris Beach State Park** (☎ 541/469-2021), the last stop along this coast. Here you'll find picnicking and camping and a good view of **Goat Island,** which is the Oregon coast's largest island.

15 Brookings-Harbor & the Oregon Banana Belt

26 miles N of Crescent City, 35 miles S of Gold Beach

Brookings and Harbor together compose the southernmost community on the Oregon coast. Because of the warm year-round temperatures, this region is known as the Oregon Banana Belt, and you'll see palm trees and other cold-sensitive plants thriving in gardens around town. Farms south of town specialize in growing Easter lilies and grow nearly all the Easter lilies sold in the United States. Other plants that thrive in this climate include coast redwoods, Oregon myrtles, and wild azaleas.

Dividing the sister towns of Brookings and Harbor is the Chetco River, one of the purest and most beautiful rivers in the state. It's best known for its fishing, but it also offers lots of great swimming holes.

ESSENTIALS

GETTING THERE   From the north, take Ore. 42 west from Roseburg to Bandon and then head south on U.S. 101. From the south, the only route to Brookings is from California via U.S. 101. There is also a narrow, winding road over the mountains to Gold Beach from Galice (near Grants Pass).

VISITOR INFORMATION   For more information on this area, contact the **Brookings-Harbor Chamber of Commerce,** 16330 Lower Harbor Rd. (P.O. Box 940), Brookings, OR 97415 (☎ **800/535-9469** or 541/469-3181).

FESTIVALS   The Brookings area is home to a native azalea that is celebrated each Memorial Day weekend with an **Azalea Festival.**

EXPLORING THE OREGON BANANA BELT

The Chetco River is known throughout Oregon as one of the best salmon and steelhead rivers in the state. It is also one of the prettiest rivers and offers opportunities for swimming, rafting, and canoeing. One interesting way to experience the Chetco River is on a combination backpacking and paddling trip with **Wilderness Canyon Adventures** (☎ **888/517-1613** or 541/247-6924; www.wilderness-canyon-ex.com), which offers several different types of trips from a day of paddling to multiday paddling/hiking trips. Rates for a 1-day paddling trip range from $70 to $80. For information on hiking in the area, which includes the high country of the Kalmiopsis Wilderness, contact the **Chetco Ranger District,** 555 Fifth St., Brookings, OR 97415 (☎ **541/469-2196**).

If you want to head out to sea to do your fishing, contact **Tidewind Sportfishing** (☎ **800/799-0337** or 541/469-0337), which operates out of Harbor and offers both salmon and bottom-fishing trips for $60 per person, as well as whale-watching excursions ($25 per person).

The area's botanical attractions are one of the most interesting reasons to pay a visit to the Brookings area. Not far from town, you can see old-growth myrtle trees (from which the ubiquitous myrtle wood souvenirs of the south coast are made) at **Alfred A. Loeb State Park,** which is 8 miles up the Chetco River from Brookings on North Bank Road. Myrtle (*Umbellularia californica*) occurs naturally only along the southern Oregon and Northern California coasts. The Brookings area is the northernmost range of the giant coast redwoods (*Sequoia sempervirens*), and just beyond Loeb State Park, you'll come to one of the largest stands of coast redwoods in Oregon. Here, the 1.2-mile **Redwood Nature Trail** loops past numerous big trees. This nature trail is connected to Loeb State Park via the ¾-mile Riverview Trail. The region's wild azaleas, celebrated each year over Memorial Day weekend, come into bloom in May. The best place to see them is at **Azalea Park** near the south end of Brookings.

To learn about the history of the area, drop by the **Chetco Valley Historical Museum,** 15461 U.S. 101 S. (☎ **541/469-6651**), which is located south of town just off the highway. The museum is in the oldest standing house in the area (built in 1857), and out front is the nation's largest Monterey cypress tree. The museum is open Wednesday through Friday from noon to 5pm, and admission is by donation.

One of the more unusual places to visit in the area is the **Brandy Peak Distillery,** Tetley Road (☎ **541/469-0194**), which is located north of Brookings off U.S. 101 (take Carpenterville Rd. for several miles up into the hills and then go right on Tetley Rd. and immediately right into the distillery). This microdistillery produces varietal marc brandies (unaged brandies), as well as barrel-aged brandies, grappas, and pear brandy. All are produced in small wood-fired pot stills. The distillery is open for tours and tastings Tuesday through Saturday from 1 to 5pm between March and November and from 10am to 6pm in December. Closed January and February. If you want to be absolutely sure you'll find someone in, call before you come.

An abundance of flowers and herbs grows at **Flora Pacifica,** 15447 Ocean View Dr. (☎ **800/877-9741** or 541/469-9741), a farm that specializes in dried flowers such as hydrangeas and artemesias. Flowers and herbs alike come together here in potpourris, dried bouquets, and wreaths. The shop is open Tuesday through Sunday from 10am to 5pm.

WHERE TO STAY

Best Western Beachfront Inn. 16008 Boat Basin Rd. (P.O. Box 2729), Harbor, OR 97415. ☎ **800/468-4081** or 541/469-7779. Fax 541/469-0283. 102 units. TV TEL. $79–$125 double. AE, CB, DC, DISC, MC, V. Pets accepted.

Located on the edge of the modern marina in Brooking's sister town of Harbor (on the south side of the Chetco River), the Beachfront Inn is the only oceanfront accommodation in this area. Most rooms are fairly large and all have ocean views, balconies, microwaves, and refrigerators. The more expensive rooms also have whirlpool tubs with picture windows over them. There are an outdoor pool and a whirlpool.

✪ **Chetco River Inn.** 21202 High Prairie Rd., Brookings, OR 97415. ☎ **541/670-1645** or 800/327-2688 (leave message). www.chetcoriverinn.com. 7 units (including 1 cottage). $115–$135 double. Rates include full breakfast. MC, V.

Set on 35 very secluded acres on the banks of the Chetco River, this contemporary B&B caters to nature lovers and anglers and makes a great weekend retreat for anyone looking to get away from it all. However, in order to get away, you'll first have to find the lodge, which is 17 miles from town up North Bank Road (the last bit on gravel). The lodge makes use of alternative energies yet is luxurious and filled with antiques. The Siskiyou National Forest surrounds the lodge property, and hiking, swimming (lots of great swimming holes right on the property), and stargazing are popular pastimes here. If you don't feel like leaving the woods, you can arrange to have dinner here at the lodge ($25 per person), but bring your own wine.

South Coast Inn Bed & Breakfast. 516 Redwood St., Brookings, OR 97415. ☎ **800/ 525-9273** or 541/469-5557. Fax 541/469-6615. 5 units (including 1 cottage). TV $84–$94 double. Rates include full breakfast. AE, DISC, MC, V.

This 1917 Craftsman bungalow was designed by the famous San Francisco architect Bernard Maybeck and is filled with the sort of beautiful architectural details that characterized the arts-and-crafts movement. Two of the guest rooms have good views, and the cottage, across the garden from the main house, offers a more private setting. The inn's newest room—also its most spacious—is dedicated to Bernard Maybeck. Guests have use of a large living room full of antiques (including an old grand piano), where a fire often crackles in the stone fireplace, although the weather here never gets really cold. There is also a sauna and whirlpool.

CAMPGROUNDS

The best base for exploring the scenic wonders of **Samuel H. Boardman State Scenic Corridor** is **Harris Beach State Park,** which is on the beach just north of Brookings. Up the North Bank Chetco River Road out of Brookings, you'll find **Loeb State Park,** which is set amid redwood and myrtle trees along the banks of the beautiful Chetco River. A bit farther up the Chetco is the Forest Service's **Little Redwood Campground,** which is the site of a very popular swimming hole. South of Brookings up the Winchuck River, you'll find the Forest Service's **Winchuck Campground.**

WHERE TO DINE

For a quick lunch, **Pasta Pasta,** 1025 U.S. 101 (☎ **541/469-9229**), serves up your choice of pasta and sauce or Italian-style sandwiches. If it's pizza you're craving, **Wild River Pizza Company,** 16279 U.S. 101 S., just south of Brookings (☎ **541/ 469-7454**), turns out a crispy one, accompanied by their own microbrews. For smoked salmon, head south of town to **The Great American Smokehouse & Seafood Co.,** 15657 U.S. 101 S. (☎ **541/469-6903**), which sells a wide variety of smoked and canned seafood and also has a sit-down restaurant. Locals swear by **The Hungry Clam,** at the Port of Brookings-Harbor (☎ **541/469-2526**), for fish-and-chips. To finish off your meal, the nearby **Slugs n' Stones n' Ice Cream Cones** (at the Port of Brookings-Harbor) sells locally made Umpqua ice cream.

Chive's. 1025 Chetco Ave. ☎ **541/469-4121.** Reservations recommended. Main courses $13–$20. MC, V. Feb–Dec Wed–Sun 5–9pm. NORTHWEST.

If you've just reached Oregon from California and are looking for your first bite of Northwest cuisine, this gem of a restaurant is a great place to stop. Leaded glass and art by local artists on the walls make this place somewhat upscale for Brookings, but you can still show up in jeans and T-shirts to try the likes of a salad with pear, endive, and watercress dressed with goat cheese and walnuts; roast breast of pheasant with soft polenta, creamed demi-glace, and sweet peas; or crisp salmon cakes with lemon-caper beurre blanc. Dishes are all artistically presented, and there are always interesting daily specials. Dessert is a high point of a meal here in more ways than one; such dishes as a sabayon (zabaglione) with marsala wine or a bread pudding with a Jack Daniels sauce shouldn't be served to minors. There's also a good selection of reasonably priced wines.

The Columbia Gorge

7

The Columbia Gorge begins just east of Portland, separating Oregon from Washington and stretching nearly 70 miles eastward to the town of The Dalles. It is to Oregon what the Yosemite Valley is to California, a dramatic landscape of mountains, cliffs, and waterfalls. But unlike the Yosemite Valley, massive floods, not glaciers, created the Columbia Gorge, with the mile-wide Columbia River that flows through it. Flanked by national forests on both the Oregon and the Washington sides, the Gorge has several towns, a population of several thousand, an interstate highway, a historic highway, and a railroad.

The Columbia River is older than the hills. It's older than the mountains too, and this explains why the waters flow not from the mountains but through them. Though the river's geologic history dates back 40 million years or so, it was a series of recent events, geologically speaking, that gave the Columbia Gorge its very distinctive appearance. About 15,000 years ago, toward the end of the last Ice Age, huge dams of ice far upstream burst and sent floodwaters racing down the Columbia. As the floodwaters swept through the Columbia Gorge, they were as much as 1,200 feet high. Ice and rock carried by the floodwaters helped the river to scour out the sides of the once gently sloping gorge, leaving behind the steep-walled gorge that we know today. The waterfalls that elicit so many oohs and aahs are the most dramatic evidence of these great floods. As early as 1915, a scenic highway was built through the Gorge, and in 1986 much of the area was designated the Columbia Gorge National Scenic Area to preserve its spectacular and unique natural beauty.

The vast gorge that the Columbia River has formed as it slices through the mountains is a giant bridge between the rain-soaked forests west of the Cascades and the desert-dry sagebrush scrublands of central Oregon. This change in climate is caused by moist air condensing into snow and rain as it passes over the crest of the Cascades. Most of the air's moisture falls on the western slopes, so the eastern slopes and the land stretching for hundreds of miles beyond lie in a rain shadow. Perhaps nowhere else on earth can you so easily witness this rain-shadow effect. It's so pronounced that as you come around a bend on I-84 just east of Hood River, you can see dry grasslands to the east and dense forests of Douglas fir over your shoulder to the west. In between the two extremes lies a community of plants that's unique to the Columbia Gorge. Springtime in the Gorge means colorful displays of wildflowers, many of which are endemic to the area.

The Columbia River is second only to the Mississippi in the volume of water it carries to the sea, but more than just water flows through the Columbia Gorge. As the only break over the entire length of the Cascade Range, the Gorge acts as a massive natural wind tunnel. During the summer, the sun bakes the lands east of the Cascades, causing the air to rise. Cool air from the west side then rushes up the river, whipping through Hood River with near gale force at times. These winds, blowing against the downriver flow of water, set up ideal conditions for boardsailing on the Columbia. The reliability of the winds, and the waves they kick up, has turned Hood River, once an ailing lumber town, into the Aspen of boardsailing.

For centuries the Columbia River has been an important route between the maritime Northwest and the dry interior. Lewis and Clark canoed down the river in 1805, and pioneers followed the Oregon Trail to its shores at The Dalles. It was here at The Dalles that many pioneers transferred their wagons to boats for the dangerous journey downriver to Oregon City. The set of rapids known as The Dalles and the waterfalls of the Cascades were the two most dangerous sections of the Columbia Gorge, so towns arose at these two points to transport goods and people around the treacherous waters. Locks and a canal helped circumvent the two sections of white water, but today the rapids of the Columbia lie flooded beneath the waters behind the Bonneville and The Dalles Dams. The ease of navigating the river today has dimmed the importance of the Cascade Locks and The Dalles, two river towns steeped in the history of the Gorge.

1 The Columbia Gorge National Scenic Area

Columbia Gorge: begins 18 miles E of Portland

Stretching from the Sandy River in the west to the Deschutes River in the east, the Columbia Gorge National Scenic Area is one of the most breathtakingly dramatic pieces of scenery in the United States. Carved by floods of unimaginable proportions and power, this miles-wide canyon is flanked on the north by Mount Adams and on the south by Mount Hood, both of which rise more than 11,000 feet high. With its basalt cliffs painted with colorful lichens, diaphanous waterfalls, and dark forests of Douglas firs rising above the Columbia River, the Gorge is a year-round recreational area where hiking trails lead to hidden waterfalls and mountain-top panoramas, mountain-bike trails meander through the forest, and boardsailors race across wind-whipped waters.

The Columbia Gorge National Scenic Area is also as controversial as it is beautiful. Over the years since this area received this federal designation, the fights over the use of private land within the Gorge have been constant. The pressure to develop this scenic marvel of the Northwest has been unrelenting, as land owners throughout the Gorge have fought against restrictions on development. To find out more about protecting the Gorge, contact the **Friends of the Columbia Gorge** (☎ **503/241-3762**), which, each spring, offers numerous guided wildflower hikes.

ESSENTIALS

GETTING THERE   I-84 and the Historic Columbia River Highway both pass through the Gorge on the Oregon side of the Columbia.

VISITOR INFORMATION   Contact the **Columbia River Gorge National Scenic Area,** 902 Wasco Ave., Suite 200, Hood River, OR 97031 (☎ **541/386-2333;** www.fs.fed.us/r6/columbia). There's also a **Forest Service Information Center** (☎ **509/427-2528**) in the lobby of the Skamania Lodge, 1141 Skamania Lodge Dr., in Stevenson, Washington.

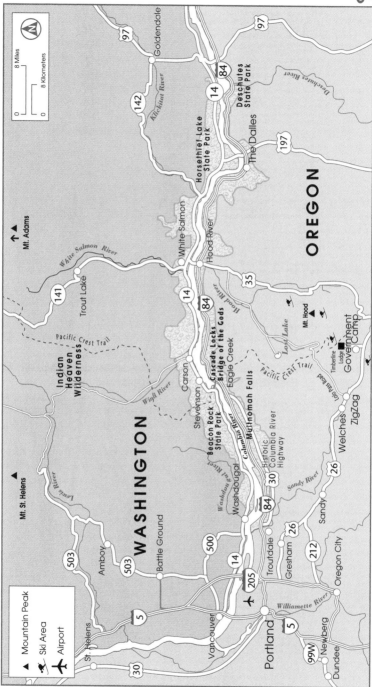

LEARNING ABOUT THE GORGE & ITS HISTORY

✪ **Columbia Gorge Interpretive Center.** 990 SW Rock Creek Dr., Stevenson. ☎ **509/427-8211.** Admission $6 adults, $5 seniors and students, $4 children 6–12, free for children 5 and under. Daily 10am–5pm. Closed Easter, Thanksgiving, Christmas, and New Year's.

This museum on the Washington side of the Gorge is your best introduction to it; the museum focuses on early Native American inhabitants and the development of the area by white settlers. Exhibits contain historical photographs by Edward Curtis and other photos that illustrate the story of portage companies and paddle wheelers. Period quotations and explanations of Gorge history put the museum's many artifacts in their proper context. A relic you can't miss is a 37-foot-high replica of a 19th-century fish wheel, which gives an understanding of how salmon runs have been threatened in the past and the present. Displays also frankly discuss other problems that the coming of civilization brought to this area. A slide program tells the history of the formation of the Gorge, and when the volcanoes erupt, the floor in the theater actually shakes from the intensity of the low-volume sound track. When it's not cloudy, the center has an awesome view of the south side of the Gorge.

A DRIVING TOUR

Though I-84 is the fastest road through the Columbia Gorge, it is certainly not the most scenic route. The Gorge, with its many natural and man-made wonders, is well worth a full day's exploration and is best appreciated at a more leisurely pace on the ✪ **Historic Columbia River Highway,** which begins 16 miles east of downtown Portland at the second Troutdale exit off I-84. Opened in 1915, this highway was a marvel of engineering at the time and, by providing access to automobiles, opened the Gorge to casual visits. But this manufactured marvel was, and still is, dwarfed by the spectacular vistas that present themselves along the route.

At the western end of the historic highway, you'll find **Lewis & Clark State Park,** which is near the mouth of the Sandy River. This park is popular with anglers and Portlanders looking to cool off in the Sandy River during the hot summer months. There is also a rock-climbing area within the park.

The first astounding view of the Gorge comes at the **Portland Women's Forum State Park** viewpoint. This is also likely to be your first encounter with the legendary Columbia Gorge winds. To learn more about the historic highway and how it was built, stop at the **Vista House,** 733 feet above the river on **Crown Point.** Inside this historic 1916 building, there are informative displays, including old photos. But most visitors can't tear their eyes away from the view long enough to concentrate on any of the exhibits. Some 30 miles of breathtaking views spread out in front of you as you gaze up and down the Columbia River. A side road near here leads 14 miles to the top of Larch Mountain.

From Crown Point, the historic highway drops down into the Gorge and passes several picturesque **waterfalls**—Latourelle Falls, Shepherd's Dell Falls, Bridalveil Falls, Mist Falls, and Wahkeena Falls—that are either right beside the road or a short walk away. If you're interested in a longer hike, there are trails linking several of the falls, as well as other trails that lead to viewpoints and deep into the adjacent wilderness area.

✪ **Multnomah Falls** is the largest and the most famous waterfall along this highway, and the state's most visited natural attraction. At 620 feet from the lip to the lower pool, it's the tallest waterfall in Oregon and the fourth tallest in the United States. An arched bridge stands directly in front of the falls part way up. This bridge is part of a steep paved trail that leads from the foot of the falls up to the top. From the top of the falls, other trails lead off into the **Mount Hood National Forest.** The historic Multnomah Falls Lodge has a restaurant, snack bar, and gift shop, as well as a **National Forest Interpretive Center** (☎ **503/695-2372**) with information on the geology, history, and natural history of the Gorge.

East of Multnomah Falls, the scenic highway passes by **Oneonta Gorge,** a narrow rift in the cliffs. Through this tiny gorge flows a stream that serves as a pathway for anyone interested in exploring upstream to **Oneonta Falls.** There are also a couple of trails here that head upstream through the forest to Triple Falls and Pony Tail Falls (the trail passes behind this latter waterfall).

Continuing east on the highway, you'll pass **Benson State Park,** which offers picnicking and swimming, and **Horsetail Falls,** which is shortly before the historic highway merges with I-84. Just after the two highways merge, you come to the exit for **Bonneville Lock and Dam** (☎ **541/374-8820**). The **Bradford Island Visitors Center** has exhibits on the history of this dam, which was built in 1927. One of the most important features of the dam is its fish ladder, which allows adult salmon to return upriver to spawn. Underwater windows let visitors see fish as they pass through the ladder. Visit the adjacent fish hatchery to see how trout, salmon, and sturgeon are raised before being released into the river. At this same exit off I-84 (and at Eagle Creek), you'll find access to the Gorge Trail, which currently is mostly paved between Cascade Locks and Bonneville Dam. This paved trail, which incorporates abandoned sections of the historic highway, will eventually extend 13 miles from Cascade Locks. The trail is open to hikers and bikers.

Beyond the dam is Eagle Creek, probably the single best area in the Gorge for a hike. The ✪ **Eagle Creek Trail** leads past several waterfalls, and if you have time for only one hike in the Gorge, it should be this one. You'll also find a campground and picnic area here.

Not far beyond Eagle Creek is the **Bridge of the Gods,** which connects Oregon and Washington at the site where, according to a Native American legend, a natural bridge used by the gods once stood. Geologists believe that the legend may have some basis in fact. There is evidence that a massive rock slide may have once blocked the river at this point.

Just beyond the Bridge of the Gods is **Cascade Locks.** It was at this site that cascades once turned the otherwise placid Columbia River into a raging torrent that required boats to be portaged around the cascades. In 1896, the Cascade Locks were built, allowing steamships to pass unhindered. When the locks were opened, they made traveling between The Dalles and Portland much easier. However, the completion of the Columbia River Scenic Highway in 1915 made the trip even easier by land. With the construction of the Bonneville Lock and Dam, the cascades were flooded and the locks became superfluous.

There are two small museums here at the locks. The **Cascade Locks Historical Museum,** Port Marina Park (☎ **541/374-8535**), which is housed in the old lock tender's house, includes displays of Native American artifacts and pioneer memorabilia, as well as the Northwest's first steam engine. It's open daily June through October, from noon to 6pm (in May and Nov, Sat and Sun noon to 5pm; closed Dec through Apr). Admission by donation.

The **Port of Cascade Locks Visitors Center,** which has displays on river travel in the past, is also the ticket office for the **stern wheeler** *Columbia Gorge* (☎ **541/ 374-8427** or 503/223-3928), which makes regular trips on the river all summer. These cruises provide a great perspective on the Gorge. Fares for the 2-hour scenic cruises are $12.95 for adults and $7.95 for children; dinner, lunch, breakfast, brunch, and other special cruises run $25.95 to $35.95 for adults and $16.95 to $25.95 for children.

Should you decide not to take the historic highway and stay on I-84, you may want to stop at **Rooster Rock State Park,** especially if it's a hot summer day. This park has a long sandy beach, and in a remote section of the park there's even a clothing-optional beach. From I-84 there's also easy access to Multnomah Falls, which is the main attraction of the Historic Columbia River Highway.

Another driving option is to cross to the Washington side of the Columbia River and take Wash. 14 east from Vancouver. This latter highway actually provides the most spectacular views of both the Columbia Gorge and Mount Hood. If you should decide to take this route, be sure to stop at **Beacon Rock,** an 800-foot-tall monolith that has a trail (mostly stairways and catwalks) leading to its summit. At one time there was talk of blasting the rock apart to build jetties at the mouth of the river. Luckily, another source of rock was used, and this amazing landmark continues to guard the Columbia. If you want to make better time, you can cross back to Oregon on the Bridge of the Gods. Continuing on the Washington side of the river, you'll come to Stevenson, site of the above mentioned Columbia Gorge Interpretive Center.

Beyond Stevenson, you come to the town of Carson, where you can avail yourself of the therapeutic waters of the **Carson Hot Springs Resort** (☎ **509/427-8292**), located just north of town. It's open daily from 7:30am to 7:30pm; charges are $12 for a soak that includes a postsoak wrap and $55 for an hour's massage. The resort has been in business since 1897 and looks every bit its age. However, it's just this old-fashioned appeal that keeps people coming back year after year to soak in the hot mineral springs (separate men's and women's soaking tubs) and get massaged. Some very basic hotel rooms ($35 to $45) and cabins ($60) are also available. If you're looking for natural hot springs, the folks here can give you directions to some that are nearby.

BOARDSAILING & OTHER ACTIVITIES

If you're looking for someplace to launch your sailboard along this stretch of the Gorge, try **Rooster Rock State Park,** near the west end of the Gorge, or **Viento State Park,** just west of Hood River.

If you're interested in hiring a guide to take you where the big ones are biting, contact **Page's Northwest Guide Service** (☎ **503/760-3373**), which will take you out fishing for salmon, steelhead, walleye, and sturgeon on the Columbia or Willamette Rivers, on Nehalem or Tillamook Bays or on other area waters ($100 to $125 per person per day). **Reel Adventures** (☎ **503/622-5372** or 503/789-6860) offers a similar fishing guide service ($125 per person per day).

If you'd like to play cowboy in the Gorge, you can go horseback riding at **Mountain Shadow Ranch** (☎ **541/374-8592**), which is also located in Cascade Locks. Expect to pay around $25 for a 1-hour ride and $45 for a 2-hour ride.

WHERE TO STAY

Best Western Columbia River Inn. 735 WaNaPa St. (P.O. Box 580), Cascade Locks, OR 97014. ☎ **800/595-7108** or 541/374-8777. Fax 541/374-2279. 63 units. A/C TV TEL. $64–$124 double. Rates include continental breakfast. AE, CB, DC, DISC, MC, V. Pets accepted ($10 fee).

Located at the foot of the Bridge of the Gods and ideally located for exploring the Gorge, this modern motel has splendid views from its river-view rooms. Many of the rooms also have small balconies, although nearby railroad tracks can make it a bit noisy for sitting out. Luckily, rooms are well insulated against train noises. For a splurge, you can opt for a spa room. Facilities include an indoor pool, a whirlpool, and an exercise room.

✪ **McMenamins Edgefield.** 2126 SW Halsey St., Troutdale, OR 97060. ☎ **800/ 669-8610** or 503/669-8610. www.mcmenamins.com. 101 units (3 with bathroom), 24 hostel beds. $85 double with shared bathroom, $125 double with private bathroom; $20 hostel bed. Rates include full breakfast. AE, DISC, MC, V.

B&Bs don't usually have 100 rooms, but this is no ordinary inn. Located 30 minutes east of downtown Portland and ideally situated for exploring the Columbia Gorge and Mount Hood, this flagship of the McMenamin microbrewery empire is the former Multnomah County poor farm. Today, after extensive remodeling, the property includes not only tastefully decorated guest rooms with antique furnishings, but a brewery, a pub, a beer garden, a restaurant, a movie theater, a winery, a wine-tasting room, a distillery, an 18-hole pitch-and-putt golf course, a cigar bar in an old shed, meeting facilities, extensive gardens, and a hostel. With so much in one spot, this makes a great base for exploring the area. The beautiful grounds give this inn the feel of a remote retreat, though you are still within a short drive of everything Portland has to offer.

Skamania Lodge. P.O. Box 189, Stevenson, WA 98648. ☎ **800/221-7117** or 509/ 427-7700. www.dolce.com. 200 units. A/C MINIBAR TV TEL. $110–$230 double; $260–$350 suite (lower rates in winter). AE, CB, DC, DISC, MC, V.

Skamania Lodge has the most spectacular vistas of any hotel in the Gorge. It's also the only golf resort in the Gorge, and although golf seems to be the preferred sport around here, the hotel is well situated whether you brought your sailboard, hiking boots, or mountain bike. The interior decor is classically rustic with lots of rock and natural wood. In the cathedral-ceilinged lobby, huge windows take in the best view on the property. Large comfortable chairs are set by the stone fireplace, so you can curl up by the fire on a cold winter night. Throughout the hotel Northwest Indian artworks and artifacts are on display. Keep in mind that this is primarily a conference hotel catering to groups and can feel too crowded for a romantic getaway.

If you should opt for a fireplace room, you won't have to leave your bed to enjoy a fire. The river-view guest rooms are only slightly more expensive than the forest-view rooms, which look out over the huge parking lot (and the forest).

Dining/Diversions: The casual Northwest cuisine served in the hotel's large rustic dining room is excellent, and the view of the Gorge is amazing. Adjacent to the dining room is a lounge with a large freestanding stone fireplace and a couple of pool tables.

Amenities: 18-hole golf course, tennis courts, indoor swimming pool, whirlpools, sauna, exercise facility, nature trails, volleyball court, bike rentals, room service, concierge, valet service, daily newspaper, baby-sitting.

CAMPGROUNDS

Camping in the Gorge isn't quite the wonderful experience you might think. With an interstate highway and a very active railway line paralleling the river on the Oregon side and another railroad and a secondary highway on the Washington side, the Gorge tends to be quite noisy. However, there are a few camping options between Portland and Hood River, and these campgrounds do what they can to minimize the traffic noises. **Ainsworth State Park,** 3½ miles east of Multnomah Falls, is most recommendable for the fact that it has showers, although the RV sites are also quite nice. In Cascade Locks, beside the dock for the stern-wheeler *Columbia Gorge,* you'll find the **Cascade Locks Marina Park,** a campground that is little more than a lawn with some picnic tables. Farther east, at exit 41 off I-84, there is **Eagle Creek Campground,** which is the oldest campground in the National Forest system and is popular for its access to the Eagle Creek Trail. At exit 51 off of I-84, there is **Wyeth Campground,** a U.S. Forest Service campground on the bank of Gordon Creek.

WHERE TO DINE

The area's best spot for a meal is the dining room of the **Skamania Lodge** (see above).

✪ **Black Rabbit Restaurant/Power Station Pub.** McMenamins Edgefield, 2126 SW Halsey St., Troutdale. ☎ **503/492-3086.** Main courses $12.25–$18.25. AE, DISC, MC, V. Mon–Sat 7–11:15am, 11:30am–2:30pm, and 5–10pm, Sun 7am–1:30pm and 5–10pm.

Both of these restaurants, one upscale though casual and the other a typical Northwest brew pub, are located on the grounds of the old Multnomah County poor farm, which is now a sprawling bed-and-breakfast, brewery, brew pub, beer garden, winery/wine bar, distillery, and pitch-and-putt golf course. Whether you're in the mood for a burger and a brew or a salmon fillet and a glass of Edgefield wine, you'll find contentment here. This is the ideal place to stop for dinner on the way back to Portland after a day of exploring the Gorge. Even in the slightly more formal Black Rabbit, you're welcome in jeans.

Multnomah Falls Lodge. I-84, exit 31. ☎ **503/695-2376.** Main courses $12–$20. AE, DISC, MC, V. Daily 8am–9pm. NORTHWEST/AMERICAN.

Built in 1925 at the foot of Multnomah Falls, the historic Multnomah Falls Lodge may be the most touristy place to eat in the entire Gorge, but the setting is excellent and the food isn't half bad. Breakfast, when the crowds haven't yet arrived, is one of the best times to eat here. Try the grilled salmon or trout and eggs. At dinner try the chicken Oneonta, which is stuffed with salmon and mushrooms, or the baked salmon Multnomah, which is served with a brown-sugar sauce. For a peek at the falls, try to get a table in the conservatory room. Otherwise, you'll have to be content with stone walls and a large fireplace for atmosphere.

Tad's Chicken 'n Dumplins. 1325 E. Historic Columbia River Hwy., Troutdale. ☎ **503/666-5337.** Call ahead wait list recommended. Main courses $11–$22. AE, MC, V. Mon–Sat 5–11pm, Sun 2–10pm. AMERICAN.

Located on the banks of the Sandy River at the western end of the Historic Columbia Gorge Highway, this rustic restaurant has been in business more than 50 years and, as its name implies, specializes in all-American chicken and dumplings. Sure you can get a steak or panfried oysters salmon, but you'd be remiss if you passed up this opportunity to fill up on this restaurant's namesake dish. Try to get a seat on the enclosed back porch, which overlooks the river. If you're coming here after dark, just watch for the classic neon sign out front.

2 Hood River: The Boardsailing Capital of the Northwest

62 miles E of Portland, 20 miles W of The Dalles, 32 miles N of Government Camp

They used to curse the winds in Hood River. Each summer, hot air rising over the desert to the east sucks cool air up the Columbia River Gorge from the Pacific, and the winds howl through what is basically a natural wind tunnel. The winds are incessant and gusts can whip the river into a tumult of whitecaps.

But things change, and ever since the first person pulled into town with a sailboard, Hood River has taken to praying for wind. Hood River is now the boardsailing capital of America, which has given this once ailing lumber town a new lease on life. People come from all over the world to catch the "nuclear" winds that howl up the Gorge. In early summer the board-heads roll into town in their "Gorge-mobiles," the 1990s equivalent of surfers' woodies, and start listening to the wind reports. They flock to riverside parks on both the Oregon and the Washington sides of the

Columbia, unfurl their sails, zip up their wet suits, and launch themselves into the melee of thousands of other like-minded souls shooting back and forth across a mile of windswept water. High waves whipped up by gale-force winds provide perfect launching pads for rocketing skyward. Aerial acrobatics such as flips and 360° turns are common sights. Even if you're not into this fast-paced sport, you'll certainly get a vicarious thrill from watching the board-heads going for air time.

Until recently, Hood River was pretty much a one-trick town, but sometimes the winds just aren't accommodating and even board-heads can get bored sitting on shore waiting for conditions to improve. The town has now become something of an out-door sports mecca, with a rapidly developing reputation for excellent mountain biking, white-water kayaking and rafting, paragliding, rock climbing, hiking, skiing, and snowboarding. In other words, Hood River is full of active people.

This town does not exist on sports alone, however; and outside town, in the Hood River Valley, are apple and pear orchards, wineries, and vineyards. Hood River also claims one of the best hotels in the state and several good restaurants. Most of the town's old Victorian and Craftsmen houses have been restored, giving Hood River a historic atmosphere to complement its lively boardsailing scene.

ESSENTIALS

GETTING THERE   Hood River is on I-84 at the junction with Ore. 35, which leads south to connect with U.S. 26 near the community of Government Camp.

Amtrak offers passenger rail service to Hood River. The station is at Cascade Avenue and First Street.

VISITOR INFORMATION   Contact the **Hood River County Chamber of Commerce,** 405 Portway Ave., Hood River, OR 97031 (☎ **800/366-3530** or 541/386-2000; www.gorge.net/hrccc), which is located by the river at exit 63 off I-84.

FESTIVALS   The **Hood River Valley Blossom Festival** is held in mid-April and celebrates the flowering of the valley's pear and apple trees, while in mid-October there is the **Hood River Valley Harvest Fest.**

BOARDSAILING & OTHER OUTDOOR ACTIVITIES

If you're here to ride the wind or just want to watch others as they race back and forth across the river, head to the **Columbia Gorge Sailpark** at Hood River Marina or the nearby **Event Site** or **The Hook,** both of which are accessed from exit 63 off I-84. Across the river in Washington, try the **fish hatchery (the Hatchery),** west of the mouth of the White Salmon River, and **Swell City,** a park about 4 miles west of the bridge. Downtown Hood River is packed with boardsailing-related shops. Classes are available through the **Rhonda Smith Windsurfing School** (☎ 541/386-WIND) and **Gorge Wind Guide Service** (☎ **541/490-4401;** www.windguide@gorge.net).

When there isn't enough wind for sailing, there's still the option to go **rafting** on the White Salmon River just across the bridge from Hood River. Companies offering raft trips on this river include **Phil's White Water Adventures** (☎ **800/366-2004** or 509/493-2641), **AAA Rafting** (☎ **800/866-RAFT** or 509/493-2511), and **Renegade River Rafters** (☎ **509/427-RAFT**). The river-rafting season runs from March to October, and a half-day trip will cost around $55 per person. White-water kayaking is also popular on the White Salmon River, and if you'd like to take some lessons or rent a kayak, contact **Cascade Adventure Center,** 6 Oak St. (☎ **541/386-4286**), which also rents sit-on-top kayaks and offers tours on the Columbia and Klickitat Rivers.

Mountain biking is also very popular in this area, and Hood River bike shops can direct you to some fun area rides. Check at **Discover Bicycles,** 205 Oak St.

(☎ 541/386-4820), or **Mountain View Cycles,** 411 Oak St. (☎ **541/386-2453**), both of which also rent bikes. Expect to pay between $6 and $8 per hour and between $30 and $40 per day.

If **fly-fishing** is your passion, drop by the Gorge **Fly Shop,** 201 Oak St. (☎ **800/ 685-7309, PIN 1019,** or 541/386-6977), which can not only fill all your angling needs and point you to where the fish are biting, but also offer guided fly-fishing trips in the area.

Hikers have their choice of trails in Mount Hood National Forest (see "Mount Hood: Skiing, Hiking & Scenic Drives," in chapter 8), the Columbia Gorge (see earlier in this chapter), or across the river (head up Wash. 141 to **Mount Adams**). At 12,276 feet in elevation, Mount Adams is the second-highest peak in Washington. For more information on hiking on Mount Adams, contact the **Gifford Pinchot National Forest,** Mt. Adams Ranger District, 2455 Wash. 141, Trout Lake, WA 98650 (☎ **509/395-2501**).

Golfers can play 18 holes at the **Hood River Golf & Country Club,** 1850 Country Club Rd. (☎ **541/386-3009**), or at **Indian Creek Golf,** 3605 Brookside Dr. (☎ **541/386-7770**).

THE FRUIT LOOP (EXPLORING THE HOOD RIVER VALLEY)

Before windsurfing took center stage, the Hood River Valley was known as one of Oregon's top fruit-growing regions, and today the valley is still Oregon's top apple- and pear-growing region. From blossom time (Apr) to harvest season (Sept and Oct), the valley offers quiet country roads to explore. Along the way you'll find numerous farm stands, wineries, museums, and interesting shops that reflect the rural heritage of the valley. Pick up a brochure called *Hood River County's Fruit Loop* at the Hood River County Chamber of Commerce visitor center (see "Visitor Information," above).

Be sure to start your tour of the Hood River Valley by stopping at **Panorama Point,** off of Ore. 35 just south of town (follow the signs). This hilltop park provides a splendid panorama of the valley's orchards with Mount Hood looming in the distance.

In the fall, fruit stands pop up along the roads around the valley. **Smiley's Red Barn,** Ore. 35 and Ehrck Hill Road (☎ **541/386-9121**), and **Rasmussen Fruit & Flower Farm,** 3020 Thomsen Rd. (☎ **541/386-4622**)—two of the biggest and best farm stands in the valley—are located adjacent to one another off Ore. 35 about 6 miles south of Hood River. Also not to be missed is the nearby **River Bend Country Store,** 2363 Tucker Rd. (☎ **800/755-7568** or 541/386-8766), where you can stock up on seasonal and organic produce and other homemade specialties. The 3-pound fruit pies are legendary around these parts. You'll find the store west of Smiley's and Rasmussen's on the opposite side of the valley. Also in the valley, you'll find numerous orchards and farms where you can pick your own fruit. Just keep an eye out for u-pick signs.

In addition to pears and apples, the Hood River valley grows quite a few acres of wine grapes. You can visit several wineries in the area and taste the local fruit of the vine. West of town, off Country Club Road (take Oak St./Cascade St. west from downtown), you'll find two wineries. **Flerchinger Vineyards and Winery,** 4200 Post Canyon Dr. (☎ **800/516-8710** or 541/386-2882), produces a good Riesling as well as Pinot Gris, Chardonnay, Petite Syrah, and a Cabernet-Merlot blend. **Hood River Vineyards,** 4693 Westwood Dr. (☎ **541/386-3772**), makes excellent fruit wines, including a d'Anjou pear wine that tastes like a grape wine. They also produce an excellent Zinfandel port.

The little hamlet of Parkdale, at the south end of the Fruit Loop, is home to the fascinating little **Hutson Museum** (☎ **541/352-6808**), which houses lapidary, archaeology, and anthropology collections, of which the rock collection and exhibits of

Native American artifacts are a highlight. The museum is open mid-April through October (call for specific hours), and admission is $1 for adults and 50¢ for children. There are also several historic buildings on the grounds. Also in Parkdale you'll find the **Elliot Glacier Public House,** 4945 Baseline Rd. (☎ **541/352-1022**), a brew pub with a great view of Mount Hood from the picnic tables out back.

Any time of year, but especially during fruit-blossom time, the **Mount Hood Railroad** (☎ **800/TRAIN-61**) offers a great way to see the Hood River Valley and its acres of orchards. The diesel locomotives operated by this scenic railroad company depart from the historic 1911 Hood River depot and pull restored Pullman coaches on 4-hour excursions. The train winds its way up the valley to Parkdale, where you can get a snack at a cafe or visit the Hutson Museum. Fares are $22.95 for adults, $19.95 for seniors, and $14.95 for children 2 to 12. In July and August, the train runs daily except Monday. In spring and fall it runs Wednesday through Sunday, and in November and December, it runs on weekends only. There are also regularly scheduled dinner, brunch, and other specialty excursions. Mid-April's Fruit Blossom Express runs when the fruit orchards are in bloom, and there are Harvest Festival excursions in mid-October. Regular excursions leave at 10am and 3pm.

OTHER ATTRACTIONS IN HOOD RIVER

At Port Marina Park, off exit 63 and down by the river, you'll find the **Hood River County Museum** (☎ **541/386-6772**), which has exhibits of Native American artifacts from this area. There are also plenty of displays on pioneer life. The museum is open April through August, Monday through Saturday from 10am to 4pm and Sunday from noon to 4pm; and in September and October, daily from noon to 4pm. Admission is by donation.

In downtown Hood River, drop in at the **Columbia Art Gallery,** 207 Second St. (☎ **541/386-4512**), to see what area artists are up to. This is a community-sponsored, nonprofit gallery. For high-end art from Northwest and national artists (including Dale Chihuly), check out the **305 Gallery,** 305 Oak St. (☎ **541/387-8880**).

WHERE TO STAY

If you're looking for a bed-and-breakfast in the area and the ones listed below are full, you can try calling **Roomfinder** (☎ **541/386-6767**), a free service provided by the Hood River Bed & Breakfast Association.

Best Western Hood River Inn. 1108 E. Marina Way, Hood River, OR 97031. ☎ **800/ 828-7873** or 541/386-2200. Fax 541/386-8905. 149 units. A/C TV TEL. June–Sept $84–$115 double, $155–$175 suite; Oct–May $64–$99 double, $105–$135 suite. AE, CB, DC, DISC, MC, V. Pets accepted.

As the only area hotel located right on the water (there's even a dock and private beach), the Best Western is popular with boardsailors. The convention hotel atmosphere (crowds of corporate types busily networking) detracts somewhat from a vacation here, but if you like comfort and predictability, this is definitely a good bet. Amenities include room service, an outdoor swimming pool, and an exercise room. The Riverside Grill serves dependable meals with a bit of Northwest imagination and a great view across the river, while a diner-style coffee shop provides casual meals.

✪ **Columbia Gorge Hotel.** 4000 Westcliff Dr., Hood River, OR 97031. ☎ **800/345-1921** or 541/386-5566. Fax 541/387-5414. www.columbiagorgehotel.com. 39 units. TV TEL. $150–$275 double (including multicourse breakfast). AE, CB, DC, DISC, MC, V. Pets accepted ($25).

Located just west of the town of Hood River off I-84 and opened shortly after the Columbia River Scenic Highway was completed in 1915, this little oasis of luxury offers the same genteel atmosphere that was once enjoyed by the likes of Rudolph Valentino and Clark Gable. With its yellow-stucco walls and red-tile roofs, this hotel would be right at home in Beverly Hills, and the hotel gardens could hold their own in Victoria, British Columbia. The hotel is perched more than 200 feet above the river on a steep cliff, so despite the attractive furnishings and gardens, it is almost impossible to notice anything but the view out the windows.

Guest rooms are all a little different, with a mixture of antique and classic furnishings. There are canopy, brass, and even some hand-carved wooden beds. Unfortunately, many of the rooms are rather cramped, as are the bathrooms, most of which have older fixtures. Recently, soaking tubs and fireplaces were added to some rooms.

Dining/Diversions: The **Columbia River Court Dining Room** serves a mix of Northwest and Continental fare at dinner, but it's best known for its five-course "farm" breakfast. Evening meals feature Northwest cuisine with an emphasis on salmon, lamb, and venison.

Amenities: Room service, daily newspaper, evening champagne and caviar social hour.

Hood River Hotel. 102 Oak Ave., Hood River, OR 97031. ☎ **800/386-1859** or 541/386-1900. Fax 503/386-6090. www.hoodriverhotel.com. 41 units. TV TEL. $59–$109 double; $85–$155 suite. Rates include continental breakfast. AE, CB, DC, DISC, MC, V. Pets accepted ($15 per day).

Located in downtown Hood River, this hotel is an economical alternative to the pricey Columbia Gorge Hotel. Built in 1913, the Hood River Hotel boasts the casual elegance of a vintage hotel. Guest rooms are all different and are furnished almost identically to those at the Columbia Gorge Hotel. Canopy beds, ceiling fans, and oval floor mirrors create a mood of elegance. Most third-floor rooms have skylit bathrooms, which makes them our favorites (these are also the only rooms with air-conditioning, which you'll appreciate in the summer). The suites have full kitchens, and, of course, river-view rooms are the most expensive. The hotel's casual dining room serves good Italian meals, and room service is also available. You'll find a whirlpool, a sauna, and an exercise room on the premises. Light sleepers should be aware of the railroad tracks behind the hotel.

Inn at the Gorge. 1113 Eugene St., Hood River, OR 97031. ☎ **541/386-4429.** 4 units. A/C TV. $78 double. Rates include full breakfast. MC, V. Closed early Oct to early May.

Though this bed-and-breakfast is housed in a 1908 Victorian home, it's still a casual sort of place catering primarily to boardsailing enthusiasts. Each of the three suites here has a kitchenette, so you can save money on your meals while you're in town. There's a storage area for boardsailing and skiing gear. The innkeepers can steer you to the best spots for your skill level.

○ **Lakecliff Estate Bed and Breakfast.** 3820 Westcliff Dr. (P.O. box 1220), Hood River, OR 97031. ☎ **541/386-7000.** Fax 541/386-1803. E-mail: Lakecliff@hotmail.com. 4 units (2 with private bathroom). $90 double with shared bathroom, $110 double with private bathroom. No credit cards. Closed Oct–Apr.

Situated high atop a cliff in a secluded forest setting on the outskirts of town, this inn was built in 1908 as a summer home and was designed by the architect of Portland's Benson Hotel and the Gorge's Multnomah Falls Lodge. The cedar-shingled main house, which is surrounded by its own 12-acre forested estate, could just as easily be in the Maine woods if not for the Gorge view out the back windows and deck. Guest rooms all have great views and are decorated in an upscale country style. One room has the bed directly under the window so you can lay under the covers and gaze out at the river far below. Three rooms also have their own fireplaces.

Meredith Motel. 4300 Westcliff Dr., Hood River, OR 97031. ☎ **541/386-1515.** 21 units. A/C TV TEL. $49–$79 double. AE, DC, DISC, MC, V. Rates include continental breakfast. Pets accepted.

Fans of retro 1950s styling won't want to miss this economical choice at the western edge of Hood River (take exit 62 and drive west on Westcliff). The vintage motel has been completely remodeled, and all the rooms now have 1950s lamps, vintage phones, and modern retro furnishings reminiscent of the 1950s. As if that weren't enough, the hotel is perched on the edge of a cliff above the Columbia River, and big picture windows put you face-to-face with the Gorge in all its grandeur.

Vagabond Lodge. 4070 Westcliff Dr., Hood River, OR 97031. ☎ **541/386-2992.** Fax 541/386-3317. www.vagabondlodge.com. 42 units. A/C TV TEL. $52–$72 double; $82 suite. Lower rates in winter. AE, DC, MC, V. Pets accepted.

If you've got a banker's tastes but a teller's vacation budget, you can take advantage of the Vagabond Lodge's proximity to the Columbia Gorge Hotel and enjoy the latter's gardens and restaurant without breaking the bank. Actually, the back rooms at the Vagabond are some of the best in Hood River simply for their views (some have balconies). However, this motel's grounds are also quite attractive. There are lots of big old oaks and evergreens, and natural rock outcroppings have been incorporated into the motel's landscaping. If you're in the mood for a splurge, ask for one of the recently remodeled suites (some have fireplaces, others have whirlpool tubs).

CAMPGROUNDS

Area campgrounds include **Toll Bridge Park,** on Ore. 35, 17 miles south of town, and **Tucker Park,** on Tucker Road (Ore. 281) just a few miles south of town. Both of these county parks are both on the banks of the Hood River. Farther south, you'll find the **Robinhood Campground** and the **Sherwood Campground,** two national-forest campgrounds also on the banks of the Hood River (these campgrounds are favored by mountain bikers). Eight miles west of Hood River off I-84 is **Viento State Park,** which gets quite a bit of traffic noise both from the interstate and from the adjacent railroad tracks. Eleven miles east of town, you'll find **Memaloose State Park,** which has the same noise problems. These two state parks are popular with boardsailors.

WHERE TO DINE

When you just have to have a bagel, the **Hood River Bagel Co.,** 13 Oak St. (☎ **541/386-2123**), is the best place in town. For espresso and a pastry or a slice of pizza, try **Andrew's Pizza & Bakery,** 107 Oak St. (☎ **541/386-1448**). **Holstein's Coffee Co.,** 12 Oak St. (☎ **541/386-4115**), is another good place for a latte. The best restaurant in town is the dining room at the **Columbia Gorge Hotel** (see "Where to Stay" above for details).

The Mesquitery. 1219 12th St. ☎ **541/386-2002.** Main courses $9–$17. AE, MC, V. Wed–Fri 11:30am–2pm and 4:30–9:30 or 10pm, Sat–Tues 4:30–9:30 or 10pm. STEAK/SEAFOOD.

Located in the uptown district of Hood River, the Mesquitery is a small and cozy grill with a rustic interior. As the name implies, mesquite grilling is the specialty of the house. Chicken and ribs are most popular, but you can also get a sirloin steak or grilled fish. At lunch there are sandwiches made with grilled meats. If you aren't that hungry, this is a good place to put together a light meal from such à la carte dishes as shrimp burritos, fish tacos, and fettuccine pesto.

Santacroces'. 4780 Ore. 35. ☎ **541/354-2511.** Main courses $10–$18. DISC, MC, V. Wed–Sat 4–10pm, Sun 2–10pm. ITALIAN.

Located adjacent to a large lumber mill south of Hood River up the Hood River Valley, this casual little place is part tavern and part great little Italian place. The pizzas here have a legendary reputation as the best for many miles around. If you're not in the mood for pizza, consider anything with the homemade spicy Italian sausage. The bracciola (rolled flank steak filled with cheeses) is another good bet.

Big City Chicks. 1302 13th St. ☎ **541/387-3811.** Reservations recommended. Main courses $8–$19. DISC, MC, V. Sun–Thurs 5–9pm, Fri–Sat 5–10pm. INTERNATIONAL.

Serving "healthy foods of the world," this uptown restaurant is out of the main tourist scene, but it's very popular with locals, who love the wide variety of dishes and reasonable prices. The menu is like an international greatest-hits list. There is pad Thai, blackened catfish, jerked snapper, hazelnut-crusted salmon, chicken *mole*, barbecued duck tacos, and lots of vegetarian dishes (such as sweet-potato and pumpkin raviolis). The restaurant is in an old house with great vintage ambiance dressed up with a bit of Miami art deco styling (think pink flamingos). Romantic and casually hip.

❀ **Sixth Street Bistro.** 509 Cascade Ave. ☎ **541/386-5737.** Reservations recommended. Main courses $8–$13. MC, V. Mon–Thurs 11:30am–10pm, Fri–Sun 11:30am–10:30pm. AMERICAN/INTERNATIONAL.

Just a block off Oak Street toward the river, the Sixth Street Bistro has an intimate little dining room and patio on the lower floor and a lounge with a balcony on the second floor. Both have their own entrance, but they share the same menu so there's a choice of ambiance. There are numerous international touches, such as chicken satay, pad Thai, and Greek salads, and also plenty of juicy burgers and interesting pasta dishes, such as farfalle puttanesca. You'll also find seasonal specials and plenty of vegetarian dishes as well.

Stonehedge Inn. 3405 Cascade Dr. ☎ **541/386-3940.** Reservations recommended. Main courses $10–$21. AE, DC, DISC, MC, V. Wed–Sun 5–9pm. CONTINENTAL.

Built as a summer vacation home in the early 1900s, the Stonehedge Inn is west of downtown Hood River down a long gravel driveway off Cascade Drive and feels as if it is deep in the wilderness. Inside the old home, there's a small lounge with a bar taken from an old tavern, and several dining rooms, all of which have a genuinely old-time feel. The menu sticks to traditional continental dishes (steak Diane, rack of lamb, steak and lobster), though there are occasional ventures into more creative territory with daily specials. Popular with an older crowd, this restaurant sticks pretty closely to familiar and reliable continental fare.

HOOD RIVER AFTER DARK
Big Horse Brew Pub. 115 State St. ☎ **541/386-4411.**

Located in a vertiginous old house above downtown, this brew pub usually has a good selection of brews, and the views from the third floor can't be beat. The pub also does decent pub food.

Full Sail Brewery/White Cap Brewpub. 506 Columbia St. ☎ **541/386-2247.**

Full Sail brews some of the most consistently flavorful and well-rounded beers and ales in the Northwest and has developed a loyal following. You have to walk past the brewery to get to the pub, at the back of an old industrial building a block off Hood River's main drag. Big windows look out over the river. Brewery tours are available.

EAST OF HOOD RIVER: WILDFLOWERS & VIEWS

East of Hood River, you'll find two more sections of the Historic Columbia River Highway (Ore. 30), one of which should be open to hikers and bikers by some time in 2000 and the other of which is open to automobiles. The former section, between Hood River and Mosier, was abandoned when I-84 was built and a tunnel on this section of the old highway was filled in. Although the tunnel was reexcavated, a rock catchment had to be built along the stretch of this route, and that has caused a delay in the opening of the old highway to the public. Check with the Hood River County Chamber of Commerce or an area bike shop to see if this route is open yet.

The second stretch of the old highway, between the towns of Mosier and The Dalles, climbs up onto the Rowena Plateau, which has sweeping vistas that take in the Columbia River, Mount Hood, and Mount Adams. In the springtime (between Mar and May), the wildflower displays here are some of the best in the state. The best place to observe the flowers is at the Nature Conservancy's **Governor Tom McCall Preserve.** On spring weekends there are usually volunteers on hand guiding wildflower walks through the preserve.

3 The Dalles

128 miles W of Pendleton, 85 miles E of Portland, 133 miles N of Bend

The Dalles (rhymes with "the pals"), a French word meaning "flagstone," was the name given to this area by early-19th-century French trappers. These early explorers may have been reminded of stepping stones or flagstone-lined gutters when they first gazed upon the flat basalt rocks that forced the Columbia River through a long stretch of rapids and cascades here. These rapids, which were a barrier to river navigation, formed a natural gateway to western Oregon.

For more than 10,000 years, Native Americans inhabited this site because of the ease with which salmon could be taken from the river as it flowed through the tumultuous rapids. The annual fishing season at nearby Celilo Falls was a meeting point for tribes from all over the West, who would come to fish, trade, and stockpile supplies for the coming winter.

White settlers, the first of whom came to The Dalles as missionaries in 1838, were latecomers to this area. However, by the 1840s, a steady flow of pioneers was passing through the region, which was effectively the end of the overland segment of the Oregon Trail. Pioneers who were headed for the mild climate and fertile soils of the Willamette Valley would load their wagons onto rafts at this point and float downriver to the mouth of the Willamette and then up that river to Oregon City.

By the 1850s, The Dalles was the site of an important military fort and had become a busy river port. Steamships shuttled from here to Cascade Locks on the run to Portland. However, the coming of the railroad in 1880, and later the flooding of the river's rapids, reduced the importance of The Dalles as a port town. Today, the city is linking itself to the Columbia Gorge and is the site of the Columbia Gorge Discovery Center. The strong winds here also attract almost as many boardsailors as those in nearby Hood River.

ESSENTIALS

GETTING THERE   The Dalles is on I-84 at the junction of U.S. 197, which leads south to Antelope, where it connects with U.S. 97.

Amtrak passenger trains stop across the Columbia River from The Dalles in Wishram, Washington.

VISITOR INFORMATION   Contact **The Dalles Area Chamber of Commerce,** 404 W. Second St., The Dalles, OR 97058 (☎ **800/255-3385** or 541/296-2231; www.gorge.net/tdacc).

LEARNING ABOUT THE GORGE
Columbia Gorge Discovery Center/Wasco County Historical Museum. 5000 Discovery Dr. ☎ **541/296-8600.** www.gorgediscovery.org. $6.50 adults, $5.50 seniors, $3 children ages 6–16. Daily 10am–6pm. Closed Thanksgiving, Christmas, and New Year's Day.

These two museums, housed in one building on the outskirts of The Dalles, serve as the eastern gateway to the Columbia Gorge. In a building constructed to resemble a Northwest Native American longhouse, you'll find exhibits on the geology and history of the Gorge. Among the most fascinating exhibits is a film of Native Americans fishing at Celilo Falls before the falls were flooded by the rising waters behind The Dalles Dam. The museum's star attraction, however, is a 33-foot-long river model with flowing water. On the surrounding museum grounds, there is a **Living History Park,** where interpreters are on hand on summer weekends to discuss the Native American traditions and pioneer experiences. There is also a short nature trail that leads past a small pond.

EXPLORING THE DALLES
After the Gorge itself, the most important attraction in the vicinity of The Dalles is actually across the river in Washington, about 18 miles east of The Dalles. The ✪ **Maryhill Museum of Art,** Wash. 14 (☎ **509/773-3733**), built between 1914 and 1926 by Sam Hill, houses a collection of Rodin sculptures, Native American artifacts, Russian icons, Fabergé artifacts, miniature French fashions, and 19th-century American and European paintings. The museum is fascinating both for its superb collections and for its remote and spectacular setting high above the Columbia River—not to be missed. The museum is open daily, March 15 to November 15, from 9am to 5pm. Admission is $6.50 for adults, $5 for seniors, and $1.50 for children ages 6 to 12.

Some of The Dalles's most important historic buildings can be seen at the **Fort Dalles Museum,** 500 W. 15th St. (☎ **541/296-4547**), at the corner of Garrison Street. Established in 1850, Fort Dalles was the only military post between Fort Laramie and Fort Vancouver. By 1867, the fort had become unnecessary, and after several buildings were destroyed in a fire, it was abandoned. Today, several of the original buildings, including a Carpenter-Gothic officers' home, are still standing. Though small, this is the oldest history museum in Oregon. April through September, the museum is open daily from 10am to 5pm; other months, the museum is open Thursday through Monday from 10am to 4pm. Admission is $3, free for children 17 and under.

Within a decade of the establishment of the fort, The Dalles became the county seat of what was the largest county ever created in the United States. Wasco County covered 130,000 square miles between the Rocky Mountains and the Cascade Range. The old **Wasco County Courthouse,** 410 W. Second St. (☎ **541/296-4798**), a two-story wooden structure built in 1859, has been preserved, and the inside looks much the way it did when it was the functioning courthouse. June through August it's open Monday, Tuesday, Friday, and Saturday from 10am to 4pm; May and September, it's open 11am to 3pm (closed other months). Admission is free.

Long before settlers arrived in The Dalles, Lewis and Clark's expedition stopped here. The site of their camp is called **Rock Fort** and is one of the expedition's only documented campsites. You'll find the historic site west of downtown near The Dalles's industrial area. Go west on West Second Street, turn right on Webber Street West, and then turn right again on Bargeway Road.

The Dalles's other historic landmark is a much more impressive structure. **St. Peter's Landmark Church,** at the corner of West Third and Lincoln streets, is no longer an active church, but its 176-foot-tall steeple is a local landmark. The church was built in the Gothic Revival style in 1898, and its spire is topped by a 6-foot-tall rooster that is the symbol of The Dalles.

If you're interested in learning more about the history and the historic buildings of The Dalles, pick up a copy of the historic walking tours brochure at the chamber of commerce. There is also a brochure on the town's many historical murals.

Just east of town rises **The Dalles Lock and Dam** (☎ **541/296-9778**), which provides both irrigation water and electricity. The dam, which was completed in 1957, stretches for 1½ miles from the Oregon shore to the Washington shore. One of the main reasons this dam was built was to flood the rapids that made this section of the Columbia River impossible to navigate. Among the numerous rapids flooded by the dam were Celilo Falls, which, for thousands of years before the dam was built, was the most important salmon-fishing area in the Northwest. Each year thousands of Native Americans would gather here to catch and smoke salmon, putting the dried fish away for the coming winter. The traditional method of catching the salmon was to use a spear or net with a long pole. Men would build precarious wooden platforms out over the river and catch the salmon as they tried to leap up the falls. You can still see traditional Native American fishing platforms near the Shilo Inn here in The Dalles. The dam's **visitor center** has displays on both the history of the river and the construction of the dam, and a small train takes visitors on guided tours. It's open mid-April to the end of September (Apr, May, and Sept, Wed through Sun from 10am to 5pm; June through Aug daily from 9am to 6pm); admission is free. To reach the visitor center, take exit 87 off I-84 and turn right on Northeast Frontage Road.

For a good view of The Dalles and the Columbia River, head up to **Sorosis Park,** on Scenic Drive, which forms the southern edge of town. East of town 17 miles, you'll find the **Deschutes River State Park** (☎ **541/739-2322**), which is at the mouth of the Deschutes River and is the eastern boundary of the Columbia Gorge National Scenic Area. The park has several miles of hiking trails, and an old railway right-of-way that parallels the Deschutes River for 25 miles has been turned into a gravel mountain-biking and horseback-riding trail. This trail is fairly flat and passes through some spectacular canyon scenery. There is also a campground in the park.

If you're interested in hiring a guide to take you **fishing** for sturgeon, steelhead, or salmon in the area, contact **Young's Fishing Service** (☎ **800/270-7962** or 541/296-5371), which offers trips on the Columbia, Deschutes, and John Day Rivers. Expect to pay around $135 to $155 for a day of fishing.

WHERE TO STAY

The Columbia House Bed & Breakfast. 525 E. Seventh St., The Dalles, OR 97058. ☎ **800/807-2668** or 541/298-4686. 4 units (3 with private bathrooms). A/C. $60–$85 double. DISC, MC, V.

With movie theme rooms (Humphrey Bogart, Marilyn Monroe, *Gone With the Wind*) and lots of art deco styling throughout, this is one of the most interesting inns in The Dalles. It is set at the back of a long driveway and perches atop a bluff overlooking the city and the Columbia River. Out back there are four large decks where guests can soak up the sunshine and views. There's also a fun basement recreation room.

Shilo Inn The Dalles. 3223 Bret Clodfelter Way, The Dalles, OR 97058. ☎ **800/222-2244** or 541/298-5502. Fax 541/298-4673. www.shiloinns.com. 112 units. A/C TV TEL. $65–$99 double. Rates include full breakfast. AE, CB, DC, DISC, MC, V. Pets accepted ($7 per night).

The Shilo Inn is a couple of miles from downtown and has the most spectacular setting of any lodging in the area. The motel is set on the banks of the Columbia River at the foot of The Dalles Dam and is adjacent to the Native American ghost town of Lone Pine. The rooms are typical motel units, so it's definitely worth spending a little extra for a river-view room. The dining room and lounge offer moderately priced meals and views of the river. Room service is available, and an outdoor pool, a fitness room, a whirlpool tub, and a sauna provide places to relax.

CAMPGROUNDS

If you're looking for someplace to pitch a tent or park an RV, try **Deschutes River State Park,** 17 miles east of The Dalles off I-84, or **Horsethief Lake State Park,** across the river near Dallesport, Washington.

WHERE TO DINE

Bailey's Place. 515 Liberty St. ☎ **541/296-6708.** Reservations recommended. Main courses $8–$20. AE, DISC, MC, V. Tues–Thurs 4:30–9pm, Fri–Sat 4:30–10pm. PRIME RIB/CONTINENTAL.

In a previous incarnation, Bailey's Place was known as Ole's Supper Club and was The Dalles' favorite fine-dining restaurant, despite its location in an industrial neighborhood. Now that the restaurant has moved to the Edward French house, built in 1865, it finally has a location befitting its menu. The prime rib au jus has made this restaurant a local legend, and it comes in sizes for hearty (10-oz.) and heartier (16-oz.) appetites. The kitchen also does a respectable job on the steaks and seafood, but if you're only here for the day, go with the prime rib. An excellent selection of very reasonably priced wines is available.

✪ **Baldwin Saloon Historic Restaurant & Bar.** First and Court Sts. ☎ **541/296-5666.** Reservations accepted only for parties of 6 or more. Main courses $5.75–$16. MC, V. Mon–Thurs 11am–9pm (until 10pm in summer), Fri–Sat 11am–10pm. AMERICAN/ CONTINENTAL.

Built in 1876, the Baldwin Saloon has one of the few remaining cast-iron facades in town. Brick walls, wooden booths, and a high ceiling (high enough to fit a loft with a piano) add to the old-time feel, as does the collection of turn-of-the-century landscape paintings and large bar nudes. Whether your tastes run to burgers or chèvre-stuffed dates, you'll find something here to please your palate. A macabre aside: The building was once a warehouse for coffins.

From the schussing of January and the kayaking of April to the wild-flowers of August and the splashes of fall foliage in October, Oregon's Cascade Range is a year-round recreational magnet. Stretching from the Columbia Gorge in the north to California in the south, the Cascades are a relatively young volcanic mountain range where picture-perfect, snowcapped volcanic peaks rise above lush green forests of evergreens. The Cascade's volcanic heritage sets this mountain range apart from others in the West, and throughout these mountains, signs of past volcanic activity are evident. Crater Lake, formed after a massive volcanic eruption, is the most dramatic evidence of the Cascades' fiery past. But you can also see evidence of volcanic activity in the cones of Mount Hood, Mount Jefferson, and the Three Sisters and the lava fields of McKenzie Pass.

As spectacular as this volcanic geology is, however, it is not what draws most people to these mountains. The main attraction is the multitude of outdoor sports that can be pursued here. Crystal-clear rivers, churned into white water as they cascade down from high in the mountains, provide numerous opportunities for rafting, kayaking, canoeing, and fishing. High mountain lakes hold hungry trout, and throughout the summer, lakeside campgrounds stay filled with anglers. The Pacific Crest Trail winds the entire length of the Cascades, but it is the many wilderness areas scattered throughout these mountains that are the biggest draw for day hikers and backpackers. At lower elevations, mountain bikers find miles of national-forest trails to enjoy. In winter, skiers and snowboarders flock to more than half a dozen ski areas and countless miles of cross-country ski trails—and because winter lingers late in the high Cascades, the ski seasons here are some of the longest in the country. Skiing often begins in mid-November and continues on into April and even May and June at Mount Bachelor. In fact, on Mount Hood, high-elevation snowfields atop glacial ice allow a year-round ski season that attracts Olympic ski teams for summer training.

The Cascades also serve as a dividing line between the lush evergreen forests of western Oregon and the dry, high desert landscapes of eastern Oregon. On the western slopes, Douglas firs and western red cedars dominate, while on the east side, the cinnamon-barked ponderosa pine is most common. These trees have been the lifeblood of the Oregon economy for much of this century, and with few virgin forests left in the state, the fight to protect the last old-growth forests has been long and litigious. Today, visitors to the Cascades will be

The Cascades

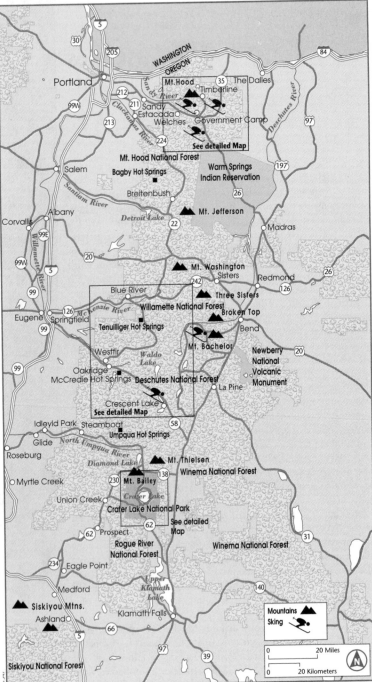

confronted at nearly every turn by the sight of clear-cuts scarring the mountainsides, yet it is still possible to find groves of ancient trees beneath which to hike and camp.

1 Mount Hood: Skiing, Hiking & Scenic Drives

60 miles E of Portland, 46 miles S of Hood River

At 11,235 feet, Mount Hood, a dormant volcano, is the highest mountain in Oregon. Sitting less than 60 miles east of downtown Portland, it is also the busiest mountain in the state. Summer and winter, people flock here in search of cool mountain air filled with the scent of firs and pines. Campgrounds, hiking and mountain-biking trails, trout streams and canoeing lakes, downhill ski areas, and cross-country ski trails all provide ample opportunities for outdoor recreational activities on Mount Hood.

With five downhill areas and many miles of cross-country trails, the mountain is a ski bum's dream come true. The country's largest night-skiing area is here, and you can even ski right through the summer at Timberline. Because the snowcapped summit can be reached fairly easily by those with only a moderate amount of mountain-climbing experience, it's also the most climbed major peak in the United States.

One of the first settlers to visit Mount Hood was Samuel Barlow, who, in 1845, had traveled the Oregon Trail and was searching for an alternative to taking his wagon train down the treacherous waters of the Columbia River. Barlow blazed a trail across the south flank of Mount Hood, and the following year he opened his trail as a toll road. The Barlow Trail, though difficult, was cheaper and safer than rafting down the river. The old trail still exists and is now a hiking and mountain-biking trail.

During the Great Depression, the Works Progress Administration employed skilled craftsmen to build the rustic **Timberline Lodge** at the tree line on the mountain's south slope. Today, the lodge is a National Historic Landmark and is the main destination for visitors to the mountain. The views from here, both of Mount Hood's peak and of the Oregon Cascades to the south, are superb and should not be missed.

Don't expect to have this mountain all to yourself, though. Because of its proximity to Portland, Mount Hood sees a lot of visitors throughout the year, and on snowy days the road back down the mountain from the ski areas can be bumper to bumper and backed up for hours. Also keep in mind that you'll need to have a Sno-Park Permit in the winter (available at ski shops around the area) and a Trail Park Permit to park at trailheads in the summer (available at ranger stations, visitor centers, and a few outdoors-oriented shops).

ESSENTIALS

GETTING THERE   Mount Hood is reached by U.S. 26 from Portland (take exit 16A off I-84) and Ore. 35 from Hood River. These highways meet just east of the town of Government Camp, which is the main tourist town on the mountain. The Lolo Pass Road is a gravel road that skirts the north and west sides of the mountain connecting these two highways.

VISITOR INFORMATION   For more information on Mount Hood, contact the **Mount Hood Information Center,** 65000 E. U.S. 26, Welches, OR 97067 (☎ 503/622-4822), or the **Mount Hood Ranger District,** 6780 Ore. 35 S., Mount Hood–Parkdale, OR 97041 (☎ 541/352-6002).

SUMMER ON THE MOUNTAIN

The historic **Timberline Lodge** (see "Where to Stay" below) is the main destination of most visitors to the mountain in the snow-free months. Besides having a fabulous view of Mount Hood, the lodge is surrounded by meadows that burst into bloom in

July and August. Here you'll find the 41-mile-long ✪ **Timberline Trail,** which circles the mountain. If you just have time for a short hike, head west from the lodge on this trail. The route east passes through dusty ash fields and then drops down into the hot, barren White River Valley. You'll find snow here any time of year, and there's even summer skiing at the **Timberline Ski Area.** The lift-accessed ski slopes are high above the lodge on the Palmer Glacier and are open only in the morning. It is also possible to ride the lift even if you aren't skiing.

In summer, you can also ride the lift at **Mt. Hood SkiBowl** (☎ 503/222-BOWL), where there are mountain-biking trails, hiking trails, and an alpine slide (sort of a summertime bobsled run). You'll also find numerous other rides and activities here.

One of the most popular hikes on Mount Hood is the trail to **Mirror Lake,** which, as its name implies, reflects the summit of Mount Hood in its waters. The trail is fairly easy and thus is very popular with families. To add a bit more challenge to the hike, you can continue on to the summit of Tom, Dick & Harry Mountain, the backside of which serves as the Mt. Hood SkiBowl in winter. The view from the summit is superb, and in late summer there are huckleberries along the trail. You'll find the trailhead right on U.S. 26 just before you reach Government Camp.

The east side of the mountain, which is accessed by Ore. 35 from Hood River, is much drier and less visited than the west side. You'll find good hiking trails in the vicinity of **Mount Hood Meadows,** where the wildflower displays in late July and August are some of the best on the mountain. The loop trail past Umbrella and Sahalie Falls is particularly enjoyable. At Mount Hood Meadows Ski Area, you'll also find summer skiing. Also on this side of the mountain, you'll find the highest segment of the Timberline Trail. This section of trail climbs up Cooper Spur ridge from the historic Cloud Cap Inn, which is no longer open to the public. To reach the trailhead, follow signs off Ore. 35 for Cooper Spur and Cloud Cap. On the east side of Ore. 35, off Forest Service Road 44, you'll also find the best mountain-biking trails in the area. Among these are the Surveyor's Ridge Trail and the Dog Mountain Trail.

If you're interested in a little adventure and an alternative route from the west side of the mountain to the Hood River area, try exploring the gravel **Lolo Pass Road,** which is usually in good enough condition to be traveled by standard passenger cars. Be sure to have a Forest Service map, since roads out here are not well marked and it's easy to get lost. Branching off from the Lolo Pass Road are several smaller roads that lead to some of the best hiking trails on Mount Hood. Also off the Lolo Pass Road, you'll find **Lost Lake,** one of the most beautiful (and most photographed) lakes in the Oregon Cascades. When the water is still, the view of the mountain and its reflection in the lake is positively sublime. Here you'll find campgrounds, cabins, picnic areas, good fishing, and hiking trails that lead both around the lake and up a nearby butte.

If you're interested in a more strenuous experience, Mount Hood offers plenty of mountain- and rock-climbing opportunities. **Timberline Mountain Guides,** P.O. Box 340, Government Camp, OR 97028 (☎ **800/464-7704;** fax 503/272-3677; e-mail: climbing@transport.com), leads summit climbs on Mount Hood and offers snow-, ice-, and rock-climbing courses. A 2-day Mount Hood mountaineering course with summit climb costs $325.

WINTER ON THE MOUNTAIN

Although snowpacks that can be slow to reach skiable depths and frequent mid-winter rains make the ski season on Mount Hood unpredictable, in an ordinary year the regular ski season runs from around Thanksgiving right through March or April. Add to this the summer skiing on the Palmer Glacier at Timberline Ski Area, and you have the longest ski season in the United States. There are five ski areas on Mount Hood,

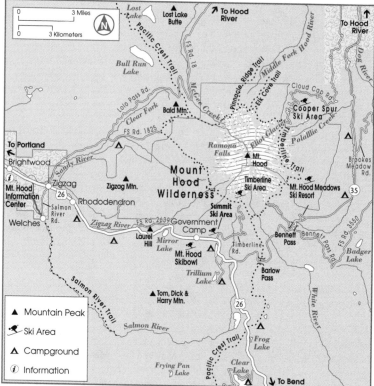

though two of these are tiny operations that attract primarily beginners and families looking for an economical way to all go schussing together. For cross-country skiers, there are many miles of marked ski trails, some of which are groomed.

The single most important thing to know about skiing anywhere in Oregon is that you'll have to have a **Sno-Park Permit.** These permits, which sell for $3 a day or $25 for the season, allow you to park in plowed parking areas on the mountain. You can get permits at ski shops in Sandy and Hood River and at a few convenience stores.

Mt. Hood SkiBowl (☎ **503/272-3206,** or 503/222-2695 for snow report; www.skibowl.com), located in Government Camp on U.S. 26, is the closest ski area to Portland; and with 1,500 vertical feet, it has more expert slopes than any other ski area on the mountain. SkiBowl also claims to be the largest lighted ski area in the United States. Adult lift ticket prices range from $17 for midweek night skiing to $35 for a weekend all-day/night pass. Call for hours of operation.

Also in Government Camp is the tiny **Summit Ski Area** (☎ **503/272-0256**), which has a double chair lift and a rope tow and only a handful of runs. However, the economical rates make this a good choice for beginners. This is also the site of a very popular snow-play hill where families come to go sledding. Lift tickets are $15 for a full day.

Timberline Ski Area (☎ **503/231-7979** in Portland, 503/272-3311 outside Portland, or 503/222-2211 for snow report) is the highest ski area on Mount Hood and has one slope that is open right through summer. This is the site of the historic Timberline Lodge. Adult lift ticket prices range from $13 for night skiing to $34 for a weekend all-day pass. Call for hours of operation.

✪ **Mount Hood Meadows Ski Resort** (☎ **503/337-2222,** or 503/227-7669 for snow report; www.skihood.com), located 12 miles northeast of Government Camp on Ore. 35, is the largest ski resort on Mount Hood, with more than 2,000 skiable acres, 2,777 vertical feet, and a wide variety of terrain. This is the closest Mount Hood comes to having a ski resort of national standing, and it is here that you'll find the most out-of-state skiers. Snowcat skiing is sometimes available, as is summer skiing. Lift ticket prices range from $18 for night skiing to $41 for an all-day pass. Call for hours of operation.

Continuing on around the mountain from Mount Hood Meadows, you'll find the small **Cooper Spur Ski Area** (☎ **503/352-7803**), the oldest ski area on the mountain, with a T-bar and rope tow and 10 short runs. Lift tickets are about $12 a day.

If you're trying to get to the mountain from Portland but don't want the hassle of driving yourself, consider **Bus/Lift** (☎ **503/287-5438**), which departs from various locations around Portland and the metro area and goes to Mount Hood Meadows and back for $20 ($50 for both bus and lift ticket). Purchase tickets at **G.I. Joe Ticketmaster** outlets (☎ **503/790-2787**). Also keep in mind that hotels in Hood River usually offer special ski packages that can make a ski vacation on Mount Hood much cheaper than you would think.

If it's **cross-country skiing** that interests you, there are plenty of trails on Mount Hood. For scenic views, head to the **White River Sno-Park,** east of Government Camp. The trails at **Glacier View Sno-Park,** across U.S. 26 from Mount Hood Ski-Bowl, are good for beginner and intermediate skiers, as are those at **Bennett Pass Sno-Park** on Ore. 35. If you're looking for groomed trails, you'll find them at Trillium Lake (after an often icy ungroomed start), at the **Mount Hood Meadows Nordic Center** ($9 trail pass) on Ore. 35, and at **Teacup Lake** (small donation requested for use of trails), which is located across the highway from the turnoff for Mount Hood Meadows. Teacup Lake is maintained by a local ski club and is the best system of groomed trails on the mountain. In the town of Sandy and at Government Camp, you'll find numerous ski shops that rent cross-country skis.

WHERE TO STAY
ON THE MOUNTAIN

Falcon's Crest Inn. 87287 Government Camp Loop Hwy. (P.O. Box 185), Government Camp, OR 97028. ☎ **800/624-7384** or 503/272-3403. Fax 503/272-3454. www. falconscrest.com. 5 units. $95–$99.50 double; $169–$179 suite. AE, DISC, MC, V.

If you're looking for a B&B within walking distance of the ski slopes, this is your best bet on Mount Hood. Tucked into the trees on the edge of Government Camp, Falcon's Crest is a sprawling chalet-style lodge. Both suites, one of which is done up in a Mexican theme, have whirlpool tubs (one outside on a deck), and though a bit incongruous in this mountain setting, the Safari Room, with its deck and view of the ski slopes, is a great choice. The inn also serves elegant six-course dinners (Cornish game hen, saltimbocca, beef Wellington) by reservation, and throughout the year many special events are staged here, including murder-mystery dinners.

Mt. Hood Inn. 87450 E. Government Camp Loop, Government Camp, OR 97028. ☎ **800/443-7777** or 503/272-3205. www.mthoodinn.com. 55 units. TV TEL. $134–$164 double. Rates include continental breakfast. AE, DC, DISC, MC, V.

Located at the west end of Government right on the highway, this modern budget hotel doesn't have a lot of character, but the adjacent Mt. Hood Brew Pub makes this a great place to stay if you enjoy craft beers after a long day outdoors. Pine furnishings give the guest rooms here a contemporary rustic feel. The king spa rooms, with two-person whirlpool tubs beside the king-size beds, are definitely the best rooms, but they're somewhat overpriced. Other rooms have refrigerators and microwaves. There is an indoor whirlpool, VCR and video rentals, and ski lockers.

✪ **Timberline Lodge.** Timberline, OR 97028. ☎ **800/547-1406** or 503/622-7979. Fax 503/622-0710. www.timberlinelodge.com. 59 units (50 with private bathroom). $65 double without bathroom, $100–$180 double with bathroom. AE, DISC, MC, V. Sno-Park Permit required in winter, but hotel will loan you one.

Constructed during the Great Depression of the 1930s as a WPA project, this classic alpine ski lodge overflows with craftsmanship. The grand stone fireplace, huge exposed beams, and wide plank floors of the lobby impress every first-time visitor. Wood carvings, imaginative wrought-iron fixtures, hand-hooked rugs, and handmade furniture complete the rustic picture.

Rooms vary in size considerably, with the smallest lacking private bathrooms. But no matter which room you stay in, you'll be surrounded by the same rustic furnishings. Unfortunately, windows in the rooms are not very large, and only odd-numbered rooms look out to Mount Hood (you can request one of these, but they won't guarantee it). But you can always retire to the Ram's Head lounge for a better view.

Dining/Entertainment: The **Cascade Dining Room** enjoys a near legendary reputation. The tables are rustic and the windows are small (which limits views), but the Northwest-style food is superb, if a bit pricey. There is also a casual snack bar in the Wy'East Day Lodge across the parking lot. The **Blue Ox Bar** is a dark dungeon of a place while the **Ram's Head Bar** is a more open and airy spot.

Amenities: Ski lifts, ski school and rentals, outdoor swimming pool, hiking trails, coin laundry, guided hotel tours.

AT THE BASE OF THE MOUNTAIN

✪ **The Resort at the Mountain.** 68010 E. Fairway, Welches, OR 97067. ☎ **800/ 669-7666** or 503/622-3101. Fax 503/622-2222. www.theresort.com. 160 units. TV TEL. June–Sept $119–$179 double, $199–$249 suite; Oct–May $99–$139 double, $159–$199 suite. AE, DC, DISC, MC, V.

Set in a clearing in the dense woods at the base of Mount Hood, this resort, though in a beautiful setting, feels less like a mountain lodge than a golf resort. If you stay here, you'll still be a bit of a drive up to Timberline or Government Camp and the area's hiking trails and ski areas. But if a round of golf in a gorgeous setting sounds tempting, this is your best choice in the Oregon Cascades (although the Bend and Sisters areas on the east side of the mountains are the state's real golf resort region). Beautifully landscaped grounds that incorporate concepts from Japanese garden design hide the resort's many low-rise buildings and make this a tranquil woodsy retreat. The guest rooms are large and all have either a balcony or a patio. Coffeemakers and special closets for ski gear are available in some rooms.

Dining: The main lodge has a formal dining room serving primarily Mediterranean and American cuisine, while a more casual dining room overlooks the golf course (open only during the golf season).

Amenities: Room service, laundry/valet service, mountain-bike rentals, 27-hole golf course, four tennis courts, outdoor swimming pool, whirlpool tub, fitness center, horseshoes, nature trails, volleyball, badminton, croquet and lawn-bowling courts, pro shop.

NORTHEAST OF THE MOUNTAIN

Mt. Hood Bed & Breakfast. 8885 Cooper Spur Rd., Parkdale, OR 97041. ☎ **800/ 557-8885** or 541/352-6885. www.mthoodbnb.com. 4 units (2 with private bathroom). TV. $102–$125 double. Rates include full breakfast. MC, V.

Located on a 42-acre working farm on the northeast side of Mount Hood, this B&B offers a quiet place to get away from it all. As an added bonus, you're only minutes away from a small ski area, and the mountain's major ski areas are less than 30 minutes away. We recommend either the Mount Hood or the Mount Adams rooms, both of which have views of their respective mountains. Guests can spend time in a barn that has a tennis court, basketball court, and sauna.

The Inn at Cooper Spur. 10755 Cooper Spur Rd., Mount Hood, OR 97041. ☎ **541/ 352-6692.** Fax 541/352-7551. E-mail: cooperspurinn@gorge.net. 15 units (including 6 cabins). A/C TV TEL. $69–$85 double; $135–$150 cabin or suite. AE, DISC, MC, V.

If you're looking to get away from it all, try an off-season stay at this surprisingly remote lodge. During ski season, though, you might find it difficult to get a reservation (and even in summer, ski teams from around the country often stay here while they train on Mount Hood's summer ski slopes). The inn consists of a main building and a handful of modern log cabins that are certainly the more enjoyable rooms. These cabins have two bedrooms and a loft area reached by a spiral staircase. There are full kitchens for those wishing to do their own cooking. The inn's restaurant serves decent meals at reasonable prices. At the end of the day you can soak yourself in one of the inn's whirlpool spas.

WHERE TO DINE
ON THE MOUNTAIN

✪ **Cascade Dining Room.** In Timberline Lodge, Timberline. ☎ **503/272-3700.** Reservations highly recommended on weekends. Main courses lunch $9–$15, dinner $16–$30. AE, DISC, MC, V. Summer 8–10am, noon–2pm, and 5–8:30pm. Hours may vary other seasons. NORTHWEST.

It may appear a bit casual from the lobby and there are no stunning views of Mount Hood even though it's right outside the window, but the Cascade Dining Room is by far the best restaurant on Mount Hood. The menu changes regularly, but you'll probably find the likes of Dungeness crab flan or smoked salmon cheesecake on the appetizer list. Main courses might include roasted salmon with raspberry-chipotle glaze, seared tuna au poivre, or vegetarian grilled portobello mushroom with a lentil roast. There's a good wine selection, and desserts showcase the variety of local seasonal ingredients such as raspberries, pears, and apples.

Mt. Hood Brew Pub. 87304 E. Government Camp Loop. ☎ **503/272-3724.** Main courses $6–$15. AE, DISC, MC, V. Sun–Thurs noon–10pm, Fri–Sat noon–11pm.

This modern brew pub on the edge of Government Camp offers good microbrews and pub food (sandwiches, pasta, pizzas), as well as decent entrees such as grilled smoked pork chops and beef tenderloin. With at least six beers on tap, and a large selection of Northwest wines, you'll certainly find something to your liking.

AT THE BASE OF THE MOUNTAIN

Calamity Jane's. 42015 U.S. 26, Sandy. ☎ **503/668-7817.** Burgers $4–$12. AE, DISC, MC, V. Daily 11am–10pm. BURGERS.

What, you ask, is a $12 hamburger? Well, at Calamity Jane's, it's a 1-pound pastrami-and-mushroom cheeseburger. That's right: 1 pound! If you think that's outrageous,

Up to Your Neck in Hot Water

Scattered up and down the length of the Oregon Cascades are numerous hot springs, both natural and developed. Of these, ✪ **Bagby Hot Springs,** southeast of Estacada, is one of the most popular. With its rustic wooden buildings and soaking tubs carved out of big logs, the springs have the feel of a backwoods hippie or hillbilly health spa. The springs are 1½ miles down an easy trail through an old-growth forest. Keep in mind two things: (1) clothing is optional here, and (2) car break-ins sometimes happen in the trailhead parking lot, so take your valuables with you or lock them in your trunk.

To reach the springs, take Ore. 224 through Estacada. A half mile past the Ripplebrook Ranger Station, turn right onto F.S. 46. In 3½ miles turn right onto F.S. 63; after another 3½ miles, turn right onto F.S. 70 and continue another 6 miles.

wait until you see the other burgers listed on the menu. There's the peanut-butter burger, the George Washington burger (with sour cream and sweet pie cherries), the hot-fudge-and-marshmallow burger—even an unbelievably priced inflation burger. Not all the burgers at this entertaining and rustic eatery are calculated to turn your stomach—some are just plain delicious. There are even pizza burgers. This place is just east of Sandy on U.S. 26.

The Rendezvous Grill. 67149 E. U.S. 26, Welches. ☎ **503/622-6837.** Reservations recommended. Main courses lunch $7.50–$10, dinner $15–$20. AE, DISC, MC, V. Daily 11:30am–9pm. MEDITERRANEAN.

Located right on U.S. 26 in Welches, this casual, upscale restaurant is a great choice for dinner on your way back to Portland after a day on the mountain. While the emphasis here is on the Mediterranean, other flavors also show up in the guise of sake-glazed salmon and crab and shrimp cakes with chipotle aïoli. The grilled steak with Whidbey's port and blue cheese sauce is a must for steak fans.

2 The Santiam Pass, McKenzie Pass & McKenzie River

Santiam Pass: 82 miles SE of Salem, 40 miles NW of Bend; McKenzie Pass: 77 miles NE of Eugene, 36 miles NW of Bend

As the nearest recreational areas to both Salem and Eugene, the Santiam Pass, McKenzie Pass, and McKenzie River routes are some of the most popular in the state. Ore. 22, which leads over Santiam Pass, is also one of the busiest routes to the Sisters and Bend areas in central Oregon. Along these highways are to be found some of the state's best white-water rafting and fishing, some of the most popular and most beautiful backpacking areas, and good downhill and cross-country skiing. In the summer, the Detroit Lake recreation area is the main attraction along Ore. 22 and is a favorite of water-skiers and lake anglers. In winter, it's downhill and cross-country skiing at Santiam Pass that brings people up this way.

Ore. 126, on the other hand, follows the scenic McKenzie River and is favored by white-water rafters and drift-boat anglers fishing for salmon and steelhead. Several state parks provide access to the river. During the summer, Ore. 126 connects to Ore. 242, a narrow road that climbs up and over McKenzie Pass, the most breathtaking pass in the Oregon Cascades.

ESSENTIALS

GETTING THERE   Santiam Pass is a year-round pass and is reached by Ore. 22 from Salem, U.S. 20 from Albany, and Ore. 126 from Eugene. McKenzie Pass is on Ore. 242 and lies to the south of Santiam Pass. It can be reached by all the same roads that lead to Santiam Pass, but it is closed during the winter months.

VISITOR INFORMATION   For more information on outdoor recreation in this area, contact the **Detroit Ranger Station,** HC73, Box 320, Mill City, OR 97360 (☎ 503/854-3366); the **McKenzie Ranger Station,** 57600 McKenzie Hwy., McKenzie Bridge, OR 97413 (☎ 541/822-3381); or the **Blue River Ranger Station,** Blue River, OR 97413 (☎ 541/822-3317). For more general information, contact the **McKenzie River Chamber of Commerce,** 44643 McKenzie Hwy. (P.O. Box 1117), Leaburg, OR 97489 (☎ 541/896-3330), which operates a visitor center at the old Leaburg fish hatchery on Leaburg Lake east of Springfield.

ALONG THE SANTIAM PASS HIGHWAY

Detroit Lake is the summertime center of activity on this route, with fishing and waterskiing the most popular activities. North of the lake, you'll find the **Breitenbush Hot Springs Retreat and Conference Center** (☎ 503/854-3314), which allows day use of its hot springs by reservation only. The day-use fee is $15 per person, and vegetarian meals are available for $8.

At Santiam Pass, you'll find the **Hoodoo Ski Area** (☎ 541/822-3337 for snow report, or 541/822-3799; www.hoodoo.com), which has three chair lifts and a rope tow, and 22 runs for all levels of experience. Lift tickets are $26 for adults and $19.50 for children. Night skiing is available. Here you'll also find the **Hoodoo Nordic Center,** which has more than 16 kilometers of groomed cross-country ski trails and charges $5 to $8 for a trail pass. Also in the Santiam Pass area, you'll find several Sno-Parks. The Maxwell, Big Springs, and Lava Lake East Sno-Parks access the best trails in the area.

UP THE MCKENZIE RIVER

The McKenzie River is one of Oregon's most popular white-water rafting rivers, and the cold blue waters offer thrills for rafters with a wide range of experience levels. **The Oregon Paddler** (☎ 888/297-9922 or 541/741-8661), **Oregon Whitewater Adventures** (☎ 800/820-RAFT or 541/746-5422), **McKenzie River Adventures** (☎ 800/832-5858 or 541/822-3806), and **Jim's Oregon Whitewater** (☎ 800/254-JIMS or 541/822-6003) all offer a variety of trips of varying lengths on the McKenzie. Expect to pay around $50 for a half day of rafting and $65 to $75 for a full day. Overnight trips can also be arranged. A tamer white-water experience can be had on the pontoon platform boats of **McKenzie Pontoon Trips** (☎ 541/741-1905).

If you're interested in seeing this area by bike, contact **Oregon Trails Adventure Vacations** (☎ 541/984-1433), which offers a variety of bike rides, both road and trail, for between $15 (a group ride) and $75 (a full-day mountain bike ride). This company can also arrange rafting trips, glider rides, and skydiving.

Surprisingly, the McKenzie River town of Blue River is home to one of the best golf courses in Oregon. **Tokatee Golf Club,** 54947 McKenzie Hwy., Blue River (☎ 800/452-6376), gets consistently high ratings and has a spectacular setting with views of snowcapped Cascade Peaks and lush forests.

Off Ore. 126, between the towns of Blue River and McKenzie Bridge, you'll find the turnoff for the **Aufderheide National Scenic Byway** (Forest Service Road 19).

This road meanders for 54 miles through the foothills of the Cascades, first following the South Fork McKenzie River (and Cougar Reservoir) and then following the North Fork of the Middle Fork Willamette River, which offers excellent fly-fishing and numerous swimming holes. At the south end of Cougar Reservoir, you'll find a trail that leads to the very popular **Terwilliger Hot Springs.** The southernmost stretch of this road is the most scenic portion and passes through a deep, narrow gorge formed by the North Fork of the Middle Fork Willamette River. Along the route, you'll find several hiking trails, including the trail up **French Pete Creek,** which was one of the first lowland old-growth forests to be protected from logging. At the southern end of the scenic byway is the community of Westfir, which is the site of the longest covered bridge in Oregon.

Between the turnoff for McKenzie Pass and the junction of Ore. 126 and U.S. 20, you'll find some of the Cascades's most enchanting water features. Southernmost of these is **Belknap Lodge & Hot Springs** (☎ 541/822-3512), where, for $4.50 an hour or $8.50 a day, you can soak in a hot mineral swimming pool. Just north of Trail Bridge Reservoir, on a side road off the highway, a 2-mile hike on a section of the McKenzie River Trail will bring you to the startlingly blue waters of the ✪ **Tamolitch Pool.** This pool is formed when the McKenzie River wells up out of the ground after flowing underground for 3 miles. Five miles south of the junction with Ore. 20, you'll come to two picturesque waterfalls—**Sahalie Falls** and **Koosah Falls.** Across the highway from these falls is **Clear Lake,** the source of the McKenzie River. This spring-fed lake truly lives up to its name, and a rustic lakeside resort rents rowboats so you can get out on the water and see for yourself. Be sure to hike the trail on the east side of the lake; it leads to the turquoise waters of **Great Springs,** which is connected to the lake by a 100-yard stream.

One of the most breathtaking sections of road in the state begins just east of **Belknap Hot Springs.** Ore. 242, which is open only in the summer, is a narrow, winding road that climbs up through forests and lava fields to **McKenzie Pass,** from which there's a sweeping panorama of the Cascades and blackened, ragged hillsides of lava. These lava fields are some of the youngest in Oregon. An observation building made of lava rock provides sighting tubes so that you can identify all the visible peaks, and a couple of trails will lead you out into this otherworldly wasteland. In autumn, this road has some of the best colors in the state. On the west side of the pass, the short **Proxy Falls** trail leads through old lava flows to a waterfall that has no outlet stream in late summer. The water simply disappears into the porous lava.

WHERE TO STAY
SANTIAM PASS ROUTE

Breitenbush Hot Springs Retreat and Conference Center. P.O. Box 578, Detroit, OR 97342. ☎ **503/854-3314.** www.breitenbush.com. 43 cabins. $55–$90 per person cabin; $50–$55 per person platform tents; $45–$50 per person campsites. Rates include all meals, use of hot springs, and daily well-being programs. AE, MC, V.

This New Age retreat center deep in the Cascade forests offers a wide range of programs (from yoga retreats to massage workshops to various single-sex retreats and programs), but it is also open to anyone simply wishing to come for a personal retreat without participating in any specific program. The cabins are very simple, and not all have private bathrooms; but it is this very simplicity that accounts for much of the mellow atmosphere. There are also large tents on platforms, as well as sites where you can pitch your own tent. There are both natural hot pools and hot tubs (clothing optional), and massages are available.

ALONG THE MCKENZIE RIVER

The Osprey Inn. 56532 North Bank Rd., McKenzie Bridge, OR 97413-9614. ☎ **541/ 822-8186.** www.osprey-inn.com. 4 units. A/C. $110–$135 double. Rates include full breakfast. 2-night minimum on weekends. Closed Nov–Mar. No credit cards.

Located about 50 miles east of Eugene, this modern riverfront B&B boasts comfortable rooms and a beautiful setting overlooking the McKenzie River. Big windows take in the scenery, and there are even a couple of gazebos down by the water. For the ultimate views, ask for the Window Room, with its 180° view. For lots of space, request the Master Suite. Paths wander the grounds, and a small creek flows across the property into the river.

○ **Belknap Lodge & Hot Springs.** 59296 N. Belknap Springs Rd., Belknap Springs, OR 97413. ☎ **541/822-3512.** Fax 541/822-3327. 12 units, 6 cabins. $70–$85 double; $45–$75 cabin. Rates for lodge include continental breakfast. MC, V.

Located on the bank of the McKenzie River, this lodge has recently undergone an extensive remodeling and renovation that has turned it into one of the most enjoyable mountain retreats in the state. Extensive lawns and perennial gardens have been planted, turning this clearing in the forest into a burst of color in the summer. Guest rooms vary in size, but all have comfortable modern furnishings. Some also have whirlpool tubs or decks overlooking the roaring river. The hot springs, which are on the far side of the river and are reached by a foot bridge, are pumped into a small pool between the lodge and the river. There is a library/breakfast room, as well as a small exercise room. The cabins are more rustic than the lodge rooms. The lodge also has campsites for tents and RVs ($17 to $18). There are plans to add a restaurant.

Holiday Farm. 54455 McKenzie River Dr., Blue River, OR 97413. ☎ **800/823-3715** or 541/822-3715. 16 cottages. $125–$150 cottage. Closed Nov–Mar. Pets accepted. AE, DISC, MC, V.

Forget about log cabins, this place is a collection of white cottages reminiscent of those found on Cape Cod. It started out as a stagecoach stop and has been around long enough to have hosted Pres. Herbert Hoover. The best cottages are those that are perched right over the river. The setting, under the big trees and beside the rushing McKenzie River, is as idyllic as you'll find in Oregon. Guests have 90 acres to roam, with 750 feet of riverfront and two private lakes for fishing and swimming. The dining room, a throwback to the early 1960s, serves three meals a day and has a small lounge and game room.

Log Cabin Inn. 56483 McKenzie Hwy., McKenzie Bridge, OR 97413. ☎ **800/355-3432** or 541/822-3432. 8 cabins. $80–$95 cabin for 2 to 4 people. 2-night minimum stay on weekends Apr–Oct. DISC, MC, V.

Situated on 6½ acres in the community of McKenzie Bridge, this log lodge was built in 1906 after the original 1886 lodge (a stagecoach stop) burned to the ground. In the lodge's heyday, its guests included President Hoover, Clark Gable, and the duke and duchess of Windsor. (More recently, Sean Penn has graced the premises.) Today, you can stay in rustic cabins, all but one of which have their own fireplaces. The one cabin without a fireplace does, however, have a kitchen, which the others do not. Although the one duplex log cabin has cramped rooms, it has a lot of woodsy character. There are also large teepees ($45 per night) that sleep up to six people for anyone interested in camping. The lodge's restaurant is renowned for its high-quality meals, which include such game as wild boar, venison, and buffalo. At under $10, Sunday brunch is a great deal.

CAMPGROUNDS

There are several campgrounds along the McKenzie River on Ore. 126. Of these, the **Delta Campground,** set under huge old-growth trees between Blue River and McKenzie Bridge, is one of the finest. Rafters and kayakers tend to gravitate to **Olallie Campground** and **Paradise Campground,** which are east of McKenzie Bridge. Between Paradise and Delta, you'll also find **McKenzie Bridge Campground.**

If you are up this way to hike, mountain bike, or do some flat-water canoeing, there is no better choice than Clear Lake's **Coldwater Cove Campground** on Ore. 126 just south of Santiam Pass junction. South of here on Ore. 126, the **Trail Bridge Campground** makes a good alternative to Coldwater Cove.

Along the popular McKenzie Pass Highway (Ore. 242), you'll find **Scott Lake Campground, Alder Springs Campground,** and **Lava Lake Campground.**

Along the Aufderheide National Scenic Byway, you'll find campgrounds at **Frissell Crossing, Twin Springs, Homestead,** and **French Pete,** all of which are on the banks of the South Fork of the McKenzie River. Toward the south end of this road is **Kiahanie Campground,** which is on the North Fork of the Middle Fork of the Willamette River and is popular with fly anglers.

WHERE TO DINE

The dining room at the Log Cabin Inn is the best place to eat along the McKenzie River. Other than this, there are a few casual roadhouses strung out along Ore. 126. For burgers, try the **Vida Cafe,** milepost 26 (☎ **541/896-3289**), or **Finn Rock General Store,** milepost 38 (☎ **541/822-3299**), which has a deck beside the river. For some of the best pies in the state, stop at the **Village Cafe/Mom's Pies,** 49647 McKenzie Hwy., Vida (☎ **541/822-3891**), where usually about a dozen types of pies are available.

3 The Willamette Pass Route

Oakridge: 41 miles SE of Eugene; Willamette Pass: 68 miles SE of Eugene

Ore. 58, which connects Eugene with U.S. 97 north of Crater Lake, is the state's fastest and straightest route over the Cascades. However, this is not to imply that there isn't anything along this highway worth slowing down for. Flanked by two wilderness areas—Waldo Lake and Diamond Peak—and three major lakes—Waldo, Odell, and Crescent—Ore. 58 provides access to a wide range of recreational activities, chief among which are mountain biking, fishing, and boating in summer and both downhill and cross-country skiing in winter.

The sister towns of Oakridge and Westfir are the only real towns on this entire route and are the only places where you'll find much in the way of services. Westfir is also the southern terminus of the Aufderheide National Scenic Byway, which winds through the Cascade foothills to just outside the town of McKenzie Bridge on Ore. 126. For information on this scenic drive, see above.

ESSENTIALS

GETTING THERE   Ore. 58 begins just south of Eugene off I-5 and stretches for 92 miles to U.S. 97.

VISITOR INFORMATION   For more information on recreational activities in this area, contact the **Oakridge Ranger Station,** 49098 Salmon Creek Rd., Oakridge, OR 97463 (☎ **541/782-2291**). For other information, contact the Oakridge/Westfir Chamber of Commerce, P.O. Box 217, Oakridge, OR 97463 (☎ **541/782-4146; www.oakridgechamber.com**).

WHAT TO SEE & DO: FROM HOT SPRINGS TO SNOW SKIING

In the Willamette National Forest outside the logging town of Oakridge are miles and miles of great mountain-biking trails that have turned the Oakridge area into one of Oregon's top mountain-biking regions. Stop by the ranger stations in Westfir and Oakridge to get maps and information on riding these trails. One of the most scenic rides is the 22-mile trail around Waldo Lake. You'll also find mountain-biking trails at Willamette Pass Ski Area, where the cross-country ski trails make great bike trails.

If you're keen to soak your weary muscles in some natural hot springs, you'll find some right beside Ore. 58 about 10 miles east of Oakridge. **McCredie Hot Springs** are neither the hottest nor the most picturesque hot springs in the state, and with traffic noise and crowds, they aren't the most pleasant either. But if you want a quick soak without having to go wandering down gravel roads, they do the trick.

Just before reaching Willamette Pass, you'll see signs for **Salt Creek Falls,** which are well worth a stroll down the short trail to the falls overlook. At 286 feet high, these are the second-highest falls in the state. Longer hiking trails also lead out from the falls parking area.

Also just before Willamette Pass is the turnoff for Forest Service Road 5897, which leads 10 miles north to **Waldo Lake,** one of the purest lakes in the world. The lake, which is just over a mile high, covers 10 square miles and is 420 feet deep. When the waters are still, it is possible to see more than 100 feet down into the lake. Because this is such a large lake, and because there are reliable afternoon winds, it is popular for sailboating and boardsailing. Powerboaters and canoeists also frequent the lake. There are several campgrounds along the east shore of the lake, while the west shore abuts the Waldo Lake Wilderness Area. The 22-mile loop trail around the lake is popular with mountain bikers and backpackers, but shorter day hikes, particularly at the south end, are rewarding. The mosquitoes here are some of the worst in the state, so before planning a trip up here, be sure to get a bug report from the Oakridge Ranger Station.

Just over Willamette Pass lie two more large lakes. **Odell Lake** is best known by anglers who come to troll for kokanee salmon and Mackinaw trout. However, it's also a good windsurfing lake, and each July it hosts the Pioneer Cup Canoe Races. Although the waters never exactly get warm, **Crescent Lake** is the area's best for swimming, notably Symax Beach, on the lake's northeast corner.

At **Willamette Pass Ski Area** (☎ **800/444-5030** for information, 541/484-5030, or 541/345-SNOW for skiing conditions; www.willamettepass.com), 69 miles southeast of Eugene on Ore. 58, you'll find 30 downhill runs and 12½ miles (20km) of groomed cross-country trails. The ski area is open daily from around Thanksgiving to mid-April. Night skiing is available on selected Friday and Saturday nights from late December to March. Adult lift tickets are $29 per day.

WHERE TO STAY

Odell Lake Lodge. P.O. Box 72, Crescent Lake, OR 97425. ☎ **541/433-2540.** E-mail: odellake@bendnet.com. 19 units (including 12 cabins). $44–$58 double; $70–$225 cabin. Pets accepted ($5 per day). DISC, MC, V.

Located at the east end of Odell Lake just off Ore. 58, this rustic cabin resort is set beneath tall trees beside the lake. Most popular in the summer, when fishing is the sport of choice, the lodge also stays open through the winter and has its own network of groomed cross-country ski trails. The lodge rooms are generally rather small, but the economical prices keep them filled. The cabins vary in size from tiny one-bedroom buildings to one with four bedrooms. All the cabins have wood stoves, and about half overlook the water. The lodge has a dining room serving three meals a day. In summer, the lodge's marina rents fishing boats (and tackle), canoes, rowboats, and sailboats.

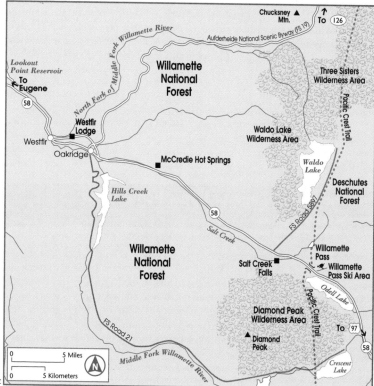

The lodge also rents mountain bikes and cross-country skis. This place is pretty basic, but the location is great. Several of the cabins have been recently remodeled, so try to get one of these.

Westfir Lodge. 48365 First St., Westfir, OR 97492. ☎ **541/782-3103.** Fax 541/782-3103. 8 units. A/C. $70–$85 double. Rates include full breakfast. No credit cards.

Housed in what was once the company headquarters for a long gone lumber mill, this bed-and-breakfast has a very Victorian feel inside and beautiful flower gardens outside. Directly across the street is the longest covered bridge in Oregon, which once connected the offices to the lumber mill itself. The bridge crosses the North Fork of the Middle Fork of the Willamette River, which is a good fly-fishing river. Set at the southern end of the Aufderheide National Scenic Byway, this inn makes an excellent base for exploring both the McKenzie River to the north and the Willamette Pass area to the east. While all the rooms have private bathrooms, only four of these are actually in the room itself; others are across the hall from the guest room. An eclectic assemblage of antiques and artifacts from the innkeepers' world travels fills the guest rooms and many public rooms.

CAMPGROUNDS

On Waldo Lake, the **Islet Campground,** with its sandy beach, should be your first choice. Second choice on the lake should be **Shadow Bay Campground** at the south end of the lake. If you have a boat, you can camp at primitive campsites along the west shore of the lake. **Gold Lake Campground,** just west of Willamette Pass on FS Road

500, is a quiet spot on a pretty lake that allows no motorboats and is fly-fishing only. Just over Willamette Pass, there are several campgrounds on Odell Lake. The **Sunset Cove Campground** is your best choice if you are here to windsurf. Otherwise, I would opt for the quieter **Odell Creek Campground** at the east end of the lake.

WHERE TO DINE
Most people heading up this way plan to be self-sufficient when mealtime rolls around, whether they're camping or staying in a cabin. If you don't happen to have a full ice chest, you'll find a couple of pizza places, a Mexican restaurant, and a couple of espresso places in Oakridge. Although none of these is particularly memorable, they're the only places to get a meal other than in the dining room of the Odell Lake Lodge or the pizza place at the Willamette Pass Ski Area.

4 The North Umpqua–Upper Rogue River Scenic Byway

Diamond Lake: 76 miles E of Roseburg, 80 miles NE of Medford

Ore. 138, which heads east out of Roseburg, leads to Diamond Lake and the north entrance to Crater Lake National Park, but it's also one of the state's most scenic highways. Along much of its length, the highway follows the North Umpqua River, which is famed among fly anglers for its fighting steelhead and salmon. As far as we're concerned, this deep aquamarine stream is the most beautiful river in Oregon and is well worth a visit even if you don't know a wooly bugger from a muddler minnow. Between Idleyld Park and Toketee Reservoir, you'll find numerous picnic areas, boat launches, swimming holes, and campgrounds.

As Ore. 138 approaches the crest of the Cascades, it skirts the shores of Diamond Lake, which though not even remotely as beautiful as nearby Crater Lake is still a major recreational destination. The lake, which is almost a mile in elevation, is set at the foot of jagged Mount Thielsen, a spire-topped pinnacle known as the "lightning rod of the Cascades." The lake offers swimming, boating, fishing, camping, hiking, biking, and, in winter, snowmobiling and skiing. Just beyond Diamond Lake is the north entrance to Crater Lake National Park.

The 24-mile-long Ore. 230 connects the Diamond Lake area with the valley of the upper Rogue River at the community of Union Creek. While this stretch of the Rogue is not as dramatic as the North Umpqua or the lower Rogue River, it has its charms, including a natural bridge, a narrow gorge, and some grand old trees.

ESSENTIALS
GETTING THERE The North Umpqua River is paralleled by Ore. 138, which connects Roseburg, on I-5, with U.S. 97, which parallels the Cascades on the east side of the mountains. This highway leads to the north entrance of Crater Lake National Park.

VISITOR INFORMATION For information on recreational activities in this area, contact the **North Umpqua Ranger District,** 18782 N. Umpqua Hwy., Glide, OR 97443 (☎ **541/496-3532**); or the **Diamond Lake Ranger District,** 202 Toketee RS Rd., Idleyld Park, OR 97447 (☎ **541/498-2531**).

WHAT TO SEE & DO: FLY-FISHING, RAFTING & A WATERFALL
Oregon abounds in waterfalls and white-water rivers, but in the town of Glide, 12 miles east of Roseburg, you'll find the only place in the state where rivers collide.

At the interesting **Colliding Rivers Viewpoint,** the North Umpqua River rushing in from the north slams into the white water of the Little River, which flows from the south, and the two rivers create a churning stew.

The most celebrated portion of the river is the 31-mile stretch from Deadline Falls, in Swiftwater Park, to Soda Springs Dam. This stretch of river is open to fly angling only. Between June and October, you can often see salmon and steelhead leaping up Deadline Falls, which has a designated salmon-viewing area down a short trail on the south bank of the river. For fly-fishing needs and advice, stop in at the **Blue Heron Fly Shop** (☎ 541/496-0448) just off Ore. 138 in Idleyld Park, or **Steamboat Inn** (☎ 541/498-2230) in Steamboat. If you want to hire a guide to take you out fishing on the North Umpqua River, try **Larry Levine's River Wolf Guide Service** (☎ 541/496-0326), **North River Guide Service** (☎ 541/496-0309), **Jerry Q. Phelps** (☎ 541/672-8324), or **Summer Run Guide Service** (☎ 541/496-3037). Rates are generally between $150 and $250 per day.

If you'd rather just paddle the river in a kayak or raft, contact **Noah's River Adventure Float Trips** (☎ 800/858-2811 or 541/488-2811), **North Umpqua Outfitters** (☎ 541/673-4599), **Orange Torpedo Trips** (☎ 800/635-2925 or 541/479-5061), or **Oregon Ridge and River Excursions** (☎ 541/496-3333), which all offer trips of varying lengths. Rates are around $65 to $95 for a 1-day trip. Oregon Ridge and River Excursions also offers half-day and full-day guided mountain-bike rides ($45 and $65), as well as multiday tours.

At the turnoff for Toketee Reservoir, you'll find the trailhead for the ½-mile hike to **Toketee Falls.** This double cascade plummets 120 feet over a wall of columnar basalt and is one of the most photographed waterfalls in the state. Also in this same area, past the Toketee Lake Campground, you'll find the **Umpqua Hot Springs** down a short trail. These natural hot springs perch high above the North Umpqua River on a hillside covered with mineral deposits. For longer hikes, consider the many segments of the 79-mile **North Umpqua Trail,** which parallels the river from just east of Glide all the way to the Pacific Crest Trail. The lower segments of this trail are also popular mountain-biking routes.

At **Diamond Lake,** just a few miles north of Crater Lake National Park, you'll find one of the most popular mountain recreation spots in the state. In summer, the popular and somewhat run-down **Diamond Lake Resort** is the center of area activities. Here you can rent boats and horses, swim at a small beach, and access the 10½-mile paved hiking/biking trail that circles Diamond Lake.

Near the community of Union Creek, west of the Crater Lake National Park on Ore. 62, are the Rogue River Gorge and a small natural bridge. The gorge, though only a few feet wide in places, is quite dramatic and has an easy trail running alongside. The natural bridge is formed by a lava tube through which flows the Rogue River.

In winter, Diamond Lake Resort serves as the region's main snowmobiling destination, but it also serves as a base camp for downhill skiers heading out with **Mount Bailey Snowcats** (☎ 800/446-4555; www.mountbailey.com), which provides access to untracked snow on the slopes of nearby Mount Bailey. A day of snowcat skiing runs between $130 and $175. Cross-country skiers will find rentals and groomed trails at the **Diamond Lake Resort Cross Country Ski Center.** There are also many more miles of marked, but not groomed, cross-country ski trails in the area, with the more interesting trails to be found at the south end of the lake. Snowmobile rentals and tours are also available here. For more information on these activities, contact **Diamond Lake Resort** (☎ 800/733-7593).

WHERE TO STAY & DINE

Diamond Lake Resort. Diamond Lake, OR 97731. ☎ **800/733-7593** or 541/793-3333. Fax 541/793-3309. www.diamondlake.net. 92 units (including 42 cabins). TV. $69–$76 double; $129–$185 cabin. AE, DISC, MC, V. Pets accepted ($5 per day).

Located on the shores of Diamond Lake near the north entrance to the national park, this resort has long been a popular family vacation spot, and with Mounts Thielsen and Bailey flanking the lake, this is one of the most picturesque settings in the Oregon Cascades. The variety of accommodations provides plenty of choices, but our favorites are the lakefront cabins, which are large enough for a family or two couples. These have great views of the lake and mountains. If you want to do your own cooking, you'll find kitchenettes in both the cabins and the studios. The lodge also offers several dining options, though most visitors opt to cook their own meals. Boat, mountain-bike, and horse rentals are available, and there's a small sandy beach and a bumper-boat area. In winter, the resort is most popular with snowmobilers but also attracts a few cross-country skiers, as well as downhillers here to snowcat ski on Mount Bailey. Unfortunately, this resort has not been that well maintained in recent years, though some units have new carpeting.

Prospect Historical Hotel/Motel. 391 Mill Creek Dr., Prospect, OR 97536. ☎ **800/944-6490** or 541/560-3664. Fax 503/560-3825. www.prospecthotel.com. 23 units. $50–$85 double. DISC, MC, V. Pets accepted.

This hotel, located in the tiny hamlet of Prospect, 30 miles from Crater Lake's Rim Village, is a combination of an 1889 vintage hotel and a modern motel. The old hotel is a big white building with a wraparound porch. The small rooms in the historic hotel have few furnishings, but they do have a country styling that gives them a bit of charm. If you stay in one of these rooms, a continental breakfast is included. The motel rooms are much larger and have televisions and telephones, and some of these rooms also have kitchenettes. The elegant dining room is well-known for its excellent meals, with main courses from hamburgers to prime rib ranging in price from $7 to $25 (closed Oct through Apr).

✪ **Steamboat Inn.** 42705 N. Umpqua Hwy., Steamboat, OR 97447-9703. ☎ **800/840-8825** or 541/498-2230. Fax 541/498-2411. www.thesteamboatinn.com. 19 units (including 5 cottages and 4 houses). $130 cabin; $165 cottages and houses; $245 suites. MC, V.

Located roughly midway between Roseburg and Crater Lake, this inn on the bank of the North Umpqua River is by far the finest lodging on the river. While the lodge appeals primarily to anglers, the beautiful gardens, luxurious guest rooms, and gourmet meals also attract a fair number of people looking for a quiet getaway in the forest and a base for hiking and biking. If you aren't springing for one of the suites, which have their own soaking tubs overlooking the river, your best bet will be one of the streamside rooms, which are referred to as cabins but really aren't. These have gas fireplaces and open onto a long deck that overlooks the river. The hideaway cottages are more spacious but don't have river views and are half a mile from the lodge (and the dining room). Dinners are multicourse affairs served in a cozy dining room, and breakfast is available all day. There's also a fly-fishing shop on the premises.

Union Creek Resort. 56484 Ore. 62, Prospect, OR 97536. ☎ **541/560-3565.** 9 units, 14 cabins. $38–$48 double; $50–$90 cabin for 2 to 6 people. MC, V.

Located almost across the road from the Rogue River Gorge, this cabin resort has been catering to Crater Lake visitors since the early 1900s and is listed on the National Register of Historic Places. Tall trees shade the grounds of the rustic resort, which is right on Ore. 62 about 23 miles from Rim Village. Accommodations include both lodge rooms and very basic cabins (many of which have kitchenettes), and most have been updated in recent years. Across the road from the cabins and lodge building is Beckie's Café, which serves home-style meals and is best known for its pies. This is your best and closest option outside the Crater Lake National Park on the west side.

CAMPGROUNDS

Along the North Umpqua River between Idleyld Park and Diamond Lake, you'll find the Bureau of Land Management's **Susan Creek Campground,** the most upscale public campground along the North Umpqua (it even has hot showers). Up Forest Service Road 38 (between mileposts 38 and 39), you'll find **Canton Creek Campground,** which is just off Steamboat Creek and **Steamboat Falls Campground.** Nearby on Ore. 138 is **Island Campground.** The larger **Horseshoe Bend Campground,** near Steamboat, is popular with rafters and kayakers on weekends and has well-separated campsites, big views of surrounding cliffs, and access to the North Umpqua Trail. Continuing east, **Eagle Rock Campground** is in deep woods. **Boulder Flat Campground,** right on the highway east of Eagle Rock, is the uppermost campground on the wild and scenic section of the river. **Toketee Lake Campground,** at Toketee Reservoir, is situated back from the lake, but there are a few sites on the river.

Diamond Lake has three U.S. Forest Service campgrounds—Diamond Lake, Broken Arrow, and Thielsen View—with a total of 450 campsites. Here you'll also find the **Diamond Lake RV Park** (☎ 541/793-3318).

Southwest of the Crater Lake National Park on Ore. 62, you'll find **Huckleberry Mountain Campground.** However, this campground is set amid spindly young trees and is devoid of atmosphere. Farther west is **Farewell Bend Campground,** which is set amid big trees on the Rogue River. The next campgrounds are **Union Creek** and **Natural Bridge,** both of which are also along the Rogue River. North of Ore. 62 on Ore. 230, you'll find the **Hamaker Campground,** on a pretty bend in the Rogue River with big trees and meadows across the river.

5 Crater Lake National Park

71 miles NE of Medford, 83 miles E of Roseburg, 57 miles N of Klamath Falls

At 1,932 feet, Crater Lake is the deepest lake in the United States (and the seventh deepest in the world). But depth alone is not what has made this one of the most visited spots in the Northwest. Ever since a prospector searching for gold stumbled on the high mountain lake in 1853, visitors have been mesmerized by its startling sapphire-blue waters. In 1902, the lake and its surroundings became a national park, and it's still the only national park in Oregon.

The crater (more precisely known as a caldera) that holds the serene lake was born in an explosive volcanic eruption 7,700 years ago. When the volcano, now known as Mount Mazama, erupted, its summit (thought to have been around 12,000 feet high) collapsed, leaving a crater 4,000 feet deep. It has taken thousands of years of rain and melting snow to create the cold, clear lake, which today is surrounded by crater walls nearly 2,000 feet high.

The drive into the park winds through forests that offer no hint of the spectacular sight that lies hidden among these mountains. With no warning except the signs leading to Rim Village, you suddenly find yourself gazing down into a vast bowl full of blue water. Toward one end of the lake, the cone of Wizard Island rises from the blue waters. This island is the tip of a volcano that has been slowly building since the last eruption of Mount Mazama.

How's the Fishing?

One of the most frequently asked questions in southern Oregon is "How's the fishing in Crater Lake?" The answer is "Not too good." However, there are some rainbows and kokanee to be caught if you're willing to hike 700 feet down to Cleetwood Cove (and back up with your catch). No fishing license is necessary to fish the lake, and there is no limit on how many fish you can take. In fact, the park service would be happy if more people fished this lake and reduced the fish population. Two things to remember, though, are that no live or organic bait is allowed in the lake, and cleaning fish in the lake is prohibited.

Once there were no fish in Crater Lake, and it is perhaps partly for this reason that this is one of the purest lakes in the world. With no inlets or outlets, the lake was cut off from any chance of naturally acquiring a fish population. However, in the late 19th century, the hand of man intervened, and fish were introduced in an attempt to attract more visitors to the lake. Over the next 50 years, rainbow, cutthroat, and brown trout, steelhead, and coho and kokanee salmon were stocked in the lake, but only the rainbows and kokanee have survived since the discontinuation of this misguided program.

Aside from the shores around Cleetwood Cove, the only other place to fish Crater Lake is from Wizard Island, where you may have good luck if you are stealthy and lucky enough. To fish from Wizard Island, take one of the early boat tours from Cleetwood Cove, get off on the island, and arrange to take one of the later boats back.

In addition to lake fishing, Crater Lake National Park offers stream fishing for several species of trout. For the most part, though, the park's streams are fairly inaccessible.

ESSENTIALS

GETTING THERE   If you're coming from the south on I-5, take exit 62 in Medford and follow Ore. 62 for 75 miles. If you're coming from the north, take Exit 124 in Roseburg and follow Ore. 138. From Klamath Falls, take U.S. 97 north to Ore. 62. In winter, only the south entrance is open. Due to deep snowpack, the north entrance usually doesn't open until sometime in late July.

VISITOR INFORMATION   For more information, contact **Crater Lake National Park,** P.O. Box 7, Crater Lake, OR 97604 (☎ **541/594-2211;** www.nps.gov/crla).

ADMISSION   Park admission is $10 per vehicle and $5 per person for pedestrians and cyclists.

SEEING THE HIGHLIGHTS

After your first breathtaking view of the lake, you may want to stop by one of the park's two visitor centers. The **Steel Information Center** is located between the south park entrance and the Rim Village, which is where you'll find the smaller and less thorough **Rim Village Visitor Center.** Though the park is open year-round, in winter, when deep snows blanket the region, only the road to Rim Village is kept clear. During the summer (roughly beginning in late June), the ✪ **Rim Drive** provides many viewpoints as it makes a 39-mile-long circuit of the lake.

Narrated boat trips around the lake are the park's most popular activity. These tours last 1¾ hours and begin at Cleetwood Cove, at the bottom of a very steep 1-mile trail that descends 700 feet from the rim to the lakeshore. Before deciding to take a

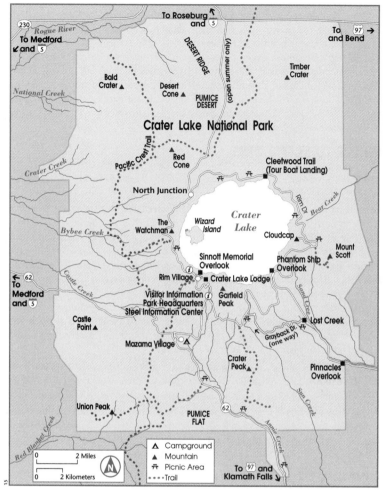

boat tour, be sure you're in good enough physical condition to make the steep climb back up to the rim. Also, be sure to bring warm clothes because it can be quite a bit cooler on the lake than it is on the rim. A naturalist on each boat provides a narrative on the ecology and history of the lake, and all tours include a stop on Wizard Island. Tours are offered from late June to mid-September and cost $15 for adults and $8.50 for children 11 and under.

Of the many miles of **hiking trails** within the park, the mile-long Cleetwood Trail is the only trail that leads down to the lakeshore. It's a steep and tiring hike back up from the lake. The trail to the top of Mount Scott, although it's a rigorous 2½-mile hike, is the park's most rewarding. Shorter trails with good views include the 0.8-mile trail to the top of the Watchman, which overlooks Wizard Island, and the 1.7-mile trail up Garfield Peak. The short Castle Crest Wildflower Trail is best hiked in late July or early August. Backpackers can hike the length of the park on the Pacific Crest Trail (PCT) or head out on a few other trails that lead into more remote, though less scenic, corners of the park.

Other summertime park activities include children's programs, campfire ranger talks, history lectures, and guided walks. To find out about these, check in *Crater Lake Reflections,* a free park newspaper given to all visitors when they enter the park.

In winter, **cross-country skiing** is popular on the park's snow-covered Rim Drive and in the backcountry. At Rim Village, you'll find several miles of well-marked ski trails, affording some of the best views in the state, weather permitting. Skiers in good condition can usually make the entire circuit of the lake in 2 days but must be prepared to camp in the snow. Spring, when the weather is warmer and there are fewer severe storms, is actually the best time to ski around the lake.

WHERE TO STAY & DINE

✪ **Crater Lake Lodge.** Mailing address: 1211 Ave. C, White City, OR 97503. ☎ **541/ 830-8700.** Fax 541/830-8514. www.crater-lake.com. 72 units. $112–$142 double. MC, V. Closed mid-Oct to mid-May.

Perched on the edge of the rim overlooking Crater Lake, this lodge was completely rebuilt in 1995 and has since become the finest national-park lodge in the Northwest. Not only are the views breathtaking, but the amenities are modern without sacrificing the rustic atmosphere that visitors expect in a mountain lodge. Among the lodge's few original features are the stone fireplace and ponderosa pine–bark walls in the Great Hall. Slightly more than half of the guest rooms overlook the lake, and although most rooms have modern bathrooms, eight have clawfoot bathtubs. The very best rooms are the corner rooms on the lake side of the lodge. The lodge's dining room serves creative Northwest cuisine and provides a view of both Crater Lake and the Klamath River basin. As at other national-park lodges throughout the country, reservations here are hard to come by. Plan as far in advance as you can.

Mazama Village Motor Inn. Mailing address: 1211 Ave. C, White City, OR 97503. ☎ **541/830-8700.** Fax 541/830-8514. www.crater-lake.com. 40 units. $89 double. MC, V. Closed Nov–May.

Though the Mazama Village Motor Inn isn't on the rim of the crater, it's just a short drive away. The modern motel-style guest rooms are housed in 10 steep-roofed buildings that look much like traditional mountain cabins. A laundry, gas station, and general store make Mazama Village a busy spot in the summer.

CAMPGROUNDS

Tent camping and RV spaces are available on the south side of the park at the **Mazama Village Campground,** where there are 200 sites ($10 to $15 per night). There are also 16 tent sites available at **Lost Creek Campground** ($10 per night) on the park's east side. These campgrounds are open from June to October. Reservations are not accepted at either campground. If you're a backpacker, there's camping in the park's backcountry; be sure to get a backcountry permit at one of the park's two visitor centers. For information on campgrounds outside the park, see "Campgrounds" in "The North Umpqua–Upper Rogue River Scenic Byway" section above.

Southern Oregon 9

Roughly defined as the region from the California border to just north of Roseburg and lying between the Coast Range and the Cascades, southern Oregon is a mountainous area that seems more akin to Northern California than to the rest of Oregon. Here the Cascade Range, Coast Range, and Siskiyou Mountains converge in a jumble of peaks.

It was gold that first brought white settlers to this area, and it was timber that kept them here. The gold is all played out now, but the legacy of the gold-rush days, when stagecoaches traveled the rough road between Sacramento and Portland, remains in picturesque towns such as Jacksonville and Oakland.

Southern Oregon is quite a hike from the nearest metropolitan areas. From Ashland, the southernmost city in the region, it's a 6-hour trip to either Portland or San Francisco. Despite this isolation, Ashland is renowned for its **Oregon Shakespeare Festival,** which annually attracts tens of thousands of theatergoers. The festival, which now stretches through most of the year, has turned a sleepy mill town into a facsimile of Tudor England. Not to be outdone, the nearby historic town of ✪ **Jacksonville** offers performances by internationally recognized musicians and dance companies throughout the summer.

But it is rugged beauty and the outdoors that draw most people to the region. Crater Lake National Park, Oregon's only national park, hides within its boundaries a sapphire jewel formed by the massive eruption of Mount Mazama less than 7,000 years ago. In this same area rise two of the most fabled **fly-fishing** rivers in the country. Ever since Zane Grey wrote of the fighting steelhead trout and salmon of the Rogue and Umpqua Rivers, fly-fishers have been casting their lines in hopes of hooking a few of these wily denizens of the Cascade Range's cold waters. (For information on Crater Lake and the North Umpqua River, see chapter 8.)

In addition to the sources of information listed below in each individual city section, you can get information on all of southern Oregon by contacting the following regional tourism associations: **Southern Oregon Visitors Association,** P.O. Box 1645, Medford, OR 97501-0731 (☎ **800/448-4856;** www.sova.org), and the **Southern Oregon Reservation Center,** P.O. Box 477, Ashland, OR 97520 (☎ **800/547-8052** or 541/488-1011; www.sorc.com), which mainly provides information and reservations for area theater, attractions, and lodging.

Southern Oregon

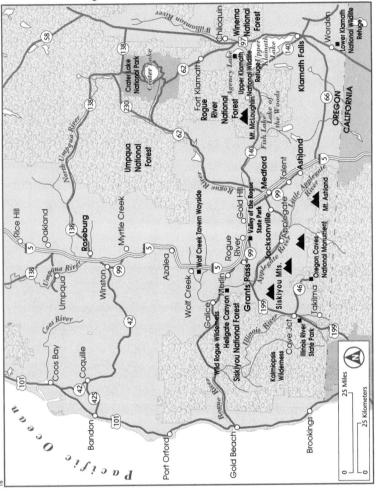

1 Ashland & the Oregon Shakespeare Festival

285 miles S of Portland, 50 miles W of Klamath Falls, 350 miles N of San Francisco

With new cocktail bars and upscale restaurants, live jazz in the clubs and cafes, more art galleries than ever before, and day spas once again taking advantage of Ashland's famed Lithia Springs mineral waters, Ashland is growing ever more cosmopolitan. Sure this is still a small town 6 hours by car from the nearest metropolitan area, but more than half a century of staging Shakespeare plays has turned it into Oregon's preeminent arts community.

It all started on the Fourth of July 1935. In a small Ashland theater built as part of the Chautauqua movement, Angus Bowmer, an English professor at Southern Oregon University, was staging a performance of Shakespeare's *As You Like It*. The Depression had dashed any hopes local businessman Jesse Winburne had of turning Ashland, a quiet mill town in the rugged Siskiyou Mountains, into a mineral-springs resort.

However, before the Depression struck, Winburne had managed to construct beautiful Lithia Park. Luckily, neither man's love's labor was lost, and today their legacies have turned the town into one of the Northwest's most popular destinations.

Each year more than 300,000 people attend performances of the Oregon Shakespeare Festival, a 9-month-long repertory festival that was born of Bowmer's love of the Bard. Though Ashland never became a mineral-springs resort, Lithia Park, through which still flow the clear waters of Winburne's dreams, is the town's centerpiece. Surrounding the town are mountains and forests that also offer a wealth of outdoor recreational activities, so there's still plenty to do when the stages are quiet and dark. This is one of the best little arts towns in America, so be prepared to fall in love.

ESSENTIALS

GETTING THERE   Ashland is located on I-5. From the east, Ore. 66 connects Ashland with Klamath Falls.

The nearest airport is the **Rogue Valley International–Medford Airport** in Medford, which is served by Horizon/Alaska Airlines and United Airlines. A taxi from the airport to Ashland will cost around $14.

VISITOR INFORMATION   Contact the **Ashland Chamber of Commerce,** 110 E. Main St. (P.O. Box 1360), Ashland, OR 97520 (☎ **541/482-3486;** www.ashlandchamber.com).

GETTING AROUND   If you need a taxi, call **Yellow Cab** (☎ **541/482-3065**). Car-rental companies with offices at the Rogue Valley International Airport are Avis, Budget, Hertz, and National. Public bus service in the Ashland area is provided by the **Rogue Valley Transportation District** (☎ **541/779-2877**).

FESTIVALS   The month-long Yuletide **Holiday Festival of Lights** held each year in December is Ashland's other big annual festival.

THE OREGON SHAKESPEARE FESTIVAL

The raison d'être of Ashland, the Oregon Shakespeare Festival is an internationally acclaimed theater festival with a season that stretches from February to October. The season typically includes four works by Shakespeare plus eight other classic or contemporary plays. These plays are performed in repertory, with as many as four being staged on any given day.

The festival complex, often referred to as "the bricks" because of its brick courtyard, is in the center of town and contains three theaters. The visually impressive outdoor **Elizabethan Theatre,** modeled after England's 17th-century Fortune Theatre, is used only in the summer and early fall. The **Angus Bowmer Theatre** is the festival's largest indoor theater. The **Black Swan** is the smallest theater and stages contemporary and experimental works.

In addition to the plays, there are **backstage tours** (tickets are $11 for adults and $8.25 for children, with lower prices in spring and fall) and a **Shakespeare Exhibit Center** (admission is $3 for adults and $2 for children) that houses a collection of props and costumes used in past productions. Throughout the festival season there are also talks and special performances. The opening of the Elizabethan Theatre is celebrated each June in Lithia Park with the elaborate Feast of Will.

For more information and upcoming schedules, contact the **Oregon Shakespeare Festival,** 15 S. Pioneer St. (P.O. Box 158), Ashland, OR 97520-0158 (☎ **541/482-4331;** www.orshakes.org). Ticket prices range from $28 to $40, with box seats at the Elizabethan going for $49; children's and preview tickets are less expensive. In spring and fall, all ticket prices are discounted 25%.

EXPLORING ASHLAND & ITS SURROUNDINGS

If you'd like to learn a bit more about Ashland's history, take a tour with **Old Ashland Walking Tours,** which offers 1-hour walking tours at 10am Monday through Saturday, June 15 to September 15; assemble at the Plaza Information booth across from Lithia Park. Tickets are $5 for adults and $2 for children.

At the **Schneider Museum of Art,** on the campus of the Southern Oregon University, 1250 Siskiyou Blvd. (☎ **541/552-6245**), art exhibits are the quality you'd expect in a big-city museum. In summer, the museum is open Tuesday through Friday from 10am to 5pm, Saturday and Sunday from noon to 4pm; during the academic year, hours are Tuesday through Saturday from 11am to 5pm.

Ashland's first claim to fame was its healing mineral waters, and today you can still relax and be pampered at one of the city's day spas. **The Phoenix,** 2425 Siskiyou Blvd. (☎ **541/488-1281**), and **Atrium Center for Body Therapies,** 51 Water St. (☎ **541/488-8775**), both offer various body treatments, skin care, and massages.

Long before Shakespeare came to town, this was farm country, and if you'd like to pay a visit to a first-class farm stand, head over to Talent, where you'll find **Meadow-Brook Farm,** 6731 Wagner Creek Rd. (☎ **541/535-2688**). Step into the past at this National Historical Landmark and organic farm. There are flower and herb gardens and a renovated barn, and you can buy lunch from the farm stand and have a picnic on the grounds. To reach the farm, take Rapp Road west from Ore. 99 in Talent.

WINE TOURING

Ashland Vineyards. 2775 E. Main St. ☎ **541/488-0088.** Apr–Oct Tues–Sun 11am–5pm; Nov–Dec and Feb–Mar Tues–Sat 11am–5pm; Jan by appt. 25¢ per taste. Closed Dec 24–Jan 1 and major holidays. From Ore. 99 south of downtown Ashland, go east on Ashland St., cross I-5, and turn left on East Main St.

Grapes used in the wines here are organically grown on the surrounding vineyards. Best for white wines such as Chardonnay and dry Sauvignon Blanc.

Weisinger's. 3150 Siskiyou Blvd. ☎ **800/551-WINE** or 541/488-5989. Jan–Apr Wed–Sun 11am–5pm; May–Oct daily 10am–6pm; Nov–Dec Wed–Sun 11am–5pm. Take Ore. 99 (Siskiyou Blvd.) south from downtown Ashland.

Located just south of town, this winery has a great view over the hills and valleys. Dry whites are a strong point here, though if you like tannins you may like Weisinger's Merlot and Petite Pompadour, a Bordeaux-style blend of Cabernet Franc, Merlot, Malbec, and Cabernet Sauvignon.

ENJOYING THE GREAT OUTDOORS

A memorable part of your visit will be a long, leisurely stroll through beautiful **Lithia Park.** This 100-acre park follows the banks of Ashland Creek starting at the Plaza. Shade trees, lawns, flowers, ponds, fountains, and, of course, the babbling brook are reminiscent of an English garden. There's no more romantic way to explore the park than by horse-drawn carriage; rides are available from **Lithia Carriage Company** (☎ **541/482-2484**).

Summertime thrill-seekers shouldn't pass up the chance to do some **white-water rafting** on the Rogue or Klamath River while in southern Oregon. Trips are offered between April and October by several companies. Try **Noah's World of Water,** 53 N. Main St. (☎ **800/858-2811** or 541/488-2811), or **The Adventure Center,** 40 N. Main St. (☎ **800/444-2819** or 541/488-2819), both of which offer trips lasting from half a day to 5 days. Prices range from $65 for a half-day trip to about $110 to $160 per day per person, depending on the length and type of the trip. The former

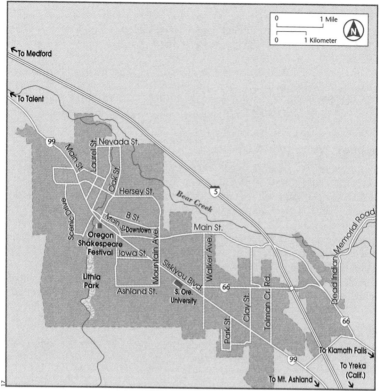

company also offers salmon and steelhead fishing trips, and the latter offers downhill bike rides from the top of Mount Ashland.

Mountain bikes can be rented at **Ashland Mountain Supply,** 31 N. Main St. (☎ **541/488-2749**), and the folks at this shop can point you in the direction of good rides.

Miles of **hiking trails,** including the Pacific Crest Trail, can be found up on Mount Ashland in the Siskiyou Rogue River National Forest.

Horseback riding is available at **Mountain Gate Stables,** 4399 Ore. 66 (☎ **541/482-8873**). Rides start at $25 for 1 hour (two-person minimum).

In the winter there's good downhill and cross-country **skiing** at **Mt. Ashland Ski Area,** 15 miles south of Ashland (☎ **541/482-2897** for information or **541/482-2754** for snow report). Day lift tickets for adults range from about $23 to $27. You can rent cross-country skis and pick up ski-trail maps at **Ashland Outdoor Store,** 37 Third St. (☎ **541/488-1202**).

SHOPPING

Ashland has the best shopping in southern Oregon. Interesting and unusual shops line East Main Street, so when the curtains are down on the stages, check the windows of downtown.

Art galleries abound in Ashland, and on the first Friday of the month, many are open late. One of our favorites for contemporary art is the **Hanson Howard Gallery,** 82 N. Main St. (☎ **541/488-2562**). And for a gallery of wearable art, stop by

The Web-sters, 11 N. Main St. (☎ 541/482-9801), a knitting and weaving store carrying beautiful sweaters. At **Footlights Theatre Gallery,** 240 E. Main St. (☎ 541/488-5538), you'll find a wall of posters available for purchase, from *Amadeus* to *West Side Story.*

For a well-rounded selection of wines and other gourmet treats, you can't beat the **Chateaulin Wine Shoppe,** next to the restaurant Chateaulin at 52 E. Main St. (☎ 541/488-9463). To further enhance your tabletop, **The Clay Angel,** 101 E. Main St. (☎ 541/482-8007), has lovely ceramics, most of which are imported from Italy.

WHERE TO STAY

It seems Shakespeare and B&Bs go hand in hand. At last count, there were close to 50 bed-and-breakfasts in town. If your reason for coming to Ashland is to attend the Shakespeare Festival, you'll find it most convenient to choose an inn within walking distance of the theaters. By doing so, you'll also be within walking distance of the town's best restaurants and shopping and won't have to deal with finding a parking space before the show. For a comprehensive list of Ashland inns, contact **Ashland's Bed & Breakfast Network,** P.O. Box 1051, Ashland, OR 97520-0048 (☎ 800/944-0329 or 541/858-1670; www.abbnet.com).

If all you're looking for is a clean, comfortable room for the night, the **Super 8 Motel—Ashland,** 2350 Ashland St., Ashland, OR 97520 (☎ 800/800-8000 or 541/482-8887), is the most reliable bet in town, charging $48 to $66 double.

IN TOWN

Antique Rose Inn. 91 Gresham St., Ashland, OR 97520. ☎ 888/282-6285 or 541/482-6285. www.wvi.com/~dhull/antiquebnb. 4 units. A/C. June–Oct $117–$159 double. Nov–May $89–$119 double. Rates include full breakfast. AE, MC, V.

Set in a quiet, shady yard on a hillside above downtown and only 3 blocks from the festival theaters, this inn is housed in an 1888 Queen Anne Victorian home that was ordered from a catalog. Throughout the inn you'll find period antiques that capture the flavor of Victorian times. The Rose Room is the best room in the house and has a beautiful fireplace and a tiny balcony with a view across the valley. However, if its a clawfoot tub you need, ask for either the Lace Room or the Mahogany Room. Breakfasts are lavish, gourmet affairs, and in the evening complimentary wine is available. The cottage next door to the main house has its own sauna and whirlpool tub. The cottage is also the only accommodation with its own phone and TV.

Best Western Bard's Inn. 132 N. Main St., Ashland, OR 97520. ☎ 800/528-1234 or 541/482-0049. Fax 503/488-3259. 91 units. A/C TV TEL. Mid-May to mid-Oct $115–$134 double, $125–$165 suite. Mid-Oct to mid-May $82–$85 double, $88–$144 suite. Rates include continental breakfast. AE, CB, DC, DISC, MC, V.

If you prefer motels to B&Bs and want to be within walking distance of downtown, the Bard's Inn should be your first choice in Ashland. The rooms are large and comfortable, and those in the new annex have patios or balconies, though these rooms can get a bit of traffic noise. The older rooms have all been refurbished and have refrigerators. An outdoor pool and hot tub provide a bit of relaxation, and there's a restaurant here as well. However, this motel's best feature is that it's only 2 blocks from the festival theaters.

Chanticleer Bed & Breakfast Inn. 120 Gresham St., Ashland, OR 97520. ☎ 800/898-1950 or 541/482-1919. Fax 541/488-4810. www.ashland-bed-breakfast.com. 6 units. A/C TEL. June–Oct $150–$250 double. Nov–Jan $75–$150 double. Feb–May $115–$200 double. Rates include full breakfast. AE, MC, V.

The Chanticleer has long been a favorite of theatergoers, and a complete renovation has left it looking better than ever. The 1920s Craftsman bungalow is only 3 blocks from "the bricks," and equally close to all the downtown shops and restaurants. European country styling gives the inn an old-world charm that allows you to immerse yourself in the Shakespeare experience. The guest rooms are decorated with antiques and have down comforters, and they look out on either the garden or the valley. Breakfasts are a lavish affair that can be served either in bed or in the dining room overlooking the mountains. Throughout the day, treats are always on hand as well. For special occasions, there is a big luxurious suite with its own fireplace, kitchen, and private back yard.

Coolidge House. 137 N. Main St., Ashland, OR 97520. ☎ **800/655-5522** or 541/ 482-4721. 6 units. A/C. Apr–Oct $120–$145 suite; $160 cottage. Nov–Mar $85–$105 suite; $125 cottage. Rates include full breakfast. 2-night minimum on weekends Apr–Oct. MC, V.

Located right on busy North Main Street only 3 blocks from the theaters, this inn sits high above the street on a hill with commanding views across the valley. The Victorian home was built in 1875 and is one of the oldest homes in Ashland. However, inside you'll find some decidedly modern amenities, as well as interesting antiques. Guest suites all have sitting rooms and large luxurious bathrooms, most of which have either a whirlpool tub or a clawfoot tub. The Parlor Suite, with its draped window seat, is the inn's most romantic room. However, if views and space are what you seek, opt for the Sun Suite or the Grape Arbor. There is a pleasant patio in the back garden.

✪ **Peerless Hotel.** 243 Fourth St., Ashland, OR 97520. ☎ **800/460-8758** or 541/ 488-1082. www.peerlesshotel.com. 6 units. A/C MINIBAR TEL. Early June to early Nov $98–$160 double; $185–$195 suite. Early Nov to mid-Feb $65–$95 double; $130–$150 suite. Mid-Feb to early June $95–$125; $145–$160 suite. Rates include expanded continental breakfast. AE, MC, V.

Located in the historic Railroad District 7 blocks from the festival theaters, this restored 1900 brick boarding house is one of Ashland's most interesting lodgings. With the feel of a small historic hotel rather than that of a B&B, the Peerless is filled with antiques and an eclectic array of individually decorated guest rooms. Of these, the West Indies suite, with its balcony, double whirlpool tub, and view of Ashland, is by far the most luxurious. However, in other rooms you'll find lush fabrics, unusual murals, stenciling, and tile work that all add up to unexpected luxury. Most rooms have either a whirlpool tub or a clawfoot tub (one even has his-and-hers clawfoot tubs). The hotel has a restaurant offering both casual and fine dining. Room service is also available.

✪ **The Winchester Country Inn.** 35 S. Second St., Ashland, OR 97520. ☎ **800/ 972-4991** or 541/488-1113. Fax 541/488-4604. www.winchesterinn.com. 18 units. A/C TEL. $99–$145 double; $135–$210 suite. Rates include full breakfast. AE, DISC, MC, V.

With its massive old shade trees, English tea gardens, and elegant internationally influenced restaurant (see "Where to Dine," below for details), the Winchester is Ashland's premier historic inn. Though it styles itself as a country inn, it's actually right in town within a few blocks of the theaters. The rooms are very comfortably furnished with antiques and modern bath fixtures, including sinks built into old bureaus in some rooms. We prefer the upstairs rooms, which get quite a bit more light than the ground floor rooms. There are also rooms in the building next door. If you want a bit more space, six suites are available, two of which are in the old carriage house. The suites also come with TVs and VCRs. A decanter of sherry in each room is a welcome touch upon returning from the theater. Throughout the year, special events are held here, including murder-mystery weekends and Christmas Dickens feasts.

Windmill Inn of Ashland. 2525 Ashland St., Ashland, OR 97520-1478. ☎ **800/ 547-4747** or 541/482-8310. Fax 541/488-1783. www.windmillinns.com. 230 units. A/C TV TEL. Early June to early Oct $89–$99 double; $119 suite. Early Oct to early June $53 double; $69 suite. Rates include continental breakfast. AE, CB, DC, DISC, MC, V. Pets accepted.

Set on the outskirts of Ashland a few miles from downtown, this hotel is the only local hotel offering resort-style amenities. Set on sprawling, attractively landscaped grounds, the inn caters primarily to groups, and because it's outside of town it's somewhat inconvenient. But most of the rooms have balconies or patios and great views of the surrounding countryside. Services include room service, complimentary morning coffee and newspaper, free airport and theater shuttle, and valet/laundry service. An indoor swimming pool, a hot tub, an exercise room, tennis courts, guest bicycles, and a jogging trail provide plenty of recreational options. However, the hotel no longer has a restaurant on the premises.

OUT OF TOWN

Country Willows. 1313 Clay St., Ashland, OR 97520. ☎ **800/WILLOWS** or 541/ 488-1590. Fax 541/488-1611. www.willowsinn.com. 9 units. A/C TEL. $95–$135 double; $135–$195 suite. Rates include full breakfast. Lower rates Nov–Mar. AE, DISC, MC, V.

Just outside town and surrounded by 5 acres of rolling hills and pastures, the Country Willows B&B offers the tranquillity of a farm only minutes from excellent restaurants and the theaters. If you're looking for a very special room, consider the recently remodeled Sunrise Suite, which is in a renovated barn behind the main house; it has pine paneling, a high ceiling, a king-size bed, a gas fireplace, and, best of all, an old-fashioned tub for two with its very own picture window and skylight. Rooms in the restored farmhouse are smaller, but some offer excellent views across the valley. Ducks, geese, and goats call the farm home, and there's a 2-mile hiking trail that starts at the back door. You'll also find a pool and whirlpool on the grounds.

Mt. Ashland Inn. 550 Mt. Ashland Rd., Ashland, OR 97520. ☎ **800/830-8707** or 541/482-8707. www.mtashland.com. 5 units. $99–$110 double; $120–$190 suite. Rates include full breakfast. DISC, MC, V.

Located on 160 acres on the side of Mount Ashland, this massive log home commands distant panoramas from its forest setting, and though the inn is only 15 minutes from downtown Ashland, you're in a different world up here. The Pacific Crest Trail, which stretches from Canada to Mexico, passes through the front yard, and just a few miles up the road is the Ski Ashland ski area. Whether you're in the area for an active vacation or a few nights of theater, this lodge makes a very special base of operations. The decor is straight out of an Eddie Bauer catalog, and in one guest bathroom there's a stone wall with a built-in waterfall. The Sky Lakes Suite is the best room in the house.

Pinehurst Inn at Jenny Creek. 17250 Hwy. 66, Ashland, OR 97520. ☎ **541/488-1002.** 6 units. $69–$89 double. Rates include continental breakfast. DISC, MC, V. Closed Jan 1– Feb 14.

Located about 25 miles from downtown Ashland, this historic roadhouse and inn, part of which is a hexagonal log structure, isn't convenient for attending the theater, but it is such a timeless place that it's worth considering if you're looking for a peaceful mountain getaway. The inn dates back to the 1920s, and though it has been updated and renovated recently, it succeeds in preserving an early-20th-century country roadhouse atmosphere. Guest rooms, which are quite simply furnished, have a genuinely old-fashioned feel to them, and in the bathrooms you'll find clawfoot tubs. At the back of the inn, there's a sun porch overlooking the meadows. Meals (dinner is also available) are served family-style in a room heated by a big wood stove. The inn also offers horseback riding.

WHERE TO DINE

If you're headed to the theater after dinner, let your waitstaff know. They will usually do whatever they can to make sure you aren't late!

EXPENSIVE

✪ **Chateaulin.** 50 E. Main St. ☎ **541/482-2264.** Reservations recommended. Main courses $14.50–$25.75. AE, DISC, MC, V. June–Oct daily 5–9:30pm; Nov–May Wed–Sun 5:30–9pm. Bar open until midnight. FRENCH.

Located just around the corner from the festival theaters, this has long been one of the finest restaurants in town. Exposed brick walls and old champagne bottles give Chateaulin a casually elegant appearance that's accented by art nouveau touches and dark-wood furnishings. The menu is almost as traditional as the decor; you can start your meal with escargots or house pâté and then move on to rack of lamb. A separate bar menu caters to smaller or après-theater appetites. The restaurant's wine list features 100 selections from Oregon, California, and France. For visitors on a budget, there is a more affordable and contemporary prix-fixe menu that changes weekly. There's also an attached wine and gourmet-foods store for classy picnic fare.

Firefly. 25 N. Main St. ☎ **541/488-3212.** Reservations recommended. Main courses $20–$30. MC, V. Summer Tues–Sun 5–8:30pm; winter Wed–Sun 5–8pm. INTERNATIONAL.

For several years now, Firefly has been one of Ashland's trendier restaurants, a big hit with visitors from San Francisco, Seattle, and Portland. At press time, popularity had dictated a move to a newer, larger, and more prestigious location—a "penthouse" space right on the Plaza. Dishes at Firefly tend to be complex and beautifully presented, as you might expect from the hefty prices. Entrees might include a mixed grill with lamb, duck, and lobster, or pork chops with bread pudding in hazelnut-tarragon sauce with fried sage. There always seems to be an eclectic selection of desserts here; one such recent standout was a delectably rich homemade pistachio ice cream with a port and fig compote.

Monet. 36 S. Second St. ☎ **541/482-1339.** Reservations recommended. Main courses $17–$26. MC, V. Mid-June to Sept daily 5:30–8:30pm; May to mid-June and Oct Tues–Sun 5:30–8:30pm; Nov–Dec and Feb–Apr Tues–Sat 5:30–8:30pm. Closed Jan. FRENCH.

For fine French cuisine with an emphasis on lighter, more contemporary preparations, it's hard to beat Monet. Owned and operated by chef Pierre Verger, Monet has been in business for nearly a decade, a testament to the popularity and quality of the restaurant's Gallic cuisine. You might find smoked salmon wrapped around avocado mousse and served with a lemon vinaigrette as a starter, and baked pork tenderloin with prunes, shallots, and Armagnac. For lighter appetites, there are always several interesting salads and an excellent French onion soup. Vegetarians also get several choices. Though the big white house (across the street from the Winchester Inn) looks rather plain from the outside, inside you'll find a somewhat formal and impeccably set dining room. On warm days, you may want to dine in the garden surrounded by many of the same flowers that grow in Monet's famous garden in France.

New Sammy's Cowboy Bistro. 2210 S. Pacific Hwy., Talent. ☎ **541/535-2779.** Reservations highly recommended. Main courses $18–$30; 4-course menu $30. No credit cards. Feb–Oct Thurs–Sun 5–9pm; Nov–Jan Fri–Sat 5–9pm. NORTHWEST.

Unmarked yet unmistakable, New Sammy's is a tiny shack of a place in nearby Talent. If it weren't for the fact that the building looks as if the owners got their paint at a Sherwin Williams going-out-of-business sale, you'd drive right past. Be bold. Open the door. Things look different inside.

The menu is as imaginative as the exterior paint job, and everything is as fresh as it gets, with lots of organic produce from local growers and delicious rustic breads. Meats are antibiotic- and hormone-free, and for dessert there's a choice of several homemade ice creams and fresh fruits. This is a mom-and-pop operation (Mom cooks and Pop serves), and tables are frequently reserved several weeks in advance; so be sure to call ahead for a reservation.

The Peerless Restaurant. 265 Fourth St. ☎ **541/488-6067.** Reservations recommended. Bistro $13–$25; fine dining $20–$30. AE, DC, DISC, MC, V. Tues–Sun 5–9pm (fine dining closed Tues). PAN ASIAN/CONTINENTAL.

With its Hawaiian/tropical decor, this upscale restaurant a few blocks from the Plaza seems decidedly out of place in the southern Oregon hills, but good food is good food no matter where it's served. The Peerless is actually two restaurants in one: a very formal gourmet dining room and a more casual (though only slightly less expensive) bistro. There's also a garden patio for summertime alfresco dining. Because The Peerless is out of Ashland's restaurant mainstream, it tends to work just a little bit harder to satisfy its customers. In the bistro, dinner might include a shrimp spring roll with spicy mango-ginger sauce for a starter, and caramelized salmon with orange-shoyu glaze for an entree. In the fine-dining wing, you might start with a Hawaiian heart of palm salad or baked escargot followed by rack of lamb in a Dijon-feta herb crust or a wild mushroom Wellington with a truffle emulsion. For a truly decadent dinner, top it all off with a Grand Marnier or chocolate soufflé.

Primavera Restaurant & Gardens. 241 Hargadine St. ☎ **541/488-1994.** Reservations recommended in summer. Main courses $20–$26; bistro menu $6.50–$14. AE, MC, V. Summer Wed–Thurs and Sun 5–8:30pm, Fri–Sat 5–9pm; fall–spring, closed Wed. Closed in Jan. MEDITERRANEAN/REGIONAL.

Housed in a former church and in business for more than a decade, Primavera serves an eclectic menu that focuses primarily on Mediterranean flavors. With both a full dinner menu and a bistro menu, there's enough variety that you can enjoy a dinner here on any budget. The menu changes regularly and is limited to a few choice treatments of beef (fillet with gorgonzola bread pudding, mustard demi-glaze, and wine-roasted onions), chicken (breast baked with lemon, garlic, and herbs), or fish (salmon baked in parchment with ginger, scallions, lemon, and garlic), as well as a vegetarian dish. The produce used here is largely organic, and they also make their own breads and ice cream. In keeping with Ashland's theatrical theme, this restaurant has adopted a very dramatic decor, with rich colors, soft lighting, and theatrically lit paintings inspired by old Ballet Russe posters. A handsome garden at the back makes a fine place to dine before attending a summertime performance. In keeping with the atmosphere, you might want to dress up.

The Winchester Inn. 35 S. Second St. ☎ **541/488-1115.** Reservations highly recommended. Main courses $16–$25; Sun brunch $6.50–$12. AE, DISC, MC, V. Summer Mon–Thurs 5–8pm, Fri–Sat 5:30–8:30pm, Sun 9:30am–12:30pm (brunch) and 5–8pm. Closed Mon from mid-Oct to end of May. INTERNATIONAL.

Located on the ground floor of Ashland's premier in-town country inn, this restaurant melds a historic Victorian setting with an eclectic international menu that visits such far-flung culinary destinations as China, Mexico, Greece, and the Mediterranean. Starters here tend toward simple preparations such as smoked salmon with ginger-chive aïoli or baked brie in a peppernut crust served with apple-pear chutney. Any time of year the teng dah beef, the inn's signature French-Vietnamese dish, offers an unusual treatment of filet mignon (marinated in soy sauce and flavored with lemon zest, nutmeg, and anise). Sunday brunch is the perfect way to finish a weekend of theater before heading home. The dining rooms overlook the inn's English tea gardens, and in summer there is dining on the porch and deck as well. During the Christmas season, there are special Dickens feasts here.

MODERATE

✪ **Cucina Biazzi.** 568 E. Main St. ☎ **541/488-3739.** Reservations recommended in summer. 4-course fixed-price dinner $19–$30. MC, V. Daily 5:30–8:30pm; hours may be shorter in winter. TUSCAN.

The owners have transformed this Ashland bungalow on the edge of downtown into a cozy Italian cottage, with romantic touches including lace curtains and candlelight. The menu here, inspired by available seasonal ingredients, changes every week or two, but you might find that the antipasto course is a salad of Tuscan white beans, mushrooms, marinated artichokes, asiago cheese, and other tempting ingredients. The pasta course might include ravioli tossed with browned butter and crisped sage or spaghetti with clams, Tuscan-style. For a main course, you usually have a choice of a chicken, fish, veal, or steak dish. For a switch on the American norm, the salad course comes last here (but before dessert—save room). For alfresco dining, there's a low-walled patio. Service is excellent.

Kat Wok. 62 E. Main St. ☎ **541/482-0787.** Reservations recommended. Main courses $7–$17. AE, MC, V. Summer Sun–Mon 5–8pm, Tues–Sat 5–9pm. Closed Mon in other months. PACIFIC RIM.

With the sort of clever ambiance you'd find in a hip new restaurant in Portland or Seattle, Kat Wok is a prime example of the new cosmopolitan atmosphere in Ashland. If you happen to enter from "the bricks," you'll think you've stumbled onto a theater's backstage. Each table is dramatically lit by a spotlight, and there are tables on a catwalklike mezzanine (hence the name). Kat Wok is popular with people of all ages who come here for light Asian-style cuisine, such as an Asian pear salad with roasted chicken, spicy stir-fried pork with a refreshing cucumber salad, or Szechwan green beans. Later in the evening, Kat Wok becomes a night club with live music.

Plaza Cafe. 47 N. Main St. ☎ **541/488-2233.** Reservations recommended. Main courses $6–$13.50. DISC, MC, V. Mon–Thurs 11am–9pm, Fri–Sat 11am–10pm, Sun 9am–9pm. REGIONAL AMERICAN.

Located just opposite the plaza in downtown Ashland, this cafe has an upscale urban atmosphere with a high ceiling and art on the brick walls. Stop in here for the likes of coconut-lime poached halibut with Chinese vegetables or a delicious black tiger shrimp kabob with peanut sauce. Salads, such as a warm spinach salad, are generous and fresh, featuring local organic produce. Prices here (including wine) are quite reasonable, and brunch is served on the weekend.

Quinz. 29 N. Main St. ☎ **541/488-5937.** Reservations recommended. Small plates $4–$9, large plates $9.50–$17. DISC, MC, V. Daily 11:30am–2pm and 5–9:30pm. MEDITERRANEAN.

With its colorful decor, convenient location opposite the plaza, and prompt service, Quinz is a good place to stop for reasonably priced Mediterranean-influenced food. The menu is fairly long and includes plenty of options for light eaters as well as the famished. You can get anything from Portuguese-style mussels steamed with andouille sausage to a grilled New York steak with garlic mashed potatoes. However, dishes that should not be missed include the Catalan-style saffron risotto, the Moroccan lamb meatballs in cumin-coriander tomato sauce, and the souvlaki. The indecisive should consider the substantial antipasti platter for two. It's enough for a light meal (especially if you have dessert). At night, there are usually fish specials, while lunch features many of the same dishes served at dinner.

INEXPENSIVE

In addition to the restaurant listed below, **Tashi Tea,** tucked away downstairs at 66 N. Pioneer St. (☎ 541/488-2744), is a quiet place for a cup of tea and light vegetarian meals.

Ashland Bakery Cafe. 38 E. Main St. ☎ **541/482-2117.** Breakfast, sandwiches, and main courses $5–$10. MC, V. Mon–Tues 7:30am–3pm, Wed–Sun 7:30am–8pm. INTERNATIONAL.

You'll find this cafe right in the hub of downtown Ashland. It's usually mobbed at breakfast with people reading newspapers and sipping coffee while patiently waiting for their smoked salmon or tofu scrambles and avocado-and-cheese omelets. At lunch or dinner it's a good place for a quick sandwich, pizza, or pasta dish. Top it off with a giant cookie from the bakery case.

ASHLAND AFTER DARK

The Oregon Shakespeare Festival may be the main draw, but Ashland is overflowing with talent begging to express itself. From experimental theater to Broadway musicals, the town sees an amazing range of theater productions. To find out what's going on while you're in town, pick up a free copy of *Sneak Preview.*

Theaters and theater companies in the area include the **Oregon Cabaret Theatre,** First and Hargadine streets (☎ 541/488-2902), a professional dinner theater; the **Theatre Arts Department of Southern Oregon University,** 1250 Siskiyou Blvd. (☎ 541/552-6346), which stages well-regarded student productions; the **Ashland Community Theatre** (☎ 541/482-7532), which stages new and old popular plays, frequently at the Town Hall, 300 N. Pioneer St.; and **Actor's Theatre,** Miracle Playhouse, 101 Talent Ave., in the nearby town of Talent (☎ 541/535-5250). The **Rogue Music Theatre** (☎ 541/479-2559), which has its home in Grants Pass, regularly brings musicals such as *Evita* and *My Fair Lady* to Ashland.

Nontheater performing-arts companies include the **Rogue Valley Symphony** (☎ 541/770-6012).

Throughout the summer there are numerous outdoor events, some free and some not, at the **Lithia Park band shell.** You can pick up a schedule of events at the Ashland Chamber of Commerce, 110 E. Main St. (☎ 541/482-3486).

2 Jacksonville & Medford: After the Gold Rush

16 miles N of Ashland, 24 miles E of Grants Pass

Jacksonville is a snapshot of southern Oregon history. After the Great Depression it became a forgotten backwater, and more than 80 buildings from its glory years as a gold-boom town in the mid-1800s were left untouched. The entire town has been restored, thanks to the photos of pioneer photographer Peter Britt, who moved to Jacksonville in 1852 and operated the first photographic studio west of the Rockies. His photos of 19th-century Jacksonville have provided preservationists with invaluable 100-year-old glimpses of many of the town's historic buildings. Britt's name has also been attached to the **Britt Festivals,** another southern Oregon cultural binge that rivals the Oregon Shakespeare Festival in its ability to stage first-rate entertainment.

Though thousands of eager gold-seekers were lured into California's Sierra Nevada by the gold rush of 1849, few struck it rich. Many of those who were smitten with gold fever and were unwilling to give up the search for the mother lode headed out across the West in search of golder pastures. At least two prospectors hit pay dirt in the Siskiyou Mountains of southern Oregon in 1851, at a spot that would soon be known as Rich Gulch. Within a year Rich Gulch had become the site of booming Jacksonville, and within another year the town had become the county seat and commercial heart of southern Oregon. Over the next half century, Jacksonville developed into a wealthy town with brick commercial buildings and elegant Victorian homes. However, in the 1880s, the railroad running between Portland and San Francisco bypassed Jacksonville in favor of an easier route 5 miles to the east. It was at this spot that the trading town of Medford began to develop.

Despite a short rail line into Jacksonville, over the years more and more business migrated to the main railway in Medford. Jacksonville's fortunes began to decline, and by the time of the Depression, residents were reduced to digging up the streets of town for the gold that lay there. In 1927, the county seat was moved to Medford, and Jacksonville was left with its faded grandeur and memories of better times.

Off the beaten path, forgotten by developers and modernization, Jacksonville inadvertently preserved its past in its buildings. In 1966, the entire town was listed on the National Register of Historic Places, and Jacksonville, with the aid of Britt's photos, underwent a renaissance that has left it a historical showcase. Together the Britt Festivals and Jacksonville's history combine to make this one of the most fascinating towns anywhere in the Northwest.

ESSENTIALS

GETTING THERE   Medford is right on I-5, 30 miles north of the California state line, and Jacksonville is 5 miles west on Ore. 238.

The **Rogue Valley International–Medford Airport,** at 3650 Biddle Rd., Medford, is served by Horizon/Alaska Airlines and United Airlines.

VISITOR INFORMATION   Contact the **Jacksonville Chamber of Commerce,** 185 N. Oregon St. (P.O. Box 33), Jacksonville, OR 97530 (☎ **541/899-8118;** www.jacksonvilleoregon.org), or the **Medford Visitor & Convention Bureau,** 101 E. Eighth St., Medford, OR 97501 (☎ **800/469-6307** or 541/779-4847; www. visitmedford.org).

THE BRITT FESTIVALS & OTHER AREA PERFORMANCES

Each summer between mid-June and early September, people gather several nights a week for folk, pop, country, jazz, and classical music concerts; theater; and modern dance performances. The Britt Festivals are a celebration of music and the performing arts featuring internationally renowned performers. The setting for the performances is an amphitheater on the grounds of Britt's estate. Located only a block from historic California Street, the ponderosa pine–shaded amphitheater provides not only a great setting for the performances, but a view that takes in distant hills and the valley far below.

Both reserved and general-admission tickets are available for most shows. If you opt for a general-admission ticket, arrive early to claim a prime spot on the lawns behind the reserved seats—and be sure to bring a picnic. For information, contact the festival at P.O. Box 1124, Medford, OR 97501-0083 (☎ **800/88-BRITT** or 541/773-6077; www.brittfest.org). Tickets range from $16 to $54.

Not wanting to lose out to its better-known neighbors, Medford recently renovated an old downtown theater and christened it the **Craterian Ginger Rogers Theater,** 23 S. Central Ave. (☎ **541/779-3000**), in honor of the famous dancer who lived in the area after her retirement. The theater stages everything from performances by the Rogue Opera (☎ **541/608-6400**) to touring Broadway shows and classical music performances.

When the Britt Festivals have closed up shop for the year, you can still catch Dixieland jazz at the annual **Medford Jazz Jubilee,** which is held in early October. For information, call ☎ **800/599-0039** or 541/770-6972.

MUSEUMS & HISTORIC HOMES

With more than 80 buildings listed on the National Register of Historic Places, Jacksonville boasts that it's the most completely preserved historic town in the nation. Whether or not this claim is true, there certainly are enough restored old buildings to make the town a genuine step back in time. Along California Street you'll find restored brick commercial buildings that now house dozens of interesting shops, art galleries, and boutiques. On the side streets you'll see the town's many Victorian homes.

Jacksonville Museum of Southern Oregon History. 206 N. Fifth St. ☎ **541/773-6536.** Admission $2 adults, $1 seniors and children 6–12. Memorial Day–Labor Day daily 10am–5pm; Labor Day–Memorial Day Wed–Sat 10am–5pm, Sun noon–5pm.

In order to get some background on Jacksonville, make this museum your first stop in town. Housed in the old county courthouse, built in 1883, the museum has displays on the history of Jacksonville, including 19th-century photos by Peter Britt. The price of admission also includes the adjacent Children's Museum, housed in the former jail.

Beekman House. 470 E. California St. ☎ **541/773-6536.** Beekman House, $2 adults, $1 seniors and children 6–12; Beekman Bank, free. Beekman House, Memorial Day–Labor Day daily 1–5pm. Beekman Bank, any time.

At the 1876 Beekman House, history comes alive as actors in period costume portray the family of an early Jacksonville banker. The turn-of-the-century Beekman Bank, 101 W. California St., is also open to the public.

Southern Oregon History Center. 106 N. Central Ave. ☎ **541/773-6536.** www.sohs.org. Free admission. Mon–Fri 9am–5pm, Sat 1–5pm.

Located in downtown Medford, this is the headquarters for the Southern Oregon Historical Society, which stages changing exhibits pertaining to the history of this region.

Butte Creek Mill. 402 N. Royal Ave., Eagle Point. ☎ **541/826-3531.** Free admission. Mon–Sat 9am–5pm.

In nearby Eagle Point, you can visit Oregon's only operating water-powered flour mill. The Butte Creek Mill was built in 1873 and its millstones are still grinding out flour. After looking around at the workings of the mill, you can stop in at the mill store and buy a bag of flour or cornmeal. Next door, the **Oregon General Store Museum,** open 11am to 4pm on Saturday, has a fascinating collection of antique items representing a turn-of-the-century grocery store. Also on this same block is the **Eagle Point Historical Museum** (☎ **541/826-4166**), in case you want to learn more about local history. The Antelope covered bridge is also here in Eagle Point.

OTHER ATTRACTIONS

Pears and roses both grow well in the Jacksonville and Medford area, and these crops have given rise to two of the country's best known mail-order businesses. **Harry and David's Country Village,** 1314 Center Dr. (☎ **877/322-8000**), is the retail outlet of a fruit company specializing in mail-order Fruit-of-the-Month Club gift packs. You'll find the store just 1 mile south of Medford at exit 27 off I-5. You can tour the Harry and David's packing house and then wander through the store in search of bargains. Associated with this store is the **Jackson and Perkins rose test garden** and mail-order rose nursery.

Each year in early autumn, the Jacksonville Boosters Club sponsors a **homes tour** that allows glimpses into many of Jacksonville's most lovingly restored old homes. Contact the Jacksonville Chamber of Commerce for details.

There are lots of great stores in Jacksonville, and one of our favorites is the **GeBzz Gallery,** 150 S. Oregon St. (☎ **541/899-7535**), which carries a diverse selection of high-quality contemporary art works.

OUTDOOR ACTIVITIES

Rafting and **fishing** on the numerous fast-flowing, clear-water rivers of southern Oregon are two of the most popular sports in this region, and Medford makes a good base for doing a bit of either, or both. **Arrowhead River Adventures** (☎ **800/227-7741** or 541/830-3388) and **River Trips Unlimited** (☎ **800/460-3865** or 541/779-3798) offer both rafting and fishing; **Rogue Excursions Unlimited** (☎ **541/826-6222**) offers fishing. A day of rafting will cost around $75 to $100, and fishing trips cost about $125 per person per day (with a minimum of two people).

If you're here in the spring, you can catch the colorful **wildflower displays** at Table Rocks. These mesas are just a few miles northeast of Medford, and because of their great age and unique structure, they create a variety of habitats that allow the area to support an unusual diversity of plants. For more information, contact the **Bureau of Land Management,** Medford District Office (☎ **541/770-2200**).

Information on **hiking** and **backpacking** in the area can be obtained from the **Rogue River National Forest,** 333 W. Eighth St. (P.O. Box 520), Medford, OR 97501 (☎ **541/858-2200;** www.fs.fed.us/r6/rogue).

For a different perspective on this region, try a **hot-air balloon ride** with **Oregon Adventures Aloft** (☎ **800/238-0700** or 541/582-1574).

WINE TOURING

You can taste local wines at the **Valley View Vineyard,** 100 Upper Applegate Rd. (☎ **800/781-WINE** or 541/899-8468), or their in-town tasting room at **Anna Maria's,** 130 W. California St., Jacksonville (☎ **541/899-1001**). Valley View is known for its red wines but also produces good dry whites. The Cotes du Rogue, a blend of Syrah, Zinfandel, Cabernet, and Merlot, is particularly tasty.

Wine connoisseurs also won't want to miss perusing the wine racks at the **Jacksonville Inn Wine Shop,** 175 E. California St., Jacksonville (☎ **541/899-1137**), where you might find a bottle of 1811 Tokay Essencia for $5,500 or a bottle of Chateau Lafite-Rothschild for $1,500. Oregon wines (and beef jerky) can also be tasted at the **Gary R. West Tasting Room,** 690 N. Fifth St., Jacksonville (☎ **541/899-1829**).

WHERE TO STAY
IN JACKSONVILLE

Historic Orth House/The Teddy Bear Inn. 105 W. Main St. (P.O. Box 1437), Jacksonville, OR 97530-1437. ☎ **800/700-7301** or 541/899-8665. Fax 503/899-9146. www. historicorthhousebnb.com. 3 units. A/C. May–Oct $120–$135 double; $175 suite. Nov–Apr $85–$100 double; $125 suite. Rates include full breakfast. MC, V.

This Italianate brick house, built in 1880, stands behind majestic old shade trees on a corner 1 block off busy California Street. The picket fence, old buggy on the lawn, and inviting front porch cry out small-town Americana. Inside, you'll find an eclectic mix of modern and antique (symbolized by the TV inside the wood stove). However, it is the inn's extensive collection of teddy bears and antique toys that are the main attraction here. With its in-room clawfoot tub, the romantic Josie's Room is a favorite.

✪ **Jacksonville Inn.** 175 E. California St., Jacksonville, OR 97530. ☎ **800/321-9344** or 541/899-1900. Fax 541/899-1373. www.jacksonvilleinn.com. 13 units (including 5 cottages). A/C TV TEL. $120–$159 double; $219–$255 cottage. Rates include full breakfast. AE, DC, DISC, MC, V.

Located in the heart of the town's restored business district in a two-story brick building part of which was built in 1861, the Jacksonville Inn is best known for its gourmet restaurant, but upstairs there are eight antiques-filled rooms that offer traditional elegance mixed with modern amenities (hair dryers, irons and ironing boards, refrigerators). Rooms are elegantly furnished and several have exposed brick walls that conjure up the inn's past. Room 1, with its queen-size canopy bed and whirlpool tub for two, is the house favorite. Modern bathrooms complement the antique furnishings. If you're looking for more privacy and greater luxury, consider the cottages, which are a couple of blocks away and have whirlpool tubs, steam showers, and entertainment centers.

✪ **The McCully House.** 240 E. California St. (P.O. Box 13), Jacksonville, OR 97530. ☎ **800/367-1942** or 541/899-1942. www.mccullyhouseinn.com. 3 units. A/C. May–Sept $105 double. Oct–Apr $95 double. Rates include full breakfast. AE, DC, DISC, MC, V.

Built in 1861, the McCully House is one of the oldest buildings currently being used as an inn in the state of Oregon, and with its classic, symmetrical lines and simple pre-Victorian styling, it looks as if it could easily be an 18th-century New England inn. If you like being steeped in local history, this is Jacksonville's best choice. In the McCully Room, you'll even find the original black-walnut master bedroom furnishings. Surrounding the inn, and enclosed by a white picket fence, is a formal rose garden with an amazing variety of roses. The inn is also one of Jacksonville's finest restaurants, and the downstairs parlors now serve as dining rooms. However, in summer, most people prefer to eat outside in the garden. Breakfasts are served in a cheery sunroom that overlooks the less-formal back garden and patio.

The Stage Lodge. 830 N. Fifth St. (P.O. Box 1316), Jacksonville, OR 97530. ☎ **800/253-8254** or 541/899-3953. 27 units. A/C TV TEL. $68–$84 double. Lower rates Oct–Apr. AE, DISC, MC, V.

Jacksonville has several bed-and-breakfast inns, but it's short on moderately priced motels. Filling the bill for the latter category is a motel designed to resemble a 19th-century stage stop, with gables, clapboard siding, and turned-wood railings along two floors of verandas. These details allow the lodge to fit right in with all the original buildings in town. The rooms are spacious and comfortable and have a few nice touches such as ceiling fans, TV armoires, and country decor.

TouVelle House Bed & Breakfast. 455 N. Oregon St. (P.O. Box 1891), Jacksonville, OR 97530. ☎ **800/846-8422** or 541/899-8938. Fax 541/899-3992. www.touvellehouse.com. 6 units. May–Sept $125–$140 double. Oct–Apr $110–$125 double. AE, DISC, MC, V.

This inn sits at the top of a 1½-acre hilly yard on the edge of town, but only 2 blocks from downtown and the Britt Festivals amphitheater. Built in 1916, the three-story Craftsman-style home is one of the largest historic homes in town. The wood-paneled great room with its large stone fireplace is a favorite gathering spot for guests, especially in the cooler months. There is also a hot tub and an outdoor swimming pool. If you don't want to climb a lot of stairs, ask for the Judge's Chamber, the only guest room on the ground floor. The third-floor Pendleton Suite, with its clawfoot tub, and the second-floor Garden Suite, with its Roman tub for two, are favorites. A gourmet three-course breakfast is served each morning.

IN MEDFORD

In addition to the B&B listed below, you'll find dozens of inexpensive chain motels clustered along I-5.

Under the Greenwood Tree. 3045 Bellinger Lane, Medford, OR 97501. ☎ **541/776-0000.** www.greenwoodtree.com. 5 units. A/C TEL. $95–$125 double. Rates include full breakfast. V. Pets accepted by arrangement.

Located just west of Medford and taking its name from the 300-year-old oaks that shade the front yard, this B&B offers a step back in time to the days of iced tea on the veranda, croquet on the lawn, and stolen kisses behind the barn. Romance is the name of the game here, with beds piled with plump pillows and lace curtains swaying in the summer breezes. During the summer, fresh-cut flower arrangements fill the house. The guest rooms are furnished with antiques, and two have separate sitting rooms. Throughout the house you'll find antique quilts and Oriental carpets, which give the inn a touch of country class. Out back there is a huge deck that overlooks the inn's 10 acres of land and its gazebo, garden, and barns, all of which you can explore. Bicycles are available for guests, and there's even some fitness equipment. A three-course breakfast and afternoon tea are served by innkeeper Renate Ellam, a Cordon Bleu–trained chef.

IN THE APPLEGATE VALLEY

✪ **Applegate Lodge.** 15100 Ore. 238, Applegate, OR 97530. ☎ **541/846-6690** or 541/846-6408. www.diron.com/applegate. A/C. 7 units. $125–$160 double (20% off in winter). MC, V.

This modern lodge, which opened in 1997, is a masterpiece of woodworking, with burnished woods (including fiddleback redwood paneling) and unique wooden details throughout. Situated on the bank of the Applegate River 16 miles outside Jacksonville, the lodge boasts one of the prettiest settings in southern Oregon. The high-ceilinged great room with a river-rock fireplace features a wall of glass looking out on the river, and across the length of the lodge is a deck where you can sit and listen to the music of the water. The guest rooms are all very large, and several of them have loft sleeping areas. Lots of peeled log furniture give the inn a solidly western feel. Right next door and under the same ownership is the ever-popular Applegate River Ranch House (see "Where to Dine" below for details). The river here is great for swimming.

WHERE TO DINE
IN JACKSONVILLE

In addition to the establishments mentioned below, **Good Bean Coffee,** 165 S. Oregon St. (☎ **541/899-8740**), is *the* place for a cup of espresso. **MacLevin's Nosherie,** 150 W. California St. (☎ **541/899-1251**), will pack up a deli-style picnic for a Britt performance (or any other occasion).

Bella Union Restaurant & Saloon. 170 W. California St. ☎ **541/899-1770.** At dinner, call ahead to be placed on wait list. Main courses $6–$15. AE, MC, V. Mon–Fri 11:30am–10pm, Sat 11am–10pm, Sun 10am–10pm, lounge until midnight daily. ITALIAN/AMERICAN.

For casual dining or someplace to just toss back a cold beer or sip an Italian soda, the Bella Union is Jacksonville's top choice. The lounge hearkens back to the days when the Bella Union was one of Jacksonville's busiest saloons, and in the back of the building is a garden patio. However, it's the main dining room up front that's most popular. Old wood floors, storefront windows, and exposed brick walls conjure up images of gold miners out on the town. Meals range from pizzas and pastas to a delicious house chicken that's marinated in Gorgonzola and walnut pesto.

Gogi's Restaurant. 235 W. Main St. ☎ **541/899-8699.** Reservations recommended. Main courses $10.50–$19. MC, V. Tues–Sat 5–9pm, Sun 10am–2pm (brunch) and 5–9pm. REGIONAL AMERICAN.

With an ambiance somewhere between the casual atmosphere of Bella Union and the formality of the Jacksonville Inn Dinner House, this newest restaurant on the Jacksonville scene is a gleaming and comfortable little bistro. The small plates, such as roasted garlic with olives and goat cheese or sautéed scallops with vegetable slaw, make good choices for sharing around the table. Other tasty standouts include filet mignon broiled with blue cheese butter, and lamb in a bourbon demi-glaze.

Jacksonville Inn Dinner House. 175 E. California St. ☎ **541/899-1900.** Reservations recommended. Main courses lunch $7–$11, dinner $9–$26. DISC, MC, V. Sun 10:30am–2pm (brunch) and 5–9pm, Mon 5–10pm, Tues–Sat 11:30am–2pm and 5–10pm. Bistro menu served daily 2pm–closing. CONTINENTAL/MEDITERRANEAN.

Old-world atmosphere, either in the dark and elegant downstairs or in the airier upstairs dining room, sets the mood for reliable continental fare. Together the cuisine and the decor attract a well-heeled clientele that likes familiar dishes perfectly prepared, such as rack of lamb, veal scaloppini, or prime rib. The bistro menu is lighter and leans toward Mediterranean influences, with such dishes as eggplant lasagna and roasted garlic pasta. Pears are a mainstay of the local economy and show up frequently in both entrees and desserts. The inn's wine shop gives diners access to a cellar boasting more than 1,500 wines.

✪ **McCully House Inn.** 240 E. California St. ☎ **541/899-1942.** Main courses lunch $8–$12, dinner $19–$23. AE, DC, DISC, MC, V. Mon–Sat 11:30am–2:30pm and 5–9:30pm, Sun 9:30am–2:30pm and 5–9:30pm. REGIONAL AMERICAN.

The McCully House is one of the oldest homes in Jacksonville, and though the dining rooms have plenty of historic atmosphere, the beautiful gardens are the place to dine on a summer evening. You might start out with mushrooms sautéed in cognac with basil pesto, followed by Dijon-crusted salmon or seafood fettuccine. Fresh fish from the Oregon coast is a strong point here, but so is the aged New York beef, and fresh herbs and vegetables from the garden round out the flavors. You can also get boxed meals to go if you are heading to a Britt Festival performance and want to take a picnic with you.

IN MEDFORD

Samovar Restaurant. 101 E. Main St., Medford. ☎ **541/779-4967.** Reservations recommended on weekends. Main courses $13–$17; lunch $5–$7.25. MC, V. Tues–Sat 11am–3pm and 5–9pm. RUSSIAN/MIDDLE EASTERN.

At this restaurant run by a Russian couple, you'll find soft lights, tablecloths, and classical music—an unexpected scene in downtown Medford. Bakery products made with whole grains, fresh produce, and low-fat poultry and meats are the mainstay ingredients for dishes such as a bracing and delicious borscht with cabbage, tomatoes, and beets (and topped with sour cream, of course). Other Russian and Middle Eastern favorites are blintzes, *piroshki* (flaky dough pies stuffed with cheese or meat), stuffed cabbage, and skewered kabobs of lamb or chicken. To top off your meal, tortes and pastries are available from the bakery to eat in or take out.

IN THE APPLEGATE VALLEY

Applegate River Ranch House. 15100 Hwy. 238, Applegate. ☎ **541/846-6082** or 541/846-6690. Reservations recommended in summer and on weekends. Main courses $11–$20. MC, V. Wed–Mon 4–9pm. STEAK/SEAFOOD.

With a deck overlooking the beautiful Applegate River, the location here just can't be beat. We like to enjoy the view with a plate of succulent oak-wood-broiled mushrooms and a glass of crisp Chardonnay. Anything broiled over the local red oak wood is delicious, from chicken to various cuts of steaks. We like to top it all off with a piece of the "hula" pie.

3 The Klamath Falls Area: Bird Watching & Native American Artifacts

65 miles E of Ashland, 60 miles S of Crater Lake

Klamath Falls, which has a history that stretches back more than 14,000 years, is set in a wide, windswept expanse of lakes and high desert just north of the California line. The large lakes in this dry region have long attracted a wide variety of wildlife (especially waterfowl), which in turn used to feed the area's Native American population. Native Americans lived on the banks of the Klamath Basin's lakes, from which they harvested fish, birds, and various marsh plants. Today, two local museums exhibit extensive collections of Native American artifacts that have been found in this area over the years.

Upper Klamath Lake and adjacent Agency Lake have shrunk considerably over the years as shallow, marshy areas have been drained to create pastures and farmland. Today, however, as the lake's native fish populations have become threatened and migratory bird populations in the region have plummeted, there is a growing movement to restore some of the region's drained marshes to more natural conditions. Though large portions of the area are now designated as national wildlife areas, farming and ranching are still considered the primary use of these wildlife lands. However, the many bird-watchers who flock to the region are quick to point out that the Klamath Falls area still has some of the best birding in the state.

The region's shallow lakes warm quickly in the hot summers here, and, partly because of the excess nutrients in the waters from agricultural runoff, they support large blooms of blue-green algae. While the algae blooms deprive the lake's fish of oxygen, they also provide the area with its most unusual agricultural activity. The harvesting and marketing of Upper Klamath Lake's blue-green algae as a dietary supplement has become big business throughout the country as people have claimed all manner of health benefits from this chlorophyll-rich dried algae.

ESSENTIALS

GETTING THERE   Klamath Falls is on U.S. 97, which leads north to Bend and south to I-5 near Mount Shasta in California. The city is also connected to Ashland by the winding Ore. 66 and to Medford by Ore. 140, which continues east to Lakeview in eastern Oregon. The **Klamath Falls Airport** is served by Horizon/Alaska Airlines and United Express. Amtrak's *Coast Starlight* trains stop here en route between San Francisco and Portland.

VISITOR INFORMATION   For more information on the region, contact the **Klamath County Department of Tourism,** 1451 Main St. (P.O. Box 1867), Klamath Falls, OR 97601 (☎ **800/445-6728** or 541/884-0666; www.klamath.org).

GETTING AROUND   Rental cars are available at Klamath Falls Airport from Hertz.

DELVING INTO LOCAL HISTORY

In addition to the two museums listed here, you might want to drive by the historic **Ross Ragland Theater,** 218 N. Seventh St. (☎ **541/844-LIVE**), an impressive art deco theater in downtown Klamath Falls. The theater stages a wide variety of performances throughout the year.

✪ **Favell Museum of Western Art and Indian Artifacts.** 125 W. Main St. ☎ **541/ 882-9996.** Admission $4 adults, $3 seniors, $2 children 6–16. Mon–Sat 9:30am–5:30pm.

Anyone with an interest in Native American artifacts or Western art will be fascinated by a visit to this unusual museum, considered one of the best Western museums in the country. On display are thousands of arrowheads, including one made from fire opal, obsidian knives, spear points, stone tools of every description, baskets, pottery, and even ancient shoes and pieces of matting and fabric. Though the main focus is on the Native Americans of the Klamath Basin and Columbia River, there are artifacts from Alaska, Canada, other regions of the United States, and Mexico. Few museums any-where in the country have such an extensive collection; the cases of artifacts can be overwhelming, so take your time. The other half of the museum's collection is Western art by more than 300 artists, including 13 members of the famous Cowboy Artists of America. Paintings, bronzes, photographs, dioramas, and wood carvings capture the Wild West in realistic, romantic, and even humorous styles. There is also the world's largest publicly displayed miniature gun collection in the world.

Klamath County Museum. 1451 Main St. ☎ **541/883-4208.** Admission $2 adults, $1 seniors and students. Summer Mon–Sat 9am–5:30pm; winter 8am–4:30pm.

More Native American artifacts, this time exclusively from the Klamath Lakes area, are on display in this museum, while a history of the Modoc Indian Wars chronicles the most expensive campaign of the American West. Also of particular interest here are the early-20th-century photos by local photographer Maud Baldwin. There's also an extensive collection of stuffed birds.

BIRD WATCHING & OTHER OUTDOOR ACTIVITIES

In this dry region between the Cascades and the Rocky Mountains, there are few large bodies of water, so the lakes and marshes of the Klamath Basin are a magnet for birds. In the winter the region hosts the largest concentration of bald eagles in the Lower 48. More than 300 eagles can be seen at the **Bear Valley National Wildlife Refuge** near the town of Worden, 11 miles south of Klamath Falls. Other avian visitors and resi-dents include white pelicans, great blue herons, sandhill cranes, egrets, geese, ducks, grebes, bitterns, and osprey. For more information on bird watching in the area, con-tact the Klamath County Department of Tourism (see above).

If you want to get out and paddle around one of the local lakes, check out the **Upper Klamath Canoe Trail,** which begins near the junction of Ore. 140 and West Side Road northwest of Klamath Falls. The canoe trail wanders through marshlands on the edge of Upper Klamath Lake. For more information, contact the **Winema National Forest,** Klamath Ranger District, 1936 California Ave., Klamath Falls, OR 97601 (☎ **541/885-3400**). Canoes and kayaks can be rented at the adjacent **Rocky Point Resort,** 28121 Rocky Point Rd. (☎ **541/356-2287**). Rates are $6 an hour or $20 for half a day. If you'd like to do a guided canoe trip around the lake, contact **Kla-math Lake Touring Company** (☎ **541/883-4622**).

If you're more in the mood for white-water thrills, **Cascade River Runners** (☎ **800/884-2113** or 541/883-6340) offers 1-day **white-water rafting** trips on the Class IV-plus Upper Klamath River. This 18-mile run includes 40 major rapids and is not for novices.

If you're truly serious about **trout fishing,** there is no better place in Oregon to get your line wet. Upper Klamath and Agency Lakes and the Wood and Williamson Rivers produce the largest rainbow trout in the West. The official record is 19 pounds, while the unofficial record is 25 pounds. If you want to hire a guide, contact

Miranda's Guide Service (☎ 541/356-2141), **Roe Outfitters** (☎ 541/884-3825), or **Williamson River Anglers** (☎ 541/783-2677). At Rocky Point Resort (see above) and **Harriman Springs Resort & Marina,** 26661 Rocky Point Rd. (☎ 541/356-2331), you can rent fishing boats.

For world-class **fly-fishing** on 6 miles of private Wood River water, consider spending time at **Horseshoe Ranch,** 52909 Ore. 62, Fort Klamath (☎ 541/381-2297). **Free Spirit Guide Service** (☎ 541/884-3222) offers guided fly-fishing trips.

Horseback rides are available through the **Running Y Stables,** 5115 Running Y Rd. (☎ 541/850-5691), which charges $27 for a 1-hour ride and $65 for a half-day ride. Pony rides are also available.

The **Running Y Ranch Resort** (☎ 888/850-0261) is also the place to head for a round of **golf.** Other area courses include the **Shield Crest Golf Course,** 3151 Shield Crest Dr. (☎ 541/884-1493), and **Harbor Links,** 601 Harbor Isles Blvd. (☎ 541/882-0609).

Northwest of Klamath Falls about 35 miles on Ore. 140, you'll find the region's main mountain recreation area. Here, in the vicinity of **Lake of the Woods** and **Fish Lake,** you'll find, in summer, the fun High Lakes mountain-bike trail, which leads through a rugged lava field. Also in the area is the hiking trail to the summit of Mount McLoughlin. In winter, this same area has cross-country ski trails. There are rustic cabin resorts and campgrounds on both Lake of the Woods and Fish Lake.

If you'd like to head out on the waters of Upper Klamath Lake, **Meridian Sail Center,** Pelican Marina, 928 Front St. (☎ 541/884-5869), offers sailboat charters starting at $40 for 2 hours. They also rent sailboats here.

WHERE TO STAY

Rocky Point Resort. 28121 Rocky Point Rd., Klamath Falls, OR 97601. ☎ **541/356-2287.** Fax 541/356-2222. 9 units. $55 double; $75 cabin. MC, V. Pets accepted ($2 per night).

This rustic fishing resort on the west shore of Upper Klamath Lake is the sort of place that conjures up childhood memories of summer vacations by the lake. Neither the rooms nor the cabins are anything special, but the setting is bewitching. Shaded by huge old ponderosa pine trees and partly built atop the rocks for which this point is named, the resort has a great view across the waters and marshes of the Upper Klamath National Wildlife Refuge. Green lawns set with Adirondack chairs go right down to the water, where there is a small boat-rental dock. The rustic restaurant and lounge, complete with moose antlers over the fireplace, boast the best views on the property. Meals are the basic American fare you would expect at such a place. The Upper Klamath Lake canoe trails originate here, and the bird watching is excellent, but fishing is still the favorite pastime here. The resort also has tent and RV sites.

Running Y Ranch Resort. 5115 Running Y Rd., Klamath Falls, OR 97601. ☎ **888/RYRANCH.** Fax 541/850-5593. www.runningy.com. 83 units. A/C TV TEL. May 15–Oct 15 $109–$132 double; $218–$264 suite. Oct 16–May 14 $82–$99 double; $164–$198 suite. AE, DISC, MC, V. Rates include continental breakfast.

Located northwest of town off Ore. 140, this golf resort and time-share condominium community is built close to the shore of Upper Klamath Lake amid ponderosa pines. Although remote, it is almost as luxurious as any of the central Oregon resorts in the Bend and Sisters areas. However, this is the newest resort community in the state and it's still under construction. The hotel has a mountain-lodge feel, though guest rooms are fairly standard in their decor. Some have balconies. As of press time, the resort's hotel didn't even have a restaurant, though there is one at the golf course and there's a snack bar across the parking lot from the hotel. With the only Arnold Palmer–designed golf course in the state, the resort is obviously aiming primarily to attract golfers. However, horseback riding, bicycling on paved and gravel trails, and canoeing through a wetland area under restoration are other resort options. There is also a pool and fitness center.

CAMPGROUNDS

Along Ore. 140 between Klamath Falls and Medford are several national-forest campgrounds. On Fish Lake, **Fish Lake Campground** and **Doe Point Campground** are in nice locations, but they both get a lot of traffic noise. Just west of Fish Lake on F.S. 37, the **North Fork Campground** provides a quieter setting on a trout stream and a scenic mountain-bike trail. **Sunset Campground** and **Aspen Point Campground** at Lake of the Woods are popular in summer with the boat-fishing and waterskiing crowd. The latter campground is near Great Meadow Recreation Area, has a swimming beach, and is right on the High Lakes mountain-bike trail.

WHERE TO DINE

For dinner with the best view in the area, make a reservation at the **Rocky Point Resort** (see above), which is 30 minutes outside Klamath Falls and is open nightly in summer. Sunday brunch is also served.

4 Grants Pass & the Rogue River Valley

63 miles S of Roseburg, 40 miles NW of Ashland, 82 miles NE of Crescent City

It's the climate, proclaims a sign at the entrance to Grants Pass; and with weather almost as reliably pleasant as California's, the town has become a popular base for outdoor activities of all kinds. With the Rogue River running through the center of town, it's not surprising that most local recreational activities revolve around the waters of this famous river. Located at the junction of I-5 and U.S. 199, Grants Pass is also the last large town in Oregon if you're heading over to the redwoods, which are about 90 miles southwest on the northern California coast. About the same distance to the northeast, you'll find Crater Lake National Park, so Grants Pass makes a good base if you're trying to see a lot of this region in a short time.

The city is slowly reviving its few blocks of historic commercial buildings, and it's worth wandering down Southwest G Street to see what's new along the historic blocks.

ESSENTIALS

GETTING THERE Grants Pass is at the junction of I-5 and U.S. 199. The **Rogue Valley International–Medford Airport** at 3650 Biddle Rd., Medford, is served by Horizon/Alaska Airlines and United Airlines.

VISITOR INFORMATION Contact the **Grants Pass-Josephine County Chamber of Commerce,** 1995 NW Vine St. (P.O. Box 1787), Grants Pass, OR 97528 (☎ **800/547-5927** or 541/476-5510; www.grantspass.com/vcb). There is also a welcome center in the downtown historic district at the corner of G Street and Sixth Street.

FESTIVALS **Boatnik,** held Memorial Day weekend, is Grants Pass's biggest annual festival and includes jet boat and hydroplane races on the Rogue River, as well as lots of festivities at Riverside Park.

OUTDOOR ACTIVITIES: RAFTING, FISHING, HIKING & MORE

Grants Pass is located midway between the source and the mouth of the Rogue River and is an ideal base for river-oriented activities. The Rogue, first made famous by Western novelist and avid fly-fisherman Zane Grey and more recently the location for scenes in the film *The River Wild,* is now preserved for much of its length as a National Wild and Scenic River. Originating in Crater Lake National Park, the river twists and tumbles through narrow gorges and steep mountains as it winds its way to the coast at Gold Beach. The most famous section of the river is 250-foot-deep **Hellgate Canyon,** where the river narrows and rushes through a cleft in the rock. The canyon can be seen from an overlook on Merlin-Galice Road, which begins at exit 61 off I-5. From the interstate it's about 10 miles to the canyon overlook.

Several companies offer **river trips** of varying length and various watercraft. You can even spend several days rafting the river with stops each night at riverside lodges. If you have only enough time for a short trip on the river, we'd recommend a jet-boat trip up to Hellgate Canyon, the most scenic spot on this section of the river. **Hellgate Jetboat Excursions,** 966 SW Sixth St., Grants Pass (☎ **800/648-4874** or 541/479-7204), operates four different jet-boat trips, with adult ticket prices ranging from $25 to $45.

Local **white-water rafting** companies offer half-day, full-day, and multiday trips, with the multiday trips stopping either at rustic river lodges or at campsites along the river banks. Rafting companies include **Rogue Wilderness,** 325 Galice Rd., Merlin (☎ **800/336-1647** or 541/479-9554); **Galice Resort,** 11744 Galice Rd., Merlin (☎ **541/476-3818**); **Orange Torpedo Trips,** 209 Merlin Rd., Merlin (☎ **800/635-2925** or 541/479-5061); and **Rogue River Raft Trips,** Morrison's Lodge, 8500 Galice Rd., Merlin (☎ **800/826-1963** or 541/476-3825). Rates are around $45 for a half day and $65 for a full day. Two-day lodge trips start around $225 per person, 3-day camp/lodge trips are about $525, and 4-day camping trips are $550.

At several places near Merlin, you can rent rafts and kayaks of different types and paddle yourself downriver. Try **White Water Cowboys,** 209 Merlin Rd., Merlin (☎ **541/479-0132**); **Galice Resort Store,** 11744 Galice Rd., Merlin (☎ **541/476-3818**); or **Ferron's Fun Trips,** 585 Rogue Rim Dr., Merlin (☎ **800/404-2201** or 541/474-2201). Rental rates vary from about $20 to $80 per day.

If **fishing** is your passion, the steelhead and salmon of the Rogue River already haunt your dreams. To make those dreams a reality, you'll want to hire a guide to take you where the fish are sure to bite. Rogue Wilderness (mentioned above), **Rogue Excursions Unlimited** (☎ **541/826-6222**), and **Geoff's Guide Service** (☎ **541/474-0602**) offer guided fishing trips of 1 to 4 days. Expect to pay about $149 per person for a day of fishing.

Golfers can play a round at the **Red Mountain Golf Course,** 324 N. Schoolhouse Creek Rd. (☎ **541/479-2297**), which is 15 minutes north of Grants Pass, or at the **Dutcher Creek Golf Course,** 4611 Upper River Rd. (☎ **541/474-2188**).

Fans of **horse racing** can bet on the ponies at **Grants Pass Downs** at the Josephine County Fairgrounds (☎ **541/476-3215**) on U.S. 199 west of town. The season runs from the weekend before Memorial Day to the Fourth of July.

OTHER THINGS TO SEE & DO

Though most people visiting Grants Pass are here to enjoy the mountains and rivers surrounding the town, history buffs can pick up a free map of the town's historic buildings at the Tourist Information Center. Two small art museums—the **Grants Pass Museum of Art,** in the historic district at 229 SW G St. (☎ **541/479-3290**), and the **Wiseman Gallery,** 3345 Redwood Hwy., at Rogue Community College (☎ 541/956-7500)—offer changing exhibits of classic and contemporary art by local and national artists.

Wildlife Images Rehabilitation and Education Center, 11845 Lower River Rd. (☎ 541/476-0222), is dedicated to nurturing injured birds of prey and other wild animals back to health and then releasing them back into the wild, if possible. The center is located 13 miles south of Grants Pass and is open for tours daily at 11am and 1pm by reservation only. Admission is by donation. One of the best things about this place is that you can get closer to the animals than you can in a zoo.

Riverside Park, in the center of town, is a popular place to play, especially in the warmer months when people come to cool off in the river.

About midway between Medford and Grants Pass and just 4 miles off I-5, you'll find one of Oregon's most curious attractions: the **Oregon Vortex and House of Mystery,** 4303 Sardine Creek Rd., Gold Hill (☎ 541/855-1543). This classic tourist trap is guaranteed to have the kids, and some adults, oohing and aahing in bug-eyed amazement at the numerous phenomena that defy the laws of physics. People grow taller as they recede. You, and the trees surrounding the House of Mystery, lean toward magnetic north rather than stand upright. Seeing is believing—or is it? Open March to May and September through mid-October, daily from 9am to 5pm; June to August, daily from 9am to 6pm (closed mid-Oct through Feb). Admission is $7 for adults, $5 for children 5 to 11.

Fourteen miles north of Grants Pass in Sunny Valley, you'll find the **Applegate Trail Interpretive Center** (☎ 888/411-1846). This small museum, which opened in 1998, documents the little-known Applegate Trail, an alternative to the Oregon Trail. To find the museum, take exit 71 off I-5 and go 2 blocks east. The museum is open daily from 10am to 5pm and admission is $5.95 for adults, $4.95 for seniors and ages 13 to 18.

WHERE TO STAY
IN TOWN

Riverside Inn Resort. 971 SE Sixth St., Grants Pass, OR 97526. ☎ **800/334-4567** or 541/476-6873. Fax 541/474-9848. www.riverside-inn.com. 174 units. A/C TV TEL. $65–$90 standard double; $88–$115 river-view double; $125–$350 suite. Lower rates Nov–Mar. AE, DC, DISC, MC, V. Pets accepted ($15).

Located in downtown Grants Pass, the Riverside Inn is, as the name implies, right on the bank of the Rogue River. A weathered wood exterior and cedar-shingle roof give the two-story inn a bit of Northwest flavor, though the setting between two busy bridges is not exactly idyllic. Luckily, a park across the river means the views from most rooms are quite pleasant. The inn sprawls across 3 blocks, and rooms vary in age and quality. Our favorites are the fireplace rooms in the west section and the whirlpool river-view suites. Avoid the rooms near the road, which can be quite noisy. Though the river-view rooms are a bit more expensive than nonview rooms, they're certainly worth the price.

The inn's restaurant and lounge offer a great view of the river and some of the best meals in town. There is also room service, valet/laundry service, and access to a nearby health club. Facilities include two outdoor swimming pools and a whirlpool. Jet-boat tours to Hellgate Canyon leave from the resort.

NORTH AND WEST OF TOWN

✪ **Morrison's Rogue River Lodge.** 8500 Galice Rd., Merlin, OR 97532. ☎ **800/ 826-1963** or 541/476-3825. Fax 541/476-4953. www.morrisonslodge.com. 13 units. $170–$300 double. Rates include all meals. DISC, MC, V. Closed Dec–Apr.

If you're in the area to do a bit of fishing or rafting, we can think of no better place to stay than at Morrison's. Perched on the banks of the Rogue, this fishing lodge epitomizes the Rogue River experience. The main lodge is a massive log building that's rustic yet comfortable, with a wall of glass that looks across wide lawns to the river. All the rooms have been recently redecorated, and though there are B&B–style accommodations in the main lodge, the cabins seem more appropriate in this setting. The spacious cabins stand beneath grand old trees, and all have good views of the river. Fireplaces will keep you warm and cozy in the cooler months. The dining room serves surprisingly creative four-course dinners. Fishing and rafting trips are the specialty here, but there are also tennis courts, an outdoor pool, a putting green, and a private beach.

Pine Meadow Inn. 1000 Crow Rd., Merlin, OR 97532-9718. ☎ **800/554-0806** or 541/471-6277. www.pinemeadowinn.com. 4 units. A/C TEL. Apr–Sept $85–$115 double. Oct–Mar $70–$95 double. Rates include full breakfast. AE, DISC, MC, V.

Situated between a meadow and a pine forest on 9 acres of land near the Rogue River, this modern farmhouse B&B is secluded yet close to town. The tranquil setting, with a hot tub and koi pond in the backyard, makes it impossible not to slow down and relax here. The guest rooms are all furnished with antiques and fresh flowers. Two rooms have mountain views, while the other two overlook the gardens and forest. Breakfasts often feature fresh organic produce from the inn's own gardens. The inn is located close to the Wild and Scenic stretch of the Rogue River and makes a good base if you are planning on doing some rafting or fishing.

○ **Wolf Creek Inn and Tavern.** 100 Front St. (P.O. Box 6), Wolf Creek, OR 97497. ☎ **541/866-2474.** 8 units. $85–$125 double ($10 less in winter). Rates include full breakfast in summer, continental breakfast in winter. MC, V.

Originally opened in 1883 on the old stagecoach road between Sacramento and Portland, the Wolf Creek Tavern is a two-story clapboard building with wide front verandas along both floors. Today the inn, which is 25 miles north of Grants Pass and just off I-5, is the oldest hotel in Oregon and is owned and managed by the Oregon State Parks and Recreation Division. The interior is furnished in period antiques dating from the 1870s to the 1930s. On a winter's night there's no cozier spot than by the fireplace in the downstairs "ladies parlor." The guest rooms are small and comfortably furnished, much as they may have been in the early 1900s. Meals are available in the inn's dining room. All in all, this inn has a genuinely timeless feel.

EAST OF TOWN

○ **Weasku Inn.** 5560 Rogue River Hwy., Grants Pass, OR 97527. ☎ **800/4-WEASKU** or 541/471-8000. Fax 541/471-7038. 16 units. $85–$150 double; $150–$295 suite/cabin. Rates include continental breakfast. AE, DC, DISC, MC, V.

Set on the bank of the Rogue River just below the Savage Rapids Dam (which is scheduled for removal sometime soon), this log lodge built in 1924 was once *the* area fishing lodge. That was back in the days when Clark Gable, Carole Lombard, Walt Disney, Zane Grey, Bing Crosby, and Herbert Hoover used to stay here. Today, after a total renovation, the lodge is once again the sort of place where such luminaries would feel comfortable. Guest rooms, on the second floor of the old log lodge, are spacious and modern and have such interesting details as bent-willow furnishings and coiled-rope lamps. The riverside cabins are done in modern lodge style with whirlpool tubs, fireplaces, and private decks. Set beneath towering trees a few miles out of Grants Pass, this inn is one of the most memorable lodgings in the state, the quintessential mountain/fishing lodge. In addition to breakfast, guests get a complimentary wine-and-cheese reception each evening.

CAMPGROUNDS

Along the Rogue River east of Grants Pass, you'll find the very busy **Valley of the Rogue State Park** just off I-5 near the town of Rogue River. West of Grants Pass, there are several county-operated campgrounds: **Indian Mary Park,** near Galice on Merlin-Galice Road (this is the nicest of these campgrounds and is in the Hellgate Canyon area); **Schroeder Park,** off Ore. 199 (the Redwood Hwy.) only a mile or so out of town; and **Whitehorse Park,** on Lower River Road about 2½ miles out of town. Near Indian Mary Park, you'll also find the **Almeda Park,** which is close to the Grave Creek trailhead of the Rogue River Trail.

WHERE TO DINE

If all you need is a pizza and a microbrew, try **Wild River Brewing & Pizza Co.,** 595 NE E St. (☎ **541/471-RIVR**). Alternatively, check out the same company's Wild River Pub, 533 NE F St. (☎ **541/474-4456**). For espresso drinks and light meals, **Coffee Cartel,** 405 NE 7th St. (☎ **541/955-8573**), has a fun atmosphere. **The Cake Shop,** 215 Galice Rd., Merlin (☎ **541/479-0188**), is open only Friday through Sunday; but if you happen to be there during that time, it's worth a stop for the Wisconsin cheese rolls. **Morrison's Rogue River Lodge,** 8500 Galice Rd., Merlin (☎ **541/476-3825**), serves the best meals on the river. For nonguests, dinners are $20 to $30. Reservations are required. See above for details.

✪ **Hamilton River House.** 1936 Rogue River Hwy. ☎ **541/479-3938.** Reservations recommended. Main courses $7.50–$15. AE, DC, DISC, MC, V. Sun–Thurs 11:30am–9pm, Fri–Sat 11:30am–10pm. REGIONAL AMERICAN.

If you're looking to soak up as much Rogue River atmosphere as you can while you're in Grants Pass, be sure to have a meal at this restaurant, located right on the bank of the river. Three levels of decks outside provide plenty of seating in pleasant weather, and even if you have to eat inside, there are big windows that let you gaze out at the river. Besides the good views, the Hamilton House does a respectable job with the food. Reliable dishes include anything with Caribbean spices, such as spicy jerk prawns or jerk chicken, or rotisserie choices such as beef with garlic rub. Roasted trout is a house specialty, as are cheesecakes and berry desserts. The lively bar really gets hopping on weekends when there's live jazz.

The Laughing Clam. 121 SW G St. ☎ **541/479-1110.** Main courses $6–$18. DISC, MC, V. Mon–Sat 11am–11pm, Sun noon–9pm. SEAFOOD/PUB.

Located in a historic building in the hip G Street neighborhood, this microbrewery is furnished in "shabby chic" and sports a bar that came around Cape Horn by ship a long time ago. They serve up tasty salads, sandwiches, and pastas, and there are also plenty of meatless and seafood selections to accompany a microbrew or glass of Oregon wine. We really like the curried coconut prawns and calamari with spicy chili mayonnaise.

Summer Jo's. 2315 Upper River Rd. Loop. ☎ **541/476-6882.** Salads and sandwiches $5.50–$8.50. AE, MC, V. Tues–Sat 11am–4pm. Closed Jan. Drive west on G St. and look for the sign; it's 1½ miles from downtown Grants Pass. SALADS/SANDWICHES.

Located out in the country and surrounded by flower and vegetable gardens, this casual restaurant provides a glimpse of the good life, Grants Pass style. If you like gardens, you'll especially enjoy a meal here in high summer when the gardens are bursting with life and color. Lunch (often busy and popular with groups) and afternoon tea are served inside or outside on the lawn. The cafe uses organically grown herbs and produce.

Pongsri's. 1571 NE Sixth St. ☎ **541/479-1345.** Main courses $6.50–$9. MC, V. Tues–Sun 11am–3pm and 4:30–9pm. THAI/CHINESE.

Located in a nondescript older shopping center between downtown Grants Pass and I-5, Pongsri's is a tiny and basic restaurant serving good Thai food. The long menu includes plenty of choices, including lots of seafood. If you like shrimp as much as we do, opt for the *tom yum kung,* a sour-and-spicy soup that's guaranteed to clear your sinuses. Vegetarians have lots of options here, too, and the lunch special for $4 to $5 just can't be beat.

NORTH OF GRANTS PASS: SWEET ROLLS AS BIG AS YOUR HEAD

If you've got a sweet tooth, you won't want to miss one of the most important stops in Oregon, exit 86 off I-5 in the community of Azalea. Fans of gooey cinnamon rolls and berry pies will find **Heaven on Earth** at 703 Quines Creek Rd. (☎ **541/ 837-3700**). They serve legendary cinnamon rolls that are as big as your head, equally hefty blackberry pies, and turnovers that will have you turning to a new diet when you're done.

5 Oregon Caves National Monument & the Illinois Valley

Cave Junction: 30 miles SW of Grants Pass, 56 miles NE of Crescent City

For many people, U.S. 199 is simply the road to the redwoods from southern Oregon. However, this remote stretch of highway passes through the Illinois Valley and skirts the Siskiyou Mountains, which together offer quite a bit in the way of recreational activities. The Illinois River, which flows into the Rogue River, is an even wilder river than the Rogue, and its Class V waters are often run by experienced paddlers looking for real white-water adventure. Because the Siskiyou Mountains are among the oldest in Oregon, they support a unique plant community. These mountains are also known for their rugged, rocky peaks, which, though not very high, can be very impressive.

ESSENTIALS

GETTING THERE   Cave Junction is on U.S. 199 between Grants Pass and the California state line. Oregon Caves National Monument is 20 miles outside Cave Junction on Ore. 46.

VISITOR INFORMATION   For more information on this area, contact the **Illinois River Valley Visitor Center,** 201 Caves Hwy., Cave Junction, OR 97523 (☎ **541/592-2631**).

EXPLORING THE CAVES

Oregon Caves National Monument. 19000 Caves Hwy. ☎ **541/592-2100.** Admission $7.50 adults, $5 children 6–11. Cave tours May and after Labor Day–Sept 30 daily 9am–5pm; June–Labor Day daily 8:30am–7pm; Oct–Apr call for hours.

High in the rugged Siskiyou Mountains, a clear mountain stream cascades through a narrow canyon, and here stands one of southern Oregon's oldest attractions. Known as the marble halls of Oregon and first discovered in 1874, the caves, which stretch for 3 miles under the mountain, were formed by water seeping through marble bedrock. The slight acidity of the water dissolves the marble, which is later redeposited as beautiful stalactites, stalagmites, draperies, soda straws, columns, and flowstone. Guided tours of the caves take about 1½ hours, and up above ground there are several miles of hiking trails that start near the cave entrance. To reach the monument, take Ore. 46 out of Cave Junction and follow the signs.

OTHER THINGS TO SEE & DO IN THE ILLINOIS VALLEY

The Illinois River, when it isn't raging through rock-choked canyons, creates some of the best **swimming holes** in the state. Try the waters at Illinois River State Park, just outside Cave Junction, or ask at the **Illinois Valley Ranger District,** 26568 Redwood Hwy., Cave Junction, OR 97532 (☎ **541/592-2166**), for directions to other good swimming holes in the area. At this ranger station, you can also pick up information and directions for **hiking trails** in the Siskiyous, where the 180,000-acre Kalmiopsis Wilderness is a destination for backpackers.

WINE TOURING

The Cave Junction area is one of the warmest regions of Oregon and consequently produces some of the best Cabernet Sauvignons and Merlots in the state. This is about as far south as you can get and still claim to be producing Oregon wines; only a few more miles and you cross into California (though it's still a long way to Napa Valley).

Foris. 654 Kendall Rd. ☎ **800/843-6747** or 541/592-3752. Daily 11am–5pm. Closed major holidays.

Full-bodied and complex red wines are the hallmark of Foris Vineyards Winery, which is one of the few wineries in the state to have a female winemaker. Of particular note here is the Klipsun Vineyards Cabernet Sauvignon, which is actually made with grapes from a celebrated Washington state vineyard. The Marechal Foch, Pinot Noir, and Cabernet Sauvignon/Merlot/Cabernet Franc blend are all outstanding. They also do very good Chardonnay and even produce port.

Bridgeview. 4210 Holland Loop Rd. ☎ **541/592-4688.** Daily 11am–5pm. From Cave Junction, go east on Ore. 46 and turn right on Holland Loop Rd.

Best known for its distinctive blue bottles, Bridgeview is one of the three largest wineries in the state and produces primarily inexpensive white wines for the masses. This place is not for wine snobs, but for those who enjoy a pleasant glass of wine with dinner. The tasting room boasts an idyllic setting beside a large pond that is stocked with trout (don't forget to feed them). Whites are usually under $10, while most reds tend to be around $20.

WHERE TO STAY

✪ **Out 'n' About Treehouse Treesort.** 300 Page Creek Rd., Cave Junction, OR 97523. ☎ **800/200-5484** or 541/592-2208. www.treehouses.com. 6 units. $45–$150 double. No credit cards.

This is by far the most unusual accommodation in southern Oregon: a complex of tree houses. Michael Garnier, the owner, fought for years with county officials over whether the tree houses were safe. The county finally agreed to let the treetop cottages remain, much to the delight of the many people who have stayed here. Choices include a Tree Room Schoolhouse, the Swiss Family Complex (complete with swinging bridge to the kids' room), the Peacock Perch, the Cabintree (actually a land-locked cabin), and the Treeplex, which consists of two "treepis" and a "Cavaltree" fort (big hits with kids). Despite the address, Out 'n' About is actually located in the community of Takilma.

Oregon Caves Lodge. 20000 Caves Hwy. (P.O. Box 128), Cave Junction, OR 97523. ☎ **541/592-3400.** Fax 541/592-6654. www.oregoncaves.com. 26 units. $74–$95 double; $125–$135 suite. MC, V.

A narrow road winds for 20 miles south into the Siskiyou National Forest, climbing through deep forests before finally coming to an end in a narrow, steep-walled canyon. At the very head of this canyon stands the Oregon Caves Lodge, a rustic six-story lodge built in 1934. Huge fir beams support the lobby ceiling, and two marble fireplaces beckon (it can be cool here any time of year). About the only thing that's missing from this alpine setting is a view (because the lodge is in a wooded canyon, there are no sweeping vistas). The guest rooms have rather unattractive furnishings and don't live up to the promise of the rest of the building. However, if you spend your time exploring the caves, hiking the hills, or lounging in the lobby, you'll hardly notice. A 1930s-style soda fountain (an absolute classic) serves burgers, shakes, and other simple meals, while in the main dining room steak and seafood dinners are available.

CAMPGROUNDS

Although there are no campgrounds in Oregon Caves National Monument, there are a couple of national-forest campgrounds nearby. On the road to the national monument, you'll find **Grayback Campground** and **Cave Creek Campground,** both of which are in forest settings on creek banks.

WHERE TO DINE

Wild River Brewing & Pizza Company. 249 N. Redwood Hwy. ☎ **541/592-3556.** Sandwiches $4–$5.50; pizzas $4–$20. DISC, MC, V. Mon–Sat 10am–10pm, Sun 11am–9:30pm. PIZZA/DELI.

If you're a fan of microbrewery ales, a pleasant surprise awaits you in the crossroads community of Cave Junction. This very casual combination pizza parlor and deli also happens to be a respectable little brewery specializing in British ales. The rich and flavorful ales go great with the pizzas, several of which are made with locally made sausage. And for fans of the unusual, there's a pizza with smoked sausage and sauerkraut and another with avocado and sprouts.

6 The Roseburg Area: Lions & Tigers & Wineries

68 miles N of Grants Pass, 68 miles S of Eugene, 83 miles W of Crater Lake National Park

Although primarily a logging mill town, Roseburg is set at the mouth of the North Umpqua River and, consequently, is well situated for exploring one of the prettiest valleys in Oregon. The surrounding countryside bears a striking resemblance to parts of northern California, so it should come as no surprise that there are a half dozen wineries in the area. The hills south of town also look a bit like Africa, which may be why the Wildlife Safari park chose to locate here. Today this drive-through wildlife park is one of the biggest attractions in southern Oregon. In downtown Roseburg, you'll find numerous old Victorian homes, and a drive through these old neighborhoods will be interesting for fans of late-19th-century architecture.

WHAT TO SEE & DO: A WILDLIFE PARK & LOCAL HISTORY

✪ **Wildlife Safari.** Off Ore. 42, just outside Winston (south of Roseburg). ☎ **800/ 355-4848** or 541/679-6761. Admission $11.95 adults, $9.95 seniors, $6.95 children 4–12, free for children 3 and under. Summer daily 9am–7pm; winter daily 10am–4pm; call for exact hours.

This 600-acre drive-through nature park looks like an African savanna and is home to wild animals from around the world. You'll come face-to-face with curious bears, grazing gazelles and zebras, ostriches, and even lumbering elephants and rhinos. In addition to the drive-through the park, you can visit the educational center or attend an animal show. Signs as you approach let you know that convertibles are not allowed in the lion or bear enclosures (but rental cars are available).

Douglas County Museum of History & Natural History. 123 Museum Dr. (exit 123 off I-5). ☎ **541/957-7007.** $3.50 adults, $1 children 4–17. Mon–Fri 9am–5pm, Sat 10am–5pm, Sun noon–5pm.

South of town at the Douglas County Fairgrounds, you'll find this surprisingly well-designed museum. The unusual, large building that houses it resembles an old mining structure or mill. Inside are displays on the history and natural history of the region. Pioneer farming and mining displays interpret the settlement of the region, but it's the very large elk that really grabs people's attention.

THE NEARBY HISTORIC TOWN OF OAKLAND

About 15 miles north of Roseburg is the historic town of Oakland, which is listed on the National Register of Historic Places. Though the town was founded in the 1850s, most of the buildings here date from the 1890s. A stroll through town soaking up the atmosphere is a pleasant way to spend a morning or an afternoon. You can pick up a self-guided walking-tour map at the **Oakland Museum,** 130 Locust St. (☎ **541/459-4531**), which is housed in an 1893 brick building and contains collections of historic photos, old farm tools, household furnishings, and clothing from Oakland's past. Admission is by donation, and the museum is open daily from 1 to 4pm.

WINE TOURING

The Roseburg area is home to half a dozen wineries, all of which are located within a few miles of I-5.

La Garza Cellars. 491 Winery Lane. ☎ **541/679-9654.** Feb–May and Oct to mid-Dec Wed–Sun noon–4pm; June–Sept daily 11am–5pm. Closed late Dec–Jan. South of Roseburg, take exit 119 off I-5 and go west ½ mile.

This small winery just off I-5 is very convenient if you just want to make a quick foray into the world of Oregon wines. They specialize in Cabernet Sauvignon but also do a dry Riesling. The reserve Cabs, though pricey (up around $40), can be excellent, and they are among the best Oregon Cabernets you'll find. Lunch is also served here, which makes this a great place to stop if you're just passing through.

Girardet Wine Cellars. 895 Reston Rd. ☎ **541/679-7252.** Apr–Oct daily 11am–5pm,;Nov–Mar Sat 11am–5pm. Closed Dec 20–Jan 30 and major holidays. Take Ore. 42 (exit 119) west from I-5 south of Roseburg and turn right on Reston Rd. before reaching Tenmile.

Although this winery is unique in Oregon for producing such obscure wines as Baco Noir and Seyval Blanc, Girardet is best known for its big, bold red wines.

Callahan Ridge Winery. 340 Busenbark Lane. ☎ **541/673-7901.** Apr–Oct daily 11am–5pm. Closed Nov–Mar (open by appt.). From Roseburg, go west on Garden Valley Rd., and turn left on Melrose Rd.

The tasting room at this winery is housed in a beautifully weathered old barn set in a grove of shady oak trees. Red wines, including Zinfandel and a Cabernet-Merlot blend, are the strong points here, but they also do very good Riesling and white Zinfandel. With the exception of the dessert wines, most wines here are $10 or less.

Hillcrest Vineyards. 240 Vineyard Lane. ☎ **800/736-3709.** Daily 11am–5pm. From Roseburg, go west on Garden Valley Rd., and turn left on Melrose Rd., right on Doerner Rd., right onto Elgarose Rd., and left onto Vineyard Lane.

This winery is worth seeking out if for no other reason than that it is Oregon's oldest continuously operating winery producing wines from vinifera (European) grapes.

Vineyards here were first planted in 1961. The winemaker here believes in releasing his wines when they're ready to drink, so expect to find wines several years older than those at other area wineries.

Umpqua River DeNino Estate Winery. 451 Hess Lane. ☎ **541/673-1975.** Apr–Oct daily noon–5pm; Nov–Mar Sat–Sun noon–5pm. Closed major holidays. From exit 129 off I-5 north of Roseburg, go west on Del Rio Rd. and left on Old Garden Valley Rd.

This small family-run winery is just about as unpretentious as a winery can be, and it manages to produce some very good wines. In particular, the organically grown Marechal Foch tends to be complex and full bodied. Their lighter white wines, including Semillon and the sweet late-harvest Sauvignon Blanc, can also be quite good.

Henry Estate Winery. Ore. 9 west of Umpqua. ☎ **541/459-5120.** Daily 11am–5pm. Closed major holidays. From exit 136 off I-5 at Sutherlin, go west on through Umpqua and cross the Umpqua River.

This winery on the bank of the Umpqua River produces primarily white wines. Grapes are grown on a special trellising system known as a Scott Henry trellis, named for the winery's founder and now used all over the world.

WHERE TO STAY
IN ROSEBURG

Windmill Inn. 1450 NW Mulholland Dr., Roseburg, OR 97470-1986. ☎ **800/547-4747** or 541/673-0901. 128 units. A/C TV TEL. $65–$79 double. Rates include continental breakfast. AE, DC, DISC, MC, V. Pets accepted.

Although this is little more than an off-ramp motel, it offers a few unexpected extras that make it your best choice in Roseburg. There is an outdoor swimming pool, a hot tub, and a sauna, along with bicycles for the use of guests, breakfast and the newspaper delivered to your door, and free local phone calls.

IN OAKLAND

The Beckley House Bed & Breakfast. 338 SE Second St., Oakland, OR 97462. ☎ **541/459-9320.** Fax 541/459-9320. 2 units. A/C. $75–$95 double. Rates include full breakfast. AE, MC, V.

If you enjoy the atmosphere in Oakland and want to stick around for the night, the Beckley House B&B is the place to stay. This Queen Anne–style Victorian home dates from the late 1800s and is furnished with period antiques. An old Victrola and lots of 1930s magazines provide vintage entertainment. The suites are fairly large and can be joined to a third room with two twin beds if you need space for four people.

WHERE TO DINE
IN ROSEBURG

Between May and the end of September, **La Garza Cellars** (see above) serves good sandwiches and light lunches Wednesday through Sunday between 11am and 4pm.

Dino's Wine Bar and Italian Deli. 404 SE Jackson St. ☎ **541/673-0848.** Main courses $7–$15. MC, V. Tues 11am–6pm, Wed–Thurs 11am–9pm, Fri 11am–10pm, Sat 5–9pm. WINE BAR/REGIONAL ITALIAN.

With its brick walls and shelves and shelves of wine bottles (both Northwest and imported) lining the back of the restaurant, Dino's has the feel of a well-stocked wine cellar. Dino, the restaurant's owner and the ultimate Italian host, is also a winemaker, producing decent wines at his own winery, the Umpqua River DeNino Estate Winery (see above). Yes, this is a place for wine lovers, but it's also a good (and romantic) place to assuage your Italian food cravings with the likes of sweet potato ravioli with sage butter or lasagna *Bolognese.*

✪ **Roseburg Station Pub & Brewery.** 700 Sheridan St. ☎ **541/672-1934.** Main courses $5–$12. AE, DISC, MC, V. Mon–Thurs 11am–11pm, Fri–Sat 11am–1am, Sun noon–10pm. PUB.

Another jewel in the McMenemins brew pub empire, the Roseburg Station Pub is an example of the way McMenemins breathes new life into historic buildings. This authentic restoration of an old train station celebrates Roseburg's rail culture and is a casual place for dinner and a microbrew. An eclectic collection of chandeliers decorates the 16-foot ceiling, and street signs from around the world punctuate the room. Original features such as the dark wainscoting have been restored to their former elegance. A straightforward menu features burgers, sandwiches, and house-specialty Terminator stout chili. Be sure to accompany your meal with one of the craft ales for which McMenemins pubs are famous.

IN OAKLAND

✪ **Tolly's.** 115 Locust St., Oakland. ☎ **541/459-3796.** Main courses lunch $7–$10, dinner $10–$27. AE, DC, MC, V. Mon 9am–5pm, Tues–Fri 9am–9:30pm, Sat–Sun 8am–9:30pm. SODA FOUNTAIN/REGIONAL AMERICAN.

Since 1964, folks from all over the region have been dropping in on Oakland to have dinner or just a root-beer float or sundae here at Tolly's. Housed in a storefront on Locust Street, Tolly's is both an elegant restaurant and an old-fashioned soda fountain. You can hop onto a stool at the counter and linger over a cold malted milk shake in a tall glass, or have a dinner of steak or perfectly prepared salmon. Check out the case for deliciously decadent desserts. Attached to the restaurant are both an antiques shop and an art gallery.

NORTH OF ROSEBURG: A SERIOUS ICE-CREAM STOP

Consider yourself very lucky if you happen to be driving north from Roseburg on I-5 on a hot summer day. Respite from the heat lies just off the interstate at the Rice Hill exit ramp, at the legendary **K-R Drive Inn** (☎ 541/849-2570), where every scoop of ice cream you order is actually a double scoop! Consider this before you order a double scoop of rocky road. The K-R is open daily from 10am to 9pm in summer, daily from 10am to 8pm in winter.

Central Oregon 10

On the west side of the Cascade Range, rain is as certain as death and taxes. But cross the invisible dividing line formed by the mountains and you leave the deluge behind. Central Oregon basks under blue skies nearly 300 days of the year—in fact, it gets so little rain that parts of the region are considered high desert. Such a natural attraction is a constant enticement to Oregonians living west of the Cascades. In summer, they head to central Oregon for hiking, fishing, rafting, and camping, and in winter they descend on the ski slopes of Mount Bachelor, Oregon's best ski resort.

"Central Oregon" does not so much refer to a geographical area as a recreational region, and it doesn't actually lie in the central part of the state. The Cascade Range is responsible for a rain-shadow effect, creating a distinct and visible dividing line between the wet west side and the dry east side. Ponderosa pines rather than Douglas firs and western red cedars dominate the eastern foothill forests of this region. Farther east, where there is even less annual rainfall, juniper and sagebrush country takes over. It is this classically Western environment that has in part led to the adoption of a Wild West theme in the town of Sisters, which is filled with false-fronted buildings and covered wooden sidewalks.

On closer inspection, however, it becomes evident that it is more than just a lack of rainfall that sets this region apart. Central Oregon's unique volcanic geography provides the scenic backdrop to all the region's many recreational activities. Obsidian flows, lava caves, cinder cones, pumice deserts—these are the sorts of features that make the central Oregon landscape unique.

Despite the dryness of the landscape here, water is the region's primary recreational draw. The Deschutes River is the state's most popular rafting river and is fabled among fly anglers for its wild red-side rainbow trout and its steelheads. West of Bend, a scenic highway loops past a dozen or so lakes, each with its own unique character and appeal. Closer to Bend, the Deschutes River cascades over ancient lava flows, forming impressive waterfalls that are favorite destinations of area hikers.

However, for solitude and scenic grandeur, most hikers and backpackers head out from Bend and Sisters into the Three Sisters Wilderness, which encompasses its snow-clad namesake peaks. Outside the wilderness, there are also many miles of mountain-biking trails that have made the Bend and Sisters areas the best mountain-biking destination in the state.

While it is the open slopes of Mount Bachelor ski area that attract most visitors in the winter, the area also has many miles of cross-country ski trails, including the state's finest Nordic center (at Mount Bachelor, of course). Snowmobiling is also very popular.

1 North Central Oregon & the Lower Deschutes River

Maupin: 95 miles N of Bend, 100 miles E of Portland, 40 miles S of The Dalles

Dominated by two rivers—the Deschutes and the John Day—north central Oregon is the driest, most desertlike part of this region. It is also the closest sunny destination for rain-soaked Portlanders.

Hot springs, canyon lands, and some of the best rafting and fishing in the state are the main draws in this part of central Oregon. For many visitors, the high desert landscape is a fascinating change from the lushness of the west side of the Cascades. For others it is just too bleak and barren. But there is no denying that the Deschutes River is the busiest river in the state. Rafters and anglers descend en masse throughout the year, but especially in summer, to challenge the rapids and the red sides under sunny skies.

Even if the Deschutes is not your destination, this region has several unusual attractions that make it worthwhile for a weekend's exploration. First and foremost of these is the Kah-Nee-Ta Resort, which, with its proximity to Portland and its warm-spring swimming pool, is a powerful enticement after several months of gray skies and constant drizzle west of the Cascades.

Not far from the resort, in the town of Warm Springs, is a fascinating modern museum dedicated to the cultures of Northwest Native Americans. A forgotten page of pioneer days can be found at nearby Shaniko, a ghost town that once made it big as a wool shipping town. Much older history, up to 40 million years of it, is laid bare in the three units of the John Day Fossil Beds National Monument. If the stark hills of the national monument don't give you enough sense of being in the desert, be sure to visit The Cove Palisades State Park, where three steep-walled canyons have been flooded by the waters of Lake Billy Chinook.

ESSENTIALS

GETTING THERE   Maupin, which is the staging site for most rafting and fishing trips on the lower Deschutes River, is at the junction of U.S. 197, the main route from The Dalles south to Bend, and Ore. 216, which connects to U.S. 26 east of Mount Hood.

VISITOR INFORMATION   For more information on this area, contact the **Greater Maupin Area Chamber of Commerce,** P.O. Box 220, Maupin, OR 97037 (☎ 541/395-2599).

RAFTING, FISHING & OTHER AQUATIC ACTIVITIES

Flowing through a dry sagebrush canyon lined with basalt cliffs, the lower Deschutes River, from the U.S. 26 bridge outside Warm Springs down to the Columbia River, is one of the most popular stretches of water in Oregon. This section of the river provides lots of Class III rapids. While 1-day rafting trips keep the masses content, at almost 100 miles in length, the lower Deschutes also provides several options for multiday rafting trips.

Popular 1-day splash-and-giggle trips are offered by dozens of rafting companies and usually start just upstream from Maupin and end just above the impressive

North Central Oregon

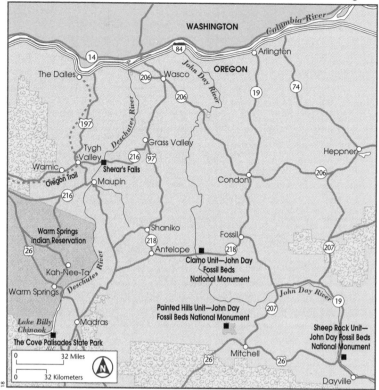

Sherar's Falls. Some companies also offer 2- and 3-day trips as well. Rafting companies operating on the lower Deschutes River include **All Star Rafting** (☎ 800/909-7238 or 541/395-2201), which also rents rafts and offers kayaking classes; **C&J Lodge** (☎ 800/395-3903 or 541/395-2404), which also operates a bed-and-breakfast inn for rafters in Maupin; **Deschutes River Adventures** (☎ 800/723-8464), which also rents rafts; **Deschutes Whitewater Services** (☎ 541/395-2232 or 541/395-2545), which also offers raft rentals and car shuttles; **Ewings' Whitewater** (☎ 800/538-RAFT); and **Rapid River Rafters** (☎ 800/962-3327 or 541/382-1514). Expect to pay around $60 to $85 for a day trip up to around $330 to $400 for a 3-day trip.

If you're just passing through the region but would like to catch a glimpse of some of the lower Deschutes River's more dramatic sections, you can visit **Sherar's Falls,** which are at the Sherar Bridge on Ore. 216 between Tygh Valley and Grass Valley. Native Americans can sometimes be seen dip-netting salmon from the waters of these falls, which can also be reached by following the river road north from Maupin for 8 miles. Just west of Sherar Bridge, you'll also find **White River Falls State Park,** where more waterfalls can be seen.

The stretch of the Deschutes River from Pelton Dam to the Columbia River is one of Oregon's most legendary stretches of **fishing** water and is managed primarily for wild steelhead and the famed red-side rainbow trout. Together these two types of fish provide fly anglers with nearly year-round action. From the mouth of the river upstream to several miles above Maupin, there are several good access points.

Fly-fishing supplies and emergency rentals are available in Maupin at the **Deschutes Canyon Fly Shop,** 599 S. Hwy. 197, Maupin (☎ 541/395-2565).

South of Madras 12 miles you'll find one of the most unlikely of settings in the state. **Lake Billy Chinook,** an artificial lake created by the construction of Round Butte Dam in 1964, now fills the canyons of the Metolius, Crooked, and Deschutes Rivers and seems lifted straight out of the canyon lands of Arizona or Utah. Here nearly vertical basalt cliffs rise several hundred feet above the lake waters, and sagebrush and junipers cling to the rocky hillsides. The lake is most popular with waterskiers and anglers who come to fish for kokanee (landlocked sockeye salmon) and bull trout (also known as dolly vardens).

Lake access is provided at **The Cove Palisades State Park** (☎ 541/546-3412), where you'll find boat ramps, a marina, campgrounds, picnic areas, and swimming beaches. There are even houseboats for rent here (see below), and at the marina you'll find a restaurant atop a hill overlooking the lake.

A NATIVE AMERICAN HERITAGE MUSEUM
✪ **The Museum at Warm Springs.** U.S. 26, Warm Springs. ☎ 541/553-3331. Admission $6 adults, $5 seniors, $3 children ages 5–12. Daily 10am–5pm.

For thousands of years the Warm Springs, Wasco, and Paiute tribes have inhabited this region, part of which is today the Confederated Tribes of the Warm Springs Reservation, and adapted to its environment. It is the history of these peoples that is presented in this impressive modern museum. Over the decades prior to the opening of the museum, the tribes amassed an outstanding collection of regional Native American artifacts, which now form the core of the museum's collection. To better display these artifacts, various styles of traditional houses have been reconstructed at the museum and serve as backdrops for displays on everything from basketry and beadwork to fishing and root gathering. There are new temporary exhibits every 3 months, including exhibitions of Native American artwork.

A GHOST TOWN & A FOSSIL EXCURSION
Between 1900 and 1911, **Shaniko** was the largest wool-shipping center in the country, and it claims to have been the site of the last range war between cattle ranchers and sheepherders. However, when the railroad line from the Columbia River down to Bend bypassed Shaniko, the town fell on hard times. Eventually, when a flood washed out the railroad into town, Shaniko nearly ceased to exist. Today the falsefronted buildings and wooden sidewalks make this Oregon's favorite and liveliest ghost town. Antiques shops, a wedding chapel, and a historic hotel make for a fun excursion or overnight getaway. Each year on the first weekend of August, the **Shaniko Days** celebration brings life to the town with stagecoach rides, shoot-outs, and plenty of crafts vendors.

Eight miles south of Shaniko is the town of **Antelope,** which gained infamy back in the early 1980s as the home of Rajneeshpuram, the U.S. commune founded by followers of Indian mystic Bagwhan Shree Rajneesh.

The **John Day Fossil Beds National Monument,** consisting of three individual units separated by as much as 85 miles, preserves a 40-million-year fossil record which indicates that this region was once a tropical or subtropical forest. From tiny seeds to extinct relatives of the rhinoceros and elephant, an amazing array of plants and animals has been preserved in one of the world's most extensive and unbroken fossil records.

To see fossil leaves, twigs, branches, and nuts in their natural state, visit the **Clarno Unit,** 23 miles southeast of Shaniko and U.S. 97. Here ancient mudflows inundated a forest, and today these ancient mudflows appear as eroding cliffs, at the base of which a ¼-mile trail leads past numerous fossils. From here it is an 85-mile drive on Ore. 218 and Ore. 19 to the national monument's **Sheep Rock Unit,** which is the site of the monument **Visitor Center.** Here you can get a close-up look at numerous fossils and sometimes watch a paleontologist at work. The visitor center is open daily in summer from 9am to 6pm (hrs. vary in other months). Just north of the visitors center you'll pass **Blue Basin,** where there's an interpretive trail.

From the Sheep Rock Unit, the monument's **Painted Hills Unit,** along the John Day River near Mitchell, is another 30 miles west on U.S. 26. Here you won't see any fossils, but you will see strikingly colored rounded hills that are favorites of photographers. The bands of color on these hills were caused by the weathering of volcanic ash under different climatic conditions.

For more information, contact the **John Day Fossil Beds National Monument,** HCR 82, Box 126, Kimberly, OR 97848 (☎ 541/987-2333; www.nps.gov/joda).

While you can't collect fossils on the national monument, you can dig them up behind the Wheeler High School in the small town of **Fossil,** 20 miles east of the Clarno Unit. You can also dig for agates, jasper, and thundereggs at **Richardson's Recreational Ranch** (☎ 541/475-2680), 17 miles southwest of Madras off U.S. 97.

WHERE TO STAY & DINE

In addition to the resort and the historic hotel listed below, you'll find three modern log cabins for rent on the shore of Lake Billy Chinook at **The Cove Palisades State Park.** These cabins rent for $45 to $65 per night for up to five people and are right beside the water. For reservations, call **Reservations Northwest** (☎ 800/452-5687). Houseboats are also available for rent at Lake Billy Chinook through The Cove Palisades State Park, for about $1,049 to $1,590 per week (reserve through park), and through **Chinook Water Chalets,** P.O. Box 40, Culver, OR 97734 (☎ 541/546-2939), for $1,150 to $2,000 per week.

C & J Lodge. 304 Bakeoven Rd. (P.O. Box 130), Maupin, OR 97037. ☎ **800/395-3903** or 541/395-2404. www.deschutesriver.com. 11 units. Rates include full breakfast. AE, MC, V.

Popular primarily with people heading out rafting on the Deschutes River, this lodge may not be your classic B&B, but it is the most comfortable place for many miles around. Guest rooms sport Oregon themes and all have private entrances. There are handmade quilts on the beds. The river-view rooms are the best and have whirlpool tubs. Dinner is available, and meals feature organically grown herbs and vegetables. C & J Lodge also offers a wide variety of rafting trips.

✪ **Kah-Nee-Ta Resort.** P.O. Box K, Warm Springs, OR 97761. ☎ **800/554-4SUN** or 541/553-1112. www.kahneetaresort.com. 169 units plus 20 teepees. A/C TV TEL. $130–$150 double; from $180 suite; $70 teepee (for 3 people). AE, CB, DC, DISC, MC, V.

Although the rooms here are not nearly as nice as those at Bend area resorts, Kah-Nee-Ta, operated by the Confederated Tribes of the Warm Springs Reservation, remains a popular getaway for a couple of reasons. First is the fact that the resort is only 120 miles from Portland and is the closest sunny-side resort for the rain-soaked citizens of the Willamette Valley. Second is the resort's pool, fed by the spring for which the Warm Springs Indians and the reservation are named. The setting, in a remote part of the Warm Springs River valley, also gives the resort a unique, isolated atmosphere. Kah-Nee-Ta offers a wide range of activities and accommodations. The main lodge sits atop a bluff that commands a brilliant vista of the high desert, while down by the river you'll find motel units as well as teepees and RV sites. Beside the river you'll also find the warm-water swimming pool. The lodge is slowly remodeling its rooms, so try to get one that's been redone.

Travelers' Tip

For reservations at Forest Service campgrounds, call the **National Recreation Reservation Service** (☎ **800/280-CAMP** or www.reserveusa.com), which charges a $7.50 reservation fee. These sites can be reserved up to 7 months in advance.

Dining/Entertainment: Two dining rooms serve a mix of American dishes and Northwest specialties. Over in the camping area by the pool are a snack bar and a more casual restaurant. During the summer months, a traditional salmon bake is held on Saturday evening and is followed by traditional Native American dancing. If you'd like to do your own dancing, check out the Appaloosa Lounge in the main lodge.

Services: Resort shuttle, bicycle rentals, kayak rentals, horseback riding, massage, fishing-rod rentals, white-water rafting trips.

Facilities: Casino, golf course, naturally heated outdoor pool plus a second pool at the main lodge, mineral baths and various spa treatments, fitness center, games room, tennis courts.

Shaniko Historic Hotel. Fourth and E Sts., Shaniko, OR 97057. ☎ **800/483-3441** or 541/489-3441. www.shaniko.com. 18 units. $56–$96 double. Rates include full breakfast. DISC, MC, V.

This restored two-story brick hotel is a surprisingly solid little place in a ghost town full of glorified shacks. However, don't start thinking that this is a fancy B&B; it's not. Most rooms are fairly small and simply furnished, and carpets are getting old, but guests don't seem to mind. No one comes out here to be pampered; they come for a bit of rustic Wild West atmosphere, and that's exactly what they get. The faded elegance hints at the wealth that once made the fortunes of area sheep ranchers, and the covered wooden sidewalk out front conjures up images of the Wild West. The bridal suite is the hotel's largest room.

CAMPGROUNDS

Downriver from Sherar's Falls, there are many undeveloped campsites along the Deschutes River. At Lake Billy Chinook, west of U.S. 97 between Madras and Redmond, are several campgrounds. The most developed are the two at **The Cove Palisades State Park.** Farther west, up the Metolius arm of the reservoir on F.S. Road 64, you'll find the Forest Service's primitive **Perry South Campground.** A little bit farther west is the **Monty Campground,** which is the lowermost campground on the Metolius River's free-flowing waters.

2 The Sisters Area

108 miles SE of Salem, 92 miles NE of Eugene, 21 miles NW of Bend

Lying at the eastern foot of the Cascades, the small Western-themed town of Sisters takes its name from the nearby Three Sisters mountains, which loom majestically over the town. Ponderosa pine forests, aspen groves, and wide meadows surround Sisters, giving it a classic Western setting that the town has cashed in on in recent years. Modern buildings sport false fronts and covered sidewalks, though the predominantly pastel color schemes are more 1990s than 1890s.

Once just someplace to stop for gas on the way to Bend, Sisters is now a destination in itself. A few miles outside of town is the Black Butte Resort, one of the state's finest golf resorts, and also nearby is the tiny community of Camp Sherman, which has been a vacation destination for most of this century. Sisters has also become Oregon's llama capital, with numerous large llama ranches around the area. One of

Central Oregon

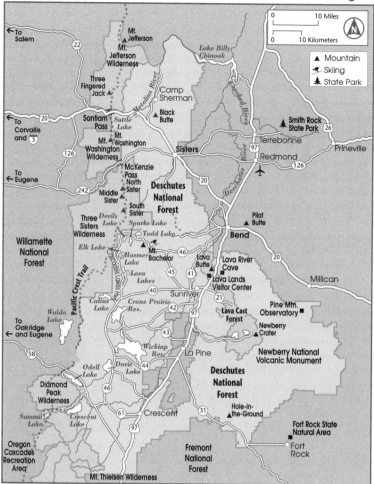

these ranches, just west of town on Ore. 242, also raises elk, which can often be seen from the roadside.

ESSENTIALS

GETTING THERE   The **Redmond Municipal Airport,** 20 miles east of Sisters, is served by Horizon Airlines and United Airlines. **CAC Transportation** (☎ **800/847-0157** or 541/389-7469) operates a shuttle between Portland and Bend, with stops at the Redmond Airport, Sisters, and Sunriver. There are also taxis operating from the airport.

VISITOR INFORMATION   Contact the **Sisters Area Chamber of Commerce,** 164 N. Elm St. (P.O. Box 430), Sisters, OR 97759 (☎ **541/549-0251;** www.sisters-chamber.com).

FESTIVALS   During the annual **Sisters Outdoor Quilt Show** on the second Saturday in July, buildings all over town are hung with quilts. The **Sisters Rodeo,** held the second weekend of June, also attracts large crowds.

ENJOYING THE OUTDOORS

While shopping may be the number one recreational activity right in Sisters, the surrounding lands are the town's real main attraction. Any month of the year, you'll find an amazing variety of possible activities within a few miles of town. One of the area's top outdoor attractions lies to the northwest of Sisters in the community of Camp Sherman. It is here that you'll find the springs that form the **headwaters of the Metolius River.** Cold, crystal-clear waters bubble up out of the ground here and, within only a few hundred yards, produce a full-blown river.

FLY-FISHING   If you need some fly-fishing supplies or want to hire a guide to take you out fishing the local waters, try **The Fly Fisher's Place,** 151 W. Main Ave. (☎ 541/549-3474). The folks here can guide you to the best **fly-fishing** spots on the Deschutes, McKenzie, and Crooked Rivers. If it's the nearly impossible waters of the Metolius River that you want to try, contact **John Judy Flyfishing** (☎ 541/595-2073) in Camp Sherman, which can set you up with gear and a guide.

GOLFING   The two area resorts, Black Butte Ranch, west of Sisters, and Eagle Crest, east of town, both have two 18-hole courses. At **Black Butte Ranch** (☎ 800/399-2322 or 541/595-1500), you'll play surrounded by ponderosa pines and aspens ($42 to $58 greens fee); while at **Eagle Crest** (☎ 541/923-4653), you get a more desertlike experience with junipers and sagebrush surrounding the fairways ($45 greens fee). There are great views at either resort.

HIKING   West and south of Sisters, several excellent and scenic trails lend themselves to both day hikes and overnight trips. Many of these trails lead into the Mt. Washington, Mt. Jefferson, and Three Sisters wilderness areas. Near Camp Sherman, you can hike to the summit of Black Butte for 360-degree views or hike along the spring-fed Metolius River. Farther west off U.S. 20, you'll find trails leading up to the base of craggy Three Fingered Jack. South of town there are trailheads leading into the Three Sisters Wilderness (the Chambers Lakes area is particularly scenic). The hike up Tam McArthur Rim is another good one if you're looking for spectacular views. Stop by the **Sisters Ranger Station** (☎ 541/549-2111) at the west end of town for information and trail maps.

To the east of Sisters outside the town of Terrebonne, there are several miles of very scenic hiking trails within **Smith Rock State Park.** The park's 400-foot crags and the meandering Crooked River provide the backdrops for hikes through high desert scrublands. Hiking trails lead through the canyon and up to the top of the rocks. The view of the Cascades framed by Smith Rock is superb.

HORSEBACK RIDING   If Sisters has put you in a cowboy state of mind, you can saddle up a palomino and go for a ride at **Black Butte Stables** (☎ 541/595-2061), which is at Black Butte Ranch west of Sisters. These stables offer a variety of rides, with an hour ride costing about $27.

MOUNTAIN BIKING   Sisters makes an excellent base for mountain bikers, who will find dozens of miles of trails of all skill levels within a few miles of town. In fact, one easy ride starts only a few blocks from downtown's many shops. Other fun rides include the Butte Loops Trail around Black Butte and the strenuous Green Ridge Trail. Stop by the **Sisters Ranger Station** (☎ 541/549-2111) at the west end of town for information and trail maps. You can rent bikes in town at **Eurosports,** 182 E. Hood Ave. (☎ 541/549-2471), for about $12 per day.

ROCK CLIMBING   East of Terrebonne, **Smith Rock State Park** is one of central Oregon's many geological wonders. Jagged rock formations tower above the Crooked River here and attract rock climbers from around the world. Before heading out here to climb, you should pick up a copy of Alan Watts's *Climber's Guide to Smith Rock* (Chockstone Press, 1992), which describes hundreds of routes among these rocks. You can pick up this book and other climbing supplies at **Redpoint Climbers' Supply,** 975 Smith Rock Way (☎ **800/923-6207** or 541/923-6207), at the corner of U.S. 97 in Terrebonne, and **Rockhard Climbing and Clothing Gear,** 9297 NE Crooked River Dr. (☎ **541/548-4786**), right outside the park entrance. This latter shop is also famous for its huckleberry ice cream. If you want to learn how to climb, contact **First Ascent Climbing Services** (☎ **800/325-5462** or 541/548-5137), which offers semi-private ($95 per day) and private ($175 per day) climbing lessons. **Vertical Ventures** (☎ **541/389-7937**) also offers rock-climbing classes at similar prices.

FOLK ART, REINDEERS & OTHER THINGS TO SEE & DO

Fans of folk art should be sure to stop by the **Petersen Rock Gardens,** 7930 SW 77th St., Redmond (☎ **541/382-5574**), 9 miles north of Bend just off U.S. 97. This 4-acre folk-art creation consists of buildings, miniature bridges, terraces, and tiny towers all constructed from rocks. The gardens, built between 1935 and 1952 by a Danish immigrant farmer, are open daily from 9am to dusk; admission is $3 adults, $1.50 ages 12 to 16, and 50¢ ages 6 to 11.

Rail-travel enthusiasts might consider an excursion on the **Crooked River Railroad Company Dinner Train,** 4075 NE O'Neil Rd., Redmond (☎ **541/548-8630**). The 38-mile, approximately 3-hour rail excursion travels from Redmond to Prineville and back. Restored dining cars are the setting for dinners or brunches that may feature train-robbery or murder-mystery themes. Fares are $59 to $69 for adults and $32 for children 4 through 12. Reservations are required.

A couple of local attractions will likely appeal to kids. **Reindeer Ranch at Operation Santa Claus** (☎ **541/548-8910**), located 2 miles west of Redmond on Ore. 126, is the largest reindeer ranch in the United States and is home to more than 100 reindeer. It's open daily and admission is free.

WHERE TO STAY

In addition to the accommodations listed below, you'll find two very nice rooms available upstairs from the **Kokanee Café** in Camp Sherman (see "Where to Dine" below). They go for $60 double.

☼ Black Butte Ranch. P.O. Box 8000, Black Butte Ranch, OR 97759. ☎ **800/452-7455** or 541/595-6211. Fax 541/595-2077. www.blackbutteranch.com. 35 units plus 70 homes. TV TEL. $85–$137 double; $163–$295 condo or home. AE, DISC, MC, V.

Located 8 miles west of Sisters on former ranch lands, the Black Butte Ranch resort community has the most breathtaking mountain views of any of Central Oregon's resorts. It's also the first resort you come to after crossing to the east side of the Cascades, and a stay here lets you avoid the traffic congestion in Bend. With its aspen-ringed meadows and expansive views, this is as beautiful a spot as you'll find in central Oregon. Add a pair of golf courses, miles of bike paths, and lots of recreational activities and you have a nearly perfect family vacation resort. The only drawback here is that you're a long way from Mount Bachelor's ski slopes in winter (though the slopes at Hoodoo Ski Area are nearby). The condos and homes are set amid open lawns between the forest and the meadows, and most have fireplaces and kitchens. Large decks and sliding glass doors let you enjoy the views no matter what the weather. If you're planning to bring the whole family, one of the vacation homes may be the best bet.

Dining/Diversions: In the Lodge restaurant, where the menu focuses on steaks and seafood, large windows provide nearly every table with a view of the mountains or adjacent lake. A cozy lounge is upstairs from the dining room. A poolside cafe provides casual family dining.

Amenities: Two 18-hole golf courses, outdoor pool, tennis courts, recreation center, sports field, 16 miles of bike and jogging trails, canoe rentals, bicycle rentals, horseback riding, pro shop, sports shop, nature walks, children's programs.

Conklin's Guest House. 69013 Camp Polk Rd., Sisters, OR 97759. ☎ **800/549-4262** or 541/549-0123. Fax 541/549-4481. www.conklinsguesthouse.com. 5 units. $90–$140 double. Rates include full breakfast. No credit cards.

Surrounded by meadows and with an unobstructed view of the mountains, Conklin's B&B is an excellent choice for anyone who has become enamored of Sisters' Western charm. The inn's country decor fits right in with the town, and a duck pond and a trout pond provide a bit of a farm feel. There's even a swimming pool, and breakfast is served in a tile-floored sunroom. Our favorite room has a big old clawfoot tub surrounded by windows that look out to the Cascades. This room also has its own little balcony.

Eagle Crest Resort. P.O. Box 1215, Redmond, OR 97756. ☎ **800/682-4786** or 541/923-2453. Fax 541/923-2453. www.eagle-crest.com. 100 units plus 200 2- to 3-bedroom town houses. A/C TV TEL. $61–$97 double; $84–$135 suite; $119–$278 town house. AE, DISC, MC, V.

Less than 20 miles east of Sister, on the banks of the Deschutes River, is another sprawling resort that attracts sun worshipers and golfers. The landscape is much drier here than around Sisters and is dominated by scrubby junipers that give Eagle Crest the feel of a desert resort. The rooms overlook the golf course rather than the mountains, which should give you an idea of most guests' priorities. Facilities here are geared primarily toward owners of homes and condos, so if you aren't a buyer, you may feel a bit left out.

Dining/Diversions: The restaurant is located on the opposite side of the golf course from the main building, so you'll have to walk or drive. The menu and decor are both very traditional.

Amenities: Two championship golf courses, putting course, indoor and outdoor pools, hot tub, indoor and outdoor tennis courts, racquetball courts, playing field, jogging trails, horseback riding, massage and other spa treatments, bicycle rentals, children's programs, games room, concierge, valet/laundry service, beauty salon.

✪ **Metolius River Resort.** 25551 SW F.S. Rd. 1419, Camp Sherman, OR 97730. ☎ **800/81-TROUT.** Fax 541/595-6281. www.metolius-river-resort.com. 11 cabins. TV. $160 double. 2-night minimum. Lower rates in off-season. MC, V.

Set on the banks of the crystal-clear, spring-fed Metolius River 14 miles west of Sisters, these contemporary cedar-shingled two-story cabins are exceptional, offering modern amenities and styling with a bit of a rustic feel. Peeled-log beds, wood paneling, river-stone fireplaces, and green roofs give the cabins a quintessentially Western appeal. Although the Metolius River is legendary as the most difficult trout-fishing stream in Oregon, the cabins here are particularly popular with trout anglers. Despite the name, this is hardly a resort. However, as a secluded getaway it just can't be beat and will be appreciated by anyone looking for peace and quiet. Great for romantic getaways too. Not far away, you'll find the springs of the Metolius, where the river comes welling up out of the ground.

CAMPGROUNDS

About a dozen Forest Service campgrounds are strung out along F.S. Road 14 north of Camp Sherman. All of these campgrounds are on the banks of the river and are most popular with anglers. The first of these, the **Camp Sherman Campground** is only ½ mile north of Camp Sherman. South of Sisters, at the end of F.S. Road 16, there are three campgrounds at or near Three Creek Lake.

WHERE TO DINE

No visit to Sisters is complete without a stop at the **Sisters Bakery,** 251 E. Cascade St. (☎ **541/549-0361**), for marionberry pastries and bear claws.

Hotel Sisters and Bronco Billy's Saloon. 190 E. Cascade St. ☎ **541/549-7427.** Reservations recommended. Meals $6–$24. MC, V. Mon–Fri 11:30am–9 or 10pm, Sat 11am–10pm, Sun 11am–9pm. AMERICAN.

Though it's no longer a hotel, the Hotel Sisters does serve up some Wild West grub in the form of belt-loosening platters of barbecued ribs, steaks, and green chili burgers. The decor, with its Victorian wallpaper and lace curtains, is a bit too fussy for a rib house, but step through the swinging saloon doors into the bar and you'll find genuine Western atmosphere, including a buffalo head on the wall.

✪ **Kokanee Café.** Camp Sherman. ☎ **541/595-6420.** Reservations highly recommended. Main courses $10–$21. MC, V. Apr–May and Oct to mid-Nov Thurs–Sun 5–9pm; June–Sept daily 5–9pm. Closed mid-Nov to Mar. NORTHWEST.

This out-of-the-way place, located about 14 miles west of Sisters adjacent to the Metolius River Resort in Camp Sherman, is one of the best restaurants in the region and serves Northwest cuisine with an Oregon slant. The interior of the log building is contemporary rustic with an open-beamed ceiling and a wrought-iron chandelier, and out back there's a deck under the ponderosa pines. The menu is short and includes fresh trout, lamb chops with mint sauce, and grilled duck breast with marionberry sauce. There are also daily chalkboard specials, often seafood prepared in whatever style is currently the rage. The always interesting dessert menu includes Oregon hazelnut cheesecake or Northwest berry pie. Lots of reasonably priced wines are available by the bottle or glass, with an emphasis on Oregon wines.

Black Butte Restaurant. Black Butte Ranch. ☎ **541/595-1260.** Reservations recommended. Main courses $13–$20. AE, DISC, MC, V. Daily 7:30am–2:30pm and 5–9pm. NORTHWEST.

This rustic yet elegant restaurant at the Black Butte Ranch resort has large windows that provide nearly every table with a view of the mountains or adjacent lake. A huge ponderosa pine trunk inside the restaurant brings even more of the outdoors in. Deftly prepared steaks, seafood, and pasta dishes range from wild mushroom, pine nut, and chicken fettuccine to panfried Northwest oysters to sirloin steak with herb and red wine sauce. Upstairs from the dining room, a cozy lounge adds to the rustic atmosphere.

3 Bend & Sunriver: Skiing, Hiking, Fishing, Mountain Scenery & More

160 miles SE of Portland, 241 miles SW of Pendleton

Situated on the banks of the Deschutes River, this town was originally named Farewell Bend but said good-bye to that name in 1905 at the insistence of postal authorities. Lumber mills supported the local economy for much of Bend's history, but today retirees, skiers, and lovers of the outdoors are fueling the town's growth.

With only about 33,000 residents, Bend is still the largest city east of the Oregon Cascades, and the surrounding area has more resorts than any other location in the state. To understand why a small town on the edge of a vast high desert could attract so many vacationers, just look to the sky. It's blue. And the sun is shining. For the web-foots who spend months under gray skies west of the Cascades, that's enough of an attraction.

However, Bend doesn't end with sunny skies; it also offers the biggest and best ski area in the Northwest: Mount Bachelor. Several other mountains—the Three Sisters and Broken Top among them—provide a breathtaking backdrop for the city, and their pine-covered slopes, many lakes, and trout streams attract hikers, mountain bikers, sailors, and anglers. A lively downtown area filled with interesting shops, excellent restaurants, and attractive Drake Park (which is named for the city's founder, A. M. Drake, and not for the ducks that are the park's major attraction) complement the outdoor offerings of the area, and it's sometimes difficult to tell which is more popular.

ESSENTIALS

GETTING THERE   Bend is at the junction of U.S. 97, which runs north and south, and U.S. 20, which runs east to west across the state. From the Portland area, the most direct route is by way of U.S. 26 to Madras and then south on U.S. 97.

The **Redmond Municipal Airport,** 16 miles north of Bend, is served by Horizon Airlines and United Airlines. **CAC Transportation** (☎ 800/847-0157 or 541/389-7469) operates a shuttle between Portland and Bend, with stops at the Redmond Airport, Sisters, and Sunriver. There are also taxis operating from the Redmond Airport.

VISITOR INFORMATION   Contact the **Bend Chamber of Commerce,** 63085 N. U.S. 97, Bend, OR 97701 (☎ 800/905-2363 or 541/382-3221; www.bendchamber.org).

GETTING AROUND   Car rentals are available from **Avis** (☎ 800/831-2847), **Budget** (☎ 800/527-0700), and **Hertz** (☎ 800/654-3131). If you need a taxi, call **Owl Taxi Service** (☎ 541/382-3311).

FESTIVALS   The **Cascade Festival of Music** (☎ 541/382-8381), held the last weekend in August in Drake Park, is Bend's biggest festival.

EXPLORING THE BEND AREA

If you'd like to have a guide show you around the area, contact **Wanderlust Tours** (☎ 800/962-2862 or 541/389-8359; www.empnet.com/wanderlust), which offers trips to many of the region's natural attractions. Tour rates range from $29 to $45.

✪ **The High Desert Museum.** 59800 S. U.S. 97. ☎ **541/382-4754.** www.highdesert.org. Admission $7.75 adults, $6.75 students and seniors, $3.75 children 5–12. Daily 9am–5pm. Closed Jan 1, Thanksgiving, and Dec 25. Take U.S. 97 3½ miles south of Bend.

Bend lies on the westernmost edge of the Great Basin, a region that stretches from the Cascade Range to the Rocky Mountains and is often called the high desert. Through the use of historical exhibits, live animal displays, and reconstructions of pioneer buildings, this museum, one of the finest in the Northwest, brings the cultural and natural history of the region into focus. In the main building is a walk-through timeline of Western history. The natural history of the region comes alive in the Desertarium, where live animals of the region can be observed in a very natural setting. Outside, the frolicking river otters and slow-moving porcupines are the star attractions. A pioneer homestead and a forestry exhibit with a steam-driven sawmill round out the outdoor exhibits. Informative talks are scheduled throughout the day, and throughout the year the museum holds classes, workshops, and lectures. At press

Bend

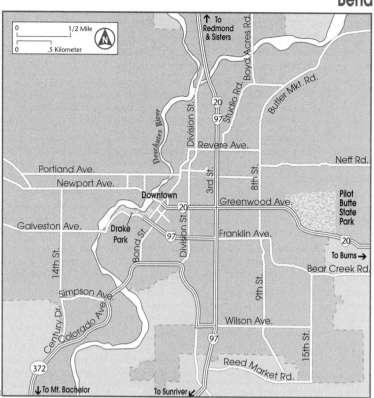

time, the museum was about to open its new Plateau Indians Hall, which features a 7,000-item collection of Indian artifacts that was donated to the museum. A new birds-of-prey center was also scheduled to be built in late 1999. The museum's cafe is a good place for lunch.

Des Chutes Historical Center. 129 NW Idaho Ave. ☎ **541/389-1813.** Admission $2.50 adults, $1 children 6–15. Tues–Sat 10am–4:30pm.

To learn more about the history of central Oregon, stop by this museum, which is housed in a 1914 stone school building at the south end of downtown.

Pine Mountain Observatory. 35 miles east of Bend off U.S. 20. ☎ **541/382-8331.** Admission $2. Memorial Day weekend–Sept Fri–Sat from 8pm.

The same clear skies that attract vacationers to central Oregon have also attracted astronomers. At this small observatory, you too can gaze at the stars and planets through 15- and 24-inch telescopes.

EXPLORING CENTRAL OREGON'S VOLCANIC LANDSCAPE

From snow-covered peaks to lava caves, past volcanic activity and geologic history are visible everywhere around Bend. For a sweeping panoramic view of the Cascade Range, head up to the top of **Pilot Butte** at the east end of Greenwood Avenue. From the top of this cinder cone, you can see Mount Hood (11,235 ft.), Mount Jefferson (10,495 ft.), Three-Fingered Jack (7,848 ft.), Mount Washington (7,802 ft.), North Sister (10,094 ft.), Middle Sister (10,053 ft.), South Sister (10,354 ft.), Broken Top

(9,165 ft.), and Mount Bachelor (9,075 ft.). All these peaks are volcanic in origin, even Mount Bachelor, which is the site of the Northwest's largest ski resort.

To the south of Bend lies a region of relatively recent volcanic activity that has been preserved as the **Newberry National Volcanic Monument.** The best place to start an exploration of the national monument is at the **Lava Lands Visitor Center,** 58201 S. U.S. 97 (☎ **541/593-2421**), 11 miles south of Bend and open from about April through October. Here you can learn about the titanic forces that sculpted this region. An interpretive trail outside the center wanders through a lava flow at the base of 500-foot-tall ✪ **Lava Butte,** an ominous black cinder cone. In summer, a shuttle bus ($2.50 for adults and children 6 through 12, $2 seniors) will take you to the summit of the cone. From here you have another outstanding view of the Cascades, and you can explore the crater on another trail.

A mile to the south, you'll find the **Lava River Cave,** which is actually a long tube formed by lava flows. The cave is more than a mile long and takes about an hour to explore. Admission is $3 for adults and $2.50 for children 13 to 17, plus $2 for lantern rentals. When lava flowed across this landscape, it often inundated pine forests, leaving in its wake only molds of the trees. At **Lava Cast Forest,** 9 miles down a very rough road off U.S. 97 south of Lava River Cave, a paved trail leads past such molds. Continuing farther south on U.S. 97 will bring you to the turnoff for the **Newberry Crater** area, the centerpiece of the monument. Covering 500 square miles, the crater contains Paulina and East Lakes, both of which are popular with boaters and anglers, and numerous volcanic features, including an astounding flow of obsidian. Today there are rental cabins and campgrounds within the national monument, and 150 miles of hiking trails.

If, after thoroughly exploring all the local volcanic features, you still want to see more geologic wonders, head south 75 miles or so to **Fort Rock State Park** and the nearby **Hole-in-the-Ground,** both of which are off Ore. 31. These unusual volcanic features were formed when lakes of molten lava encountered groundwater and exploded with great violence. The walls of Fort Rock rise straight out of the flat landscape and form almost a full circle. Hole-in-the-Ground is a mile-wide crater 200 to 300 feet deep.

HITTING THE SLOPES & OTHER WINTER SPORTS

If downhill skiing is your passion, you probably already know about the fabulous skiing conditions and myriad runs of ✪ **Mount Bachelor Ski & Summer Resort** (☎ 541/382-2442 for information, or 541/382-7888 for a snow report; www.mtbachelor.com), located 22 miles west of Bend on the Cascades Lakes Highway. With a 3,100-foot vertical drop, 60 runs, 11 lifts, 6 day lodges, and skiing from November to July, it's no wonder that this is the training area for the U.S. Ski Team.

Lift tickets can be purchased for the day or on a point system that allows you to make a few runs and come back another day or share the rest of your points with a friend. All-day lift tickets are $43 for adults, $22 for children 7 to 12, and free for children 6 and under.

Cross-country skiers will also find plenty of trails to choose from. Just be sure to stop by a ski shop and buy a **Sno-Park** permit before heading up to the cross-country trailheads, the best of which are along the Cascades Lakes Highway leading to Mount Bachelor ski area. At the ski area itself, there are 90 miles of groomed trails. Passes to use these trails are $11 for adults and $5.25 for children. Ski shops abound in Bend, and nearly all of them rent both downhill and cross-country equipment. If you're heading to Mount Bachelor, you can rent equipment there, or try the **Powder House,**

311 SW Century Dr. (☎ **541/389-6234**), on the way out of Bend heading toward Mount Bachelor.

The **Mount Bachelor Super Shuttle** (☎ **541/382-2442**) operates between Bend and the ski resort and leaves from the corner of Colorado Avenue and Simpson Street, where there's a large parking lot. The shuttle costs $1 each way.

If you've had enough skiing, how about a **dogsled ride?** At **Oregon Trail of Dreams** (☎ **800/829-2442** or 541/382-2442; www.mtbachelor.com) you can take a 1-hour dogsled ride and then learn about the care of sled dogs. Rates are $60 for adults, $30 for children over 80 pounds, and $10 for children under 80 pounds. All-day and overnight trips are also available.

Easy 1-mile **snowshoe nature walks** are led by ranger-naturalists on weekends and holidays at 10am and 1:30pm starting from the **West Village Ski & Sport Building** on Mt. Bachelor. Meet half an hour before the walk; snowshoes are provided. For more information call ☎ **541/388-5664.**

SUMMER ACTIVITIES

Both hiking and mountain biking are available at Mount Bachelor in the summer, when a chair lift operates to the 9,065-foot top of the mountain; the fare is $11.50 for adults, $10.25 for seniors, $5.75 for children 7 to 12, and free for children 6 and under. From here you may either ride the chair or hike down. Bike rentals are available for biking around the mountain ($15 per day).

FISHING   If fishing is your passion, you've come to the right place. The Deschutes River flows right through downtown Bend, and some good trout waters can be found both upstream and downstream of town. The lakes of the Cascade Lakes Highway west of Bend are, however, the most popular fishing destinations in the area. Of these, Hosmer Lake, with its catch-and-release fly-fishing only, is perhaps the most fabled fishing spot. If you're not familiar with these rivers and lakes, you may want to hire a guide to show you where to hook into a big one. Try contacting **Garrison's Fishing Guide Service** (☎ **541/593-8394**) or **Fishing on the Fly** (☎ **800/952-0707** or 541/389-3252). Expect to pay between $150 and $165 for a day of fishing. Fly-fishing supplies are available at **The Fly Box,** 1293 NE Third St. (☎ **541/388-3330**).

GOLF   For many of central Oregon's visitors, Bend's abundance of sunshine means only one thing—plenty of rounds of golf at more than 20 area golf courses. Of the resort courses in the area, the three courses at **Sunriver** (☎ **800/962-1769** or 541/593-1000)—Crosswater, Meadows, and Woodlands—are the most highly regarded. Expect to pay anywhere from $55 to $135 depending on which course you play and when.

Right in Bend, you'll find more reasonable prices at the Riverhouse resort's **River's Edge Golf Course,** 3075 N. U.S. 97 (☎ **541/389-2828**), where 18 holes will cost you about $29 to $39 in the summer. **Awbrey Glen Golf Club,** Mt. Washington Drive (☎ **800/697-0052** or 541/388-8526), and **Widgi Creek,** Century Drive (☎ **541/382-4449**), are the two most highly regarded semiprivate clubs in the area. Greens fees for both are about $75. **Mountain High Golf Course,** China Hat Road (☎ **541/382-1111**), is yet another area 18-hole course open to the public. The greens fee is $48.

HIKING   Hiking is one of the most popular summer activities here, but keep in mind that high-country trails may be closed by snow until late June or early July.

Just to limber up or for a quick breath of fresh air, head up to the north end of Northwest First Street, where you'll find a 3-mile-long trail along the Deschutes River. However, our favorite trail is the ✪ **Deschutes River Trail,** which parallels the

Deschutes for several miles. To reach this trail, head 10 miles west on the Cascade Lakes Highway (Century Drive), and after the Inn of the Seventh Mountain, turn left on F.S. 41 and follow the signs to Lava Island Falls.

The **Three Sisters Wilderness,** which begins just over 20 miles from Bend or Sisters, offers secluded hiking among rugged volcanic peaks. Permits are required for overnight trips in the wilderness area and are currently available at trailheads. Currently, you'll also need a permit (available at the Bend and Sisters ranger stations) to park at area trailheads. Contact the **Bend/Fort Rock Ranger Station,** 1230 NE Third St. (☎ 541/388-5664), or the **Sisters Ranger Station** (☎ 541/549-2111) in Sisters for trail maps and other information.

HORSEBACK RIDING   Down in Sunriver, you can get saddled up and ride the meadows and ponderosa pine forests at **Saddleback Stables** (☎ 541/593-6995), which offers a variety of rides with an hour's ride costing about $23.

✪ MOUNTAIN BIKING   Mountain biking is fast becoming one of the most popular activities in central Oregon. When the snow melts, the cross-country ski trails become mountain-bike trails. Contact the **Bend/Fort Rock Ranger Station,** 1230 NE Third St. (☎ 541/388-5664), to find out about trails open to mountain bikes. The most scenic trail open to mountain bikes is the Deschutes River Trail mentioned above.

Guided mountain-bike rides in Newberry National Volcanic Monument are offered by **High Cascade Descent Guide Service** (☎ 800/296-0562 or 541/389-0562). They offer the Paulina Plunge, an easy downhill ride that includes stops at waterfalls and a natural water slide; the cost is $40. Guided rides are also offered by **Pacific Crest Mountain Bike Tours** (☎ 800/849-6589 or 541/593-5252), with rates ranging from $35 to $75.

WHITE-WATER RAFTING   The Deschutes River, which passes through Bend, is the most popular river in Oregon for white-water rafting, although the best sections of river are 100 miles north of here (see the "North Central Oregon & the Lower Deschutes River" section, above, for details). However, numerous local companies offer trips both on the lower section of the Deschutes and on the stretch of the upper Deschutes between Sunriver and Bend. This latter stretch of the river is known as the Big Eddy run, and though it is short and really has only one major rapid, it is a quick introduction to rafting. **Sun Country Tours** (☎ 800/770-2161 or 541/382-6277), **Cool Runnings Rafting** (☎ 877/389-5327 or 541/389-5327), and **Rapid River Rafters** (☎ 800/962-3327 or 541/382-1514) offer full-day trips on the lower Deschutes for $75 to $90. At the **Inn of the Seventh Mountain** (☎ 541/389-5166), you can arrange to do the Big Eddy run for only $33 (Sun Country Tours offers this trip as well). Rates for children are generally lower than those for adults.

A SCENIC DRIVE ALONG THE CASCADE LAKES HIGHWAY

During the summer, the ✪ **Cascade Lakes Highway** is the most popular excursion out of Bend. Formerly known as Century Drive because it was a loop road of approximately 100 miles, this National Forest Scenic Byway is an 87-mile loop that packs in some of the finest scenery in the Oregon Cascades. Along the way are a dozen lakes and frequent views of the jagged Three Sisters peaks and the rounded Mount Bachelor. The lakes provide ample opportunities for boating, boardsailing, fishing, swimming, and picnicking.

At the **Central Oregon Welcome Center,** 63085 N. U.S. 97 in Bend (☎ 541/382-3221), you can pick up a guide to the Cascade Lakes Highway. From mid-November to late May, this road is closed west of Mount Bachelor because of snow.

River Twister

Moving river waters are categorized on a scale of I to VI, with Class I waters being swift but lacking any real rapids and Class VI being those waterfalls that not even crazy people paid to advertise beer and questionable sports products would attempt. So how do you categorize a tornado? That's a question that Ed Wheeler, river guide for Cascade River Adventures, is probably still pondering.

On July 26, 1996, Wheeler was leading a boatload of six clients through the Deschutes River's popular Big Eddy run just upstream from Bend when a giant dust devil (or miniature tornado, depending on who you listen to) dropped onto the river. The twister sucked up water to a height of somewhere between 150 and 200 feet and barreled down the river straight for Wheeler's 1,000-pound raft. Everyone in the boat was more fascinated than fearful of this strange phenomenon, and no one thought to try to get out of its way. When the twister slammed into the raft, it lifted the boat 10 feet into the air, spun it around twice, and threw rafters and equipment into the river before depositing the raft back in the water, upside down. So powerful was the twister that it even sucked people's shoes right off their feet. Luckily no one was hurt, and everyone agreed it was the raft trip of a lifetime.

The first area of interest along the highway is **Dutchman Flat,** just west of Mount Bachelor. This minidesert is caused by a thick layer of pumice that can support only a few species of plants. A little farther and you come to **Todd Lake,** a pretty little lake that is off the highway a bit and can be reached only by a short trail. Swimming, picnicking, and camping are all popular here.

The next lake along this route is **Sparks Lake,** a shallow, marshy lake that has lava fields at its southern end. A trail meanders through these forested lava fields with frequent glimpses of the lake. The lake is a popular canoeing spot, though you'll need to bring your own boat. At the north end of the lake, you'll find the trailhead for a popular mountain-biking trail that heads south to Lava Lake. Across the highway from the marshes at the north end of the lake is the **trailhead for Green Lakes,** which are in the Three Sisters Wilderness at the foot of Broken Top Mountain. This is one of the most popular backpacking routes in the region and offers spectacular scenery. The hike to Green Lakes can also be done as a day hike. West of the Green Lakes trailhead is an area known as **Devils Garden,** where several springs surface on the edge of a lava flow. On a boulder here you can still see a few **Native American pictographs.** Apollo astronauts trained here before landing on the moon.

With its wide open waters and reliable winds, **Elk Lake** is popular for sailing and boardsailing. There are cabins, a lodge, and campsites around the lake. **Hosmer and Lava Lakes** are both well-known as good fishing lakes, while spring-fed **Little Lava Lake** is the source of the Deschutes River. **Cultus Lake,** with its sandy beaches, is a popular swimming lake. At the **Crane Prairie Reservoir** you can observe osprey between May and October. The **Twin Lakes** are examples of volcanic maars (craters) that have been filled by springs. These lakes have no inlets or outlets.

WHERE TO STAY
EXPENSIVE

✪ **Pine Ridge Inn.** 1200 SW Century Dr., Bend, OR 97702. ☎ **800/600-4095** or 541/389-6137. Fax 541/385-5669. www.pineridgeinn.com. 20 units. A/C TV TEL. $110–$165 double; $160–$275 suite. Rates include full breakfast. AE, DC, DISC, MC, V.

This small luxury inn on the outskirts of town provides an alternative accommodation for anyone who wants first-class surroundings but doesn't need all the facilities (and crowds) of the area's family-oriented resorts. This is an ideal choice for romantic vacations and honeymoons, but it is also a favorite of business travelers who need to be close to town. The inn is set on a bluff high above the Deschutes River, and though this particular stretch of river is not too attractive, you still get a river view (and pay extra for it, too). Whether you get a regular room or a suite, you'll have tons of space, including such features as sunken living rooms and fireplaces. Lots of antiques and artworks by regional artists give the inn a very distinctive style.

Dining: Although the inn doesn't have a restaurant, there is a complimentary afternoon wine and cheese tasting.

Amenities: Access to a nearby athletic club, concierge, valet/laundry service, in-room massages, baby-sitting.

MODERATE

Best Western/Entrada Lodge. 19221 Century Dr., Bend, OR 97702. ☎ **800/528-1234** or 541/382-4080. Fax 541/382-4080. 79 units. A/C TV TEL. $59–$89 double. Rates include continental breakfast. AE, CB, DC, DISC, MC, V. Pets accepted.

Located a few miles west of Bend on the road to the Mount Bachelor ski area, this motel is in a tranquil setting shaded by tall pine trees. Stay here and you'll be just a little bit closer to Mount Bachelor in winter and the region's many lakes and hiking and mountain-biking trails in summer. Although you'll have to drive back into town or to a nearby resort for meals, it's worth that small inconvenience to get such a pleasant setting at economical rates. The Deschutes National Forest borders the property, and the popular Deschutes River Trail is only a mile away. Facilities include an outdoor pool and a whirlpool.

Inn of the Seventh Mountain. 18575 SW Century Dr., Bend, OR, 97702. ☎ **800/452-6810** or 541/382-8711. Fax 541/382-3517. www.7thmtn.com. 419 units. A/C TV TEL. $59–$130 double; $155–$302 condo. AE, DC, DISC, MC, V.

As the closest accommodations to Mount Bachelor, this sprawling resort is especially popular with skiers. However, summer is still the high season here, and during the warm months, families descend on the property to avail themselves of the seemingly endless array of recreational activities calculated to keep the whole family contentedly exhausted. The guest rooms are done in a country decor and come in a wide range of sizes. Many have balconies and/or kitchens. Our favorites are the rooms perched on the edge of the wooded Deschutes River canyon.

Dining/Diversions: Two restaurants, one serving creative meat-and-potato meals and the other a more casual sort of place, provide options at mealtimes. The fireside lounge is popular for après-ski gatherings.

Amenities: Note that there's no golf course on the premises, but there are several close by. Indoor and outdoor pools, whirlpools, sauna, tennis courts, tennis clinics, access to nearby health club, roller-skating/ice-skating rink, hiking/jogging trails, miniature golf course, playing fields, volleyball, basketball, horseshoes, playgrounds, horse stables, in-room massages, children's summer camp, teen program, arts-and-crafts classes, white-water rafting, float trips, canoe trips, horseback riding, hayrides, bike rentals, concierge, baby-sitting.

Lara House Bed & Breakfast. 640 NW Congress St., Bend, OR 97701. ☎ **800/766-4064** or 541/388-4064. Fax 541/388-4064. www.moriah.com/larahouse. 6 units. $55–$125 double. Rates include full breakfast. DISC, MC, V.

This large 1910 vintage home sits on a big lot diagonally across the street from downtown Bend's Drake Park and Mirror Pond and is also only 2 blocks from the downtown commercial district, where you'll find lots of good restaurants. Guest rooms are all very spacious and are complemented by a comfortable living room with a fireplace and a sunroom that overlooks the large yard. There's also a hot tub.

✪ **Mount Bachelor Village Resort.** 19717 Mount Bachelor Dr., Bend, OR 97702. ☎ **800/452-9846** or 541/389-5900. Fax 541/388-7401. www.empnet.com/mbvr. 120 units. A/C TV TEL. $75–$95 double; $105–$335 suite. Minimum stay 2 nights. AE, MC, V.

Set along the top of a narrow ridge overlooking the Deschutes River, this neatly manicured resort on the road to Mount Bachelor is a somewhat more relaxed version of the family ski-and-summer resorts so common in central Oregon. The resort is located close enough to town to make going out for dinner convenient but far enough out in the pine forests to feel away from it all. This is a condominium resort; most of the accommodations have separate bedrooms, and many have fireplaces and kitchens. For the best views, request a River Ridge condo, right on the edge of the bluff. These rooms are newer and are quite simply some of the nicest rooms in the area, with private outdoor hot tubs on the view decks and whirlpool tubs in the bathrooms.

Dining/Diversions: The restaurant in the athletic club just down the hill from the condos offers innovative meals, and there's also a second, more casual dining room.

Amenities: Outdoor pool, two whirlpools, nature trail, four tennis courts, use of large athletic club on the resort's grounds, bike rentals.

INEXPENSIVE

Bend Riverside Motel. 1565 NW Hill St., Bend, OR 97709. ☎ **800/284-2363** or 541/389-2363. Fax 541/617-1832. www.bendriversidemotel.com. 194 units. A/C TV TEL. $58–$120 double. AE, CB, DC, DISC, MC, V. Pets accepted ($5 per night).

Located on the banks of the Deschutes and bounded by Pioneer Park, this renovated older motel is tucked into a quiet corner of the city only a few blocks from most of Bend's best restaurants. This place has the best location of any budget motel in Bend, and consequently it is very popular and can be crowded and noisy at times. Keep in mind that rooms here are not standard-issue motel rooms and can be somewhat unpredictable. The cheapest rooms lack views and are rather cramped, but for less than $30 more you can get a waterfront room with a great view of the Deschutes River. Some units also have fireplaces and kitchens. Facilities include an indoor pool, a whirlpool, a sauna, and a tennis court.

✪ **The Riverhouse.** 3075 N. U.S. 97, Bend, OR 97701. ☎ **800/547-3928** or 541/389-3111. www.riverhouse.com. 220 units. A/C TV TEL. $69–$79 double; $79–$189 suite. AE, CB, DC, DISC, MC, V. Pets accepted.

Located at the north end of town on the banks of a narrow stretch of the Deschutes River, the Riverhouse is one of the best hotel deals we know of in the state; and with its golf course and other resort facilities, it's an economical choice for anyone who wants resort amenities without the high prices. Try to get a ground-floor room; these allow you to step off your patio and almost jump right into the river. However, the rooms on the upper floor have a better view of this rocky stretch of river. All in all, this is the best deal in Bend. Book early.

The hotel's main dining room is a steak house with a view of the river. There is also a poolside cafe and a lounge that features a variety of live entertainment. Facilities include an 18-hole golf course, indoor and outdoor pools, whirlpools, a sauna, an exercise room, and a pro shop.

IN SUNRIVER

The resort community of Sunriver is Oregon's most popular summer destination resort and has hundreds of condos, cabins, and vacation homes at a wide range of prices. Contact **Sunset Management** (☎ **800/541-1756** or 541/593-5018; www.sr-sunset.com), **Coldwell Banker/First Resort Realty** (☎ 800/544-0300 or 541/593-1234; www.sunriverinfo.com), or **Sunray Property Management** (☎ **800/531-1130** or 541/593-3225; www.sunrayinc.com).

❀ **Sunriver Lodge & Resort.** P.O. Box 3609, Sunriver, OR 97707. ☎ **800/547-3922** or 541/593-1000. Fax 541/593-5458. 211 units. A/C TV TEL. $115–$159 double; $189–$229 suite. 2- to 5-bedroom condos and homes also available. Lower rates off-season. AE, CB, DC, DISC, MC, V.

This sprawling resort is less a hotel than a town unto itself, and with a wealth of activities available for active vacationers, it is the first choice of families vacationing in the area. Most of the accommodations overlook both the golf course and the mountains. Our favorite rooms are the loft suites, which have stone fireplaces, high ceilings, and rustic log furniture; although the newest rooms, added in 1999, are very luxurious. Lots of pine trees shade the grounds, and 30 miles of paved bicycle paths connect the resort's many buildings (two bicycles come with every room). But no matter how impressive the other facilities are, it is the three golf courses here that attract the most business.

Dining/Entertainment: The resort's main dining room displays Northwest creativity, with entree prices in the $10 to $20 range. The adjacent lounge offers a cozy fireplace, and downstairs there's a casual cafe. A separate lounge features live music on weekends. Golfers have two choices for quick meals or a drink. Guests can also dine at The Grille at Crosswater.

Services: Concierge, room service, aerobics classes, tennis clinics, horseback riding, massages, children's programs, white-water rafting; bicycle, fishing-gear, and canoe rentals.

Facilities: Three golf courses, 2 pools, 28 tennis courts, indoor miniature golf, ice-skating rink, pro shop, nature center (with summer star-gazing programs).

CAMPGROUNDS

The closest campground to Bend is **Tumalo State Park,** 5 miles northwest of Bend off U.S. 20. The biggest campground in the area is **La Pine State Park,** which is accessible from U.S. 97 between Sunriver and La Pine.

Of the many campgrounds along the Cascade Lakes Highway, **Todd Lake Campground,** 25 miles west of Bend, is our favorite because it is enough of a walk from the parking lot to the campsites to discourage most car campers. **Devil's Lake Campground,** also a walk-in campground, is another favorite of ours. Farther south, there are lots of campgrounds on the many lakes along this road. Two of our favorites are the **Mallard Marsh** and **South** campgrounds, both of which are on beautiful Hosmer Lake. The campgrounds at **Lava Lake** and **Little Lava Lake** are also fairly quiet, and the view from Lava Lake is the finest at any campground on this stretch of road.

WHERE TO DINE
IN BEND

Coffee addicts will want to spend time at the **Café Paradiso,** 945 NW Bond St. (☎ 541/385-5931), a popular hangout that combines elegance and funkiness, or **Desert High Espresso,** 2205 NE Division St. (☎ 541/330-5987), located in an unusual stone building that is something of a folk-art construction. The facade of the building is sort of a public rock-collection exhibit. For good handcrafted ales and pub food, the **Bend Brewing Co.,** 1019 Brooks St. (☎ **541/383-1599**), is a great alternative to the Deschutes Brewery and Public House (see below). The **Rimrock Café** at

The High Desert Museum, 59800 S. U.S. 97 (☎ **541/382-4754**), is an excellent place for lunch.

Baja Norte. 801 NW Wall St. ☎ **541/385-0611.** Main courses $3–$7. MC, V. Daily 11am–9pm. MEXICAN.

This colorful Mexican fast-food spot makes its own tortillas and fills them with tasty fillings. You can get chunky fish tacos or thick quesadillas covered with various toppings (we like the artichoke quesadilla). The icy margaritas are a big hit in summer. The meals are big, so bring a good appetite. The crowd here is generally young and athletic.

✪ Broken Top Club Restaurant and Lounge. 62000 Broken Top Dr. ☎ **541/383-8210.** Reservations recommended. Main courses $17–$24; lunch $7–$8. AE, MC, V. Tues–Fri 11:30am–2pm and 6–10pm, Sat 6–10pm. NORTHWEST.

Golf courses are among the top attractions of the Bend area, so it should come as no surprise that the city abounds in good golf-course restaurants. This is among the finest of them, offering a posh, rustic ambiance, good food, and a superb view of Broken Top Mountain. (There's a golf-course view as well.) For a peak experience, make sure your reservation coincides with sunset. The menu here emphasizes regional flavors, and includes the likes of grilled salmon served over sun-dried tomato-herb polenta and a cambozola cheese velouté and pecan-crusted venison with cranberry conserves. If you're in the mood for something lighter, there's also a separate appetizer menu. The wine list is long and includes quite a few reasonably priced wines.

Hans. 915 NW Wall St. ☎ **541/389-9700.** Reservations recommended for dinner. Pizza and sandwiches $8–$10; pasta and entrees $13–$17. MC, V. Tues–Sat 11am–9pm. ITALIAN.

With its white linens and warmly painted walls, this pleasantly stylish little restaurant conjures up a European bistro. We like the rosemary garlic chicken and chevre pizza and the angel-hair pasta with rock shrimp, fennel, and Greek olives. Meat eaters will appreciate charbroiled New York steak with black peppercorns, topped with a bleu-cheese and walnut relish. For dessert, the decadent selection of cakes and tortes will likely catch your fancy.

✪ Deschutes Brewery and Public House. 1044 NW Bond St. ☎ **541/382-9242.** Main courses $6–$17. MC, V. Daily 11am–9pm. REGIONAL AMERICAN.

For good handcrafted ales (we're partial to the Obsidian Stout) and a range of pub food more creative and tastier than you'd expect, bustling Deschutes Brewery is the place. The buffalo wings here are the best we've ever had, and sweet and spicy hoisin-glazed ribs get two thumbs up. Not only do the cooks do an exemplary job on the normal pub menu, but they also prepare more complex daily specials, such as seared blue marlin crusted with pistachios, served with raspberry sauce and wild rice. Mustard, pastrami, root beer, and ginger ale are all made in-house. Bring the family—even the ones who don't drink beer.

Pine Tavern Restaurant. 967 NW Brooks St. ☎ **541/382-5581.** Reservations recommended. Main courses $11.50–$20. AE, DISC, MC, V. Mon–Sat 11:30am–2:30pm and 5:30–9:30pm, Sun 5:30–9:30pm. AMERICAN/NORTHWEST.

Opened in 1936, the Pine Tavern Restaurant has been a local favorite for generations, and neither the decor nor the view has changed much over the years. Knotty pine and cozy booths give the restaurant an old-fashioned feel, while a 250-year-old ponderosa pine growing up through the center of one dining room provides a bit of grandeur. Most people ask for a table in the back room, which overlooks Mirror Pond. The menu is designed to appeal to a wide range of tastes and includes such comfort foods as meat loaf and filet mignon, but also more creative dishes such as a steelhead fillet with goat cheese and marionberry vinaigrette, as well as cherry pork Madeira. Many of the dishes meet American Heart Association guidelines, and the restaurant is popular with families.

IN SUN RIVER

✪ **Meadows Restaurant.** Sunriver Resort. ☎ **541/593-3740.** Reservations highly recommended. Main courses $15.50–$27. AE, CB, DC, DISC, MC, V. Daily 6:30am–2pm and 5–10pm. AMERICAN/INTERNATIONAL.

Boasting the best view in Sunriver and some of the best food as well, the main dining room of Sunriver Resort is the place to go if you're looking to get dressed up for the evening. As befits the setting, the menu here offers a lot of game meat, including elk carpaccio, roasted elk, and buffalo ribeye. Of course, you can also get well-prepared steaks and regional seafood such as razor clams and Dungeness crab cakes. Throw in some barbecued pork ribs, Thai prawns, and Northwest paella, and you have a menu sure to please most everyone in your party.

Trout House Restaurant. Next to the Marina in Sunriver. ☎ **541/593-8880.** Reservations recommended. Main courses lunch $5–$11, dinner $9–$22. DISC, MC, V. Daily 8am–3pm and 5–9pm. NORTHWEST/AMERICAN.

One of the best things about this little restaurant is that it's located smack dab on the Deschutes River. It's a great place for a waterfront breakfast, lunch, or dinner, but be sure to make reservations during the summer since dining here is a very popular activity with Sunriver visitors. Seafood predominates, with trout available at all three meals. Razor clams (in season), panfried oysters, and blackened salmon with a tequila, lime, and sour-cream sauce can assuage a hunger earned by canoeing on the river or playing an exhausting round of golf. Also open daily from 3 to 4pm for appetizers.

Eastern Oregon

So different is eastern Oregon from the wet west side of the Cascades that it is often difficult to remember that it is still the same state. Indeed, the dry eastern ranch lands, deserts, canyons, and mountain ranges of this region have more in common with the landscapes of neighboring Idaho and Nevada. Yet, Oregon it is, and though it is remote, the fascinating geography makes it an interesting region to explore when you've had enough of the verdant landscapes west of the Cascades.

With huge cattle ranches sprawling across the countryside (cattle greatly outnumber people in these parts) and the Pendleton Round-Up attracting cowboys and cowgirls from around the country, this region is Oregon's Wild West out east. This part of the state is also steeped in the history of the Oregon Trail, and while it was to the Willamette Valley that most wagon trains were heading, it is here that signs of their passing 150 years ago still abound. All across this region, **wagon ruts** left by those stalwart overlanders can still be seen, and the history of the Oregon Trail immigrants is chronicled at several regional museums. While the first pioneers never thought to stop and put down roots in this region, when gold was discovered in the Blue Mountains in the 1860s, fortune seekers flocked to the area. Boom towns flourished and as quickly disappeared, leaving the land to the cattle ranchers and wheat farmers who still call this area home.

Today, however, the region also attracts a handful of outdoors enthusiasts. They come to hike and horseback ride in the Eagle Cap Wilderness of the Wallowa Mountains, to bird-watch in the Malheur National Wildlife Refuge, to snow ski in the Blue Mountains, to explore the deepest canyon in the United States, and to raft and fish the Snake, Owyhee, and Grande Ronde Rivers. On the north side of the Wallowa Mountains, the small town of Joseph has even become a center for Western art, with several bronze foundries casting sculptures sold all over the country.

Because this region is so far from the state's population centers, it is little visited by west-siders, who rarely venture farther east than the resorts of central Oregon. Eastern Oregon is also so vast, and the road distances so great, that it does not lend itself to quick weekend trips. At the very least, it takes a 3-day weekend to get out to Joseph and the Wallowa Mountains or the Malheur National Wildlife Refuge. Should you make it out to this part of the state, leave yourself plenty of time for getting from point A to point B.

1 Pendleton

125 miles E of The Dalles, 52 miles NW of La Grande, 40 miles S of Walla Walla, Washington

If not for its famous woolen mills, few people outside the region would be familiar with the Pendleton name. But because the blankets and clothing long manufactured by the **Pendleton Woolen Mills** (here and at other mills around the region) have gained such a reputation, the name has become as much a part of the West as Winchester, Colt, and Wells Fargo. Today, Pendleton blankets and clothing are as popular as ever, and the town's mill is one of its biggest attractions.

But what brings more visitors to town than even the mill is a single annual event—the **Pendleton Round-Up.** Located at the western foot of the Blue Mountains in northeastern Oregon, Pendleton prides itself on being a real Western town; and as the site of one of the largest and oldest rodeos in the West, it has a legitimate claim. Each year in mid-September, the Round-Up fills the town with cowboys and cowgirls, both real and urban. For the rest of the year, Pendleton sinks back into its quiet small-town character and begins preparing for the next one.

Once the homeland of the Cayuse, Umatilla, Walla Walla, and Nez Perce Indians, the Pendleton area began attracting settlers in the 1840s, as pioneers who had traveled the Oregon Trail started farming along the Umatilla River. In the 1850s, gold strikes created boomtowns in the nearby mountains, and Pendleton gained greater regional significance. Sheep ranching and wheat farming later became the mainstays of the local economy, and by the turn of the century, Pendleton was a rowdy town boasting dozens of saloons and legal bordellos. Today Pendleton is a much quieter place, one that few people notice as they rush by on the interstate. But those who do pull off find a quiet town whose downtown historic district is filled with attractive brick buildings and some stately old Victorian homes.

ESSENTIALS

GETTING THERE   I-84 runs east to west through Pendleton. From the south take U.S. 395; from the north, Ore. 11, which leads to Walla Walla, Washington. **Horizon Airlines** has service to the **Eastern Oregon Regional Airport,** which is located about 4 miles west of downtown Pendleton.

VISITOR INFORMATION   Contact the **Pendleton Chamber of Commerce,** 501 S. Main St., Pendleton, OR 97801 (☎ **800/547-8911** or 541/276-7411; www.pendleton-oregon.org).

GETTING AROUND   **Hertz** rental cars are available at the Eastern Oregon Regional Airport.

THE PENDLETON ROUND-UP

The Pendleton Round-Up, held the second week of September each year, is one of the biggest rodeos in the country and has been held since 1910. In addition to daily rodeo events, there's a nightly pageant that presents a history of Native American and pioneer relations in the area. After the pageant, there's live country-and-western music in the Happy Canyon Dance Hall. A country-music concert and a parade round out the events. The Hall of Fame, 1205 SW Court Ave. (under the south grandstand), holds a collection of cowboy and Indian memorabilia. The city is packed to overflowing during Round-Up week, so if you plan to attend, reserve early. Tickets sell for $10 to $18, and some types of tickets sell out a year in advance. For more information, contact the **Pendleton Round-Up Association,** P.O. Box 609, Pendleton, OR 97801 (☎ **800/45-RODEO** or 541/276-2553).

Eastern Oregon

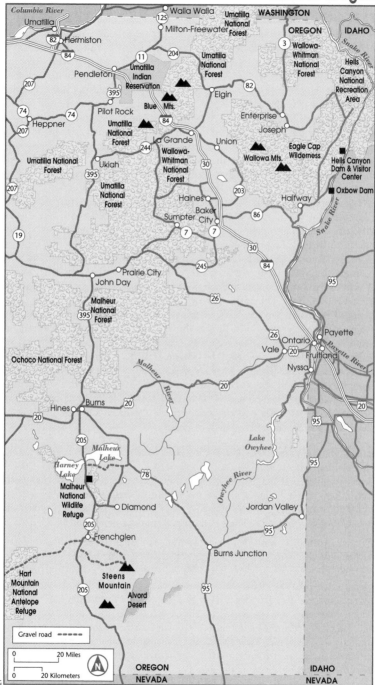

EXPLORING PENDLETON

If you happen to be in town any other week of the year, there are still a few things worth doing. This is the hometown of **Pendleton Woolen Mills,** the famed manufacturer of Native American–inspired blankets and classic wool sportswear. At the mill here in Pendleton, the raw wool is turned into yarn and then woven into fabric before being shipped off to other factories to be made into clothing. Tours are offered Monday through Friday at 9am, 11am, 1:30pm, and 3pm. Also at the mill is a salesroom that's open Monday through Saturday from 8am to 5pm.

At one time there were supposedly 10 miles of underground passages and rooms under the streets of Pendleton. Over the years, these spaces were home to speakeasies and saloons, opium dens, and the living quarters of Chinese laborers who were forbidden to be aboveground after dark. On walking tours operated by **Pendleton Underground Tours,** 37 SW Emigrant Ave. (☎ **800/226-6398** or 541/276-0730), you can learn all about this shady underside of old Pendleton, the entertainment capital of the Northwest, where gamblers, drinkers, and Chinese laborers rubbed shoulders. After exploring the underground, you'll visit a former bordello, whose rooms have been decorated much the way they once might have looked. Tours are offered daily from 9am to 5pm; tickets are $10 for adults and $5 for children 12 and under.

At the **Umatilla County Historical Museum,** 108 SW Frazer Ave. (☎ **541/ 276-0012**), you can learn about the region's more respectable history. The museum is housed in the city's 1909 vintage railway depot and contains exhibits on the Oregon Trail and Pendleton Woolen Mills, as well as a display of beautiful Native American beadwork. The museum is open Tuesday through Saturday from 10am to 4pm; admission is $2 for adults and $1 for seniors and children ages 12 to 18.

If you're looking for glimpses of the **Oregon Trail,** head 20 miles west of Pendleton to the town of Echo, where you can see wagon ruts left by early pioneers. There's an interpretive exhibit in town at Fort Henrietta Park on Main Street; then 2.7 miles west of town on Ore. 320 you can see wagon ruts in Echo Meadows. A mile of ruts can also be seen about 5.5 miles west of town north of Ore. 320. On Ore. 207 north of Ore. 320, there is another Oregon Trail marker.

EAST OF TOWN: NATIVE AMERICAN HISTORY AND A CASINO

East of Pendleton, at exit 216 off I-84, you'll find a complex of attractions that has been developed over the past few years by the Confederated Tribes of the Umatilla Indian Reservation. Included here are the **Wildhorse Casino Resort,** 72777 Ore. 31 (☎ **800/654-WILD**), which offers 24-hour gambling, including slot machines, poker, blackjack, and keno. There is also a golf course, a motel, and an RV park.

✪ **Tamástslikt Cultural Institute.** 72789 Ore. 331. ☎ **541/966-9748.** Admission $6 adults; $4 seniors, students, and children; free for children under 5. Daily 9am–5pm. Closed Thanksgiving, Christmas, and New Year's Day.

Opened in 1998, this modern museum is Oregon's fourth Oregon Trail interpretive center. This one differs from others by focusing on the impact the trail had on the Native Americans of this region. The exhibits incorporate artifacts, life-size dioramas, and audio and video presentations to document the effect pioneer settlement had on the indigenous Cayuse, Walla Walla, and Umatilla Indians who were living in the region when the first settlers arrived. A tour of the museum begins with an exhibit on how the three tribes lived in the days before the arrival of the outsiders. Another exhibit documents the arrival of horses in the region and the way these animals changed the lives of the region's tribes. Other exhibits focus on the coming of missionaries, the advent of Indian schools, and treaty negotiations. The last exhibit focuses on the future of the three tribes.

WHERE TO STAY

In addition to the B&B and hotel below, there's a **Motel 6,** 325 SE Nye Ave., Pendleton, OR 97801 (☎ **800/4-MOTEL6** or 541/276-3160), charging $38 to $43 double; and the **Best Western Pendleton Inn,** 400 SE Nye Ave., Pendleton, OR 97801 (☎ **800/528-1234** or 541/276-2135), charging $64 to $90 double. Both are located at Ore. 11 off I-84.

The Parker House Bed and Breakfast. 311 N. Main St., Pendleton, OR 97801. ☎ **800/700-8581** or 541/276-8581. www.parkerhousebnb.com. 5 units (all with shared bathroom). TEL. $75–$85 double. Rates include full breakfast. AE, MC, V.

Looking very out of place in this Northwest cow town, this Italianate villa seems lifted from the southern California coast. Built in 1917, the home is only 2 blocks from downtown Pendleton and is surrounded by colorful perennial gardens. As befits the villalike surroundings, a formal atmosphere reigns. The Gwendolyn Room, with its fireplace and semiprivate balcony, is the best room in the house; and in the Mandarin Room, you'll find the original Chinese wallpaper and Asian styling. In all the guest rooms you'll find plenty of antiques. Guest rooms share a bathroom, but what a bathroom it is, with the original multiple-head shower and lots of big old porcelain fixtures. Breakfasts are elaborate and filling, with fresh-baked breads and unusual entrees.

Wildhorse Casino Resort. 72777 Ore. 331, Pendleton, OR 97801. ☎ **800/654-WILD.** www.wildhorseresort.com. 100 units. A/C TV TEL. $65–$70 double; $89 suite. AE, DISC, MC, V. Pets accepted ($10 fee).

Located east of town, this hotel is, as the name implies, part of a casino. However, whether you're interested in gambling or not, it makes a good place to stay in the area. Not only are the rooms modern and comfortable, but there is an indoor swimming pool, a whirlpool spa, and an adjacent golf course. Also near is the Tamástslikt Cultural Institute. Of course, there's also the casino, with its casual restaurant. The hotel is 4 miles east of Pendleton and has nice views of the nearby foothills of the Blue Mountains.

Working Girls Hotel. 17 SW Emigrant Ave., Pendleton, OR 97801. ☎ **800/226-6398** or 541/276-0730. 5 units. $50–$70 double. MC, V.

Pendleton likes to play up its Wild West heritage, and there was a time when brothels were legal here. The historic building that now holds the Working Girls Hotel was just such an establishment, and while female companionship doesn't come with the rooms anymore, you will get comfortable accommodations. Although the rooms all have private bathrooms, only one of these is actually in the room; all others have their bathrooms directly across the hall. The hotel is operated in conjunction with Pendleton Underground Tours, and hotel guests get a discount on the tour.

WHERE TO DINE

Crabby's Underground Steakhouse and Saloon. 220 SW First St. ☎ **541/276-8118.** Reservations not accepted. Main courses $6–$15. DC, DISC, MC, V. Mon–Sat 4pm–2am. STEAK.

Down a flight of stairs and behind a heavy wooden door that used to lead to a walk-in freezer is a dark and friendly saloon with stone walls that look as if they were blasted from the bedrock. Back during Prohibition a lot of saloons went underground, but today this is the only one in town that evokes Pendleton's wilder days. Crabby's is known as much for its prime-rib and steak dinners as for the cold drinks it serves. In the evenings, there is sometimes live music (mostly country).

The Great Pacific Wine and Coffee Company. 403 S. Main St. ☎ **541/276-1350.**
Sandwiches $2.50–$5. AE, MC, V. Mon–Thurs 8:30am–6pm, Fri 8:30am–7pm, Sat
8:30am–6pm. DELI.

If you happen to be in town at lunch or need an espresso to get you the rest of the way
across the hot Oregon plains, this is the place. Sandwiches come on croissants or
bagels, and there are also daily soups. Cookies, muffins, truffles, and other sweets
round out the menu.

2 La Grande, Baker City & the Blue Mountains

La Grande: 260 miles E of Portland, 52 miles SE of Pendleton;
Baker City: 41 miles SE of La Grande, 75 miles NW of Ontario

Though pioneers traveling the Oregon Trail in the 1840s found good resting places in
the Powder River and Grande Ronde Valleys, where Baker City and La Grande now
stand, few stayed to put down roots in this remote region. It would not be until the
1860s that pioneers actually looked on these valleys as a place to live and make a
living. However, those first pioneers who just passed through the region left signs of
their passing that persist to this day. Wagon ruts of the Oregon Trail can still be seen
in this region, and outside of Baker City stands the most interesting and evocative of
the state's museums dedicated to the Oregon Trail experience.

By 1861, however, the Blue Mountains, which had been a major impediment to
wagon trains, were crawling with people—gold prospectors. A gold strike in these
mountains started a small gold rush that year, and soon prospectors were flocking to
the area. The gold didn't last long, and when mining was no longer financially feasible,
the miners left the region. In their wake, they left several ghost towns, but the prosperity of those boom times also left the region's larger towns with an enduring legacy
of stately homes and opulent commercial buildings, many built of stone that was
quarried in the region. Today, the historic commercial buildings of Baker City, the
ornate Victorian homes of Union, and the Elgin Opera House are reminders of past
prosperity. Although the gold has played out, signs of those raucous days, from gold
nuggets to ghost towns, are now among the region's chief attractions.

One of the most arduous and dangerous sections of the Oregon Trail—the crossing
of the Blue Mountains—lies just west of present-day La Grande. These mountains
are no longer the formidable obstacle they once were, but they are still among the
least visited in Oregon. The Blues, as they are known locally, offer a wide variety of
recreational activities, including skiing, soaking in hot springs, hiking, mountain
biking, fishing, and camping. With their numerous hotels and restaurants, both La
Grande and Baker City make good bases for exploring this relatively undiscovered
region.

ESSENTIALS
GETTING THERE   Both La Grande and Baker City are on I-84. La Grande is at
the junction of Ore. 82, which heads northeast to Joseph and Wallowa Lake. Baker
City is at the junction of Ore. 7, which runs southwest to John Day, and Ore. 86,
which runs east to the Hells Canyon National Recreation Area.

VISITOR INFORMATION   Contact the **Baker County Visitors and Convention
Bureau,** 490 Campbell St., Baker City, OR 97814 (☎ **800/523-1235** or 541/
523-3356; www.neoregon.com/visitBaker.html), or the **La Grande/Union County
Visitor & Conventions Bureau,** 1912 Fourth St., Suite 200, La Grande, OR 97850
(☎ **800/848-9969** or 541/963-8588; www.eoni.com/~visitlg).

OREGON TRAIL SITES

Oregon Trail history is on view west of La Grande, in downtown Baker City, and just north of Baker City. At the **Oregon Trail Interpretive Park at Blue Mountain Crossing,** at exit 248 off I-84, you'll find a ½-mile trail that leads past wagon ruts in the forest. Informational panels explain the difficulties pioneers encountered crossing these rugged mountains. On most weekends between Memorial Day and Labor Day, there are living history programs as well.

Oregon Trail Regional Museum. 2480 Grove St., Baker City. ☎ **541/523-9308.** Admission $2.50 adults, 50¢ children ages 6–12. Late Mar to late Oct, daily 9am–5pm.

In a large building that once housed Baker City's public swimming pool, this museum is filled with pioneer memorabilia, including a large collection of stagecoaches and an extensive mineral collection.

✪ **Oregon Trail Interpretive Center.** Ore. 86, Baker City. ☎ **800/523-1235** or 541/ 523-1843. $5 adults, $3.50 seniors and youths, free for children under 6, or $10 per vehicle, whichever is less. Apr–Oct daily 9am–6pm. Nov–Mar daily 9am–4pm. Closed Jan 1 and Dec 25.

Today, atop sagebrush-covered Flagstaff Hill just north of Baker City, stands a monument to what became the largest overland migration in North American history. Between 1842 and 1860, an estimated 300,000 people loaded all their worldly belongings onto wagons and set out to cross the continent to the promised land of western Oregon. Their route took them through some of the most rugged landscapes on this continent, and many perished along the way.

This museum commemorates the journeys of these hardy souls, who endured drought, dysentery, and starvation in the hopes of a better life at the end of the Oregon Trail. Through the use of diary quotes, a life-size wagon-train scene, artifacts from the trail, and interactive exhibits that challenge your ability to make the trip, the center takes you through every aspect of life on the trail. Outside, a trail through the sagebrush leads to ruts left by the wagons on their journey west.

EXPLORING BAKER CITY

At the Baker City Visitors & Convention Bureau, you can pick up a brochure that outlines a **walking tour** of the town's most important historic buildings, including the restored **Geiser Grand Hotel,** which, when it first opened, was one of the finest hotels in the west. (See "Where to Stay" below for details.) However, an even better way to learn about this town's colorful past is on a horse-drawn trolley tour with **Oregon Trail Trolley,** which operates on Fridays, Saturdays, and holidays throughout the summer. At press time, this company had just changed hands and a phone number was not available. Call the **Baker County Visitors and Convention Bureau** (☎ **800/523-1235** or 541/523-3356) for information.

If you'd like to take a look inside one of Baker City's restored old homes, drop by the **Adler House Museum,** 2305 Main St. (☎ **541/523-9308**), a stately Victorian. Everything on the second floor, from wallpaper to furniture, is original, dating to the 1890s. The first floor has been refurbished and decorated the way it might have looked. The museum is open from May 1 to October 1; Thursday through Saturday it's open from 1 to 4pm, and on Sunday it's open from 11am to 2pm. Admission is $5 per person (children 6 and under are free).

Baker City's fortunes were made by gold mines in the Blue Mountains, and if you'd like to see some samples from those golden years, stop in at the **U.S. Bank** on Main Street in Baker City. The gold collection here includes a nugget that weighs in at 80.4 ounces.

An Almost Grand Old Opera House

In the town of **Elgin,** 18 miles north of La Grande on Ore. 82, you can take in a film, play, or concert at the restored **Elgin Opera House,** 104 N. Eighth St. (☎ **541/437-3456**), which was built in 1912. The opera house is in the same building that once housed the Elgin City Hall.

OUTDOOR ACTIVITIES
SPRING THROUGH FALL

If you're interested in **bird watching,** head out to the **Ladd Marsh Wildlife Area,** 6 miles south of La Grande off I-84 at the Foothill Road exit. This wetland is home to Oregon's only breeding population of sandhill cranes.

The **hot springs** of this region have been attracting people since long before the first white settlers arrived, and you can still soak your sore muscles in thermal waters at **Lehman Hot Springs,** in Ukiah, 38 miles west of La Grande on Ore. 244 (☎ **541/427-3015**), which is in a remote forest setting. Here you'll find a large hot swimming pool perfect for an afternoon of lounging around. There are also two smaller and hotter soaking pools (the first of these is too hot to actually get into), as well as an unheated swimming pool (which sees very little use). Also on the premises are campsites and a couple of rustic cabins ($85 and $95), and nearby are hiking, mountain-biking, cross-country ski, and snowmobiling trails. The springs are open Tuesday through Sunday in summer from 10am to 9pm (call for hrs. the rest of the year). Admission is $5.

In summer, there are plenty of nearby trails to hike or mountain bike on. Contact the **Wallowa-Whitman National Forest,** La Grande Ranger District, 3502 Ore. 30, La Grande, OR 97850 (☎ **541/963-7186**), or **Baker Ranger District,** 3165 Tenth St., Baker City, OR 97814 (☎ **541/523-4476**), for details.

WINTER SPORTS AND ACTIVITIES

With the highest base elevation and the most powderlike snow in the state, **Anthony Lakes Mountain Resort** (☎ **541/562-1039** or 541/856-3277), 40 minutes west of Baker City, is a good little ski area—small, but with a good variety of terrain. Daily lift tickets are $24. You'll also find good groomed cross-country ski trails here, and the area is very popular with snowmobilers.

Winter is also the best time of year to see some of the region's Rocky Mountain elk. Each year from December through February, the Oregon Department of Fish & Wildlife feeds a large herd of elk at the **Elkhorn Viewing Area** in North Powder, about halfway between La Grande and Baker City. You can usually see between 150 and 200 elk. On weekends between 11am and 2:30pm, **T and T Tours** (☎ **541/856-3356**) takes visitors out to the feeding area by horse-drawn wagon. Tours last about a half hour and cost $4 per person. To reach Elkhorn, take exit 285 off I-84 and follow the Wildlife Viewing signs. For more information, contact the **Oregon Department of Fish & Wildlife** (☎ **541/898-2826**).

THE ELKHORN MOUNTAIN SCENIC LOOP

Rising up on the outskirts of Baker City is the Elkhorn Range of the Blue Mountains. A paved loop road winds up and around the south side of these mountains, providing scenic vistas, access to the outdoors throughout the year, and even a couple of sparsely inhabited ghost towns. Start this loop by heading south out of Baker City on Ore. 245 and then take Ore. 7 west to **Sumpter,** which is 30 miles from Baker City.

As you approach Sumpter, you'll notice that the valley floor is now covered with large piles of rocks. These are the tailings from the Sumpter Dredge, preserved as the **Sumpter Dredge State Heritage Area** (☎ 541/894-2486), which is currently undergoing restoration. Between 1935 and 1954, the ominous-looking dredge laid waste to the valley floor as it sat in its own little pond sifting through old streambed gravel for gold. Although you can stop and view the dredge any time of year, between May and October it is possible to board the strange machine (open daily from 9am to 4pm), which now has a few interpretive exhibits on board. By late summer of 2000, the restoration should be complete. Admission is by donation.

In its wake, the dredge left 6 miles of tailings that formed hummocks of rock and gouged-out areas that have now become small ponds. Although such a mining-scarred landscape isn't usually considered scenic, the Sumpter Valley is today surprisingly alive with bird life attracted to the ponds.

A favorite way of visiting the Sumpter Dredge is aboard the **Sumpter Valley Railroad** (☎ 541/894-2268), which operates a classic steam train on a 5-mile run from west of Phillips Reservoir to the Dredge. This railway first began operation in 1890 and was known as the stump dodger. Excursions are operated on Saturdays, Sundays, and holidays from Memorial Day weekend to late September; round-trip fares are $9 for adults and $6.50 for children 6 to 16.

Gold kept Sumpter alive for many decades, and a bit of gold-mining history is still on display in this rustic mountain town, which, though it has a few too many people to be called a ghost town, is hardly the town it once was. In the boom days of the late 19th and early 20th century, this town boasted several brick buildings, hotels, saloons, and a main street crowded with large buildings. However, when a fire destroyed the town in 1917, it was never rebuilt. Today, only one brick building and a few original wooden structures remain. At **The Gold Post** (☎ 541/894-2362), you can see old photos of Sumpter as well as various artifacts from the town's gold-mining heyday.

Continuing west on a winding county road for another 14 miles will bring you to ✪ **Granite,** another ghost town that also has a few flesh-and-blood residents. The weather-beaten old buildings on a grassy hillside are the epitome of a Western ghost town, and most buildings are marked. You'll see the old school, general store, saloon, bordello, and other important town buildings.

Beyond Granite, the road winds down to the North Fork of the John Day River and then heads back across the mountains by way of the Anthony Lakes area. Although Anthony Lakes is best known for its small ski area, in summer there are hiking trails and fishing in the area's small lakes. The vistas in this area are the best on this entire loop drive, with rugged, rocky peaks rising above the forest. Also in this same area, you'll catch glimpses of the irrigated pastures of the Powder River Valley far below.

Coming down onto the valley floor, you reach the tiny farming community of Haines, which is the site of the **Eastern Oregon Museum,** Third Street (☎ 541/856-3233), a small museum cluttered with all manner of artifacts of regional historic significance. It's open April to October only, daily from 9am to 5pm; admission is by donation. Here in Haines you'll also find the Haines Steakhouse (see below), a favorite of area residents.

WHERE TO STAY
IN LA GRANDE

In addition to the B&B listed below, there are several inexpensive chain motels in La Grande, including the **Super 8 Motel,** 2407 E. R Ave., La Grande, OR 97850 (☎ 541/963-8080), charging $52 to $57 double.

Stang Manor Bed & Breakfast. 1612 Walnut St., La Grande, OR 97850. ☎ **800/ 286-9463** or 541/963-2400. www.stangmanor.com. 4 units. $75–$80 double; $90 suite. Rates include full breakfast. MC, V. Children 10 and older only.

This Georgian colonial mansion, built in the 1920s, looks a bit like the White House and is the best accommodation in La Grande. It's filled with beautiful woodwork and comfortable guest rooms, a couple of which have the original bathroom fixtures, including a footed bathtub. The best deal here is the three-room suite, which has a fireplace and a sun porch that has been converted into a sleeping room. Breakfasts are elegant affairs served in the formal dining room.

IN UNION

The Union Hotel. 326 N. Main St. (P.O. Box 569), Union, OR 97883 ☎ **541/562-6135.** www.theunionhotel.com. 9 units. $40–$90 double. DISC, MC, V.

Although Union today is a sleepy town, it was once the county seat and a booming little place. This grand little hotel first opened its doors in 1921, but in more recent years it was a decrepit apartment house. An ongoing renovation has turned it into one of eastern Oregon's more interesting historic hotels. Surrounded by lawns and shade trees, the three-story brick hotel now goes a long way toward conjuring up Union's lively past. The lobby, with its white tile floor, could be straight out of a movie set, while the upstairs guest rooms are decorated in various themes. To make the most of a stay here, consider staying in the room with the whirlpool tub. Although Union is 14 miles from La Grande, the location is still fairly convenient for exploring this region.

IN BAKER CITY

In addition to the hotel and B&B listed below, you'll find several inexpensive chain motels in Baker City. These include the **Quality Inn,** 810 Campbell St., Baker City, OR 97814 (☎ **800/228-5151** or 541/523-2242), charging $49 to $69 double; and the **Super 8 Motel,** 250 Campbell St., Baker City, OR 97814 (☎ **888/726-2466** or 541/523-8282), charging $52 to $57 double.

A'Demain Bed & Breakfast. 1790 Fourth St., Baker City, OR 97814. ☎ **541/523-2509.** 2 units. TV. $60–$75 double. Rates include full breakfast. MC, V.

Set on a shady, tree-lined street just 4 blocks from Main Street, this Victorian B&B has a quintessentially small-town feel. An octagonal turret anchors one corner of the house, and if it captures your attention as much as it did ours, you'll want to stay in the upstairs room, which includes the entire second floor of the house, with the turret alcove. This suitelike room also includes a small balcony. The downstairs room is quite a bit smaller.

✪ **Geiser Grand Hotel.** 1996 Main St., Baker City, OR 97814. ☎ **888/GEISERG** or 541/523-1889. Fax 541/523-1800. 30 units. A/C TV TEL. $85–$109 double; $109–$259 suite. Rates include continental breakfast (Mon–Fri only). AE, DC, DISC, MC, V. Pets accepted ($10).

Built in 1889 at the height of the region's gold rush, the Geiser Grand is by far the grandest hotel in eastern Oregon. With its corner turret and clock tower, the hotel is a classic 19th-century Western luxury hotel. The hotel shut down in 1968 after the cast of the movie *Paint Your Wagon* stayed here, but after a 3-year renovation, the hotel reopened in 1997. In the center of the hotel is the Palm Court dining room, above which is suspended the largest stained-glass ceiling in the Northwest. Throughout the hotel, including in all the guest rooms, ornate crystal chandeliers add crowning touches to this historic hotel. Guest rooms also feature 10-foot windows, most of which look out to the Blue Mountains. Although the Oriental suite is the most opulent in the hotel, the two cupola suites are the most luxurious and evocative of the past. These two suites also are the only rooms with whirlpool tubs. Breakfast is served in a separate and sunny dining room. Prices for meals are very reasonable. Room service is available, and there is a saloonlike lounge as well.

CAMPGROUNDS

You'll find several national-forest campgrounds along the Elkhorn National Scenic Byway, including **Union Creek Campground,** which is on the shore of Phillips Reservoir southeast of Baker City. Others can be found near Anthony Lakes.

WHERE TO DINE
IN LA GRANDE

If you're in need of a good cup of espresso, drop by **One Smart Cookie,** 1119 Adams Ave. (☎ 541/963-3172), which, as you might guess, also specializes in cookies.

Foley Station. 1011 Adams Ave. ☎ **541/963-7473.** Reservations recommended for dinner. Main dishes $8–$19. MC, V. Wed and Sun 7–10:30am and 11am–3pm, Thurs–Sat 7–10:30am, 11am–3pm, and 5–9pm. AMERICAN/NORTHWEST.

Although the focus at this surprisingly upscale little restaurant is on breakfasts and lunches, it is also open for dinner 3 nights a week. Here you'll find more contemporary dishes than are available anywhere else in town. A recent menu included Tequila halibut and rock shrimp sauté, prime rib with Yorkshire pudding, and pesto-baked brie with caramelized onions. You can design your own burger (or how about an emu burger?). Lunch dishes include crab-cake sandwiches and white gazpacho with bay shrimp.

Mamacita's. 110 Depot St. ☎ **541/963-6223.** Main courses $6.25–$11.75. No credit cards. Tues–Fri 11am–2:30pm and 5–9pm, Sat–Sun 5–9pm. MEXICAN.

With its colorful downtown setting, this small low-key Mexican place is more college hangout than local Mexican joint. The menu is short but varied. Fire-eaters should try the hot salsa verde.

Ten Depot Street. 10 Depot St. ☎ **541/963-8766.** Reservations recommended. Main courses $6.50–$29. AE, MC, V. Mon–Sat 5–10pm. STEAK/SEAFOOD.

Housed in a historic brick commercial building and under the same ownership as Mamacita's, this restaurant has a classic turn-of-the-century feel, complete with a saloon on one side. Although the steaks are what most people crave, the salads are large and flavorful, and there are even some vegetarian dishes. There's a $5.95 blue-plate special on weeknights, and other inexpensive nightly specials.

IN THE BAKER CITY AREA

By far the most elegant restaurant in town is the **Palm Court** of the historic Geiser Grand Hotel. This restaurant serves standard American fare at economical prices, but the setting is classic Wild West hotel. All three meals are available; see above for details. For pub food and microbrews, there's **Barley Brown's Brew Pub,** 2190 Main St. (☎ 541/523-4266).

Baker City Cafe/Pizza à Fetta. 1915 Washington Ave. ☎ **541/523-6099.** Pizzas $13–$22. MC, V. Mon–Fri 9am–2pm and 5–8pm, Sat 11am–3pm. PIZZA.

When you've just got to have a pizza and you want more than pepperoni or sausage, this is the place. You can dress your pie with the likes of blue cheese, feta, Montrachet, sun-dried tomatoes, kalamata olives, or pancetta. Pasta and sandwiches are also available. You'll find this place just off Main Street.

Chinese History in Eastern Oregon

In the town of John Day, the fascinating little ✪ **Kam Wah Chung & Co. Museum** (☎ **541/575-0028**), on Northwest Canton Street adjacent to City Park, is well worth a visit. It preserves the home and shop of a Chinese doctor who, for much of the first half of this century, administered to his fellow countrymen who were laboring here. The building looks much as it might have at the time of the doctor's death and contains an office, a pharmacy, a general store, and living quarters. It's open May to October only, Monday through Thursday from 9am to noon and 1 to 5pm, and on Saturday and Sunday from 1 to 5pm. Admission is $3 for adults, $2.50 for seniors, $1.50 for children 6 to 18, and free for children 12 and under.

You'll find more Chinese history in Baker City, where an old Chinese cemetery can be seen on Allen Street, just east of exit 304 off of I-84. The Pendleton Underground tour in Pendleton (see section 1 above) also focuses on the region's Chinese history.

The Phone Company. 1926 First St. ☎ **541/523-7997.** Reservations recommended. Main courses $13–$19. AE, DISC, MC, V. Mon–Thurs 11:30am–2pm and 5–9pm, Fri 11:30am–2pm and 5–10pm, Sat 5–10pm (shorter hours in winter). AMERICAN.

Located in, you guessed it, the old phone company building, this is one of Baker City's two formal restaurants and is a favorite for both business lunches and romantic evenings out. Simply prepared steaks, prime rib, pasta, and seafood make up the bulk of the menu offerings in this dark and vaguely country cute establishment. There are also daily specials.

Front Street Café & Coffee Co. 1840 Main St. ☎ **541/523-0223.** Meals $5.50–$12. MC, V. Mon–Wed and Sat 7am–3pm, Thurs–Fri 7am–8pm. SANDWICHES/MEXICAN.

Sort of a new "old-fashioned" country diner, this antique-filled cafe has exposed brick walls, a black-and-white tile floor, and lots of antique decorations. Gourmet sandwiches, large filling salads, hearty breakfasts, Mexican dishes, and espresso are the lunch and breakfast staples. Thursday is pasta night and Friday is prime-rib night.

Haines Steakhouse. 910 Front St., Haines. ☎ **541/856-3639.** Reservations recommended. Main courses $6–$20. AE, DC, DISC, MC, V. Mon and Wed–Fri 5–10pm, Sat 4–10pm, Sun 1–9pm. STEAK.

Thick, juicy steaks are the specialty of the house here, but it's the decor as much as the food that attracts people. Log walls and booths, a chuck-wagon salad bar, buffalo and elk heads mounted on the walls, and even a totem pole and an old buggy keep diners amused as they eat. A longtime favorite in the area.

3 Joseph, Enterprise & the Wallowa Mountains

Joseph: 355 miles E of Portland, 80 miles E of La Grande, 125 miles N of Baker City

The Wallowa Mountains, which stand just south of the town of Joseph, are a glacier-carved range of rugged beauty that has been called both the Alps of Oregon and the Little Switzerland of America. Though the range is small enough in area to drive around in a day, it is big on scenery and contains the largest designated wilderness area in the state: the **Eagle Cap Wilderness.**

In the northeast corner of the mountains lies Wallowa Lake, which was formed when glacial moraines blocked a valley that had been carved by the glaciers. With blue waters reflecting the rocky peaks, the lake has long attracted visitors. In the fall, the lake also attracts bald eagles that come to feed on spawning kokanee salmon, which turn a bright red in the spawning season.

In recent years, the town of Joseph, just north of Wallowa Lake, has become a center for the casting of Western-themed **bronze sculptures,** and there are now several art galleries and foundries in the area. With its natural beauty, recreational opportunities, and artistic bent, this corner of the state today has more to offer than any other area in eastern Oregon.

ESSENTIALS

GETTING THERE   Ore. 82 connects Joseph to La Grande in the west, and Ore. 3 heads north from nearby Enterprise to Lewiston, Idaho, by way of Wash. 129.

VISITOR INFORMATION   For more information, contact the **Wallowa County Chamber of Commerce,** 107 SW First St. (P.O. Box 427), Enterprise, OR 97828 (☎ 800/585-4121 or 541/426-4622; www.eoni.com/~wallowa/).

FESTIVALS   The rowdy **Chief Joseph Days Rodeo,** over the last full weekend in July, and the **Alpenfest,** on the third weekend after Labor Day, are the biggest annual events in the area.

BRONZE FOUNDRIES AND ART GALLERIES

Though the lake and mountains are the main attractions of this area, the presence of several bronze foundries in Joseph and Enterprise has turned the area into something of a Western art community. Along Main Street in Joseph, you'll find several art galleries that specialize in bronze statues and Western art.

A good place to start is at the impressive **Manuel Museum,** 400 N. Main St. (☎ 541/432-7235), at the west end of town. In addition to housing bronzes by artist David Manuel, the combination gallery/museum includes an outstanding collection of Native American artifacts and a large collection of old wagons. Guided foundry tours are also available. Admission is $6 for adults, $5 for seniors, and $2 for children.

Between May and late fall, foundry tours ($5 per person) are offered by **Valley Bronze of Oregon,** 018 Main St. (☎ 541/432-7445), which is the second-largest bronze foundry in the country and has its foundry at 307 W. Adler St. (☎ 541/432-7551). **Parks Bronze,** 331 Golf Course Rd., Enterprise (☎ 541/426-4595), offers foundry tours Monday through Friday ($5 per person). Other bronze galleries in town include the **Bronze Gallery of Joseph,** 603 N. Main St. (☎ 541/432-3106), and the **Wildhorse Gallery,** 508 N. Main St. (☎ 541/432-4242).

LOCAL HISTORY

At the **Wallowa County Museum,** 110 S. Main St. (☎ 541/432-6095), you can see pioneer artifacts, displays on the Nez Perce Indians, and other items donated to the museum by local families. This old-fashioned community museum is housed in a former bank building and is open daily from 10am to 5pm from the last weekend in May through the third weekend in September. On Saturdays in summer they stage reenactments of an 1896 bank robbery.

OUTDOOR ACTIVITIES

Down at the south end of Wallowa Lake, you'll find **Wallowa Lake State Park** (☎ 541/432-4185), where there is a swimming beach, picnic area, and campground. Adjacent to the park is the **Wallowa Lake Marina** (☎ 541/432-9115), where you can rent canoes, rowboats, paddleboats, and motorboats (open May through Sept). This end of the lake has an old-fashioned mountain resort feel, with pony and kiddy rides, go-cart tracks, miniature golf courses, and the like. However, it is also the trailhead for several trails into the Eagle Cap Wilderness.

For a different perspective on the lake, ride the **Wallowa Lake Tramway** (☎ **541/432-5331;** www.wallowa-tramway.com) to the top of 8,200-foot Mount Howard. This is the steepest tramway in America and provides great views both from the gondolas and from the summit of Mount Howard. The views take in Wallowa Lake and the surrounding jagged peaks. The tramway operates from late May through September (and between Christmas and New Year's), daily from 10am to 4pm (in July and Aug until 5pm); the fare is $14.95 for adults and $8.95 for children 10 and under. There are 2 miles of walking trails on the summit, and food is available at the **Summit Grill & Alpine Patio.**

Because most hikes on the north side of the Cascades start out in valleys and can take up to a dozen miles or so to reach the alpine meadows of the higher elevations, there aren't a lot of great day hikes here. The **backpacking,** however, is excellent. If you're looking for **day hikes,** try taking the tramway to the top of Mount Howard, where there are easy trails with great views. If you'd like to head into the **Eagle Cap Wilderness** to the popular **Lake Basin** or anywhere else in the Wallowas, you'll find the trailhead less than a mile past the south end of the lake. For more information on hiking in the Wallowas, contact the **Wallowa Valley Ranger District,** 88401 Ore. 82, Enterprise, OR 97828 (☎ **541/426-4978**).

Horse packing into the Wallowas is a popular activity, and rides of a day or longer can be arranged through **Eagle Cap Wilderness Pack Station,** 59761 Wallowa Lake Hwy., Joseph, OR 97846 (☎ **800/681-6222** or 541/432-4145; www.neoregon.net/wildernesspackstation), which offers trips into the Eagle Cap Wilderness during the summer and into Hells Canyon during the spring. Expect to pay around $150 per person per day for a guided trip. **Millar Pack Station,** 69498 Sherrod Rd., Wallowa, OR 97885 (☎ **541/886-4035**), offers similar pack trips at similar prices.

If you'd like to try **llama trekking** and let these South American beasts of burden carry your pack, contact **Hurricane Creek Llama Treks,** 63366 Pine Tree Rd., Enterprise, OR 97828 (☎ **800/528-9609** or 541/432-4455). Most trips last 5 to 6 days and cost between $740 and $850.

This region also offers some of the best **trout fishing** in Oregon, and if you'd like a guide to take you to the best holes, contact **Eagle Cap Fishing Guides,** P.O. Box 865, Joseph, OR 97846 (☎ **800/940-3688** or 541/432-9055; www.wallowa.com/eaglecap), or **The Joseph Fly Shoppe,** 203 N. Main St., Joseph, OR 97846 (☎ **541/432-4343;** www.eoni.com/~flyshop). This latter company also offers whitewater kayaking trips and instruction. Expect to pay anywhere from $140 to $200 for a day of fishing.

If you'd like to try pedaling a **mountain bike** in the area (including in Hells Canyon), contact **Crosstown Traffic Bicycles,** 102 W. McCully St., Joseph (☎ **541/432-2453**), which charges $75 for a daylong ride.

In winter, the Wallowas are popular with cross-country and backcountry skiers. Check at the ranger station in Enterprise for directions to trails. You'll also find a small downhill ski area and groomed cross-country trails at **Ferguson Ridge,** which is 9 miles southeast of Joseph on Tucker Down Road. **Wing Ridge Ski Tours,** P.O. Box 714, Joseph, OR 97846 (☎ **800/646-9050** or 541/426-4322; www.wingski.com), leads experienced skiers on hut-to-hut ski tours for around $395 to $495 for a 6-day/5-night trip. The huts can also be rented for $30 per night.

WHERE TO STAY

Chandlers' Bed, Bread, and Trail Inn. 700 S. Main St. (P.O. Box 639), Joseph, OR 97846. ☎ **800/452-3781** or 541/432-9765. www.eoni.com/~chanbbti. 5 units (3 with private bathroom). $60 double with shared bathroom, $80 double with private bathroom. Rates include full breakfast. MC, V.

"I Will Fight No More Forever"

The Wallowa Mountains and Hells Canyon areas were once the homeland of the Nez Perce people. The Nez Perce land, which encompassed rolling hills covered with lush grasses, was perfect for raising horses, and sometime in the early 1700s the tribe came to own horses that were descended from Spanish stock and had been traded northward from the American Southwest. They began selectively breeding this strange new animal, emphasizing traits of speed and endurance. Their horses were far superior to those used by other tribes and became known as Appaloosas. The area where these horses were first bred is now the Palouse Hills country of eastern Washington.

The Nez Perce had befriended explorers Lewis and Clark in 1805 and remained friendly to white settlers when other Indian tribes were waging wars. This neutrality was rewarded, however, with treaties that twice cut the size of their reservation in half. When one band refused to sign a new treaty and relinquish its land, the stage was set for one of the great tragedies of Northwest history.

En route to a reservation in Idaho, several Nez Perce braves ignored orders from the tribal elders and attacked and killed four white settlers to exact revenge for the earlier murder by whites of a father of one of the braves. This attack brought on the ire of settlers, and the cavalry was called in to hunt down the Nez Perce. Tribal elders decided to flee to Canada, and, led by Chief Joseph (also known as Young Joseph), 700 Nez Perce, including 400 women and children, began a 2,000-mile march across Idaho and Montana on a retreat that lasted 4 months.

Along the way several skirmishes were fought, and the cavalry finally succeeded in defeating the Nez Perce only 40 miles from Canada. At their surrender, Chief Joseph spoke the words for which he has long been remembered: "Hear me my Chiefs, I am tired; my heart is sick and sad. From where the sun now stands, I will fight no more, forever."

The town of Joseph is named after Chief Joseph, and on the outskirts of town you'll find the grave of his father, Old Joseph. Young Joseph is buried on the Colville Indian Reservation in central Washington. Not far from Joseph, near Lewiston, Idaho, you can learn more about the Nez Perce at **Nez Perce National Historical Park.**

Located right in Joseph, Chandler's is a contemporary home with cedar-shingle walls and a boardwalk that leads through a rock garden to the front door. Inside you'll find a high-ceilinged living room with open-beam construction, folk art, quilts, and an "early attic" decor. Three of the rooms have mountain views, and there are also three sitting areas for guest use. In warm weather, breakfast is served in a gazebo in the garden. There's also a hot tub with a view atop a raised deck to one side of the garden.

Eagle Cap Chalets. 59879 Wallowa Lake Hwy., Joseph, OR 97846. ☎ **541/432-4704.** Fax 541/432-3010. www.neoregon.net/eaglecapchalets/. 37 units. TV. $40–$95 double; $100–$115 2- and 3-bedroom. AE, DC, DISC, MC, V. Pets accepted except during summer months.

Set under tall pines just a short walk from hiking trails and the lake, Eagle Cap Chalets has a wide variety of rooms, as well as an indoor pool and whirlpool spa and a very basic miniature golf course. Consequently, this place is very popular with families and groups. The rooms here vary from motel style to rustic-though-renovated cabins.

Siding on all the buildings makes them appear to be built of logs. The cabins and condos have kitchens. In the early fall, there always seem to be deer hanging out on the lawns here.

George Hyatt House. 200 E. Greenwood St., Enterprise, OR 97828. ☎ **800/95-HYATT** or 541/426-0241. www.moriah.com/hyatt/. 4 units. $95 double. Rates include full breakfast. MC, V.

Located on the courthouse square in downtown Enterprise, this elegant 1898 Victorian home is surrounded by colorful gardens that make it a veritable oasis in this often-brown landscape. The two porches are ideal spots from which to enjoy the gardens and tranquil setting. The four guest rooms are furnished with a variety of antiques that conjure up Victorian times. Two of the rooms have clawfoot tubs, but the best room is the Queen Anne Room, which includes the house's tower, which was removed in the 1970s and then rebuilt in 1994.

✪ **Ramshead Cottage at Wallowa Lake.** 84591 Pine Ridge Rd. (P.O. Box 874), Joseph, OR 97846. ☎ **541/432-2002.** Fax 541/432-2002. www.oregontrail.net/~dsteiger/. 1 two-bedroom cottage. $115 double, $150 4 people. No credit cards.

Located in the shady pine forest at the south end of Wallowa Lake, this modern cedar-shingled cottage is operated by Lynn and Doris Steiger, who for years ran a B&B in the wine country outside Portland. The interior decor is rustic yet very comfortable, and the cottage shows the thoughtful touches you expect from a B&B—antique furnishings, an excellent library, quality linens. Light fir floors and pine paneling are found throughout (as opposed to the dark paneling usually found in older mountain cabins), and an abundance of windows keeps the rooms bright. The upstairs suite has a living room with a small kitchen, while the downstairs has a Murphy bed and a private deck. From the cottage, it's just a short walk to either the lake or the start of the trails that lead into the Eagle Cap Wilderness.

✪ **Wallowa Lake Lodge.** 60060 Wallowa Lake Hwy., Joseph, OR 97846. ☎ **541/432-9821.** Fax 541/432-4885. www.wallowalake.com. 30 units (including 8 cabins). May to mid-Oct $78–$135 double; $85–$175 cabin. Mid-Oct to Apr $60–$105 double; $70–$115 cabin. 2-night minimum in cabins during summer. DISC, MC, V.

This rustic two-story lodge at the south end of Wallowa Lake was built in 1923 and is surrounded by big pines and a wide expanse of lawn that attracts deer in late summer and early fall. Big comfortable chairs fill the lobby, where folks often sit by the stone fireplace in the evening. The guest rooms are divided between those with carpeting and modern bathrooms and those with hardwood floors, original bathroom fixtures, and antique furnishings (our favorites). All but two of the latter type have two bedrooms each, and two rooms have balconies overlooking the lake. The cabins are rustic but comfortable and have full kitchens. The dining room serves a limited menu of well-prepared dishes in the $12.50 to $21.50 range. Hazelnut pancakes with marionberry butter are a breakfast specialty.

A GUEST RANCH IN THE WILDERNESS

Minam Lodge. High Country Outfitters, P.O. Box 3384, La Grande, OR 97850. ☎ **888/454-4415** or 541/432-9171. 6 units. $95 per person per night ($50 per night for children ages 6–12); dormitory beds $50 per night; campsites $10. Rates include all meals. MC, V.

Located on the Minam River and surrounded by the Eagle Cap Wilderness, Minam Lodge is accessible only on foot, on horseback, or by small plane. This rustic and very remote getaway is for those who enjoy horseback riding, hiking, fishing, and hunting. The rustic log cabins are set atop a low hill and have wood stoves for warmth and good-sized windows to let in the sunshine and the views. Horseback rides to and from the lodge are $65 each way, and guided trail rides are available ($17 for 1 hr. up to $85 for a full day). Guided overnight pack trips and packages are also available.

A CAMPGROUND

At the south end of Wallowa Lake, you'll find a campground under the trees at **Wallowa Lake State Park.** In addition to campsites, the park has two yurts for rent for $27 a night. For campsite reservations, call **Reservations Northwest** (☎ **800/452-5687**).

WHERE TO DINE

In addition to the restaurants listed below, you'll find good meat-and-potatoes meals at the **Wallowa Lake Lodge** (see "Where to Stay" above for details). If you're just looking for some baked goodies or a light lunch, check out the **Wildflour Bakery,** 600 N. Main St., Joseph (☎ **541/432-7225**), which is set behind an attractive perennial garden and has a deck out front and wooden booths inside.

Old Town Cafe. 8 S. Main St., Joseph. ☎ **541/432-9898.** Main dishes $4.25–$7. No credit cards. Fri–Wed 7am–2pm. INTERNATIONAL.

This tiny cafe sits right in the middle of Joseph and serves up satisfying portions of excellent food. The menu is very limited, which seems to give the owners plenty of opportunity to perfect their offerings. For breakfast don't miss the breakfast burrito, especially if you are heading out for a day of hiking. These burritos are huge! At lunch, the bottomless bowl of soup is a big hit. Marionberry pie and giant cookies round out the offerings.

✪ **Terminal Gravity Brewery & Pub.** 803 School St., Enterprise. ☎ **541/426-0185.** Main courses $5–$8. No credit cards. Wed–Sat 3:30–11pm, Sun 3:30–9pm. INTERNATIONAL.

Although it's small, this brewery on the east side of Enterprise has been getting raves across the state for its excellent beers. However, you can also get good food in the tiny brew-pub dining room. There are only a couple of tables and a few barstools (with a few more tables upstairs), but the food is some of the best in this corner of the state. The chili is among the best we've ever had. Each night there is a single dinner special; otherwise, there are only a handful of other basic dishes on the menu.

Vali's Alpine Restaurant and Delicatessen. 59811 Wallowa Lake Hwy. ☎ **541/432-5691.** Reservations required. Main courses $7.50–$12. No credit cards. Tues–Sun 9–11am and 5–8pm. Closed weekdays from Labor Day to Memorial Day. EASTERN EUROPEAN.

Just past the Wallowa Lake Lodge you'll find this little restaurant, which specializes in the hearty fare of Eastern Europe. Only one dish is served each evening, so if you like to have options, you won't want to eat here. Stuffed cabbage (Tues), Hungarian goulash (Wed), chicken paprikash (Thurs), beef kabobs (Fri), steak (Sat), and schnitzel (Sun) should help you stay warm on cold mountain evenings. Luckily, the apple strudel is served every night. Hungarian gypsy music plays on the stereo, and at breakfast there are fresh homemade doughnuts.

4 Hells Canyon & the Southern Wallowas

South access: 70 miles NE of Baker City; North access: 20 to 30 miles E of Joseph

Sure, the Grand Canyon is an impressive sight, but few people realize that it isn't the deepest canyon in the United States. That distinction goes to Hells Canyon, which forms part of the border between Oregon and Idaho. Carved by the Snake River and bounded on the east by the Seven Devils Mountains and on the west by the Wallowa Mountains, Hells Canyon is as much as 8,000 feet deep. While it's not quite as spectacular a sight as the Grand Canyon, neither is it as crowded. Because there is so little road access to Hells Canyon, it is one of the least visited national recreation areas in the West.

The Hells Canyon area boasts a range of outdoor activities, but because of blazing hot temperatures in summer, when this rugged gorge lives up to its name, spring and fall are the best times to visit. Despite the heat, though, boating, swimming, and fishing are all popular in the summer.

ESSENTIALS

GETTING THERE The south access to Hells Canyon National Recreation Area is reached off of Ore. 86 between 9 and 48 miles northeast of the town of Halfway, depending on which route you follow. Northern sections of the national recreation area, including the Hat Point Overlook, are reached from Joseph on Ore. 82, which begins in La Grande.

VISITOR INFORMATION For more information, contact the **Hells Canyon National Recreation Area,** 88401 Ore. 82, Enterprise, OR 97828 (☎ **541/426-4978**).

EXPLORING THE REGION

Much of Hells Canyon is wilderness and is accessible only by boat, on horseback, or on foot. Few roads lead into the canyon, and most of these are recommended only for four-wheel-drive vehicles. If you are driving a car without high clearance, you'll have to limit your exploration of this region to the road to Hells Canyon Dam and the scenic byway that skirts the eastern flanks of the Wallowa Mountains. If you don't mind driving miles on gravel, you can also head out to the **Hat Point Overlook** east of Joseph.

Southern river-level access begins in the community of Oxbow, but the portion of the Snake River that has been designated a National Wild and Scenic River starts 27 miles farther north, below Hells Canyon Dam. Below the dam, the Snake River is turbulent with white water and provides thrills for jet boats and rafts. To get this bottom-up view of the canyon, take Ore. 86 to Oxbow, cross the river into Idaho, and continue 22 miles downriver to **Hells Canyon Creek Visitor Center** (☎ **541/785-3395**), which is located 1 mile past the Hells Canyon Dam. This center has informative displays on the natural history of Hells Canyon and is open May through mid-September daily from 7:30 to 11:30am and from 12:30 to 4:30pm. At the information center, there is also access to the river via a long flight of stairs.

To get a top-down overview of the canyon, drive to the **Hells Canyon Overlook,** 30 miles northeast of Halfway on Forest Road 39. From here you can gaze down into the canyon, but you won't be able to see the river.

You'll find many miles of **hiking trails** within the national recreation area, but summer heat, rattlesnakes, and poison oak keep all but the most dedicated hikers at bay. For information on trails here, contact the information center for the recreation area (see above).

The best way to see Hells Canyon is by **white-water raft** or in a **jet boat.** Both sorts of trips can be arranged through **Hells Canyon Adventures,** 4200 Hells Canyon Dam Rd. (P.O. Box 159), Oxbow, OR 97840 (☎ **800/422-3568** or 541/785-3352; www.hellscanyonadventures.com). Jet-boat tours range from $30 for a 2-hour tour to $95 for a 6-hour tour. A day of white-water rafting runs $140. Multiday white-water rafting trips are also offered by **Freewater Expeditions** (☎ **800/818-7423**). A 3-day trip will run you around $650, while a 6-day trip runs around $1,000.

Horseback trips into the southern Wallowas are offered by **Cornucopia Wilderness Pack Station,** Route 1, Box 50, Richland, OR 97870 (☎ **541/893-6400,** or in summer 541/742-5400), with rates around $200 per person per day for fully catered and guided trips. Horses can also be rented here on an hourly or daily basis.

You can also opt to explore the southern Wallowas with a llama carrying your gear. Contact **Wallowa Llamas,** 36678 Allstead Lane, Halfway, OR 97834 (☎ **541/742-2961;** e-mail: wallama@pdx.oneworld.com), for more information. Trips range in price from $350 to $990.

While in this area, you can learn about bison at **Clear Creek Buffalo Ranch** (☎ **800/742-4992** or 541/742-2238). This ranch outside the town of Halfway offers tours during which you get to see their bison up close, learn more about bison and their cultural significance to the Plains Native peoples, and then have a buffalo dinner. Tour and dinner runs $25. Tours alone are $6.

WHERE TO STAY

Clear Creek Farm Bed and Breakfast Inn. 48212 Clear Creek Rd., Halfway, OR 97834. ☎ **800/742-4992** or 541/742-2238. Fax 541/742-5175. www.neoregon.com/ccgg. 8 units. $130–$169 double. Rates include full breakfast. MC, V.

Located in the hills on the outskirts of Halfway, this modern farmhouse B&B is part of a buffalo ranch. However, the inn is far more comfortable and contemporary than you might expect from a buffalo ranch. A veranda wraps around three sides of the inn, and there are beautiful flower gardens all around. Most rooms have mountain or meadow views, and the Garden Room has a clawfoot tub. In addition to the rooms in the main house, there are three rustic cabins that have private bathrooms (which are, however, in a separate bathhouse building). With no insulation and in some cases only screens on the windows, these cabins are just a step above camping and are open only during the warmer months. Meals (including buff bourguignonne and buff fillets) can be arranged for an additional charge, and ranch privileges are also available at an additional charge.

✪ **Pine Valley Lodge.** N. Main St. (P.O. Box 712), Halfway, OR 97834. ☎ **541/742-2027.** www.neoregon.net/pinevalleylodge. 6 units (2 with private bathroom), 1 cabin (sleeps 6 to 10 people). $65–$75 double with shared bathroom, $95–$105 double with private bathroom. Rates include deluxe continental breakfast. No credit cards. Pets accepted ($10).

This amazing little lodge and restaurant, composed of four old buildings in downtown Halfway, is a Wild West fantasy created by two very creative artists. With handmade furniture and Western collectibles scattered all about, the main lodge is a fascinating place to just wander around. Two small guest rooms that combine rustic furnishings with the artistic endeavors of the owners are on the second floor. Next door is the Blue Dog, with more rustic Western furnishings and four rooms (which can also be combined to form two suites). Outdoorsy types will like the bunkhouse, aka the Love Shack, which truly is a shack, though with a lot of charm. All in all, this place is unique. The lodge's Halfway Supper Club is located across the street in an old church that was built in 1891 (see below for details).

WHERE TO DINE

✪ **The Halfway Supper Club/Babette's Maybe Baby Bakery.** N. Main St., Halfway. ☎ **541/742-2027.** Reservations recommended. Main courses $12–$22. No credit cards. Fri–Sun 6–8pm; bakery Thurs–Sun 10am–2:30pm. CONTINENTAL/FUSION COUNTRY CUISINE.

Located in an old church that was built in 1891, this restaurant is part of the wonderfully eclectic and rustic Pine Valley Lodge (see above), and it serves the most creative cuisine in this corner of the state. The meals, which include the likes of lamb chops with rosemary and lemon and coq au vin (here known as hunter's chicken), are served amid handmade furniture and painted pillows and wall coverings by the owners. This place is well worth a drive if you're staying anywhere in the vicinity. The Maybe Baby Bakery does good lunches as well as baked goodies.

5 Ontario & the Owyhee River Region

Ontario: 72 miles SE of Baker City, 63 miles NW of Boise, 130 miles NE of Burns

Ontario, the easternmost town in Oregon, lies in the Four Rivers region, at the confluence of the Owyhee, Snake, Malheur, and Payette Rivers. Irrigated by waters from the massive Owyhee Reservoir, these wide, flat valleys are prime agricultural lands that produce onions, sugar beets, and, as in Idaho, plenty of potatoes. This region is also where much of the world's zinnia seeds are grown. During the summer, zinnia fields color the landscape in bold swaths. If you're curious to see the flower fields, head out of Ontario on Ore. 201.

The biggest attraction in the region is the **Four Rivers Cultural Center,** which focuses on the various cultures that have made the region what it is today. However, nearby there is also some Oregon Trail history to be seen. South of Ontario lies one of Oregon's most rugged and remote regions. This corner of the state is rugged high desert, and along the banks of the Owyhee River and Succor Creek you can see canyons and cliffs that seem far more suited to a Southwestern landscape.

ESSENTIALS

GETTING THERE   Ontario is on the Idaho line at the junction of I-84 and U.S. 20/26, all of which link the town to western Oregon.

VISITOR INFORMATION   For more information on the Ontario area, contact the **Ontario Visitors & Convention Bureau,** 676 SW Fifth Ave., Ontario, OR 97914 (☎ **888/889-8012** or 541/889-8012; www.ontariochamber.com).

A CULTURAL MUSEUM

Four Rivers Cultural Center. 676 SW Fifth Ave. ☎ **888/211-1222** or 541/889-8191. Admission $4 adults, $3 seniors and children 3–12. Daily 10am–5pm (10am–6pm in summer). Closed Thanksgiving, Christmas, and New Year's Day.

While this remote corner of Oregon may seem an unlikely place for a multicultural museum, that is exactly what you'll find at the Four Rivers Cultural Center. The museum focuses on four very distinct cultures that have called, and still do call, this region home. The Paiutes were the original inhabitants of the area, and an exploration of their hunting-and-gathering culture is the first exhibit. In the mid–19th century, the first pioneers began arriving in the area and quickly displaced the Paiutes. By the late 19th century, many Mexican cowboys, known as vaqueros or buckaroos, had come north to the region to work the large cattle ranches. At the same time, Basque shepherds settled in the area and tended large herds of sheep in the more remote corners of the region. The fourth culture focused on is that of the Japanese, who were forced to live in internment camps in the area during World War II. After the war, many of them stayed on.

EXPLORING THE REGION

For more Oregon Trail history, head 18 miles west of Ontario to the small farming community of **Vale.** Here you'll find the **Rinehart Stone House,** 283 S. Main St. (☎ **541/473-2070**), which was built in 1872 and was a stage stop and an important wayside along the route of the Oregon Trail. Today it houses a small historical museum that is open March 1 through November 1, Tuesday through Saturday from noon to 4pm; admission is free.

Note

Ontario is on Rocky Mountain time, not Pacific time.

Large historic murals cover numerous walls around Vale, and a good way to see them is by horse-drawn buggy operated by **Wilcox Horse & Buggy** (☎ 888/TRY-VALE or 541/473-9251). The 1-hour evening tours operate June through September and cost $10 per person. Six miles south of Vale, at Keeney Pass, you can see **wagon ruts** left by pioneers traveling the Oregon Trail.

South of Ontario 15 miles, you'll find **Nyssa,** the "Thunderegg Capital of Oregon." **Rockhounding** is the area's most popular pastime, and thundereggs (also known as geodes) are the prime find. These round rocks look quite plain until they are cut open to reveal the agate or crystals within. You'll find plenty of cut-and-polished thundereggs in the rock shops around town. If you'd like to do a bit of rockhounding yourself, you can head south to **Succor Creek State Park,** a rugged canyon where you'll find a campground, picnic tables, and thundereggs waiting to be unearthed.

If you have a four-wheel-drive or high-clearance vehicle, you can continue another 30 minutes to **Leslie Gulch,** an even more spectacular canyon with walls of naturally sculpted sandstone. If you're lucky, you might even see bighorn sheep here. Few places in Oregon have more of the feel of the desert than these two canyons, and just as in the desert Southwest, here too rivers have been dammed to provide irrigation waters and aquatic playgrounds. **Lake Owyhee,** 45 miles south of Ontario off Ore. 201, is the longest lake in Oregon and offers boating, fishing, and camping. The Owyhee River above the lake is a designated State Scenic Waterway and is popular for **whitewater rafting.** If you're interested in running this remote stretch of river, contact **Cascade River Runners** (☎ 800/884-2113 or 541/883-6340), **Destination Wilderness** (☎ 800/423-8868 or 541/549-1336), or **Oregon Whitewater Adventures** (☎ 800/820-RAFT or 541/746-5422), all of which occasionally run this river. Below the Owyhee Dam, 12 miles southwest of the town of Adrian, you'll find a signed **"Watchable Wildlife" area** offering excellent bird watching. You might also spot beavers, porcupines, mule deer, and coyotes.

WHERE TO STAY

For the most part, Ontario is a wayside for people traveling along I-84, and, as such, the city's accommodations are strictly off-ramp budget motels. Motel options include a **Best Western Inn,** 251 Goodfellow St., Ontario, OR 97914 (☎ 800/828-0364 or 541/889-2600), charging $57 to $78 double; a **Super 8 Motel,** 266 Goodfellow St., Ontario, OR 97914 (☎ 800/800-8000 or 541/889-8282), charging $53 to $59 double; and a **Motel 6,** 275 NE 12th St., Ontario, OR 97914 (☎ 800/466-8356 or 541/889-6617), charging $38 to $42 double.

At nearby **Farewell Bend State Park** (☎ 541/869-2365), 25 miles northwest of Ontario on I-84, you'll find not only campsites but also covered wagons that can be rented for overnight stays ($27 per night). Don't look for horses to hitch up, though; these wagons stay put. For campsite and covered-wagon reservations, call **Reservations Northwest** (☎ 800/452-5687).

WHERE TO DINE

In downtown Ontario, you'll find a couple of basic Mexican restaurants and some places specializing in steaks, but that's about it. When you just have to have a latte or a mocha, head to **Coyote Coffee Company,** 146 SW Fourth Ave. (☎ 541/889-HOWL), in a tiny cottage a block off Oregon Street, which is downtown Ontario's main street.

6 Southeastern Oregon: Land of Marshes, Mountains & Desert

Burns: 130 miles SE of Bend, 130 miles SE of Ontario, 70 miles S of John Day

Southeastern Oregon, the most remote and least populated corner of the state, is a region of extremes. Vast marshlands, the most inhospitable desert in the state, and a mountain topped with aspen groves and glacial valleys are among the most prominent features of this landscape. While cattle outnumber human inhabitants and the deer and the antelope play, it's bird life that's the region's number one attraction. At **Malheur National Wildlife Refuge,** birds abound almost any month of the year, attracting flocks of bird-watchers, binoculars and bird books in hand.

Because this is such an isolated region (Burns and Lakeview are the only towns of consequence), it is not an area to be visited by the unprepared. Always keep your gas tank topped off and carry water for both you and your car. Two of the region's main attractions, **Steens Mountain** and the **Hart Mountain National Antelope Refuge,** are accessible only by way of gravel roads more than 50 miles long. A visit to the Alvord Desert will also require spending 60 or more miles on a gravel road.

ESSENTIALS

GETTING THERE   The town of Burns is midway between Bend and Ontario on U.S. 20. Malheur National Wildlife Refuge, Steens Mountain, and Hart Mountain National Antelope Refuge are all located south of Burns off Ore. 205.

VISITOR INFORMATION   For more information on this area, contact the **Harney County Chamber of Commerce,** 18 W. D St., Burns, OR 97720 (☎ **541/ 573-2636;** www.harneycounty.com).

EXPLORING THE REGION

Because water is scarce here in the high desert, it becomes a magnet for wildlife wherever it appears. Three marshy lakes—Malheur, Harney, and Mud—south of Burns cover such a vast area and provide such an ideal habitat for bird life that they have been designated the ✪ **Malheur National Wildlife Refuge.** The shallow lakes, surrounded by thousands of acres of marshlands, form an oasis that annually attracts more than 300 species of birds, including waterfowl, shorebirds, songbirds, and raptors. Some of the more noteworthy birds that are either resident or migratory at Malheur are trumpeter swans, sandhill cranes, white pelicans, great blue herons, and great horned owls. Of the more than 58 mammals that live in the refuge, the most visible are mule deer, antelope, and coyotes.

The refuge headquarters is 32 miles south of Burns on Ore. 205, but the refuge stretches for another 30 miles south to the crossroads of Frenchglen. The **visitor center,** where you can find out about recent sightings and current birding hot spots, is open weekdays only, while a **museum** housing a collection of nearly 200 stuffed-and-mounted birds is open daily. Camping is available at two campgrounds near Frenchglen. For more information on the refuge, contact **Malheur National Wildlife Refuge,** HC-72, Box 245, Princeton, OR 97721 (☎ **541/493-2612;** www.r1.fws.gov/malheur).

Steens Mountain, a different sort of desert oasis, is 30 miles southeast of French-glen on a gravel road that's usually open only between July and October. Even then the road is not recommended for cars with low clearance, but if you have the appropriate vehicle, the mountain is well worth a visit. Rising to 9,733 feet high, this fault-block mountain was formed when the land on the west side of a geological fault line rose in relationship to the land on the east side of the fault. This geologic upheaval caused the east slope of Steens Mountain to form a precipitous escarpment that falls away to the Alvord Desert a mile below. The panorama out across southeastern Oregon is spectacular. The mountain rises so high that it creates its own weather, and on the upper slopes the sagebrush of the high desert gives way to juniper and aspen forests. From Frenchglen, there's a 66-mile loop road that leads to the summit and back down by a different route.

More wildlife-viewing opportunities are available at the **Hart Mountain National Antelope Refuge,** which is a refuge for both pronghorns, the fastest land mammal in North America and not really an antelope at all, and California bighorn sheep. The most accessible location for viewing pronghorns is the refuge headquarters, 49 miles southwest of Frenchglen on gravel roads. Bighorn sheep are harder to spot but tend to keep to the steep cliffs west of the refuge headquarters. Primitive camping is available near the headquarters at **Hot Springs Campground.** For more information, contact the **Hart Mountain National Antelope Refuge,** P.O. Box 111, Lakeview, OR 97630 (☎ **541/947-3315**).

WHERE TO STAY & DINE

Frenchglen Hotel. Frenchglen, OR 97736. ☎ **541/493-2825.** Fax 541/493-2825. E-mail: fghotel@ptinet.net. 8 units (all with shared bathroom). $55–$58 double. DISC, MC, V. Closed Nov 16–Mar 14.

Frenchglen is in the middle of nowhere, so for decades the Frenchglen Hotel (now owned by the Oregon State Parks) has been an important way station for travelers passing through this remote region. The historic two-story hotel is 60 miles south of Burns on the edge of Malheur National Wildlife Refuge. Though the historic setting will appeal to anyone with an appreciation for pioneer days, the hotel is most popular with bird-watchers. The guest rooms are on the second floor and are small and simply furnished. This hotel is often booked up months in advance. Three meals a day will cost $20 to $27 per person, and the hearty dinners are quite good.

Hotel Diamond. HC-72, Box 10, Diamond, OR 97722. ☎ **541/493-1898.** 8 units (3 with private bathroom). A/C. $55–$65 double with shared bathroom, $80–$90 double with private bathroom. MC, V.

Located 54 miles south of Burns off Ore. 205, the Hotel Diamond, built in 1898, is on the opposite side of the Malheur Wildlife Refuge from Frenchglen. The hotel was completely restored in the late 1980s, and in 1998 two more rooms with private bathrooms were added. There's a big screened porch across the front and a green lawn complete with a croquet court and horseshoe pits. Family-style dinners are available for $10 to $15 with reservations at least 24 hours in advance. The hotel prefers that room and meal reservations be made by phone, not by mail.

✪ **McCoy Creek Inn.** McCoy Creek Ranch, HC 72, Box 11, Diamond, OR 97722. ☎ **541/493-2131.** Fax 541/493-2131. 4 units. $75 double. Rates include full breakfast. DC, MC, V.

Of the three lodges in this area, the McCoy Creek Inn is the most remote and most luxurious. Set on a working cattle ranch that has been run by the same family for five generations, the inn consists of three rooms in the main house plus one more in the bunkhouse. McCoy Creek runs right through the property and its canyon is full of wildlife. You can hike the trails, splash in the stream, or feed the farm animals (if you're so inclined). Steens Mountain rises up from the ranch and the Malheur National Wildlife Refuge is nearby. A hot tub provides the perfect end to a long day of exploring the high desert.

Appendix A:
Oregon in Depth

1 The Natural Environment

At 97,073 square miles (roughly 1¹/₂ times the size of New England), Oregon is the 10th-largest state in the Union, and it encompasses within its vast area an amazing diversity of natural environments—not only lush forests, but also deserts, glacier-covered peaks, grasslands, alpine meadows, and sagebrush-covered hills. Together, these diverse environments support a surprisingly wide variety of natural life.

The **Oregon coast** stretches for nearly 300 miles from the redwood country of Northern California to the mouth of the Columbia River, and much of this length is only sparsely populated. Consequently, this coastline provides habitat not only for large populations of seabirds, such as cormorants, tufted puffins, and pigeon guillemots, but also for several species of marine mammals, including Pacific gray whales, Steller sea lions, California sea lions, and harbor seals.

Each year between December and April, more than 20,000 **Pacific gray whales** pass by the Oregon coast as they make their annual migration south to their breeding grounds off Baja California. These whales can often be seen from shore at various points along the coast, and numerous whale-watching tour boats operate out of different ports. In recent years, more and more gray whales have been choosing to spend the summer in Oregon's offshore waters, and it is now possible to spot these leviathans any month of the year. More frequently spotted, however, are **harbor seals** and Steller and California **sea lions,** which are frequently seen lounging on rocks. Sea Lion Caves and Cape Arago State Park, both on the Oregon coast, are two of the best places to spot sea lions.

The **Coast Range,** which in places rises directly from the waves, gives the coastline its rugged look. However, even more than the mountains, it is **rain** that gives this coastline its definitive character. As moist winds from the Pacific Ocean rise up and over the Coast Range, they drop their moisture as rain and snow. The tremendous amounts of rain that fall on these mountains have produced dense forests that are home to some of the largest trees on earth. Although the south coast is the northern limit for the coast redwood, the **Douglas firs,** which are far more common and grow throughout the region, are almost as impressive in size, sometimes reaching 300 feet tall. Other common trees of these coastal forests include sitka spruce, western hemlocks, Port Orford cedars, western red cedars, and the evergreen myrtle trees. The wood of these latter trees is used extensively for carving, and myrtle wood shops are common along the southern Oregon coast where myrtle trees grow.

More than a century of intensive **logging** has, however, left the state's forests of centuries-old trees shrunken to remnant groves scattered in largely remote and rugged areas. How much exactly is still left is a matter of hot debate between the timber industry and environmentalists, and the battle to save the remaining old-growth forests continues, with both sides claiming victories and losses with each passing year.

Among this region's most celebrated and controversial wild residents is the **northern spotted owl,** which, because of its requirements for large tracts of undisturbed old-growth forest and its listing as a federally endangered species, brought logging of old-growth forests to a virtual halt in the 1990s. Concern next focused on the **marbled murrelet,** a small bird that feeds on the open ocean but nests exclusively in old-growth forests. Destruction of forests is also being partially blamed for the demise of trout, salmon, and steelhead populations throughout the region.

Roosevelt elk, the largest commonly encountered land mammal in the Northwest, can be found throughout the Coast Range, and there are even designated elk-viewing areas along the coast (one off U.S. 26 near Jewell and one off Ore. 38 near Reedsport).

Behind the northern section of the Coast Range lies the **Willamette Valley,** which because of its mild climate and fertile soils, was the first region of the state to be settled by pioneers. Today, the Willamette Valley remains the state's most densely populated region and is home to Oregon's largest cities. However, it also contains the most productive farmland in the state.

In 1999, eight species of salmon and steelhead in the Willamette River drainage were listed as threatened under the Endangered Species Act. By the end of the year, Portland and other metropolitan areas in the valley were struggling to determine what impact this listing would have on development in the region.

To the east of the Willamette Valley rise the mountains of the 700-mile-long **Cascade Range,** which stretches from Northern California to southern British Columbia. The most prominent features of the Cascades are its **volcanic peaks:** Hood, Jefferson, Three Fingered Jack, Washington, the Three Sisters, Broken Top, Thielsen, and McLoughlin. The eruption of Washington's Mount St. Helens on May 18, 1980, reminded Northwesterners that this is still a volcanically active region. The remains of ancient Mount Mazama, which erupted with great violence 7,700 years ago, are today preserved as **Crater Lake National Park.** Near the town of Bend, geologically recent volcanic activity is also visible in the form of cinder cones, lava flows, lava caves, and craters. Much of this volcanic landscape is now preserved as **Newberry National Volcanic Monument.**

The same moisture-laden clouds that produce the near rain-forest conditions in the Coast Range leave the Cascades with frequently heavy snows and, on the highest peaks (Mount Hood, Mount Jefferson, the Three Sisters), numerous glaciers. The most readily accessible glaciers are on **Mount Hood,** where ski lifts keep running right through the summer, carrying skiers and snowboarders to slopes atop the Palmer Glacier, high above the historic Timberline Lodge. It is the winter snowpack in these mountains that provides the water for the state's largest cities. This snowpack can also be the source of floodwaters, as was the case in February 1996 when downtown Portland came within inches of flooding and many other communities along the Willamette River incurred millions of dollars of damage.

East of the Cascades, less than 200 miles from the damp Coast Range forests, the landscape becomes a desert. The **Great Basin,** which reaches its

How to Speak Northwestern

All across Oregon there are dozens of linguistic land mines waiting to trip up visitors to the region—place names that aren't pronounced the way they're spelled or that simply are so strange that no one could ever figure out how to pronounce them without a little coaching. So we include here an Oregon primer of place names to help non-natives speak like locals and thus blend into the Oregon landscape. Think of the following knowledge as verbal camouflage.

Cape Arago   Cape *Air*-uh-go

Champoeg   Sham-*poo*-ee

Coquille   Ko-*keel*

Deschutes (River)   Duh-*shoots*

Heceta   Huh-*see*-tuh

Siuslaw   Sigh-*oos*-law

The Dalles   The Dals (rhymes with "pals")

Umatilla   You-muh-*til*-uh

Wallowa (Mountains)   Wuh-*lou*-uh

Willamette (River)   Wuh-*la*-mit

Yachats   *Yah*-hots

Yaquina   Yuh-*quin*-uh

northern limit in central and eastern Oregon, comprises a vast, high desert region that stretches to the Rockies. Through this desolate landscape flows the **Columbia River,** which, together with its tributary the Snake, forms the second-largest river drainage in the United States. During the last Ice Age, roughly 13,000 years ago, glaciers repeatedly blocked the flow of the Columbia, forming huge lakes behind dams of ice. These vast prehistoric lakes repeatedly burst the ice dams, sending massive and devastating walls of water flooding down the Columbia. These floodwaters were sometimes 1,000 feet high and carried with them ice and rocks, which scoured out the **Columbia Gorge.** The gorge's many waterfalls are the most evident signs of such floods.

Today, the Columbia is dammed not by ice, but by numerous large, modern **dams** that have become the focus of one of the region's hottest environmental battles. The large dams, mostly built during the middle part of this century, present a variety of barriers both to returning adult salmon and to young salmon headed downstream to the Pacific. Though many of the dams have fish ladders to allow **salmon** to return upriver to spawn, salmon must still negotiate an obstacle course of degraded spawning grounds in often clear-cut forests, slower river flows in the reservoirs behind the dams, turbines that kill fish by the thousands, and irrigation canals that often confuse salmon into swimming out of the river and into farm fields. Overfishing for salmon canneries in the late 19th century struck the first major blow to salmon populations, which have been steadily dwindling ever since. Compounding the problem has been the use of fish hatcheries to supplement wild salmon populations (hatchery fish tend to be less vigorous than wild salmon). A salmon recovery plan was adopted in the 1990s to attempt to save threatened runs of native salmon, but farmers, electricity producers, shipping companies, and major users of hydroelectric power have continued to fight the requirements of the recovery plan, which include lowering water levels in reservoirs to speed the downstream migration of young salmon. In the late 1990s, the focus turned to the removal of some of the dams on the Snake River, which proved to be a very controversial idea. However, despite these dire straits for the fish populations of the state, hatchery fish still provide almost enough fish to keep the state's sport anglers happy.

South-central and southeastern Oregon are the most remote and unpopulated regions of the state. However, this vast desert area does support an abundance of wildlife. The **Hart Mountain National Antelope Refuge** shelters herds of pronghorn antelope, which are the fastest land mammal in North America. This refuge also protects a small population of California bighorn sheep. At **Malheur National Wildlife Refuge,** more than 300 species of birds frequent large shallow lakes and wetlands, and at the **Lower Klamath National Wildlife Refuge,** large numbers of bald eagles gather. Several other of the region's large lakes, including Summer Lake and Lake Abert, attract large populations of birds.

2 Oregon Today

For the past decade, Oregon has been one of the fastest-growing states in the nation, as high-tech industries have moved manufacturing here and Californians, fed up with that state's pollution, crime, congestion, and high cost of living, have moved north in search of a better quality of life. Oregon is today riding a boom that has fueled rapid growth, especially in the high-tech industries. Intel, the microchip maker that has found its way inside almost everyone's computer, has several large plants in the Portland area, and its presence has encouraged dozens of other high-tech companies to locate there and elsewhere in the Willamette Valley. This economic growth has, unfortunately, begun to undermine the very values that drew many here in the first place. Urban sprawl, congested roads, and sky-rocketing housing costs are all changing the character of Oregon. However, Oregonians are working hard to preserve the state's unique character and to keep Portland as livable as it has always been. From almost anywhere in the state, it's possible to look up and see green forests and snow-capped mountains, and a drive of less than 2 hours from any Willamette Valley city will get you to the mountains or the Pacific Ocean's beaches.

Oregonians don't let the weather stand between them and the outdoors. The temptation is too great to head for the mountains, the river, or the beach, no matter what the weather. Consequently, life in Oregon's cities tends to revolve less around cultural venues and other urban pastimes such as shopping than around parks, gardens, waterfronts, rivers, mountains, and beaches. Portland has its Forest Park, Rose Garden, Japanese Garden, and Waterfront Park. Eugene has its miles of riverside parks, bike paths, and even a park just for rock climbing. In Hood River, the entire Columbia River has become a playground for boardsailors, and when the wind doesn't blow, there are always the nearby mountain-bike trails and rivers for kayaking. In Bend, mountain biking and downhill skiing are a way of life. These outdoor areas are where people find tranquillity, where summer festivals are held, where locals take their visiting friends and relatives, and where they tend to live their lives when the fun isn't being interrupted by such inconveniences as work and sleep.

This is not to say, however, that the region is a cultural wasteland. Both Portland and Eugene have large, modern, and active performing-arts centers. During the summer months, numerous festivals take music, theater, and dance outdoors. Most impressive of these are the Oregon Shakespeare Festival and the Britt Festivals, both of which are staged in southern Oregon. Many other festivals feature everything from chamber music to alternative rock.

With urban areas of the Willamette Valley experiencing a very rapid population growth in recent years, politics have developed a very pronounced urban-rural split in Oregon. Citizens from the eastern part of the state argue that Salem and Portland are dictating to rural regions that have little in common with the cities, while urban dwellers, who far outnumber those living outside the Willamette Valley, argue that majority rule is majority rule. This split has pitted conservative voters (often from rural regions) and liberal voters (usually urban) on a wide variety of issues, and the reality of Oregon politics is now quite a bit different from the often-held perception of a state dominated by liberal, forward-thinking environmentalists and former hippies. Medical use of marijuana and assisted suicide, both of which were legalized in Oregon in the late 1990s, both continue to generate much controversy.

3 Oregon History 101

Dateline

- **13,000 B.C.** Massive floods, as much as 1,000 feet deep, rage down Columbia River and carve the Columbia Gorge.
- **10,000 B.C.** Earliest known human inhabitation of Oregon.
- **5,000 B.C.** Mount Mazama erupts violently, creating a caldera that will later fill with water and be known as Crater Lake.
- **A.D. 1542** Spanish exploratory ship reaches what is now the southern Oregon coast.
- **1579** Englishman Sir Francis Drake reaches the mouth of the Rogue River.
- **1602** Spain's Martín de Aguilar explores the coast of Oregon, probably as far as Coos Bay.
- **1792** Robert Gray becomes the first explorer to sail a ship into a great river he names the Columbia, in honor of his ship the *Columbia Rediviva.*
- **1805–06** Expedition led by Meriwether Lewis and William Clark crosses the continent and spends the

continues

EARLY HISTORY The oldest known inhabitants of the state lived along the shores of the huge lakes in the Klamath Lakes Basin some **10,000 years ago.** Here they fished and hunted ducks and left records of their passing in several caves. These peoples would have witnessed the massive eruption of **Mount Mazama,** which left a hollowed-out core of a mountain that eventually filled with water and was named Crater Lake. Along the coast, numerous small tribes subsisted on salmon and shellfish. In the northeast corner of the state, the **Nez Perce Indians** became experts at horse breeding even before Lewis and Clark passed through the region at the start of the 19th century. In fact, the appaloosa horse derives its name from the nearby Palouse Hills of Washington.

However, it was the **Columbia River tribes** that became the richest of the Oregon tribes through their control of **Celilo Falls,** which was historically the richest salmon-fishing area in the Northwest. These massive falls on the Columbia River east of present-day The Dalles witnessed the annual passage of millions of **salmon,** which were speared and dip netted by Native Americans, who then smoked the fish to preserve it for the winter. Today, Native Americans still fish for salmon as they once did, perched on precarious wooden platforms with dip nets in hand. However, Celilo Falls are gone, inundated by the pooling water behind **The Dalles Dam,** which was completed in 1957. Today little remains of what was once the Northwest's most important Native American gathering ground, a place where tribes from hundreds of miles away congregated each year to fish and trade. At the **Columbia Gorge Discovery Center** in The Dalles, you can see film footage of people fishing at Celilo Falls before its inundation.

Even before this amazing fishing ground was lost, a far greater tragedy had been visited upon Northwest tribes. Between the 1780s, when white explorers and traders began frequenting the Northwest coast, and the 1830s, when the first settlers began arriving, the Native American population of the Northwest was reduced to perhaps a tenth of its historic numbers. It was not war that wiped out these people, but European **diseases**—smallpox, measles, malaria, and influenza. The Native Americans had no resistance to these diseases, and entire tribes were soon wiped out by fast-spreading epidemics.

THE AGE OF EXPLORATION Though a Spanish ship reached what is now southern Oregon in **1542,** the Spanish had no interest in the gray and rainy coast. Nor did famed British buccaneer **Sir Francis Drake,** who in 1579 sailed his ship the *Golden Hind* as far north as the mouth of the Rogue River. Drake called off his explorations in the face of what he described as "thicke and stinking fogges."

Though the Spanish laid claim to all of North America's west coast, they had little interest in the lands north of Mexico. However, when the Spanish found out that Russian fur traders were establishing themselves in Alaska and along the North Pacific coast, Spain took a new interest in the Northwest. Several Spanish expeditions sailed north from Mexico to reassert the Spanish claim to the region. In **1775,** Spanish explorers **Bruno de Heceta** and **Francisco de la Bodega y Quadra** charted much of the Northwest coast, and though they found the mouth of the Columbia River, they did not enter it. To this day four of the coast's most scenic headlands—Cape Perpetua, Heceta Head, Cape Arago, and Cape Blanco—bear names from these early Spanish explorations.

It was not until **1792** that an explorer, American trader **Robert Gray,** risked a passage through treacherous sandbars that guarded the

winter at the mouth of the Columbia River.

- **1810** Americans attempt first settlement at the Columbia River's mouth.
- **1819** Spain cedes all lands above 42° north latitude.
- **1824–25** Russia gives up claims to land south of Alaska; Fort Vancouver founded by Hudson's Bay Company on Columbia River near present-day Portland.
- **1834** Methodist missionary Jason Lee founds Salem, which later becomes the state capital.
- **1840** First settlers move to what is now Oregon.
- **1842** Jason Lee founds first school of higher learning west of the Mississippi.
- **1843** First wagons cross the continent on the Oregon Trail; Asa Lovejoy and William Overton stake claim on land that will soon become Portland.
- **1844** Oregon City becomes the first incorporated town west of the Mississippi.
- **1846** The 49th parallel is established as the boundary between American and British territories in the Northwest.
- **1848** Oregon becomes first U.S. territory west of the Rockies.
- **1851** Portland is incorporated; gold is discovered in southern Oregon.
- **1860** Gold is discovered in eastern Oregon.
- **1905** Lewis and Clark Exposition attracts worldwide attention to Oregon.
- **1915** Columbia Gorge scenic highway is constructed.
- **1935** Angus Bowmer stages *As You Like It* in Ashland and plants the seed of the Oregon Shakespeare Festival.
- **1940s** Kaiser shipyards in the Portland area become the world's foremost shipbuilders.

continues

- **1945** Oregon becomes the only state to have civilian war casualties when six children are killed by a Japanese balloon bomb.
- **1957** The Dalles Dam is completed; backwaters inundate Celilo Falls, the most productive Native American salmon-fishing grounds.
- **1974** In a bold step toward making Portland a more livable city, a freeway along the city's downtown waterfront is removed.
- **1980s** Oregon's timber industry suffers a severe economic downturn.
- **1995** Sen. Bob Packwood resigns after the Senate Ethics Committee recommends his expulsion for sexual misconduct.
- **1996** February floodwaters come within inches of spilling out of the Willamette River and into downtown Portland.
- **1998** Portland moves its much-heralded Urban Growth Boundary for the first time since it was created in the 1970s.
- **1999** Eight species of salmon and steelhead in the Willamette River are listed as federally threatened species.
- **1999** The freighter *New Carissa* runs aground off Coos Bay.

mouth of the long speculated upon Great River of the West. Gray named this newfound river **Columbia's River,** in honor of his ship, the *Columbia Rediviva*. This discovery established the first American claim to the region. When news of the Columbia's discovery reached the United States and England, both countries began speculating on a northern water route across North America. Such a route, if it existed, would facilitate trade with the Northwest.

In **1793,** Scotsman **Alexander MacKenzie** made the first overland trip across North America north of New Spain. Crossing British Canada on foot, MacKenzie arrived somewhere north of Vancouver Island. After reading MacKenzie's account of his journey, Thomas Jefferson decided that the United States needed to find a better route overland to the Northwest. To this end, he commissioned **Meriwether Lewis** and **William Clark** to lead an expedition up the Missouri River in hopes of finding a single easy portage that would lead to the Columbia River.

Beginning in **1804,** the members of the Lewis and Clark expedition paddled up the Missouri, crossed the Rocky Mountains on foot, and then paddled down the Columbia River to its mouth. A French Canadian trapper and his Native American wife, Sacajawea, were enlisted as interpreters, and it was the presence of Sacajawea that helped the expedition gain acceptance among Western tribes. After spending a very dismal, wet winter of **1805–06** at the mouth of the Columbia, the expedition headed back east. Discoveries made by the expedition added greatly to the scientific and geographical knowledge of the continent. A reconstruction of **Fort Clatsop,** the expedition's dreary winter camp at the mouth of the Columbia, is now a national memorial and one of the most interesting historical sites in the state. Outside of The Dalles, a campsite used by Lewis and Clark has also been preserved.

In **1819,** the Spanish relinquished all claims north of the present California-Oregon state line, and the Russians gave up their claims to all lands south of Alaska. This left only the British and Americans dickering for control of the Northwest.

SETTLEMENT—Fur Traders, Missionaries & the Oregon Trail Only 6 years after Lewis and Clark spent the winter at the mouth of the Columbia, employees of John Jacob Astor's Pacific Fur Company managed to establish themselves at a nearby spot they called Fort Astoria. This was the first permanent settlement in the Northwest, but with the War of 1812 being fought on the far side of the continent, the fur traders at **Fort Astoria,** with little protection against the British military presence in the region, chose to

❷ Did You Know?

- Oregon was home to America's first policewoman, Lola Greene Baldwin, who joined the Portland force in 1908.
- Matt Groenig, creator of "The Simpsons," got his start in Portland.
- Portland is home to the world's smallest dedicated park—Mill Ends Park—which measures only 24 inches in diameter.
- Oregon is one of the few states with no sales tax.
- Astoria, in the very northwest corner of the state, is the oldest American community west of the Mississippi.
- Oregon's Crater Lake is the deepest lake in the U.S.
- Hells Canyon is the deepest gorge in North America.
- Oregon is home to the world's shortest river, the 120-foot-long D River.
- Port Ortford, Oregon, is the westernmost incorporated town in the contiguous 48 states.

relinquish control of their fort. However, in the wake of the war, the fort returned to American control, though the United States and Britain produced no firm decision about possession of the Northwest. The British still dominated the region, but American trade was tolerated.

With the decline of the sea-otter population, British fur traders turned to beaver and headed inland up the Columbia River. For the next 30 years or so, fur-trading companies would be the sole authority in the region. Fur-trading posts were established throughout the Northwest, though most were on the eastern edge of the territory in the foothills of the Rocky Mountains. The powerful **Hudson's Bay Company** (HBC) eventually became the single fur-trading company in the Northwest.

In 1824, the HBC established its Northwest headquarters at **Fort Vancouver,** 100 miles up the Columbia near the mouth of the Willamette River; and in 1829, the HBC founded Oregon City at the falls of the Willamette River. Between 1824 and 1846, when the 49th parallel was established as the boundary between British and American northwestern lands, Fort Vancouver was the most important settlement in the region. A reconstruction of the fort now stands outside the city of Vancouver, Washington, across the Columbia River from Portland. In Oregon City, several homes from this period are still standing, including that of John McLoughlin, who was chief factor at Fort Vancouver and aided many of the early pioneers who arrived in the area after traveling the Oregon Trail.

By the **1830s,** the future of the Northwest had arrived in the form of American **missionaries.** The first was Jason Lee, who established his mission in the Willamette Valley near present-day Salem (today the site is Willamette Mission State Park). Two years later, in 1836, Marcus and Narcissa Whitman, along with Henry and Eliza Spaulding, made the overland trek to Fort Vancouver, then backtracked into what is now eastern Washington and Idaho, to establish two missions. This journey soon inspired other settlers to make the difficult overland crossing.

In 1840, a slow trickle of American settlers began crossing the continent, a 2,000-mile journey. Their destination was the Oregon country, which had been promoted as a veritable Eden where land was waiting to be claimed. In 1843, **Marcus Whitman,** after traveling east to plead with his superiors not to shut down his mission, headed back west, leading 900 settlers on the **Oregon Trail.** Before these settlers ever arrived, the small population of retired trappers, missionaries, and HBC employees who were living at Fort Vancouver and in nearby Oregon City had formed a provisional government in anticipation of the land-claim problems that would arise with the influx of settlers to the region. Today, the best places to learn about the experiences of the Oregon Trail emigrants are at the **Oregon Trail Interpretive Center** outside Baker City and the **End of the Oregon Trail Interpretive Center** in Oregon City. In many places in the eastern part of the state, Oregon Trail wagon ruts can still be seen.

In **1844,** Oregon City became the first incorporated town west of the Rocky Mountains. This outpost in the wilderness, a gateway to the fertile lands of the Willamette Valley, was the destination of the wagon trains that began traveling the Oregon Trail, each year bringing more and more settlers to the region. As the land in the Willamette Valley was claimed, settlers began fanning out to different regions of the Northwest so that during the late 1840s and early 1850s many new towns, including Portland, were founded.

Though the line between American and British land in the Northwest had been established in 1846 at the 49th parallel (the current Canadian-American border), Oregon was not given U.S. territorial status until **1848.** It was the massacre of the missionaries at the Whitman mission in Walla Walla (now in Washington state) and the subsequent demand for territorial status and U.S. military protection that brought about the establishment of the first U.S. territory west of the Rockies.

The discovery of **gold** in eastern Oregon in **1860** set the stage for one of the saddest chapters in Northwest history. With miners pouring into eastern Oregon and Washington, conflicts with Native Americans over land were inevitable. Since 1805, when Lewis and Clark had first passed this way, the **Nez Perce tribes** (the name means "pierced nose" in French) had been friendly to the white settlers. However, in 1877 a disputed treaty caused friction. Led by **Chief Joseph,** 700 Nez Perce, including 400 women and children, began a march from their homeland to their new reservation. Along the way, several angry young men, in revenge for the murder of an older member of the tribe, attacked a white settlement and killed several people. The U.S. Army took up pursuit of the Nez Perce, who fled across Idaho and Montana, only to be caught 40 miles from the Canadian border and sanctuary.

INDUSTRIALIZATION & THE 20TH CENTURY From the very beginning of white settlement in the Northwest, the region based its growth on an extractive economy. Lumber and salmon were exploited ruthlessly. The history of the timber and salmon-fishing industries have run parallel for more than a century and have led to similar results in the 1990s.

The trees in Oregon grew to gigantic proportions. Nurtured on steady rains, such trees as Douglas fir, Sitka spruce, western red cedar, Port Orford cedar, and hemlock grew tall and straight, sometimes as tall as 300 feet. The first sawmill in the Northwest began operation near present-day Vancouver, Washington, in 1828. Between the 1850s and the 1870s, Northwest sawmills supplied the growing California market as well as a limited foreign market. When the transcontinental railroads arrived in the 1880s, a whole new market opened up, and mills began shipping to the eastern states.

Lumber companies developed a cut-and-run policy that leveled the forests. By the turn of the century, the government had gained more control over public forests in an attempt to slow the decimation of forest lands, and sawmill owners were buying up huge tracts of land. At the outbreak of World War I, more than 20% of the forest land in the Northwest was owned by three companies—Weyerhaeuser, the Northern Pacific Railroad, and the Southern Pacific Railroad—and more than 50% of the workforce labored in the timber industry.

The timber industry has always been extremely susceptible to fluctuations in the economy and has experienced a roller-coaster ride of boom and bust throughout the 20th century. Boom times in the 1970s brought on record-breaking production that came to a screeching halt in the 1980s, first with a nationwide recession and then with the listing of the **northern spotted owl** as a threatened species. When the timber industry was born in the Northwest, there was a belief that the forests of the region were endless. However, by the latter half of this century, big lumber companies had realized that the forests were dwindling. Tree farms were planted with increasing frequency, but the large old trees continued to be cut faster than they could be replenished by younger trees. By the 1970s, environmentalists, shocked by the vast clear-cuts, began trying to save the last old-growth trees. The battle between the timber industry and environmentalists is today still one of the state's most heated debates.

Salmon was the mainstay of the Native Americans' diet for thousands of years before the first whites arrived in the Oregon country, but within 10 years of the opening of the first salmon cannery in the Northwest, the fish population was decimated. In 1877, the first fish hatchery was developed to replenish dwindling runs of salmon. Salmon canning reached a peak on the Columbia River in 1895. Later, in the 20th century, salmon runs would be further decimated by the construction of numerous dams on the Columbia and Snake Rivers. Though fish ladders help adult salmon make their journeys upstream, the young salmon heading downstream have no such help, and a large percentage is killed by the turbines of hydroelectric dams. One solution to this problem has been barging and trucking young salmon downriver. Today the salmon populations of the Northwest have been so diminished that entire runs of salmon have been listed as threatened or endangered under the Endangered Species Act. Talk is now focusing on the removal of certain dams that pose insurmountable barriers to salmon. However, there is great resistance to this, and long, drawn-out legal battles seem inevitable.

The **dams** that have proved such a detriment to salmon populations have, however, provided irrigation water and cheap electricity that have fueled both industry and farming. Using newly available irrigation water, potato and wheat farms flourished in northeastern Oregon after the middle of this century. The huge reservoirs behind the Columbia and Snake River dams have also turned these rivers into waterways that can be navigated by huge barges, which often carry wheat downriver from ports in Idaho. Today, the regional salmon recovery plan is attempting to strike a balance between saving salmon runs and meeting all the other needs that have been created since the construction of these dams.

Manufacturing began gaining importance during and after World War II. In the Portland area, the **Kaiser Shipyards** employed tens of thousands of people in the construction of warships, but the postwar years saw the demise of the Kaiser facilities. Recent years have seen a diversification into **high-tech industries,** with such major manufacturers as Intel, NEC, Epson, and Hewlett-Packard operating manufacturing facilities in the Willamette Valley.

However, it is in the area of **sportswear** manufacturing that Oregon businesses have gained the greatest visibility. With outdoor recreation a way of life in this state, it comes as no surprise that a few regional companies have grown into international giants. Chief among these is **Nike,** which is headquartered in the Portland suburb of Beaverton. Other familiar names include Jantzen, one of the nation's oldest swimwear manufacturers; Pendleton Woolen Mills, maker of classic plaid wool shirts, Indian-design blankets, and other classic wool fashions; and Columbia Sportswear, which in recent years has become one of the country's biggest sports-related outerwear manufacturers. If you like to play outside, chances are you own some article of clothing that originated here in Oregon.

4 Eat, Drink & Be Merry

While there is no specifically Oregon cuisine, there is a regional cooking style that, while somewhat diluted by various international influences in recent years, still can be distinguished by its pairings of meats and seafood with local fruits and nuts. This cuisine features such regional produce as salmon, oysters, halibut, raspberries, blackberries, apples, pears, and hazelnuts. A classic Northwest dish might be raspberry chicken or oysters with a hazelnut crust. In the state's hinterlands, this is often labeled "Portland-style food" to distinguish it from far less creative meat-and-potatoes meals.

Salmon is king of Oregon fish and has been for thousands of years, so it isn't surprising that in one shape or another, it shows up on plenty of menus throughout the state. It's prepared in seemingly endless ways, but the most traditional method is what's known as alder-planked salmon. Traditionally, this Native American cooking style entailed preparing a salmon as a single fillet, splaying it on readily available alder wood, and slow-cooking it over hot coals. The result is a cross between grilling and smoking. Today, however, it's hard to find salmon prepared this traditional way. Much more readily available, especially along the Oregon coast, is traditional smoked salmon. You'll find such smoked salmon for sale at gourmet food shops (often vacuum-packed so that it doesn't need refrigeration until opened); at better grocery stores; and in restaurants, prepared a variety of ways. However, for freshness and quality, coastal smokehouses can't be beat. We make it a point of never passing a smokehouse without stopping to sample the wares. Smoked oysters are usually also available.

With plenty of clean cold waters in many of its bays and estuaries, Oregon raises large numbers of **oysters,** especially in Tillamook and Coos Bays. Then there are the mussels and clams. Of particular note are **razor clams,** which can be tough and chewy if not prepared properly, but which are eagerly sought after along north-coast beaches when the clamming season is open. After salmon, though, **Dungeness crab** is the region's other great seafood offering. Though not as large as an Alaskan king crab, the Dungeness is usually big enough to make a meal for one person. Crab cakes have become a staple of seafood menus across the state in recent years.

The Northwest's combination of climate and abundant irrigation waters has also helped make this one of the nation's major fruit-growing regions. Hood River Valley and the Medford area are two of the nation's top pear-growing regions, and just a few miles east of Hood River, around The Dalles, cherries reign supreme, with the blushing Rainier cherry a regional treat rarely seen outside the Northwest. The Willamette Valley, south of Portland, has become the nation's center for the production of berries, including **strawberries, raspberries,** and numerous varieties of **blackberries.** All these fruits show up in the summer months at farm stands all over the state, making a drive through the Northwest at that time of year a real treat. Pick-your-own farms are also fairly common throughout the Northwest. So famed are Oregon's fruits that the Harry and David's company has become a mainstay of the mail-order gift industry, shipping regional produce all over the country.

When hunger strikes on the road, Oregon offers what seems to be a regional potato preparation that just might be the only truly Northwestern cuisine. **Jo-jos** are potato wedges dipped in batter and fried. Traditionally served with a side of ranch dressing for dipping, these belly bombs are usually purchased as an accompaniment to fried or baked chicken.

One last Northwest food we should mention is the **wild mushroom.** As you'd expect in such a rainy climate, mushrooms abound here. The most common wild mushrooms are morels, which are harvested in spring, and chanterelles, which are harvested in autumn. In recent years, Oregon has been the site of modern-day range wars as armed mushroom hunters have combed the state's forests for these often-valuable fungi. Gun battles have ensued over control of prime mushroom-picking grounds, drawing national attention to this lucrative trade. In hopes of turning the outlaw lifestyle of the mushroom hunter into a more law-abiding pursuit, the National Forest Service, which oversees much of the land from which mushrooms are harvested, has been imposing stricter controls on pickers. The crash of the Japanese economy also slowed the mushroom wars, since the Japanese were among their main buyers.

We don't suggest heading out to the woods to pick your own unless you or your companions are experienced mushroom hunters. However, you will find wild mushrooms showing up on menus of better restaurants throughout the region, so by all means try to have some while you're here.

Oregon's thriving **wine** industry has for quite a few years now been producing award-winning varietal wines. Oregon is on the same latitude as the French wine regions of Burgundy and Bordeaux and produces similar wines. Oregon **Pinot Noirs** are ranking up there with those from France, and Chardonnays, Rieslings, and other varietals are getting good press as well. Unfortunately, the wet autumn weather in western Oregon, where most of the state's wine grapes are grown, can adversely affect wines here, so it pays to know your vintages (and your wineries, for that matter). **Wineries** throughout the state are open to the public for tastings, with the greatest concentrations to be found southwest of Portland in Yamhill County, just west of Salem, and northwest of Roseburg. Better restaurants throughout the state tend to stock plenty of Oregon wines. Fruit wines are also produced here and, contrary to what most people think, are not always cloyingly sweet. Fruit-based distilled liqueurs are also an up-and-coming product in the state, and some of the apple brandies are excellent.

With more **microbreweries** per capita than any other state in the nation, Oregon is at the center of the national obsession with craft beers, and new brew pubs continue to open across the state. Such local breweries as Bridgeport, Full Sail, and Widmer, which have long been at the forefront of the state's craft brewing industry, have grown so large that the term "microbrewery" no longer applies to them. While Portland is still the state's (and the nation's) microbrewery mecca, brew pubs can now be found throughout the state. From the tiny northeastern town of Enterprise to Cave Junction down in the southwest corner of the state, brewmeisters are crafting an amazing variety of distinctive brews. Perhaps part of the reason for the popularity of brewing in Oregon is that hops, one of the main ingredients in beer, are grown here in the Willamette Valley.

While local wines may be the state's preferred accompaniment to dinner and microbrews the favorite social drink, it is **coffee** that keeps Oregonians going through long gray winters—and even through hot sunny summers, for that matter. While Seattle gets all the press for its espresso obsession, this dark and flavorful style of coffee is equally popular throughout Oregon. There may still be a few small towns in the state where you can't get an espresso, but you certainly don't have to worry about falling asleep at the wheel for want of a decent cup of java. In parking lots throughout the state, tiny espresso stands dispense all manner of coffee concoctions to the state's caffeine addicts.

5 Recommended Books

NONFICTION   The best introduction to Oregon and the Northwest, both past and present, is probably Timothy Egan's *The Good Rain* (Vintage Departures, 1991), which uses a long-forgotten Northwest explorer as the springboard for an examination of all the forces that have made the Northwest what it is today.

Nineteenth-century explorers Meriwether Lewis and William Clark spent the winter of 1805–06 in present-day Oregon (and had a miserable time). *The Journals of Lewis and Clark* (Houghton Mifflin, 1997) is a fascinating account of their difficult 1804 to 1806 journey across the continent, and it includes a wealth of observations on Native Americans and North American flora and fauna. David Freeman Hawke's *Those Tremendous Mountains: The Story of the Lewis and Clark Expedition* (W.W. Norton and Company, 1998) is a more readable form of the journals and also has a considerable amount of background information.

For a complete history of the Northwest, try *The Pacific Northwest: An Interpretive History,* by Carlos A. Schwantes (University of Nebraska Press, 1996).

The pioneer period is the subject of *Women's Diaries of the Westward Journey* (Schocken Books, 1992), a collection of writings of women pioneers moving West compiled by Lillian Schlissel. *The Well-Traveled Casket: A Collection of Oregon Folklife,* by Tom Nash and Twilo Scofield (University of Utah Press, 1992), captures the folk and folklore of the Northwest's African American, Hispanic, Chinese, Native American, and Basque immigrants who came here as farmers, miners, loggers, and fishermen.

If you're interested in learning more about the Oregon wine industry, read Paul Pintarich's *Boys Up North: Dick Erath and the Early Oregon Wine Makers* (Graphic Arts Center Publishing, 1998), which chronicles the early years of contemporary Oregon wine making.

The rains of the Pacific Northwest are legendary, and in *Rains All the Time* (Sasquatch Books, 1997), David Larkin documents several centuries of commentaries on the region's dampness. Fun reading.

If it's just Oregon in pictures that you want, look for a copy of the beautiful coffee-table book *Oregon III* (Graphic Arts Center Publishing, 1987), a compilation of scenic photos by Ray Atkeson, the state's former Photographer Laureate.

FICTION   Oregon has not inspired a great deal of fiction. The best-known work of Oregon fiction is probably Ken Kesey's *Sometimes a Great Notion* (Penguin Books, 1977), which presents an evocative portrayal of a logging family and was made into a feature film starring Paul Newman and Henry Fonda. More recently, Kesey set his novel *The Last Go Round* (Penguin Books, 1995) among the cowboys and bucking broncos of the Pendleton Round-Up, circa 1911. The life of a 19th-century mountain man is the subject of Don Berry's

Trask (Comstock Editions, 1984), which, though out of print, is well worth searching out.

Ernest Callenbach's *Ecotopia* (Bantam Books, 1990) is a novel of the near future in which the Northwest secedes from the United States to pursue its own environmentally conscious beliefs (unfortunately, much has changed in the Northwest since the idealistic early 1970s, when this novel was written). In *The River Why* (Bantam Books, 1984), David J. Duncan writes of the search for self along the rivers of Oregon. This could best be described as a sort of "Zen and the Art of Fly-Fishing."

Fans of detective fiction may want to look for the Eldon Larkin mysteries by Vince Kohler: *Rainy North Woods* (St. Martin's Press, 1990), *Rising Dog* (St. Martin's Press, 1992), and *Banjo Boy* (St. Martin's Press, 1994) are all set along the Oregon coast.

TRAVEL & THE OUTDOORS   The outdoors is a way of life in Oregon, and enjoying it might require a specialized guidebook to get you to the best places. If you're a generalist when it comes to the outdoors, *Frommer's Great Outdoor Guide to Washington & Oregon* (Macmillan Travel, 1999), by this book's co-author, Karl Samson, is a very useful and usable guide to a wide variety of outdoor activities in western Oregon and western Washington.

Appendix B:
Useful Toll-Free Numbers & Web Sites

Airlines

Aer Lingus
☎ 800/474-7424 in the U.S.
☎ 01/886-8888 in Ireland
www.aerlingus.ie

Air Canada
☎ 800/776-3000
www.aircanada.ca

Air New Zealand
☎ 800/262-2468 in the U.S.
☎ 800/663-5494 in Canada
☎ 0800/737-767 in New Zealand

Alaska Airlines
☎ 800/426-0333
www.alaskaair.com

American Airlines
☎ 800/433-7300
www.americanair.com

America West Airlines
☎ 800/235-9292
www.americawest.com

British Airways
☎ 800/247-9297
☎ 0345/222-111 in Britain
www.british-airways.com

Canadian Airlines International
☎ 800/426-7000
www.cdnair.ca

Continental Airlines
☎ 800/525-0280
www.continental.com

Delta Air Lines
☎ 800/221-1212
www.delta-air.com

Frontier Airlines
☎ 800/432-1359
www.frontierairlines.com

Hawaiian Airlines
☎ 800/367-5320
www.hawaiianair.com

Horizon Air
☎ 800/547-9308
www.horizonair.com

Northwest Airlines
☎ 800/225-2525
www.nwa.com

Qantas
☎ 800/474-7424 in the U.S.
☎ 612/9691-3636 in Australia
www.qantas.com

Southwest Airlines
☎ 800/435-9792
www.iflyswa.com

Trans World Airlines (TWA)
☎ 800/221-2000
www.twa.com

United Airlines
☎ 800/241-6522
www.ual.com

US Airways
☎ 800/428-4322
www.usairways.com

Virgin Atlantic Airways
☎ 800/862-8621 in Continental U.S.
☎ 0293/747-747 in Britain
www.fly.virgin.com

Car-Rental Agencies

Advantage
☎ 800/777-5500
www.arac.com

Alamo
☎ 800/327-9633
www.goalamo.com

Avis
☎ 800/331-1212 in Continental U.S.
☎ 800/TRY-AVIS in Canada (800/879-2847)
www.avis.com

Budget
☎ 800/527-0700
www.budgetrentacar.com

Dollar
☎ 800/800-4000
www.dollarcar.com

Enterprise
☎ 800/325-8007
www.pickenterprise.com

Hertz
☎ 800/654-3131
www.hertz.com

National
☎ 800/CAR-RENT (800/227-7368)
www.nationalcar.com

Payless
☎ 800/PAYLESS
www.paylesscar.com

Rent-A-Wreck
☎ 800/535-1391
www.rent-a-wreck.com

Thrifty
☎ 800/367-2277
www.thrifty.com

Major Hotel & Motel Chains

Best Western International
☎ 800/528-1234
www.bestwestern.com

Clarion Hotels
☎ 800/CLARION (800/252-7466)
www.hotelchoice.com

Comfort Inns
☎ 800/228-5150
www.hotelchoice.com

Courtyard by Marriott
☎ 800/321-2211
www.courtyard.com

Days Inn
☎ 800/325-2525
www.daysinn.com

Doubletree Hotels
☎ 800/222-TREE (800/222-8733)
www.doubletreehotels.com

Econo Lodges
☎ 800/55-ECONO (800/553-2666)
www.hotelchoice.com

Fairfield Inn by Marriott
☎ 800/228-2800
www.fairfieldinn.com

Toll-Free Numbers & Web Sites

Hampton Inn
☎ 800/HAMPTON (800/426-7866)
www.hampton-inn.com

Hilton Hotels
☎ 800/HILTONS (800/445-8667)
www.hilton.com

Holiday Inn
☎ 800/HOLIDAY
www.basshotels.com

Howard Johnson
☎ 800/654-2000
www.hojo.com

Hyatt Hotels & Resorts
☎ 800/228-9000
www.hyatt.com

ITT Sheraton
☎ 800/325-3535
www.sheraton.com

La Quinta Motor Inns
☎ 800/531-5900
www.laquinta.com

Marriott Hotels
800/228-9290
www.marriott.com

Microtel Inn & Suites
☎ 888/771-7171
www.microtelinn.com

Motel 6
☎ 800/4-MOTEL6 (800/466-8536)
www.motel6.com

Quality Inns
☎ 800/228-5151
www.hotelchoice.com

Radisson Hotels International
☎ 800/333-3333
www.radisson.com

Ramada Inns
☎ 800/2-RAMADA (800/272-6232)
www.ramada.com

Red Lion Hotels & Inns
☎ 800/547-8010
www.redlion.com

Residence Inn by Marriott
☎ 800/331-3131
www.residenceinn.com

Rodeway Inns
☎ 800/228-2000
www.hotelchoice.com

Sleep Inn
☎ 800/753-3746
www.sleepinn.com

Super 8 Motels
☎ 800/800-8000
www.super8motels.com

Travelodge
☎ 800/255-3050
www.travelodge.com

Wyndham Hotels and Resorts
☎ 800/822-4200 in Continental U.S. and Canada
www.wyndham.com

Index

378

Index

Foris (Cave Junction), 13, 304

Fort Astoria, 158, 360–61

Fort Clatsop National Memorial (Astoria), 6, 158, 163, 360

Fort Dalles Museum (The Dalles), 252

Fort Henrietta Park (Echo), 334

Fort Rock State Park, 322

Fort Stevens State Park, 159, 161, 224

Fort Vancouver National Historic Site, 107, 108, 361

Fossil (town), 313

Fossil Beds National Monument, John Day, 310, 312–13

Four Rivers Cultural Center (Ontario), 350

Free Flight Bird and Marine Mammal Rehabilitation Center (Bandon), 222

Frenchglen, 353

French Pete Creek, 265

Fruit Loop, Hood River Valley, 246–47

Fruit stands, 110, 123–24, 246, 364–65

Fun Run Express (Garibaldi), 177

Gambling. *See* Casinos

Gardiner, 211

Garibaldi, 173, 176–77

Gaston, 120–21, 128

Gay and lesbian travelers, 28, 107

Gearhart, 163, 164, 165–66

Geiser Grand Hotel (Baker City), 9, 337, 340–41

Ghost towns, 6, 310, 312, 339, 351

Gifford Pinchot National Forest, 246

Gilbert (A. C.) Discovery Village (Salem), 129, 131

Girardet Wine Cellars (Roseburg), 306

Gleneden Beach, 9, 184, 188, 189

Glide, 270–71

Goat Island, 233

Gold Beach, 8, 229–33

Golden and Silver Falls State Natural Area, 218

Gold Lake, 269–70

Gold Post (Sumpter), 339

Golf, 24
  Bandon, 221–22
  Bend, 323
  Blue River, 264
  Charleston, 218
  Eugene, 148
  Florence, 208
  Gold Beach, 230
  Grants Pass, 299
  Hood River, 246
  Lincoln City, 186
  Manzanita, 173
  Neskowin, 182
  Newport, 197
  Portland, 91
  Seaside, 164
  Sisters, 316
  Tillamook, 178

Government Camp, 257–62

Governor Tom McCall Preserve, 251

Grand Ronde, 128

Granite, 6, 339

Grant House Folk Art Center (Vancouver), 107

Grants Pass, 19, 298–303

Grants Pass Downs, 299

Grants Pass Museum of Art, 299–300

Great Basin, 320–21, 355–56

Great Meadow Recreation Area, 298

Great Springs, 265

Green Lakes, 325

Gresham, 20, 49

Grey, Zane, 2, 15, 229, 277, 299

Grotto, the (Portland), 21, 88

Haines, 339, 342

Halfway (town), 8, 11, 348, 349–50

Hallie Ford Museum of Art (Salem), 130

Hammond, 160

Hang gliding, 24, 180, 264

Harbor (town), 234–36

Harbor Vista County Park, 209

Harris Beach State Park, 27, 233, 236

Harry and David's Country Village (Medford), 290

Hart Mountain National Antelope Refuge, 352, 353, 357

Hatfield Marine Science Center (Newport), 194

Haystack Rock, 167

Hebo Lake, 179

Heceta Beach County Park, 207

Heceta Head Lighthouse, 7, 205, 206

Hellgate Canyon, 299, 302

Hells Canyon National Recreation Area, 2, 336, 344, 347–49

Helvetia Vineyards & Winery (Hillsboro), 115

Hendricks Park and Rhododendron Garden (Eugene), 146

Henry Estate Winery (Roseburg), 307

Higgins, Greg, 10, 65, 68

High Desert Museum (Bend), 5–6, 16, 320–21

High Pass Winery (Junction City), 147

Hiking, 4–5, 24–25
  tours, 21, 24–25, 26
  Ashland, 281
  Bend, 323–24
  Brookings area, 234–35
  Bullards Beach, 221
  Cape Lookout, 4, 24, 180
  Cape Perpetua, 202–3
  Cascade Head, 183
  Columbia Gorge, 240, 241
  Crater Lake, 275
  Deschutes River Trail, 5, 323–24
  Drift Creek Falls Trail, 186
  Ecola State Park, 4, 24, 164, 168, 170
  Gold Beach, 230
  Grants Pass, 299
  Hells Canyon, 348
  Hood River, 246
  Illinois Valley, 304
  Jacksonville, 291
  McKenzie River Trail, 4, 265
  Mount Bachelor, 323–24
  Mount Hood, 4, 258
  Munson Creek County Park, 178
  Oregon Dunes, 4, 212
  Oswald West State Park, 4, 24, 172, 179
  Pacific Crest Trail, 24, 255, 275, 281
  Portland, 24, 52, 84, 91
  Saddle Mountain, 24, 172
  Seaside, 164
  Silver Falls, 24, 129, 134

FROMMER'S® COMPLETE TRAVEL GUIDES

FROMMER'S® DOLLAR-A-DAY GUIDES

Australia from $50 a Day
California from $60 a Day
Caribbean from $70 a Day
England from $70 a Day
Europe from $60 a Day
Florida from $60 a Day

Hawaii from $70 a Day
Ireland from $50 a Day
Israel from $45 a Day
Italy from $70 a Day
London from $85 a Day
New York from $80 a Day

New Zealand from $50 a Day
Paris from $85 a Day
San Francisco from $60 a Day
Washington, D.C.,
  from $60 a Day

FROMMER'S® PORTABLE GUIDES

Acapulco, Ixtapa &
  Zihuatanejo
Alaska Cruises & Ports of Call
Bahamas
Baja & Los Cabos
Berlin
California Wine Country
Charleston & Savannah
Chicago

Dublin
Hawaii: The Big Island
Las Vegas
London
Maine Coast
Maui
New Orleans
New York City
Paris

Puerto Vallarta, Manzanillo
  & Guadalajara
San Diego
San Francisco
Sydney
Tampa & St. Petersburg
Venice
Washington, D.C.

FROMMER'S® NATIONAL PARK GUIDES

Family Vacations in the
  National Parks
Grand Canyon

National Parks of the
  American West
Rocky Mountain

Yellowstone & Grand Teton
Yosemite & Sequoia/
  Kings Canyon
Zion & Bryce Canyon

FROMMER'S® GREAT OUTDOOR GUIDES

New England
Northern California

Southern California & Baja
Washington & Oregon

FROMMER'S® MEMORABLE WALKS

Chicago
London

New York
Paris

San Francisco
Washington D.C.

FROMMER'S® IRREVERENT GUIDES

Amsterdam
Boston
Chicago
Las Vegas

London
Los Angeles
Manhattan

New Orleans
Paris
San Francisco

Seattle & Portland
Vancouver
Walt Disney World
Washington, D.C.

FROMMER'S® BEST-LOVED DRIVING TOURS

America
Britain
California

Florida
France
Germany

Ireland
Italy
New England

Scotland
Spain
Western Europe

THE UNOFFICIAL GUIDES®

SPECIAL-INTEREST TITLES